Advanced Place[ment]
World History Test
Preparation Guide

to accompany

Traditions and Encounters
A Global Perspective on the Past

Third Edition

by
Jerry H. Bentley and Herb F. Ziegler

written by

Dixie Johnson Grupe
Hickman High School

Sigrid Reynolds
Washington High School

Boston   Burr Ridge, IL   Dubuque, IA   Madison, WI   New York   San Francisco   St. Louis
Bangkok   Bogotá   Caracas   Kuala Lumpur   Lisbon   London   Madrid   Mexico City
Milan   Montreal   New Delhi   Santiago   Seoul   Singapore   Sydney   Taipei   Toronto

Higher Education

Published by McGraw-Hill, an imprint of The McGraw-Hill Companies, Inc., 1221 Avenue of the Americas, New York, NY 10020. Copyright © 2007. All rights reserved. No part of this publication may be reproduced or distributed in any form or by any means, or stored in a database or retrieval system, without the prior written consent of The McGraw-Hill Companies, Inc., including, but not limited to, in any network or other electronic storage or transmission, or broadcast for distance learning.

This book is printed on acid-free paper.

2 3 4 5 6 7 8 9 0 079 09

ISBN-13: 978-0-07-329211-3
ISBN-10: 0-07-329211-7

The Internet addresses listed in the text were accurate at the time of publication. The inclusion of a Web site does not indicate an endorsement by the authors or McGraw-Hill, and McGraw-Hill does not guarantee the accuracy of the information presented at these sites.

www.mhhe.com

TABLE OF CONTENTS

Consider this....

Today, if you watched the news on television, read a newspaper article, or downloaded a podcast on an electronic device, you probably heard a story: something important happened to someone, somewhere. Over time, the technology we use to tell our stories has changed, but not the basic premise: we are interested in other people's lives, especially how their stories impact our own.

Whether you fully understand the story you heard depends on what you already know about the people involved, where the story took place, and what events occurred that set the story in motion. This book is about the essential background knowledge you need to make sense of our most important human story, our history.

Advanced Placement World History is a course designed to provide you with the ultimate human "backstory," the peoples and processes that over time have created the world in which we live. The course is also designed to assess and reward your learning upon successful completion of a comprehensive national exam taken in early May. A good performance on that exam can result in potential college credit of up to five hours at some colleges and universities. The exam itself is prepared by The College Board, a not-for-profit association whose mission it is to help students find opportunity and success in college, and a Test Development Committee which includes college and university professors and high school teachers who teach AP World History every day; they design the curriculum and write the exam.

The exam consists of 70 multiple choice questions and three specific types of essay questions: one uses historical documents to assess your ability to read, think, and write critically; another requires you to describe and analyze changes and continuities in human history; and the third requires you to compare and contrast a common theme in diverse places. You get 185 minutes to do all that!

Once you take the exams, your essays are graded over a ten-day period in June by AP World History teachers and college and university professors who read every word that you (and more than 70,000 of your peers) have written. These teachers and professors first read several hundred sample essays to set the standards of excellence for each individual essay question. Once those standards are set, they spend eight hours a day reading your work every day until they are finished. Each grader knows AP World History content and the standards of excellence in scholarship required to achieve a solid score; each essay is scored individually on a nine-point scale. Every year, they read thousands of essays from thousands of students; these trained exam readers can easily recognize students who are prepared in content and skills. This book's purpose is to help you prepare and to help you succeed. So here goes . . .

Section I of this book explains course expectations and exam parameters and includes preparation suggestions to help you maximize your studies and your time. Each chapter in Section II contains chapter content summaries with ten practice Chapter Multiple Choice questions as well as three Comprehensive Multiple Choice questions which require you to synthesize knowledge from other chapters. Pay careful attention to the analysis and reference for all of these questions. Section III includes Model Essay questions and responses, ideas on how to approach, plan, and organize each type of essay, and detailed analyses of three high-quality essays. Section IV contains two complete practice exams and a thorough analysis of every question and response.

SECTION I

INTRODUCTION TO ADVANCED PLACEMENT WORLD HISTORY AND EXAM*

BEFORE YOU GET STARTED

There is a lot of history to learn before the national exam. Even if you memorized 100 details every day from now until the exam, and could retain 80 percent of those details, you would not be prepared for what the exam assesses. The national exam is not about random details or lists; it is about the "evolution of global processes and their interaction" with different types of human societies. This means that the national exam is about major concepts and your ability to select and apply historical examples from across the world to support them. However, it also means you must demonstrate your mastery of historically significant facts and details in the 70 multiple choice questions, as well as demonstrate your ability to recall, analyze, and evaluate those facts in the three essay questions which are set in specific time periods and locations. This text resource is written with those premises in mind.

To help you learn the content and be successful on the national exam, we have four suggestions:

1) Rely on the course themes.
2) Understand the concepts of periodization and region.
3) Anticipate the parameters of the exam and its format.
4) Be motivated to work at a steady pace.

COURSE THEMES

There are six overarching themes which guide this course and exam and should guide your learning and exam preparation. No single theme is more important than another and no single chapter deals equally with all themes.

Theme #1: Continuity and Change-Over-Time

This theme looks at the dynamics of change and continuity. What changes and what stays the same? What causes these big changes? What elements stay the same over several historical periods and across several cultures and which ones change? What causes some elements to change and others to continue?

Theme #2: Interactions of Cultures

This theme looks at how peoples from different cultures consistently interact through trade, war, diplomacy, and international organizations. Like theme #1, this theme appears more often as you progress through the text.

Theme #3: Effects of Technology, Economics, and Demography on People and the Environment

You will consistently see this theme throughout this course. It includes population growth and decline, disease, labor systems, manufacturing, agriculture, migrations, and weaponry. These subjects frequently appear as topics for the multiple choice and the essay questions.

Theme #4: Social and Gender Structure

This theme also appears early in the text and continues through the final chapters. How is society organized and how do gender structures affect society? What is the basis for social class structure in each society? How does economic position affect social class? What are the roles for men and women in this society and how do those roles affect how society is organized? Frequently, there are questions asking you to compare and contrast elements of this theme between cultures and over time.

Theme #5: Culture, Intellectual Developments, and Belief Systems

This is a major theme: the ways people live, what they think about, and what they believe in. Many multiple choice questions are drawn from this theme and it is often used as the content for all three types of essay questions.

Theme #6: Political Identity, Political Institutions, and Political Organizations

This theme is the most traditional for a history course. How do people organize themselves? How is power gained, maintained, and lost? How does one political tradition compare and contrast with another? How do political structures develop and change over time?

COURSE THEMES IN THIS BOOK

These six themes are used throughout most AP World History texts and clearly in the textbook around which this guide is based: *Traditions and Encounters: A Global Perspective on the Past* by Jerry Bentley and Herb Ziegler. The textbook authors used these themes to decide what to include and emphasize. This preparation book goes even further than the text to help you focus on the themes by identifying the major theme(s) addressed in each section. Under each section title, the main theme of the section is identified in parentheses and bold italics. For example, it might say: (*Changes and Continuities*).

Each section will include other ideas, but this theme will be most directly addressed. You should use these identified themes to make your own charts or other graphic organizers. If you are keeping a list of vocabulary terms, the themes will help you organize those terms into meaningful groups. These clearly identified themes in each section should help you make sense of the content in each chapter and connect several chapters together. Of course, these identified themes should be most useful as you are gathering content for an essay.

PERIODIZATION

Although themes are an essential way to promote your learning from the textbook and to organize your thinking for the exam questions, the other major organizing principle for this course is *periodization,* which means that history is divided into "chunks" of time which make sense. For example, if you were going to tell your own life story, you could go day-by-day-by-day, but that would tell little about who you are and how you came to be. "I was born on April 25, 1989. On day one, I breathed, napped, and ate. On day two, I breathed, napped, ate, and cried. On day three . . . " If you told your story around important periods of your life, we would know you much better. "The first five years of my life were focused around learning to live in my household with three brothers, a dog, and my mother. My three brothers always tried to get me in trouble because they never wanted a baby sister. One time, they even tried to sell me at their lemonade stand. To this day, I do not like lemonade and I am suspicious of my brothers . . . " Your story would go on to tell about your dog and then your mother. We could remember the three big events from that period and then be able to compare and contrast those events with the events in the next big period in your life. Eventually, we would be able to discuss the changes in your life across several of those periods and posit some reasons for those changes.

The concept of periodization in this course and on the national exam works exactly like this somewhat silly personal example. Big "chunks" of time containing specific historic events provide the organizing principles for dealing with change and continuity throughout the course. This concept is especially important on the essay portion of the national exam which includes three essay questions: a question using historical documents, a question which asks you to compare and contrast two elements, and a question which asks you to analyze a theme which changes over time. To answer any of those essays well, you must know what time periods the essay question asks about.

The key periods are divided chronologically from about 8000 B.C.E. to the present and a particular percentage of the exam content is ascribed to each period.

8000 B.C.E.–600 C.E.	19–20%	(Foundations Period)
600 C.E.–1450	22%	(Post-classical Period)
1450–1750	19–20%	(Early Modern Era)
1750–1914	19–20%	(Modern Era)
1914–present	19–20%	(Contemporary Era)

Periodization makes it possible to organize this huge amount of course content.

Each essay question will be set in a specific period; for example, "Discuss the continuities and changes in global trading systems from 1450–1750." To succeed on this exam, it is essential for you to understand what big events typify each period. Use the timelines at the end of each text chapter to mark key events in each period.

PLACES

The national exam will also require you to know what nations, states, or empires are encompassed in what regions for both the multiple choice questions and the three essays. While it is impossible to list every country in every region, the most commonly misidentified nations and their regions are

North Africa: Egypt, Libya, Algeria, Tunisia, Morocco
West Africa: Ghana, Nigeria, Senegal, Togo, Benin
East Africa: Kenya, Tanzania, Somalia, Ethiopia, Mozambique,
Equatorial Africa: Congo, Rwanda, Sudan
Southern Africa: Angola, Republic of South Africa, Zimbabwe
Middle East: Turkey, Israel, Egypt, Jordan, Saudi Arabia, Iran, Iraq
East Asia: China, Japan, Korea
South Asia: India, Pakistan, Afghanistan
Southeast Asia: Thailand, Viet Nam, Laos, Cambodia, Indonesia, Philippines
Latin America: Mexico, Honduras, Brazil, Argentina, Chile, Peru, Cuba

The essay questions frequently ask you to choose two examples from a list of regions. For example: "Compare and contrast demographic changes during the period 1914–2000 in TWO of the following regions: South Asia, East Asia, West Africa, North America, Latin America."

If you wrote a beautiful, well-constructed, well-supported response using Japan and China, you would only earn 3 points instead perhaps of 8 or 9 because Japan and China are in the same region: East Asia. Or you might write a well-constructed, well-supported essay using Kenya and Egypt and earn 0 points because those nations are not in the regions given as choices. So, you must know the regions and the places they include.

Be careful: cultural areas shift over time and you must read the text and national exam carefully for both time and place contexts. A great essay on the wrong topic or wrong place or wrong time gets you no points.

EXAM PARAMETERS, FORMAT, AND SCORING

The AP World History Exam is long; you will spend three hours and five minutes taking the test. Plus, it takes a while to fill out the pre-exam paperwork and explain the directions, so the time is actually closer to four hours. For many students, this is the longest sustained time they have spent on an exam in their school experience. Therefore, it is very important that you are physically ready to sustain the kind of focus necessary to do your best. Most testing sites offer a brief break between the multiple choice and the essay portion of the exam, but a good night's sleep, some food in your stomach, and clear expectations are essential to your success. Of course, even with the best of intentions, you must be prepared with solid world history content and writing. The best way to score well on this exam is to think, read, and write consistently throughout the year. There is no way to cram for this exam and earn the best possible score.

There are two major sections to this exam. The Multiple Choice section counts as 50 percent of your score and the Essay Section counts as the other 50 percent.

Multiple Choice Questions

In this section you will be given 70 multiple choice questions to complete in 55 minutes. The questions will come from all time periods covered in the course and each period gets 13 to 15 questions, with perhaps a few extra questions covering the post-classical period. Some of the questions are cross-chronological; they span one or more periods. You should anticipate a range of questions across the entire time span of the course: 8000 B.C.E. to the present. The multiple choice questions will always have five possible answers and will basically follow a chronological sequence. You will be marking your answers on a computer answer sheet, so it is extremely important to periodically check that you are markng in the correct spot.

To guess or not to guess? Here is the answer . . .

Do not guess if you have absolutely no idea what the question means. Random guessing is not a good idea because 25 percent of the questions answered incorrectly will be deducted from questions answered correctly.

However, if you have some knowledge of the question and can eliminate one or more of the choices, then you are better off to choose an answer from the remaining choices.

Here are two possible multiple choice questions. Even though this content may be unfamiliar to you, it is important to get a sense of how to read and reason through multiple choice questions that are written at a level beyond simple knowledge or recall.

Read and answer these two questions as if they were part of the real exam and then carefully consider the discussion of process and correct answers that follow.

1. Which of the following statements best describes BOTH Hinduism and Buddhism?
    a. Both Hinduism and Buddhism depended on the services of brahmins to escape the cycle of reincarnation.
    b. Both Hinduism and Buddhism used Sanskrit rather than vernacular languages to teach others.
    c. Both Hinduism and Buddhism relied on monastic organizations and preaching to attract followers.
    d. Both Hinduism and Buddhism sought to escape the cycle of incarnation through the following of dharma.
    e. Both Hinduism and Buddhism were based on the idea that life is suffering and believers must work collectively to escape that suffering through self-denial.

2. The split between the Sunni and the Shia branches of Islam was originally focused on
   a. a disagreement over who should control the Ka'ba and Mecca.
   b. a dispute as to who should protect the Dome of the Rock in Jerusalem.
   c. a conflict over the language of the Qu'ran and the Hadith.
   d. the luxurious lifestyle of the Abbasids who insisted in moving their capital to Damascus.
   e. a disagreement over succession as the Shia wanted Ali and his descendents to serve as caliphs.

To answer Question #1 correctly, you have to know some basic information about the two religions and then you have to read the choices carefully to select the statement that best applies to both Hinduism and Buddhism. Choice "a" is incorrect, because Buddhism teaches that one does not escape from the cycle of reincarnation through the assistance of another person, but only through following the Middle Way. Choice "b" is also incorrect because one reason for the appeal and spread of Buddhism in India after the fifth century B.C.E. was that its monks used the language of the people to reach greater numbers of people. Choice "c" is incorrect because Hinduism does not have a monastic tradition nor a tradition of conversion. Choice "e" is incorrect because while the First Noble Truth in Buddhism is that life is suffering, an individual does not conquer suffering through self-denial, but through following the Middle Way. That leaves only choice "d" as a credible option; both traditions do teach the idea of dharma, though they define it differently.

To answer Question #2 correctly, you must both understand the basic tenets and history of Islam, but you must also know something about the two major sects in Islam: Sunni and Shia. While there are pieces of accurate information in all five of the choices, only choice "e" is completely correct and directly responds to the statement, "The split between the Sunni and the Shia branches of Islam was originally focused on. . ." Remember that for an answer to be correct, it must be fully correct and it must complete the statement or answer the question posed.

The multiple choice questions are rarely about recalling specific, discrete pieces of information which you have learned in your AP World History course. Instead, they require you to apply what content knowledge you've gained through your class and your readings to questions you have never seen before. The multiple choice questions are never easy, but the stronger your content knowledge, and the more consistent your strategy through practice, the more doable these questions become.

Essay Questions

The other half of your exam grade comes from your performance on the three specific types of essay questions. Like the multiple choice questions, these essay questions are designed to assess the range and scope of your world history knowledge, but these questions also require you to be able to communicate that knowledge in a clear and specific manner. You have 130 minutes to accomplish all three of these tasks and that includes a mandatory 10 minute reading and planning period before you can begin to write. You need both strong content knowledge and an intimate understanding of the scoring guides for these three types of essays to do well on this portion of the exam. The content for these questions is drawn from across the time and scope of this course—8000 B.C.E. to the present—and includes all world regions and course themes.

For example, the first essay you will be asked to write is a Document Based Question, known in AP jargon as a DBQ. Both the AP United States History Exam and the AP European History Exam require a DBQ, but the requirements for the AP World History DBQ are *markedly different* than those two exams. Pay attention to the specifics here.

An AP World History DBQ is designed to evaluate your ability to formulate and support a response based on between 4 and 10 documents which are provided to you. You are given ten minutes to read these documents and plan your essay before you are allowed to start writing your response; you should anticipate taking about 40 minutes to write this type of an essay. There are no deliberately misleading or irrelevant documents and everything you need to answer the question is provided in the documents. Practice,

practice, practice this type of essay, because knowing the format and structure of an AP World History DBQ is really all you need to be successful on this type of essay.

For example, you might see a DBQ which asks you to "Analyze the social results of European and Japanese industrialization." You might be given eight documents, which could include charts and pictures as well as written texts. You would begin by carefully reading the question to fully understand what it is asking and then begin a careful reading of the documents provided. Next, you would consider in what ways the documents answer that question; usually at this point, students make a chart on the documents page which divides the documents into groups. We *always* recommend three groups. Once the reading time is over, you would begin to write your essay, based on the documents provided and your request for additional documents which would help you better answer the question. Ultimately, every student produces a different DBQ essay, so the test scorers are looking for your ability to use the documents to produce an accurate, well-supported essay which follows the prescribed criteria.

The DBQ is designed to be answered without having any outside knowledge, but of course the more you know about world history, the easier this essay is to write. But no matter what content they ask about, if you demonstrate the required format and desired structure, you will score well. Without those elements, despite all you know about a topic, you will not score well on the DBQ.

The second essay you will see will be a Change-Over-Time Essay, although it is really better to think of it as a Continuity-and-Change-Over-Time question. This essay will ask about the dynamics of change and continuity concerning some large global issue such as gender roles, migrations, military aggression, etc. Think about those AP World History themes, periods, and regions listed above; they form the parameters of this type of question.

For example, you might see a question which asks you to "Pick one of the following regions and discuss changes and continuities in gender roles from 1450 to the present: West Africa, East Asia, Eastern Europe, Latin America."

Unlike the DBQ, this types of essay requires a span of historical knowledge regarding one theme in one region. You might select Latin America and talk about the roles for men and women in the Aztec empire before the coming of the Europeans, the changing roles for men and women during Spanish colonization including the coming of Christianity, and the impact of industrialization on changing gender roles in Latin America in the twentieth century. That type of approach sustains the gender role theme over three eras and gives European colonization, Christianity, and industrialization as reasons for the changes. Note that this is NOT a cause-and-effect essay or a then-and-now essay; you will need to develop and support three distinct periods, eras, or topics within this type of question to deal fully with what elements change and what elements stay the same. This type of essay question is often the most difficult one on the exam as it requires range and depth of knowledge and a clear understanding of acceptable format.

The last type of essay you will find on the exam is the Comparative Essay and while you may have more familiarity with writing this type of essay than the other two, beware. Sometimes you will have a choice in this question's content and other times you will not.

For example, you might see a question which asks you to "Compare and contrast the Haitian and French Revolutions." Or, you might also see a question which gives you some choice, i.e., "Compare and contrast labor systems c. 1450–1900 in TWO of the following regions: West Africa, North America, South America, Eastern Europe."

Even with choice of region, this is not a simple question. You must address both comparisons and contrasts within the labor systems of two regions during a prescribed time period: that requires ample content knowledge of two regions in one period. Further, to earn a top score on this type of essay, you must analyze the reasons for those comparisons and contrasts. Content knowledge and a clear understanding of the scoring criteria are necessary for success here as in the other two essays.

With effort and practice, you can complete all three essays in the 130 minutes allotted. This book is designed to help you meet this challenge. Part III includes a Model Essay for each type of essay you will be required to write, a planning guide to construct each essay type, and a detailed analysis of how each essay will be scored. Plan some study time in that section before you take the national exam. It is essential to your success.

How do all these numbers turn into the score you receive in the mail sometime in July? Your multiple choice score counts one half of your total exam score; your three essays together make up the other half of your score. That means each essay counts as one third of your essay portion; you cannot skip an essay and score well, no matter how great your other two essays are. The exam readers score each essay on a nine-point scale and then the College Board statisticians determine how those nine-point raw scores mesh with your Multiple Choice Score; then they translate that score into a composite score on five-point scale. A 5 means you did an excellent job on the multiple choice and all three essays and you are considered "extremely well-qualified" for college credit. A 4 means you did a good job on the multiple choice and the essays and you are considered "well-qualified" for college credit. A 3 means you did an acceptable job on both the multiple choice and essays and are "qualified" to earn college credit. A 2 means you are considered "possibly qualified" for college credit and a score of 1 carries no recommendation. Individual colleges and universities decide how much credit is awarded for each score. Check the websites for those colleges and universities you are interested in to see what scores they accept and how many hours you may earn.

HOW TO USE THIS RESOURCE

Those individuals who gain the best scores on the AP exam are those who have been conscientious in their preparation. They enrolled in a well-taught AP World History course, paid attention in class, created good notes, wrote a lot of essays, read the chapters, and studied for tests. This manual will help you clarify issues, remind you of content, and give you additional practice, but it cannot teach you everything you should have learned throughout a year of study.

However, you will be able to use this manual to supplement your learning during the year. It follows the pattern and pacing of the Bentley and Ziegler textbook, *Traditions and Encounters: A Global Perspective on the Past,* so you can use it to check as you finish each chapter or section. You can use it to practice those essential essay writing techniques or you can use it to practice the content and time your multiple choice testing skills. If you are enrolled in an AP World History class which uses this text, you can use it to prepare for your teacher's unit exam or semester finals.

If you don't use this textbook or are not currently enrolled in an AP World History course, this resource can still be useful to you. You can use the chapter summaries to flesh out your understanding of certain topics not covered in your text or covered in a different way. For example, you could jot notes or connections from your previous learning in the margins of each chapter summary or use sticky notes to record your thinking or questions to use during a review. Certainly, anyone can use the multiple choice questions included at the end of each chapter summary and in the two practice exams. It is important to get practice with all types of multiple choice questions, especially those written by someone whose wording or style is not familiar to you. And, of course, you should use this book to guide your review before the national AP Exam.

Each chapter in Part II contains a chapter summary paralleling the chapters in *Traditions and Encounters: A Global Perspective on the Past* by Jerry Bentley and Herb Ziegler. Each chapter summary contains several parts which should be useful for you whether or not you use that particular text.

1) "Before you get started." These sections give you an overview of the chapter and how it fits with other chapters. It might include a strategy to help you learn the content.

2) All major section and subsection headings mirror the ones of the main textbook. That way, if you have specific questions, or if you need more information after reading the summary, you know where to look in your text.

3) Each subsection includes a specific theme identified in parentheses. Each of these themes fits with an AP World History theme.

   For example: *(Theme: Technology)*

   These identified themes should help you identify, plan, and write essays throughout the school year.

4) Certain words are printed in boldface. Those are specific words, terms, people, events, or concepts which you can anticipate will figure prominently in AP multiple choice questions or essay questions. They form the basis of the index found at the back of this resource.

5) "Finished reading the chapter? Be sure you can . . ." You will find this section at the end of each chapter summary. Use these as a self-check for the chapter's content; they are directly tied to the AP World History curriculum.

6) Chapter Multiple Choice Questions. You can use these questions for a self-check after you've read the textbook chapter or even after reading the chapter summaries in this book. The answers follow at the end of each chapter summary and we've included the page numbers in your text if you need further clarification.

7) Comprehensive Multiple Choice Questions. At the end of each chapter summary, after the Chapter Multiple Choice Questions, you will find three Comprehensive Multiple Choice questions which reflect a similar style to those you will see on the national AP World History Exam. These questions tend to be more complex, more global, and more challenging than the chapter multiple choice questions.

8) Primary Source Questions. At the end of almost every chapter summary, you will find some primary source, either a text or a work of art, and some thought questions. Use these questions to practice those skills you will need on the DBQ portion of the exam. Potential responses to these Primary Source Questions are included at the end of each chapter summary.

ONE LAST COMMENT

Motivation is an internal phenomenon most influenced by success; the more successful someone is at a task, the more likely he or she is willing to keep trying. We've tried to organize this resource to help you be successful in your own preparations or in your world history class and of course on the national AP Exam. We hope you earn that college credit.

Finally, we think the most valuable aspect of this course is that you will learn a lot about the history of the world, which enables you to become a better, more educated citizen capable of making intelligent and thoughtful decisions. Besides, with some of the money you save by earning that college credit now, in a few years you could be traveling to all the places you've been reading about.

SECTION II

CHAPTER REVIEWS WITH MULTIPLE CHOICE QUESTIONS, PRIMARY SOURCES, AND ANALYSIS

PART I

THE EARLY COMPLEX SOCIETIES,
3500 TO 500 B.C.E.

CHAPTER 1

BEFORE HISTORY

Before you get started: Let the AP themes be your guide to help you determine importance in this and every chapter to come.

1) Dynamics of Continuity and Change
2) Patterns of Interactions: Trade, War, and Diplomacy
3) Technology, Economics, and Demography
4) Systems of Social and Gender Structure
5) Cultural, Intellectual, and Religious Developments
6) Political Organization and Functions of States

After finishing each chapter summary, you should be able to apply the information to each of these themes, which govern the curricular focus and will be addressed in the questions on the AP Exam.

One of the most challenging aspects of this course is the vocabulary. Learning history is like learning a foreign language. You must memorize, see, hear, practice, and apply the words frequently. We have bold-faced the most important terms. Sometimes it helps to know their origins. In this chapter, *paleo* is Greek for "old" and *lithic* refers to stone; thus the paleolithic was the Old Stone Age. Likewise, *neo* in neolithic means "new" as in New Stone Age, when there was a change in tools and lifestyles. Only a limited amount from this period may appear on the test; nevertheless, it is important to note the period as a base-line for comparison with the following one.

THE EVOLUTION OF *HOMO SAPIENS*

The Hominids
(Theme: Technology)

Between four and one million years ago, the earliest hominids appeared in east Africa. Archaeologists named them *australopithecines*. They were quite small, appear to have walked upright, and fashioned hand tools of stone. Around one million years ago, they vanished and the genus *Homo* arose. *Homo erectus* had bigger brains and fashioned more sophisticated tools. They also used fire to cook food, as defense, and to keep warm. These people lived in small bands and hunted large animals, so it is presumed that they had high intelligence and good language skills.

Homo Sapiens
(Theme: Migration)

About two hundred thousand years ago, *Homo sapiens* ("consciously thinking man") supplanted *Homo erectus*. The brain was very large and particularly well developed in the areas that control consciousness and reflective thinking. The adaptability of *Homo sapiens* to different environmental settings prompted the **migration** of early humans to the temperate zones of all continents and later allowed habitation of the coldest regions, because they could make their own clothing and shelters. Between sixty and fifteen thousand years ago, people traveled along land bridges that existed between continents due to a global cooling period. It is believed that during this period, individuals and family units moved from southeast Asia to Australia and from northeast Asia to the Americas. Even more sophisticated tools were made and caves and huts were used as dwellings. They hunted very large mammals and it is speculated that they may have had an influence in the disappearance of several species. They competed very effectively with other species, likely due to their intelligence.

PALEOLITHIC SOCIETY

The paleolithic period begins with the first hominids and ends about twelve thousand years ago. Its principle feature was **hunting and gathering**.

Economy and Society of Hunting and Gathering Peoples
(Themes: Economics and Social Structure)

Paleolithic societies depended on foraging to feed themselves. Successful hunting and gathering depended upon manmade tools and sophisticated language abilities for the cooperative hunting of large animals. Tools to kill animals and prepare the meat and skins for clothing were fashioned of stone and bone. From cave paintings it is apparent that men hunted while women augmented their diets by collecting seeds and fruits. Since the lifestyle required a **nomadic life**, bands typically had thirty to fifty members. A paleolithic society had little wealth and therefore probably had relative social equality among its members.

Paleolithic Culture
(Themes: Intellectual and Religious Developments)

The earliest sites of modern humans, so-called Neandertals, contain evidence of reflective thinking about the nature of human existence and the world around them. Archaeologists have found abundant evidence of culture at ancient settlements and gravesites in Europe dating from two hundred thousand to thirty-five thousand years ago. The artifacts found at these sites indicate **elaborate burial practices** with flowers and possessions scattered around the individual. On the basis of the burial practices, archaeologists have suggested a belief in an afterlife, but it is also possible that the Neandertals simply wanted to honor their dead. Later the Cro-Magnon, physically identical to modern humans, also left art for scholars to contemplate in the settlement sites and along rock faces and cave walls. Some clay statues, known as **Venus figurines**, have been found that exhibit prominent sexual features. Anthropologists believe this indicates an interest in fertility. The Cro-Magnon people invented bows and arrows, spear-throwers, and harpoons, and they adorned themselves with elaborate jewelry. Rock and cave paintings found around the world provide some insight into paleolithic hunting practices. These paintings were done with ground pigments made from many natural substances that were applied to rock with moss, frayed twigs, and brushes made from hair.

Although not mentioned in the textbook, one must note that there have been isolated populations in parts of the world that have persisted in the paleolithic lifestyle well into the twentieth century. Anthropologists have studied many of these societies and passed on the information to archaeologists to help determine how ancient peoples might have lived.

THE NEOLITHIC ERA AND THE TRANSITION TO AGRICULTURE

The **neolithic period** lasted from about twelve thousand years ago to six thousand years ago and is characterized by the appearance of agriculture and larger settlements.

The Origins of Agriculture
(Themes: Economics and Technology)

As humans looked to ensure a more steady food supply, it seems probable that women began to collect seeds and grow plants. The earliest evidence of agriculture, the cultivation of wheat, appears in sites in the Middle East around 9000 B.C.E. Somewhat later, inhabitants of the southeast border of the Sahara began domesticating cattle, sheep, and sorghum. Between 8000 and 6000 B.C.E., west Africans began to grow yams, okra, and black-eyed peas. Rice cultivation in southern China began as early as 6000 B.C.E.with soybeans and millet soon afterward in northern China. Chickens and pigs appear to have been domesticated during this time as well. Two thousand years later, the Mesoamericans learned to grow maize and the Andes people began to grow potatoes. The early Americans had hunted many large species to extinction so only llamas, alpacas, and guinea pigs were domesticated by the people of the Andes.

This brings up the question of **independent invention** and **cultural diffusion.** Earlier historians believed that there could only be one site of origin for any invention or idea. When it appeared in another region, historians assumed that it had been borrowed from an earlier or neighboring culture. However, as there appear to be many sites for the primary origin of agriculture, they now recognize the independent origin of many cultural traits. Cultural diffusion, or the exchange of ideas, does appear to be what occurred when wheat domesticated in the Middle East was adopted by the Chinese around 3000 B.C.E., or when rice cultivation moved to the Indian subcontinent from China around 1500 B.C.E. However, this is secondary to the independent origin of agricultural techniques with different plants.

Early methods of agriculture such as **"slash-and-burn"** techniques resulted in the expansion of peoples into new regions as the fertility of previous sites began to decline. Ironically, neolithic agriculture required more work than paleolithic hunting and gathering even though the food source became fairly reliable and abundant. Furthermore, long-distance migrations of humans slowed down as they settled around grain fields.

Early Agricultural Society
(Themes: Economics and Technology)

Once people had settled into sustained agricultural communities with an expanding food supply, the human population began to increase, from fourteen million in 3000 B.C.E. to 100 million by 500 B.C.E. The earliest agricultural settlement sites are **Jericho** in present-day Israel (8000 B.C.E.) and **Çatal Hüyük** in present-day Turkey (7000 B.C.E.). These villages soon became towns with as many as eight thousand individuals engaged in activities in support of and outside of agriculture. There is evidence of **pottery**, basketry, **textiles**, leather goods, and jewelry making at the Çatal Hüyük site. Pottery was enormously useful for storage as it did not deteriorate as fast as baskets. However, the Middle East was not the earliest site for pottery. One site in Japan may have produced pottery as early as 10,000 B.C.E. Copper **metallurgy** appears in the Middle East by 6000 B.C.E. Domesticated animals provided food and clothing, but during the neolithic period, women began to spin and weave cloth from animal fur. The differences in numbers and quality of artifacts at house sites in Çatal Hüyük has led archaeologists to theorize that **wealth and social distinctions** began to appear during this period.

Neolithic Culture
(Themes: Religious and Intellectual Developments)

The early farmers began to gain expertise about the natural processes of the earth and the universe. As they gained more knowledge of the seasons and astronomical movements, they began to develop rudimentary calendars. The new knowledge of the natural world affected religion as well. Basic religious values seem to have continued with the earlier fertility worship but they added an interest in the life cycle and the idea of regenerated life as seen in their fields. Thousands of sculptures of gods and goddesses have been found. It is believed that many deities were associated with birth and death whereas other gods and goddesses were associated with animals.

The Origins of Urban Life
(Themes: Demographics, Social Structure, and Trade)

As some settlements thrived due to environmental advantages, they grew into cities that had political and economic prominence over the surrounding region. More complex social and economic relationships appeared as **professional classes** emerged who spent no time at all on agriculture. Priests, political managers, and artists could focus on their work without concern for basic subsistence. Cities affected whole regions as well as their near neighbors. Marketplaces in cities attracted long-distance traders. The increased need to feed the growing populations required military and political control over ever-larger areas. Eventually, their cultural conditions were extended to the new areas as well. Cities arose independently in river valleys like the **Tigris-Euphrates** region of modern day Iraq, the **Nile River** in Egypt, the **Yellow River** valley of northern China, and the **Indus River** valley of northwest India.

Finished reading the chapter? Be sure you can . . .

- Give two or three examples of the human response to climate and geography.
- Describe major migrations in early human history.
- Differentiate between the paleolithic and neolithic eras.
- Describe the agricultural transition.
- Give examples that illustrate the difference between independent origin and cultural diffusion.

Chapter Multiple Choice Questions

1. What specifically separates early neolithic lifestyles from paleolithic lifestyles?
   a. use of meat
   b. use of shelters
   c. use of clothing
   d. use of fire
   e. use of plants

2. What was the chief reason that people settled into agricultural communities?
   a. They wanted to reduce the amount of work to obtain food.
   b. They needed to stop nomadic migrations.
   c. They wanted to be assured of a more regular food source.
   d. It allowed more families to live together.
   e. They could build better shelters for protection from the elements.

3. With regard to the origin of specific agricultural practices, it can be said that agriculture
   a. occurred independently in different regions throughout the world.
   b. was passed from one group to another throughout the world.
   c. developed at the same time in different regions.
   d. was a side effect of intensified trade relationships in cities.
   e. was shared by the originators when they migrated to distant regions.

4. While the earliest development of agriculture occurred in the Middle East, it was not long before it also appeared in
   a. east Asia.
   b. eastern Africa.
   c. south Asia.
   d. central America.
   e. Europe.

5. Although most neolithic peoples domesticated animals for food and clothing, one region never developed a tradition of herding. Which region was this?
   a. Europe
   b. Africa
   c. east Asia
   d. south Asia
   e. North America

6. What made pottery the earliest craft associated with the neolithic period?
    a. Clay was easily available in the Middle East.
    b. Storage baskets had many drawbacks.
    c. They could be used for irrigation as well.
    d. There had been little need to store food in earlier societies.
    e. Pots could be artistic as well as functional.

7. It is presumed by historians that women played the catalyst role in specific areas of neolithic life. The two areas were
    a. herding and cooking.
    b. pottery and religion.
    c. agriculture and textiles.
    d. jewelry making and painting.
    e. social distinctions and education.

8. The first evidence of social stratification appears in
    a. cave paintings.
    b. house sites and graves.
    c. sculpture.
    d. early writings.
    e. stories in current communities.

9. Which metal was the earliest to be successfully mined and fashioned into tools?
    a. iron
    b. bronze
    c. tin
    d. copper
    e. gold

10. The most successful neolithic farming communities began to increase their trade and subsequently
    a. merged peacefully with neighboring communities.
    b. conquered their neighbors creating large kingdoms.
    c. attracted more people.
    d. fell prey to outside conquerors.
    e. practiced more trade than agriculture.

Comprehensive Multiple Choice Questions

1. Which of the following most accurately describes the development of professions?
    a. Nomads settled into permanent communities and needed technology produced by professionals immediately.
    b. Since settled peoples require pots to store grain, they allowed members to become potters as soon as they harvested the first crop.
    c. Migratory peoples brought their priests with them. Once they settled down, the priests were exempt from farming.
    d. Nomads began to farm and settle into communities. Professions developed as the community could release some members from farm labor.
    e. Neolithic potters found sources of clay in the Middle East. They settled into farming communities to provide the farmers with storage containers.

2. An important issue that is debated by historians relates to cultural borrowing or independent origin. In which of the following areas is diffusion the most likely process?
    a. the development of professions
    b. a specific crop found in two places
    c. the idea of class structure
    d. the role of women in society
    e. the way in which people harvest crops

3. The interaction between people and the environment led to similar adoptions of housing, clothing, and agriculture, but what area of a neolithic society would be LEAST affected by the natural world?
    a. religion
    b. childrearing
    c. tools
    d. social status
    e. wealth

Primary Source Questions

A Note on Primary Sources: On the AP Exam, there can be primary sources in the multiple choice section as well as the document-based question. Not all documents will be written, so it is useful to examine the textbook's illustrations and maps closely. It will be helpful to learn to recognize art from different regions.

1. **Examine the two cave paintings on page 20 of your textbook.**
    a. What do the captions say about gender roles? Could there have been any exceptions?
    b. Describe who might have drawn them (point of view).
    c. Do these paintings indicate anything about specific crops or animals?
    d. What else do they indicate about the culture?

2. **Turn to the pottery vessel from Haçilar in Anatolia on page 25 of your textbook.**
    a. Describe the vessel.
    b. Who might have made it? A man? A woman? A professional? An off-duty farmer?
    c. What does it say about work, values, and technological advances?

3. **Refer to Map 1.3, Origins and Early Spread of Agriculture, on pages 22–23 of your textbook.**
    a. Where were the following crops first planted? Millet, potatoes, yams, wheat, peanuts, tomatoes, citrus fruits.
    b. Which regions had no domesticated animals but developed crops?
    c. Which continents did not develop any crops or domesticated animals?

Chapter Multiple Choice Answers

1. **e:** Historians associate the neolithic period with the early stages of agriculture. (p. 19)

2. **c:** The growth of edible crops and domesticated animals ensured a more regular food supply. (p. 19)

3. **a:** Agriculture emerged independently in different regions from 9000 B.C.E. to 3000 B.C.E. (p. 20)

4. **b:** By 9000 B.C.E., agriculture had developed in southwest Asia. (p. 21)

5. **e:** The people of the Americas had hunted all large animals to extinction except in the Andes where llamas were raised. (p. 21)

6. **e:** Paleolithic peoples did not need to store food for long periods, and in nomadic life, pots were too heavy to carry around. (p. 24)

7. **c:** It is believed that women began to nurture plants and also were responsible for the spinning and weaving of animal fibers. (pp. 19, 25)

8. **b:** At Çatal Hüyük, differences in wealth and social status are seen in the quality of house decorations and items in graves. (p. 25)

9. **d:** Soft and malleable even when cold, copper tools are found in many neolithic sites. (p. 25)

10. **c:** Cities developed gradually as towns with the best locations attracted more people. (p. 27)

Comprehensive Multiple Choice Answers

1. **d:** Hunters and gatherers must settle down before they can grow enough food to allow any member of society to be exempt from agriculture. (pp. 24, 25)

2. **b:** Food crops such as rice to India and wheat to China were probably diffused through trade. People must develop their own tools to harvest each specific crop. The role of women generally developed within a single society while class structure and specialized labor occur almost simultaneously. (p. 21)

3. **b:** Nursing and watching over youngsters occurred whether women were engaged in crafts or farming. It was only affected by availability of food. Religion was directly influenced by seasonal changes of the natural world. Tools had to be fashioned from whatever resources were available, such as stone, bone, wood, and metal. Social status was connected to wealth which was derived from the accumulation of farming resources by one individual or family. These properties would be affected by proximity to water, natural fertility of the soil, and availability of rain. (p. 25)

Primary Source Answers

1. Women planted crops and men herded animals. It is possible that young children helped out in either area regardless of gender. From what we understand about early neolithic societies, it is likely that these were drawn by members of the society who had some time on their hands but did not necessarily dedicate their time to art. The animals appear to be cattle, but the crops are indistinguishable. Obviously, these occupations are community activities, not sole occupations. Neither group wears many clothes. Some of the herders are sitting, so it appears that the cattle are very tame and that tending the crops is much more labor-intensive. Thus women have harder jobs than men. (p. 20)

2. This is a pot that has been fashioned into the shape of an animal. Both women and men have been known to be potters but it is not possible to tell the gender of the potter. The sophistication of the design indicates that most likely a professional with practiced skills fashioned the pot. In this neolithic society, labor has become specialized, animals are favored as design motifs, and people are wealthy enough to afford to replace pottery since the head and neck of this vessel would be prone to breakage. (p. 25)

3. a. east Asia, Andean South America, southwest Asia, Amazon River valley, North America, southeast Asia
   b. North America and southeast Asia
   c. Europe and Australia
   (pp. 22–23)

CHAPTER 2

EARLY SOCIETIES IN SOUTHWEST ASIA AND THE INDO-EUROPEAN MIGRATIONS

Before you get started: The AP guidelines point out that students should be able to compare two of the following early civilizations: Mesopotamia, Egypt, the Indus River Valley culture, the Yellow River culture, and the two American societies. It is unlikely that you will be asked to compare Egypt to Mesopotamia because they are in the same region. So, think about similarities and differences as you study. Consider starting a chart or other graphic organizer to help you see the comparisons.

Mesopotamia has some of the earliest archaeological traces of the neolithic period as well as the grand remains of mighty empires. Its location was conducive to agriculture but also subject to natural disasters such as floods and earthquakes. It is the sole early civilization dependent on two rivers rather than one, the Tigris and Euphrates in modern-day Iraq. The Greek roots for Mesopotamia are *Meso* for middle and *potamia* for rivers. In this chapter cultures demonstrate two key concepts in religion: **polytheism** meaning multiple gods and **monotheism** meaning a single god.

THE QUEST FOR ORDER

As the human population grew rapidly due to increased agricultural yield, the administration of cities and states became necessary to handle the political and social affairs of large urban areas.

Mesopotamia: "The Land between the Rivers"
(Themes: Migration and Political Structures)

Around 4000 B.C.E., **Mesopotamia** developed the earliest urban culture in the region between the Tigris and Euphrates rivers. Elaborate **irrigation systems** from the two river sources allowed the Mesopotamians to develop the arid area. Successful farming around the world's earliest city, **Sumer**, fostered its population growth to approximately 100,000 by 3000 B.C.E. Other Semitic groups, such as the Hebrews and Phoenicians, migrated to and settled in the region. Eventually, a dozen Sumerian cities emerged that worked together but were politically separate. Ruled by absolute monarchs, each **city-state** was engaged in tax collection and governance of its population. Primary functions of the state included building palaces, **ziggurats** (temples), irrigation systems, and defensive walls. These projects were so elaborate that they required enormous numbers of laborers who had to be drafted by the state.

The Course of Empire
(Themes: Patterns of Interactions and Political Structures)

As Mesopotamian city-states came into conflict with each other, some extended their control over weaker cities and developed into larger states. The late period of Mesopotamian city-states was punctuated by frequent warfare. Later, other **Semitic peoples** conquered the Sumerian cities and formed regional empires. The primary early Semitic ruler was Sargon of Arkad in the twenty-third century B.C.E., but the more important later ruler was the **Babylonian King Hammurabi** who improved administration with an extensive legal code built on previous regional laws. The foundation of the code was **lex talionis,** or the law of retribution, with punishments tied closely to offenses. So, the loss of an eye between equals demanded the loss of the offender's eye. But the loss of an eye between different classes required more punishment for the lower-class offender and less for the upper-class offender. In reality, judges had some latitude to make their own decisions, but it set a strong precedent for the rule of law.

THE FORMATION OF A COMPLEX SOCIETY AND SOPHISTICATED CULTURAL TRADITIONS

The formation of social classes occurred as the population became very diverse and long-distance trade increased. Small groups of individuals began to accumulate wealth and power that distinguished them from other groups. Social, economic, and political power lay in the hands of males thus forming a patriarchal society. The Mesopotamians devised a system of writing that revolutionized administration and trade.

Economic Specialization and Trade
(Themes: Technology and Economics)

One early development in labor specialization occurred when the Mesopotamians learned how to combine tin and copper into **bronze**. By 4000 B.C.E., they had begun to fashion bronze into weapons. Later on, they developed bronze farm implements that replaced the wood and stone tools. But the expense of the relatively scarce tin and copper required to make bronze gave way to more easily mined and more durable **iron.** With iron technology, the Assyrians were able to conquer the entire region. Mesopotamians also devised extremely efficient transportation with their invention of the **wheel**. They improved sailing vessels so much that by 2300 B.C.E. Mesopotamians traded regularly with distant regions of the Indus Valley, Egypt, and Afghanistan.

The Emergence of a Stratified Patriarchal Society
(Theme: Gender Structure)

Continued accumulation of wealth led to more pronounced **class distinctions** in Mesopotamian cities. **Royal** family members had hereditary status and early monarchs were even considered the children of gods. The **nobility** formed around the monarch with **priests and priestesses** closely connected to them. The role of priests was to intercede with the gods on behalf of the people. But the large temple complexes also brought in revenue and benefited both farmers and craftsmen attached to the religious lands. The lower classes consisted of **free commoners and slaves** with an intermediary class known as **dependent clients** who owned no property but were not slaves. All three lower classes were drafted into building the large construction projects but also engaged in agriculture. The commoners and dependent clients were taxed heavily to support the state and religion. Slaves were prisoners of war, indebted individuals, and convicted criminals who generally worked as domestic servants in wealthy households.

Mesopotamia was a **patriarchal society**. Men dominated public and home life and, legally, had the ability to sell their wives and children into slavery. Other laws also favored men over women. Nevertheless, individual women advised kings, managed large estates, and obtained a formal education that enabled them to become scribes. Women were also shopkeepers, bakers, and weavers. Eventually, men tightened control over women and decreased interactions between women and men outside their families to protect the family fortunes. By 1500 B.C.E., married women began to wear veils outside the home. Much later, this custom was adopted by Muslims in the region.

The Development of Written Cultural Traditions
(Theme: Intellectual Developments)

Around 4500 B.C.E., the Mesopotamians began to develop the world's earliest written language for their commercial transactions and tax collection. The writing tool of **cuneiform** was a wedged-shaped stick used to make marks on tablets of wet clay. Early symbols were pictographs but later phonetic symbols were added. Since cuneiform writing required years of study and education, most educated people became scribes or government officials. The development of writing enabled the Mesopotamians to devise more sophisticated mathematics and sciences as well as to transpose their oral legends like the *Epic of Gilgamesh* into writing. With the advent of advanced math and astronomy, a calendar was devised that broke the year into twelve months and hours into sixty minutes each consisting of sixty seconds. These conventions remain with us today. The Mesopotamians also used complex math to survey their vast agricultural lands.

THE BROADER INFLUENCE OF MESOPOTAMIAN SOCIETY

The Mesopotamians influenced many cultures outside their boundaries by the unique quality of their ideas and occasionally by force. Other societies adopted components of the Mesopotamian culture but maintained their own traditions as well.

Hebrews, Israelites, and Jews
(Themes: Cultural Developments and Changes and Continuities)

The **Hebrews** were **nomadic pasturalists** who lived between Mesopotamia and Egypt but took on more of the cultural attributes of Mesopotamia than Egypt. For instance, early Hebrew law was derived from the principles of Hammurabi's code and tribal governance was abandoned for monarchies. Among the accomplishments of the Hebrews, the world's first permanent adoption of **monotheism** in place of polytheism is most notable. Early Hebrews had recognized the same gods as the Mesopotamians, but after 900 B.C.E., **Moses** embraced a single god, Yahweh. The development of a **written Hebrew script** allowed the history of the people, its belief system, and its legal code to be recorded in the **Torah.** Conquered by the Egyptians, Assyrians, and Babylonians, the Israelites eventually settled in Judea, maintained their monotheistic religion, and became known as **Jews**. Their religion later influenced both Christianity and Islam.

The Phoenicians

Settled in coastal cities along the Mediterranean, the **Phoenicians** developed a thriving trade network. Overland and maritime trade of timber and high-quality manufactured goods resulted in enormous prosperity for this small group. They were particularly well known for a desirable purple dye derived from a shellfish. Eventually, their **advanced ship technology** allowed them to trade as far away as the British Isles and down to the Gulf of Guinea. Like the Hebrews, they adopted Mesopotamian culture, although they remained polytheistic. Their primary contribution to world culture was the development of a twenty-two–symbol writing system based on phonemes where each symbol represented a sound in the Phoenician language. Eventually, the Greeks and Romans would adopt and enlarge upon the world's first completely **phonetic language.**

THE INDO-EUROPEAN MIGRATIONS

The Mesopotamians developed relationships with diverse groups beyond the Middle East. The most significant of these were Indo-Europeans whose migrations across Eurasia profoundly affected world history.

Indo-European Origins
(Themes: Migration and Changes and Continuities

Indo-Europeans were originally herders from the Russian steppes. They domesticated horses about 4000 B.C.E. and once they obtained metallurgy and wheels from the Mesopotamians, they devised carts and chariots. With horse power and speed, the Indo-Europeans spread widely across Eurasia. They considered themselves superior and called themselves "nobility" or **Aryans**.

Indo-European Expansion and Its Effects

As the Indo-European population increased, they spread further away from their homelands. Intermittent migrations occurred over two thousand years of early history. An Indo-European group, the Hittites, spread into the Middle East and conquered regions as far away as Egypt. They adopted the cuneiform writing and the polytheistic gods of Mesopotamia. They greatly refined iron metallurgy and introduced the war chariot. Some also went as far as western China. And many went to Europe, invading the British Isles and the Baltic region as well as the more central areas of Europe. They depended upon agriculture or herding but did not build large states. However, Celts dominated the areas north of the Mediterranean in trade, religion, and agriculture. They also spread into India. The primary legacy of the Indo-Europeans was their language, the ancestor of most European languages and Sanskrit.

Finished reading the chapter? Be sure you can . . .

- Explain the effect of the Tigris and Euphrates geography on Mesopotamian culture.
- Describe the political and class structure of Mesopotamia.
- Discuss the origin and development of monotheism.
- Discuss the origin and development of written language.
- Describe gender relations in Mesopotamia.
- Explain Mesopotamian adoption of metallurgy.
- Identify Mesopotamian art style and subject matter.

Chapter Multiple Choice Questions

1. The most favorable environmental condition that prompted the growth of cities was
   a. a dry climate.
   b. high mountains.
   c. access to fresh water.
   d. rivers.
   e. seasonal climate change.

2. As populations increased, Mesopotamian cities were obligated to protect the welfare of their citizens by
   a. expanding control to the neighboring agricultural areas.
   b. building defensive walls to hold off Indo-European armies.
   c. developing religions so that gods protected the inhabitants of the cities.
   d. refusing to allow canals in urban areas.
   e. organizing smaller political units within the city.

3. While sharing the same language and customs, relations between the late Mesopotamian city-states were
   a. cooperative and neighborly.
   b. kept at a minimum due to distance.
   c. subject to overwhelming authority of Sumer.
   d. degenerated into constant conflict.
   e. easily sustained by trade.

4. In order to maintain an orderly state, Babylonian King Hammurabi developed laws from
   a. earlier Babylonian traditions.
   b. unwritten regional precedents.
   c. his personal ideas of legality.
   d. Mesopotamian legal traditions.
   e. Hebrew legal traditions.

5. Conquering armies were dependent upon new metal technology to best their opponents. Bronze metallurgy took the place of copper because
    a. tin deposits were more common than copper.
    b. bronze is stronger than copper.
    c. most warriors could better afford bronze.
    d. copper could not be used for tools.
    e. bronze was more prized in art.

6. Later the Hittites gained an advantage over Egypt when they used iron technology. Iron metallurgy replaced bronze because
    a. only iron could be made into weapons.
    b. mining for iron is done on the surface of the earth.
    c. bronze is a relatively rare metal.
    d. iron was less expensive.
    e. iron could be used as ballast for Phoenician ships.

7. Mesopotamian long-distance trade expanded to include most areas of the Mediterranean and parts of the Indian Ocean due to
    a. its geographic location.
    b. its alliance with Egypt and India.
    c. the development of improved sailing ships.
    d. reliance on camels for desert travel.
    e. easy access to river travel.

8. Regarding social stratification, Mesopotamians were
    a. egalitarian with just three classes.
    b. dependent on bureaucracy for status.
    c. more fair to their slaves than the dependent clients.
    d. disinterested in an inherited class of nobles.
    e. divided into several distinct classes.

9. Monotheism is the cornerstone of Judaism, Christianity, and Islam. It developed in Mesopotamia due to
    a. the recognition of a single god by Hammurabi.
    b. the beliefs of a separate ethnic group in Mesopotamia.
    c. cultural diffusion from the Egyptian pharoah, Akhenaton.
    d. the acceptance of a single god by the priests.
    e. the development of Christianity.

10. The place of women in Mesopotamian society was
    a. the legal equivalent of slaves.
    b. approximately equal to men.
    c. legally subservient but allowed to participate in public life.
    d. economically subservient to men but legally equal.
    e. a solely domestic role of wife and mother.

Comprehensive Multiple Choice Questions

1. What area of Mesopotamian life deeply influenced both Phoenicians and Hebrews?
    a. weaponry and the art of war
    b. manufacture and distribution of trade items
    c. a society deeply influenced by urban living
    d. a tradition of writing that enabled both worship and trade
    e. adoption and retention of essential religious practices

2. Increased patriarchal forms of gender status appear to evolve in accordance with the sophistication of society. Compared with earlier communities, the high status of males may be the result of
   a. the relative importance of wealth in a society.
   b. men's physical ability to act as farmers.
   c. an innate resentment of women as nurturers.
   d. a failure to recognize women as manufacturers.
   e. the lack of equal education.

3. The relationship between settled peoples such as the Sumerians and nomadic groups such as the Indo-Europeans was a state of interdependency that was chiefly reliant on
   a. tolerance and acceptance of differences in customs, such as legal codes and women's status.
   b. acceptance and adaptation of aspects of technology, religion, and social order by the nomads.
   c. a willingness on the part of the nomads to settle down into separate communities.
   d. a strict separation of the societies outside of trade and commerce.
   e. the adoption of the settled society's belief system with a rejection of the nomad's religion.

Primary Source Questions

1. **Refer to the painting, the Royal Standard of Ur, 2700 B.C.E., on page 30 of your textbook.**
   a. What type of professions are represented?
   b. Who might have drawn this?
   c. Does dress indicate different social status? Does anything else?
   d. Does the painting demonstrate any other cultural values?

2. **Examine the basalt stele of Hammurabi, c. 1750 B.C.E., on page 37 of your textbook.**
   a. What does the stele have in common with the Royal Standard of Ur?
   b. How has the style of dress changed from the Royal Standard?
   c. What impression does Hammurabi make? Why would this impression be important?

Chapter Multiple Choice Answers

1. **c:** The early Mesopotamians developed methods to irrigate their agricultural fields with water from the Tigris and the Euphrates. (p. 33)

2. **a:** Since the citizens were dependent on crops from outside the city walls, Mesopotamian governments expanded to include farming areas surrounding the cities. (p. 34)

3. **d:** Cities competed constantly with each other for political power. (p. 36)

4. **d:** Hammurabi borrowed liberally from Mesopotamian predecessors. (p. 37)

5. **b:** Bronze implements are stronger than copper or tin. (p. 39)

6. **d:** Iron deposits are more common than tin or copper deposits. (p. 40)

7. **c:** Invention of the wheel and improved sailing vessels facilitated long-distance trade. (p. 40)

8. **e:** Mesopotamian society was divided into a nobility, a priestly class, free commoners, dependent clients, and slaves. (p. 41)

9. **b:** The Hebrews under Moses embraced the concept of one god, Yahweh. (p. 46)

10. **c:** Regardless of legal status, women served as advisers to rulers, scribes, shopkeepers, midwives, and textile producers. (p. 42)

Comprehensive Multiple Choice Answers

1. **d:** Evidence that the Hebrews adopted writing can be found in the compiled teachings of the Torah; the Phoenicians adapted cuneiform into a simplified set of phonetic symbols. (pp. 47, 49)

2. **a:** As societies became more complex and accumulation of wealth determined family status, women became increasingly restricted in society. (p. 42)

3. **b:** The most important nomadic groups associated with the Mesopotamians were the Hittites and the Hebrews. They adopted components of Mesopotamian innovations such as iron metallurgy and legal codes but later revised them into more appropriate societal needs such as war chariots and Hebrew law. (pp. 45, 53)

Primary Source Answers

1. It is evident that there are servants, porters, wealthy men, cattlemen, fishermen, a horse trader, and one foreigner (with the beard and the hat). It is likely that this was painted by a court artist specifically for the king. All are dressed similarly in short skirts except the foreigner. The only indication of status is that two men are sitting in chairs. Apparently, the fashion is for all men to be shaved on their faces and their heads. The foreigner indicates long-distance trade. The artistic style of the Mesopotamians is linear with all people and animals in profile. Finally, large eyes seem to have importance. (p. 30)

2. In both art pieces, the figures are in profile and the higher-status person is sitting. It is apparent that the Babylonians wore full body covering and had facial hair and hats, like the foreigner in the Royal Standard. Hammurabi's figure is wider, more open, and emanates power. Since the stele was a memorial to Hammurabi's laws, he needed to appear authoritative. (pp. 30 and 37)

CHAPTER 3

EARLY AFRICAN SOCIETIES AND THE BANTU MIGRATIONS

Before you get started: No matter how fascinating you found ancient Egyptian culture to be in middle school, it will be a very minimal part of the AP Exam so don't overdo your memorization of its terms. Nevertheless, it is included in the AP guidelines as one of the classical cultures that you may compare with another. As for the sub-Saharan history of Bantu Africa, our knowledge is expanding all the time. Where there was once the belief that Africa was a dark continent until discovered by Europeans, we now know that it has marvelous archaeological sites that can corroborate the essential truths in many oral history traditions. These sites demonstrate dynamic kingdoms with early technological knowledge and complex class structures. Furthermore, once Islam arrived, some so-called Arab writers have been rediscovered as educated African Muslims. The study of African history today is as dynamic as that of any region in the world.

EARLY AGRICULTURAL SOCIETY IN AFRICA

While Egypt was the most prominent of early African culture, its southern neighbor, Nubia, up the Nile River, was just as complex and sophisticated if less prosperous.

Climatic Change and the Development of Agriculture in Africa
(Themes: Demographics, Political Structures, and Changes and Continuities)

By 10,000 B.C.E., the Sahara had became a grassland with rivers and lakes that sustained Sudanic peoples. Within a thousand years they had settled down to grow sorghum, followed by the cultivation of yams, gourds, watermelons, and cotton. They took on the **domestication of sheep and goats** from the Middle East. By 500 B.C.E. they had organized themselves into small monarchies with semi-divine kings. Their religion reflected the values of an agricultural society. Soon after, climatic change made the region hotter and drier so that people were forced to gather around the two remaining bodies of water, Lake Chad and the Nile River. When the **Nile's annual spring floods** receded, a layer of fertile soil was left that sustained agriculture in its valley.

Egypt and Nubia: "Gifts of the Nile"
(Themes: Economics and Technology)

The lower Nile had a much larger floodplain than the upper Nile so Egyptians were able to take better advantage of the annual flooding than the Nubian people to the south. As Sudanic peoples moved north into the region, they brought cattle and donkeys, as well as African crops while the Egyptians borrowed grains like wheat and barley from the Mesopotamians. Eventually, **irrigation** methods improved and the Egyptians were able to expand their farming to higher areas away from the Nile. These fields required plowing and systems of dikes. And by 4000 B.C.E., there were large numbers of Egyptian villages along the Nile.

The Unification of Egypt
(Themes: Political Structures, Changes and Continuities, and Patterns of Interactions)

Both Egyptians and Nubians began as small bickering kingdoms, not unlike Mesopotamian city-states. But around 3100 B.C.E., a minor official named **Menes** unified Egypt into one large state with a centralized government. The **Old Kingdom pharoahs** were considered gods and deserving of massive tombs, so they built the pyramids to honor their remains. The Old Kingdom lasted until 2040 B.C.E. and was followed by the **Middle Kingdom.**

Nubian states remained small and decentralized but closely intertwined with the Egyptian state. There were five military campaigns to conquer the Nubians. Pushed south by the attacks, later Nubian leaders established the strong state of Kush 700 kilometers south of Aswan. Interactions between the kingdom of Kush and Egypt became more cordial with trade, diplomatic regions, and Egyptian exploration. Nubian mercenaries became common in Egyptian armies and were assimilated into Egyptian society.

Turmoil and Empire
(Themes: War, Political Structures, and Changes and Continuities)

Usually protected by vast deserts and the Mediterranean, Egypt was invaded once by the **Hyksos**, a Semitic people, at the end of the Middle Kingdom. Eventually the Egyptians drove them out and formed the **New Kingdom** in 1550 B.C.E. The Egyptian bureaucracy vastly expanded in complexity during this period while the new pharaohs built many temples, palaces, and statues instead of pyramids. The New Kingdom reached imperial status when it conquered the coastal regions of the Mediterranean and down through Nubia. After the New Kingdom, Egypt began to decline and the upper Nile fell to Nubian forces in 1100 B.C.E. Assyrians from Mesopotamia invaded the northern Nile valley in the seventh century B.C.E., starting a pattern of continual foreign domination.

THE FORMATION OF COMPLEX SOCIETIES AND SOPHISTICATED CULTURAL TRADITIONS

Specialized labor and social stratification emerged with the growth of cities along the Nile. Due to its advantageous location, Egypt was a very prosperous society with complex religious and writing systems.

The Emergence of Cities and Stratified Societies
(Themes: Changes and Continuities and Gender and Social Structures)

Several large cities developed in Egypt that served as political, cultural, and economic centers. Among them **Memphis** and **Thebes** were notable for their role in politics. The Egyptians recognized one supreme ruler, the Pharoah, so unlike Mesopotamia they never developed a noble class. Instead, the military and bureaucracy took over high social positions. The society also included an urban middle class as well as peasants and slaves. Nubian society developed similarly.

Egyptian women were relegated to lesser roles at home and in public although they had more authority than Mesopotamian women. Nevertheless, some Egyptian women gained power as regents to young rulers and one, **Queen Hapshetsut**, even attained the throne as a co-ruler. But a woman as ruler was so disconcerting for Egyptians that artists depicted her with a beard. Women in Egypt also became priestesses and, in some cases, educated scribes. In Nubia, however, there appear to have been many female rulers.

Economic Specialization and Trade
(Themes: Economics and Technology)

The Egyptians were slow to adopt metal tools and weapons, and only did so after the invasion of the Hyksos. Sub-Saharan Africans independently developed techniques of iron mining and metallurgy as early as 900 B.C.E. Most travel in Egypt occurred by boat but long-distance trade routes across land also existed. Later, the Egyptians adopted wheeled vehicles from the Middle East. Thriving trade networks developed to obtain luxury goods from Nubia, the eastern coast of the Mediterranean, and down through the Red Sea to Ethiopia. Prized Egyptian goods such as cotton, pottery, and wine were traded in Nubia and Ethiopia for African ivory, ebony, animal skins, gold, and slaves. The Egyptians had to import trees from the Middle East because they had few of their own.

Early Writing in the Nile Valley
(Theme: Intellectual Developments)

Egyptian writing, possibly borrowed from the Mesopotamians, appeared in Egypt around 3200 B.C.E. Written on paper-like **papyrus** sheets and carved into monuments, **hieroglyphs** were so cumbersome that an abbreviated form existed for everyday records. Eventually, the Egyptians adopted the Greek alphabet. Numerous papyrus manuscripts exist because of Egypt's exceptionally dry weather. As in Mesopotamia, professional scribes had a prestigious position in society. Early Nubian writing was in hieroglyph form. Eventually, Nubian scribes developed an alphabetic script of their own.

The Development of Organized Religious Traditions
(Theme: Religious Developments)

The Egyptians were **polytheistic** although some deities such as sun gods **Amon** and **Re** became more important. The cult of **Osiris**, lord of the underworld, became associated with the Nile's annual flooding and the crop cycle of seed generation, harvest, and replanting. Massive temple complexes that employed hundreds of people supported the worship of specific gods. A brief period of monotheism occurred during the reign of Akhenaten in 1473 B.C.E. but that was quickly suppressed by later pharaohs with the guidance of the priesthood. Mummification existed to help the Egyptians into immortality. At first it was only available to the pharaohs but by the New Kingdom many wealthy families had also taken up the practice. The Nubians also worshipped multiple deities and eventually adopted some of the Egyptian gods.

BANTU MIGRATIONS AND EARLY AGRICULTURAL SOCIETIES OF SUB-SAHARAN AFRICA

Bantu-speaking peoples are presumed to have migrated into most regions of sub-Saharan Africa and established agricultural communities.

The Dynamics of Bantu Expansion
(Theme: Demographics)

The **Bantu** language originated in west Africa around 4000 B.C.E. The earliest speakers settled along rivers and cultivated **yams** and **oil palms**. With the ability to travel by canoe and a growing population due to successful agricultural practices, Bantu speakers began to spread across Africa and, by 1000 B.C.E., they inhabited most of the regions south of the equator. Their progress was not in mass migrations but rather incremental and intermittent spurts of migration. After 1000 B.C.E., **iron metallurgy** hastened the rate of migration because the Bantu had the increased technology to clear forests and prepare soil for agriculture. Today, the language itself has differentiated into more than five hundred distinct languages, each representing a different ethnic group.

Early Agricultural Societies of Sub-Saharan Africa
(Themes: Economics, Political Structures, Social Structure, and Religious Developments)

Along with the language, Bantu methods of agriculture were spread into sub-Saharan Africa, bringing new crops and domesticated animals to wide regions of Africa. Most Bantu speakers lived in agricultural communities of several hundred individuals ruled by chiefs. Within the society, there were also **age sets**, groups of individuals about the same age, who wielded considerable political and military power.

Bantu speakers believed in a creator god but primarily worshipped their ancestors and local spirits. It was necessary to keep these deities happy or disaster might occur. Bantu religious beliefs were quite flexible so when Bantus encountered different religious beliefs, components were incorporated into the belief system.

Finished reading the chapter? Be sure you can . . .

- Explain the effect of the Nile on Egyptian culture.
- Describe the social and political structures of Egypt.
- Explain the basic tenets of Egyptian polytheism and its integration into politics.
- Describe the extent of Egyptian trade and its trading partners.
- Identify Egyptian art style and subject matter.

Chapter Multiple Choice Questions

1. Egyptians viewed the Nile as a
   a. persistent barrier to trade.
   b. source of destructive floods.
   c. problem that could be solved by technology.
   d. benevolent source of a prosperous society.
   e. protective obstacle to invaders.

2. Egypt was unified under Menes when he formed a
   a. decentralized government.
   b. series of city-states.
   c. coalition with the Nubians.
   d. defensive alliance with other Egyptian kingdoms.
   e. centralized government born of conquest.

3. Rulers in the New Kingdom demonstrated their power and authority by
   a. building pyramids.
   b. constructing a network of roads.
   c. building temples and palaces.
   d. eliminating the nobility.
   e. destroying all traces of earlier pharoahs.

4. Since Egypt had an all-powerful divine ruler, rather than inherited nobility, the Egyptian ruling class was comprised of
   a. wealthy merchants.
   b. the military and bureaucrats.
   c. relatives of the pharoah.
   d. a priestly class.
   e. civil servants.

5. Despite the frequent presence of female regents and the acceptance of women in other public roles, Queen Hapshepsut unsettled Egyptian society so much that
   a. the military overthrew her.
   b. priests refused to deify her.
   c. peasants rejected her.
   d. artists depicted her as a male.
   e. neighboring kingdoms refused to acknowledge her.

6. Egyptians engaged in long-distance trade
   a. well before unification by Menes.
   b. only after the invasion of the Hyksos.
   c. with the advent of unification.
   d. as the pharoahs of the New Kingdom required more precious items than before.
   e. to gain rare tools used in agriculture.

7. In what way was Egyptian writing less cumbersome than cuneiform?
    a. Hieroglyphs are phonetic while cuneiforms are pictographs.
    b. There are fewer symbols to learn for proficiency.
    c. The ease of reading hieroglyphs negated the necessity for scribes.
    d. Hieroglyphs are written on papyrus rather than clay tablets.
    e. Hieroglyphs could be used for informal events.

8. Unlike the Hebrew beliefs in Mesopotamia, Egyptian monotheism was
    a. a long, slow development revolving around a series of kings.
    b. unsustainable due to its competition from the priests of other dieties.
    c. promoted by one man rather than a group of people.
    d. borrowed from neighbors of the upper Nile in Nubia.
    e. an adaptation of earlier beliefs that only the sun god existed.

9. The origin of the Bantu language is believed to be in
    a. east Africa where it is a descendant of Arab languages.
    b. the Sahara under the influence of the Egyptians.
    c. south Africa among the hunter-gatherers of the Kalahari.
    d. Sudanic Africa as the Nubians expanded their power.
    e. west Africa where populations grew enough to spread out.

10. What was the pattern of the expansion of Bantu culture?
    a. primarily through conquest of neighboring communities
    b. primarily through trade with the regions of Sudanic Africa
    c. by mass migrations of people escaping climate changes
    d. in small bursts of expansion coinciding with an increased food supply
    e. intermittently through colonization in regions of agricultural prosperity

Comprehensive Multiple Choice Questions

1. While Mesopotamia met its primary challenge by decentralizing, Egypt's response was to unify and remain so during most of its history. What was this challenge?
    a. to satisfy increasing stratification in the social structure
    b. the necessity of developing a large defensive military
    c. efforts to support large scale agriculture
    d. management of complex government bureaucracies
    e. control of several different ethnic groups

2. Egyptian history is traditionally organized around three kingdoms. What institutional patterns changed between the three?
    a. Government structure moved towards decentralization.
    b. Administrations began to build enormous dams to control flooding on the Nile.
    c. Egypt moved toward a nobility to accommodate successful bureaucrats.
    d. Egyptian governments moved toward expansion into neighboring lands.
    e. Art styles began to incorporate more Mesopotamian and Nubian motifs.

3. It is apparent from archaeological sites that sub-Saharan peoples developed iron metallurgy independently. What would possibly lead historians to the conclusion that iron metallurgy was not a borrowed technology from southwest Asia?
   a. The remains are dated from successive time periods proving that the knowledge traveled from one region to another.
   b. There were known trade routes through the Sudan that could have brought iron metallurgy to the region.
   c. Early iron production sites in Africa are far beyond the Nile River valley and date to a period close to its adoption in Egypt.
   d. The amount of iron ore and the numbers of early sites indicate spread across sub-Saharan Africa by 500 B.C.E.
   e. Since the Egyptians obtained iron technology from the Hittites, it must have spread from Egypt to Nubia and into the Bantu-speaking regions of Africa.

Primary Source Questions

1. **Examine the funerary sculpture from Upper Egypt, 2200–2000 B.C.E., on page 67 of your textbook.**
   a. From this painting, what can you surmise about the relationship between Egyptians and Nubians?
   b. To what extent did Egypt tolerate foreigners?
   c. Who may have painted this?

2. **Examine Map 3.3, Bantu Migrations, 2000 B.C.E.–1000 C.E., on page 81 of your textbook.**
   a. Describe the pace of the origin of the Bantu.
   b. How did the migration of the language and culture proceed?
   c. Was this a rapid migration?

Chapter Multiple Choice Answers

1. **d:** The Egyptians had a highly productive agriculture dependent on annual flooding. Greek historian Herodotus referred to Egypt as a "Gift of the Nile." (p. 62)

2. **e:** Menes, a minor official from upper Egypt, conquered the northern kingdoms of the Nile River valley and formed a centralized government from Memphis. (p. 63)

3. **c:** New Kingdom pharoahs did not build pyramids as Old Kingdom pharoahs had, but built other monumental structures to demonstrate strength and authority. (p. 67)

4. **b:** Egyptians did not have an inherited nobility but individuals could attain high status as a member of the military or the bureaucracy. (p. 71)

5. **d:** It was necessary to add a traditional male beard to her costume in paintings. (p. 72)

6. **a:** As early as 4000 B.C.E., Egyptians were trading intermittently up the Nile with the Nubians. (p. 73)

7. **d:** Papyrus is similar to paper so it could be transported and stored more easily than clay tablets. (p. 75)

8. **b:** Once Akhenaton had died, the traditional worship of Amon-Re resumed its status. (p. 78)

9. **e:** Population increase due to successful farming probably drove the expansion of Bantu peoples into other regions. (p. 81)

10. **e:** The Bantu migration pattern resembles Indo-European expansion in its gradual spread of culture and language as groups settled into new areas. (p. 81)

Comprehensive Multiple Choice Answers

1. **c:** Both societies were dependent upon massive agricultural efforts to support burgeoning populations. Unification in Egypt allowed one authority to tighten control over its agricultural policies. The New Kingdom's elaborate bureaucracy even included separate departments to deal with agricultural affairs, while in Mesopotamia, Sumer developed into a city-state in order to protect its agricultural lands. (pp. 67, 34)

2. **d:** The Old Kingdom was focused on unification even though it invaded the Nubians on the Upper Nile several times. The Middle Kingdom expanded trade and diplomacy with cultures as far away as Syria but the New Kingdom conquered portions of the eastern Mediterranean and became an imperial power. (p. 67)

3. **c:** Although the textbook does not explain why African iron production was not a borrowed technology, you can deduce that all the other answers would explain borrowing rather than independent origin. Only C posits a conclusion that time and distance count in terms of independent origin. If the distance is very great and the time is relatively short, independent origin is a more likely scenario. (p. 73)

Primary Source Answers

1. Painted by a professional artist, this funerary art indicates that Egypt worked closely with Nubia. Egypt appears to have been a tolerant society that allowed the intermarriage of its citizens with foreigners. It is also apparent that Egyptians afforded their foreign mercenaries the same lifestyle as their own citizens. (p. 67)

2. The origin of the Bantu is southwest of Lake Chad in west Africa. Bantu culture migrated east to the region of Lake Victoria and southward along the coasts of east and west Africa. No, this migration occurred over 3000 years. (p. 81)

CHAPTER 4

EARLY SOCIETIES IN SOUTH ASIA

Before you get started: You have made it through three chapters and the details may begin to be overwhelming. Do not panic and do not try to memorize everything; remember the course themes listed at the start of Chapter 1? If not, go back and review them. Those big categories should structure your thinking as you read and provide a scaffold for your new learning.

By the time you finish working through this chapter, you should be able to discuss examples from Harappan and Aryan societies for each theme. Try making your own chart or visual organizer to record your thinking. Remember, this course is based on large pictures and examples, not every minute detail. Use the boldfaced words to create a vocabulary of terms you can use to address each theme.

HARAPPAN SOCIETY

The earliest known urban society in India, known as **Harappan society,** developed c. 7000 B.C.E. along the Indus River. The availability of fresh water and fertile silt for crops produced increasing agricultural output of wheat, barley, and cotton as well as land suitable for herding cattle, sheep, and goats; the ensuing rapidly growing population spread throughout the Indian subcontinent by 3000 B.C.E. The developments in Harappan society are difficult for scholars to trace because the earliest Harappan settlement remains lie under the water table and because there are no deciphered written records. Harappan society declined after 1900 B.C.E.; scholars are still unclear as to reasons for its demise.

Foundations of Harappan Society and Culture
(Themes: Trade, Political Structure, and Cultural Developments)

Harappan society, which embraced much of modern-day Pakistan and northern India, was considerably larger than either Mesopotamian or Egyptian society. Its agricultural economy, which relied on the somewhat erratic flooding of the Indus River, produced food and cotton which were traded both domestically and with the peoples of Persia and Mesopotamia by following the Arabian Sea coastline.

Despite the size and splendor of the two largest cities, **Mohenjo-daro** and **Harappa,** scholars have no evidence concerning the Harappan political system. Archeological evidence from those two cities suggests that they had large populations and served as economic and political centers.

Harappan economic wealth reached its high point between 2500 B.C.E. and 2000 B.C.E. Archaeological evidence reveals a diverse economic, occupational, and social structure. Without access to a deciphered written language, scholars depend on statues, illustrations, and carved seals to understand Harappan society. Like all known early civilizations, their **polytheistic religion** appears to have centered around creation and procreation.

Harappan society began to decline c. 1900 B.C.E. Ecological degradation, especially deforestation and desertification, as well as natural catastrophes, severely reduced agricultural output; by 1500 B.C.E, most Harappan cities had collapsed.

THE INDO-EUROPEAN MIGRATIONS AND EARLY ARYAN INDIA

As Harappan society declined, **nomadic** and **pastoral peoples** who called themselves **Aryans** migrated through the Hindu Kush and established small herding and agricultural communities throughout northern India. There is little indication that this movement was an invasion or in any significant way contributed to the destruction of Harappan society. The interaction of Aryan and Dravidian peoples laid the foundations of modern Indian society.

The Aryans and India
(Theme: Demographics)

Historically, the Aryans were pastoralists who practiced very limited agriculture. They measured their wealth in sheep, goats, and, especially, cattle, even using them to calculate the price of other goods. Horses were also valued in Aryan culture, though the Aryans had to import them from central Asia. Unlike the Harappans, the early Aryans did not have a written language but relied on oral tradition using Sanskrit to preserve extensive collections of religious and literary works known as the Vedas, a term which means "wisdom." The *Rig Veda*, the most important of these works, was committed to writing c. 600 B.C.E. Today, scholars use the Vedas to understand early Aryan society in India, the Vedic age.

Life during the Vedic age was characterized by competition for land and resources as reflected in the chief god of the Aryan pantheon, Indra. The Aryans fought the Dravidians, and among themselves, attacking cities and ruining essential irrigation systems. The Aryans did not have a state or common government but were controlled by chiefdoms dominated by a **raja** who governed in collaboration with a council of village elders. Raiding for cattle and horses was common.

As part of the early Indo-European migration c. 1500 B.C.E., the Aryans established themselves in the Punjab, then spread east and south establishing communities throughout the Indian subcontinent. During this era, they learned how to work with iron to make axes and plows that increased their food production, spurred their population growth, and encouraged them to push further into India. By 1000 B.C.E., they had settlements between the Himalayan foothills and the Ganges River and by 500 B.C.E., they had migrated as far south as the northern Deccan plateau. The Aryans established permanent communities throughout these regions, began to rely more on agriculture, and gradually lost their tribal political organization. The traditional chiefdoms developed into regional kingdoms that built permanent capitals, depended on professional administrators, and became the most common form of political organization on the subcontinent.

Origins of the Caste System
(Theme: Social Structure)

The Aryans' social hierarchy, which rested on sharp, hereditary distinctions between individuals and groups according to their occupations and roles in society, served to maintain order and stability and became the foundation of the caste system. This strict system of social order developed gradually as growing social complexity and interaction with the Dravidians prompted the Aryans to shift from their traditionally simple distinctions of herders, cultivators, warrior chiefs, and priests to a hierarchy based on Aryan or Dravidian ancestry. The Sanskrit term for these social distinctions is *varna,* which suggests that the original distinctions made have been based on skin color, though over time color distinctions became less clear.

By 1000 B.C.E., there were four main varnas: (1) *brahmins* who were the priests, (2) *kshatriyas* who were the warriors and aristocrats, (3) *vaishyas* who were the cultivators, artisans, and merchants, and (4) *shudras* who were the landless peasants and serfs. Another category was added at the end of the Vedic age, the **untouchables,** whose duties were so unpleasant or dirty that they were strictly separated from the other varnas. By the end of the Vedic age, caste distinctions served as the principal foundation of social stability.

Over time, the varna hierarchy expanded to include thousands of subcastes known as *jati* that were strictly tied to occupation. Elaborate behavioral rules developed for each jati with severe consequences for violation of jati rules. Achieving upward mobility, though very difficult and thus infrequent, did dissipate some tensions.

Development of Patriarchal Society
(Theme: Gender Structures)

Aryan social order during the Vedic era was also characterized by a strict *patriarchal system.* Gender distinctions were maintained by the Aryan tradition of recognizing descent through the male line. Women had no public authority, could only inherit land if there were no male heirs, could not preside over family religious rituals, and received almost no formal education. The *Lawbook of Manu* describes these rules for proper moral behavior and social relationships, stressing that the most important duties for women were to bear children and maintain the home. The practice of *sati,* the sacrifice of widows on their husband's funeral pyre, though never widely practiced in India, was considered a powerful illustration of a woman's devotion to her husband. It is an extreme example of patriarchy.

RELIGION IN THE VEDIC ERA

The foundations of Hinduism are found in the fusion of Aryan and Dravidian traditions.

Aryan Religion
(Theme: Patterns of Interactions)

The Aryans were polytheistic with gods for the sun, the sky, the moon, fire, health, and other natural phenomena. *Indra,* the Aryan god of war and weather, was the most important of those gods, reflecting the difficulties of survival in Vedic society. From his heavenly palace, *Varuna,* another important Vedic god, oversaw the behavior of humans and preserved the order of the universe; his role was to ensure ethical behavior with the threat of disease, suffering, and death for evildoers and entrance to heaven called the World of the Fathers for virtuous souls.

Early Aryans practiced extensive ritual sacrifice as a way to gain divine support, win military battles, produce large families, ensure long life, and guarantee abundant cattle herds. These sacrifices could become quite elaborate, requiring hundreds of animals from the Aryans' herds, constant prayer and attention from the Brahmins (priests), and the ingestion of drugs by participants to manifest the gods' appearance and their positive response.

Over time, Aryan religious practice changed dramatically. By 800 B.C.E., **ascetic practices,** mystical interactions with religious texts, living in nature, and study with a revered teacher, became the more ideal form of religious practice. This evolution of religious thought included changes in beliefs as well as in practice as the Aryans drew inspiration from traditional Dravidian religion. The ideas of transmigration and reincarnation intrigued the Aryans and fostered an interest in understanding the fate of souls after death.

The Blending of Aryan and Dravidian Values
(Themes: Religious Developments and Changes and Continuities)

The *Upanishads* began to appear in the late Vedic Age, 800–400 B.C.E. These works, which often took the form of dialogues between a sage and his disciples, sought to explore ultimate truth and knowledge in an ideal world that transcends this earth by introducing the concepts of *samsara* and *karma* to explain how each person exists as part of *Brahman,* the universal soul. Brahman is the permanent foundation of all living things, according to the Upanishad's explanations, and, unlike the physical world, is unchanging, eternal, and the only genuine reality. The authors of the Upanishads believed individual souls were born into the physical world many times and in many forms but their highest goal was to escape this cycle of birth, death, and rebirth and join with Brahman.

The state of rejoining Brahman was known as *moksha;* it signified the soul's permanent liberation from reincarnation. Though difficult, moksha could be attained through asceticism and meditation, which would separate the individual from the physical world of change, illusion, and incarnation. Later, both

Greek philosophers and Christian theologians would seek to explain a separation between the physical world and a spiritual realm.

The Upanishads called for **high ethical standards** by discouraging any and all personal traits which indicated an excessive attachment to the material world and insufficient focus on union with the universal soul. They advocated personal integrity, self-knowledge, and a respect for all living things. Yet, these teachings from the Upanishads can be interpreted as a cynical ideology designed to justify the social inequalities of the caste system by encouraging individuals to observe their caste and jati rules despite hardships and inequities in hopes of enjoying a more positive incarnation in the future.

Finished reading the chapter? Be sure you can . . .

- Describe the basic features of early Harappan civilization including geography, culture, social structure, states, and political identity.
- Compare and contrast Harappan civilization with Egypt and Mesopotamia especially in terms of social, political, and gender structures. (See Chapters 2 and 3)
- Analyze the changes in demography in the Indus Valley with the decline of Harappan civilization and with the coming of the Aryans as part of the Indo-European invasions c. 1500 B.C.E.
- Describe the nature of patriarchy in Harappan and Aryan traditions.
- Explain the basic features of Dravidian and Aryan religious structures which became the basis of Hinduism.

Chapter Multiple Choice Questions

1. Why is it difficult for scholars to follow the development of Harappan society in great detail?
   a. Constant invasion destroyed large cities and significant documents.
   b. Silt deposits and desertification have made earliest settlements unexplorable.
   c. Aryan invasions destroyed all written records of Harappan civilization.
   d. Erratic flooding forced constant movement between cities.
   e. Their pictographic written language is still undeciphered.

2. The Indus River was most like what other river in its origins and its deposition of silt?
   a. Tigris
   b. Euphrates
   c. Nile
   d. Jordan
   e. Congo

3. The most likely cause for the decline of Harappan society after 1900 B.C.E. was
   a. invasion by Aryan pastoralists.
   b. the trade war with Egypt.
   c. constant civil war between the two largest cities.
   d. deforestation and desertification.
   e. disease and plague resulting from overpopulation.

4. The Vedas were originally
   a. transmitted orally between generations using Sanskrit.
   b. spoken in Prakrit which later evolved into Hindi.
   c. written on papyrus leaves and preserved in tombs.
   d. carved into clay tablets using cuneiform characters.
   e. business records, like all forms of early writing.

5. Which statement is true about relations between the Aryans and the Dravidian peoples in the period 1500–500 B.C.E.?
    a. The religious differences between the two peoples caused constant strife.
    b. The similarity in social structure helped create ties between the two groups.
    c. The competition for land and resources caused intermittent conflict.
    d. The presence of a single strong ruler provided protection for the Dravidians and contained the Aryans.
    e. The matrilineal traditions of each group made intermarriage ideal.

6. The Aryan political structure changed from the rajas who ruled with a council to kingdoms ruled by regional chiefs as a result of
    a. their interaction with the larger Dravidian cities.
    b. the Aryans settling into permanent agricultural communities.
    c. the strict social restrictions of the caste system.
    d. the need for protection from nomadic invasions.
    e. the threat of nomadic invasions from northern Asia.

7. During the early Vedic era, social distinctions were based on
    a. Dravidian or Aryan ancestry.
    b. the number of cattle a family owned.
    c, the ability to read and write Sanskrit.
    d. a person's mother's family line.
    e. an individual's occupation and roles in society.

8. The Aryan patriarchal social order was described in the *Lawbook of Manu* which advised
    a. women to obey the laws of dharma so they could achieve moksha with their husbands and families.
    b. men to instruct their wives in the tradition of sati to ensure good karma for generations.
    c. men to discipline their wives, harshly if necessary, to protect their family's reputation in the community.
    d. women that their most important duty was to bear children and maintain wholesome homes for their families.
    e. women to commit sati as a way of cleansing their karma.

9. According to the Upanishads, what would bring understanding of Brahman?
    a. proper instruction using dialogs between a sage and students
    b. ritual sacrifice of sheep and goats but not cows
    c. specific rites and practices taught by the eldest male in the family
    d. marriage into a higher varna, the creation of large families and especially the birth of sons
    e. study at a center of higher learning like a college or university

10. How did the teachings regarding samsara and karma affect the caste system?
    a. Both promoted the ideals of hard work and upward mobility which undermined the concept of the caste system.
    b. Both explained why individuals were born into certain castes and encouraged individuals to observe their caste duties in hopes of achieving an honorable future incarnation.
    c. Samsara explained the superficial nature of the material world while karma justified the needs of the untouchables for salvation.
    d. Samsara explained the inequalities within society while karma offered liberation from the physical pains of the caste system.
    e. By the time the caste system had fully developed, samsara and karma were no longer valid teachings.

Comprehensive Multiple Choice Questions

1. During the period 3500–500 B.C.E., many Indo-European peoples built powerful states based on iron weaponry and horse-based military technology. Which of the following Indo-European peoples was the exception to this model?
   a. Medes
   b. Persians
   c. Celts
   d. Aryans
   e. Hittites

2. The gender relationships in Vedic India were LEAST like what other river valley civilization?
   a. Mesopotamia
   b. Egypt
   c. Hwang He
   d. Phoenicia
   e. Assyria

3. The Nile and the Indus rivers are similar in that both
   a. draw their waters from the melting waters of the Hindu Kush and Himalayas.
   b. consistently flood in predictable cycles and amounts.
   c. change course and form new channels to the sea.
   d. deposit large amounts of silt as they move through the lowlands.
   e. rise in the highlands and flow north before emptying into the Mediterranean Sea.

Primary Source Questions

1. **Read *Sources from the Past: The* Rig Veda *on the Origins of Castes,* on page 98 of your textbook.**
   a. How does this poem reflect the interests of the Brahmins who composed it?
   b. Why might this hymn include so much animal imagery?

2. **Read *Sources from the Past: The* Mundaka Upanishad *on the Nature of Brahman* on page 102 of your textbook.**
   a. How is the Brahman described as not human?
   b. How is metaphor used as a means to describe Brahman?

Chapter Multiple Choice Answers

1. **e:** While the first portion of choice "b" is a correct statement, the desertification element is not true; this statement would be correct if it said "a rising water table" instead of "desertification." The best answer provided is "e" because the lack of a key to unlock the Harappan writing system forces historians to rely primarily on archeological evidence and keeps the wealth of written records hidden. (p. 88)

2. **c:** Though not predictable like the Nile, the Indus River begins in highlands by the accumulation of snow and rain moisture, flows rapidly toward the lower elevations, and deposits its rich silt as it moves through the lowlands. (p. 89)

3. **d:** Ecological degradation is considered to be the primary reason for the decline of Harappan society, specifically deforestation and corresponding desertification. Your textbook clearly discounts "a" as a choice on page 94. (p. 92)

4. **a:** Like all early peoples, religious texts were originally transmitted orally and often in a sacred language. For the Aryans, this was Sanskrit. (p. 94)

5. **c:** While there were some religious differences between the two peoples, it was competition for basic resources that caused clashes between the Aryans and the Dravidians. (pp. 94–95)

6. **b:** While the Aryans were nomadic, having a warrior leader, a raja, made a great deal of political sense as raiding and warfare were quite common among these boisterous people. Becoming sedentary however, changed the needs and nature of their pattern of political leadership as the council of elders became recognized as the more useful structure for political authority. (pp. 95–96)

7. **e:** Because the stem of the question specifies "early Vedic era" the correct choice must be "e." The time period specified is crucial to selecting the right choice for the question asked. (p. 96)

8. **d:** While parts of each choice are correct in describing aspects of Aryan social order, only choice "d" is completely correct as it refers directly to descriptions in the *Lawbook of Manu*. (p. 99)

9. **a:** A pattern seen in many religions over time is a growing dissatisfaction with rituals that seem sterile or sacrifices that become hollow and a replacement of these practices with the teachings of wise men and sometimes women. The Upanishads reflect this change in Vedic tradition c. 800 B.C.E. Later, as you learn about early Judaism, early Christianity, and Protestantism, as well as Hinduism and Buddhism, you will see a similar pattern. (pp. 100–101)

10. **b:** Answers "a," "c," and "d" are clearly wrong as samsara teaches that upon death, individual souls go temporarily to the World of the Fathers before being reborn to earth in a new incarnation and karma is the record of one's deeds, good and bad, on earth. Answer "b" is correct because it religiously justifies the caste system and offers the promise of rewards for earning good karma. (pp. 100–101)

Comprehensive Multiple Choice Answers

1. **c:** Horses and iron metal working became the standard for most states built by Indo-European peoples of this era; certainly this was true of the Aryans. The Celts were the exceptions. (pp. 53–55 and 93–94)

2. **b:** While all of the societies listed were patriarchial, the Assyrians and the Phoenicians were not river valley civilizations. However, Egyptian women, though living in a patriarchial system, were, at times, in positions of great political and religious authority. Further, a few Egyptian women attained a formal education and some worked as scribes; this was not an opportunity women enjoyed in the other river valley civilizations. (pp. 71–72)

3. **d:** Though both rivers begin in highland regions, the Nile begins in the African highlands. The fertile silt deposited by both rivers throughout their lowlands made farming possible for millennia in both river valleys. (p. 89)

Primary Source Answers

1. a.   When considering perspective in this source, it is important to note that the Brahmins who composed the hymn were the ones who were made from Purusha's mouth. The concept that they were to serve as a "voice" for religious teachings and that they were created first among humans reinforces their position at the top of the caste system. (p. 98)

b.   The Aryans were originally pastoralists so the emphasis on horses, cattle, goats, and sheep seems a natural reflection on their earliest culture. Also, the survival of animals was essential to the survival of the later farming Aryans as well. (p. 98)

2.   a.   Brahman is described as beyond thought and invisible; he is said not to have human form or human ties of color or family. He is described as eternal and all knowing. Human beings are just the opposite. Perhaps he is described in this decisively nonhuman manner to make it clear that Brahman is beyond all human attributes and behaviors. (p. 102)

b.   Metaphor is a commonly used means of explaining the complex; it allows humans to understand something new or difficult by making comparisons with things we understand. We understand fire, flames, and sparks, so we can begin to understand Brahman in that way. We understand wind that blows and we understand rivers that flow. Because Brahman is too immense to be fully understood through sacrifice, rites, or even worship, metaphors can help us understand. (p. 102)

CHAPTER 5

EARLY SOCIETY IN EAST ASIA

Before you get started: This chapter may be difficult since Chinese names and spellings can be complicated. If you have not already developed a system to learn AP World History vocabulary, a flashcard system might help you learn significant terms, names, people, inventions, locations, and concepts. As you develop your own library of flashcards, you can quiz yourself and then switch cards with friends to practice with theirs. Try the flashcard strategy with this chapter and see if it helps.

Other than the new Chinese words and terms, many of the ideas in this chapter parallel the previous chapter on South Asia: the significance of geography in the foundation of the earliest civilization, the development of a governing tradition, the origins of patriarchy and its philosophical justifications, the emerging cultural and intellectual accomplishments, and the interactions between nomadic and sedentary societies. Be thinking about comparisons you can make between this chapter and the previous ones.

POLITICAL ORGANIZATION IN EARLY CHINA

Agriculture developed in China c. 7000 B.C.E. along the **Chang Jiang** and **Huang He** rivers with domestication of rice in the south and millet in the north. By 3000 B.C.E., people in both river valleys were living together in organized communities which managed their own affairs but communicated, traded, and interacted with other towns and villages along the rivers' banks. By the end of the third millennium, the larger regional states of **Xia, Shang,** and **Zhou** emerged to bring much of China under their authority and to lay the political foundation of a distinctive Chinese society.

Early Agricultural Society and the Xia Dynasty
(Themes: Environment and Political Structures)

The *Huang He* takes it name from the vast quantities of **loess** which it gathers along the route from its source in the high mountains of Tibet to its mouth as it empties into the Yellow Sea. More than 2,900 miles long, the Huang He is also known as *China's Sorrow* as its unpredictable flooding can devastate fields, villages, granaries, and anything else in its path.

Despite periodic devastation, the river has supported the development of complex societies along its banks. Unlike Egypt or Mesopotamia, adequate rainfall made vast irrigation systems unnecessary, but early Chinese people needed to work together to dredge the river to deepen its bed, thus reducing the frequency of devastating floods. The need to coordinate these public work projects as well as to maintain order and resolve disputes as populations became more concentrated provided the basis for the earliest governments in China.

The three most ancient Chinese dynasties—Xia, Shang, and Zhou—were hereditary states that extended control over increasingly larger regions. Archaeologists have only recently begun to study the Xia dynasty, which they believe first emerged c. 2000 B.C.E. Ancient legends credit Xia's founder Yu with establishing the precedent for hereditary monarchical rule in China, effective flood control projects, and the development of metallurgy.

The Shang Dynasty
(Themes: Technology, Trade, and Political Structures)

Much more is known about the **Shang Dynasty** than the Xia, because the Shang left written records as well as an extensive amount of material remains, especially bronze works. Bronze metallurgy, as well as horses, chariots, and other wheeled vehicles, had come to China with Indo-European migrants c. 2000

B.C.E. The Shang Dynasty dominated bronze production by controlling access to copper and tin ores and by employing artisans to make large quantities of weapons for the government only. This large arsenal of bronze weapons, a large army, and the confiscation of surplus agricultural production made it easy for the Shang government to subdue much of northeastern China.

Shang society revolved around several large cities including Ao and Yin. Shang kings had a large corps of political allies who supported the king in exchange for a share of the kingdom's agricultural output and access to metal works. Several large cities, highly fortified with thick, tall walls, testify to the centralized political power and central rule of Shang kings. This power is further reflected in Shang royal tombs which include thousands of objects demonstrating the abundance and diversity of Shang material culture, trade items from other regions in Asia, and human sacrificial remains. Shang rulers ruled by proclamation or decree and trusted their military forces and political allies to enforce their will; they do not appear to have developed a law code.

The Zhou Dynasty
(Themes: Political Structures and Technology)

The **Zhou Dynasty** developed along the Wei River in northwestern China. They emerged first as allies of the Shang against nomadic invaders from the north, but their toughness and ability to organize their allies more successfully than the Shang led to their victory. Eventually, the Zhou overcame the corrupt Shang king who, according to legend, had succumbed to wine, women, and greed. The Zhou dynasty ruled China from 1122 B.C.E. until 256 B.C.E.

The concept of **Mandate of Heaven** developed during the Zhou dynasty and continued to dominate Chinese political thinking well into the twentieth century. The emperor's rule reflected his role as "son of heaven" and as long as he governed conscientiously, the cosmos would enjoy harmonious stability. If the ruler failed in his duties, however, the heavens would withdraw their mandate and transfer it to a more deserving individual.

The size of the Zhou state made it impossible to govern from a central court, so the Zhou relied on a decentralized administration of loyal subordinates who provided the Zhou with allegiance, tribute, and military support in exchange for power in each smaller region. At first this decentralized system worked well and subordinate rulers delivered taxes and tribute and even married into the Zhou line. However, over time, these subordinates began to solidify their own power independent of and eventually in competition with the Zhou rule.

The Zhou emperors could not easily control the local production of bronze and, with the introduction of easily produced iron technologies to China c. 1000 B.C.E., the Zhou lost their monopoly on weapons production.

The last years of the Zhou Dynasty are known as the **Period of Warring States.** The Zhou were attacked by nomadic people from the west; their former subordinate states first refused to defend the Zhou territory and eventually attacked each other in an attempt to establish themselves as a new political order. The **Qin** were among these ambitious former subordinates and were ultimately successful in establishing a new central government for China.

SOCIETY AND FAMILY IN ANCIENT CHINA

The introduction of agriculture, the establishment of sedentary communities, and the ensuing accumulation of wealth within families created the foundations for social distinctions and patriarchy in China.

The Social Order
(Themes: Social Structure, Labor Systems, and Gender Structure)

The ruling elites of the Xia, Shang, and Zhou dynasties included the royal family and allied noble families. These most honored members of Chinese society lived well off the agricultural surplus and taxes provided by their subjects and their conspicuous consumption of bronze set them apart from less privileged classes. These nobles controlled the production of bronze weaponry as well as highly prized and aesthetically beautiful bronze utensils and vessels, the remains of which can be seen in recently excavated tombs from those eras.

Next in the social hierarchy were the hereditary aristocrats who rose from the political allies of the Shang and Zhou rulers. This social class filled administrative or military leadership positions in the empire and possessed extensive landholdings which were worked by commoners or sometimes slaves. These aristocrats often lived in cities where they obtained at least an elementary education and developed an elaborate tradition of etiquette.

During the Xia, Shang, and Zhou eras, there was a small class of free craftsmen and artisans including jewelers, jade workers, embroiderers, manufacturers of silk, and, of course, bronze workers. Their standards of living varied, but those who were favored by the aristocrats might live well by the standards of the era.

Not much is known about the merchants and traders of the era. Trade routes between China and the regions of India and southwest Asia were clearly established by 2000 B.C.E. and remnants of goods and products from those regions have been found in royal tombs and other archeological sites throughout China. During the Shang dynasty, Chinese maritime technology, including large oar-propelled vessels as well as sailing ships, connected China with Korea and other east Asian regions. Chinese mariners were using the celestial bodies for navigation by the time of the Zhou dynasty.

Peasants and slaves provided the bulk of labor during the Xia, Shang, and Zhou eras. Peasants owned no land, but provided agricultural and military labor for their aristocratic lords in exchange for land to cultivate, a portion of the harvest, and the promise of protection. Though these agricultural peasants had limited tools, relying mostly on wooden and stone- or bone-tipped sticks, the light, fertile loess soil was easily cultivated. Iron technology was introduced by the sixth century B.C.E. and peasant farmers quickly adopted these much-improved implements. Slaves, most of whom were enemy warriors captured during battles between competing states, performed much of the hard labor which required a large labor force. During the Shang dynasty, slaves also were used as human sacrifices during religious rites.

During these three eras, Chinese women managed the household and produced children. Aristocratic women had special responsibilities for maintaining a refined home and a setting for the formal and informal actions of governments. Peasant women worked the land with their husbands as well as being responsible for winemaking, weaving, and the cultivation of silkworms.

Family and Patriarchy
(Themes: Social and Gender Structures)

The Chinese family served as the principal institution for socialization of children and as the preserver and perpetuator of cultural traditions. In ancient China, these two roles were vested in the extended family and within a strong patriarchal tradition. The ***veneration of ancestors*** in Chinese families has its origins in neolithic times as the family was considered an institution that linked departed generations to the living. A family could expect to prosper only if all its members—living and dead—worked cooperatively toward common interests, so the extended family exercised tremendous power over the public and private lives of its members. The family patriarch, the eldest male member, possessed tremendous authority. He presided at rites and ceremonies honoring ancestors' spirits and he mediated relations between the living and the dead. During neolithic times, men's public authority was determined by the female line of descent, but by the end of the Shang era that tradition was replaced by an intense patrilineal focus. As larger states emerged, women increasingly lost their status in Chinese society.

EARLY CHINESE WRITING AND CULTURAL DEVELOPMENT

Unlike Egyptian, Mesopotamian, or Indian culture, organized religion did not play a major role in ancient Chinese society. The Chinese did not recognize a personal supreme deity who regularly intervened in daily life. Instead, the concept of *tian* was an impersonal power responsible for bestowing or revoking the Mandate of Heaven, not for monitoring or judging individual behavior. Therefore, no large priestly class developed in China as it did in other ancient civilizations. Instead, writing, begun during the Xia era but developed during the Shang dynasty, served as the foundation for Chinese cultural traditions as a way of expressing human ideas and reflections and as an indispensable tool of government.

Oracle Bones and Chinese Writing
(Theme: Cultural Developments)

Earliest known Chinese writing served the interests of rulers as scribes at the Shang court kept records on bamboo or silk strips. However, it is inscriptions kept on specially prepared broad bones which demonstrate the power and prominence of writing during the Shang era. Diviners would use these *oracle bones* to determine an answer to an important question of state such as whether or not to attack an enemy. Most of these surviving artifacts relate to issues of state or government. Oracle bones also provide insight into early pictographic Chinese writing which did not include an alphabetic or phonetic component and which has identifiable parallels even in contemporary Chinese characters.

Thought and Literature in Ancient China
(Theme: Cultural Developments)

The use of writing expanded during the Zhou dynasty to include poetry, history, etiquette, and moral and philosophical essays; many of these books served as textbooks for Chinese schools and students of government. The most famous of these books, the ***Book of Songs***, contains poems on both serious and light-hearted topics and demonstrates the beginnings of a Chinese literary tradition. Many of these non-utilitarian texts were destroyed by the **Qin dynasty**, as it feared such works would encourage independence of mind.

ANCIENT CHINA AND THE LARGER WORLD

Treacherous geography hindered, but did not stop, interaction with China. China's neighbors to the north, west, and south developed intense relationships with Chinese agricultural society.

Chinese Cultivators and Nomadic Peoples of Central Asia
(Theme: Patterns of Interaction)

The arid environment of the *steppe* shaped the lifestyle of nomads who herded there and impacted the lives of farmers who survived on its fringe. When the Indo-Europeans domesticated and began to ride horses c. 4000 B.C.E., they pushed deeper into the steppe and were able to sustain large herds of cattle, sheep, goats, yaks, and horses. After learning metallurgy c. 2900 B.C.E., these hearty people began to build heavy wagons which further extended their range into the Eurasian steppe. By 1000 B.C.E., these nomadic people served as the link between farming cultures in the west and in the east as they herded their flocks from region to region following pasturelands and water holes. The nomads depended on the agricultural communities to supply them with grains and finished products such as metals and textiles and they in turn supplied the farmers with horses while serving as a trading conduit for products and ideas.

Despite being tied by trade and communication needs, relationships between these nomads and the farmers were often hostile. Often the nomads would raid the agricultural settlements and seize their wealth; this was especially true in China during the Xia and Shang dynasties. Even the Zhou nearly crumbled under these nomadic assaults.

The nomads did not adopt Chinese traditions as their lives were tied to the steppe's geographic and resource limitations. While they did enjoy the agricultural goods and products, they maintained the position of leadership by charismatic warrior chiefs and did not build towns or cities, nor adopt other Chinese government or social traditions.

The Southern Expansion of Chinese Society
(Themes: Migration and Demographics)

Chinese influence spread south from the Chang Jiang region into modern **Taiwan, Vietnam, and Thailand** during this era. The moist climate and the rivers' ample water source made it possible for people in this region to easily grow rice, sometimes even two crops a year. This intense cultivation depended on the construction and maintenance of elaborate irrigation systems and resulted in agricultural surpluses. The ensuing population growth encouraged migration into surrounding hills and mountains and throughout southeast Asia as well as the emergence of cities and states throughout the Yangzi region. By the Zhou era, this southern region had adopted northern Chinese political and social traditions and was eventually conquered by the Zhou military to become part of the emerging larger Chinese society.

Finished reading the chapter? Be sure you can . . .

- Explain the connections between geography and climate on the relationships between the nomadic peoples of central Asia and the Chinese cultivators.
- Explain the significance of bronze and then iron technologies in China during the Xia, Shang, and Zhou dynasties.
- Compare and contrast the basic features of the Yellow River valley civilization with those of Mesopotamia, Egypt, and the Indus Valley civilizations, especially cultural developments and state and social structure.
- Discuss the major political developments as well as social and gender structures in China c. 3500–500 B.C.E.

CHAPTER MULTIPLE CHOICE QUESTIONS

1. The phrase "Yellow River" refers to
   a. the loess gathered in the Huang He.
   b. the unpredictable nature of the Chang Jiang.
   c. the vast volume of water carried by the Wei River.
   d. the source of the Yangzi River at the Yellow Sea.
   e. the degree of pollution caused by a dense population.

2. Which of the following Chinese dynasties is considered the first to bring China under unified control?
   a. Xia
   b. Shang
   c. Zhou
   d. Qin
   e. Han

3. What technology is credited with the rise and success of the Shang dynasty?
    a. iron metallurgy
    b. bronze metallurgy
    c. crop terracing
    d. jade crafting
    e. horse stirrups

4. Pounded earth building is a technology first employed with great success in cities such as Ao and Yin during
    a. the Xia dynasty.
    b. the Shang dynasty.
    c. the Zhou dynasty.
    d. the Qin dynasty.
    e. the Han dynasty.

5. One reason the Zhou dynasty was able to topple the Shang dynasty, was that the Zhou
    a. ruled by proclamation or decree rather than by law code.
    b. proved more capable at preventing flooding on the Huang He.
    c. made stronger alliances with the northern nomads.
    d. organized their allies more effectively than the Shang.
    e. had strong support among the priestly class.

6. One reason the Zhou dynasty fell was that it
    a. could not protect such a large empire from invasions from the north.
    b. could not prevent people migrating to the south for better farmland.
    c. lost their hold on bronze and iron metallurgy.
    d. failed to adequately maintain dikes and levees along the Huang He.
    e. burned all the books necessary to keep organized tax records.

7. The elite of the Shang and Zhou dynasties considered possession of what items a mark of status?
    a. oracle bones
    b. bronze serving vessels
    c. jade figurines
    d. iron swords
    e. terra-cotta warriors

8. Why were wooden tools used in China even after bronze technology was available?
    a. Tradition dictated that the earth must be tilled with wooden implements only. Also, bronze was believed to be unclean.
    b. The peasants preferred wooden tools over bronze ones because they were easier to handle and could be traded more easily.
    c. The Emperor refused to share bronze technology with the non-aristocratic classes.
    d. Bronze was reserved for making elaborate ritual vessels and burial urns.
    e. Wooden tools were strong enough to till the loess and bronze tools were too expensive.

9. Why did the victorious Qin emperor order all books not of a utilitarian nature destroyed?
    a. He feared they might inspire doubts about his government and encourage independent thinking.
    b. He believed it was part of his responsibility under the Mandate of Heaven to purify the thinking of his subjects.
    c. He hoped the destruction of out-of-date ideas might spur China to work harder to produce great literature.
    d. He wanted his own writings to be more widely read and accepted by the educated intellectuals.
    e. He believed the books taught ideals opposed to the veneration of ancestors.

10. The nomadic peoples of central Asia provided what for the farmers with whom they traded?
    a. metal tools and weapons
    b. horses
    c. bronze religious vessels
    d. oracle bones which could be used as medicine
    e. silk cloth

Comprehensive Multiple Choice Questions:

1. The Shang rulers in China used the bronze weapons and horse-drawn chariots to overpower the Xia. This use of technology to subdue a rival is comparable to
    a. the Egyptians conquering the Hyksos.
    b. the Hebrews overshadowing the Phoenicians.
    c. the Sumerians overpowering the Babylonians.
    d. the Phoenicians decimating the Assyrians.
    e. the Aryans overtaking the Harappans.

2. The need to organize effective flood control projects during the Xia dynasty is similar to the same need in
    a. Egypt and Mesopotamia.
    b. Mesopotamia and Phoenicia.
    c. Phoenicia and Palestine.
    d. Egypt and Palestine.
    e. Nubia and Congo.

3. What effect did the growth of the Chinese state have on women's roles?
    a. Women became more powerful as they could be the mothers of emperors.
    b. Women became more powerful because they controlled the bronze trade.
    c. Women became less powerful because men no longer won their right to political authority through the female line of descent.
    d. Women became less powerful because they could not handle the requirements of heavy farm labor.
    e. Women became less powerful as they were no longer allowed to attend formal, imperial schools.

Primary Source Questions

1. **Read *Sources from the Past: Peasant's Protest* on page 120 of your textbook.**
    a. Why did the peasants choose rats as an image for their aristocratic landlords?
    b. What criticisms did the peasants make of their landlords?
    c. What avenues for their grievances did the peasants have in Zhou China?

2. **Read *Sources from the Past: Family Solidarity in Ancient China* on page 122 of your textbook.**
    a. What metaphors does the speaker use to state his message?
    b. According to the poem, what is the benefit in valuing one's brother?
    c. In what ways does this poem illustrate the patriarchal nature of Chinese society in ancient times?

Chapter Multiple Choice Answers

1. **a:** Loess is the extremely fertile, powdery yellow soil which the Huang He picks up along its 2,900-mile journey from the Tibetan Plateau to the Yellow Sea. (p. 110)

2. **d:** The Xia, Shang, and Zhou dynasties ruled China as hereditary states. It was under the Qin dynasty that China was first brought under unified rule. (p. 111)

3. **b:** The Shang Dynasty was built on the monopoly of bronze production which provided them with superior weapons to use against their rivals. Iron metallurgy did not reach China until c. 1000 B.C.E. (p. 112)

4. **b:** This pounded earth technology is important evidence of Shang authority in the Yellow River regions of northern China. Ten thousand laborers working more than twenty years to construct these buildings and walls means the Shang had great power and an impressive system of centralized rule. (p. 115)

5. **d:** Developing in the Wei River valley of northern China, the Zhou battled the Shang in the east and the nomads from the north. The Zhou used their battle experience and their ability to build alliances to eventually rise above the Shang. (p. 115)

6. **c:** The technological shift from expensive bronze weapons to more readily produced and durable iron weapons meant that subordinates and enemies of the Zhou now could make their own weapons and therefore effectively resist the Zhou central government. (p. 118)

7. **b:** The high cost of copper and tin necessary to make bronze made the conspicuous consumption of bronze the mark of the ruling elite in the Shang and early Zhou dynasties. Elaborate weapons and exquisite utensils and vessels testify to the rich material culture of these social elites. (p. 119)

8. **e:** Bronze technology had been available for several centuries, but it was too expensive for peasant use and because of the light texture of the loess, wooden tools would suffice. Iron technology increased dramatically as farm equipment after 600 B.C.E. (p. 121)

9. **a:** While this emperor, Qin Shihuangdi, established the large-scale political organization which would dominate Chinese history in the centuries to come, he was very concerned about the effects of individualized, free thinking and was determined to prevent any ideas which might question or challenge his determination to centralize his rule. Not only did he attempt to destroy all books of poetry, history, or philosophy, he even attempted to eradicate scholars who already possessed this knowledge by burying 460 of them alive. Don't worry, he did not survive long; he accidentally poisoned his own self. You will read more about him in Chapter 8. (p. 127)

10. **b:** The relationship between sedentary people and nomadic people is an important aspect of this course; it fits right into the Patterns of Interaction theme. The nomads of central Asia could produce great herds of horses on the abundant grasses of the steppe; the Chinese farmers needed these horses and they also wanted the trade connection with the west that the nomads provided. (p. 128)

Comprehensive Multiple Choice Answers

1. **e:** The Aryans used their metallurgical skills and their access to horses to overpower the people of the Indus Valley; the Shang did the same in the Hwang He region c. 1766 B.C.E. (pp. 94, 113)

2. **a:** Flood control projects imply the presence of mighty rivers. Only choice "a" refers to places with such powerful rivers. Neither Phoenicia or Palestine had such significant rivers. (p. 112)

3. **c:** During Neolithic times, Chinese men held political authority based on their female line of descent. As the authority and powers of the dynasties grew, this tradition of female lineage was abandoned. It is true that certain mothers of emperors were important from the Zhou dynasty forward, but the effect on women's roles throughout the rest of Chinese society was negligible. Women's authority or power decreased as the power of the state grew. (p. 123)

Primary Source Answers

1. Rodents are one of the most persistent and destructive threats to farmers' productivity. Rats, in particular, eat the stored food, thus stealing the farmers' livelihood; they also represent potential death by spreading disease. The Chinese farmers could not directly accuse their uncaring, unkind, and unresponsive landlords of these crimes, but they could use the metaphor of rodents to make their point. There was no official or office to which these peasants could plead his or her situations. The peasants owned no land of their own and were tied to their lords for land, security, and a portion of the harvest. When the lord did not fulfill his role, the peasants had few alternatives but to continue their suffering or to move to the protection of another lord in another land, as the verse indicates. (p. 120)

2. The speaker uses the "flowers on the cherry tree," "the wagtail on the level height," "dishes in array," and "drink to satiety" as images to set up the comparison to the joys and benefits of brothers. The poem's speaker explains that valuing one's brother is the most essential relationship. It is one's brother who will grieve with you, who will support you in times of quarrel or threat, who will help you in times of crisis, and who will remain with you throughout eternity. While it is tempting to expand "brothers" to include all family members, the poet is careful to delineate wife and children as separate entities, so the term brother must be precise as well. Brother meant brother, not sister or sibling, in patriarchal China. Finally, this poem reflects the value placed on family and ancestor veneration and it foreshadows the Confucian teachings regarding filial piety and the five essential relationships. (p. 122)

CHAPTER 6

EARLY SOCIETIES IN THE AMERICAS AND OCEANIA

Before you get started: Do not be frightened by the opening pages of this chapter in the Bentley/Ziegler textbook; there is much more to early societies in the Americas and Oceania than sex and blood. . . . Okay, now that you are interested, you should know that this chapter is really mostly about migration, geography, trade, and culture. This chapter has a lot of content that is not required for the national exam, so it is really important to keep those themes in mind to help you sort the information into "need to know" and "nice to know" categories. A chart or another type of graphic organizer here will help you keep the details in order and in perspective.

EARLY SOCIETIES OF MESOAMERICA
(Theme: Migration)

As sea levels dropped during the **Ice Ages**, humans took advantage of the exposed land bridges to migrate into new lands and establish cultures there. Human groups migrated to the Americas long after people had established communities throughout the eastern hemisphere but before people understood or practiced agriculture. By the time the Ice Ages ended, about 18,000 years ago, people had become well established in the Americas, the islands of southeast Asia, and Australia. Humans continued to migrate throughout the Americas and Oceania resulting in population pressures and the use of technology such as large sailing canoes. By 700 C.E., people had established communities throughout most of the habitable world.

The high sea levels made it difficult, but not impossible, for these people in the Americas and Oceania to interact with their neighbors near and far. Particularly after the discovery of agriculture in northern and southern America, population pressures, trade, and the need for additional new resources led to the development of increasingly complex social forms.

The Olmecs
(Themes: Trade and Cultural Developments)

The first complex society in the Americas was the **Olmecs**. These people, who modern researchers named after the rubber trees in the region, built a complex society on the rich agricultural harvests of their ancestors. Beans, chili peppers, avocados, squash, gourds, and eventually **maize** provided these people of Mesoamerica with ample food sources. Turkeys and small dogs were also domesticated and used for food, but the larger animals of Mesoamerica were not subject to domestication; there were no horses, mules, cattle, or pigs in this region until the Europeans arrived in the sixteenth century. No large domesticated animals also meant animal energy for transportation was impossible and therefore the wheeled cart was unnecessary. The Mesoamericans managed very well using human power for labor and trade.

Olmec society was probably **authoritarian** as archeological remains show huge construction projects such as pyramids, temples, altars, and tombs which would have demanded coordination of large numbers of workers over vast periods of time. The necessity for drainage systems to divert abundant water also indicates that the Olmecs had some social class system which allowed for the construction of such large public works.

The most compelling evidence that the Olmec people labored for the elite at least part of the year are the sculptures of colossal human heads carved from huge slabs of black basalt. These most distinctive Olmec artistic creations are believed to have required thousands of laborers to quarry, transport, carve, and set in place in each of the Olmec capital cities.

Trade was also important to Olmec culture. Imported jade was turned into decorative objects, imported **obsidian** was used to create wickedly sharp knives and axes, and abundant rubber was used to make balls and other objects which the Olmecs could trade along with their basalt carvings, ceramics, and animal skins.

The demise of the Olmecs is somewhat mysterious, as they left no written language other than their calendar inscriptions. It appears, perhaps, that civil conflicts and a loss of religious faith might have caused the Olmecs to abandon their cities. Historians and archaeologists have only been studying the Olmecs for about sixty years, so there is clearly much more to learn about them.

Heirs of the Olmecs: The Maya
(Themes: Trade and Political Structures)

The **Maya,** who occupied southern Mexico, Guatemala, Belize, Honduras, and El Salvador, were the earliest heirs to Olmec tradition. Like the Olmecs, the Mayans used a huge labor force to build immense ceremonial centers. The first Maya center was in the highlands of Guatemala where the fertile soil was excellent for agriculture. From this site, early Maya traded their agricultural surplus throughout Guatemala and central Mexico. This center eventually came under the economic and political domination of **Teotihuacan** in central Mexico and the center of Maya culture moved into the Mesoamerican lowlands including the Yucatan Peninsula.

The infertile and poorly drained Mesoamerican lowlands required that the Mayas build **terraces** to trap the fertile silt which was being washed away by the many rivers of the region. This terrace technology which artificially retained the rich earth, made it possible for the Mayas to dramatically increase their agricultural output—maize, cotton, and especially the **cacao** bean. Cacao, used by the Maya elite as a stimulant and even as currency, made the Maya wealthy.

The Maya political organization was based on scores of small city-kingdoms, in addition to several large ceremonial centers, some like **Tikal,** with populations over 40,000. These centers, which evolved into large complex cities, boasted enormous paved plazas and scores of public buildings including pyramids, temples, and palaces. Maya kings took great powerful names, often including the word *jaguar,* the most fearsome animal of the Mesoamerican forests.

Maya culture was martial. The Maya city-kingdoms frequently fought each other over resources and land with the hope of capturing prisoners who could be used as slaves or for ritual sacrifice. Between the ninth and eleventh centuries C.E., the Maya state of Chichen Itza in the northern Yucatan peninsula tried to establish a more unified Maya nation and began to absorb war captives and integrate them into their society rather than enslave or sacrifice the prisoners. Other Maya centers began to decline and be deserted by their people by the eighth century C.E., but Chichen Itza survived a few more centuries until it too was smothered by the encroaching tropical jungles of the Mesoamerican lowlands.

Maya Society and Religion
(Themes: Social Structures, Cultural and Religious Developments)

Maya society was based on an elaborate social hierarchy: kings and ruling families, literate priests, landowning nobility, merchants who came from the noble classes, professional architects and sculptors, specialized artisans, a large class of peasants, and a large class of slaves.

The Maya script is considered to be the most flexible and elaborate of all the early American systems of writing. It contains both **ideographics** and **syllabic elements,** and was used to keep astronomical, genealogical, and political records as well as to record poetry, history, and religious texts. Though the Mayas wrote thousands of books, only four survived the sixteenth-century Spanish attempt to destroy traditional Maya religion. Most Maya writing today is found in inscriptions on temples and other buildings. Though modern historians and archaeologists have only learned to decipher those scripts within the past sixty years, it appears that the Mayas were expert at astronomical observation, prediction, and calculation thanks in large part to their invention of the concept and symbol for zero which they used to manipulate the large numbers needed in their complex calculations. This abstract mathematical reasoning was demonstrated in their amazingly accurate **calendar** which had both religious and practical purposes.

Surviving Maya literature includes the *Popol Vuh* which explains how the gods created humans out of maize and water to become flesh and blood and how the gods further kept the world going including the agricultural cycle in exchange for honors and sacrifices which humans must perform for them. The shedding of blood was crucial in Mayan religious rituals because it is associated with rain and agriculture; the practice was believed to be pleasing to the gods and could guarantee the rains would come, the crops would be bountiful, and the culture would survive.

Bloodletting occurred in sport as well. The Maya used the Olmec tradition of the ball game as a ritual in political and religious affairs in addition to its compelling entertainment factor. Skull racks surrounding the ball fields testify to the deadly nature of the game.

Heirs of the Olmecs: Teotihuacan
(Themes: Cultural Developments and Trade)

Teotihuacan society developed in the fertile lake region of the northern Mexican highlands beginning c. 500 B.C.E. but flourished between 400–600 C.E. Relying on the abundant supply of fresh water, fertile soil, fish, and wildlife, this area was a natural haven for the establishment of a productive agricultural society. At its high point the capital city, Teotihuacan, had a population of almost 200,000 people and boasted a pyramid almost as large as Khufu's in Egypt. All books and writings from this civilization have disappeared, but archaeological remains of huge temples and palaces, scores of streets and neighborhoods, and numerous market centers indicate that this society was complex and authoritarian in political structure. Historians also believe it may have been a **theocracy,** of sorts, as surviving paintings and murals all have religious themes and subjects.

Exquisite obsidian tools and detailed orange pottery were produced and prized in Teotihuacan and traded throughout Mesoamerica and into North America as well. Teotihuacan established colonies and built a military force to protect its trade routes and sources of raw materials; this rationale is different than the martial Maya of the south. Perhaps this lack of either military preparedness or offensive aggression accounts for the destruction of this civilization c. 500 C.E. when outside aggressors began to encroach on the city. By the middle of the eighth century C.E., the city, its books and records, and even its monuments were destroyed and the people deserted the remains.

EARLY SOCIETIES OF SOUTH AMERICA

Hunting and gathering peoples made their way from Central America to South America c. 12,000 B.C.E. The Andes highlands provided deer, llama, and alpaca and the cool coastal regions provided fish as well as ample natural supplies of squash, gourds, and wild potatoes to keep these non-farmers well nourished. As the climate began to change after 8000 B.C.E. however, the natural occurring supplies of food could not meet the population needs so these human communities began to experiment with agriculture. Agriculture proved highly successful in these regions and thus the populations grew; complex, organized cultures developed; and large cities and states were established over the next nine thousand years.

Early Andean Society and the Chavin Cult
(Themes: Changes and Continuities, Migration, and Religious Developments)

Early Andean society occupied the region that is now Peru and Bolivia. Though contemporary with early Mesoamerican cultures, the difficult geography and lack of pack animals made communication or trade between these regions extremely unlikely. Certainly agricultural products like maize and squash spread southward and Andean gold, silver, and copper were gradually handed northward, but regular and consistent commerce between the two regions was not feasible. The challenges of Andean geography even made transportation or communication within the region difficult.

Between 2500 and 2000 B.C.E., many small, but permanent, farming settlements took root along the Pacific coast. Farmers cultivated beans, peanuts, and sweet potatoes for food, and cotton for fishing nets and textiles. Protein from the Pacific allowed communities to grow and prosper. By 2000 B.C.E., farming had spread to the Andes, where many varieties of the potato supported increasing complex agricultural communities.

The arrival of maize c. 1000 B.C.E. appears to have suddenly created quite a change in this region. The **Chavin Cult** is the term modern historians and archaeologists give to the period between 900 and 800 B.C.E. as they try to explain the sudden building of large temple complexes and elaborate works of art, the creation of thousands of intricate stone carvings of animals, the development of gold, silver, and copper metallurgy, and a population boom. They speculate that the Chavin Cult developed to promote fertility and abundant harvests. It certainly seems to have worked as large ceremonial centers were built during this period which later would emerge as great cities.

Early Andean States: Mochica
(Themes: Political Structures and Changes and Continuities)

The earliest Andean states, which developed on the western side of the mountains, were created as conquerors unified individual valleys and organized them into integrated societies. By building irrigation systems so that the lower valleys could support agriculture, and by establishing trade and exchange networks through difficult terrain, leaders of early Andean states sought to create integrated economic zones. Surviving architecture and artifacts testify that this process was carried out with coercion and warfare by warrior leaders of regional states. Without written records, these remains are the only insight into this region.

The most well studied of these early Andean regional states is **Mochica,** which had its base along the Moche River in the coast and valleys of northern Peru from 300–700 C.E. Though leaving no written language, the Mochica left a remarkable artistic record which describes their culture as highly religious, distinctly individualistic, socially diverse, and economically complex.

EARLY SOCIETIES OF OCEANIA

Human migrations to Australia and New Guinea using canoes outfitted with sails began about 60,000 years ago when sea levels were lower due to the Ice Ages' climate changes. These people also moved onto the surrounding islands in the following centuries. By 3000 B.C.E., seafaring traders from Asia had established trading ports in New Guinea and were venturing further and further east into the islands of the western Pacific. By the middle of the first millennium C.E., they had established communities on virtually all of the habitable islands of the Pacific Ocean.

Early Societies in Australia and New Guinea
(Themes: Migration and Changes and Continuities)

People reached Australia and New Guinea long before the advent of agriculture. For thousands of years, hunters and gathers must have traveled between the two islands, taking advantage of the lower sea levels during the Ice Ages. Once the Ice Ages ended and the high waters returned to separate the two islands, the people of each place took very different paths. The **aboriginal peoples of Australia** happily maintained their hunting and gathering traditions until the forceful settlement of the Europeans in nineteenth and twentieth centuries. The **aboriginal people of New Guinea**, however, interacted with outsiders much, much earlier than their Australian counterparts. About 5000 years ago, seafaring people from southeast Asia, who spoke languages known as **Austronesian,** visited the coast of New Guinea, traded with the indigenous people, and even established trading communities of their own. Coming from agricultural communities in Asia, these settlers introduced root crops like taro and yams as well as domesticated animals including chickens and pigs, all of which caught on quickly with the New Guinea aborigines. As always, the introduction of agriculture quickly brought population growth, specialization of labor, growth of permanent settlements, and the development of complex social and material culture. The Austronesian-speaking traders soon turned their attention to establishing settlements further and further out into the Pacific Ocean.

The Peopling of the Pacific Islands
(Themes: Migration and Trade)

It was the Austronesian-speaking people who possessed the sophisticated maritime technology and the agricultural expertise to establish human settlements on the islands of the Pacific. By 1500 B.C.E., they had established trading colonies in **Vanuatu,** by 1000 B.C.E., they reached **Tahiti,** by the early centuries C.E. they had reached **Hawai'i,** and by 700 C.E. they were in **New Zealand.** Another group of the Austronesians sailed westward into the Indian Ocean as far as the island of **Madagascar.**

The earliest known Austronesian-speaking peoples are known as the **Lapita,** named after a beach in New Caledonia where twentieth-century archaeologists discovered some of their artifacts: terra-cotta pottery specifically decorated with a distinctive stamped geometric design. The Lapita traded this pottery and their highly prized obsidian across the wide expanses of the Pacific for nearly 1000 years between 1500 and 500 B.C.E.

After 500 B.C.E, Lapita trading networks declined, probably because their settlements had grown large enough to provide for themselves. Local hereditary chiefdoms developed and physical contests for leadership roles appeared common. The possibility of migration to surrounding islands appears to have been used to ease tensions and avoid widespread bloodshed.

Over time, descendants of the Lapita built elaborate societies with complex social classes including chiefs, priests, administrators, soldiers, and servants, especially on the large islands like Hawai'i. There, chiefs and their nobles organized public life in their districts, led public ritual services, and maintained the irrigation systems necessary to grow crops; these chiefs and aristocrats eventually came to be seen as semi-divine or divine by their island subjects.

Finished reading the chapter? Be sure you can . . .

- Relate the geography and climate of the Americas and Oceania with the development of human society in each area.
- Explain the relationship between agriculture and the environment in America and Oceania.
- Compare and contrast the social structure, state, and cultures of Mesoamerican and Andean American civilizations with at least one other you've already studied in Chapters 2 through 5.
- Discuss the major trading patterns within and among peoples of the Americas and Oceania.
- Explain the migrations of people into the Americas and throughout Oceania.

Chapter Multiple Choice Questions

1. The shedding of blood was critical to Mayan culture because
   a. the Mayans constantly fought the Olmecs and they believed the gods would only reward them with victory if they slaughtered their enemies.
   b. the bloodletting rituals were associated with rain and agriculture upon which the Mayan culture was based.
   c. the Mayans needed to control their population so it did not outstrip the resources of their farmlands.
   d. the Mayans inherited the tradition from the Olmecs who were bloodthirsty nomads from the north.
   e. the Mayans believed that bloodletting would bring a savior who would reward them with victories over their enemies.

2. By what year had human migrations established communities throughout every habitable part of the world?
   a. 8000 B.C.E.
   b. 3000 B.C.E.
   c. 100 C.E.
   d. 700 C.E.
   e. 1500 C.E.

3. Why did Mesoamericans have no need for wheeled vehicles?
   a. They had ample domesticated pack animals to carry heavy burdens, so they did not need wheeled vehicles.
   b. They did not travel or trade to far places, so human power was adequate for their needs.
   c. They had remained hunters and gatherers, so they did not accumulate much material wealth which needed to be transported.
   d. They did not have many domesticated large animals which would have been necessary to make wheeled vehicles useful.
   e. The swampy nature of much of Mesoamerica made wheeled vehicles not useful.

4. The distinctive artistic creations of Olmec culture were
   a. colossal basalt sculptures of human heads.
   b. great pyramids which served as tombs for their rulers.
   c. huge cities with pounded walls which could withstand constant assault from their enemies.
   d. fertility statues which resembled the Venus of Willendorf.
   e. elaborate seven-story buildings which served as the political and religious centers of the cities.

5. Which American people established the most flexible and sophisticated systems of writing?
   a. Olmecs
   b. Mayans
   c. Teotihuacan
   d. Mochica
   e. Chavin Cult

6. What product did the Maya produce that could be both consumed as a stimulant, traded, and used as currency?
   a. corn
   b. coffee
   c. cacao
   d. sugar
   e. tobacco

7. A king named Great Jaguar Paw or Shield Jaguar or Bird Jaguar was most likely a king of what Mesoamerican civilization?
   a. Olmecs
   b. Toltecs
   c. Mochica
   d. Chavin Cult
   e. Maya

8. Why did agriculture take root after 3000 B.C.E. in New Guinea but not in Australia?
   a. The Australians were not interested in trade so they did not have any contact with agricultural producers.
   b. The Austronesian merchants who settled in New Guinea brought agriculture to that island, but the peoples of Australia had little sustained contact with these settlers.
   c. The land in Australia was too hostile for agriculture but the river valleys of New Guinea made agriculture easy.
   d. The people of New Guinea did not have the same religious prohibitions against trade, as did the Australian people.
   e. The rapidly expanding population of Australia did not need the benefits of agriculture, as did the smaller population of New Guinea.

9. The primary reasons for the spread of Austronesian peoples throughout the Pacific were
   a. population pressures and internal conflicts.
   b. religious missionaries and political threats.
   c. fear of disease and warfare.
   d. the benefits of agriculture and monopoly on trad.
   e. the push to expand empires and establish a tribute system.

10. What seafaring technology made it possible for Austronesian-speaking peoples to travel throughout the Pacific?
    a. astrolabe
    b. outrigger canoe
    c. compass
    d. rudder
    e. triangular sail

Comprehensive Multiple Choice Questions

1. The reason that Andean society showed greater cultural, political, and economic regional diversity than did Mesoamerican society was that
   a. the difficult geographic barriers in the Andes Mountains made unity and uniformity impossible.
   b. the Mesoamerican society had more sophisticated technology and social organizations than did the people of the Andes.
   c. the Mochica needed prisoners of war from outside their culture to sacrifice to the gods.
   d. the Chavin Cult remained separate from other Andean people to preserve its secret rites.
   e. the Mesoamerican empires demanded many prisoners to sacrifice and so spread their traditions in an attempt to gain victims.

2. The relationships between Mayan city-states is most similar to the relationships between city-states in
   a. Egypt c. 3000 B.C.E.
   b. Egypt c. 1500 B.C.E.
   c. Harappan civilization c. 2000 B.C.E.
   d. Aryan settlements c. 1500 B.C.E.
   e. Sumer c. 2800 B.C.E.

3. Which of the following societies developed a writing system which is still undeciphered?
   a. Maya
   b. Aboriginal Australians
   c. Olmecs
   d. Harappans
   e. Shang

Primary Source Questions

1. **Examine the Maya mural on page 140 of your textbook.**
   a. What does this mural indicate about the material wealth of Maya culture?
   b. How does this mural reflect Mayan social structure?

2. **Read *Sources from the Past: The* Popol Vuh on the Creation of Human Beings on page 143 of your textbook.**
   a. What elements of Maya culture are evident in this excerpt?
   b. What comparisons and contrasts exist between the *Popol Vuh* and the *Rig Veda* on page 98?

Chapter Multiple Choice Answers

1. **b:** The Mayans believed that since the gods had shed their blood to nourish the earth, the people should do the same to please the gods and ensure agricultural bounty. (p. 133)

2. **d:** While there are not many specific dates required on the AP test, you are expected to have a sense of chronology especially as you discuss continuity and change. Circa 8000 B.C.E .is the beginnings of agriculture, c. 3000 B.C.E. is the development of writing in Mesopotamia, c. 100 C.E. is the first century of the Pax Romana, and c. 700 C.E. is the time when humans had spread to most of the habitable world. (p. 134)

3. **d:** The absence of large domesticated draft animals meant the early Mesoamerican peoples had to rely on human laborers and porters for labor and transportation of goods. Later, in the fifteenth century C.E., when horses and cattle arrived with the Spanish, Mesoamerican culture would be significantly changed. (p. 133)

4. **a:** These huge statues can stand ten feet tall and weigh more than twenty tons. They are evidence of the power of Olmec rulers to command the services of more than 1000 laborers to quarry, transport, and sculpt these likenesses. (p. 137)

5. **b:** Mayan writing was both ideographic and syllabic which made it possible for it to be both spoken and written. (p. 141)

6. **c:** This answer will be obvious if you read all parts of the question: "consumed as a stimulant, and used as currency." The AP Exam often includes questions such as this that deal with commodities and trade within a culture. (p. 138)

7. **e:** The jaguar was the most feared animal of the Mesoamerican forest and hence many Mayan kings took the name in their titles as a sign of their ferocity. (p. 138)

8. **b:** The Austronesian-speaking traders who came to the islands of New Guinea brought agriculture as they established their settlements; they did not settle in Australia and thus had little sustained contact. In addition, the people of Australia maximized the foraging wealth of their land and did not need agriculture to support their indigenous society. (pp. 149–150)

9. **a:** The possibility of migration helped to ease the ills of population growth and provided an alternative to warfare on many of the islands in the Pacific. The lure of new islands for settlement in a sense acted as a safety valve for Austronesian societies. (p. 153)

10. **b:** The astrolabe was developed in the Hellenistic world and the compass, the triangular sail, and rudder were Chinese inventions. With the stabilizing benefits of the outrigger, the Austronesians were able to navigate using the stars, winds, currents, and other natural formations. (p. 150)

Comprehensive Multiple Choice Answers

1. **a:** High mountains, deep valleys and rivers which emptied swiftly into the Pacific Ocean made transportation and communication very difficult in this region. Coupled with the technology and social organization of the time, the geographic challenges of the region made it impossible for early civilizations in the Andes to impose order or dominate a large region. (p. 148)

2. **e:** Sumerian city-states frequently fought each other over resources and power, as did the Mayan city-states. The other choices here either did not have a city-state structure, or we do not have evidence of a history of consistent aggression between them. (pp. 36, 138–139)

3. **d:** The Maya script was only begun to be deciphered about fifty years ago, and the writings from Shang China about 120 years ago. There are no written records from the Aboriginal Australians and the Olmecs left only calendar inscriptions. The Harappans left many written records, but the script is still undecipherable. (pp. 88, 125, 137, 141, 148)

Primary Source Answers

1. The complexity and wealth of Maya culture are thoroughly represented in this mural. There are at least seven different types of instruments and musicians represented including horn players of various kinds, drummers, and players of other percussion instruments. There are several musicians with each kind of instrument as well as individuals whose job it is to shield the musicians from the sun with elaborate umbrellas. Such diversity reflects the depth of material wealth found in Maya culture. The priests in the middle of the mural reflect a similar diversity in their clothing, especially their hats or crowns. The placement of the musicians under the priests, who appear to be under a god or other supernatural being, is parallel to the social hierarchy of Maya culture. (p. 140)

2. The importance of agriculture and the closeness to nature can be seen throughout this excerpt. The fact that people are made from corn with water and the "grease" from the hands of the goddess Xmucane illustrates the essential connection between Maya culture and agriculture. The naming of the first people demonstrates the connection with the animal world, specifically the jaguar for men and then bird and sea-life names for the first women.

The most striking comparison between the two excerpts is the role of sacrifice. In the *Rig Veda*, the sacrifice was Purusha, a primeval being who existed before the universe. From specific parts of this being each of the varnas was created with specific roles for each varna. In the *Popol Vuh*, the first humans were made by "sacrifice alone, by genius alone" by the gods known as the Maker, Modeler, Bearer, Begetter, and the Sovereign Plumed Serpent.

The most striking contrast between the two stories is the way social classes come to be. In the *Rig Veda*, the varnas are determined at the time human life first began by the designated parts of Purusha's body. In the *Popol Vuh,* social classes come as the result of the ladies of rank who give birth to the "peoples of the tribes, small and great": the implication is that social classes will exist in Maya society, but not with the direct tie to all time and place which is essential to the *Rig Veda* description. (p. 143)

PART II

THE FORMATION OF CLASSICAL SOCIETIES, 500 B.C.E TO 500 C.E.

CHAPTER 7

THE EMPIRES OF PERSIA

Before you get started: This summary of Chapter 7 is short because Persia is not included in the specific AP guidelines. Thus we have omitted primary sourcework as well as AP style questions at the end of the chapter summary. Nevertheless, there are certain patterns of empire-building, societal traditions, and religion that influenced later societies. You should have some familiarity with these aspects and it may be possible to use Persia to gain the "global context" points in the expanded core of the essays. By the way, Achaemenid refers to the initial ruling family of Persia and is virtually interchangeable with the term *Persians.*

THE RISE AND FALL OF THE PERSIAN EMPIRES

Persia lies in the arid area between Mesopotamia and the nomadic tribes of central Asia, so it was subject to intermittent invasions and migrations from the east. Nevertheless, in the sixth century B.C.E., the Persians began conquests that would put the area under imperial control for the next millennium.

The Achaemenid Empire
(Theme: Political Structures)

The settlers of **Persia** were Indo-European ethnic groups organized into clans who became loosely connected to Mesopotamian overlords. As descendants of central Asian tribes, the Persians had a military tradition. With the prowess borne of this tradition, Achaemenid ruler **Cyrus** conquered a vast region between India and Egypt by 530 B.C.E. He was a clever and wily military leader who undoubtedly would have conquered more regions but was killed in battle on the northeast border. His son, Cambyses, completed the conquest by gaining Egypt.

A young kinsman, **Darius,** extended the empire into northwest India and the western shore of the Black Sea. But it is his skill as an administrator that is most notable. Darius built a new capital at Persepolis which became the center of a sophisticated bureaucratic state. He also set up an efficient administration of twenty-three *satrapies* (provinces) creating a fine balance between central and local control. The provincial rulers, *satraps*, were constrained by the presence of imperial troops and tax collectors while traveling bureaucrats also monitored their actions. In common with later administrators of far-flung empires, he **standardized taxation and coinage**. While he did not set up a standardized legal system, legal scholars examined the laws in conquered areas to make sure that they did not conflict with Persian law. The other achievement of the Achaemenid emperors was the development of a network of roads providing communication with large parts of the empire. The **Persian Royal Road** stretched for 1600 miles from the Aegean Sea to Iran. It is helpful to recognize a repeat of these administrative patterns in the successful empires of China and Rome.

Decline and Fall of the Achaenamid Empire
(Themes: Political Structures and Changes and Continuities)

Eventually, differences between the Persians and its subject peoples became too difficult to overcome. Unfortunately, the tolerance for other traditions exhibited by Cyrus and Darius was not continued by Xerxes, the successor to Darius. His Persian policies led to rebellions which culminated in the **Persian Wars** with Greece. A long period of warfare with Greek city-states resulted in defeat. And, in 334 B.C.E., Macedonian conqueror **Alexander the Great** invaded Persia and defeated the Persians three years later. Persia was then divided into three regions ruled by Alexander's generals, one of which persisted until Arab warriors defeated it in 651 C.E.

The Seleucid, Parthian, and Sasanid Empires
(Theme: Political Structures and Changes and Continuities)

The Seleucids, named after Alexander's general, Seleucus, retained the Achaemenid administration but faced resistance to their foreign rule. Internal rebellions and central Asian invasions diminished their holdings so that the Romans easily defeated their remnants in the first century B.C.E. Those same invaders from central Asia became the next rulers of the central region of Persia. The Parthians ruled with a somewhat less centralized government for two centuries. In 224 C.E., the Sasanids of Persian origin claimed the lands and began to rebuild the elaborate bureaucracy of the Achaemanids. Regular conflict in their border areas weakened the Sasanids so that in 651 C.E., Arabs defeated the last ruler and instituted an Islamic state. But even in defeat, Persian governmental traditions continued when the Arabs adopted them.

IMPERIAL SOCIETY AND ECONOMY

Classical societies like the Persians became much more complex requiring increased numbers of bureaucrats, craftsmen, and slaves to function.

Social Development in Classical Persia
(Theme: Social Structure)

Similar to centralized Egypt, the demands of imperial administration required a large class of **bureaucrats** at the top of society to act as tax collectors and record keepers. To tie together the vast reaches of the empire with all its different cultures, the bureaucracy also needed large numbers of translators. Similar to earlier Mesopotamian societies, **free classes** and **slaves** formed the bulk of Persian society. Free classes had few privileges beyond their freedom. These consisted of craftsmen, artisans, merchants, and the lowest civil servants. Priests and priestesses formed a significant portion of the population of Persian cities as well. In rural areas, peasants and landless cultivators were included in the free classes. Not only did they farm the lands but they built elaborate irrigation systems including the underground channels known as *qanats*, some of which have persisted to the modern period. A large class of slaves also worked in rural and urban areas. Most were prisoners of war but some were unfortunate debtors owned by private individuals; the state itself owned slaves, as did the temple communities, to use as laborers on massive building projects.

Economic Foundations of Classical Persia
(Theme: Economics)

Despite the arid regions of central Persia, the conquered regions of the Persian empire were exceptionally fertile agricultural areas so there was great agricultural prosperity in the empires. Cereal grains, fruits, and vegetables were in abundance. Given its enviable position between eastern and western Asia, **long-distance trade** flourished particularly after the fall of the Acheamenid Empire.

RELIGIONS OF SALVATION IN CLASSICAL PERSIAN SOCIETY

The original religion of the Persians was probably close to that of the Aryans in India but a new faith appeared in the classical era that influenced Judaism, Christianity, and Islam.

Zarathustra and His Faith
(Theme: Religious Developments)

In the late seventh or early sixth centuries B.C.E., Zarathustra developed a theology based on the dualism of good and evil represented by two gods. Zarathustra is believed to be a historical person but the details of his life are not well understood. *Magi* or priests transmitted his teachings through oral traditions that later were written as the *Gathas*. Zarathustra named one main good deity, Ahura Mazda, and six lesser deities who conflicted with an evil spirit, Angra Mainyu. Followers of **Zoroastrianism** could be assured of entrance to heaven by following a life of "good words, good thoughts, good deeds." The religion spread widely throughout the Persian empire and persisted in some areas well beyond the fall of classical Persia. As a religion of salvation, some specific Zoroastrianism teachings influenced Jewish, Christian, and Islamic theology.

Religions of Salvation in a Cosmopolitan Society
(Theme: Religious Developments)

Although Alexander attempted to obliterate Zoroatrianism, it persisted through oral tradition and had a revival in the Sasanid dynasty. Later Islamic conquerors also persecuted the Zoroastrians until most converted and the remainder moved to India where small communities of believers remain to this day. Meanwhile, the tolerant rule of the Persians had allowed Judaism, Buddhism, Manichaeism, and Christianity to gain a foothold in Persian realms. And it was through these small communities that Zoroastrian beliefs moved into the other religions. These beliefs included a beneficent creator god, the conflict between good and evil, and the idea that human beings should strive to be moral so that when the day of judgment came, they would not be found wanting. Thus, the Persians had a profound effect on major religions today.

Chapter Multiple Choice Questions

1. What group did the early Achaemenids most closely resemble?
   a. Mesopotamians
   b. Greeks
   c. Arabs
   d. Aryans
   e. Egyptians

2. Cyrus and Cambyses conquered the regions originally held by the
   a. Greeks and Egyptians.
   b. Egyptians and Mesopotamians.
   c. Arabs and Indians.
   d. Greeks and Babylonians.
   e. Aryans and Nubians.

3. While Darius conquered further regions, he is known more as an administrator for his work with
   a. taxation and centralization.
   b. colonization and dictatorship.
   c. roads and sea routes.
   d. rulers and military elite.
   e. commoners and the regimental soldiers.

4. What is the definition of a satrap?
   a. an imperial bureaucrat
   b. the military leader of a province
   c. an imperial provincial governor
   d. the local ruler of a province
   e. quasi-independent provinces

5. How strict was Persian rule over its conquered peoples?
   a. Not very; most local rulers only had to exact tribute from their citizens.
   b. Fairly strict, as all provinces were ruled with military discipline.
   c. Somewhat strict since the Achaemenids distrusted foreigners.
   d. Pretty lenient although it kept close control by use of traveling investigators.
   e. Very strict as they replaced all local officials with Persians.

6. What was the unintended result of the standardization of coinage?
   a. People moved more freely from one region to another.
   b. It was easier to assess taxes.
   c. It promoted a sense of nationalistic pride.
   d. It allowed foreign traders access to more goods.
   e. It facilitated trade throughout the empire.

7. The Achaemenids fell due to a combination of
   a. a weakening army and succession problems.
   b. growing intolerance of other cultures and internal rebellions.
   c. attacks from central Asians and weak bureaucracy.
   d. bureaucratic infighting and a discontented population.
   e. satrap challenges and weak rulers.

8. The Seleucids, Parthians, and Sasanids were different ethnic groups but they all shared one attribute that allowed them to continue strong imperial rule. What was it?
   a. They founded new cities to serve as administrative capitals.
   b. They continued Darius's administrative policies.
   c. They faced little resistance from the Persian population.
   d. They used Persian administrators as satraps.
   e. They had few neighbors with imperial ambitions.

9. Like Mesopotamia and Egypt, Persian society was highly stratified. As in these cultures, most people in rural areas were engaged in
   a. building temple complexes and new cities.
   b. manufacturing trade items for the export market.
   c. domestic servitude to the upper classes on their large country properties.
   d. cultivation of grain crops exclusively since slaves could be used in irrigation duties.
   e. agriculture and the maintenance of an adequate water supply for the crops.

10. What aspect of Zoroastrianism is the most significant with respect to world history?
    a. It sustained the Persian empire and served as a justification for their rule.
    b. It became one of the many foreign religions that found a home in India.
    c. Parts of its tenets were adopted by monotheistic religions.
    d. Its temple complexes served as the backbone of Persian prosperity.
    e. Zoroastrianism is the founding faith of Judaism, Christianity, and Islam.

Chapter Multiple Choice Answers

1. **d:** As part of the Indo-European migration, the Achaemenids shared language and military traditions with the Aryans. (p. 160)

2. **b:** Cyrus conquered the Mesopotamian region as well as Anatolia and to the edge of India. His son conquered Egypt in 525 B.C.E. (pp. 161–162)

3. **a:** Darius set up a system of imperial government from his capitol in Persepolis that was highly centralized and chiefly engaged in tax collection. (p. 163)

4. **c:** A satraps was a provincial governor who was usually Persian. However, mostly local bureaucrats served under him. (p. 163)

5. **d:** The Persians allowed the provinces to decide their own laws as long as they did not conflict with Persian law. Yet, Darius used surprise investigations to keep control over the provinces. (p. 163)

6. **e:** Although Darius borrowed the idea of standard coinage from the Lydians to improve tax collection, it promoted trade across the Persian empire. (p. 164)

7. **b:** After the relatively tolerant regimes of Cyrus and Darius, Xerxes asserted Persian domination over the provinces. This led to revolts which culminated in the disastrous Persian Wars. (p. 165)

8. **b:** The successors to the Achaemenids all used the administrative framework set in place by Darius although the Parthians allowed clan leaders to serve as satraps. (pp. 166–168)

9. **e:** Farmers in all three regions spent a good part of their time ensuring the harvest of their crops by managing the water supply, whether scarce or plentiful. In the case of the Persians, arid fields required sophisticated solutions like the *qanat*. (pp. 170–171)

10. **c:** Jewish communities adopted some aspects of Zarathustra's faith having to do with morality and the forces of evil as well as the idea of a time of judgment for all humans. These ideas later were inherited by Christians and Muslims. (p. 177)

CHAPTER 8

THE UNIFICATION OF CHINA

Before you get started: Chinese names and terms should become easier and more familiar with this chapter. In Chapter 5, you learned the essential concepts of the dynastic cycle and ancestor worship that persist throughout Chinese history. Now, you will build on that base. You may continue to use flashcards for the new terms, if you wish. The key to understanding this stage of Chinese history is learning the achievements of the short Qin dynasty and seeing how the Han dynasty continues them. A note for the name Confucius: this is the latinization of "Kong Fuxi" and is still the more typical spelling.

IN SEARCH OF POLITICAL AND SOCIAL ORDER

The late Zhou Dynasty disintegrated into a period of political chaos leading to the **Period of Warring States** (403–221 B.C.E.). As it deteriorated, some notable cultural achievements occurred, especially in the area of philosophy. **Confucianism, Daoism,** and **Legalism** were three competing schools of thought that developed out of the chaos.

Confucius and His School
(Themes: Intellectual Developments and Political Structures)

In the sixth century B.C.E., **Kong Fuxi (Confucius)** developed a philosophy that had moral, social, and political dimensions. Despite a disappointing career, his teachings developed a following and those disciples compiled his sayings into a written work known as the ***Analects***. His view of life was entirely practical as he did not deal with religion or abstract philosophy. Rather, he focused on the moral and ethical behavior of the individual. According to Confucius, there were three important qualities in a superior individual (*junzi*) and those were courtesy (*ren*), propriety (*li*), and filial piety (*xiao*). And, it is the presence of highly moral citizens that produces an effective society and government. Confucius encouraged his followers to study classic texts from the Zhou. The study of those classics, along with others, remained a fixture of Chinese education until the twentieth century.

Confucian ideas had been expressed in general terms so the philosophy evolved with the input of later disciples. **Mencius** in the fourth century B.C.E. put more emphasis on the benevolent aspect of *ren* while **Xunxi,** even later, saw the less positive side of humans and emphasized *li*. Despite their differences, both placed an emphasis on how to produce an orderly society.

Daoism
(Theme: Intellectual Developments)

Daoists looked at the same Warring States period and came up with an opposite philosophy. They emphasized a withdrawal from society because there was no real solution to the problems. Instead, they advocated learning to live in passive harmony with the world. If everyone worked on following the *dao* or "the way of the cosmos," society would fix itself. The ideal citizen practiced *wuwei*, complete withdrawal from the active world, and emphasized pursuit of self-knowledge. They believed that following the natural principles that governed the world, like diet and meditation, would restore balance and harmony. The traditional founder of Daoism was a philosopher named **Laozi**; however, historians believe that he is a composite of several different thinkers of the era. Particularly interesting is that Confucians found parts of Daoism very appealing and since neither philosophy requires exclusivity, Chinese scholars often were faithful Confucian bureaucrats as well as devoted followers of Daoism in their private lives.

Legalism
(Themes: Intellectual Developments and Political Structures)

Neither Confucianism nor Daoism solved the problems of the Warring States; it was **Legalism** that unified and calmed China. Legalists were representatives of the Qin state who believed that the only answer to chaos was harsh governance. They believed the basis of an orderly society was agriculture and the military, so they emphasized soldiers and peasants while de-emphasizing other classes. Men were discouraged from becoming merchants, scholars, or educators. Harsh penalties were imposed on criminals and dissenters and even entire families could be punished along with the offender. Legalism was used effectively in the Qin and early Han dynasties. In later dynasties, there continued to be tension between ruling on the model of the moral behavior of Confucianism or the harsh rule of law in Legalism. Legalism was effective but history was written by the Confucians, so Legalists have been harshly criticized in the annals of Chinese history.

THE UNIFICATION OF CHINA

The harsh policies of Legalism allowed the Qin state to unify China. While it lasted a very short time, its governmental structure persisted into the twentieth century and its cultural unity continues to this day.

The Qin Dynasty
(Themes: Political Structures and Changes and Continuities)

The **Qin** state built up the loyalty of its common citizens with land reform and produced a powerful army with the profits of its agriculture. Then, it systematically conquered surrounding states. By 221 B.C.E., its ruler, **Qin Shihuangdi,** was able to pronounce himself as the First Emperor of the new Qin dynasty. Like the Egyptians and Persians, the Qin then developed a strong centralized administration over a vast area. Qin Shihuangdi divided China into provinces but kept strict central control over them. He built **roads** to facilitate communications and governance. He **standardized weights and measurements**, as well as coinage and laws to further unify the state. While each region's spoken language remained incomprehensible to others, Qin Shihuangdi ordered the **standardization of Chinese script**. One thing to note is how other large empires like Rome will institute many of the same policies.

While the Chinese must have welcomed orderly governance after the wars between states, his tactics drew significant criticism from the Confucians and Daoists. The First Emperor responded with executions and **book-burnings**. Many classics completely disappeared and others had to be reconstructed in the Han dynasty. He conscripted millions of workers for public projects. Thousands died reinforcing defensive walls on the northwest border. These walls later became components of the **Great Wall.** Furthermore, some seven hundred thousand other laborers were conscripted to build the **elaborate tomb** for Qin Shihuangdi. Every student should be able to identify the rows of life size terra-cotta soldiers that were discovered in the modern excavations of his tomb. The harshness of the Qin regime led to its downfall soon after the burial of the First Emperor and traditional Chinese scholars remembered him as China's most cruel ruler.

The Early Han Dynasty
(Themes: Political Structures and Changes and Continuities)

Among the peasant rebels who defeated the Qin Dynasty was a talented commander named **Liu Bang.** He was able to consolidate control over competing forces by sheer persistence and the immense loyalty of his army. In 206 B.C.E., he declared himself the first emperor of the Han dynasty. At first, he allowed the provinces to operate fairly independently but when they failed to support the Han during an invasion, he returned to the Qin model of centralized control. The Han dynasty lasted for more than four hundred years from 206 B.C.E. to 220 C.E. It is so revered by the Chinese that they refer to themselves as the "people of Han."

The most successful Han emperor was **Han Wudi,** who followed the Legalist principles and governmental policies of the Qin. An energetic and talented administrator, Han Wudi built a more elaborate bureaucracy, added more canals and roads, and founded a university. Confucianism returned to its central position in the Han government with the education and examination of scholar-bureaucrats based on Confucian ideals. So, while he relied on Legalism to sustain his empire, he promoted Confucianism to obtain his bureaucratic workforce. The Han had faced a persistent problem from nomads from the northwest, the Xiongnu. They had a highly disciplined army and ruled a confederation of Turkish nomads across central Asia. The Han tried economic and diplomatic means to appease the Xiongnu but neither bribes of tribute nor marriages between the two peoples had any lasting effect. Han Wudi added the conquest of the Xiongnu to his conquests of Korea and Vietnam and rightly became known as the Martial Emperor.

FROM ECONOMIC PROSPERITY TO SOCIAL DISORDER

Eventually, dissatisfaction over land policies led to social and economic problems in the later Han. Banditry and rebellion were signs that the dynasty was losing its Mandate of Heaven. Unable to produce a solution for disgruntled citizens, the Han dynasty failed by the third century C.E.

Productivity and Prosperity during the Former Han
(Themes: Social Structure, Economics, and Trade)

The structure of the Chinese household changed little from the Zhou, with the average household size of five inhabitants. The Han saw families as the essential unit of an orderly society. The Confucian *Classic of Filial Piety* demonstrates the importance that the Han attached to the patriarchal structure with children obedient to their elders. Women were admonished to be humble, obedient, and subservient in the *Admonitions for Women.*

Iron metallurgy and **silk production** added to the prosperity of the Han. While iron weapons and armor contributed to the Han military prowess, Chinese silk was valued as a trade item as far away as Rome. Commodities flowed along the silk roads from east Asia to the Mediterranean. During the Han, the Chinese invented **paper,** a less expensive medium than silk scrolls. Agricultural yields and general prosperity were so great that the population tripled to sixty million by 9 C.E.

Economic and Social Difficulties
(Theme: Changes and Continuities)

Han Wudi's military expeditions required higher taxation and he eventually had to resort to confiscation of businesses and properties to obtain the revenue. This policy discouraged investors which caused the economy to suffer. Furthermore, the gap between rich and poor widened causing increased social tension. This disparity was exacerbated by inequitable land distribution as profitable land became concentrated in the hands of the wealthy. The reaction by the poor was banditry and rebellion but the Han leaders were reluctant to alienate the large landholders by addressing the problem. Despite the short-lived reform efforts of the usurper Wang Mang who seized the Han throne, proclaimed a new dynasty, and was ousted, further chaos ensued as landowners refused to give up their property and drought devastated agriculture.

The Later Han Dynasty
(Theme: Changes and Continuities)

Despite renewed centralized power, the Later Han emperors continued the failure to address land distribution and in the late second century C.E., the rebellions of peasant societies like the **Yellow Turbans** further weakened the Han. The dynasty then deteriorated into competing factions of bureaucrats, eunuchs, and imperial family members within the imperial administration. Internal weakness demonstrated by the infighting ultimately led to its division into regional states.

Finished reading the chapter? Be sure you can . . .

- Compare the three Chinese philosophies.
- Describe Qin unification, accomplishments, and the reasons for its downfall.
- Describe the patriarchal structure.
- List the important economic accomplishments of the Han.
- Explain the tensions between the elite and common classes.
- Explain why the Han dynasty deteriorated.

Chapter Multiple Choice Questions

1. Chinese schools of thought came out of a period of
   a. domestic harmony.
   b. chaotic disunity.
   c. centralized power.
   d. dynastic stability.
   e. unified authority.

2. Daoism and Confucianism differ on the topic of
   a. family values.
   b. the existence of a god.
   c. reincarnation.
   d. social involvement.
   e. heaven and hell.

3. How did the Qin state became dominant in China?
   a. through cooperation with neighboring states
   b. by genocide aimed at other strong states
   c. by the gradual conquest of other states
   d. through its diplomacy that encouraged allies to help
   e. by offering social reform to the peoples of other states

4. Among the many accomplishments of the First Emperor, which one persisted into the Han dynasty?
   a. formation of administrative districts
   b. adherence to Legalism
   c. persecution of dissenters
   d. suppression of Confucianism
   e. elaborate burial procedures

5. Despite his scorn for other classes, Qin Shihuangdi failed to consider the concerns of the average peasant. Which of the following most aggravated them?
   a. taxation policy that favored the scholars
   b. paranoia that led to the persecution of officials
   c. massive conscription for public works
   d. economic policies that favored trade
   e. policy of persecution of educated people

6. While the Qin was already weakened by earlier dissent and rebellions, what allowed Liu Bang, the founder of the Han dynasty, to produce its ultimate defeat?
   a. better equipment
   b. larger armies
   c. charismatic leadership
   d. little competition
   e. a devoted army

7. Han Wudi is recognized as the strongest Han emperor. What would be his most important contribution to the administrations of later dynasties?
   a. the conquest of northern Korea and Vietnam
   b. the formation of a Confucian educational system
   c. the continuation of Qin road building
   d. the example of how to defeat central Asian nomads
   e. the establishment of imperial monopolies on iron and salt

8. Despite the change in dynasties, domestic life changed very little. Chinese patriarchy continued and was supported by
   a. the Confucian classics.
   b. the Daoist principles.
   c. the governmental enforcement.
   d. the Legalist ideas.
   e. the imperial edicts.

9. Several technologies improved trade and commerce for the Han, including
   a. compasses.
   b. bronze tools.
   c. sericulture.
   d. wheeled vehicles.
   e. improved ships.

10. The Han Dynasty began its decline when it could not solve the problem of
    a. military weakness.
    b. enormous taxation.
    c. drought and plague.
    d. land distribution.
    e. weak rulers.

Comprehensive Multiple Choice Questions

1. The Zhou concept of the Mandate of Heaven required the ruler to govern well in order to maintain social stability. Which of the following groups most clearly represent a failure on the part of the Han ruler?
   a. the Xiongnu nomads
   b. the scholar-officials produced by universities
   c. the eunuchs within the imperial court
   d. the Yellow Turbans
   e. the dissatisfied peasants

2. While Qin Shihuangdi used Legalism to maintain tight control and force unity on China, other policies unified the Chinese more directly and lasted much longer.
   a. the participation by peasants from around China in building the Great Wall
   b. the standardization of weights, measurements and scripts
   c. the high enrollment in Qin Shihuangdi's army forces
   d. the improved road systems built for military use
   e. both b and c

3. During the chaotic Period of Warring States the Chinese looked to different philosophies for stability. Neither Confucianism nor Daoism includes the worship of any deities. What might be one reason a true religion with dieties does not originate in China?
   a. The Chinese are inherently practical people who desire guidelines for daily life rather than promises of eternal life.
   b. Veneration of ancestors as practiced since ancient times fulfilled the need for protective spirituality.
   c. By killing scholars and burning books, Qin Shihuangdi managed to convince the Chinese that it was safer to have no beliefs.
   d. Daoism promotes meditation that serves the same purpose as prayer.
   e. Outside of human warfare, there are no natural disasters in China that would produce a set of protective deities.

Primary Source Questions

1. **Read *Sources from the Past, Confucius on Good Government,* post-sixth century B.C.E., on page 184 of your textbook.**
   a. Who wrote this?
   b. Who are the questioners and the Master?
   c. Do outside influences inspire people?
   d. What does a ruler have to do to gain the confidence of his people?
   e. What analogy does the Master use?

2. **Read *Sources from the Past, Laozi on Living in Harmony with Dao,* post-sixth century B.C.E., on page 188 of your textbook.**
   a. Who wrote this piece? (Point of view that is not the translator.)
   b. What is the important message for government officials?
   c. What analogy does Laozi use?

3. **Examine the Wheeled Chariot Model bronze, Qin and Han Dynasty, on page 195 of your textbook.**
   a. What does the chariot indicate about the status of officials in China?
   b. What can you determine about the artist?
   c. What does this sculpture say about technology in the Qin and Han?
   d. As an art piece, how would you recognize this as Chinese?

Chapter Multiple Choice Answers

1. **b:** Confucianism, Daoism, and Legalese all appeared during the Period of the Warring States (403–221 B.C.E.) (p. 182)

2. **d:** Instead of social activism, Daoists were devoted to introspection. (pp. 186, 187)

3. **c:** By the third century B.C.E., the kingdom of Qin had absorbed most other Chinese states by attacking each one. (p. 190)

4. **a:** Despite a brief period of social chaos, the Han dynasty returned to the centralized government of the Qin, including the continuation of administrative districts. (p. 194)

5. **c:** Peasants forced to work on Qin public work projects resented leaving families and lands. They formed the core of rebellions against the Qin dynasty. (p. 193)

6. **e:** Liu Bang was neither charismatic nor unchallenged, but he followed the brilliant advice of loyal soldiers. (p. 194)

7. **b:** Han Wudi established a university based on Confucian principles that was designed to train the bureaucrats that every dynasty needed. (p. 195)

8. **a:** *The Classic of Filial Piety* promoted obedience to superiors, and orderly families were seen as the basis of an orderly society. (p. 197)

9. **c:** Sericulture or the production of valuable silk fabrics helped to boost trade along the silk roads. (p. 198)

10. **d:** The Later Han never solved the problem of land distribution that had disrupted the Early Han, so disgruntled peasants turned to rebel groups such as the Yellow Turbans. (p. 201)

Comprehensive Multiple Choice Answers

1. **d:** Although all these groups represented some challenges to Han emperors, it was the organized power of the Yellow Turbans that directly challenged the dynasty and seriously undermined its credibility with the people of China. (pp. 201–202)

2. **e:** Although the army and public works projects brought many Chinese together, it was the standardization policies and improved road system that allowed trade to flourish thus tying all regions more closely together. (pp. 192–194)

3. **b:** Veneration of ancestors continued throughout Chinese history so it is easy to see that a pragmatic approach to social order would be appealing. While Confucians promote a structure for society, veneration of ancestors provides the framework for the family. Just as one could practice both Daoism and Confucianism, it was possible to follow all three for complete spiritual protection. (p. 186)

Primary Source Answers

1. As in all Confucian works, this was written by a Confucian follower. The questioners are other followers, perhaps rulers, and the Master is Confucius (Kong Fuxi). People are inspired by their own virtue and sense of shame. The ruler must be kind and grave, and must advance good people in government. The relationship is as "a wind to grass"; that is to say, the people must bend to the will of the ruler. (p. 184)

2. A follower of Daoism wrote this piece. Governments should practice moderation and uprightness. The Sage remarked that water was the softest thing but it easily surrounds and defeats hard items. (p. 188)

3. The status of officials is indicated by the presence of four horses with fine harnesses and a finely crafted two-wheeled cart. The artist is very skilled since the sculpture uses two types of metallurgy. The technology is advanced as can be seen in the silver and bronze but also in the refinement of the wheeled vehicle. It is recognizable as Chinese by its realistic quality, its chunky horses, and its composition of bronze. The driver appears to be dressed in a typical Chinese dress with a high, rolled collar and his hair appears to be dressed in the topknot of that period. The flat-angled roof of the cart is also reminiscent of roofs on Chinese houses. (p. 195)

CHAPTER 9

STATE, SOCIETY, AND THE QUEST FOR SALVATION IN INDIA

Before you get started: Remember that you learned about castes and the beginnings of Hinduism in Chapter 4. Now, you will build on that as you learn that Buddhism has its roots in Hinduism and the appearance of *jati* or subcastes augments the caste system. On the AP Exam, you are not expected to know Jainism or the different types of Buddhism, but you should understand the basic tenets of Buddhism and its origin.

THE FORTUNES OF EMPIRE IN CLASSICAL INDIA

Between 1500 and 600 B.C.E., a series of **Aryan kingdoms** consolidated into several regional kingdoms. Although two dynasties enjoyed brief control over the subcontinent, India never established a tradition of one large, centralized state as seen in China.

The Mauryan Dynasty and the Temporary Unification of India
(Theme: Political Structures)

When Alexander the Great withdrew from Northwest India, he left a vacuum that was eventually filled by the ruler of an Indian kingdom, **Chandragupta Maurya.** The **Mauryans** expanded their empire into present-day Afghanistan and well into central and eastern India by 321 B.C.E. However, the dynasty never captured the southern tip of India. Chandragupta's government was based on a set of administrative principles in a book called the *Arthashustra* written by his close adviser, Kautalya. Like the Qin dynasty in China, his administration was quite harsh and incorporated the use of numerous spies.

The apex of the Mauryans was the reign of Chandragupta's grandson, **Ashoka.** In 268 B.C.E. Ashoka began his campaign to conquer the last state in the northern region of the subcontinent. Once he had subdued the kingdom, Ashoka turned from conqueror to administrator. He was a skilled governor who utilized a strong bureaucracy under his direct control. **Edicts** were carved in many stone pillars to express his wishes. Ashoka encouraged agriculture with irrigation systems and trade with road-building projects. Travelers were impressed to find inns, wells, and shade trees along these routes. Eventually, Ashoka converted to **Buddhism** and became intensely supportive of the religion. His promotion helped Buddhism to flourish during his reign. But when Ashoka died in 232 B.C.E., his policies failed to be sustained and the dynasty fell into decline. The costs of sustaining a huge army and a large administration were so heavy that by 185 B.C.E., there was no Mauryan empire.

The Emergence of Regional Kingdoms and the Revival of Empire
(Themes: Political Structures and Changes and Continuities)

Many small, successful kingdoms succeeded the Maurya for the next four hundred years until the advent of the **Guptas** in 320 C.E. Their territory included much of the former Mauryan empire but nevertheless remained smaller. Under Chandra Gupta (no relation to Chandragupta Maurya) and his two successors, the Guptas controlled every area except the Deccan Plateau and the southern tip of India. More similar to the Persians than the Mauryans, the Guptas left governance in the provinces to local allies. Their rule produced a stability that lasted for almost two centuries. White Hun invasions from the northwest split the Gupta empire into its original regions and the last Gupta rulers lost their power to regional rulers. Then, once again, India became a continent of many kingdoms.

ECONOMIC DEVELOPMENT AND SOCIAL DISTINCTIONS

The success of iron metallurgy and great harvests allowed India to develop more urban centers and fostered more trade. However, both of these developments also intensified the caste system.

Towns and Trade
(Theme: Economics)

Indian craftsmen provided numerous manufactured products for the common and elite classes. Many towns in India provided marketplaces to distribute goods from thousands of workshops. Long-distance trade was carried out primarily through the northwest region, following the roads built by the Persians, and maintained by Alexander and Chandragupta. The endpoints of direct Indian trade along this route were China in the east and Persia in the west. Increasingly, merchants turned to the Indian Ocean for trade. Merchant ships benefited from the **monsoon seasons** that brought winds from the southwest in the spring and summer and winds from the northeast during the fall and winter. Along the seacoast were ships that went as far away as the Red Sea and there is evidence that the Romans had trading posts in western India.

Family Life and the Caste System
(Theme: Social Structure)

Despite the ideal of the extended family living in one household, most Indians lived with their **nuclear families.** Only the highest castes with wealth came close to the ideal. Women's positions became even more subordinate to men. Women were viewed as weak in the Hindu epics, ***Ramayana*** and ***Mahabharata.*** And, the evidence that the patriarchy became more dominant is that the number of **child brides** betrothed to men in their twenties increased. Nevertheless, it is still highly probable that women dominated domestic issues.

The **caste system** continued with its four major groups but a new social order began to emerge. As trade and industry took off, groups of merchants and craftsmen formed guilds to set prices and provide aid to their members. The guilds functioned as more subcastes or *jati,* with primary responsibility to all members of their occupation. Thus, social stability and security became a function of local groups rather than governmental bodies. Another unusual change occurred in the social order during this time. Tremendous wealth generated by increased manufacturing often gave more influence to members of the two lower castes (the *vaishyas* and *shudras*) than the two upper castes (*brahmins* and *kshatriyas*.) But, both of these developments solidified the absolute power that castes had over life in India.

RELIGIONS OF SALVATION IN CLASSICAL INDIA

During the fifth and sixth centuries B.C.E., new religions emerged that offered the hope of salvation for the dispossessed. In following these new religions, millions of converts rejected the Hinduism that was promoted by the brahmin caste.

Jainism and the Challenge to the Established Cultural Order
(Theme: Religious Developments)

Jainism is not mentioned in the AP guidelines; however, you should know that it was a very strict form of Hinduism that eschewed all forms of violence. It was so strict that few people outside of Jainist monks were able to follow its tenets successfully. However, the Jainists did not follow the rules of caste so it was a popular religion. Indeed, there remain two million Jainists in India today and the religion influenced both Mohandas Gandhi and Martin Luther King Jr. in the twentieth century.

Early Buddhism
(Themes: Religious Developments)

The founder of Buddhism, **Siddhartha Gautama,** grew up in a high-caste family protected from any sadness by an overprotective father. When he was older, he saw the world outside the walls of his home and discovered old age, illness, and poverty. Shocked out of his complacent lifestyle, he took to the life of a wandering monk as he contemplated the nature of suffering. Eventually, under a bo tree, he discovered enlightenment and became the **Buddha—"the enlightened one."** He began preaching his ideas and soon attracted many followers dedicated to him and his teachings.

The Buddha outlined the **Four Noble Truths** of enlightenment: All life has suffering; desire is the cause of suffering; to eliminate desire will bring an end to suffering: and the only way to eliminate it is to follow the **Noble Eightfold Path**. The eight paths to enlightenment are right belief, right resolve, right speech, right behavior, right occupation, right effort, right contemplation, and right meditation. Thus followers should live a moderate lifestyle with quiet contemplation and self-control. A faithful adherent will eventually eliminate desire and will attain spiritual independence or *nirvana* as an escape from the cycle of reincarnation. The Four Noble Truths and the Eightfold Path constitute the *dharma* or the basic doctrine of Buddhism.

Buddhism was enormously appealing to members of lower castes because the route to *nirvana* did not rest with the priestly caste, the *brahmins*, but could be attained by anyone. So, similar to the Jainists, Buddhists eschewed caste differences. Furthermore, Buddhists used the vernacular language to preach rather than the elite Sanskrit of Hinduism. And, once Buddha's followers organized themselves into communities of **monks,** they spread Buddhism into distant lands. The Mauryan emperor Ashoka's conversion and subsequent support of the religion further aided its spread throughout India and into central Asia. Buddhism also proved appealing to women with Buddhist nuns choosing the ascetic life during the era of the Buddha himself. By tradition, the first Buddhist nun was his own stepmother, Pajapati.

Mahayana Buddhism
(Theme: Religious Developments)

While you do not need to know the types of Buddhism, it is useful to have some awareness of the general direction that the branches took. Like Jainism, true devotion to the Buddha was difficult and required a life of **asceticism**. So, somewhere between the third century B.C.E. and the first century C.E., additions to the religion allowed easier adherence to its tenets. Buddhists began to worship the Buddha; the concept of *boddhisatvas* or enlightened individuals appeared and Buddhists began to accept wealthy gifts from individuals in return for a promise of salvation. All these expanded the practice of Buddhism to a wider audience and it eventually became the most popular religion in India.

The Emergence of Popular Hinduism
(Theme: Religious Developments)

Three epics of Hinduism during this period, the *Mahabharata*, the *Ramayana*, and the *Bhagavad Gita*, reinforced the caste system by emphasizing the active life and adherence to caste over the ascetic life. This message opened Hinduism to common people who were accustomed to the caste system and gradually Hinduism overtook Buddhism as the most popular religion in India. The Gupta dynasty further supported Hinduism by favoring the *brahmins* and their educational programs. Buddhism persisted in India for the first millenium C.E., but as it retreated into a purely monastic endeavor supported by rich patrons, it lost its popular appeal. By the time Islam arrived in India, Buddhism had practically disappeared.

Finished reading the chapter? Be sure you can . . .

- Describe the development of Buddhism and its tenets.
- Compare Hinduism and Buddhism and how they influenced societal norms.
- Describe the complexities of the later caste system that include *jatis* and its support from Hinduism.
- Describe the role of women in Hindu and Buddhist tradition.

Chapter Multiple Choice Questions

1. Before the advent of the Mauryan Dynasty c. 320 B.C.E., India was
    a. split into many city-states.
    b. completely controlled by Alexander of Macedonia.
    c. divided into several large kingdoms.
    d. divided into two major realms, one Hindu and one Buddhist.
    e. recovering from the harsh regime of another dynasty.

2. In what way did Chadragupta Maurya rule?
    a. He left the governance to smaller kingdoms.
    b. He followed a strong philosophy of governance.
    c. He allowed local control of government.
    d. He encouraged Buddhism as the sole state religion.
    e. He conquered Sri Lanka and personally ruled there.

3. Ashoka's accomplishments were numerous and included promotion of Buddhism and the economy as well as
    a. communicating extensively with his people by written edicts.
    b. encouraging Indian Ocean trade over land routes.
    c. allowing his vassals to maintain independent armies.
    d. promoting a single official language so that all Indians would be able to read his edicts.
    e. rejecting a capital city in favor of numerous governmental seats throughout India.

4. The Gupta empire was primarily different from the Maurya in size. What was another significant difference?
    a. its rural economic focus
    b. the status of women
    c. its emphasis on Buddhism
    d. its intolerance to new religions
    e. its dependence on local governance

5. During the period between 321 B.C.E. and 550 C.E., India went through enormous economic growth in
    a. the border towns that could trade with the Persians.
    b. the small towns becoming large cities through trade.
    c. the rural areas where farmers turned to crafts instead.
    d. local trade in the northern regions of the subcontinent.
    e. long-distance trade by land routes and sea routes.

6. The caste system became more intricate due to the influence of
    a. Ashoka, who demanded strict adherence to caste.
    b. the *jatis* formed from the emerging guilds.
    c. Buddhism which promotes the caste system.
    d. the Mauryan emperors who only communicated through Brahmins.
    e. long-distance traders who adopted the caste system to fit into society.

7. What does Buddhist doctrine hold as the root of all suffering?
   a. disease
   b. aging
   c. violence
   d. desire
   e. castes

8. Buddhism appealed to many common people because
   a. the life of a monk or a nun was fairly easy to follow.
   b. it downplayed social caste, and emphasized individual freedoms.
   c. most people were looking for an opportunity to worship one god.
   d. it accepted the prevailing social order.
   e. it was promoted by the Guptas.

9. After his conversion to Buddhism, what was Ashoka's greatest support of Buddhism?
   a. support for its missionary efforts
   b. elimination of social castes
   c. persecution of Hindus
   d. promotion of Jainist principles as a secondary faith
   e. religious tolerance throughout India

10. Hinduism went through a transformation as Buddhism became more popular when
    a. strict adherence to the caste system began to liberalize.
    b. Ashoka built Hindu temples to promote tolerance.
    c. gurus promoted salvation through the *Brahmins.*
    d. organized communities of monks began to find *Brahmin* patrons.
    e. recognition of the active life became a route to salvation for all, no matter what caste.

Comprehensive Multiple Choice Questions

1. The ultimate goal in both Buddhism and Hinduism is to escape the cycle of reincarnation, but in what way do their goals differ?
   a. It is a difference in name only; *nirvana* and *brahman* are the same thing.
   b. Buddhists believe in salvation while Hindus believe in heaven.
   c. For Buddhists, it is spiritual independence while for Hindus it is spiritual union.
   d. Hindus pursue karma while Buddhists pursue dharma.
   e. Hindus will come to the place of the deities while Buddhists will float in the void.

2. From Aryan society to the kingdom period of the Mauryans, the prestige of the four main castes changed. The lower two castes became as influential if not more so than the upper castes. How did these reflect the values of their societies?
   a. Aryan societies mostly valued political and spiritual power while Mauryan societies also valued commercial endeavors.
   b. Aryan society was forming the Hindu religion while later Mauryans were strengthening Buddhism.
   c. Aryan societies allowed high-caste women more opportunities than did the Mauryans.
   d. Aryan society valued military prowess while Mauryans valued administrative expertise.
   e. Aryan societies valued teachers and priests more than the Mauryans.

3. The decline of the Zhou dynasty in China paralleled that of India's Gupta dynasty. What were the primary similarities?
   a. They were threatened by internal rebellions and overthrown by military insurrections.
   b. They spread themselves too thinly in continued conquests of neighboring states.
   c. Their territories were gradually taken from them by their neighbors.
   d. They were overwhelmed by internal financial problems when their currencies became devalued.
   e. Invasions from central Asian nomads allowed provincial governors to form independent states.

Primary Source Questions

1. **Read** *Sources from the Past: Caste Duties According to the* **Bhagavad Gita, on page 227 of your textbook.**
   a. Who might have written this piece? (point of view)
   b. How could this instruction for the warrior caste (*kshatriya*) apply to all castes?
   c. How did the *Bhagavad Gita* contribute to the popularity of Hinduism?

2. **Examine the gold coin, northern India, first/second century C.E., on page 215 of your textbook.**
   a. Can you determine why Buddha might be on the face of a coin?
   b. How do you know this is the Buddha?

3. **Examine the stupa at Sanchi, India, second century B.C.E., on page 221 of your textbook.**
   a. Describe the shape of the main building.
   b. Why did Ashoka have it built and who actually built it?
   c. Can you guess what the shape represents?

Chapter Multiple Choice Answers

1. **c:** After the Aryans, several small kingdoms were able to expand into larger regional kingdoms. (p. 208)

2. **b:** Chadragupta Maurya followed the advice of his adviser, Kautalya, who detailed every aspect of governance in his book, the *Arthashastra.* (p. 209)

3. **a:** As a means of communication with his citizens, Ashoka arranged for rocks and pillars to be carved with his edicts. (p. 210)

4. **e:** Unlike Ashoka who followed closely the actions of every local official, the Guptas let their allies govern the distant places in their empire. (p. 212)

5. **e:** As China and the Mediterranean region prospered, India was able to establish long-distance trade over the networks forged by the Persians and Alexander. (p. 214)

6. **b:** Guilds or *jatis* associated with different occupations added another layer of social control to the caste system. (p. 216)

7. **d:** In the Four Noble Truths, the Buddha taught that desire was the cause of all suffering. (p. 219)

8. **b:** The Buddhists did not recognize social distinctions and *nirvana* was available to all without the services of the *brahmins.* (p. 220)

9. **a:** Ashoka encouraged the spread of Buddhism throughout India with direct aid to missionaries in Bactria and Sri Lanka. (p. 221)

10. **e:** When the recognition that active lives did not preclude salvation transformed Hinduism, it regained its status as the most popular religion in India. (p. 226)

Comprehensive Multiple Choice Answers

1. **c:** Both will indeed escape reincarnation but Buddhists will attain *nirvana* which is a state of spiritual independence while Hindus will attain union with the universal soul, *Brahman*. (pp. 101, 220)

2. **a:** Traditional Aryan values pointed to the upper castes as being more important for their role in ruling a primarily agricultural society. Mauryan society had become quite urbanized so that there were many more merchants and craftsmen accumulating wealth and prestige. (p. 217)

3. **e:** The Zhou kings appointed allies and relatives to control various regions and then exercised very little control over them. The governors built up political, military, and economic power so once the capital of the Zhou government had been conquered by a nomadic army, the governors became independent of central authority. Similarily, the Guptas were disinterested in strict supervision of regional subordinates. They allowed the separate regions to govern themselves. Once the White Huns had invaded and weakened the central authority, the regional governors gradually took power for themselves. (pp. 117, 213)

Primary Source Answers

1. Written by numerous Hindu authors, the *Bhagavad Gita*'s high praise for the *kshatriya* dedication to battle can be applied to each caste. The *brahmins* were expected to be devoted to teaching and preaching. The *vaishyas* would be rewarded for prosperity in trade and the *shudra* would find salvation with a dedicated life in farming. With each caste member accepting a highly defined place in society, the new Hinduism promoted salvation through living an active life devoted to caste duties. Since most lives were already absolutely defined by caste, the promotion of devotion to caste as a means of salvation appealed to most Indians. (p. 227)

2. Since Buddhism had been highly promoted by Ashoka two hundred years before, it is likely that Buddhism had many followers in northern India at this date. It is probable that the ruler of this kingdom was Buddhist. It is possible to recognize this figure as the Buddha because the spelling on the side of the coin is so close to the English spelling that you can read it. This indicates that the Indo-European languages are closely connected. Furthermore, the standing figure is depicted in the long robes of a monk as in most early depictions. And he has very long earlobes, a symbol of superb perception, which is a feature of representations of the Buddha. (p. 215)

3. The stupa is a domed building in the shape of a bell. Ashoka was the foremost promoter of Buddhism but he would not have built it. Rather, it would have been built by laborers under the direction of engineers and perhaps monks. The shape of a stupa is meant to represent the sitting Buddha; thus it is the base as the rounded body with a small square as his head and the spire as his crown. The stupa shape on any building in Asia is representative of Buddhism. (p. 221)

CHAPTER 10

MEDITERRANEAN SOCIETY: THE GREEK PHASE

Before you get started: This is probably a chapter you think you know something about already: Zeus, Mount Olympus, Hercules, Troy, Alexander . . . Rely on that prior knowledge, but don't let it get in your way. For the AP Exam, that type of background information may help you a bit, but it is not the content you are expected to know for the multiple choice nor for any of the three essays. What you will need to draw from this chapter and the next is content predominantly tied to the themes of trade and the interaction of cultures, political culture and organizations, and cultural and intellectual developments. Hollywood movies won't be much help.

EARLY DEVELOPMENT OF GREEK SOCIETY

Early Greek history is based on small, autonomous city-states which developed in hard-fought isolation with roots in ancient cultures like Mesopotamia, Egypt, and Phoenicia. Over time, however, these city-states began to trade with each other and then venture out into the Aegean and eventually Mediterranean Seas which they used as a highway to link Europe, Asia, and Africa. This highway allowed the spread of Greek goods and, more importantly, ideas and values throughout the Mediterranean basin, Europe, and southwest Asia.

Minoan and Mycenaean Societies
(Themes: Trade and Patterns of Interactions)

Minoan society developed on **Crete** c. 2000 B.C.E. and thrived there until it fell under foreign domination c. 1100 B.C.E. The Minoans developed a written language as yet undecipherable, known as Linear A based on syllables rather than words or pictures. They traded olive oil and wine, established colonies, mined copper, created beautiful frescoes, and built luxurious palaces and homes.

Mycenaean society developed from Indo-European roots in Peloponnesus, the southern part of the Balkan Peninsula. Sometimes considered the "thugs of the Mediterranean," the Mycenaeans first traded with the Minoans, but eventually overpowered them, taking over their palaces, goods, and trade routes. These aggressive Greek ancestors even adapted Minoan writing to their own language and developed a syllabic script known as Linear B, which is also yet to be deciphered. The Mycenaeans fought a war with the city of Troy c. 1200 B.C.E. that served as the inspiration for Homer's epics, the *Iliad* and the *Odyssey*. By 1100 B.C.E., even the tough Mycenaeans had fallen apart under constant foreign invasion.

The World of the Polis
(Themes: Political Structures and Cultural Developments)

The Greek **polis**, or city-state, developed out of the political chaos of the eleventh century B.C.E.; these local government institutions first served as forts which people would use for refuge in times of danger. Over the centuries, however, the **poleis** became cultural and economic centers as well as political bases for classical Greek civilization. Each polis was independent and so a range of political institutions developed across the Balkan Peninsula and the Aegean Islands. Frequently, a **tyrant**, one who takes power by force rather than inherits it, ruled the polis. The modern connotation of the word *tyrant* should not be confused with its original Greek meaning; the Greek tyrants were often very popular and not always oppressive despots.

Sparta and **Athens** are the two most famous Greek poleis and they reflect the diversity of life in each Greek polis. Sparta, located in a fertile region in Peloponnesus, relied on its military power to control that region and to maintain public order. The Spartans forced the original Peloponnesian inhabitants to work as slaves called **helots** to effectively cultivate this agricultural region. Because the helots rapidly outnumbered the Spartans, the polis became a military state in which the Spartans increasingly devoted resources to maintaining power and discipline. Equality among Spartan citizens was highly valued, so citizens led materially simple, austere, and frugal lives. Distinction within Spartan society was earned by physical strength, discipline, and military talent. Women, like men, were expected to be physically strong as their role was to produce solid Spartan soldiers.

The Athenian polis, located in a region called Attica, developed much different traditions than did the Spartans. Athens's political structure was based on democratic principles and citizen participation in decision-making, though citizens were only defined as free adult males, not women, slaves, or foreigners. Over time, aristocratic Athenian landowners accumulated more and more wealth through maritime trade, and began to force citizen landowners with small holdings to sell their land, often resulting in high debt and even slavery for the former small land holders. The actions of leaders like Solon and Pericles reduced these tensions and prevented brutal class warfare.

GREECE AND THE LARGER WORLD

The poleis prospered and expanded by establishing trading centers and colonies along the shores of the Mediterranean and Black Seas. This expansion brought them into conflict with the Persians and into contact with and eventual domination by Alexander of Macedon. This expansion and conquest resulted in immense commercial and cultural exchange from India to Egypt.

Greek Colonization
(Themes: Migration and Demographics)

Growing populations in the Greek poleis spurred the development of colonies throughout the Mediterranean basin and the Black Sea. This growth was not controlled by any centralized imperial state, but was promoted by population pressures in the individual polis. Settlers in these colonies often did not take guidance or direction from the original polis, but instead developed their own independent political, social, and economic structures. These colonies emerged as diverse trading centers for local or regional products including fish, fur, metals, honey, gold, amber, and slaves. At the same time, each colony was instrumental in spreading Greek language and cultural traditions far beyond the Greek mainland.

Conflict with Persia
(Theme: Patterns of Interactions)

The Greek conflict with Persia had significant international and domestic consequences. Persian Kings Darius and later Xerxes sought to gain control over Greek cities on the Ionian coast and then to punish the Greeks for rebellion. Though the Greeks were victorious at the battle of Marathon and later at Salamis, the skirmishes between the two powers continued for more than a century.

Once the Persian threat diminished, the independent Greek poleis began to turn on each other. The **Delian League,** once formed to unite the Greeks against the Persians, was increasingly dominated by the Athenians, who felt free to use its treasury to finance massive public building projects in their polis; this behavior by the arrogant Athenians caused much resentment among other League members and ultimately resulted in a disastrous civil conflict, the **Peloponnesian War.**

The Macedonians and the Coming of Empire
(Themes: Political Structures and Changes and Continuities)

While the Greeks were busy squabbling among themselves, the Macedonians to the north were becoming increasingly powerful due in large part to the win-at-all-costs leadership of Philip II. Philip picked off his opponents one by one and by the time the Greek poleis recognized the threat posed by their "barbaric" neighbors, it was too late to mount any significant unified resistance. By 338 B.C.E. Philip controlled all of Greece and turned his attention to his larger goal: Persia. His mysterious assassination in 336 B.C.E. meant his dream would be realized by his young son, Alexander.

One of the great, complex personalities in history, Alexander inherited his Macedonian father's relentless and brutal ruthlessness and his Greek mother's brilliant and wily intelligence. He quickly won control of Ionia and Anatolia, then Syria, Palestine, and Egypt. By 330 B.C.E., the twenty-six-year old Alexander had defeated the Persians and had taken the title of Emperor of the Persians. Unfailingly ambitious, Alexander invaded India, capturing the exotically wealthy region of Punjab and would have gladly continued to the "ends of the earth" had his army not clamored to return home. Alexander's sudden death in Mesopotamia in 323 B.C.E. cut short his plans for exploration and expansion. Historians still debate his potential impact but agree that his efforts spread Greek and Macedonian traditions further and further away from their Balkan beginnings.

The Hellenistic Empires
(Themes: Patterns of Interactions and Changes and Continuities)

The time between Alexander's death and the expansion of the Roman Empire in the east is known as the **Hellenistic era**. Alexander's empire was divided into three large states: the **Antigonid empire** which included Greece and Macedon, the **Ptolemic empire** which included Egypt and parts of northern Africa, and the **Seleucid empire** which stretched from Anatolia to Bactria. These large, cosmopolitan empires facilitated trade and the spread of cultural and religious ideals across parts of Europe, Africa, and Asia. The Seleucid empire, which was the largest of these divisions, provided the greatest channel for the spread of Greek influence. Greek and Macedonian settlers quickly migrated to cities in the former Persian empire where they formed a large imperial bureaucracy and a wealthy merchant class. The resulting Mediterranean-style urban society influenced places as distant as Bactria and India.

THE FRUITS OF TRADE: GREEK ECONOMY AND SOCIETY

The challenges of Greek geography forced the early Greeks to depend on maritime trade.

Trade and the Integration of the Mediterranean Basin
(Themes: Trade and Patterns of Interactions)

Greece's rocky and fertile soil made it difficult to grow grain, but the terrain and climate were well suited for grapes and olives whose value as trading items was quickly recognized. The Greeks used their easy access to the Mediterranean and thus Asia, Africa, and Europe, to trade their products for much-needed food and much-desired luxuries. The development of Greek colonies through the Hellenistic era expanded this trading network and the commercial and economic organizations which made it feasible.

Trade provided an opportunity for positive interactions between and among the poleis and their colonies. The tradition of Pan-Hellenic festivals reminded the Greeks of their shared language and religious traditions and promoted the arts and athletics; they established a sense of collective identity among these independent-thinking people.

Family and Society
(Themes: Social and Gender Structures)

The Greeks had a strong patriarchal society. Male family members headed households and held virtual life-and-death power over their subordinate family members. Upper-class women spent much of their time in the family home and ventured outside only under the watchful eye of a servant or chaperone. Frequently, upper-class women could read and write, and some, like the controversial poetess Sappho, became quite famous. Women in merchant families might operate a small shop or business, but in most poleis, women could not own property. Being a priestess of a religious cult was the only public position open to women. Ironically, in martial Sparta, women enjoyed the most freedom to move freely in public places, participate in athletic games, and join in public festivals; yet even there, only male citizens determined polis policy.

THE CULTURAL LIFE OF CLASSICAL GREECE

Classical Greek cultural life was guided by the principles of human reason; it is evident in the art, literature, and philosophy produced during this era. Even the written language they developed by adding vowels to the established Phoenician alphabet produced a flexible, easy-to-learn system for recording human speech.

Rational Thought and Philosophy
(Themes: Cultural and Intellectual Developments)

Though there were many great Greek thinkers, the most significant three for beginning scholars are Socrates, Plato, and Aristotle. Socrates is remembered for his focus on questioning to uncover truths about human ethics and morality. Plato is known for his theory of Forms and Ideas. Aristotle, who was once the tutor of Alexander the Great, believed that philosophers should rely on their senses and their reason to sort out the mysteries of the world. He wrote extensively about the natural world as well as politics, ethics, and psychology and his works earned him the distinction, "the master of those who know." Plato and especially Aristotle were influential in later Christian and Islamic thinking.

Popular Religion and Greek Drama
(Themes: Religious and Cultural Developments)

Philosophy like that espoused by Socrates, Plato, and Aristotle was not part of popular culture. Instead, most Greeks turned to the traditions of popular religion for guidance on proper behavior and to understand human nature. The **polytheistic** Greeks, like most early people, began by attributing supernatural powers to the elements of nature such as the sun, wind, and rain. Over time, these powers were vested in deities whose stories illustrated the reasons or causes for natural phenomena and human problems. Through the gods, the Greeks sought to explain the world and the forces that shape it. Religious cults such as the Cult of Demeter, or the Cult of Dionysus, offered rare opportunities for women to openly participate in lives outside the home.

Over time, the Cult of Dionysus became the foundation of **Greek drama** which developed from wild, frenzied rites hidden in the woods into much tamer public performances centered in the poleis. These plays explored the limitations and possibilities of human nature as well as comedic criticism of public officials and institutions.

Hellenistic Philosophy and Religion
(Themes: Religious and Cultural Developments)

The civic character of Greek philosophy and religion was eclipsed by the growth of the Hellenistic empires. Hellenistic philosophers dealt with questions of the individual need for peace and tranquility. Stoicism was the most significant of these Hellenistic philosophies; it taught the duty of people to aid others and to lead virtuous lives. Salvation cults also developed promising eternal bliss for people who followed the prescribed rites and doctrines of the cult. They promised security for people who were searching in the complex Hellenistic world.

Finished reading the chapter? Be sure you can . . .

- Explain how the geography and climate of Greece affected the development of Greek society.
- Trace the major political developments in Greece from the Minoans through Alexander.
- Explain how trade transformed classical and Hellenistic Greece.
- Describe social and gender roles in classical Greek society.
- Analyze the Greek approaches to science, drama, religion, and philosophy, especially Aristotle.

Chapter Multiple Choice Questions

1. Since their written language is yet to be deciphered, archaeologists examine vivid frescoes, often showing beautiful young people at play or wealthy couples at home or even ships laden with luxurious cargo, to reveal life in
   a. the Athenian society.
   b. the Spartan society.
   c. the Minoan society.
   d. the Mycenaean society.
   e. the Trojan society.

2. Tyrants came to power in many Greek poleis as a result of
   a. inheritance.
   b. warfare between the poleis.
   c. appointment by Greek kings.
   d. direct elections.
   e. popular support.

3. A key difference between helots in Sparta and chattel slavery is that
   a. helots could not be bought and sold as property.
   b. helots could serve in the Spartan army.
   c. helots were not mistreated.
   d. helots had some rights as citizens of Sparta.
   e. helots could earn their citizenship after a number of years of service.

4. Athens reached its democratic zenith under the leadership of
   a. Alexander.
   b. Solon.
   c. Pericles.
   d. Aristotle.
   e. Socrates.

5. What was the main motivation for Greek colonization throughout the Mediterranean basin?
   a. the strained resources of the mountainous Balkan Peninsula
   b. the desire to spread Greek polytheistic religion
   c. the belief in democracy as the most desirable form of government
   d. the fear of potential Persian expansion into the region
   e. the need to escape the plagues of the fifth century

6. The most significant long-term result of the Persian Wars was
   a. the Greek victory at Marathon which laid the foundations for the modern Olympics.
   b. the Greek Victory at Salamis which demonstrated the superiority of Greek naval technology.
   c. the integration of Greek and Persian religious and cultural traditions.
   d. the splintering of Greek unity after the Persian defeat which set the stage for the rise of Macedon.
   e. the spread of Alexander's empire across Persia, India, and into China.

7. Which of the following public professions was open to women in classical Greece?
   a. Priestess
   b. Physician
   c. Lawyer
   d. Teacher
   e. Archon

8. Which of the following civilizations had the greatest impact on the Greek's written language?
   a. Egyptian
   b. Babylonian
   c. Phoenician
   d. Latin
   e. Hebrew

9. Greek theater has its strongest connection to
   a. the Eleusinian mysteries.
   b. the rites of Demeter.
   c. the philosophy of Aristotle.
   d. the cult of Dionysus.
   e. the philosophy of Socrates.

10. What did salvation cults of the Hellenistic era promise believers which was NOT available through Greek philosophy or traditional religion?
    a. an ethical system for living
    b. the promise of a rewarding afterlife
    c. a community of believers
    d. the freedom from polis control
    e. an explanation of natural phenomena

Comprehensive Multiple Choice Questions

1. A key difference between the Greek city-states and the city-states of Mesopotamia, or the city-states of Mesoamerica, was that
   a. most of the Greek city-states developed direct democracies.
   b. many of the Greek city-states allowed some freedoms for women.
   c. many of the Greek city-states were ruled by kings.
   d. most of the Greek city-states were ruled by cruel leaders called tyrants.
   e. many of the Greek city-states were under the collective rule of local nobles.

2. Unlike many slaves in _____ which were used for human sacrifice, slaves in _____ were provided the agricultural labor necessary to feed the polis.
   a. China, Athens
   b. Harappan society, Sparta
   c. Maya culture, Sparta
   d. Maya culture, Mycenaean culture
   e. Sparta, Athens

3. Despite their many differences, the Hellenistic philosophers would have most agreed with the _____ regarding duty because of the Greek focus on fulfilling one's duties to reason and logic in order to achieve a sense of inner peace and tranquility.
   a. Hindu thinking in the *Upanishads*
   b. Taoist thinking in the *Tao Te Ching*
   c. Confucian thinking in the *Book of Songs*
   d. Egyptian thinking in the *Book of the Dead*
   e. Sumerian thinking in the *Epic of Gilgamesh*

Primary Source Questions

1. **Read *Sources from the Past: Arrian on the Character of Alexander of Macedon,* on page 243 of your textbook.**
   a. Why does Arrian spend time describing Alexander's appearance?
   b. What key adjectives does Arrian choose to describe Alexander's behavior?
   c. How does he justify Alexander's faults?

2. **Examine the Pompeii mosaic of Plato on page 251 of your textbook.**
   a. How are elements of Greek culture revealed in this mosaic?

Chapter Multiple Choice Answers

1. **c:** Minoan script known as Linear A has not yet been deciphered, so archaeologists are forced to rely on the remains of material culture to reconstruct Minoan life on Crete. (p. 232)

2. **e:** This word carries a different meaning today than it did during the classical Greek era. It simply meant someone who came to power by irregular means such as popular support rather than birthright or actions by another polis; there was no single Greek king to make such appointments. (p. 235)

3. **a:** Chattel slavery is the concept that slaves are a commodity. They can be bought or sold as property and do not exist as people. The helots in Sparta could not be bought and sold, but they also were not free to leave the land they worked. In some ways, the helots were closer to serfs than slaves. (p. 235)

4. **c:** Pericles built on Solon's reforms which had opened councils to any citizen regardless of lineage; he also supported appointment of commoners to public offices, financed building projects throughout the polis which created jobs and loyalty, and promoted the arts to bring renown and prestige to his city. (p. 237)

5. **a:** With no major rivers to replenish the soil, and rocky, mountainous conditions across the peninsula, the Greeks constantly had to import grain. As the number of Greeks increased colonies came to be seen as a population outlet as well as an opportunity to promote trade and commerce. (p. 237)

6. **d:** Though the Greeks were victorious at Marathon and Salamis, it was the disintegration of the Delian League and the ensuing Peloponnesian War which made the rise of Philip II and, hence, Alexander possible. (pp. 239–240)

7. **a:** In the strongly patriarchal society, Greek women were allowed only very limited public interaction. A woman from a wealthy family might serve as a priestess for a religious cult, but no other public professions were open to her. (p. 248)

8. **c:** The Phoenicians had developed a written syllabic, phonetic language which was easy to learn and thus a huge asset to business and trade. The Greeks who relied on maritime trade for survival recognized the benefits of the Phoenician system over the Egyptian hieroglyphics or Babylonian cuneiform, added their own symbols for vowel sounds, and developed a flexible and beautiful written language. (p. 249)

9. **d:** Over time, the practices of the cult of Dionysus moved from secretive wild woods settings into the center of the polis. Greek theater grew out of the presentation of plays much more suited for these tamer, public audiences. (p. 253)

10. **b:** Eternal bliss is a powerful motivator. The promise of salvation was not available through the traditional popular Greek gods, or the teachings of classical Greek philosophy. The salvation cults with their eastern roots attracted disciples throughout the Hellenistic world. (p. 254)

Comprehensive Multiple Choice Answers

1. **e:** While the city-states of Mesopotamia and Mesoamerica were governed by kings, Greek poleis developed independently and this independence is reflected in the range of political institutions developed in Greece. While there were some poleis governed by kings, many were under the collective rule of local nobles. (pp. 35, 138, 235)

2. **c:** The Maya used prisoners of war as slaves and frequently as human sacrifices. Helots, Spartan slaves, were used to produce food for the polis as male Spartan citizens were serving in the military for most of their lives. (pp. 138, 139, 235)

3. **a:** Though there are many differences between Greek and Hindu philosophy, the two share a common interest in fulfilling the roles of duty and responsibility in order to achieve some level of inner peace and tranquility. For the Greeks, the benefits of such goals are focused in this world, and for the Hindus the benefits come with rebirth into a higher varna or perhaps even moksha. Choice "c" may have been a tempting answer, except that *The Book of Songs* predates Confucius. (pp. 254, 104)

Primary Source Answers

1. Arrian describes Alexander as having "great personal beauty," "invincible power of endurance," and a "keen intellect." Those three attributes were highly prized by the Greeks who believed that one's outer beauty was a reflection of one's inner strengths. He describes Alexander's behavior as "noble," "inspiring," and "bold," also attributes highly desired by the Greeks and by the Romans to whom he was writing. He explains that Alexander was honest, free to share his wealth with friends, and sharp enough to seize the unexpected moment. He accounts for Alexander's flaws by explaining that passion of the moment could temporarily overpower rational thinking, by blaming his youth for bad decisions, and by explaining that Alexander's drunkenness was really just about the company of friends, not that he was a " heavy drinker." Finally, Arrian asks if anyone who criticizes Alexander is really above reproach himself? (p. 243)

2. There are many aspects of Greek culture revealed in this mosaic. First, only men are seen interacting in the mosaic; there are no women in the center or even in the background of the work which is a clear reflection of the patriarchal nature of Greek society. Women were secluded at home and would not be a subject of such an elaborate work nor would have been seen interacting with men in public settings like this. Second, the men are engaged in thinking and conversation rather than physical labor. Certainly most Greek men had to physically work for a living, but the aristocrats and intellectuals valued the ability and opportunity to think and converse with their peers about intellectual and philosophical topics as demonstrated here by the scrolls and the subjects' hand gestures and placement. Finally, the gregarious nature of the Greeks is seen by the animated interaction of these seven men and their placement in the work. They are interacting together as a group with highly individualized stances and physical features. (p. 251)

CHAPTER 11

MEDITERRANEAN SOCIETY: THE ROMAN PHASE

Before you get started: This chapter is a continuation of the previous chapter on Greece; notice how the Bentley/Zeigler text links Greece and Rome together as both being part of Mediterranean society c. 800 B.C.E.–300 C.E. Think about connections between these two Mediterranean civilizations and use both chapters for comparing and contrasting with civilizations discussed in previous chapters; Han China and Rome are a frequent comparison/contrast required on the AP Exam. The details regarding Rome you have gathered from film or fiction may help you visualize this chapter, but do not let those sweaty gladiators and pounding chariots dominate your understanding of Roman political structures, engineering and technology, social and gender structures, and religious developments.

FROM KINGDOM TO REPUBLIC

Though Rome began as a small, agricultural city-state, it soon developed into a monarchy, then a republic, an empire, and, eventually, the dominant Mediterranean power.

The Etruscans and Rome
(Theme: Migration)

Colorful tales are told regarding the founding of Rome. The stories relate that the city was founded by descendents of Aeneas, the surviving Trojan prince: Brothers Romulus and Remus compete for the right to found the city; Romulus wins and builds his city on seven hills overlooking the Tiber River. More likely, the city was founded by Indo-European migrants who crossed the Alps c. 2000 B.C.E. attracted by the warm weather, pasturelands, and agricultural valleys. These invaders intermarried with the indigenous neolithic farmers to form the basis of early Roman society.

The next people to migrate across the Alps and onto the Italian peninsula were the Etruscans. Originally from Anatolia, the Etruscans quickly built cities across northern Italy, where they produced fine bronze, iron, gold, and silver products to trade throughout the western Mediterranean. The Etruscans built enduring roads and bridges and created the city of Rome, which prospered through trade. Challenges from the outside and a rising Roman aristocracy caused the overthrow of the last Etruscan king in 509 B.C.E.

The Roman Republic and Its Constitution
(Themes: Social Structure and Political Structures)

The Romans avoided destructive class struggle by establishing a **republican form of government** which first provided a voice in government for the wealthy aristocrats known as the **patricians,** and soon included a voice for the common Roman citizens known as the **plebeians.**

The government structure included two executives known as **consuls;** a **Senate**, dominated by the aristocrats; **two assemblies,** one for the patricians and one for the plebeians; and, eventually, the office of **tribune** which included up to ten men whose job it was to speak for the plebeians. The office of **dictator** was established to make executive decisions in times of crisis, but his time in office was limited to six months. This interwoven structure provided a stable government for almost five hundred years.

The Expansion of the Republic
(Theme: Demographics)

The period from the fourth through second centuries B.C.E. was a time of growth for the Roman republic. First, Rome consolidated its power in Italy, through military and political means. Their policy toward conquered peoples across the peninsula was to allow them to trade freely throughout the republic, to govern their own affairs so long as they remained militarily loyal to Rome, to intermarry with Romans, and sometimes to even gain Roman citizenship. Second, Rome established itself as the dominant power in the western Mediterranean, after victory in a series of bloody wars with Carthage, a former Phoenician colony in North Africa which was a major naval and trading empire. Finally, Roman domination of the Mediterranean was secured with the defeat of the Antigonids and the Seleucids in the east.

FROM REPUBLIC TO EMPIRE

Expansion brought wealth, power, and problems to Rome. Unequal distribution of wealth and strained governmental capacity caused the end of the republic and the creation of an imperial government.

Imperial Expansion and Domestic Problems
(Themes: Social and Political Structures)

Lands conquered by Rome often fell into the hands of wealthy families who established **latifundia,** enormous plantations which used the large land size and slave labor to produce products at a much cheaper cost than could the traditional, smaller Roman landowners. The wealthy families used this economic edge to push smaller landowners out of business and gobble up their lands as well. Many of these former small landowners were forced into the cities and sometimes even into slavery when they could not pay their bills. These squeezing phenomena caused social conflict and eventually civil war in Rome.

Tiberius and Gauis Gracchus were two brothers who tried to address this problem with a policy of land reform and redistribution. Obviously unpopular with the upper, wealthy, ruling classes, both men were assassinated before their redistribution plans could be realized. For the next one hundred years, dissatisfied Roman citizens sought leadership from politicians and generals who promised protection and justice. Gaius Marius sided with those who favored justice and land reform and Lucius Sulla promised to protect the conservative aristocratic classes and their property. Years of terror and civil war resulted as poor Romans joined the personal armies of ambitious generals. The rise of **Julius Caesar** brought brief years of peace but also the end of the republic, and it further foreshadowed the rise of imperial Rome.

The Foundation of Empire
(Theme: Political Structures)

Julius used his talents as a shrewd general and his keen understanding of people to make himself the master of the Roman state, if only for a brief while. Capitalizing on victories in Egypt, Greece, and Gaul, Caesar used that wealth to promote building and entertainment in Rome, which pleased and pacified many of his poor subjects. He also confiscated land from conservative opponents to redistribute among his army's veterans, and he extended Roman citizenship to people in the conquered provinces. These actions brought him great public support, but thoroughly alienated and frightened Roman elite classes who plotted and carried out his assassination in the Forum in 44 B.C.E.

Caesar's death led to thirteen years of civil war, which ultimately marked an end to any remnant of the republic and firmly established Octavian, Caesar's nephew and adopted heir, as leader of Rome. Granted the powerful title of **Augustus,** Octavian built a "monarchy disguised as a republic" where he personally controlled all important government functions including leading the military. His empire was strong and stable, but certainly not republican in any way.

Continuing Expansion and Integration of the Empire
(Theme: Cultural and Intellectual Developments and Technology)

The **Pax Romana,** initiated by Octavian and continuing for more than two hundred years after his death, was a period of domestic peace and foreign expansion for Rome. At its high point, the Roman empire stretched from Britain, across all the shores of the Mediterranean, and into Mesopotamia and Egypt. In Europe especially, the growth of cities and urban culture was dramatic.

The Romans accomplished this integration of their empire by building an **extensive road system,** using much of the technology they had first learned from the Etruscans. Wide, well-maintained, and safe roads facilitated trade and communications, which perpetuated the empire's power and wealth.

The political stability of this era also produced an expansive and influential **legal tradition.** To bring order, stability, and rationality to their empire, the Romans developed a system of law applied throughout the empire, which promoted such enduring ideas as innocent until proven guilty, the right of the accused to confront his accusers, and the principles of judicial review and judicial precedents.

ECONOMY AND SOCIETY IN THE ROMAN MEDITERRANEAN

The expansion of Roman rule and trade brought economic and social changes for people throughout the Mediterranean basin; this expansion was sustained through the use of slave labor and the confines of a patriarchal society.

Trade and Urbanization
(Themes: Trade, Technology, and Demographics)

Commercial agriculture played a pivotal role in the economic integration and expansion of the Roman empire. Because of well-built roads, security of travel, and a consistent and enforced system of laws, merchants could be assured of a steady supply of high-demand products and luxury goods. Commercial farmers could be assured of markets and dependable prices for their crops. Consumers, especially in Roman cities, could be assured of an array of goods and services not available in the Mediterranean before the rise of the Roman empire.

Roman advances in engineering resulted in the construction of **aqueducts,** which brought huge amounts of fresh drinking water from the mountains into Roman cities. This dependable supply of water made urban life possible. The invention of **concrete** made huge public building projects possible and affordable. Sewage and plumbing systems, public baths, hippodromes, and arenas became part of every major Roman city. Though still financed by large-scale agriculture, Roman expansion meant the creation of a growing urban society.

Urban growth occurred in all parts of the empire. In the east, where there was an urban tradition, cities continued to expand. In the west, cities, founded and built for government and administrative purposes, stimulated and sustained economic growth and social development.

Family and Society in Roman Times
(Themes: Gender and Social Structures and Labor Systems)

The concept of **pater familias** permeated Roman society. Under this patriarchal tradition, the eldest male ruled the household, deciding virtually all matters for family members, free servants, and slaves, even including questions of life and death. However, women frequently ran the households and increasingly played significant roles in determining family finances and inheritance.

Increasing wealth had significant effects on Roman society. The newly wealthy often flaunted their wealth with extravagant expenditures on palaces, gardens, and flamboyant parties. The increasing poor and slave populations were sometimes appeased with "bread and circuses," but other times took their complaints into the streets. Riots and rebellions were not uncommon in large Roman cities especially if food prices fluctuated.

Slavery was an essential component of the Roman empire's economic success. By the second century C.E. more than one-third of the population of the Roman empire were slaves. Slaves were under the strict authority of their masters who had the right to sell them, punish them, and even kill them. Some urban slaves had the potential to lead economically successful lives and perhaps even be rewarded with **manumission**, their freedom, after years of service. Rural slaves endured much harsher conditions as they labored on the latifundia.

THE COSMOPOLITAN MEDITERRANEAN

Cultural and religious traditions were also affected by the integration of the Mediterranean region during the Roman empire. Roads and communication networks encouraged the spread of religious ideas beyond their original foundations throughout the empire; Christianity is one such example.

Greek Philosophy and Religions of Salvation
(Themes: Patterns of Interaction and Religious Developments)

Like most neolithic peoples, the earliest Romans were **polytheistic**, worshipping gods associated with forces in nature and fertility. Through their interaction with the Etruscans and later the Greeks, the Romans added other gods to their **pantheon** and other practices to their traditional rites.

From the Hellenistic Greeks, the later Romans drew on the teachings of the **Stoics**, especially the ones related to morals and ethics. In the first century B.C.E., Cicero focused especially on justice and public duty which helped to make Stoicism the most prominent moral philosophy in Rome.

The Roman populace was increasingly interested in the **religions of salvation** prominent throughout the eastern Mediterranean basin in Hellenistic times. Merchants, soldiers, and government administrators encountered these ideas and carried them throughout the empire. Persian-based Mithraism and the Egyptian cult of Isis proved especially popular.

Judaism and Early Christianity
(Theme: Religious Developments)

Though the Jewish kingdom of David and Solomon had survived under various imperial regimes, the Jews struggled whenever an imperial power sought to promote some state cult. Strict monotheists, the Jews refused to participate in state-sanctioned activities, no matter how minor or shallow the ceremony. The Jews considered such behavior to be blasphemy, and at times refused to pay taxes or obey any Roman laws that conflicted with their own. This opposition eventually led to open rebellion and war, resulting in the exile of Jews from their homeland in 70 C.E. under the Roman Emperor Titus.

While some Jews openly fought the Romans, others sought salvation through isolation or through a God-delivered spiritual leader. **Christianity** emerged in this context as some Jews sought to form a community around **Jesus of Nazareth**, a charismatic leader who taught peace, devotion to God, and love for fellow human beings. The Romans, concerned about another Jewish uprising and fearful about Jesus' proclamation that the "kingdom of God is at hand," arrested and executed him in the early 30s C.E.

Jesus' execution did not quell the crowds nor end the movement. After his death, his closest followers proclaimed that he had risen from the grave, that he was the **"Son of God,"** and that belief in him offered eternal reward. These promises, plus the compilation of his teachings, began to spread Jesus' appeal far beyond the borders of Palestine; men like **Paul of Tarsus** spread the teachings using the infrastructure of the Roman empire. Roman roads, trade, and communication systems once again encouraged the rapid spread of new ideas.

With no central authority for the first two centuries, Christianity developed in the Roman empire with a variety of divergent practices and theologies. Like their Jewish predecessors, many Christians refused to acknowledge Roman state cults and came into direct conflict with Roman law; thus Roman persecution of Christians was not uncommon in the first two centuries of the modern era. Despite these threats, the egalitarian appeals of Christianity appealed to many Romans: urban poor, lower social classes, slaves, and especially women. By the third century C.E., Christianity was the most dynamic and influential faith in the Mediterranean.

Finished reading the chapter? Be sure you can . . .

- Trace the major demographic changes in Rome from its founding until c. 300 C.E.
- Describe and analyze the major political developments in Rome from its founding through the end of the western empire.
- Describe the impact of Roman patriarchy on gender roles, social structures, and labor systems.
- Analyze the significance of trade within Rome and throughout its empire.
- Explain how Christianity emerged as a dynamic and influential faith in the Mediterranean basin.

Chapter Multiple Choice Questions

1. The early Roman republic dealt with pressures from the plebeians for a voice in government by
   a. creating a militaristic government modeled on the Spartan tradition of force and authority.
   b. creating the office of tribune who had the power to intervene in all political affairs.
   c. creating the office of dictator to rule Rome in times of crisis and put down plebeian rebellions.
   d. making the Senate more egalitarian and open to plebeians and patricians alike.
   e. persecuting the plebeian leaders as a way of intimidating the masses.

2. The Roman policy toward its conquered subjects is called "generous" because
   a. it allowed them to vote in the assemblies, to petition the tribunes, and to depose the dictator if he was deemed too harsh.
   b. it allowed them to maintain their culture, and gave them the right to trade in Rome and perhaps become Roman citizens.
   c. compared to the Persian empire, Roman rule was more humane and less restrictive to religious freedoms.
   d. the Romans were only interested in the economic wealth of regions they controlled, so they did not require taxes or political loyalty from their conquered subjects.
   e. it did not use the same deportation and hostage-taking strategies to gain control of conquered regions as did the Greeks.

3. Rome ultimately benefited from the defeat of Carthage because
   a. Carthage was a huge naval and trading empire and the Romans were able to absorb and expand that empire and exploit its resources.
   b. Carthage had been raiding Roman cities and outposts along the Mediterranean coast and the banks of the Tiber River for more than 200 years.
   c. Carthage had inherited the Athenian trading network and was using it to pirate Roman sea vessels, especially those sailing from Gaul.
   d. Carthage had joined with the Etruscans to build roads and bridges which rivaled Roman trade routes.
   e. Carthage benefited from fertile soil to produce much grain which the Romans could not produce in their own fields.

4. The most serious political and social tensions in Rome during the last years of the republic and the first years of the empire focused on
   a. voting rights and patterns.
   b. military leadership and pay.
   c. patterns of land distribution.
   d. who should serve as dictator.
   e. patrician versus plebeian conflicts.

5. One reason Octavian escaped Caesar's fate was that he
   a. had more military victories than his uncle in Gaul and Britain and so had more popular support.
   b. aligned with Marc Antony and Cleopatra at Actium to defeat the enemies of Rome.
   c. made alliances with Sulla and Marius to pacify the Roman elites who feared liberal ideas.
   d. converted to Christianity which brought him renewed public support.
   e. wisely preserved the façade of the republic while cautiously consolidating his power.

6. During the Pax Romana, where was the greatest growth seen in the number of newly founded cities?
   a. in Egypt, as the Romans relied on the export of grain from that fertile land
   b. in Syria, as it lay on the trade routes to the east and into Asia
   c. in the Black Sea region, as the Romans traded for furs and glassware
   d. in Spain, Gaul, and Britain where cities were first built for government and administrative purposes
   e. in north Africa with the addition of lands formerly controlled by Carthage

7. In what context were Roman slaves most likely to receive manumission?
   a. after a successful revolt, such as the one led by Spartacus in 73 B.C.E.
   b. after years of service as an urban slave around the age of thirty
   c. after successfully completing thirty years of service on the latifundia
   d. after participating in a successful gladiatorial competition
   e. after earning enough money to buy their freedom

8. Why were Roman commoners especially attracted to the Hellenistic era religions of salvation?
   a. The religions of salvation provided a purpose or model for how to live and the promise of a rewarding afterlife.
   b. The religions of salvation were more understandable and simpler to follow than the polytheistic Roman traditions.
   c. The religions of salvation were based on logic and rationality which the Romans highly prized.
   d. The religions of salvation had their origins in early Roman culture and therefore carried the powerful weight of tradition.
   e. The religions of salvation accepted the Roman gods and modeled their gods on the traditional Roman pantheon.

9. Why did the Jews find it so difficult to abide by Roman law?
   a. The Romans demanded that everyone in their empire worship the Roman gods and observe Roman religious traditions and rites.
   b. The Jews had never been under occupation before, so they had no experience with religious traditions other than their own.
   c. The Jewish religion forbids the worship of any other gods but Yahweh and therefore Jews would not participate in the Roman state cults.
   d. The Jews did not want to pay taxes to Rome without some representation in the Roman government.
   e. The Jews feared the loss of their military power under Roman occupation and therefore refused to surrender their arms as required by Roman law.

10. Despite repression by the Roman government, Christianity had great appeal to what group of people throughout the empire?
    a. merchants and traders because Christianity promoted honest and fair business practices
    b. slaves and women because Christianity promised spiritual freedom and eternal reward regardless of status
    c. Soldiers because Christianity valued duty, honor, and loyalty above all other values
    d. elite, wealthy Romans because Christianity taught the value of hard work and effort to achieve material and spiritual success
    e. Roman emperors because it allowed them to claim the right to rule from God

Comprehensive Multiple Choice Questions

1. Many early civilizations relied on slavery for economic and/or religious purposes. Which of the following civilizations was most dependent upon slave labor in its economic realm?
    a. Egypt
    b. Inca
    c. Maya
    d. Zhou China
    e. Rome

2. Rome's most enduring impact was experienced in what region?
    a. Egypt and north Africa because Rome brought roads to these desert nations which made unification much easier
    b. Greece because Roman religion absorbed the Greek pantheon and justified polytheism
    c. Mesopotamia because Roman law replaced the Code of Hammurabi and introduced the concept of trial by jury of one's peers
    d. Eastern Europe because Roman polytheism replaced the cult of Isis and other cults of salvation
    e. Western Europe because Roman rule stimulated trade and agricultural production resulting in urban growth

3. The Roman concept of the "paterfamilias" as a means of providing order in society was most closely tied to what other civilization's patriarchal structure?
    a. Han China
    b. Maya culture
    c. Pre-Vedic India
    d. New Kingdom Egypt
    e. Hellenistic Greece

Primary Source Questions

1. **Examine the Marble Relief sculpture of Roman Temple Construction on page 258 of your textbook.**
    a. What elements of Roman culture are evident in this work?

2. **Read *Sources from the Past: Tacitus on Corruption in the Early Roman Empire* on page 270 of your textbook.**
    a. What does Tacitus mean by "the rising tide of flattery"?
    b. What techniques does Augustus use to gain popular support while at the same time whittling away at Roman rights?
    c. What problems existed with this technique after Augustus's death?

Chapter Multiple Choice Answers

1. **b:** The office of tribune was created in response to plebian pressure and its holders were to represent plebian interests in the Roman republic. (p. 262)

2. **b:** The generous policy toward conquered peoples is a key reason for the successful expansion of the Roman republic beyond its city-state borders. The liberal occupation policy and the potential for Roman citizenship made upward economic mobility possible for many people in these regions. (p. 264)

3. **a:** Carthage and Rome fought over trade routes and naval stations across the western Mediterranean. After the Roman defeat of Carthage, control of grain from Sicily and luxury products from north Africa came under Roman control. (p. 264)

4. **c:** Problems associated with the latifundia and social class conflict all revolved around the increasing consolidation of landholding into the hands of a few wealthy families. Roman citizens whose families had owned small farms for generations found themselves unable to compete with these large plantations and were frequently forced to sell out or be sold into slavery for debts. (p. 266)

5. **e:** Octavian understood why Caesar had been popular and also why he had been assassinated. The heir capitalized on both by outwardly supporting the republic while accumulating powers for himself. He reorganized the army and appointed commanders who owed allegiance directly to the emperor and not to private individual generals. (p. 268)

6. **d:** The effects of urbanization in the Roman empire were most dramatic in western Europe as this region was overwhelmingly rural before the arrival of the Romans. These newly built cities soon joined the expansive Roman trade network. (p. 274)

7. **b:** Though not mandatory, it was not uncommon for some urban slaves to be freed around the age of thirty if they had served their masters well. (p. 277)

8. **a:** The traditional Roman pantheon was a compilation of gods and goddesses who came into Rome along with their conquered followers. This polytheistic pantheon did not offer Romans and others during the Hellenistic period much direction or guidance as to how to live and cope with the changing urban world. Religions of salvation did, and they further promised hope for a glorious life after death. (p. 279)

9. **c:** The most elemental aspect of the Jewish faith is unquestionable monotheism. The Roman promotion of the cult of state, no matter how benign, was totally unacceptable to practicing Jews. (p. 280)

10. **b:** Though Christianity did promote honesty and loyalty, it was the promise of spiritual freedom and eternal reward that proved its greatest appeal for people in the empire. (p. 283)

Comprehensive Multiple Choice Answers

1. **e:** Although all these civilizations used slavery with an economic and sometimes religious purpose, Rome had the largest percentage of slaves working in urban and rural settings. It is estimated that by the second century C.E. up to one-third of the empire's population were slaves. (p. 275)

2. **e:** Though the Roman Empire had an impact throughout its realm, places like Egypt, Greece, and Mesopotamia had a long tradition of powerful empires. The Roman pantheon did not replace the cults of salvation anywhere including eastern Europe. Western Europe, however, was transformed from a rural, agricultural region to a region fully included in the urban, trade-oriented Roman empire. Even after the fall of Rome, some of those Roman-inspired cities managed to survive until their tenth-century economic revival. (p. 269)

3. **a:** Each of the civilizations listed was a patriarchal society, but the Roman idea that the eldest male ruled the household and made decisions for all the people in his extended family is most closely linked to the Confucian traditions of Han China. (pp. 185, 274)

Primary Source Answers

1. This work illustrates many aspects of Roman culture. First, it is constructed in the Greek temple tradition which the Romans so admired. Using "post and lintel" techniques rather than the Roman engineered arch, it reflects the Roman adaptation of Greek visuals in architecture, especially the use of Corinthian-style columns and carved friezes. Of course, the Romans added many layers of decoration and ornamentation which classical Greeks would have found overdone and gaudy. Second, the temple is constructed using a powerful crane powered by workers who were probably slaves. Slaves as an urban labor force were the norm for such Roman construction projects. Certainly the placement of the emperor surrounded by his predecessors at the top of the relief is meant to convey the proximity of the emperor to the gods and his ties to previous emperors which conveys an important message about his legitimacy. (p. 258)

2. a.   Tacitus is warning that because earlier Roman historians feared the emperors, they described them more positively than was accurate. Then, once the emperor died and his successor was crowned, historians had to write negatively to escape persecution from the new emperor. The result was incorrect history, which Tacitus says he wants to avoid in his writing on Augustus.

   b.   Augustus was very clever; he used people's basic greed to win their favor and to take away their rights, for example, bonuses for the army and cheap food for the people as a way to win their approval. Obedience to Augustus brought people wealth and social status and his rule brought peace which he says people often choose over freedoms.

   c.   When Augustus died, there was the potential for unrest as some Romans began to talk about a return to the republic with its rights but also with its problems. That talk was promptly squashed through assassinations, fear, and greed. Any objectors to Tiberius were either too afraid of the repercussions of any opposing or questioning statement or too seduced by the desire to retain their economic and social positions to question Tiberius's authority. (p. 270)

CHAPTER 12

CROSS-CULTURAL EXCHANGES ON THE SILK ROADS

Before you get started: Though this chapter in the Bentley/Zeigler text is only 24 pages long, in many ways the content is the heart of the Foundations Unit as it pulls together all six of the AP themes:

1) Dynamics of Continuity and Change
2) Patterns of Interactions: Trade, War, and Diplomacy
3) Technology, Economics, and Demography
4) Systems of Social and Gender Structure
5) Cultural, Intellectual, and Religious Developments
6) Political Organization and Functions of States

The focus of your work in this chapter should be theme one: *Dynamics of Continuity and Change*. Remember, you will be asked to write a Continuities-and-Changes-Over-Time essay on the national exam and the topic could come from this chapter. The key to success on that type of question is (1) to address three distinct periods within the parameters of the prompt, (2) to develop examples of continuity which you can sustain and support in all three periods, and (3) to fully explain examples of change, one for each period. Ideally, you will include all three elements in your thesis, which should be the last sentence of your introductory paragraph. For many students this type of essay is the most difficult to write because it demands ample, accurate content knowledge and experience writing essays in a strict format.

So, this might be one chapter to read twice and to outline before the national exam. You will see this content in some portion of the exam: multiple choice, DBQ, Comparison/Contrast, or Continuity and Change. This is an important chapter to master.

LONG-DISTANCE TRADE AND THE SILK ROADS NETWORK

Long-distance trade profoundly affected both classical civilizations and their nomadic neighbors throughout the eastern hemisphere. It brought wealth and access to foreign products that enabled local producers to specialize in items best suited to their regions, enabled the spread of religious ideas far beyond their original homelands, and facilitated the transmission of devastating diseases which dramatically altered social, political, and economic traditions in all adjacent regions.

Trade Networks of the Hellenistic Era
(Themes: Trade and Changes and Continuities)

Trade can be a risky business, but much of that risk was reduced during the classical era. The construction of roads and bridges and the development of large imperial states provided some ease of movement and some protection for merchants who sought to sell products from one region to another. With the reduction of risk came an increase in volume and accessibility of exotic goods throughout the eastern hemisphere.

Greek merchants and bankers were attracted to Bactria and Persia within the Seleucid empire. The Ptolemies in Egypt maintained their land routes east into Africa, while also building new ports on the Red Sea and the Mediterranean. Most significantly, the Ptolemies also learned about the rhythm of the **monsoon winds** that blew from the southwest in the summer and northeast in the winter. Arab and Indian merchants had capitalized on these dependable winds for generations; now Hellenistic traders were able to establish regular links between Arabia, India, east Africa, and Egypt, and then link those expeditions with ones across the Mediterranean to Europe. Though expensive to protect and support, these trade routes had a huge payback in the wealth of goods transported and in the taxes Hellenistic governments collected.

Spices, luxury fabrics, precious metals, jewels, grain, oils, and slaves were valuable commercial items for merchants and governments alike.

The Silk Roads
(Themes: Political Structures, Trade, and Changes and Continuities)

The **Han empire** controlled China and maintained order in much of central Asia. The **Parthian empire** ruled Persia and Mesopotamia. The **Romans** ruled the Mediterranean world and the **Kushan empire** provided protection and stability in northern India. These classical civilizations anchored the developing overland trade routes known as the **silk roads** which linked the extreme ends of the Eurasian landmass.

The silk roads also included **water routes and sea lanes** which linked the Eastern hemisphere through a series of ports along the vast Asian and African coasts from the South China Sea to the Red Sea.

An array of agricultural and manufactured products traveled over these silk roads. Silk, of course, was in high demand for its beauty and the Chinese jealously guarded its secret production technology. Spices from China and central Asia served as condiments as well as ingredients in perfumes, medicines, and magic potions. Cotton textiles as well as pearls, coral, and ivory were exported to the west. Horses and high-quality jade produced in central Asia were prized in both the eastern and western ends of the trade route. From the west came glassware, jewelry, woolen and linen textiles, bronze items, olive oils, wine, and works of art.

Merchants did not usually travel from one end of the silk roads to the other, though there were a few exceptions. Small foreign merchant communities developed along the silk roads and coastlines. Usually trade happened in stages. Governments jealously guarded movement of merchants within their empires to assure they could fully assess and collect taxes and tariffs on the goods crossing their territories.

CULTURAL AND BIOLOGICAL EXCHANGES ALONG THE SILK ROADS

Both missionaries and pathogens relied on opportunities for easy movement along the silk roads. The transmission of ideas and diseases had huge impacts on classical civilization.

The Spread of Buddhism and Hinduism
(Themes: Religious Developments and Changes and Continuities)

Buddhism was the most prominent faith of silk road merchants from 200 B.C.E.–700 C.E. Promoted first by the Indian emperor Ashoka, the faith spread with Indian merchants into Ceylon, Bactria, Iran, Central Asia, southeast Asia, and China. In China, Buddhism remained mostly a merchant faith and did not have much appeal for the native Chinese until Buddhist monks and missionaries capitalized on unrest in China during the fifth century C.E. to spread their faiths. After that, Buddhism spread quickly through China and into Japan and Korea.

Hinduism was also spread by Indian merchants through the sea lanes of the Indian Ocean throughout southeast Asia. Java, Sumatra, the Malay Peninsula, as well as parts of modern Vietnam and Cambodia, embraced the Hindu cults of Shiva and Vishnu, some even adopting Sanskrit as the means of written communication.

The Spread of Christianity
(Themes: Religious Developments and Changes and Continuities)

Early persecution of Christians by the Roman government was based on the Christian refusal to observe state cults or to participate in state-sponsored religious ceremonies and on the behavior of Christian missionaries, which the Roman government saw as disruptive and occasionally violent. The Christian missionaries, however, capitalized on the ease of travel and communication within the Roman empire. By the end of the third century C.E., Christian communities flourished throughout the Mediterranean basin, Anatolia, Syria, Palestine, Egypt, north Africa, and into southwest Asia. Christianity, along with Judaism and Zoroastrianism, remained widespread in southwest Asia through the coming of the Islamic faith in the seventh century C.E.

Christian practices were heavily influenced by the practices of converts in Mesopotamia and Iran. Asceticism and withdrawal from secular society became dominant aspects of Christian practice and influenced the formation of Christian monasteries and separate communities in the western Mediterranean basin.

Nestorian Christianity developed in the east, after the teaching of Greek theologian Nestorius, who stressed the human nature of Jesus rather than the divine. Christians in the Mediterranean opposed this emphasis, and many Nestorians in the west moved eastward carrying with them the western structure of Christianity. Nestorian Christian merchants established communities in central Asia, India, and China by the seventh century C.E..

The Spread of Manichaeism
(Themes: Religious Developments and Changes and Continuities)

Like Buddhism, Hinduism, and Christianity, the spread of **Manichaeism** relied on the trade routes of classical civilizations. Developed in the third century C.E., and spread by Mani, this faith had its roots in **Zoroastrianism** and included elements of Christianity and Buddhism in its theology. Mani believed that syncretism, the process of an existing tradition adopting elements of a new tradition into its theology, would meet the changing cosmopolitan needs of the classical world. The faith promoted a strict ascetic lifestyle, turning away from the material and physical temptations of classical civilizations, and promised individual salvation and eternal association with the forces of light and good.

Throughout the eastern hemisphere, imperial governments saw a danger to public order in Manichaeism and sought to exterminate this foreign religion and its believers. The Roman and Sasanid empires were largely successful in this goal, but Manichaeism managed to survive in the plains of central Asia where it was readily adopted by many nomadic Turkish peoples who traded with silk road merchants.

The Spread of Epidemic Disease
(Themes: Demographics and Changes and Continuities)

Pathogens for diseases such as smallpox, measles, and bubonic plague traveled easily along the silk roads and had devastating effects on the population. Despite sketchy population records, it seems clear that both the Roman empire and Han China lost a quarter to a third of their populations as a result of epidemic diseases that moved along the silk roads.

These demographic changes had social and economic effects. Both empires moved away from international trade in imperial markets and focused increasingly on **regional exchange of goods**. Social structures changed and cities became less desirable places to live. The demise of the Han and Roman empires are directly linked to the changes brought by diseases which traveled along the silk roads.

CHINA AFTER THE HAN DYNASTY

Internal problems weakened the Han dynasty, dissolving the central government by the early third century C.E.

Internal Decay of the Han State
(Themes: Political Structures and Changes and Continuities)

The perennial issue of land distribution, coupled with the growing influence of conflicting factions within the imperial household, occupied the attention of the last Han rulers. Widespread unrest and peasant unrest such as the **Yellow Turban Rebellion** in 184 C.E. plagued the late Han dynasty. Those problems, plus the usurping of central political power by wily generals, lead to the end of the Han era and the division of Chinese lands into three large kingdoms: **Wei, Wu,** and **Shu.** Not surprisingly, northern nomads took advantage of China's disunity to gain and maintain control of the northern borderlands for more than three hundred years.

Cultural Change in Post-Han China
(Themes: Cultural Development, Religious Developments, and Changes and Continuities)

War and nomadic invasions characterized life in China after the fall of the Han dynasty in 220 C.E. The devastation of China's heartland resulted in population loss and migration out of the cities. China was increasingly populated by nomadic invaders who eventually established permanent settlements, adopted agriculture, and began to intermarry with native Chinese. Over time, these people and their descendents adopted aspects of Chinese culture and the differences between native Chinese and northern nomadic peoples lessened. This process of **sinicization** is a consistent theme in China's history. In other words, invaders assimilate to Chinese culture.

Religious changes also resulted from the fall of the Han. Confucianism, which had helped to justify the Han imperial rule, lost its credibility in the face of China's chaos and seemed increasingly irrelevant. With lessened competition from Confucianism, **Daoism** now offered some hope of salvation, and a growing emphasis on elixirs and potions promised good health and perhaps immortality. **Buddhism,** which had been present in China for several centuries thanks to silk road merchants, found a broader foothold in China after the Han fall. Nomads, who now settled in China, had been familiar with Buddhist tenets and practices. Buddhist missionaries and monks stepped up their conversion efforts in the void left by the fall of the Han empire. By the sixth century C.E., Buddhism was well entrenched in China and laid the foundation for restoration of a unified political order.

THE FALL OF THE ROMAN EMPIRE

As in Han China, the collapse of the Roman empire in the west in 476 C.E. was the result of long-term internal troubles and growing external pressures which coincided with major religious and cultural changes.

Internal Decay in the Roman Empire
(Themes: Political Structures and Changes and Continuities)

The problems of ruling such a huge empire had burdened Roman emperors for generations. The "barracks emperors" represented the attempts by military leaders to seize and hold power; almost all of them died violent deaths at the hands of their troops or a new rival. The epidemics of the third century further weakened imperial control and many regions of the empire moved away from commercial economies and back toward local, self-sufficient economies. **Diocletian's** attempts to restructure the empire by dividing it into two parts and appointing a co-emperor forestalled the disintegration for a few generations, but not for long. Likewise, **Constantine** managed to hold back the fall of Rome by recognizing that the wealth of the empire lay in the east and by moving his capital to the former Greek city of Byzantium, a strategic site and much more easily defendable than the city of Rome. Building a new capital on old ruins and renaming it after himself, **Constantinople,** brought some hope that the Roman empire might survive a while longer.

Germanic Invasions and the Fall of the Western Roman Empire
(Themes: Demographics, Political Structures, and Changes and Continuities)

Migratory Germanic people also formed a threat to the Roman empire; they brought an end to the western Roman empire in the fifth century C.E., but the eastern Roman empire lasted until the fifteenth century C.E. In the west, pressure from the **Huns,** nomadic warriors from the steppe lands west of China, pushed the Germanic peoples who had lived on the borders of the Roman empire for generations, into the empire itself. These groups, especially the **Visigoths**, had lived in border regions for centuries and had adopted agriculture and Christianity, and had even fought as mercenaries in the Roman army. But relentless pressure from the Huns, led by **Attila,** pushed groups like the **Visogoths, Ostrogoths, Vandals,** and **Franks** into the Roman empire, seeking safety from these virtually unstoppable warriors. Once inside the borders of the Roman empire, these Germanic peoples first established settlements in the less densely populated areas within the western Roman empire, eventually dominated Spain, France, Britain, and north Africa, and by 476 B.C.E. controlled Rome itself.

Cultural Change in the Late Roman Empire
(Themes: Cultural Developments and Changes and Continuities)

Christianity, and hence the Roman empire, underwent many changes during the last centuries of the western Roman empire. Emperor Constantine issued the **Edict of Milan** which gave legal protections to Christians in the empire in the early fourth century C.E. By the end of that century, Emperor Theodosius proclaimed Christianity the official religion of the empire. Augustine of Hippo worked to reconcile Christianity with Greek and Roman philosophical traditions, thus making the faith appealing to educated Romans. His efforts in particular helped to move Christianity away from its original appeal to ordinary, working-class Romans, women, and slaves, to include the empire's intellectual elites.

This growing appeal of Christianity necessitated standardization of the faith and development of a structural hierarchy. The church-sponsored Council of Nicaea and the Council of Chalcedon proclaimed that Jesus was both fully human and fully divine at the same time. A hierarchy of religious authorities was established which included **patriarchs in Jerusalem, Antioch, Alexandria, and Constantinople** as well as the Bishop of Rome, later known as the **Pope**. Though at first roughly equal in authority, the western European church soon accepted the Pope and his subordinate bishops as the leaders of western Europe, just in time to fill the gaps left by the fall of the Roman empire in the west.

Finished reading the chapter? Be sure you can . . .

- Analyze the impact of silk road trade networks on the Hellenistic and Asian worlds.
- Analyze the impact of religious and biological changes occurring as a result of silk road contacts.
- Compare and contrast the collapse of the Han Empire and the western Roman empire.
- Explain the demographic changes in Asia and Europe c. 200–600 C.E.
- Discuss the continuities and changes c. 8000 B.C.E.–600 C.E. in trade, technology, demography, social and gender structures, cultural, intellectual, and religious developments, and political structures and functions.

Chapter Multiple Choice Questions

1. What two developments c. 100–500 C.E. spurred the development of long-distance trade?
   a. the building of large, imperial states and the construction of roads and bridges
   b. the end of tribal warfare and the emergence of salvation religions
   c. the spread of popular government and the development of navigation technologies
   d. the emergence of a common currency and the creation of large city-states
   e. the development and diffusion of Christianity and Islam

2. How did knowledge of the monsoons facilitate trade?
   a. Merchants needed to know when hurricane season was coming so they could avoid travel during that dangerous season.
   b. Governments could plan when ships would arrive, so they could have tax collectors ready to assess tariffs.
   c. Mariners could use this knowledge to establish trade links and sail safely throughout the Indian Ocean basin.
   d. The Romans realized it was much cheaper to travel by sea than overland, especially to China.
   e. Luxury products could be more carefully handled in ship holds with knowledge of impending storms.

3. What was the most prominent faith among silk road merchants from 200 B.C.E.–700 C.E.?
   a. Animism
   b. Buddhism
   c. Christianity
   d. Islam
   e. Hinduism

4. Aspects of eastern practices can best be seen in western Christianity c. 300–700 C.E., through the
   a. belief that ascetism and withdrawal from secular society were the ideal manifestations of a Christian life.
   b. practices of baptism and communion as daily duties for devout believers.
   c. refusal of Christian believers to worship the emperor or pay taxes to Rome.
   d. work of eastern merchants to spread Christianity along silk road trade routes.
   e. diaspora of Jews and their strict reliance on dietary and marriage laws.

5. Manichaeism was feared by imperial states because it
   a. was seen as a threat to public order and was suspected as a threat from an outside nation.
   b. promoted violence among the dissatisfied slave classes and contributed to slave revolts.
   c. was based on a strong missionary and conversion movement similar to the cult of Isis.
   d. denied the divinity of the emperors and supported individual freedom of conscience.
   e. sought to reinstate the traditional Roman pantheon and the authority of the republic.

6. Which of the following statements is true regarding the effects of epidemic diseases along the silk roads?
   a. Trade within the empires declined and the imperial economies shrank.
   b. New products were developed to fight disease and carefully traded along the silk roads.
   c. Persia escaped the fate of China and Rome.
   d. Though decimated by disease, populations sprang back quickly.
   e. People were encouraged to explore and settle in new lands.

7. The key reason for the collapse of the Han dynasty was
   a. the invasions by nomads from the north.
   b. the plagues and diseases which came to China along the silk roads.
   c. the backlash resulting from the attempted eradication of Confucian thinking.
   d. a military coup led by dissatisfied generals and the assassination of the last emperor.
   e. the conflicts over land distribution and fighting among imperial families.

8. Adopting Chinese foods, intermarrying with native Chinese people, studying Chinese philosophy and poetry, taking on Chinese names are all examples of what process which characterizes foreign interaction in China?
   a. cultural diffusion
   b. sinicization
   c. syncretism
   d. international intervention
   e. globalization

9. What was Constantine's primary motivation in moving the capital to Byzantium?
   a. It was a strategic site which linked the western empire with the increasingly wealthy east.
   b. It made it easier to protect the vast empire with a more centralized capital city.
   c. He wanted to build a new city to honor the Christian God, as he had just converted to Christianity.
   d. He wanted to show his freedom from Diocletian's influence and power.
   e. The city of Rome had been sacked by the Visigoths and it was too expensive to rebuild on that site.

10. The most important individual responsible for the inclusion of Roman educated intellectuals into early Christianity was
    a. Augustine of Hippo.
    b. Plato.
    c. Constantine the Great.
    d. Emperor Theodosius.
    e. Saul of Tarsus.

Comprehensive Multiple Choice Questions

1. Which of the following statements best reflects the cause for BOTH the fall of the western Roman empire and the fall of Han China?
   a. The collapse of imperial power coincided with the demographic impact of epidemic disease and external threats.
   b. Invasion by fierce northern nomads brought diseases which undermined the existing social order.
   c. New religious traditions threatened the existing social order and challenged the rulers' divinity.
   d. The inequitable distribution of land coupled with the introduction of new religious ideas undermined the existing social order.
   e. An unchecked military and constant threat of invasion prompted the people to abandon tradition and demand protection from local warlords.

2. One key difference between the fall of Rome and the fall of Han China is that
   a. war and nomadic invasion decimated the Chinese capital city, but Rome avoided destruction.
   b. Buddhism became less popular in China, while Christianity remained strong in Rome.
   c. Confucian tradition provided continuity during the demise of the Han, but Christianity declined dramatically in the face of pagan pressures.
   d. Han China was formally divided into three large kingdoms but Rome survived in its eastern realm for more than a thousand years.
   e. peasant unrest and insurrection plagued the late Han dynasty, but Rome had resolved its land distribution issues through the use of latifundia.

3. Prior to the fifth century, the impact of eastern Christianity can best be seen in the western Roman empire in the
   a. popularity of the religions of salvation and prayer rites.
   b. adoption of eastern ascetic practices in the formation of Christian monasteries.
   c. practices of communion and confession in religious services.
   d. reverence for Mary in a way similar to the cult of Isis.
   e. practices of animal sacrifice and self-mortification.

Primary Source Questions

1. **Examine Map 12.2, The spread of Buddhism, Hinduism, and Christianity, 200 B.C.E.–400 C.E. on page 297 of your textbook.**
   a. What prevented the spread of these faiths into eastern Europe?
   b. What prevented the spread of these faiths into Africa, other than Egypt, Ethiopia, and the north?

2. **Read *Sources from the Past: St. Cyprian on Epidemic Disease in the Roman Empire* on page 301 of your textbook.**
   a. What does St. Cyprian mean by the phrase "greatness of heart"?
   b. Why does the author explain that believers should view disease as a reward?
   c. How might the historical circumstances have influenced St. Cyprian's treatise?

Chapter Multiple Choice Answers

1. **a:** The expansion of large, imperial states reduced the areas in the eastern hemisphere outside "civilized" control and then encouraged the construction of roads and bridges to connect these growing empires for military and administrative purposes. Merchants simply capitalized on these developments. (p. 288)

2. **c:** The reliability of the monsoon winds and the establishment of regular links and ports reduced the mariners' travel risks and thus their transportation costs. (pp. 289–290)

3. **b:** Buddhism was readily adopted by merchants and residents, and Buddhists built monasteries in oasis towns along the silk roads of central Asia to both spread the faith and support their trade routes. (p. 295)

4. **a:** Christian asceticism and the withdrawal of believers from secular society is a reflection of earlier eastern religious practice. Christians in the west were impressed by these practices and used the ideas as the foundation for western Christian monastic life. (p. 298)

5. **a:** Manichaeism was largely exterminated in the Sasanid and Roman empires because it was seen as a threat to public order and because it was viewed as a threat to imperial control from an outside nation. (p. 300)

6. **a:** Large population losses, including many of the silk road merchants themselves, dramatically altered trade patterns and economic spheres. The loss of taxes and tariffs upon which large imperial governments depended had devastating and long-term effects on the empires' survival. (p. 302)

7. **e:** While disease and northern nomads continued to threaten the Han dynasty and did contribute to its demise, it was the seemingly unsolvable crisis of land distribution and the constant, distracting bickering in the imperial household that ultimately caused the end of the Han dynasty. (pp. 302–303)

8. **b:** The process of sinicization is one way historians explain the continuing survival of Chinese culture despite foreign invasion. Over time, the power of Chinese culture simply absorbs invaders and their own cultures into it. (p. 304)

9. **a:** Constantine moved the capital to Byzantium because of its strategic location both in terms of protection and trade. By the late fourth century C.E., the wealth of the empire lay in the east, especially as a trading center. Western Rome was being continually threatened by outside invasion; Constantine's move was a response to the circumstances of the times. (p. 306)

10. **a:** Prior to the work of Augustine of Hippo, Christianity's appeal was to the Roman disenfranchised: working class, women, and slaves. Augustine's efforts to reconcile Greek and Roman philosophy with the faith made it acceptable and persuasive to the empire's intellectual elites. (p. 309)

Comprehensive Multiple Choice Answers

1. **a:** The combination of imperial weakness, demographic changes brought on by disease, and the increasing success of nomadic invaders combined to bring an end to both the western Roman empire and Han China. While the other choices have elements which are correct, only choice "a" combines the elements for both empires' collapse. (pp. 302, 305)

2. **d:** When the Han dynasty was formally abolished in 202 C.E., it was divided into three large kingdoms which had difficulty withstanding nomadic migrations. Rome in the west fell in 476 C.E., but remained in the east as the Byzantine empire until 1453. (pp. 303, 305)

3. **b:** After the fifth century C.E., the rift between eastern and western Christianity would grow increasingly large and, eventually, the split between eastern and western Christianity would be formalized by the great schism of east and west in 1054 C.E. However, in the early days of Christianity, western Christians were inspired by eastern traditions of self-denial and removal from secular society as a sign of devoutness. (pp. 283. 298)

Primary Source Answers

1. a.   Prior to 400 C.E., the peoples of northern and eastern Europe practiced their traditional pagan religions and lived a nomadic lifestyle; there was limited sustained positive interaction with the Romans through trade. Christianity would not take hold here until the conversion of the Franks in the north at the end of the fifth century, and in the east through the missionary work of Cyril and Methodius in the ninth century.

   b.   The geography of Africa and its limited trade connections with Europe and Asia stalled the spread of these three religious traditions. The Sahara desert, the elevation, topography and river flow, and the vast distances delayed the Eurasian exploration of sub-Saharan Africa and the ensuing spread of these faiths. After the seventh century, Islam will enter Africa carried by merchants to ports and markets in the east and west of the African continent. Though Buddhism and Hinduism will not follow the Islamic movement, Christianity will re-seek a continental conversion during the nineteenth and twentieth centuries. (p. 297)

2. a.   "Greatness of heart" is a carefully chosen phrase which demonstrates one of St. Cyprian's goals in writing this treatise: to explain how epidemic disease is actually an opportunity for true Christians to demonstrate the depth of their faith. He explains further in the treatise that this is an opportunity for Christians to care for the sick and to demonstrate fearlessness toward death after which they will be rewarded.

b.   He explains the disease as a "win-win" situation for true believers. They will be rewarded with an opportunity to demonstrate their faith, regardless of the outcome of the battle with the disease. He is careful to point out that non-Christians have no such opportunity for "liberation."

c.   St. Cyprian wrote this document prior to Constantine's Edict of Milan (313 C.E.) and prior to Theodosius's decision to make Christianity the official religion in the Roman empire. Christians had experienced waves of persecution especially under Nero and Diocletian, so St. Cyprian was trying to reassure believers of their reward when faced with the plague and to respond to pagan critics who sought to blame Christianity for the epidemic. His motivations were based on his desire to defend and protect his faith and its adherents. (p. 301)

PART III

THE POSTCLASSICAL ERA,
500 TO 1000 C.E.

CHAPTER 13

THE COMMONWEALTH OF BYZANTIUM

Before you get started: There is good news and bad news about this chapter: The good news is that you will not find much specific detail from this chapter on the multiple-choice portion of the national exam. The Byzantine empire lasted more than one thousand years and the Byzantines were all about complex detail: in government, economics, religion, gender roles, even in art. Today, people use the word "Byzantine" as a sophisticated adjective meaning unnecessarily convoluted or complex. So, it is good you will not be expected to know one thousand years of those details.

However, the bad news is that because the Byzantine empire lasted more than one thousand years, it interacted with regions about which you are expected to know a lot of details: developments in Europe, interregional networks and contacts, emergence of new empires and political systems. Further, on the national exam, you could be asked to compare political and social institutions in western and eastern Europe. The boldfaced words in this chapter summary are there to help you choose what is most important rather than because they might specifically appear on the national exam.

So, while you might be tempted to skip this chapter because it is not specifically mentioned in the College Board Course Outline, do not. Instead, keep these four guiding questions in mind as you read.

1. How did the Byzantine Empire interact with western Europe?
2. How did the Byzantine Empire interact with the rising Islamic world?
3. How did Christianity come to be divided into eastern and western traditions?
4. How did the Byzantine Empire interact with eastern Europe?

In other words, don't sweat the details, but keep focused on the bigger picture.

THE EARLY BYZANTINE EMPIRE

The Byzantine empire, sometimes called the **Byzantine Commonwealth,** existed for nearly one thousand years as the "economic and political powerhouse of the postclassical era." During that millennium, it dominated the wealthy and productive eastern Mediterranean region, led to the formation of large, multicultural zones of trade and communication, and sustained interactions with Slavic, Arab, European, and Asian peoples and traditions. Geographically, Byzantium's location offered ready sea and overland access to Asia, Europe, and Africa and an easily defendable site overlooking the **Bosporus Strait** including a magnificent harbor which allowed huge trading vessels ease of entry. The capital city, first known by the Greek name "Byzantion," was renamed **Constantinople** in 340 C.E. by the Roman Emperor Constantine and then renamed **Istanbul** by the conquering Ottoman Turks in 1453.

The Later Roman Empire and Byzantium
(Theme: Political Structures)

The early Byzantine empire, more accurately called the **eastern Roman empire,** struggled against pressure from the **Sasanid Dynasty in Persia** and the migratory peoples of the east and north. But, it survived the fall of Rome in the west in 476 C.E. and served as the "powerhouse of the eastern Mediterranean basin" into the thirteenth century.

Two elements of Byzantine tradition seem most responsible for its survival and longevity: the concept of **Caesaropapism** and the development of an elaborate government bureaucracy. **Caesaropapism** imbued the emperor with absolute secular power as well as immense religious power as he appointed the **patri-**

arch of the Eastern Christian Church. The Byzantine government bureaucracy was large and intricate. Further, this bureaucracy was essential in enforcing the complex Byzantine legal tradition.

Justinian and His Legacy
(Theme: Political Structures)

Justinian is memorable for three reasons: his wife, his building, and his laws. **Theodora**, his wife, was his active advisor in politics, diplomacy, and theology. She encouraged the military suppression of rebellion, the rebuilding of Constantinople, the construction of the **Church of Hagia Sophia**, and the recodification of Roman law to fit the demands of the Byzantine world. **Justinian's Code**, known as "**Corpus iuris civilis**" (*Body of the Civil Law*), served as the source of legal inspiration in the Byzantine empire for nearly one thousand years and influenced civil law codes throughout western Europe as well.

Islamic Conquest and Byzantine Revival
(Themes: Patterns of Interactions, Technology, and Political Structures)

Byzantium was threatened by the rise of powerful and expansive Muslim states beginning in the seventh century. By the early eighth century, the Byzantines lost control of Syria, Palestine, Egypt, and north Africa and even faced possible loss of Constantinople itself. The use of "**greek fire**" by the Byzantines allowed her to retain control of Anatolia, Greece, and the Balkan region.

Byzantine rulers also responded to the threat of the Muslim empire by reorganizing its political structure through the development of the **theme system.** Each imperial province, known as a theme, was placed under the jurisdiction of a general who assumed full military defense and civil administration responsibilities. The general then recruited his army from the free peasants in the theme who were rewarded with allotments of land in exchange for their services. Each general was appointed by the imperial government which kept a close eye on his actions. This system allowed for quick mobilization of armies and wove society together in an interdependent social hierarchy.

Basil the Bulgar Slayer used terror to expand the Byzantine empire back into Syria, Armenia, Italy, the Danube region, Crete, and Cyprus.

Byzantium and Western Europe
(Theme: Patterns of Interaction)

Relations were strained between the Byzantine empire and western Europe. Though both Christian, differences in church language, ecclesiastical practices, and secular ties provoked conflict between these two branches of Christianity. The Byzantine maintained their claim to the remains of the Roman empire in the west despite the rising power of Germanic groups, especially **Charlemagne** and the Franks. The rise of the **Holy Roman Empire** after 962 severed and antagonized both formerly connected empires.

BYZANTINE ECONOMY AND SOCIETY

The location at a crossroads for trade, the abundant agricultural surpluses, and the tradition of a strong craft and artisan class provided a strong economic base for the Byzantine empire.

Rural Economy and Society
(Themes: Economics and Social Structures)

Constantinople was the largest city in Europe for nearly 800 years. First Egypt, then Anatolia and the Danube basin produced enough grain to feed populations in large Byzantine cities. This robust agricultural economy was made possible largely through a large class of free peasants who served as the backbone of the Byzantine army and who also owned and worked their small farms. Though the Byzantine government worked in the sixth through tenth centuries to limit landholdings of wealthy families on large estates as a way of protecting small landowners, over time landholding was consolidated into fewer and fewer hands and the former free peasants became an increasingly smaller class within Byzantine society. The decline of the free peasantry reduced the imperial tax coffers and diminished the number of potential soldiers in the themes.

Industry and Trade
(Themes: Economics and Trade)

The agricultural productivity of the land and the importance of Constantinople as a trade center guaranteed that the Byzantine empire would remain prosperous despite the worsening plight of the free peasants. Byzantine craftsmen maintained their historic reputation for producing glassware, textiles, gems, jewelry, fine gold, and silver metalwork. After the sixth-century Byzantines smuggled silkworms and **silkworm technology** out of China, the government in Constantinople worked hard to control the production and supplies of silk to European markets.

Byzantium served as the center of trade for western Eurasia working in direct commercial relationships with all of northern Europe, the Black Sea region, Persia, Syria, Egypt, and Palestine. The Byzantine gold coin, the bezant, became the standard currency of the Mediterranean basin for six hundred years. Banks and business partnerships developed to encourage trade and make huge profits from the goods which flowed through the empire on their way east and west.

The Byzantine empire revived the silk roads of classical times and served as the western anchor of these Eurasian trading networks. Silks, precious gems and metals, spices, timber, furs, honey, and slaves all passed through the Byzantine empire. The collection of taxes and tariffs from these goods and the value added to raw materials turned into luxury products made the Byzantines very wealthy.

Urban Life
(Themes: Social and Gender Structures)

Constantinople was the heart of the Byzantine empire. At the heart of "the City," the opulent imperial palace reflected the empire's wealth. Aristocrats also built elaborate homes for their extended families, servants, and slaves including **separate apartments for women** who were frequently excluded from festivities and parties in order to preserve their "honor."

Artisans and merchants frequently lived above their shops, while government workers and lower level employees lived in multistoried apartment houses. The poor lived in multifamily tenements. In these classes, women were part of the economic realm of the family.

Like their Roman ancestors, the City provided entertainment for her citizens. Horse races, baths, taverns, restaurants, theaters, circuses, and gaming houses provided entertainment and distractions.

CLASSICAL HERITAGE AND ORTHODOX CHRISTIANITY

The philosophy and literature of classical Greece had a major influence on Christianity in Byzantium. By the mid-eleventh century, differences in doctrine, ritual, and church authority had lead to a formal split between **Eastern Orthodox Christianity** and **Roman Catholic Christianity**.

The Legacy of Classical Greece
(Themes: Changes and Continuities and Intellectual Developments)

Though the common people of the Byzantine empire spoke Greek, in the earliest centuries of the Byzantine empire the business of government was conducted in Latin. After the sixth century, however, Greek became the official language of government, religion, and education. Most people in the Byzantine empire were literate. The size of the Byzantine government demanded educated workers, so the government sponsored primary schools to teach reading and writing which were essential skills for the imperial bureaucracy. The state also sponsored a school of higher learning in law, medicine, and philosophy. Aristocrats hired their own tutors to provide private instruction for their sons and daughters. Merchants and people of other middle-class occupations almost always had some primary education. Greek classics and the humanities were the basis of Byzantine scholarship.

The Byzantine Church
(Theme: Religious Developments)

Caesaropapism defined the relationship between church and state in Byzantium; emperors treated the church as part of their government. They appointed the patriarch of Constantinople and instructed church officials to preach obedience to imperial authority as obedience to God. The use of **icons** in ceremony and worship had long been a part of religious practice in the Orthodox Church. Emperor Leo III tried to eradicate their use as items of contemplation as he feared the icon itself was being worshipped; he sparked a controversy that plagued the Byzantine church for more than one hundred years. Byzantine theologians sought to reconcile Christian theology and classical Greek philosophy through a series of councils and conferences designed to clarify theological matters. The most famous of these meetings was the **Council of Nicaea** in 325 C.E.

Monasticism and Popular Piety
(Theme: Religious Developments)

Orthodox Christianity has a strong tradition of **asceticism** and **monasticism**. The "pillar saints" and the ascetic monks who followed St. Basil sought mystical union with God through meditation and prayer. Some orthodox monks and nuns served God by providing social services such as providing food and medical care in times of crisis.

Tensions between Eastern and Western Christianity
(Themes: Religious Developments and Changes and Continuities)

With the spread of Islam in the seventh century, only Constantinople and Rome remained as the principal centers of Christian authority, but the two soon clashed over religious and theological issues: the use of icons, what type of bread to use during communion, whether priests should marry or even shave, the precise relationship between God, Jesus, and the Holy Spirit, autonomy of individual regions, and the language of the Mass. The split between the Greek Orthodox Church and the Roman Catholic Church was finalized in 1054 C.E. with the **great schism of east and west.**

THE INFLUENCE OF BYZANTIUM IN EASTERN EUROPE

By the eleventh century, Byzantium was in a period of decline. Surrounded by Islamic and western European societies, Byzantium turned its political, social, and cultural attention to Russia and eastern Europe where it had an enduring impact on the Slavic peoples of that region.

Domestic Problems and Foreign Pressures
(Theme: Patterns of Interaction)

After the eleventh century, the corruption of the theme system through intermarriage of theme administrators with local nobility produced an elite class which mounted rebellions against imperial power, undermined local economies, and reduced the amount of land available to the free peasants. The results were fewer recruits available for military service and lower tax revenues for the imperial government.

Coupled with domestic problems, the rise of western powers like the Normans threatened the Byzantine empire. The **fourth crusade** and the near destruction of Constantinople in 1204 permanently weakened the empire. The eleventh century also saw invasion from the east by the **Saljuqs** who captured most of

Anatolia; the rest of that region came to be held by the western European crusaders. Loss of the agricultural and human wealth in Anatolia dealt a death blow to the Byzantines. When Constantinople fell to the **Ottoman Turks** in **1453**, the thousand-year-old Byzantine empire ended.

Early Relations between Byzantium and Slavic Peoples
(Theme: Patterns of Interaction)

Orthodox Christianity and the ensuing development of the **Cyrillic alphabet** helped to promote and sustain relations between Byzantium and the Slavic peoples of eastern Europe: Serbs, Croats, Bulgarians, and Moravians.

Byzantium and Russia
(Theme: Patterns of Interaction)

The city of **Kiev**, located on the trade route linking Scandinavia and Byzantium, emerged as a thriving city in the ninth century. In 989, **Prince Vladimir of Kiev** and his subjects converted to Orthodox Christianity and opened the doors for Byzantine influence throughout his realm. The **Russian Orthodox Church** was created by the Kievian princes who sought to cement their own caesaropapist positions. The Cyrillic alphabet and ensuing literacy as well as icons and "onion domes" reflect this cultural tie. Moscow is sometimes called the **third Rome**.

Finished reading the chapter? Be sure you can . . .

- Explain the emergence and reasons for longevity of the Byzantine empire.
- Discuss the developments and shifts in trade, technology, and cultural exchange during the years of the Byzantine empire.
- Explain the divisions between eastern and western Christianity.
- Compare and contrast developments in political, economic, and social institutions in both eastern and western Europe. (You will need to read Chapter 17 for this one.)

Chapter Multiple Choice Questions

1. Which of the following was a geographic advantage enjoyed by Constantinople?
    a. It was situated high on an easily defensible peninsula.
    b. The Golden Horn was a magnificent natural harbor.
    c. It could control the Bosporus Strait which connected the Black Sea and the Sea of Marmora.
    d. It was at the crossroads of trade from Europe, Asia, and Africa.
    e. All of the above.

2. The Byzantine concept of "theme" was developed to
    a. protect the Byzantine empire from ninth century invasions by the Franks, led by Charlemagne.
    b. organize Byzantine law into reasonable categories which would make it easier to administer.
    c. prevent the concept of "caesaropapism" which allowed the emperor's power to go unchecked.
    d. enable Byzantine military forces to organize quickly and to provide a sustainable political and social order throughout the empire.
    e. promote the opportunities for women like Theodora to serve as ministers and officials in the Byzantine bureaucracy.

3. A key economic result of the decline of the free peasants in the Byzantine empire was
   a. a decrease in the tax income collected by the imperial government.
   b. a decrease in the unemployment rate in large cities.
   c. an increase in civil unrest lead by the women and slaves.
   d. an increase in the number of men available to serve in the military.
   e. an increase in lawlessness and banditry in western Europe.

4. Byzantine businessmen made profits by
   a. forming corporations and selling stock in their economic endeavors.
   b. forming partnerships which allowed them to pool their resources and limit their risks.
   c. charging high interest rates on loans to companies which were involved in risky business deals.
   d. trading the bezant for older coins from the western Roman empire.
   e. financing overseas expeditions to create new markets for luxury goods.

5. The iconoclast controversy, begun by Emperor Leo III in 726, demonstrated
   a. the need to reform Church structure and theology according to the Pope's directives.
   b. the willingness of Byzantine emperors to involve themselves in religious and theological matters.
   c. the power of the monasteries and "pillar saints" to capture public attention.
   d. the continuing influence of classical Greek tradition and philosophy in the Orthodox church.
   e. all of the above.

6. Byzantine asceticism and monasticism was characterized by all of the following EXCEPT:
   a. perching for years atop tall pillars
   b. the abandonment of personal property
   c. living communally
   d. strict obedience to the church officials in Constantinople
   e. living as a hermit in a desert or cave

7. The Council of Nicaea was called in 325 C.E. to define Christian teaching on
   a. the distinct powers of the Pope and patriarch.
   b. the godly and human nature of Jesus.
   c. the roles for men and women in the Church.
   d. strict obedience to imperial authority.
   e. the proper language to be used in religious services.

8. The Byzantine decline after the eleventh century was due to all of the following EXCEPT:
   a. the disastrous attempts by Basil the Bulgar Slayer to expand the empire
   b. the pressure on Anatolia from the nomadic Saljuqs
   c. the corruption of the theme system and the decline of free peasantry
   d. the damage caused by the fourth crusade
   e. the sack of Constantinople in 1204 C.E.

9. What effect did the Cyrillic alphabet have on Orthodox Christianity?
   a. It made it easier for people to read the Bible and therefore question the church's teachings.
   b. It made it more difficult for people to read the Bible since it was written in Latin and people were learning Cyrillic.
   c. It stimulated conversion to Orthodox Christianity and promoted literacy among the Slavs.
   d. It drove a wedge between people who could read and people who were illiterate.
   e. It made rulers like Vladimir of Kiev less powerful as he could no longer base his power on caesaropapism.

10. The iconoclast controversy illustrated the influence of a secular ruler in a state's religion. It was a divisive one-hundred-year period of violence in what faith?
    a. Manichaeism
    b. Islam
    c. Roman Catholicism
    d. Chan Buddhism
    e. Byzantine Christianity

Comprehensive Multiple Choice Questions

1. The complex government bureaucracy, the absolute rule by an emperor, and the lavish and ornate royal palaces of Byzantium are MOST similar to
    a. China, in the later Han dynasty.
    b. Rome, under Julius Caesar.
    c. the Aryan rajas during the Vedic age.
    d. the Olmecs in the first century B.C.E.
    e. China, during the Shang dynasty.

2. What effect did the development of Islam have on Constantinople's influence on Christianity?
    a. It made Constantinople less influential in Christianity as many people converted to Islam.
    b. It made Constantinople less influential in Christianity as Christians turned to the patriarchs in Alexandria and Jerusalem for guidance.
    c. It made Constantinople more influential because many people converted to Christianity to escape the Arab armies.
    d. It made Constantinople more influential in the east as the influence of the patriarchs in Jerusalem, Alexandria, and Antioch declined.
    e. Constantinople remained secondary to Rome in influence until the crusades.

3. Why did Kiev rise as the prime trading center in the mid-ninth century?
    a. The discovery of gold, furs, amber, and oil in Russia led to a northern shift in trading centers.
    b. The fall of Constantinople in 1453 left a trade vacuum which Kiev was able to fill.
    c. It was strategically located on the Dneiper River which linked trade routes between Scandinavia and Byzantium.
    d. The development of the Cyrillic alphabet and the ensuing rise in literacy made the Slavic peoples better-educated traders and merchants.
    e. The western European sack of Constantinople during the fourth crusade weakened the Byzantine trading empire.

Primary Source Questions

1. **Read *Sources from the Past: The Wealth and Commerce of Constantinople* on page 329 of your textbook.**
    a. What observations does Benjamin of Tudela make which support his premise that "wealth like that in Constantinople is not to be found in the whole world"?
    b. How might Benjamin of Tudela's background have influenced his observations?

2. **Read *Sources from the Past: Anna Comnena on the Suppression of Bogomil Heretics* on page 334 of your textbook.**
    a. How does Anna Comnena use vivid word choice to influence her readers?
    b. Why is the emperor's choice of pyres a clever idea?
    c. Why might you question the veracity of the last sentence?
    d. How might the author's background inform her perspective on the evils of the Bogomil heretics?

Chapter Multiple Choice Answers

1. **e:** The strategic location of Constantinople and the Byzantine empire cannot be overemphasized. Its prime location and geographic assets account for much of the longevity enjoyed by the empire. (p. 318)

2. **d:** The concept of themes as an organizing principle within the Byzantine empire developed in response to outside military threats and internal problems with local government administration. (p. 324)

3. **a:** Large estate owners were able to obtain tax concessions and exemptions which reduced the money coming in to the imperial tax coffers. Decline in the free peasantry reduced the Byzantine tax base. (p. 326)

4. **b:** The use of cooperative partnerships provided great opportunities for profit and limited the risk to any individual merchant. (pp. 327–329)

5. **b:** Leo's involvement in eradicating the reverence of icons as a historic religious practice sparked a hundred years of conflict within the Orthodox Church and throughout the empire; his efforts in "the breaking of icons" clearly demonstrates the close connections between state and church in the Byzantine empire. (p. 332)

6. **d:** Life as a hermit or as a monk was based on the search for mystical union with God through self-denial, meditation, and prayer. Monks in particular went to great lengths to separate themselves from the formal, elaborate life of theologians and ecclesiastical bureaucrats. (pp. 333–335)

7. **b:** The Council of Nicaea was an important attempt by the Christian church to clarify essential dogma. The nature of Jesus was a difficult and complex issue which nearly tore the church apart and did result in persecution of Christians who retained their beliefs despite council decisions. (p. 331)

8. **a:** Byzantium was at a high point politically, militarily, and economically as a result of Basil's leadership. Basil was a disaster to all who opposed him, but he represented a pinnacle in Byzantine power. (pp. 336–338)

9. **c:** The Cyrillic alphabet represented the sounds of Slavic languages more accurately than did the Greek or Roman alphabet. This ease of sound and form made it much easier for missionaries like Cyril and Methodius to convert the Slavs to Orthodox Christianity and it made it much easier for people to learn to read and write. (p. 339)

10. **e:** The iconoclast controversy is essential to understanding the relationship between the Byzantine emperor and the Byzantine church. Lasting more than a century, the controversy underlined the willingness of Byzantine emperors to directly involve themselves in religious and theological matters. (p. 332)

Comprehensive Multiple Choice Answers

1. **a:** The Byzantine emperors held absolute power including their influence in ecclesiastical affairs. They used the wealth of their empire to create an elaborate bureaucracy to manage their highly centralized state and they built ornate palaces to enhance their lofty status. Likewise, under the leadership of Han Wudi, China established a highly centralized bureaucracy, built ornate palaces, and ruled as absolute throughout his lifetime. (pp. 94–95, 112–113, 136–137, 194–195, 267, 320)

2. **d:** Constantinople and Rome emerged as the two principal centers of Christianity as Islam spread in the Middle East and north Africa. With the decline of the powerful patriarchs in Alexandria, Antioch, and Jerusalem, the center of Christianity shifted west to Constantinople and Rome. (p. 335)

3. **c:** Kiev rose as a trading center in the ninth century because of its location. Although answers "d" and "e" are correct statements, they do not respond to the question. (pp. 339–340)

Primary Source Answers

1. a. The document's author is very careful to describe the material wealth he sees in great detail. He mentions gold, silver, and rich textiles in addition to foodstuffs and wine. He also includes details about the architectural feats such as the Hagia Sophia and the Hippodrome as evidence of Constantinople's wealth. He further includes a description of the range and assortment of people he sees from places all over the world who live in Constantinople.

   b. As a rabbi from Spain, Benjamin of Tudela would be well educated and as a world traveler he would have many experiences with other places and people to use as the basis for evaluating the wealth he sees in Constantinople. (p. 329)

2. a. The author uses descriptive language to portray these non-orthodox believers as evil. She uses vivid phrases like "ravenous wolf" and "serpent lurking in its hole" to intensify her message that these people are evil. She talks about the women as being of "bad character" and the evil being like "some consuming fire." She then portrays her father as having been patient, but simply no longer being able to bear the evil embodied in these "heretics."

   b. The choice of pyres is clever because if the heretics had been wrongly accused and were actually Christians, they should choose the cross and not fear death because they would enter heaven as believers. It is also a clever ploy by the emperor because educated Christians would see the parallel between this situation and the one faced by Solomon when two mothers claimed a single child. By the inescapable choice of two pyres, the Byzantine emperor is clearly portraying himself to be as wise as Solomon; his daughter understood the biblical allusion as would her readers.

   c. One has to wonder why, if the emperor was willing to pursue and imprison these heretics, he would be concerned with their physical comforts. Perhaps the author is continuing to portray her father as a man of mercy at the expense of the truth regarding their deaths while imprisoned.

   d. As the daughter of the emperor, the author is expected to be supportive of her father and of his role as emperor. The principle of caesaropapism was clearly part of his authority and she would want to do everything possible to support his authority including slanting her words, observations, and conclusions. (p. 334)

CHAPTER 14

THE EXPANSIVE REALM OF ISLAM

Before you get started: The Islamic world is one of the most important topics of this course because it has had such profound effects on the cultures of many continents and an enormous impact on global trade and commerce. You may find the Arabic words difficult to remember so it would be time to pull out your flashcards again. However, words such as *algebra* and *sakks* ("checks") are derived from Arabic and the innovations they represent have spread to Europe and beyond. Ironically, one innovation that we think of, Arabic numerals, are not in fact Arabic but derived from India. This is an example of the extraordinary effect the Islamic world has had as an intermediary between Europe and the rest of the globe as well as its adoption of useful cultural knowledge from the places where it spread. The changes in Islamic traditions that occurred as the religion spread are wonderful examples of the change-over-time theme emphasized in the AP guidelines. One other thing to keep in mind is the status of women. Despite its reputation for veiling and seclusion, you will discover that Islamic society has given women a great deal more freedom to pursue business and to influence politics than many other regions.

A PROPHET AND HIS WORLD

Islam's origin in the Arabian desert where bedouin nomads have lived for thousands of years has affected its values. Family and dependence on extended kinship groups in a harsh environment magnified the importance of loyalties that continued to exist long past the advent of Islam. As the Roman empire collapsed and its protection of trade routes disappeared, the Arab peninsula became the **crossroads of trade** between the Mediterranean basin and the Indian Ocean. Goods from the sea lanes of the Indian Ocean traveled overland to the Mediterranean ports making cities like Mecca important stops on the route.

Muhammad and His Message
(Theme: Religious Developments)

Muhammad was born into an important merchant family around 570 C.E. After his parents died, Muhammad came into the custody of his male relatives who provided him with an education but little else. When he left home, he was employed by a woman who, in 595 C.E., also became his wife. As she had some wealth from her deceased husband, his status in Meccan society rose. Muhammad went on to become a successful merchant in the region. Through business, he met many groups from other cultures and it is presumed that he was influenced by his associations with Jewish merchants and Arab converts to Christianity. Around 610 C.E., Muhammad had a spiritual transformation that caused him to reject the polytheism of his ancestors and affirm his faith in one god, **Allah**, who would reward the righteous and punish the wicked. He experienced many visions of the archangel Gabriel that he understood to be revelations from Allah which prompted him to speak of his faith to others. He followed the instructions and slowly gained a group of followers in Mecca.

By the 650s, the revelations that Muhammad had received and voiced had been written down by his followers. The compilation was issued as the **Quran** and reveals a powerful, poetic message of faith and understanding of Allah's wishes for the world. It has served as the authoritative foundation for Muslim doctrine and social organization. Later, Muhammad's own sayings were complied into the *hadith* which combined with the *sharia* (Islamic law) to augment followers' understanding of Islam.

Muhammad's Migration to Medina
(Theme: Religious Developments)

As more people followed Muhammad's faith, conflict arose between them and the elite of **Mecca.** Muhammad's message of Allah as the one true god challenged and worried the polytheists. Furthermore, the wealthiest businessmen took it as a personal insult and felt that it threatened their position since Muhammad preached against excessive wealth. It was also an economic threat to the caretakers of the shrines to various gods who made their money from the fees they charged to pilgrims. The best known of these shrines, the **Ka'ba**, a large black rock, would later become the center of the Muslim pilgrimage. Muhammad and his followers became so threatened that they fled to **Medina** in 622 C.E. (the *hijra* or "**migration.**") This date became the beginning of the Islamic calendar. In Medina, Muhammad organized his followers (the *umma*) and provided them with a comprehensive code of laws and social customs. The *umma* led by Muhammad then mounted a military campaign against their enemies on the Arab peninsula. In a more benevolent spirit, Muhammad looked after the welfare of widows, orphans, and the poor. Later, charity became a moral obligation of all Muslims. As his community increased, Muhammad became recognized as the last **prophet**, the final messenger after the prophets of the Jewish Torah and Christian Bible. He recognized Jesus as a prophet and acknowledged the Jewish Yahweh and Christians' God as the same god as Allah.

The Establishment of Islam in Arabia
(Theme: Religious Developments)

In 630 C.E., the followers of Islam attacked and successfully conquered **Mecca.** They forced the inhabitants to adopt Islam and destroyed all shrines except the Ka'ba. They built **mosques** ("places of worship") on the sites of the former shrines and devised a government based on Muslim principles. In 632 C.E., Muhammad led the first pilgrimage to Mecca and the sacred Ka'ba. The annual *hajj* became the fifth of the **Five Pillars of Islam.** It was joined by (1) the acknowledgement that there is only one god and his prophet is Muhammad, (2) the necessity of praying to Allah daily facing Mecca, (3) the observation of a month of prayer and fasting during **Ramadan,** and (4) the obligation of almsgiving to the poor and destitute. The Five Pillars formed a simple and effective foundation to bind all the *umma* across all regions into a community of faith. Some later Muslims took on the *jihad* as an additional sign of faithfulness. The word *jihad* means "struggle" and is usually interpreted as a personal spiritual and moral fight against evil and unbelief. Some have also extended it into a physical war against unbelievers.

The body of holy laws known as the *sharia* developed in the centuries after Muhammad's death. Based on the Quran and Muhammad's sayings, it offers guidance on every aspect of moral and social behavior such as marriage, inheritance, slavery, business, governance, and crime.

THE EXPANSION OF ISLAM

After Muhammad's death, the choice of a successor was difficult and controversial. Clans and towns initially broke away but soon the Islamic leadership readjusted and embarked on reconquest and expansion across the southern boundaries of the Mediterranean.

The Early Caliphs and the Umayyad Dynasty

Remarkably, Islam continued to expand despite a serious rift between the successors to the prophet. Since there could be no more prophets, his advisers appointed Abu Bakr, a close friend and disciple, to serve as the *caliph* ("deputy"). He became head of state as well as religious leader, chief juror, and commander of the military. Under his command, they reconquered the lapsed communities and forced them to convert. This expansion continued well beyond Arabia and into the Byzantine and Sasanid (Persian) empires. Despite their small numbers, the Muslim soldiers were able to defeat larger armies across wide areas. By 718, they had even reached and conquered parts of northwest India, across North Africa, and into the Iberian peninsula.

The first four *caliphs* had been appointed by the most powerful clans but this led to intense rivalries between clans and factions. From these disagreements arose the **Shia** sect followed by a minority of Muslims today, chiefly in Iran and Iraq. A cousin and son-in-law of Muhammad had been fourth caliph for a brief period but was assassinated by his enemies. His surviving followers organized themselves in support of the caliphate as an inherited position of Muhammad's descendents. They soon developed new holy days in honor of their martyrs as well as other traditions. They have served as an alternative to the **Sunni,** the majority sect of Islam since then.

The Umayyad caliphate was primarily interested in conquest so they made a policy on how to deal with the religions of conquered peoples. Like the Persian and Roman governments, the caliphate allowed the retention of people's faith but unlike the other empires, they required the payment of a tax (*jizya*) in order to continue their religious practices. The imposition of the tax and favoritism shown to Arabs were viewed negatively by the conquered peoples.

The Abbasid Dynasty
(Theme: Political Sructures)

The **Abbasids** took control of the caliphate with the help of the Persians. It was a far more cosmopolitan regime that did not show special favor to Arabs and in that way, more closely resembled the Romans and Persians. Although the Abbasids did not have a policy of conquest, *dar al-Islam* ("the Islamic world") continued to grow with the conquests of regional Islamic armies. The Abbasids administrated from *Baghdad,* a newly built city in present-day Iraq. The *ulama* or religious officials and *qadis* ("judges") administered public policy and justice based on the Quran and the Sharia. The Abbasids kept a standing army and established a bureaucracy for finances, taxation, coinage, and postal services. They appointed regional governors and maintained an excellent road system. (Yes, you have heard this all before, in the Persian and Roman empires.) By the ninth century, the Abbasid dynasty was a center for commerce and banking as well as industry. Its caliph, Harun al-Rashid, had such wealth that he tossed coins to indigents and sent an elephant to the court of Charlemagne in western Europe. Soon after, the dynasty weakened from regional civil wars, peasant rebellions, and foreign conquests as the caliphs became mere figureheads until its ultimate demise at the hands of the Mongols in 1258 C.E.

ECONOMY AND SOCIETY OF THE EARLY ISLAMIC WORLD

In dar al-Islam, basic economic foundations remained the same—agricultural societies with peasants tilling the ground—but it also included a vibrant urban economy and a thriving trade network.

New Crops, Agricultural Experimentation, and Urban Growth
(Themes: Technology, Economics, and Demographics)

Crops from different regions were carried throughout dar al-Islam and proved useful in new areas. Staples such as sugarcane, rice, and new varieties of wheat; vegetables such as spinach, artichokes, and eggplants; fruits such as citrus, bananas, coconuts, and watermelons; and industrial crops like indigo, cotton, and henna were grown throughout the region. The effects were an increased food supply and the establishment of a **textile** industry. New methods of agriculture also moved across the Islamic world; new methods of irrigation, fertilization, and crop rotation became the subject of agricultural manuals. Agricultural growth spurred the growth of cities with populations of several hundred thousand people. Cities as distant as Toledo, Cairo, Delhi, and Bukhara prospered from the economic success of agriculture and industry. (Look up those cities on a map.) One of the newest industries was the **manufacture of paper**, an innovation borrowed from the Chinese. Cheaper and easier to use than vellum made of calfskin, paper led to an expansion in the number of written materials in dar al-Islam.

The Formation of a Hemispheric Trading Zone
(Themes: Patterns of Interaction, Trade, and Technology)

From its earliest roots in the life and times of Muhammad, commerce had a special place in the Islamic world. Muhammad said that honest merchants stood alongside martyrs to the faith on the judgment day. The Islamic world's position at the center of trade routes between Europe and Asia offered great opportunities and prosperity. Muslim merchants took advantage of the old roads of the Persian and Roman empires as well as new roads maintained by the caliphate. The same highways provided opportunities for missionaries and pilgrims as well. The development of an adequate camel saddle allowed many more goods to traverse the deserts and high plains. Inns developed along those routes that catered to both human and camel. Innovations in maritime travel increased the sea trade. **The lateen or triangular sail** borrowed from Indian and Chinese ships allowed more direct routes while the **astrolabe** from the Hellenistic Mediterranean allowed them to calculate latitude. Arab and Persian ships sailed throughout the Indian Ocean and beyond to Chinese ports. **Banking** developed with a system of loans and sakks ("checks") that enabled merchants to work in distant regions. Different types of group investments developed to spread the risks and profits of long-distance trade. Thus Islamic trade was extraordinarily far-reaching and profitable with products such as silks and ceramics from China; gold, salt, and slaves from west Africa; and amber, furs, and trade from Scandinavia and Russia flowing into the Abbasid empire.

The Changing Status of Women
(Theme: Gender Structure)

Arab women had many rights not seen in other regions well before Muhammad's time. They could inherit property, divorce husbands, and engage in business. The Quran furthered these privileges by forbidding infanticide and allowing women to possess their own dowries. Women were seen as equal to men in the eyes of Allah with Muhammad's generosity and kindness to his own wives serving as an example for all men. However, the Quran and the sharia also reinforced male dominance by recognizing descent through the male line, putting male family members in charge of women's social and sexual lives, and allowing Muslim men to have as many as four wives. When Islam expanded into the Mesopotamian and eastern Mediterranean regions, it took on some of the patriarchal aspects of those societies. The **veiling of women** and **household seclusion** comes from Mesopotamian and Persian traditions. Although the Quran granted specific rights and privileges to women, later interpretations of it have limited those rights and placed women under the control of male guardians. Thus, when Islam spread to other regions, it picked up cultural traditions with more profound patriarchal traditions.

ISLAMIC VALUES AND CULTURAL EXCHANGES

The **Arabic** language holds a privileged position as the only true language of the Quran. Nevertheless, as Muslim missionaries spread the word of Islam through the teachings of the Quran, they allowed many pre-Islamic traditions to be retained by the affected cultures.

The Formation of an Islamic Cultural Tradition
(Themes: Cultural and Intellectual Developments)

The *sharia* as a body of civil and criminal law formed a unifying bond across the Islamic world. The *ulama* and *qadis* resolved disputes according to a unified code of law while *madrassas* ("schools of higher learning") promoted a sense of unity in education and understanding of Muslim law and theology. Groups of missionaries went to and beyond all areas of the Islamic world to proselytize. *Sufi* **mystics** were among the most effective with their goal to bring increased spirituality to Islam rather than strict adherence to formal religious teachings. Ecstatic worship in the forms of passionate sermons, dancing, and singing worried more strict adherents of Islam but proved enormously popular in most Islamic communities. The *sufis* were also remarkably tolerant toward the new converts who wished to follow some of their indigenous beliefs as well. They attracted many converts in lands with well-established Christian, Hindu, and Zoroastrian traditions, such as India and Persia, through their tolerance, their personal ascetic lifestyles, and their simple message. In addition to *sufis, qadis,* and the *ulama,* pilgrims on the *hajj* passed through many lands and brought their faith and devotion as examples to other peoples.

Islam and the Cultural Traditions of Persia, India, and Greece
(Themes: Cultural and Intellectual Developments and Patterns of Interaction)

As the Islamic world expanded into other regions, it brought its faith and traditions to those societies but it also adopted traditions that it encountered. Persian adaptations were made in the areas of administrative techniques and kingship responsibilities. Persian also became the language of poetry, literature, and history. India lent the Muslims easier symbols for mathematics with its **Hindi numerals** that later became known in Europe as Arabic numerals. This allowed the development of advanced math such as **algebra, trigonometry,** and **geometry** as well as simplifying bookkeeping. Astronomy and medicine were improved by Indian knowledge as well. The Muslims truly admired the philosophical writing of the Greeks. Some writers were able to synthesize Greek philosophy with Islamic theology. In the twelfth century, rational thought based on Aristotle was admired and reinterpreted by Ibn Rushd in Spain which shaped Islamic philosophy and later influenced European universities. Madrassas rejected rational philosophy and it fell out of favor but never completely disappeared in the Islamic world. Aspects of **Greek mathematics, science, and medicine** were also picked up by the Muslims. Greek mathematics augmented the Indian advances while anatomy and physiology were incorporated into Islamic medical knowledge. The Muslim scholars used all these new acquisitions in knowledge to produce a flowering in the body of Islamic thought that dealt with the natural world.

Finished reading the chapter? Be sure you can . . .

- Map the spread of Islam and describe the three major ways it spread.
- Compare Islam with other major religions and belief systems reviewed in previous chapters.
- Describe how Islam contributed to the economic and cultural bonds of the Islamic world.
- Relate how Islamic law and succession affected the caliphate.
- Describe the origin and spread of Islamic arts, literature, science, and technology.
- Describe and analyze the evolution of women's roles in Islamic society.
- Trace the development of trade routes through the Islamic world.

Chapter Multiple Choice Questions

1. What in Muhammad's background may have influenced his acceptance of monotheism?
   a. Muhammad's family had always been monotheistic.
   b. The Arab peninsula had equal numbers of monotheists and polytheists.
   c. Muhammad's wife had been raised as a monotheist.
   d. Muhammad was engaged in long-distance trade where he came into contact with monotheists.
   e. Muhammad's uncle adopted monotheism during his youth.

2. According to Islamic tradition, the Quran was compiled from
   a. many different sources, including polytheistic writings.
   b. revelations from Allah to Muhammad.
   c. writings by followers who recorded Muhammad's sayings.
   d. the Jewish Old Testament.
   e. the Christian New Testament.

3. In what way did the expansion of the Islamic faith progress through the rest of the Arab peninsula?
   a. by rapid and peaceful means due to its message of peace
   b. in violent warfare as Islam challenged both polytheists and the ruling elite
   c. as a steady growth passed from merchant to merchant
   d. fairly swiftly as converts were attracted to the actions of the sufi mystics
   e. it was not successful until the growth of *madrassas*

4. Adherence to the Five Pillars of Islam are the foundation of Muslim faith. Which one was the first and most important one upon which all the others are based?
    a. dedication to daily prayers facing Mecca
    b. acknowledgment of Allah as the only deity and Muhammad as his prophet
    c. almsgiving to the poor by all who have the means to afford it
    d. the Ramadan fast, with exceptions made for the young and infirm
    e. the hajj for all who are able to get to Mecca

5. The origin of the split between the Shia and Sunnis was indicative of
    a. succession problems.
    b. religious issues.
    c. economic differences.
    d. disagreements over the role of women.
    e. disputes over territorial holdings.

6. With the assistance of the *ulama* and *qadis,* how was the Abbasid empire administered?
    a. It was decentralized into local governments.
    b. It was remarkably separate from the Islamic religion.
    c. It was split between two administrators, a secular leader and a religious leader.
    d. It developed under the guidelines of the Quran and sharia.
    c. It blended Shia beliefs into Sunni administration.

7. Within *dar al-Islam*, economics proved very successful. What was responsible for this success?
    a. European and Indian traders increased the number of valuable imports to the region.
    b. Its base was a strictly agricultural economy.
    c. It decreed a uniform governmental policy across regions.
    d. It rejected agriculture for the promotion of industry.
    e. It was a zone of commerce and communication.

8. Women's roles in Islamic societies were eventually defined by
    a. their male relatives.
    b. the interaction between religion and region.
    c. Muhammad's sayings in the *hadith.*
    d. the Quran alone.
    e. the *ulama* and the *sharia.*

9. Islam quickly expanded through military means but why were Sufi missionaries so successful later on?
    a. They combined fervent worship with strict adherence to local customs.
    b. Without goods to carry, they traveled farther than merchants.
    c. They combined deep personal devotion to Islam with a tolerance for regional culture.
    d. They converted many monarchs who convinced their people to follow.
    e. They took the best parts of Islam and blended them with the best parts of the local religion.

10. As the Arabs moved into India, they adopted Indian methods of mathematics, science, and medicine. What is their best known and most widely spread borrowed idea?
    a. the concept of zero
    b. Hindi numerals
    c. techniques of bookkeeping
    d. yogic health habits
    e. heliocentrism

Comprehensive Multiple Choice Questions

1. Both Islam and Buddhism are missionary religions. Outside of the message, what aspect of the sufis and monks would have the most appeal to new converts?
    a. The possibility of leading an ascetic lifestyle.
    b. The opportunity to travel widely while following the missionaries.
    c. The possibility of escaping from one's social class.
    d. The profoundly pious example set by the missionaries.
    e. The attraction of new ways of thinking and living.

2. Both the caliphate and the Mauryan empire in India had successful administrations in their early years. When one compares the administrations, what basic difference exists?
    a. While the caliphs were tolerant of other religions, the Mauryans were not.
    b. While Ashoka encouraged agriculture, the caliphate's focus was more commercial.
    c. The Mauryans had one capital city while the caliphate operated from two.
    d. The caliphate had no standing army while the Mauryans did.
    e. The Mauryans had a secular government while the caliphate was a theocracy.

3. Like Buddhism and Christianity, Islam can be described as a derivative religion. Each grew out of another religious tradition through the efforts of one individual. In what way was Islam different from the others?
    a. Neither of the others had practical rules for living daily lives.
    b. The spread of Islam was vastly more successful in a shorter period of time.
    c. Only Islam was spread through military conquest and missionary efforts.
    d. Islam was more focused on the material world than the spiritual world.
    e. Only Islam had schools as centers of religious learning.

Primary Source Questions

1. **Read *Sources from the Past: Benjamin of Tudela on the Caliph's Court at Baghdad*, twelfth century, on page 358 of your textbook.**
    a. Since you may not know who Benjamin of Tudela was, do you notice anything about his tone?
    b. Briefly describe the life of the caliph in Baghdad.
    c. To what extent was the caliph "a benevolent man," as mentioned by Benjamin of Tudela?

2. **Examine the thirteenth-century manuscript illustration on page 360 of your textbook.**
    a. How would you know that this painting was Muslim?
    b. Describe the artistic style in a way that would make you recognize it in the future.

Chapter Multiple Choice Answers

1. **d:** Muhammad appears to have a good knowledge of Christianity and Judaism through his association with them as a long-distance merchant in the Arab peninsula. (p. 348)

2. **b:** The revelations that Muhammad received were compiled by his followers into one book. His later sayings were recorded also and are known as the *hadith*. (p. 348)

3. **b:** Muhammad and his followers were driven out of Mecca by competing forces and had to rely on war to assume control of the peninsula. (p. 349)

4. **b:** Without the acknowledgment of Allah and Muhammad, none of the other tenets can be practiced. (p. 351)

5. **a:** After Muhammad's death, the first caliph named by his followers was a close friend and adviser. After the fourth caliph who was a relative of Muhammad was assassinated, the argument concerning the true "deputy" split over the best-suited and the descendents of Muhammad. (p. 355)

6. **d:** The *ulama* were religious authorities while the *qadis* were judicial magistrates. Both worked hand in hand to solidify the government under the tenets of Islamic law. (p. 357)

7. **e:** The Islamic world served as an expanded region across continents that shared trade, the Arabic language, and exchanged crops, commodities, and ideas. (p. 359)

8. **b:** Once Islam had spread to the eastern Mediterranean regions, the roles of women as defined by the Quran and the *sharia* changed to include the more restrictive customs of those regions such as veiling. (p. 365)

9. **c:** Sufi mystics impressed people with their personal piety and willingness to overlook continued practice of local religions. (p. 367)

10. **b:** Hindi numerals that simplified Islamic bookkeeping later spread to Europe where they became known as Arabic numerals. (p. 369)

Comprehensive Multiple Choice Answers

1. **d:** Both the sufis and Buddhist monks preached and encouraged adherence to the tenets of the two religions. While each religion had its appeal and a practical application to daily life, it was the example of the devout missionaries themselves that attracted the most converts. (pp. 220, 366)

2. **e:** While Ashoka certainly promoted Buddhism, he was not the head of the faith in addition to his duties as emperor. On the the other hand, the caliphs were considered to be Muhammad's lieutenants so they were the administrative head of *dar al-Islam* as well as the premier religious leaders. (pp. 210, 353)

3. **b:** Within the first hundred years after the death of Muhammad, Islam had spread to encompass the Iberian peninsula in the west through northern Africa and the Middle East and to the central Asian steppes in the east. It took two hundred years for Buddhism to leave the subcontinent under Ashoka's patronage and still was not the dominant religion in India. Paul of Tarsus brought Christianity to Rome within its first century but it was not the dominant religion of the Roman empire until the end of its third century. (pp. 221, 282, 354)

Primary Source Answers

1. You should not be alarmed if you do not know many of the sources in the document-based question. However, you need to learn how to glean as much as you can from what you read. Tone is one way that point of view is judged. Benjamin of Tudela's tone is one of admiration, even astonishment. It is apparent that he was a traveler from abroad and he is stunned by what he has found. This type of insight and identification is enough to earn a partial point for point of view on the DBQ. Benjamin of Tudela was a Jew from Muslim Spain who traveled to Baghdad in the twelfth century C.E. The caliph lives in a world of luxury and abundance with servants and officials to obey his every wish. He is very benevolent to the sick indigents and the mentally ill but the manner in which he deals with the members of his own family is notable for its harshness. Fear of rebellion has resulted in the confinement, albeit luxurious, of all his competing male relatives. That indicates a major problem in succession to the caliphate that will be mentioned in later chapters. (p. 358)

2. The most obvious symbol of Islam is the mosque in the upper-right-hand corner. Note the dome and the minaret or prayer tower. The camels and turbans also indicate travelers in the Islamic world. You might note the absence of veils so do not assume that when Muslim women are depicted, they will be veiled. The decorative flourishes added to the flowers framing the travelers point to an exquisite attention to detail. Obviously, the costuming of the figures, the curved door frames, and the camels also indicate the Islamic world. Finally, the crowded aspects and vibrant colors would be easily recognized and are seen in the other manuscript illustrations in this chapter. (p. 360)

CHAPTER 15

THE RESURGENCE OF EMPIRE IN EAST ASIA

Before you get started: If you have not already sketched a BIG chart with the Chinese dynasties down the side and the themes of political institutions, technologies, gender roles, cultural achievements, social structures, and religious influences across the top, start now. You can count on a significant number of the multiple choice questions on the AP Exam to relate to China, and you can also be reasonably sure that China will figure into the DBQ, the Comparison/Contrast, or the Continuity or Change–Over-Time questions.

Check out the test materials available on AP Central; China is included in a significant way each year. You can be certain that China will be there on this year's exam as well. One out of six people in the world today live in China; it is important.

THE RESTORATION OF CENTRALIZED IMPERIAL RULE IN CHINA

China reestablished its political, economic, and cultural hegemony during the post-classical era by restoring **centralized rule**, by **developing technologies** which expanded agricultural and manufacturing output, and by using armed forces and diplomats to influence culture in Korea, Vietnam, and Japan.

The Sui Dynasty
(Themes: Political Structures and Technology)

In the late sixth century, **Yang Jian** reestablished centralized imperial rule in China through the use of tight political discipline and military force. He and his successors in the short-lived **Sui Dynasty** ordered the construction of granaries, dykes, and levees, rebuilt defensive walls and fortifications, sent military forces to central Asia and Korea, required compulsory labor, and levied high taxes to pay for all these endeavors.

Emperor **Sui Yangdi**'s construction project, the **Grand Canal,** established the foundation for cultural and political unity in China as it integrated the economies of both the north and the south of that vast nation. Extending more than 1,200 miles and flanked by wide roads running parallel to its course, the Grand Canal made it possible to transport food and finished products across China and then to other east Asian markets. The canal, though economically beneficial for China for more than a thousand years, was built with **conscripted labor** and through high taxes, both of which fueled resentment toward Sui Yang Di.

The Tang Dynasty
(Theme: Political Structures)

The **Tang dynasty,** which lasted nearly three hundred years, transformed Chinese society. Though he came to power through murder and deception, **Emperor Tang Taizong** ruled China with the best attributes of a Confucian scholar: a belief in duty and the goal of what was best for his subjects. Policies of maintaining transportation and communication systems, of distributing land according to the **equal-field principle,** and of relying on a **bureaucracy of merit**—all policies begun during the thirty-year Sui dynasty—resulted in a Tang reign characterized by unusual stability and prosperity throughout China.

The Tang dynasty used its military muscle to expand into Manchuria and central Asia and to extend its influence further into **Korea** and **Vietnam** making it one of the largest empires in China's history. The Tang emperors used a system of **tributary relationships** to institutionalize relationships with their neighbors, to foster trade and cultural exchanges and to promote diplomatic relations in east Asia. The **kowtow,** ritual prostration before the emperor and the elaborate exchange of gifts, developed as part of these annual tribute ceremonies. The Tang dynasty was seriously weakened by internal rebellion in the mid-eighth century and had to invite the **Uighurs,** a nomadic Turkish people, into China to rid the empire of rebels. The nomads were successful in decimating the rebellion but they exacted a huge price, the right to sack **Chang'an** and **Luoyang;** the Tang empire never fully recovered. During the ninth century, rebellions led by military commanders who revolted with support of the peasants further undermined imperial power as the emperor was forced to grant progressively greater power to local military leaders. The **Mandate of Heaven** was withdrawn in 907 as the Tang emperor abdicated.

The Song Dynasty
(Theme: Political Structures)

China remained under warlord control until the rise of the Song dynasty (960–1279) beginning with martial emperor **Song Taizu.** Using his strong army, Song Taizu challenged the local warlords and consolidated control throughout China. After completing his military conquest, the emperor convinced his winning generals to retire to a life of leisure and then he set about establishing a strong and expanding Confucian government bureaucracy based on merit which even had charge of military forces.

This huge, centralized government did have some drawbacks. First it was extremely expensive to pay an increasing number of government bureaucrats; this lead to two destructive peasant revolts. Second, a military led by government bureaucrats was no match for the threatening northern nomads who gradually chipped away at the Song boundaries until all that was left by the early twelfth century was the Southern Song. That small empire was no match for the coming Mongols in 1279.

THE ECONOMIC DEVELOPMENT OF TANG AND SONG CHINA

The economic growth begun in the Tang and Song dynasties stimulated trade and production throughout much of the eastern hemisphere for more than seven hundred years.

Agricultural Development
(Themes: Economy and Technology)

A major result of the Sui and Tang expansion into Vietnam was the introduction to China of various new food sources, especially a **fast-growing rice** which made it possible for Chinese farmers in the south to harvest two crops a year. This doubling of the rice output, plus the introduction of improved agricultural techniques such as **heavy iron plows, extensive irrigation systems, use of manure and organic materials to fertilize the soil,** and **terraced mountain farming** vastly expanded China's agricultural output.

This increased agricultural output had a dramatic impact on population growth, urbanization, and social structures. By 1200, China's population topped 115 million due to increased food production and a highly effective system of food distribution. China's cities also grew in size and number during the Sui, Tang, and Song dynasties. **Chang'an** during the Tang dynasty had a population of two million and **Hangzhou** during the Song Dynasty had a population of more than a million people. Furthermore, life in these and other Chinese cities became increasingly urban with thousands of shops, restaurants, hotels, taverns, gardens, teahouses, brothels, and other urban entertainments. Traditionally patriarchal China became even more so during these dynasties as families sought to secure their growing wealth. This goal of solidarity promoted two key practices: increased **ancestor reverence** and **footbinding.** Ancestor reverence, though long a part of Chinese social tradition, came to include elaborate rituals venerating deceased ancestors. Footbinding, like veiling in the Islamic world, was most popular in the ruling and elite classes where women's labor was not necessary for family survival.

The changing economy and technology during this era also changed the lives of farmers who increasingly took advantage of readily available rice and grains and shifted to **commercial market-oriented cultivation** of crops best suited to their regions. Families supplemented their diets with rice purchased from the money they could make growing specific fruits and vegetables.

Technological and Industrial Development
(Themes: Technology and Trade)

Ample supplies of food produced and distributed throughout most of the Tang and Song eras made it possible for the Chinese to develop significant technological and industrial interests including **porcelain, metallurgy, gunpowder,** and **printing.** Beautiful Chinese porcelain became a product in high demand throughout southeast Asia, India, Persia, and east Africa. Improved grades of **iron and steel** went into the production of farm implements and weaponry as well as large construction projects such as bridges and pagodas. Nomads from the north quickly adopted these iron weapons and used them against the Song. Ironically **gunpowder,** developed by Daoist alchemists searching for the elixir of life, was used in early flamethrowers and in primitive bombs. The diffusion of this technology to the west resulted in the development of metal barrel cannons and eventually guns. Printing became widespread during the Tang dynasty first with **block printing**, then with the development of **moveable type**. The Chinese soon realized that block printing was much more efficient for them as 40,000 characters made setting the moveable type too time-consuming. The development of printing produced cheap, high-volume readily available texts.

Chinese ingenuity and market sense affected their **naval technology** as well. During the Tang dynasty, Chinese mariners began to participate in long-distance trade in the Indian Ocean. Fueled by a desire for spices and exotic products of southeast Asia, the Chinese developed the **magnetic compass** which soon was used by seafarers throughout the Indian Ocean basin.

The Emergence of a Market Economy
(Themes: Economy and Trade)

During the Tang and Song eras, China's economy became more tightly integrated than ever before, thanks to increased agricultural production, population growth, urbanization, industrial production, and improved transportation systems. With successful government programs to manage food distribution and guard against military usurping of the iron industry, China's economy grew rapidly, so that Chinese merchants often found themselves short on copper currency. To deal with this problem, they developed such innovation as **"flying cash,"** letters of credit accepted between cooperating creditors, promissory notes, checks, and eventually paper money. These innovations promoted and sustained commercial interactions in a society short of currency.

The printing of private paper money could and eventually did cause problems. When short-term economic downturns or poor business management left merchants unable to honor these notes, disorder and even riots would occur. By the eleventh century, however, the government forbid private parties from issuing paper money. Government currency included serial numbers and warnings to counterfeiters. Sometimes even the government would mismanage the production of paper money, but by the **Qing** dynasty, the government instituted tight fiscal controls over the issuance of printed money. Yet, even with management abuses, paper money was a powerful stimulus to the Chinese economy during the Tang and Song eras.

China's economic surge during the Tang and Song dynasties promoted trade and urbanization both in China and throughout much of the eastern hemisphere. Goods traveled across land and sea to supply markets and to meet consumer demands for exotic and luxury goods. Items such as feathers, pearls, tortoise shells, incense, melons, and horses became attractive status items, often because of their scarcity. Likewise Chinese silk and porcelain became status symbols throughout central Asia, India, Persia, and east Africa.

CULTURAL CHANGE IN TANG AND SONG CHINA

The Establishment of Buddhism
(Themes: Religious Developments and Patterns of Interaction)

Buddhism, which came to China over the silk roads, developed as a **syncretic faith:** a result of the interaction of Confucian and Daoist traditions with Mahayana Buddhism set in the context of Tang and Song Chinese culture.

Though Buddhism first arrived in China with Indian merchants trading with the Han dynasty, it was not until the Tang and Song eras that Buddhism took hold in China. After the fall of the Han dynasty, support for Confucianism waned and several foreign religions established communities in China, including Nestorian Christians, Manichaeans, Zoroastrians, and Muslims. These **religions of salvation** mostly were followed by foreign merchants and converts from the nomadic societies. Buddhism found its earliest Chinese converts in oasis cities around the city of Dunhuang, in the western region of Gansu. There Chinese converts decorated cave walls with images of Buddha and Buddhist **bodhisattvas,** assembled libraries of religious works, and operated scriptoriums to produce Buddhist texts. All these efforts helped Buddhism gain a following in China.

The Chinese were attracted to Buddhism because of its high moral standards, its intellectual sophistication, and its promise of salvation. Wealthy coverts donated land which monks farmed and whose bounty was shared with nearby Chinese peasants. Confucians, though sharing a tradition of using written texts, found Buddhism too abstract and impractical for their concerns. Confucians also disliked the Buddhist emphasis on celibacy and a monastic lifestyle which was in direct opposition to the Confucian focus on the family and filial piety. Daoists did not like the Buddhist reliance on religious texts and the ideal of striving for perfection by living an ascetic lifestyle.

Buddhism responded to this opposition by tailoring its message to fit the Chinese tastes. **Dharma** was discussed as the **Dao; nirvana** was translated as **wu wei.** Celibacy and a monastic lifestyle were supported by the idea that a Chinese family could send one son to the monastery and earn salvation for ten generations. The development of **Chan** Buddhism, also known as **Zen** Buddhism in Japan, focused on intuition, moments of clarity, and sudden flashes of insight; the connection to Daoism is evident. These concessions to traditional Chinese philosophy produced a syncretic faith which promoted the spread of Buddhism throughout China.

Daoists and Confucians resented Buddhism as alien and wasteful. Confucians in particular were able to influence the Tang emperors to close monasteries and expel the Buddhists along with other foreign faiths. The Tang emperors, motivated more by greed for wealthy land resources than by religious conviction, did not thoroughly enforce their expulsion edicts and did not fully eradicate foreign faiths from China. Buddhism in particular survived and came to affect Confucian thinking in the Song dynasty.

Neo-Confucianism
(Themes: Religious Developments and Patterns of Interaction)

The Song emperors chose to support Confucianism by sponsoring the studies of Confucian scholars and subsidizing printing and dissemination of Confucian writings rather than actively persecuting the Buddhists. Ironically, these Song era Confucian scholars developed an appreciation for Buddhist interest in individual and cosmic issues previously ignored by earlier Confucians. **Neo-Confucianism** developed out of these Buddhist interests in the nature of the human soul and the individual's relationship with the cosmos. Writings by men such as Zhu Xi adapted Buddhist concepts to Confucian values and helped to expand neo-Confucian thinking into philosophical, political, moral, and intellectual life in Vietnam, Korea, and Japan.

CHINESE INFLUENCE IN EAST ASIA

In the postclassical era, Korea, Vietnam, and Japan each developed a deep but unique interpretation of Chinese cultural and political values while maintaining their own distinctive identities.

Korea and Vietnam
(Themes: Patterns of Interaction and Changes and Continuities)

Though the Tang armies conquered much of Korea in the seventh century, the Korean Silla dynasty avoided occupation by developing a highly beneficial **tribute relationship** with China. As a **vassal state**, Korean emissaries regularly delivered gifts to Chinese emperors and performed the required kowtow in exchange for valuable gifts from the Chinese court and the even more valuable opening of Chinese markets to Korean merchants, products, and goods. Korean ministers observed the workings of the Chinese imperial court and bureaucracy and sought to organize the Korean court on similar lines. Aristocratic Koreans found value in Confucian traditions, though they never established a bureaucracy based on merit, as did the Chinese, while Chan Buddhism's promise of individual salvation found willing converts among non-elite Koreans.

Unlike Korea, China's relationship with Vietnam was much more hostile. While the Tang armies were able to subdue the Vietnamese people in the north and then launch successful efforts to absorb them into some Chinese traditions, the people of the south mounted a series of revolts against Tang authorities which proved successful by the tenth century. While the Vietnamese readily adopted Chinese agricultural methods and irrigation techniques and developed schools and administrative structures modeled on Chinese methods, they retained many indigenous religious traditions. Vietnamese women had always been active in southeast Asian society and in a variety of economic realms and would not bow to the more patriarchal Chinese society.

Early Japan
(Themes: Patterns of Interaction and Changes and Continuities)

Japan was first populated by nomads from northeast Asia who traveled to the archipelago using land bridges exposed during the Ice Ages about two hundred thousand years ago. Later, immigrants arrived from Korea bringing rice cultivation, bronze and iron working, and horses. The population of the islands grew and aristocratic clans emerged to dominate several small states which ruled the region.

Chinese influence from the Tang and Song eras spread to Japan in the eighth century as one of the Japanese aristocratic clans sought to exert influence over the others by seeking to centralize Japanese government and to establish an imperial house modeled on the Chinese system. This era, known as the Nara Period (710–794 C.E.) was the high point of Chinese influence in Japan.

The Japanese adopted Chinese Confucian and Buddhist traditions but continued to maintain their indigenous religion, **Shinto.** When the capital of Japan was moved from Nara to nearby Heian (modern Kyoto), the new Japanese imperial state continued to draw inspiration from China but was careful to develop elaborate Japanese political and cultural traditions. During this **Heian period,** the tradition of Japanese emperors ruling as ceremonial figureheads and symbols of authority rather than true absolute rulers emerged. This pattern of a split between the publicly recognized imperial authority and a separate agent of effective rule helps to account for the remarkable longevity of Japan's imperial house.

The pattern of accepting Chinese tradition and then its elaboration in a distinctive Japanese way is seen in Japanese writing and literature. Chinese-style pictographic language was adapted to spoken Japanese. Japanese court officials learned and relied on Chinese script to handle imperial business. Japanese women, who rarely received this Chinese-style education, wrote many literary works. Muraski Shikibu's *The Tale of the Genji* chronicles the ultrarefined life at the Heian court and offers a meditation on the passing of life's joys, sorrows, and relationships. In the mid-twelfth century, the Taira and the Minamoto clans fought a bloody civil war for control of Japan. The victorious Minamoto clan installed a **shogun,** a military governor who ruled instead of the emperor at Kamakura, near Tokyo; the clan dominated Japanese political life for the next four centuries.

Medieval Japan
(Themes: Patterns of Interaction and Changes and Continuities)

Japan's medieval period (1185–1573 C.E.) refers to the age between Chinese influence and the rise of Japanese centralized government in the sixteenth century. During this time, Japan developed a decentralized political system in which provincial lords controlled land, economics, and justice throughout the islands, thus there was little need for Chinese-style imperial bureaucracy. Instead, the military talent and discipline of the **samurai** played the most distinctive role in political and military affairs. The local lords relied upon these professional soldiers to enforce their authority and extend their claims into other regions of Japan. The lords supported the samurai with agricultural surplus and labor services from the peasants working under their rule. Thus freed from economic constraints, the samurai were free to devote themselves to hunting, riding, archery, and martial arts.

Finished reading the chapter? Be sure you can . . .

- Analyze the Sui, Tang, and Song political and economic revolutions.
- Describe the initiatives of the early Ming dynasty.
- Explain diverse effects of the establishment of Buddhism and the development of Neo-Confucianism in China.
- Evaluate the Chinese accomplishments in the arts, sciences, and technologies.
- Analyze the Chinese influence in Korea, Vietnam, and Japan.
- Compare and contrast Japanese and European feudalism (Chapters 17 and 20 will be necessary here).

Chapter Multiple Choice Questions

1. Along with China, what other two empires are considered the anchors of the postclassical world?
   a. Rome and Greece
   b. Rome and the Carolingian Empire
   c. Byzantium and the Abbasid Empire
   d. the Abbasid Empire and the Persian Empire
   e. the Umayyad Empire and the Abbasid Empire

2. The nomads from the north of China proved the greatest threat to the demise of which Chinese dynasty?
   a. Sui
   b. Tang
   c. Song
   d. Yuan
   e. Ming

3. Why was the Grand Canal such an essential part of China's economic health?
   a. It helped to stop flooding of the Hwang He and therefore allow for more food production.
   b. It was a practical and economic way to transport foods like rice from the Yangzi River valley to residents of northern regions.
   c. It allowed otherwise unemployed Chinese laborers to earn a living wage and support their families.
   d. It allowed luxury goods to move quickly to port markets on the Yellow Sea.
   e. It supported an extensive fishing industry which brought much-needed protein into the southern Chinese diets.

4. The maintenance of transportation and communication networks, the distribution of land according to the equal-field system, and the reliance on a bureaucracy of merit are all reasons which of the following dynasties succeeded?
   a. Shang
   b. Zhou
   c. Sui
   d. Tang
   e. Song

5. Why did the Chinese continue to use block printing rather than move toward using moveable type developed during the eleventh century?
   a. Printing was considered an art form and tradition dictated that methods should not change.
   b. Block printing was part of the Daoist concept of yin and yang; to change it was to destroy the necessary balance in the universe.
   c. The scholar-gentry had been trained in block printing and were resistant to altering their means of earning a living.
   d. The aesthetics of block printing far surpass those of moveable type.
   e. Chinese written language is based on more than 40,000 characters, so moving individual ideographs within each document was too time consuming.

6. Why was Buddhism especially supportive of printing technology?
   a. Buddhists saw a strong economic potential in the sacred book market.
   b. Buddhism was fighting with Christianity for converts and saw pamphlets and flyers as a way to attract followers.
   c. Buddhism supported printing because it provided jobs for monks who otherwise could not earn a living.
   d. Buddhism favored the adoption of printing because copying and distribution of sacred text was considered a highly meritorious act.
   e. Buddhism was anti-printing as replicating Buddhist texts was seen as a sin of the ego and greed.

7. In the eleventh century, why did the Chinese government choose to restrict the private production of paper money and assume it as a duty of government?
   a. The Chinese government did not like paper money and hoped they could stamp it out by restricting its supply.
   b. The Chinese government wanted to stimulate trade by issuing more currency through checks and promissory notes.
   c. The Chinese government was fearful that Arab merchants would develop their own paper currency and try to use it in Chinese ports and markets.
   d. The Chinese government wanted to preserve the convenience of paper money, but to reduce problems caused by forgery and inadequate currency backing.
   e. The Chinese government relied on Confucian principles regarding duty and responsibility which taught that the government had the responsibility to manage the economy.

8. How did the fall of the Han dynasty encourage the introduction of new, non-Chinese religions into China?
   a. With the revocation of the Mandate of Heaven, there was no institution to stop the spread of alien religions.
   b. The last Han emperor had been interested in religions of salvation and so introduced the ideas to the bureaucrats and it filtered down to Chinese citizens.
   c. The Confucian tradition lost credibility after the fall of the Han, and the era of warlords and nomadic invaders promoted the spread of foreign religions into China.
   d. The Han dynasty had actively sought to eradicate Buddhist monasteries from China, and with its demise the Buddhists saw an open door into China's elite society.
   e. The new Sui emperor converted to Buddhism and wanted his people to follow his religious transformation.

9. Which of the following was NOT a result of Chinese interaction with Vietnamese culture?
    a. Vietnamese women lost their traditional domination of local and regional markets as a result of China's powerful patriarchal tradition.
    b. Vietnamese authorities established an administrative system and bureaucracy based on Chinese traditions.
    c. Vietnamese ruling classes prepared for their careers by pursuing a Confucian education.
    d. Buddhism came to Vietnam from China as well as from India.
    e. Vietnamese farmers adapted Chinese agricultural methods and irrigation systems.

10. During which period in Japanese history was Chinese influence most profound?
    a. Nara period
    b. Heian period
    c. Kamakura period
    d. Muromachi period
    e. Tokugawa period

Comprehensive Multiple Choice Questions

1. Why was economic expansion during the Chinese Tang and Song dynasties linked to military expansion?
    a. Military expansion into Vietnam introduced the Chinese to faster-growing rice, which made it possible to grow two rice crops a year in southern China.
    b. Military expansion into Manchuria and Korea made it possible for the Chinese to harness new energy sources in the water buffalo and the ox.
    c. Military expansion into the nomadic north made it possible for Chinese farmers to farm their land in safety and security and guarantee food harvests from their fields.
    d. Military expansion into Korea and Japan introduced a new strain of drought-resistant wheat into northern China.
    e. Military expansion into Vietnam introduced terraced farming to China, which greatly increased the amount of land under cultivation in mountainous southern China.

2. The ritual of the kowtow was significant throughout east and central Asia for all of the following reasons EXCEPT:
    a. it institutionalized relations between China and foreign lands
    b. it fostered trade with China and the other nations of Asia
    c. it promoted cultural exchanges between China and her neighbors
    d. it established the protocol of diplomatic contacts
    e. it established Chinese control in the subordinate lands

3. The development of gunpowder in China began
    a. as a Chinese response to northern nomadic invasion.
    b. as Daoist alchemists sought to discover an elixir to prolong life.
    c. as a power source for Europeans who were experimenting with metal-barreled cannons.
    d. as an outgrowth of the profitable chinaware industry.
    e. under the military directives of Shi Huangdi.

Primary Source Questions

1. **Examine the painting of workers building dikes to hold back a river on page 378 of your textbook.**
    a. Why might the artist have chosen the colors used in this work?
    b. Analyze the relationship between people and nature reflected in this painting.
    c. What does this work indicate about construction technology in seventeenth-century China?

2. **Read** *Sources from the Past: The Poet Du Fu on Tang Dynasty Wars* **on page 381 of your textbook.**
   a. How does the poem's author use imagery in the work?
   b. How would you describe the tone of this poem? What evidence in the poem leads you to that conclusion?

Chapter Multiple Choice Answers

1. **c:** Greece and Rome were part of the classical world. Western Europe was in the early medieval period during this era and though it traded some with the east, western Europe could not be considered an anchor of the postclassical world. The Persian empire and the Umayyad empire are also outside the time period addressed in the question. While you do not have to know a lot of dates on the AP Exam, you must have a sense of periodization, chronology, and relationship between eras. (p. 376)

2. **c:** Though the nomads were always a threat to the sedentary Chinese to varying degrees, the Song rulers had been unable to stop first the Khitan and then the Jurchen nomads. Finally, the Song were no match for the Mongols. (p. 382)

3. **b:** The Grand Canal, completed during the Sui dynasty, integrated the economies of northern and southern China and helped to bring a range of food products from the agriculturally rich south to the northern regions of China. (p. 377)

4. **d:** While elements of these three policies developed in previous dynasties, only the Tang were able to apply them effectively, systematically, and consistently. (p. 379)

5. **e:** The use of moveable type was unwieldy and inefficient for a language that had more than 40,000 characters. (p. 387)

6. **d:** Mahayana Buddhists saw great merit in copying and distributing sacred texts; this was especially true in Japanese monasteries. (p. 388)

7. **d:** In 1024, when the Song emperor issued the first government-supported paper currency, bureaucrats recognized the need to control the currency supply by adequately backing it and by reducing the risk of counterfeiting. (p. 389)

8. **c:** The fall of the Han empire undermined Confucian ideals of public order and honest, effective government as the ensuing era of warlords and nomadic invasion demonstrated the non-usefulness of such ideals. Further, the decentralization of power which followed allowed religions such as Christianity, Manichaeism, Zoroastrianism, Buddhism, and eventually Islam to gain footholds in local areas. (pp. 391–392)

9. **a:** Women throughout southeast Asia, including Vietnam, had traditionally dominated local and regional markets. Unlike their Chinese counterparts, Vietnamese women were thoroughly involved in society and economics. They retained this independence despite Chinese cultural influences. (p. 397)

10. **a:** The new capital city at Nara was modeled on the Chinese capital, Chang'an. The Nara period was characterized by an imperial structure and high culture modeled after the Tang ruling family. (p. 397)

Comprehensive Multiple Choice Answers

1. **a:** The fast-ripening rice the Chinese found during their military excursions into Vietnam grew extremely well in the fertile soils of south China. The increased supply of food coupled with the use of the well-maintained canal and transportation systems of the Sui and Tang dynasties stimulated economic growth throughout China. (p. 383)

2. **e:** The kowtow, though dramatic, was much more a ceremonial demonstration of Chinese influence in tribute states than an actual representation of Chinese primacy in those supposedly subordinate lands. (p. 380)

3. **b:** Developed during the Tang and Song eras, gunpowder was part of the Daoist quest for ways to maximize one's "chi" or vital energy. The alchemists' search for the "elixir of life" resulted in the discovery of gunpowder. (p. 387)

Primary Source Answers

1. a. The colors in this work are dusky yellows and browns with only a slight bit of color used on the clothing of some of the workers. The artist may have deliberately chosen these colors for an aesethic element, but also the color palette reflects the loess carried in the Hwang He (Yellow River) in northern China. The river is yellow as is the earth with which the people are building the dikes.

   b. It is impossible to look at this work and not be struck by the small size of the people and the enormous size of nature. The water and land take up more than two-thirds of the painting. Nature is massive and the individual is very small; even a large number of people seem dwarfed by the scope of nature, both water and land. Further, the people are working to contain nature, perhaps to subdue it, but there is no indication that they will be able to conquer it.

   c. The people are using buckets, poles, and hammers to build. They also appear to be using wood to support the base of the dikes. This technology requires a lot of manpower. The picture shows most individuals working with other people, as a single individual cannot provide enough power to accomplish the task. The caption indicates that conscripted laborers were used on such projects and the picture certainly supports that statement. (p. 378)

2. a. The poem uses sound as imagery: rattle, whinny, crying, questions, wailing, "the sound of their sorrow goes up to the clouds." The poet also uses powerful visuals as imagery: stare, turbaned white hair, the "blood of men spills like the sea," "strong women bent to the ploughing," "drive them like chickens and dogs," "old white bones," "like the dark sky of a stormy day."

   b. The tone of the poem is both sad and angry. The comments that introduce the poem use the word "bitter" to describe the perspective. That tone is clear in the shift that occurs in the last line of the first column. After sorrowfully describing the sounds and sights of war that have wounded the people, the poet says, "And still the heart of Emperor Wu is beating for war." This shift signals a series of painful questions which the poet poses to the Emperor : "Do you know that . . ." "Dare they complain?" "How could they pay?" (p. 381)

CHAPTER 16

INDIA AND THE INDIAN OCEAN BASIN

Before you get started: The introduction of Islam into India marks an important change in India's history. The important question is whether Islam and Hinduism can live together. Modern India, at the time of independence from Britain, decided it could not and so split into India and Pakistan in 1947. You will see that change in India comes from the northwest through Afghanistan, as did the Aryan societies, but now sea ports also open the subcontinent to change. Understanding southeast Asia can be confusing. It is such a diverse place and it takes on many cultural changes from other regions. We will simplify it down to only a few essential concepts.

ISLAMIC AND HINDU KINGDOMS

After the Gupta dynasty collapsed in the sixth century, India divided into many regional authorities much like Europe after the fall of Rome.

The Quest for Centralized Imperial Rule
(Themes: Political Structures and Changes and Continuities)

The many small kingdoms of northern India were almost at constant war until the period of the Mughal dynasty in the sixteenth century. However, there was one brief period of centralization under **Harsha**, a dynamic warrior who was able to lead his armies to successful conquest of the northern third of the subcontinent. Once he conquered the regions, Harsha, a Buddhist who promoted tolerance of all faiths, became particularly well known for his benevolent acts. He provided health care for all his subjects, promoted the building of hospitals, and promoted the arts. His generosity was noted by travelers such as the Chinese pilgrim Xuanzang. Yet Harsha never managed to completely control all the principalities of his empire so, after his assassination, the empire he built fell back into small kingships.

The Introduction of Islam to Northern India
*(Themes: Patterns of Interactions, War, and Religious Developments
and Changes and Continuities)*

Islam arrived in India by three different avenues. Military expeditions of Arab forces had conquered parts of northwest India by 711 C.E. The Sind thus became a part of the Arab empire with its policies of conversion to Islam or payment of taxes to allow practice of the local religion. Coastal regions welcomed **Muslim merchants** and, over eight centuries, along with intermarriage to local women, enclaves of Muslims were scattered throughout coastal cities. Other invasions and migrations through the northwest passes brought central Asians with their form of Islam. In the eleventh century, **Mahmud of Ghazni** made seventeen incursions into India to plunder and demolish its temples, hastening the disappearance of Buddhism from its place of origin. But there were few Muslim converts from his actions. His descendents continued to press into India and established the Muslim state known as the **Sultanate of Delhi**. While the sultanate often attacked Hindu regions in the south, they had little success and Islam was never more than a minority religion in the regions they did control. Nevertheless, by then Islam was permanently ensconced in northern India.

The Hindu Kingdoms of Southern India
(Themes: Political Structures and Changes and Continuities)

The southern two-thirds of India managed to avoid the intense conflicts of the north. Small Hindu kingdoms, loosely held, dominated the political scene but the occasional warfare was not as pervasive or damaging as that in the north. During this period, two kingdoms managed to control larger portions of the south. The **Chola kingdom** across the southern tip of India maintained control for four centuries while the **kingdom of Vijayanagar** occupied a smaller area of the western Deccan plateau for a century. Despite their devotion to the Hindu faith, southern Indian kingdoms tolerated and encouraged the Muslim merchants.

PRODUCTION AND TRADE IN THE INDIAN OCEAN BASIN

Agricultural surplus in India allowed the growth of industry and trade in the postclassical period. Merchant and artisan guilds became more important but the caste system remained in place.

Agriculture in the Monsoon World
(Theme: Economics and Demographics)

A comprehension of the **monsoon system** is essential for understanding the agriculture of India. Spring and summer brought the moist southwest winds off the Indian Ocean to water the crops in the wet season; while in the dry season the northeast fall and winter winds blew cold, dry air from the mountains that left the land parched. The only solution for successful agriculture was **irrigation.** Particularly in southern India, large dams, reservoirs, and canals were constructed which required enormous human effort to build and maintain. The increased agricultural productivity led to enormous gains in the population. At the fall of the Gupta, India had 53 million inhabitants. By 1500 C.E. India's population was at 105 million. And, as with all gains in population, migration of individuals to the cities of India increased. By the fourteenth century, four hundred thousand people lived in Delhi.

Trade and the Economic Development of Southern India
(Themes: Economics and Religious Developments)

Despite the many political units in southern India, trade was strong and industry was increasing. Staple crops of rice, barley, millet, and wheat could be grown throughout India but specialized items such as iron, copper, salt, and **pepper** could only be obtained in some regions. Extensive trade developed around these commodities as well as sugar and **saffron.** The political chaos of the north meant that the southern kingdoms prospered from their ability to produce large quantities of commodities to trade to the north.

Temples in the south served as the centers of community, agricultural endeavors, and trade. As they prospered financially, the Hindu temples grew more powerful.

Cross-Cultural Trade in the Indian Ocean Basin
(Themes: Economics, Patterns of Interaction, and Trade)

Prosperity in India was not just a result of internal production but also benefited from the wealth of the Indian Ocean trade. With a very early understanding of the monsoon seasons, Indian Ocean mariners traveled throughout the coastal regions. Large **dhows** from the Arab and Indian world and the even larger **junks** from China were dependent on the direction of the wind, so trade occurred in stages. Significant numbers of warehouses were set up in India, a central location, for storage of goods from each half of the Indian Ocean basin. Then ships would pick up their cargo and return to their half of the ocean with the appropriate monsoon. As central to the trade system, Indian cities were remarkably cosmopolitan with Hindu, Buddhist, Jewish, and other merchants commingling in commerce and living arrangements. **Arab** and **Persian merchants** largely controlled the shipping in the western region while the **Malays** and **Chinese mariners** sailed to points east of India. Regional specialization in commodities grew along with trade so that regions began to produce a greater quantity of a small number of trade items. Cotton textiles, steel production, and leather tanning were among India's specialties while silk, porcelain, and lacquerware were the purview of the Chinese. Horses, dates, and incense came from the Middle East with slaves, ivory, and gold from east Africa. Some cities and kingdoms prospered enough from trade to maintain their independence from larger empires.

Caste and Society
(Theme: Changes and Continuities)

The caste system adapted to the changes in trade and religion by becoming more complex, as it had in the classical times with the addition of *jatis*. Turkish peoples and Muslim merchants with their own codes of ethics were given their own place as they were absorbed into the system. The position of *jatis* intensified with the prosperity from commerce and caste distinctions became more prominent in southern India as the Hindu temples increased their power.

THE MEETING OF HINDU AND ISLAMIC TRADITIONS

Jainism and Buddhism lost followers as Hinduism and Islam increased their positions. Today, there remain very small communities of Jainists and Buddhists, but they largely disappeared from their land of origin. Hinduism with its enormous numbers of gods and goddesses strongly contrasted with the absolute stance of Islamic monotheism, but both prospered in India.

The Development of Hinduism
(Theme: Religious Developments)

Islamic armies destroyed large numbers of Buddhist sites in northern India so Hinduism benefited from Buddhism's declining numbers. Individuals and families began to choose favorite gods within the Hindu pantheon and devote themselves to the worship of them. By intense worship of specific deities, Hindus hoped to become unified with them for ultimate salvation. These **devotional cults** became enormously popular in southern India with Shiva and Vishnu gaining the widest following. Scholars took popular Hinduism and attempted to devise a philosophy that explained the relationship of the temporal world to the spiritual world.

Islam and Its Appeal
(Theme: Religious Developments)

At first, outside of coastal trading cities, Islam remained mainly a religion of the conquerors. There was little incentive for conversion to such a foreign theology brought by fearsome outsiders. But gradually, conversion increased because of Islam's message of equality for all caste members. Often the conversion was by entire caste or villages rather than individuals but that did not improve their social standing. The sufi mystics particularly appealed to Indians with their tolerance of Indian cultural values. During the twelfth century, the **bhakti movement** in southern India attempted to blend the two. It encouraged traditional Hindu faith but focused on the monotheism and equality found in Islam. While this syncretic movement was not very successful, it did serve to connect the two communities.

THE INFLUENCE OF INDIAN SOCIETY IN SOUTHEAST ASIA

Over a thousand year period, the peoples and governments of southeast Asia were profoundly affected by Hindu merchants who first brought them Indian political structures and religions, and, later, by Muslim merchants.

The States of Southeast Asia
(Themes: Trade, Cultural and Religious Developments, Political Structures)

In the early part of the first millenium C.E., Indian merchants were a common sight in southeast Asia. They traded their products with the local elites for spices, pearls, and animal skins. Rulers used their trade wealth to gain political power. They adopted Indian traditions while retaining many of their own and often sponsored Hinduism or Buddhism in their kingdoms. Hindu ideas about kingship and political power were particularly appealing. They did not, however, adopt the Hindu caste system. In places such as

Funan in modern day Vietnam, **Angkor** in modern day Cambodia, and among the islands of **Sumatra** and **Java,** kings used the Sanskrit term *raja* to refer to themselves and introduced Indian court rituals. Large **Hindu and Buddhist temple complexes** such as Angkor Wat were built but the people often worshipped their native deities as well.

The Arrival of Islam
(Theme: Religious Developments and Changes and Continuities)

Islam became more prominent in the tenth century with conversion of areas of the Malayan peninsula and present-day Indonesia. As with the earlier adoption of Hinduism and Buddhism, local traditions were retained but so were some Hindu and Buddhist traditions. But there was a pragmatic reason for conversion. The rulers' adoption of Islam allowed them better communication with Muslim traders and also supported their political power. Sufi missionaries hastened its adoption with their deep spiritualism and tolerance as they had in India and across central Asia. By the fifteenth century, the Islamic kingdom of **Melaka** grew powerful by controlling commerce that moved between the Indian Ocean and the South China Sea. After an earlier adoption of Hinduism, it enthusiastically sponsored the Islamic faith in regions further south and to the east.

Finished reading the chapter? Make sure you can . . .

- Describe the effects of the monsoon system on agriculture and trade.
- Analyze issues of governance which caused India to remain largely decentralized.
- Differentiate between the development of northern and southern India.
- Identify Indian Ocean trade routes and the main participants.
- Recognize the attempts at syncretic religion in the bhakti movement.
- Analyze India's political and religious effects on southeast Asia.

Chapter Multiple Choice Questions

1. Harsha dominated northern India in the sixteenth century as a conqueror and later an administrator. To what extent did Harsha centralize northern India?
   a. He founded a small kingdom that occupied northwest India.
   b. He was successful in unification of the northern third and administered it with help from local rulers.
   c. He was unsuccessful at administering his empire beyond central India.
   d. He unified southern India under one government.
   e. He centralized his empire as well as the Romans.

2. While later Islamic conversions occurred regularly in northern India, Islam was not successfully introduced by Mahmud of Ghazni and his forces because
   a. the invaders were not very devout followers of their faith.
   b. the invaders were not interested in proselytizing.
   c. the inhabitants were willing to be martyrs to their faith.
   d. the harshness of the invasions deterred people from following the religion of the invaders.
   e. the inhabitants had just converted to Buddhism and were unwilling to switch.

3. Historians generally treat southern India separately from northern India. At this time, southern India differed from northern India primarily in their
   a. steady adherence to Hinduism.
   b. acceptance of one strictly centralized government.
   c. lack of good trade routes.
   d. lack of a monsoon climatic pattern.
   e. mass conversions to Islam.

4. India and the Indian Ocean trade routes were dependent upon the climatic variations of the monsoon seasons. What areas did the monsoon system affect the most?
   a. governance and social caste
   b. trade and agriculture
   c. manufacturing and agriculture
   d. trade and governance
   e. religion and trade

5. Since the Indian Ocean trade was generally divided into two separate spheres, what was the primary ethnic identity of the sailors in the western half of the ocean?
   a. Chinese and Malay
   b. Austronesian
   c. Persian and Arab
   d. southern Indian
   e. African

6. As Hindus of northern India converted to Islam, how did the caste system adapt to the arrival of Muslim merchants?
   a. The merchants remained outside the caste system.
   b. The Indian merchants absorbed them into their own caste.
   c. They were placed at the lowest rung of society.
   d. They never stayed long enough to be a part of the system.
   e. They became a distinct caste within the system.

7. Through India's early history, Hinduism evolved constantly with challenges from other religions and changes in politics. At this time, Hinduism in southern India evolved out of a worship of all the gods into
   a. devotional cults to specific gods.
   b. the worship of two gods exclusively.
   c. a worship of local deities more than the Indian pantheon.
   d. a near acceptance of monotheism.
   e. a syncretism of Buddhism, Hinduism, and Islam.

8. Eventually, many Hindus in northern India converted to Islam. To what extent did they follow Islam?
   a. They were devout Muslims and followed all Five Pillars.
   b. They only worshipped when their rulers decreed it.
   c. There was a suppression of the caste system.
   d. While they followed Islam, their secular lives exhibited little change.
   e. Most new Muslims followed a syncretic blend of Islam and Hinduism.

9. Indian religions traveled to southeast Asia via merchants and missionaries. Why did southeast Asian monarchs convert readily to Hinduism and Buddhism?
   a. The lower classes had already done so and the kings were just following their lead.
   b. The religions reinforced the idea of kingship.
   c. The Muslim merchants had influence in ruling circles.
   d. The monarchs were open to all avenues of salvation.
   e. Their citizens demanded it.

10. As in most other places, Islam's conversion rate in southeast Asia was enhanced by the work of
    a. devout Muslim ministers.
    b. rulers' adoption of it.
    c. the conquest of islands by Arab sailors.
    d. the complete rejection of all earlier religious beliefs.
    e. the arrival of the sufi missionaries.

Comprehensive Multiple Choice Questions

1. Why was the establishment of Buddhism in China markedly different than its establishment in southeast Asia?
   a. Buddhist monks went to China but only Buddhist merchants went to southeast Asia.
   b. While rulers in southeast Asia encouraged the adoption of Buddhism, the Chinese emperors rejected it.
   c. Buddhists in China were the only foreign religion while in southeast Asia there was Hinduism as well.
   d. Chinese Buddhism incorporated Daoist ideas while southeast Asian Buddhists built on a base of Hinduism.
   e. Buddhists in China built no buildings while those in southeast Asia built large temple complexes.

2. To meet the challenges of new ideas and foreign influences, religious and social institutions of India remained essentially the same but grew increasingly complex. Which of the following are examples of this trend?
   a. Harsha's promotion of Hinduism and the increase in castes after the invasion of Mahmud of Ghazni
   b. Buddhists accepting nuns as well as monks while finding a place in the caste system
   c. the addition of subcastes from an increase in commerce and the appearance of devotional cults
   d. the synthesis of Buddhism and Hinduism with the incorporation of Muslim castes
   e. the increase in female deities indicating that the place of women in society was improved

3. The political pattern of northern China is somewhat different from that of southern India. Both devolved into small competetive Hindu kingdoms but two southern kingdoms of this period endured longer than Harsha's empire. Which of the following differences could possibly explain why the southern kingdoms had more stability?
   a. Southern India did not have the same constant threat of invasion to fracture its defenses.
   b. Due to better workmanship, south India's crafts were more in demand in the world market.
   c. The monsoons and easy access to world markets helped produce more prosperity.
   d. The Chola and Vijayanagar kingdoms had tightly administered centralized governments.
   e. Political power was more stable in south India because Hindu beliefs promoted ideas of royalty.

Primary Source Questions

1. **Examine the photographs on page 410, southern India, and page 427, southeast Asia.**
   a. What similarities do you notice?
   b. What are the differences that are evident?
   c. Looking in the text, what connects them?
   d. What does this style of architecture say about the societies?

2. **Read *Sources from the Past: Cosmas Indicopleustes on Trade in Southern India*, sixth century, on page 417 of your textbook.**
   a. What is the tone of this piece?
   b. What is the extent of trade in Ceylon?
   c. How much of the trade is purchased for use in Ceylon?

Chapter Multiple Choice Answers

1. **b:** Despite control of the northern third of India, Harsha was constantly traveling his empire to strengthen alliances with local rulers. When he was assassinated, his empire immediately devolved into kingdoms. (p. 407)

2. **d:** The invaders were more interested in plundering than conversion so the local inhabitants found nothing attractive in the customs of the invaders. Later invaders from central Asia will be more determined to convert the residents of northern India. (p. 408)

3. **a:** While two rulers in southern India briefly converted to Islam, they soon returned to Hinduism. Islam was only initially evident as a faith in Muslim merchants. (p. 410)

4. **b:** The monsoon wind pattern affected agriculture by providing periods of great rains followed by periods of drought. Merchants in the Indian Ocean depended on the monsoons to power their sailboats in each east-west direction depending upon the time of the year. (pp. 411, 413)

5. **c:** The Arabs and Persians carried most of the western trade in ships known as *dhows*. (p. 414)

6. **e:** The caste system was incredibly flexible and a separate place in the caste system was made for both Turkish immigrants to the north and Muslim merchants in the south. (p. 417)

7. **a:** Dedication to one or two gods in devotional cults centered around a specific shrine or temple reinvigorated and popularized in Hinduism. (p. 419)

8. **d:** Northern Indians converted to Islam in mass numbers, sometimes entire castes at one time. But the message of salvation and equality made little difference to their daily lives. (p. 422)

9. **b:** Epics like the *Ramayana* provided support for the value of monarchies. (p. 424)

10. **e:** Since the southeast Asians desired to retain many of their early beliefs, the sufi mixture of piety and tolerance proved to be very appealing. (p. 427)

Comprehensive Multiple Choice Answers

1. **d:** Buddhist monks and merchants who traveled to China found a welcome reception from emperor Tang Taizong and were able to set up monasteries in western China beside communities of Nestorian Christians, Manichaeans, and Zoroastrians. Buddhists in southeast Asia were welcomed by the rulers, tolerated the local traditions, and built monasteries. While Chinese Buddhists never competed with Hindus, Hinduism was well established in southeast Asia by the time Buddhism arrived. Angkor Wat, the Khmer temple complex, demonstrates this with the addition of Buddhist components to a Hindu base. In China, Buddhist philosophy had to find a way to appeal to the pragmatic Confucians so it equated Buddhist values with passive Daoist principles. (pp. 392, 426)

2. **c:** The caste system expanded to include the commercial guilds and Muslim converts as *jati*. Likewise, devotional cults developed in Hinduism where Hindu deities could be associated with local spirits or features, particularly in southern India. While Islam and Hinduism were paired in the bhakti movement, Buddhism remained a derivative of but distinct from Hinduism. Furthermore, while the Muslims did become an additional caste, Buddhists remained apart from caste considerations. (pp. 417–419)

3. **a:** While Harsha's government fell due to the lack of an heir and the strength of its local rulers, the unsettled legacy of constant invasions did not allow another individual to gain power over the northern kingdoms until the invaders themselves established the sultanate of Delhi. The dominant southern kingdoms had fairly loose internal control but managed to persist for several centuries. Southern India's economy was extremely prosperous but northern India had many resources to participate in the world market of the overland routes as well. (pp. 408–409)

Primary Source Answers

1. Comparing two buildings with related cultural backgrounds will allow you to identify distinctive architectural styles. They are obviously very large and the shape of both buildings is linear with rectangular bases. The overall presentation is very balanced. Each has a central section that has a prominent second level. Each one also has protruding domes or cones along the second level. There are multiple separate entrances along the lower level. Both buildings have intricate ornamentation on the surfaces. They differ in their composition according to available local materials. This also accounts for the color difference. Furthermore, the shape of the domes are different with the southern Indian domes more rounded than the southeast Asian ones. Angkor Wat also has rectangular shapes under the domes. Of course, one was used for elephants and the other for worship. They are connected through trade and their religions since the Khmer adopted both Hinduism and Buddhism from their trade with India. This is an example of *cultural diffusion*. This style of architecture points to wealthy societies with a sophisticated knowledge of engineering. (pp. 410, 427)

2. Unlike Benjamin of Tudela's tone of amazement (Chapter 14), Cosmas Indicapleustes has a neutral and objective tone despite being a stranger in Ceylon. You may state this in the document-based question especially if you note that he is not overwhelmed and must come from a place of extensive trade himself. Ceylon is something of a fulcrum of trade in the Indian Ocean with multiple valuable products from all points east and west passing through it. The Ceylonese purchased horses from Persia. It may be presumed that a small percentage of the other products also stayed in Ceylon. (p. 417)

CHAPTER 17

THE FOUNDATIONS OF CHRISTIAN SOCIETY IN WESTERN EUROPE

Before you get started: As a child, you probably heard of many of the people, places, and events in this chapter, thus it may be an easier one than the last one in terms of vocabulary and terminology. Build on your prior knowledge, but do not let your storybook memories obscure your careful reading. Medieval western Europe had kings, yes, but not exactly like the ones you recall from fairy tales. Yes, there were knights, but it was not so glamorous a job as you might recall; being a serf usually meant a rough life without many perks and certainly being a damsel-in-distress rarely had a real-world romantic ending.

Up to 30 percent of the national exam is drawn from western European content, so think about comparisons and contrasts you could make with other places during this era, especially eastern Europe (Chapter 13), the Islamic world (Chapter 14), the Tang, Song and Ming dynasties in China (Chapter 15), and India and the Indian Ocean realm (Chapter 16). Further, because the Continuities and Change-Over-Time essay could draw from this region, consider how western Europe changed from its pre-Roman days, through the Roman era, and during this post-Roman medieval era.

Finally, this history of western Europe really continues in Chapter 20 with the high middle ages; make a note to come back and review this chapter when you get there—your understanding from both chapters will be much more complete that way.

THE QUEST FOR POLITICAL ORDER

The period from 500–1500 C.E. in western Europe is known as the "middle ages": the years between 500–1000 are called the **medieval period.** During the medieval period, western Europe developed an agricultural economy with a decentralized political order in which most political authority was invested in local and regional governments. The Roman Catholic church emerged as the dominant source of cultural authority.

Germanic Successor States
(Theme: Migration)

After the fall of the Roman empire in the west in 476 C.E., Germanic peoples gradually displaced Roman authority and institutions. The **Visigoths** conquered Spain, the **Ostrogoths** and then the **Lombards** dominated Italy, the **Burgundians** settled in southern and eastern Gaul, and the **Angles and Saxons** established control in Britain. The **Franks** who settled in north and western Gaul emerged as the most powerfully influential of these Germanic groups. They developed an agricultural-based, decentralized society which "shifted the [European] center of gravity" from Italy to France.

The Franks and the Temporary Revival of Europe
(Theme: Political Structures)

Out of all these Germanic groups, the Franks emerged as the dominant military and political power in western Europe. Beginning in the fifth century C.E. under the rule of **Clovis** and continuing through the ninth century under **Charlemagne,** the Franks used their religious ties with the Roman Catholic church to build and secure their authority. Charlemagne, in particular, worked to reestablish centralized rule throughout much of western Europe. Extremely intelligent and wise to human motivations, Charlemagne used his military, judicial, and intellectual powers to build a centralized empire and was granted the title of **Roman Emperor** on Christmas Day in 800 C.E.

Decline and Dissolution of the Carolingian Empire
(Themes: Invasions and Political Structures)

After Charlemagne's death, internal disunity and external invasions brought the Carolingian empire to an end. Charlemagne's son and grandsons dismembered his empire in less than thirty years. The invasions of the **Muslims** from the Mediterranean, the **Magyars** from Hungary, and the **Vikings** from northern Europe completed the destruction of centralized rule in western Europe. The Vikings, Norse mariners who mounted invasions all along the European coastlines from the ninth through the eleventh centuries, were motivated by population pressures in Scandinavia and by their firm resistance to conversion attempts by Christian missionaries. Using shallow draft boats and a detailed knowledge of tides and locations of settlements, the Vikings raided coastal and inland sites using rivers as highways for rapid and unexpected assaults on monasteries, villages, and even cities throughout northern and southern Europe.

The Establishment of Regional Authorities
(Themes: Political Structures and Changes and Continuities)

The Carolingian empire was no match for the Muslims, Magyars, and Vikings. Instead, regions within the former empire responded in individualized ways. In England, smaller kingdoms established by the Angles and the Saxons were led by King Alfred to conquer Danish kingdoms on the north of the island. They then built fortresses and a navy to withstand Viking invasions, thus laying the foundation for a future nation of England. In Germany, King Otto of Saxony led the fight against the Magyar invasion, formed the basis for a German identity, and even earned the title of **Holy Roman Emperor.** France devolved into a region of small principalities run by counts and other subordinates of the decaying Carolingian rulers. The Vikings even established their own settlements in northern France. The end of the invasions and the establishment of a stable, decentralized political order laid the foundation for social, economic, and cultural development in western Europe.

EARLY MEDIEVAL SOCIETY

Feudalism is the term traditionally used to describe the political and social order of medieval Europe. Today, it is considered more accurate to describe it as a range of ways to maintain order, rather than a single monolithic system.

Organizing a Decentralized Society
(Theme: Political Structures)

After Charlemagne's death, European nobles built a system to protect their lands and maintain order in a decentralized society. They built military and political relationships with other prominent individuals within their territories. As time went on, these relationships between lords and retainers were formalized, often with church approval and sanction, becoming increasingly complex and complicated as lands and titles became hereditary.

Serfs and Manors
(Themes: Social Structure and Labor Systems)

Though the governing elite handled the business, political, and legal affairs in western Europe, it was the people who cultivated the land to produce an agricultural surplus who made this complex feudal system possible. **Serfs,** not fully free nor fully slave, cultivated land owned by the lords and their retainers in exchange for protection and small plots of land to cultivate. Serfs usually had the right to work land and pass it along to their offspring so long as they fulfilled their obligations to the landlords which could include working the lords' land three days a week, planting and harvesting, and returning a portion of the bounty from their own crops, as well as weaving, milling, building, sewing, or brewing as the lord required.

To suit such needs, the **manor** developed as the principal form of agricultural organization in western Europe. The manor included the land, crops, animals, tools, and serfs necessary to produce the agricultural surplus which kept the system functioning. The lord acted as the government, providing justice and limited services for his subjects. Over time, the manors came to be largely self-sufficient communities and developed impressive craft skills. Local small markets for goods and services not easily manufactured on the manors developed around regional monasteries and cathedrals.

The Economy of Early and Medieval Europe
(Themes: Technology, Trade, and Demographics)

By the early middle ages in western Europe, trade had slowed with the disintegration of cities and transportation infrastructure, and with repeated invasions of the Germanic peoples, the Muslims, the Magyars, and the Vikings. Yet, by the tenth century C.E., political stability led to a renewed trading relationship with the eastern hemisphere. The advent of the **moldboard plow,** the construction of **watermills,** and the development of a useful **horse collar**, allowed cultivators to put more land to use and to experiment with new crops and crop rotation systems. Though there was sufficient agricultural surplus to support life on the manor and small local communities, there was not enough surplus to support large urban centers as in Roman times. Local markets and itinerant peddlers traded from settlement to settlement, bringing goods from the east to the small markets of western Europe. By 1000 C.E., new crops such as hard durum rice, spinach, eggplants, lemons, oranges, and melons all made their way west to Europe.

In the regions of the North Sea and the Baltic Sea, **maritime trade** continued to grow. The **Norsemen,** descendents of earlier Viking invaders, established ports from Russia to Ireland; these ports linked Europe with the borders of the Islamic world. For example, the silver traded from the Abbasid empire for European honey, fish, and furs, was the principal source of minted coins in early medieval Europe.

The population loss experienced in western Europe after the demise of the Roman empire was a result of disease, invasion, and uncertainty of daily life in medieval times. By 1000 C.E. however, European population had again reached the Roman height and was poised for a period of rapid expansion.

THE FORMATION OF CHRISTIAN EUROPE

The adoption of Roman Christianity, finalized by the conversion of the Frankish king, Clovis, ensured western Europe would inherit crucial cultural elements from Rome including language and institutions.

The Politics of Conversion
(Themes: Religious Developments and Political Structures)

The Franks and the Roman church found benefits to both church and state through their relationship. For the Franks, close connections to the church provided an educated workforce for their bureaucracy and legitimacy for their growing empire. For the Church, the Franks, especially Charlemagne, helped to convert reluctant **pagans,** especially the Lombards and Saxons, to Roman Christianity.

The Papacy
(Themes: Religious Developments and Political Structures)

Strong papal leadership also contributed to the growth and power of Roman Christianity. **The Great Schism of East and West in 1054** permanently forged separate identities for the Roman Catholic and the Eastern Orthodox churches. Pope Gregory I ensured the survival of the Roman Catholic church and the city of Rome by (1) consistently asserting papal primacy—the idea that the Bishop of Rome was also the ultimate authority in the Christian church, (2) emphasizing the sacraments, especially penance and thus the need for an educated clergy, (3) promoting an active missionary movement especially in England, France, and Germany, and (4) promoting **monasticism** as a way to serve God and church.

Monasticism
(Themes: Religious Developments and Political Structures)

Though Christian monasticism began in Egypt, in Europe it increasingly became a way for devout individuals to pursue a life of holiness rather than worldly success. At first, early Christian monasteries developed their own rules but under guidance from St. Benedict of Nursia and his *Rule*, the goals of poverty, chastity, and obedience became prime virtues for monks and for their religious sisters lead by St. Scholastica.

Such discipline brought converts and newfound wealth to the monasteries. Monasteries helped to bring order to the countryside and to provide the labor and direction necessary to expand agricultural production. Monasteries also provided a range of social services including hospitality for travelers, establishing and supporting orphanages, and providing medical care and nursing. Monasteries also served as the source for educated individuals who were necessary for effective government in early medieval Europe. Finally, monasteries helped to spread Christianity and its virtues among western Europe's rural peasant population.

Finished reading the chapter? Be sure you can . . .

- Trace the restructuring of western European economic, social, and political institutions from 600 to 1450 C.E.
- Compare and contrast reasons for the division of Christianity into eastern and western churches. (Remember Chapter 9?)
- Describe and analyze European feudalism. (Eventually, you will have to compare European and Japanese feudalism; you'll need parts of Chapters 15 and 27 to do that.)
- Explain the motivations for and the impact of Viking explorations.

Chapter Multiple Choice Questions

1. Charlemagne hoped to build a western European empire which might rival his contemporaries
   a. the Abbasids and Byzantines.
   b. the Byzantines and the Umayyads.
   c. the Qin and the Guptas.
   d. the Mauryans and the Song.
   c. the Olmecs and the Incas.

2. Which of the following pairings is INCORRECT?
   a. Visogoths: Spain
   b. Lombards: Italy
   c. Angles: Britain
   d. Franks: Northwestern Europe
   e. Saxons: Denmark

3. Which is the MOST important reason for the rise of the Franks as the dominant Germanic group in Europe circa the fifth through ninth centuries?
   a. Their strong military was undefeatable even by the Moors in Spain.
   b. Clovis' conversion and allegiance to Roman Catholicism lead to support from the Pope and the Roman Catholic church.
   c. Clovis' wise and just rule throughout his realm made him a model for other kings to emulate.
   d. Charlemagne's intellectual and cultural standards were recognized even by his enemies.
   e. The use of *missi dominici* provided unrivaled justice throughout the Frankish kingdom.

4. Which of the following statements is TRUE regarding a serf's life on a manor?
   a. They could not be bought and sold like slaves.
   b. They owned only a small piece of land on the manor.
   c. They could appeal their legal cases to the King, if necessary.
   d. Their spouses were chosen by the lord.
   e. All of the above.

5. Why was the moldboard plow an essential element in the production of an agricultural surplus in western Europe in eighth century C.E.?
   a. It made it possible to aerate the soil and break up networks of weeds.
   b. It made it possible to farm lands that had previously been unsuitable for agriculture due to rocks and heavy soil.
   c. When used with heavy draft animals, it had enough energy to pull through moist northern soils.
   d. Its successful use stimulated other agricultural innovations.
   e. All of the above.

6. What effect did the technology of watermills have on western European life?
   a. It began a process of water pollution which eventually destroyed fresh water sources for the manors.
   b. It forced many serfs off the manors as there was no longer a need for their labor.
   c. It freed human and animal labor for other work.
   d. It made animal-powered technology obsolete.
   e. It promoted the use of heavier draft animals as they could stand the water pressure.

7. Towns in the Roman empire had served as commercial centers integrating the economic activities of distant regions, while towns in western Europe c. 500–1000 C.E. served as
   a. economic gathering places for the sale or exchange of locally produced goods.
   b. centers of intellectual and cultural exchange of new ideas and concepts.
   c. social and religious refuges for wandering hermits and prophets.
   d. economic centers for the collection of tribute and taxes owed to the Holy Roman Emperor.
   e. political capitals for kings and emperors to use in their bureaucracies.

8. The fact that the population of western Europe took eight centuries to recover from the demise of the western Roman empire reflects that
   a. people were reluctant to have children in such an uncertain world.
   b. the Viking practice of kidnapping for ransom was widespread.
   c. disease and uncertainty limited agricultural surplus for 800 years.
   d. the church closely monitored population numbers and growth.
   e. the children of serfs could be sold off the manor at the whim of the lord.

9. Which of the following individuals is credited with establishing a standard for monastic life?
   a. St. Augustine of Hippo
   b. St. Benedict of Nursia
   c. Charlemagne
   d. Clovis
   e. St. Gregory of Tours

10. What effect did monasteries have on the expansion of agricultural production in early modern Europe?
    a. They slowed expansion of agricultural production because they insisted on living a life of extreme poverty and asceticism.
    b. They slowed expansion of agricultural production because they focused only on prayer and service to God.
    c. They contributed to the expansion of agricultural production because they organized much of the labor needed to clear forests, drain swamps, and prepare lands for cultivation.
    d. They contributed to the expansion of agricultural production by building commercial farms and employing freed serfs as agricultural laborers.
    e. Monasteries built their own farms and were concerned only with subsistence agriculture and not with the needs of those outside the monasteries.

Comprehensive Multiple Choice Questions

1. What characteristic did medieval European monasteries share with Buddhist monasteries in Asia and Muslim charitable religious foundations?
    a. All three required poverty, chastity, and obedience of their believers.
    b. All three worked with local, decentralized governments for support.
    c. All three provided a variety of social services to people in surrounding communities.
    d. All three were constantly invaded, looted, and pillaged for their wealth.
    e. All three retained libraries and scriptoria to preserve Latin writings.

2. Which of the following statements is TRUE about the agricultural surplus in western Europe during medieval times?
    a. After the introduction of the moldboard plow, the agricultural surplus grew rapidly enough to support a few large cities like Paris and London.
    b. The agricultural surplus produced in the easier-to-farm regions around the Mediterranean made city growth in France and Italy possible.
    c. The manors required all the food grown there to feed the increasing number of serfs displaced by the watermill technology.
    d. The agricultural surplus was sufficient to sustain lords and their retainers, but not large city populations of artisans, merchants, and professionals.
    e. There was no agricultural surplus in western Europe until after the introduction of new food sources from the Islamic and Viking worlds.

3. Politically, Medieval Europe c. 1000 C.E. is MOST like which of the following:
    a. India, during the postclassical era
    b. China, under the Tang dynasty
    c. China, under the Song dynasty
    d. the Abbasids in Baghdad
    e. the Byzantines in eastern Europe

Primary Source Questions

1. **Read *Sources from the Past: Gregory of Tours on the Conversion of Clovis* on page 438 of your textbook.**
    a. What evidence in the excerpt sounds exaggerated, altered, or embellished?
    b. Why might Gregory have embellished the story of Clovis' conversion to Christianity?

2. **Read *Sources from the Past: Life on an Early Medieval Manor* on page 448 of your textbook.**
   a. What does this excerpt tell you about the economics of the manor?
   b. Why might this capitulary make such a point about accounting?
   c. What can you say about the purpose or reason for this capitulary?

Chapter Multiple Choice Answers

1. **a:** Only the empires listed in choice "a" are Charlemagne's contemporaries. (p. 433)

2. **e:** The Saxons emerged from the regions including Denmark and Germany, but they migrated to Britain along with the Angles c. fifth century C.E. (p. 435)

3. **b:** Clovis and his Frankish successors could not have retained their power without the support of the church. Conversion to Roman Catholicism helped them earn legitimacy from western European Christians as well as the hierarchy of the Roman Catholic church. (p. 437)

4. **a:** Serfs were dependent on the lord for much of their livelihood and undoubtedly lived a difficult life, but unlike chattel slaves, they could not be bought and sold. (pp. 445–446)

5. **e:** The much more serviceable moldboard plow with iron tips dramatically changed farming and hence life in western Europe. It was now possible to farm land which had previously been unfarmable and to do so with the aid of draft animals. (pp. 446–447)

6. **c:** Water power was a ready and renewable power source which freed humans and animals for other work on the manor. (p. 447)

7. **a:** Manors and local communities produced most of the goods and services people in western Europe needed during this era. Towns were only sparsely populated economic hubs for local exchange. (p. 447)

8. **c:** Disease and the threats to life from invasion, weather, or banditry kept the population figures for western Europe falling from fourth to the eighth centuries. Those numbers began to turn around by the ninth and tenth centuries and reached their original third-century level c. 1000 C.E. (p. 449)

9. **b:** St. Benedict's *Rules* set the standards for virtuous monks in the medieval world. His tenets of poverty, chastity, and obedience became the standards for ethical and spiritual behavior in monasteries across Europe. (pp. 452–453)

10. **c:** Particularly in France and Germany, abbots of monasteries organized teams of laborers to prepare new lands for cultivation. (p. 453)

Comprehensive Multiple Choice Answers

1. **c:** All three religious traditions provided a variety of social services such as orphanages, travel hostels, medical clinics, and hospitals. (p. 453)

2. **d:** Europe remained a rural society until well into the modern era despite the introduction of new technologies and food sources after 1000 C.E. Europe did produce an agricultural surplus prior to 1000 C.E., but it was only sufficient to sustain political elites, not to support large cities. (p. 447)

3. **a:** Medieval Europe was not like China, or the Abbasids, or like the Byzantines in its political structure form. Each of those regions was centralized and increasingly ruled from an imperial authority. From the end of the Gupta empire to the rise of the Mughals, India in the postclassical age remained a politically divided land. (p. 434)

Primary Source Answers

1. a. There are several places in this excerpt where it sounds too perfect or too idealized to be real. First, Clovis's prayer to God sounds more written than spoken; it is long and complex and it is difficult to believe that someone faced with a huge battlefield loss would compose and later recall such an articulate prayer. Second, rarely do the power of words actually stop a conflict in mid-battle. Also, it seems too perfect for the enemy king to be killed at just the most opportune moment in the battle. Finally, the spontaneous conversion of the Franks at the moment just prior to their king's speech is probably fictionalized for effect.

   b. As a high official in the Roman Catholic church, Gregory was interested in converting people to Christianity. Persuasive stories which include dramatic events have the power to sway people's opinions. He undoubtedly wanted to convince others to convert, and using the "star appeal" of a famous and highly regarded king is a very effective way to convince someone else to act. If even a battle-hardened king can bow down before God and be rewarded, then certainly any one else could as well. (p. 438)

2. a. This excerpt tells us many things about life on the manor. First, it provides a wealth of detail about the type of crops, animals, and products produced there: an impressive array of grains, nuts, fruits, and vegetables; a large variety of animals including pigs, oxen, cattle, fish, poultry, and horses; a huge assortment of products such as soap, wine, mead, beer, lard, tallow, candles, wool, cheese, wax, and honey. Second, it is clear that specialization of labor and an economic hierarchy existed when it is recorded that some living quarters are to be amply stocked with many material items including bedding, metal containers, tools, and weapons. The author even lists the various occupations needed to ensure a comfortable lifestyle for the lords.

   b. With all this material wealth and the seemingly basic nature of humans to want more and more, Charlemagne clearly is aware that there is a potential for stealing or at least for sloppy recordkeeping. He is careful to ask for both how much is given to him and how much is left to the manor to be sure he is receiving his designated percentage and that his subjects do not receive more than theirs.

   c. It seems as though the purpose of this **capitulary** was to both clearly and fully outline what material wealth the manor possessed and to be equally clear about who gets what parts of that wealth. Perhaps Charlemagne also wanted his subjects to know that he was well informed about the wealth on the manor and therefore would not be easily misled or deceived by any shoddy records. (p. 448)

PART IV

AN AGE OF CROSS-CULTURAL INTERACTION, 1000 TO 1500 C.E.

CHAPTER 18

NOMADIC EMPIRES AND EURASIAN INTEGRATION

Before you get started: For fun and excitement in history, it doesn't get much better than the Mongols. Our perceptions of them have been mightily influenced by the European terror of the hordes but you will find that Chingghis and his family were capable of magnificent administration of settled regions as well as psychologically terrifying attacks across Asia. We spell his name differently now but it's the same Genghis that your parents remember, only much more astute. You will need to employ a few tricks to remember the short history of this small ethnic group that ruled the world. One confusing aspect is when the Mongol empire splits into four sections, but if you make a diagram and note the main differences in names and administration of the regions, the post-Chingghis history will be clarified. Two Turkish nomadic groups in central Asia expanded into settled regions as did the Mongols. But while Tamarlane of Samarkand is a mere footnote in global history, the descendents of Osman will prove to govern much longer than the Mongols, through the end of World War I.

TURKISH MIGRATIONS AND IMPERIAL EXPANSION

The Turks were a nomadic group of clans who spoke a similar language and roamed the regions of central Asia from China to Persia. They eventually dominated Persia, Anatolia, and India.

Nomadic Economy and Society
(Themes: Economics, Gender and Social Structures, and Religious Developments)

The Asian steppes are primarily high grasslands without rain and rivers to sustain settled communities, so the peoples of central Asia followed a **nomadic life.** They drove their herds of sheep, horses, cattle, goats, and camels as they searched for adequate forage. As with most nomads, they returned to the same places at the same times of the year. They subsisted primarily on animal products such as the meat, hide, and milk of their stock although in some areas they also grew small crops of millet and vegetables. They used wool to produce felt that covered their portable huts known as *yurts* and even made mare's milk into an alcoholic drink. To obtain commodities they were unable to produce, the nomads eagerly sought trade with settled peoples and participated in the long-distance caravans along the **silk roads.**

The class structure of the nomads was simple, consisting of **commoners** and **nobles,** but it was a much more fluid arrangement than settled societies in Europe. The noble rank was gained through **charismatic leadership** during war; conversely, that status could be lost through poor leadership. The nobility was not responsible for peacetime decisions that affected the entire group. Rather, governance was assumed by each clan according to its needs. All were dependent on diplomatic skills to form alliances between the loosely knit clans. Eventually, some of the alliances grew into large confederations with allegiance to one *khan.*

The horse was the backbone of the nomad's military success. Since their numbers were so few, initial nomadic conquests were largely due to their superior cavalry. Their upbringings prepared them for warfare on horseback and they demonstrated tactical superiority in their use of well-organized units of horsemen. With this advantage, the Turks began to expand into settled regions in the tenth century.

Although barely mentioned in your textbook, nomadic women in Asia were more akin to African women than other societies. They had status and some autonomy, and had been raised to do all chores, occasionally engaging in military actions as well. Mongol women could own property and divorce their husbands. Although **polygamy** was the norm and interclan conflict often brought brides through kidnapping, as had happened to Temujin's own mother, Mongol women were recognized for their abilities to trade, to control their lives when most of the men were gone for long periods, and to serve as advisers to husbands and clans. Khubilai Khan counted his mother, **Sorghaghtani Beki**, and his second wife, **Chabi**, as his best advisers while his niece, Khutulun, performed well in battle. Furthermore, succession was occasionally determined by how politically astute one's mother was, as in the case with Sorghaghtani Beki.

Turkic religion was a form of **shamanism** in which religious leaders were believed to possess supernatural powers to divine the will of deities and nature as well as intercede on behalf of people. While maintaining their native beliefs, many later adopted Buddhism, Nestorian Christianity, and Manichaeism. Eventually, they also developed a written script to facilitate trade transactions and follow their new religions. Even later, many Turks converted to Islam and brought that religion to the settled areas that they had conquered.

Turkish Empires in Persia, Anatolia, and India
(Themes: Patterns of Interaction and Changes and Continuities)

The Turkish nomads were adept at expansion into the settled regions of southwest Asia. In the tenth century, Turkish armies moved into the Middle East initially as mercenaries of the Abbasid caliphate. Eventually the caliphs were mere figureheads to the Turkish sultans. In Anatolia, they defeated the Byzantines and welcomed converts to Islam at the same time that they took on political administration of the region. **Mahmud of Ghazni** raided regions of northwest India for treasure, but later groups of Turks established themselves as the sultanate of Delhi. After Hindu and Buddhist sites had been plundered, many were abandoned so that later Turks found the region ripe for conversion to Islam.

THE MONGOL EMPIRES

Allies of the Turkish peoples, the Mongols of east central Asia did not expand as early as the Turks. In the twelfth century, Chinggis Khan consolidated the Mongol armies into the greatest expansionary force that the world has ever known. While the Mongol expansion could not be sustained for more than a few generations, its influence on Asia and Europe was significant.

Chingghis Khan and the Making of the Mongol Empire
(Themes: Political Structures, Patterns of Interaction, and Changes and Continuities)

In 1167, **Temujin** was born into a noble family but by the time he was ten years old, his father had been poisoned by rivals and the family had sunk into poverty. Personally courageous and charismatic, Temujin managed to ally himself with powerful clans. His **steppe diplomacy** skills soon united the Mongols into a single confederation and he became known as **Chingghis Khan ("universal ruler")**. Because of Chingghis' difficult experiences earlier in life, he mistrusted the tribal system so he appointed commanders based on their skills and personal loyalty rather than their status. As a symbol of his power over the unified Mongols, he established the first Mongol capital of **Karakorum** though he rarely lived there himself.

The Mongol armies numbered about ten percent of their population which was considerably smaller than other armies. As a strategy to expand their military might, the Mongols incorporated conquered armed forces into its army. As the Turkish nomads had, the Mongols depended upon their **cavalries** as the backbone of their forces. On occasion, they were known to travel 100 kilometers a day and typically could shoot arrows from horseback with dead accuracy at 200 meters. The Mongol success can also be attributed to their use of **psychological warfare.** If a community resisted, it was cut down in the most brutal way, but if a city surrendered immediately, they were treated with relative generosity. Of course, there are numerous descriptions of the acts of brutality towards resisters, including using them as human shields.

At first, Chingghis Khan attacked other nomadic groups in central Asia but then he set his eye on large empires such as China and Persia. Chingghis captured most of northern China by 1220 and established a Mongol city, **Khanbalik**, on the site of present-day Beijing. After the ruling shah of Persia brutalized Mongol ambassadors, Chingghis Khan took his revenge by seizing Persia. But in continued retribution, the Mongols destroyed the *qanat* irrigation system and numerous Persian cities. Soon after, Chingghis Khan died, leaving an immense empire and very little administration beyond collection of tribute.

The Mongol Empires after Chinggis Khan
(Themes: Political Structures and Changes and Continuities)

Succession was never easy among the Mongols since the position was determined by general agreement, and Chinggis Khan left many sons and grandsons. After significant power struggles, the Mongols divided the empire into four regions. The wealthiest region was China which became ruled by the so-called **Great Khans.** The central region was known as the **Khanate of Chagatai** after one of Chinggis's sons. Russia came under the control of the **Khanate of the Golden Horde** and Persia was known as the **Ilkhanate of Persia.**

Mongol rule in China was solidified by one of the most talented grandsons, **Khubilai**, the khan described by Marco Polo. He conquered the southern regions of China and showed an active interest in both culture and administration, naming his administration the **Yuan dynasty**. He promoted Buddhism and was interested in the welfare of his subjects. His biggest disappointment was his failure to conquer Japan and southeast Asia. The inability to use traditional Mongol cavalries probably hampered his efforts in southeast Asia, and typhoons (known as **kamikaze or "divine wind"** by the Japanese) defeated his naval fleets close to Japan.

The Golden Horde Mongols in Russia attempted expansion into Europe as far as eastern Germany but ultimately settled into the grassland regions north of the Black Sea. They exacted tribute from the Russians but considered the vast forests unattractive for home sites. It was only in the fifteenth century that the Russians challenged the Mongols, and even into the eighteenth century the Crimean region was ruled by Mongol descendents. In Persia, Khubilai's brother Hulegu conquered both the Persians and the Baghdad caliphate but was stopped by Egyptian forces in Syria.

The Mongol rule in Persia contrasted greatly with its administration of China. The Persians were allowed to keep some autonomy serving as lower administrators. If they collected the taxes and maintained order, they stayed in their positions. Interestingly, this is very much the policy that the ancient Persians had maintained in their conquered areas. The Mongols followed another Persian practice of tolerance for all religions. Eventually, the Mongols themselves converted to Islam and were virtually absorbed into Persian society. Mongol rule in China was shorter and less benign. The Mongols maintained a strong separation from Chinese society. They eliminated the Confucian examination system and chose administrators from outside the Chinese bureaucracy. But like the Persian ilkhanate, the Great Khans tolerated all religions. An example of this tolerance can be seen in Khubilai's favorite wife Chabi who was a Nestorian Christian. While earlier Mongol rulers in China maintained their shamanistic beliefs, later rulers became infatuated with Tibetan Buddhism as it had elements of magical and supernatural beliefs that mirrored shamanism. However, part of this attraction also lay in the Tibetan wooing of the Mongols. They even declared the khans to be the reincarnation of Buddha himself.

The Mongols and Eurasian Integration
(Themes: Economics and Demographics)

The Mongols encouraged trade throughout the empire by ensuring the safety of travelers. Diplomatic missions between European and Asian lands increased and missionaries found it easier to proselytize their beliefs. Several European ambassadors made it as far as Khanbalik, and the Persian Mongols sent one of their own diplomats, **Rabban Sauma**, to Italy and France. Muslims, Buddhists, and Nestorian Christians spread their faiths along the silk roads. One policy of the Mongols was to import talented craftsmen and administrators from newly conquered regions to China and Persia. As the introduction to this chapter depicts, thousands of talented foreigners lived and worked in the Mongol cities of Asia, including **Marco Polo.**

Decline of the Mongols in Persia and China
(Theme: Changes and Continuities)

Along with significant financial problems in Persia, the ilkhanate became unstable due to continual succession quarrels. It finally collapsed with the absence of an heir in 1335, leaving a decentralized political scene. In China, Mongol deterioration was similarly complicated by financial pressures as well as a pattern of political disputes and infighting. The Yuan dynasty also faced the problem of a **bubonic plague** epidemic. Beginning in southwest China in the 1330s, it was inadvertently helped in its spread by the safety of the silk roads. As in other areas of Eurasia, the plague killed up to half of the exposed population and created economic hardship in addition to the human misery. Furthermore, Chinese rebels began to create problems for the Mongols by the 1340s and overthrew them by capturing Khanbaliq in 1368. However, the Golden Horde and khanate of Chagatai persisted into the eighteenth century.

AFTER THE MONGOLS

Despite the decline of the Mongols, nomadic Turkish influences continued in central Asia. During the late fourteenth and early fifteenth centuries, Tamerlane built a short-lived but large empire.

Tamerlane the Whirlwind
(Themes: Patterns of Interaction and Changes and Continuities)

Known as "**Timur the Lame**," Tamerlane used Chingghis Khan as his role model. Born near Samarkand, his origins were similarly from a minor noble family and he made his own fortune without the help of others. His charismatic personality attracted many warriors and by 1370 he had defeated the Mongol khanate of Chagatai. From there, he mounted successful campaigns against Persia, Afghanistan, the Golden Horde in Russia, and the sultanate of Delhi. As he prepared for invasion of China, he sickened and died. Like Chingghis Khan, Tamarlane was disinterested in administration and his realm ruled through alliances. Succession was even more difficult for Tamarlane's family than for the Mongols, and his empire disintegrated within one hundred years.

The Foundation of the Ottoman Empire.
(Themes: Patterns of Interaction and Changes and Continuities)

Nomadic peoples continued to influence Asia and Europe through the Ottoman Turks. After the Persian defeat to the Mongols, numerous Turks migrated to the Anatolian peninsula. They had several charismatic leaders but the most important was **Osman** who began to build an empire out of the weak Byzantine territories. Establishing a foothold in the Balkans, the Ottomans moved south to capture **Constantinople.** Although Tamerlane temporarily hindered Ottoman expansion, Constantinople was captured by **Mehmud the Conqueror** in 1453. Eventually, the Ottomans ruled over a vast empire across northern Africa, into southeast Europe and most of the Middle East.

Finished reading the chapter? Be sure you can . . .

- Outline the chief characteristics of central Asian nomadic societies.
- Compare the effects of the Mongols on settled societies.
- Compare the silk roads before and after the Mongol expansion.
- Compare the achievements of the Mongols with those of the Turks.
- Explain why the Mongol expansion stopped.
- Compare Mongol influence in Persia, Russia, and China.

Chapter Multiple Choice Questions

1. Nomadic Turks and Mongols affected Asian history by conquering most of
   a. India, China, and southeast Asia.
   b. China, northern India, Anatolia, and Russia.
   c. Russia, China, and India.
   d. Anatolia, India, and central Asia.
   e. Eastern Europe, Anatolia, and central Asia.

2. The attainment of nobility status in nomadic societies was dependent upon
   a. a strict social hierarchy including a peasant class.
   b. the arbitrary decisions of the leaders in governmental councils.
   c. the extent to which one's relatives achieved nobility.
   d. the personal record of achievement by the individual.
   e. recognition and adoption by noble families.

3. What did the Mongols do when they encountered other religions?
   a. They forced conversion to steppe shamanism.
   b. They adopted all religions into a unique syncretic blend.
   c. They encouraged tolerance and occasionally converted.
   d. They persecuted monotheists but allowed polytheists.
   e. They rejected other faiths on the basis of their resistance to the Mongols.

4. What characteristic did Mahmud of Ghazni share with Tamarlane?
   a. an interest in administration over wide regions
   b. they desired to emulate Chingghis Khan
   c. they came from the same region of today's Afghanistan
   d. more interest in conquest and plunder than governance
   e. they tolerated all religions of the regions they conquered

5. To what did Temujin owe his elevation to Chingghis Khan?
   a. his inherited status from a noble family
   b. his conquest of other Mongol clans
   c. his conquest of China and Persia
   d. his extraordinary loyalty to his extended family
   e. his compelling personality and ability to forge alliances

6. What did Mongol rule in the Ilkhanate of Persia have in common with the Yuan dynasty?
   a. importation of foreign administrative officials
   b. distrust and disdain for the conquered populations
   c. tolerance for the local religions
   d. an interest in maintaining all schools of knowledge
   e. eventual absorption into the culture

7. What stopped Mongols from the complete conquest of the Middle East?
   a. They were stopped by the Persians.
   b. They were defeated by Egyptian slave armies.
   c. Chingghis Khan died before they even attacked.
   d. They were defeated by the Ottomans.
   e. Interclan rivalry ended the westernmost thrust of Mongol armies.

8. To what extent did the Mongols encourage trade?
    a. As a nomadic group, they had an abiding interest in supporting all trade.
    b. While they protected the silk roads in western China, they neglected those of central Asia.
    c. They protected both the land routes in Asia and the sea lanes of the Indian Ocean.
    d. They allowed others to trade while forbidding their own people to do the same.
    e. They welcomed traders from the Middle East and India while they dismissed the traders of central Asia.

9. One trait that the Mongols and Tamarlane shared in the decline of their empire was
    a. the disintegration of their armies.
    b. the defeat by neighboring peoples.
    c. a decline of interest in the nomadic life.
    d. the failure to protect the economies of its regions.
    e. significant problems in succession.

10. In contrast to the Romans at the time of Augustus, Mongol khans chose to
    a. divide the conquered areas into separate rules.
    b. build and secure roads for good communication.
    c. allow and tolerate foreign religions.
    d. rely on mercenary armies to control its borders.
    e. ignore the necessary protection of trade routes.

Comprehensive Multiple Choice Questions

1. Which of the following statements most accurately reflects a major difference between the expansion of the Mongols in the thirteenth century and the expansion of the Arabs in the seventh century?
    a. Mongol diplomacy relied most heavily on military might while Arab expansion relied on astute diplomacy.
    b. Mongol expansion tended to avoid larger cities along the silk roads while Arab expansion attacked major cities first and depended on them to control the rural areas.
    c. Mongol expansion was dependent on cavalry while Arab expansion depended on infantry.
    d. Mongol expansion was a stunningly successful extension of the type of military actions that central Asian nomads had always attempted while Arab expansion occurred without a previous history of expansion.
    e. Mongol expansion was fueled by the ideas of one individual while Arab expansion was fueled by the ideas of many.

2. Which of the following statements about Mongol rule in China is most accurate?
    a. The Mongols scorned their Chinese subjects so much that they removed farmland from cultivation and used it for grazing Mongol livestock.
    b. The Mongols did not use the Chinese administration, preferring imported administrators.
    c. The Mongols persecuted Confucian scholar-officials by incarcerating prominent administrators.
    d. The Mongol leaders of China preferred the steppes and ruled from the Mongol capital of Karakarum.
    e. Preferring Buddhism for themselves, the Mongols outlawed Confucianism.

3. Similar to the Arab conquest of Persia, which of the following resulted from the conquest by the Mongols?
    a. Persia imparted some of its religious, social, and political traditions to its conquerors.
    b. Persian society lost the characteristics of its traditional social hierarchy.
    c. Persians resisted foreign political control with small revolts in rural areas.
    d. Persians accepted the religion of both conquerors and rejected Zoroastrianism.
    e. Persian leaders served as high government officials under both Arabs and Mongols.

Primary Source Questions

1. **Examine the siege of Baghdad illustration, 1258, on page 473 of your textbook.**
   a. What is the point of view of the painter?
   b. Describe the style of the painting.
   c. Are there Mongols within the gates of the city? How do you know?
   d. What can you tell about the lifestyle of its inhabitants?

2. **Read *Sources from the Past: Marco Polo on Mongol Military Tactic*s, late thirteen century, on page 469 of your textbook.**
   a. What is Marco Polo's point of view?
   b. What is the organization of Mongol armies?
   c. How do armies sustain themselves in order to move so fast?
   d. What does Marco Polo describe as a different strategy in battle from European armies?

Chapter Multiple Choice Answers

1. **b:** The Turks under Mahmud of Ghazni and Tamarlane twice conquered northern India and under Osman held the Anatolian peninsula. The Mongols held China, Persia, and Russia under their control in addition to the regions between these areas. [pp. 466, 470 (map), 477 (map)]

2. **d:** Nomadic societies of Asia had two classes but the social hierarchy was not rigid. Unlike India or Europe, status could be gained or lost on the basis of talent. (p. 463)

3. **c:** The Mongolians tolerated and showed an interest in the religions they encountered. Khubilai Khan promoted Buddhism while the Persian ilkhanate eventually converted to Islam. (p. 472)

4. **d:** Neither Mahmud nor Tamarlane did more than conquer other regions. (pp. 465, 477)

5. **e:** As mentioned before, nomadic status was related to talent and Temujiin demonstrated a gift for war as well as alliance building. (p. 467)

6. **c:** This is a bit of a trick question since Confucianism is not a religion with deities, but a moral belief system. Khubilai rejected Confucian scholarship but tolerated all religions. (p. 472)

7. **b:** The Mongols were stopped in Syria by an Egyptian army of slaves known as the Mamluks. (p. 472)

8. **a:** Since the Mongols could only produce animal products, they engaged in trade enthusiastically. So when they held territory with major trade routes, they protected them. (p. 473)

9. **e:** The nomadic method of succession depended on the proper identification and acceptance of the most talented offspring. Since many of the leaders took many wives, there was often a bewildering array of male descendents, all with a claim to the leadership role. The result was that succession was determined by treachery, murder, and outright warfare. None of these are conducive to a stable transition of power. (pp. 475, 477)

10. **a:** The Roman empire was not split into two sections until the emperor Diocletian in the late third century, while the Mongol empire was split into four regions soon after the death of Chingghis Khan. (pp. 268, 470)

Comprehensive Multiple Choice Answers

1. **d:** Central Asian nomads had been a threat to civilized society since the Xiongnu threatened Han China in the third to first century B.C.E. and the Huns threatened eastern Europe in the second and third centuries C.E. The Arabs had interclan rivalries but were primarily engaged in trade after the classical land routes in central Asia became too dangerous. Neither voided large cities and both were highly dependent on cavalry as their primary strategy. Both expansions were instigated by the ideas of Chingghis Khan and Mohammad. Diplomacy was necessary for Chingghis to bind the Mongol clans into one fighting force but Mohammad brought other clans under his control through military victories. (pp. 346, 461)

2. **b:** The Mongols stayed separate from their Chinese subjects and preferred to use administrators imported from other conquered regions. They abolished the Confucian examination system, but they did not actively persecute Confucians. Although later Mongol leaders converted to Tibetan Buddhism, the Mongols did not favor any religion over others but sought to provide a place of tolerance for all religions. (p. 472)

3. **a:** The Mongol rulers of Persia eventually converted to Islam and became fervent followers while Arab conquerors picked up the tradition of veiling women, administrative techniques used to govern dar al-Islam, and Persian as the language of Islamic literature. Persian social class structure remained the same. Most Persians did reject Zoroastrianism during the Arabic government but Islam was the dominant religion by the time of the Mongols. While Persian revolts did help overthrow the Umayyad dynasty, ilkhanate failures were primarily fiscal. And while Persian administrators served in lower positions in government, the ilkhanate depended upon imported talent for the highest postions. (p. 472)

Primary Source Answers

1. The painters were Persian and because painters rarely have the time and safety to do such intricate work during wartime, this was most likely painted during the Mongol occupation. Also, because of the tolerant occupation, the painters would have painted a positive view of the Mongols, despite the fact that Chingghis ravaged the countryside. The style is colorful and intricate with curvilinear horses. The perspective is not realistic as can be seen in the depiction of the walled town and the size of the army figures contrasted with the city. The painting has an almost cheerful tone. There are Mongols within the gates, as seen by their distinctive headdresses, so the inhabitants stand behind windows and corners watching the victors but there are no scenes of looting and carnage. This may be because they surrendered quickly or it may also be due to the point of view. The inhabitants are Muslim as seen in the veiled woman. In the center there appears to be a Mongol commander on horseback meeting the central authority figure of the town, also on horseback. Notice the painting detail on page 468 as a Persian rendition of the Mongols as well. Note the pointed helmets and similar curvilinear horses and swords. (p. 473)

2. Marco Polo spent seventeen years in China so the army that he is describing is the mature Yuan dynasty army of Khubilai Khan. He lived and worked in the court so he had a very favorable view of the Mongols. Mongol armies were based on an efficient decile system of command, leaving every commander responsible for ten men. Mongol armies moved swiftly at all times and used horse blood to sustain them when they wanted to move even faster. The Mongols used the retreat to ambush their enemies and saw no shame in it. It is apparent that European armies would not retreat unless necessary and would consider this a dirty trick. (p.469)

CHAPTER 19

STATES AND SOCIETIES OF SUB-SAHARAN AFRICA

Before you begin: You might want to do a quick review of Chapter 3 to refresh your thinking about Africa. This chapter is very readable as it is directly tied to the AP themes and content. The period 1000–1500 C.E. is often a time frame used in the essay portion of the national exam, as there are numerous comparison/contrast or changes and continuities question possibilities. Read carefully and keep those AP themes in mind.

EFFECTS OF EARLY AFRICAN MIGRATIONS

African migrations began c. 3000 B.C.E. with the intermittent and incremental Bantu migration and were generally complete by 1000 C.E. as Bantu-speaking people came to occupy most of Africa south of the equator.

Agriculture and Population Growth
(Theme: Demographics)

Bantu peoples established agricultural societies and displaced indigenous hunters and gatherers in almost all parts of Africa. By 500 B.C.E., Bantus were making iron farm tools which helped expand their southern cultivation zones where they grew yams, millet, and sorghum. Indian Ocean merchants brought Asian yams, taro, chicken, and, most importantly, bananas to Madagascar from southeast Asia. The cultivation of bananas enriched African diets and resulted in the expansion of cultivatable lands and a population increase.

African Political Organization
(Theme: Political Structures)

Though **kin-based societies** survived in much of sub-Saharan Africa until the mid-nineteenth century, after the first millennium regional states and kingdoms became increasingly prominent.

By 1000 C.E., African migration slowed and Bantu societies governed themselves mostly through family and kinship groups rather than relying on elaborate bureaucracies. Male heads of families participated in a village's ruling council. The head of the most prominent family served as **chief** and represented the settlement as it dealt with neighboring settlements. A group of villages, based on ethnic loyalties, made up a district, but there usually was no head or chief of a district. Village chiefs resolved district issues. The terms **stateless societies** or **segmentary societies** are often used to refer to this type of social organization.

After 1000 C.E. though, these kin-based societies faced difficult challenges as population growth strained land resources. Ensuing conflicts encouraged Bantu communities to formally organize first their military and then their governments. The west African kingdoms of **Ife** and **Benin** developed as complex city-states during this time. Near modern-day Republic of the Congo and Angola, the Kingdom of Kongo emerged as the most tightly centralized Bantu kingdom and as a prosperous trading nation transporting copper, raffia cloth, and nzimbu shells from the Atlantic Ocean. Its central government was based on a king and officials who administered the nation's judicial, political, and military affairs while provincial governors supervised district rulers who oversaw the local village rulers. This organization effectively ruled for nearly four hundred years, until the arrival of the Portuguese slave traders.

ISLAMIC KINGDOMS AND EMPIRES

Merchants brought Islam to sub-Saharan Africa—over land along the camel routes to west Africa and across the sea lanes to east Africa. Islam would profoundly influence religious, cultural, political, social, and economic development throughout the continent.

Trans-Saharan Trade and Islamic States in West Africa
(Theme: Economics and Changes and Continuities)

Though the Sahara desert had never been an absolute barrier to trade and communication, only a few nomadic peoples and a handful of merchants regularly crossed it. The introduction of the **camel** from Asia and the development of a **useful saddle** in the seventh century B.C.E., along with the conquest of north Africa by the Arabs in the eighth and ninth centuries C.E., encouraged the development of trade across the Sahara.

The kingdom of **Ghana** developed as a regional state during the fourth and fifth centuries C.E. By the late eighth century when the Muslim merchants arrived, Ghana had developed as a market for copper, iron-ware, cotton textiles, salt, grain, and carnelian beads. After the Muslim merchants came trade and traffic across the desert increased dramatically as west Africa became the center for trade in gold, in high demand as a result of surging trade throughout the eastern hemisphere. Through her capital city, **Koumbi-Sahel,** Ghana controlled the trade and taxes on gold which her kings procured from the river regions of Gambia, Niger, and Senegal. Ghana's kings used that wealth to enrich and strengthen their realms. Merchants in Ghana also **traded ivory and slaves for horses and salt,** which was especially important for survival in the tropics.

Ghanaian kings used these taxes to finance large armies to protect their sources of gold, to maintain order throughout the kingdom, and to defend Ghana from nomadic invasions across the Sahara. By about the tenth century, the kings of Ghana converted to Islam which further improved relations with Muslim desert nomads, and with north African merchants and rulers. The Ghanaian kings did not impose Islam on their subjects and even maintained some elements from their traditional religious practices; those Ghanaians involved in trade frequently adopted Islam as well.

Ghana collapsed under perpetual attack from northern nomadic raiders. At the same time, the kingdom of **Mali** emerged, lead by the lion prince, **Sundiata,** who reigned from 1230 to 1255. Through acts of legendary bravery, he used his dominant cavalry to secure his kingdom which included ancient Ghana as well as the regions of Niger, Senegal, Mauritania, Gambia, Guinea-Bissau, Guinea, and Sierra Leone. Mali benefited immensely from the trans-Saharan trade. It built a huge capital city at Niana as well as market cities like **Timbuktu, Gao,** and **Jenne.**

Sundiata's nephew, **Mansa Musa,** ruled Mali at its high point. His pilgrimage to **Mecca** in 1324–1325 is legendary in its size and wealth and in its effect on the spread of Islam throughout his realm. He returned to west Africa an even more devout believer, establishing mosques and schools throughout Mali.

Mali was overrun by the **Songhai empire** in fifteenth century, but the tradition of centralized government and the impact of Islam would survive.

The Indian Ocean Trade and Islamic States in East Africa
(Theme: Patterns of Interaction and Changes and Continuities)

Just as the sub-Saharan trade helped to build empires in the west, the wealth generated by the Indian Ocean trade financed the coastal city-states and interior kingdoms of east Africa. Merchant mariners had linked east Africa to the larger trading world since as early as 500 B.C.E., but it was not until the tenth century C.E. that Islamic merchants began regular, sustained interaction with the indigenous Bantu people in eastern Africa. These coastal dwellers, at first largely hunters and gatherers, formed the basis of the new **Swahili culture.**

Swahili, an Arabic word meaning "coasters," refers to the people who lived along the east African coast from Mogadishu to Sofala; over time, the Swahili developed a unique language and culture which mixed Bantu and Arabic traditions. By the eleventh and twelfth centuries, the Swahili were regularly trading gold, slaves, ivory, and other exotic goods from the African interior for pottery, glass, and textiles brought to Africa from Persia, India, and China by Muslim maritime merchants. This trading economy was based in cities lining the east African coast: Mogadishu, Lamu, Malindi, Mombasa, Zanzibar, Kilwa, Mozambique, and Sofala. Each city-state was governed by a powerful king. The tangible wealth of these cities was substantial as they boasted multiple-storied houses made of stone and coral, huge mosques, and large public buildings. **Kilwa** was one of the most impressive of these cities; travelers like **Ibn Battuta** remarked on the vast material wealth he saw in the city and on the level of scholarship he appreciated in her people.

Zimbabwe was a central African kingdom which also was influenced by the wealth from east African trade; the term actually simply refers to the dwelling of a chief. In the fifth and sixth centuries C.E. there were many of these wooden residences in central east Africa. By the early thirteenth century, a magnificent stone complex was built near Nyanda in modern Zimbabwe, indicating an increasingly wealthy, complex, highly organized society. The impressive stone enclosures were home to more than 18,000 people by the late fifteenth century as the kingdom's influence stretched deep into south-central Africa. From these great structures of towers and palaces, kings controlled and taxed trade between the interior and the coast and organized the flow of gold, slaves, and local products.

As in west Africa, wealthy merchants converted to Islam, though they frequently maintained their indigenous traditions as a means of maintaining their social leadership positions. The conversion of these cultural elites enhanced their political power as they gained additional legitimacy and recognition from Islamic states in Asia.

AFRICAN SOCIETY AND CULTURAL DEVELOPMENT

The diversity of African society by the eleventh century C.E. makes generalities difficult. There are some social forms and cultural patterns which appear widely, however.

Social Classes
(Themes: Social and Gender Structures)

The societies in kingdoms, empires, and city-states like Kongo, Mali, and Kilwa resemble the social structures in the settled, agricultural lands of Eurasia. In the smaller states and kin-based societies, however, kinship, sex and gender expectations, and **age groupings** determined social position. The importance of the extended family and the lack of a concept of land as private property served as foundations of social and economic organization in kin-based societies. People identified first as a member of a family.

Sex and gender also had a major influence on social roles. Workers like tanners or blacksmiths were almost always men while women in those families might work as potters. Heavy labor was considered man's work and women handled most domestic chores and took primary responsibility for raising children. Both men and women participated in agriculture.

Public authority was usually a man's realm although some women did rise to positions of power. Aristocratic women had influence in public affairs as a result of their family connections. Women were involved in markets and participated in both local and long-distance trade. Some African societies even allowed women to participate as soldiers.

Islam did little to alter the lives of African women. Since the faith spread first to the upper classes, and then slowly to other classes, most African women retained their traditional gender roles, living and working openly and unveiled.

Age grouping as a means of organizing society is a distinctive African tradition which served to establish social ties across lines of family and gender. Members of **age sets** or **age grades** performed tasks appropriate to their development and bonded to form tight circles of friends and political allies which continued throughout a person's life.

Slave holding and **slave trading** has been an African tradition since antiquity. As in most societies, slaves came as prisoners of war, debtors, criminals, and suspected witches. Most slaves in Africa worked as agricultural and construction laborers or as porters or miners. Slaves were a form of personal wealth as they enabled a family to increase their agricultural production and hence their wealth.

After the ninth century, the demand for slaves increased, as did the demand for all other African "goods." The demand for slaves in Persia, India, Southwest Asia, and the Mediterranean basin outstripped the supply available from eastern Europe, previously the main source of slaves. **Slave raiding** developed to meet this demand as rulers of large-scale states and empires began to attack the less defended smaller kingdoms and kin-based societies. The **Zanj revolt,** the most famous slave rebellion in Mesopotamia in the late ninth century, provides some information on the slave trade of this era and demonstrates the importance of African slavery as a feature of Muslim society. Figures estimate as many as ten million Africans may have been sold as slaves to the Islamic world from 750–1500 C.E. This trade laid the foundation for the much larger Atlantic slave trade to develop after 1500.

African Religion
(Theme: Religious Developments)

Religious beliefs varied among the peoples of sub-Saharan Africa. While most had **monotheistic beliefs,** those beliefs changed or were altered as the people encountered other religious traditions. Traditional African religion was **practical** rather than theological in its focus and it strongly emphasized **morality and ethics** as essential to maintaining an orderly world. Most people recognized a **divine force**, usually male, who was responsible for creating and often sustaining life. He was generally regarded as **omniscient and omnipotent.** Lesser gods, frequently associated with natural features such as rain, wind, and trees,were believed to interact freely with humans bringing good or ill. Religious rituals, such as prayer, animal sacrifice, and other ceremonies, frequently focused on honoring the deities, spirits, or ancestor's souls to win their favor. **Diviners** were intelligent men and sometimes women who understood their communities and sought to resolve problems through **consulting oracles** or **prescribing medicines.**

The Arrival of Christianity and Islam
(Theme: Religious Developments)

Christianity and Islam, both foreign religions of salvation, were adapted by some Africans. Christianity reached Egypt and north Africa during the first century C.E. **Alexandria** became an early center of Christian thought and home to such scholars as **St. Augustine of Hippo.** Christianity expanded into sub-Saharan Africa after the fourth century with the conversion of the kings of Axum in Ethiopia. There was resurgence in the thirteenth century and retained its privileged status until 1974. Ethiopian Christianity retained many basic elements of Christian theology and ritual, but like all foreign religions in Africa, it also included the interests of its African believers. This syncretism can be seen in the construction of the **Rock Churches at Lalibela**, Ethiopia, during the twelfth century C.E.

Likewise, Islam reflected the interests of its local converts. While ruling elites and merchants in sub-Saharan west and coastal east Africa certainly converted in part for the economic benefits, they also took their new faith quite seriously, building mosques and schools, and going on **hajj.** Even the most devoted African converts continued to accommodate their new faith with their traditional culture in terms of dress, gender relations, and ancestor rituals.

Finished reading the chapter? Be sure you can . . .

- Describe the emergence of new empires and political systems in sub-Saharan Africa.
- Explain the rise of Islam as a unifying cultural and economic force in sub-Saharan Africa.
- Analyze the development and shifts in interregional trade and cultural exchange in the Trans-Saharan and Indian Ocean trade routes.
- Analyze the role and functions of cities in west and east Africa.
- Compare the European and sub-Saharan contacts with the Islamic world. (You'll need Chapters 17 and 20 for this one.)

Chapter Multiple Choice Questions

1. How did the geographic conditions of sub-Saharan Africa affect its trade and communication networks in the post-classical era?
   a. Ample harbors surrounding the continent and an extensive river system made water travel and communication the most efficient.
   b. The Sahara desert made it difficult to travel over land and cataracts in major rivers made it difficult to travel inland by water.
   c. Though the Sahara desert was a formidable challenge to overland travelers, easy access through mighty rivers such as the Nile and the Limpopo allowed for ease of travel to many parts of sub-Saharan Africa.
   d. The desert-like climate of much of Africa made communication and transportation systems nearly impossible to develop.
   e. The dense jungles of central Africa prevented the building of rail and canal systems until the twentieth century.

2. How did the introduction of bananas from southeast Asia impact life in sub-Saharan Africa?
   a. Bananas enabled the Bantu to expand into heavily forested regions where yams and millet would not grow.
   b. Bananas were easy to grow so more people could make a living as farmers than ever before.
   c. Bananas were mostly cultivated by women which altered the traditional patriarchal Bantu society.
   d. Bananas did not transport well to regional markets so the economy of sub-Saharan Africa became much more localized.
   e. Bananas were not readily accepted as a new crop because people in sub-Saharan Africa already grew a wide variety of foods and did not need a new crop.

3. Which of the following statements BEST characterizes sub-Saharan African political organization in the post-classical era?
   a. Bantu societies had little or no government as they were ruled as "segmentary societies."
   b. Bantu societies were dependent on an elaborate hierarchy of bureaucrats and officials to administer their affairs.
   c. Bantu societies were dominated by Arab-based Muslim caliphates for much of their early history.
   d. Bantu societies governed themselves mostly through families and kinship groups.
   e. Bantu societies were nomadic and were ruled in a clan structure much like Mongol rule.

4. Which central African kingdom developed the most tightly centralized government system c. 1300–1650?
   a. Kingdom of Angola
   b. Kingdom of Benin
   c. Kingdom of Kongo
   d. Kingdom of Ife
   e. Kingdom of Nigeria

5. What group is largely responsible for the introduction of Islam to sub-Saharan Africa?
   a. aristocrats
   b. warriors
   c. merchants
   d. slaves
   e. women

6. Why did west African kings convert to Islam?
   a. The kings were forced to convert under threat from Arab nomads who had themselves recently converted to Islam and felt it was necessary to spread the faith even by the sword.
   b. Christianity had not been favorable to trade and the kings desperately needed money to support their large armies and lavish lifestyles.
   c. They found their indigenous religion and traditions unfulfilling and no longer useful in their increasingly complex worlds.
   d. Missionaries like Al-Bakri had shown the kings the spiritual and economic benefits of conversion.
   e. Converting to Islam improved relations with Muslim merchants from north Africa and brought the west African kings recognition and support from Muslim states in the north.

7. What was the dominant political structure in east Africa by the thirteenth century C.E.?
   a. small kinship-based societies
   b. stateless or segmented societies
   c. prosperous city-states
   d. confederated regions
   e. multinational empires

8. Which of the following statements is true regarding conversion to Islam in BOTH west and east Africa?
   a. Islam was spread by the sword in both regions by both cavalry and naval forces.
   b. Islam supplanted Christianity as the dominant religion in the region.
   c. The elites converted first and then forced rapid conversion on other social classes.
   d. The lower social classes converted first and then slowly the elites accepted the new faith because it helped their business interests.
   e. The elites converted first, and then gradually many of the lower social classes converted while retaining aspects of their traditional beliefs.

9. Which of the following statements is TRUE regarding the relationship between traditional African religions and the "foreign faiths" of Christianity and Islam?
   a. Elements of traditional African religions, especially the honoring of deities, spirits, or ancestors' souls, found their way into Christianity and Islam as practiced by many Africans.
   b. Traditional African religions, especially the Diviners, fought hard to eradicate these foreign faiths and ironically were destroyed in the process.
   c. The elites abandoned traditional African religions in favor of the more modern foreign faiths that were considered religions of salvation.
   d. Christianity proved more flexible than Islam in adapting to the traditional African religious beliefs.
   e. Islam proved more flexible than Christianity in adapting to the traditional African religious beliefs.

10. What term can be used to describe both Christianity and Islam but NOT traditional African religions?
    a. monotheism
    b. religion of salvation
    c. ethical
    d. polytheistic
    e. mystery cult

Comprehensive Multiple Choice Questions

1. The terms *stateless society* and *segmentary society* are best applied to
   a. the form of social organization found in Nigeria prior to the tenth century.
   b. the form of social organization found in Ghana in the eleventh through thirteenth centuries.
   c. the form of social organization found in Zimbabwe in the twelfth through fifteenth centuries.
   d. the form of social organization found in Mali in the fourteenth century.
   e. the form of social organization found in the Kingdom of Kongo in the fourteenth through seventeenth centuries.

2. Why was west African gold in such high demand in the eastern hemisphere c. 800–1100?
   a. Wars in the eastern hemisphere made it difficult for people to access other sources of gold.
   b. The Umayyad empire built an elaborate capital in Baghdad which required much gold for ornamentation.
   c. Gold was used for currency in western Europe which was undergoing a trade revolution.
   d. The economic development and trade boom throughout the eastern hemisphere raised the demand for gold.
   e. The Byzantine empire refused to trade with the Muslim world, so the Muslims needed another source.

3. Islam in Africa
   a. had a major impact on traditional roles for women who had to withdraw from their traditional economic roles to fulfill Islamic law.
   b. had a major impact on economic interactions between gold and salt sellers in east Africa.
   c. had a significant impact on the traditional African religious practices relating to honoring ancestral spirits.
   d. had little impact on women who continued to openly fulfill their economic roles in society.
   e. had little impact on the cultural elites who refused to convert to Islam to retain their traditional positions of power and prestige in sub-Saharan African society.

Primary Source Questions

1. **Examine the bronze plaque from Benin on page 482 of your textbook.**
   a. What is the plaque made of? What does that tell you about the society which produced it?
   b. What is the subject of the work? What message or idea does it convey?
   c. What other observations can you make which reflect Benin culture c. 1000 C.E.?

2. **Read *Sources from the Past: Ibn Battuta on Muslim Society at Mogadishu* on page 495 of your textbook.**
   a. What evidence does Ibn Battuta give of the material wealth in Mogadishu?
   b. Why would hospitality be so ritualized in Swahili society?
   c. How did religion factor into this interaction?

Chapter Multiple Choice Answers

1. **b:** The formidable Sahara desert, cataracts on major rivers, and the absence of many natural harbors prevented sub-Saharan Africa from developing extensive and permanent trade and communications networks. Choice "e" might be a partially correct statement, but it does not apply to the period and the era of construction. (p. 483)

2. **a:** The introduction of bananas as a foodstuff brought many changes to sub-Saharan Africa including making it possible for Bantu-speaking people to move into places where their traditional foods of yams and millet would not grow. Other changes included an increasing population and a diet higher in nutritional value. (p. 485)

3. **d:** The terms *stateless society* or *segmentary society* are used to describe African political organization during much of the postclassical era. These terms describe a society run by small-scale communities based on kinship groups. Decision-making was handled by male heads of families who constituted a village ruling council. The most prominent of these men served as chief and represented the village in contact with neighboring villages. (p. 485)

4. **c:** The Kingdom of Kongo was a highly complex, tightly centralized political, military, judicial, and economic authority for over three centuries until it was undermined by Portuguese slave traders in the mid-seventeenth century. (p. 486)

5. **c:** Islam arrived in sub-Saharan Africa in the west by merchants in trans-Saharan caravans, and in the east by Indian Ocean maritime traders. (p. 487)

6. **e:** The wealth gained from increasing trade with Arab Muslim merchants from the north and the increased political legitimacy gained as a result of the kings' conversion made Islam a compelling choice. The west African kings did not have to abandon their indigenous traditions and indeed used those to maintain their social and political legitimacy. (p. 489)

7. **c:** The trade generated in east Africa in the eleventh and twelfth centuries transformed Swahili culture and built a materially wealthy society based in prosperous city-states like Kilwa, Lamu, and Zanzibar. (pp. 493–494)

8. **e:** Despite many misperceptions about the spread of Islam in sub-Saharan Africa, it was the elites who generally converted first, certainly with some economic motives, and then the lower social classes who may have been attracted by economic benefit as well or who may have been attracted by the egalitarian aspects of the faith. Africans in both regions continued with some aspects of their traditional culture and religions even after conversion. (pp. 489–490, 496)

9. **a:** One of the key reasons both Christianity and Islam survived and grew in sub-Saharan Africa was the flexibility of traditional African religions and the willingness of the first-converted elites to maintain their traditional ties even after conversion. (p. 500)

10. **c:** Both Christianity and Islam are religions which focus on the afterlife and the "saving" of souls. Traditional African religion, like Christianity and Islam, is monotheistic and has a strong emphasis on ethics. (p. 501)

Comprehensive Multiple Choice Answers

1. **a:** Stateless or segmentary societies were a widely prevalent system of social organization in Bantu areas based on rule through family or kinship groups. The other choices all represent increasingly complex political structures of kingdoms and empires. (p. 485)

2. **d:** This is the most comprehensive response because Muslim merchants flocked to Ghana in this era to search for gold for consumers in the Mediterranean basin and elsewhere in the Muslim world. (p. 488)

3. **d:** Islam accommodated traditional African traditions as they related to gender roles. Women continued to fulfill their economic responsibilities and to observe their traditional fashions of dress, despite occasional comments from non-African Muslims. (p. 503)

Primary Source Answers

1. The bronze plaque reveals much about Benin culture c. 1000 C.E. It indicates that Benin culture had the ability to make alloys; in this case bronze, a mixture of tin and copper. Civilizations are traditionally defined by these advanced technological abilities. Hence, we can know that Benin must have been a complex society which produced enough agricultural surplus to allow for the specialization of labor necessary to produce this plaque. The work shows political and military power with the leader or chief in the center forefront, flanked by two heavily armed soldiers. The soldiers in the background indicate the depth of support the chief enjoys and sends a message that he is mighty and commands many soldiers. Every inch of the surface is decorated in some way with vegetation as well as geometric patterns. The direct, almost challenging expression on the chief's face as well as the faces of his soldiers portrays a sense of determination and seriousness which might make a challenger reconsider any attempts at confrontation. (p. 482)

2. This excerpt has numerous examples of material culture. Battuta carefully includes a description of the camels, sheep, and goats which appear to be abundant. He also includes a list of fine textiles which he admires: Egyptian cotton, silk "Jerusalem material"; all of which he calls cloths which "have no rival." He has a choice of places to stay which indicates that people must have large enough homes to comfortably host guests. Hospitality is ritualized in a commercial economy because merchants must feel secure about doing business with people in a particular place which is not home to them. Formality and hospitality are a way to build trust and the expectation that rules will be obeyed and followed. Tradition also prevents conflicts as everyone knows and agrees to abide by the "rules" for good business behavior. Religion seems tied to commerce and essential to understanding the traditions in Mogadishu. God is frequently referred to as reasons for meeting people or as an opportunity to share a time of worship together. The fact that the Shaikh spoke to Battuta in Arabic rather than Swahili directly demonstrates the significance of a shared religion in the interactions of these men from different parts of the world. (p. 495)

CHAPTER 20

WESTERN EUROPE DURING THE HIGH MIDDLE AGES

Before you get started: Think of the crusades and Gothic cathedrals as you study this chapter. As you saw in Chapter 17, Europe went through a chaotic period of early feudalism. Nevertheless, the early medieval period left a legacy of regional loyalties, improved farming technology, and a strong Catholic church. Europeans of this later period continued to be fierce and frequent fighters and some theories on European domination of the modern world attribute it to their almost constant state of warfare. However, despite regular warfare, we see economic bonuses from participation in the world trade network and a flowering of cultural life. In comparison with the major dynasties in China, there are many confusing changes in political power but you only need to know a few high (and low) points. Don't forget that for comparison while Europeans were mixing it up with their neighbors, the Islamic world prospered under the Abbasids and later, the Mongols dominated Asia.

THE ESTABLISHMENT OF REGIONAL STATES

While German princes established the confederation of states known as the **Holy Roman Empire**, western monarchs consolidated power over France and England. On the Iberian Peninsula, there are five regional kingdoms and the Italian cities work towards independence from regional authority. These states frequently clashed with one another but were very effective at organizing their own territories.

The Holy Roman Empire
(Themes: Political Structures and Changes and Continuities)

The German king of Saxony, Otto, defeated so many of his neighbors that by 962, the pope proclaimed him the Holy Roman Emperor. However, there was enormous tension between the succeeding emperors and popes as the emperors sought to control the Catholic church and the popes attempted to exert their own authority over all monarchs. During the **Investiture Contest Controversy**, clashes between church and state came to a head when Pope Gregory VII excommunicated Holy Roman Emperor Henry IV for attempting to name the bishops in his own region. Henry IV backed down by pleading to the Pope barefoot in the snow and the Catholic church maintained its strong authority over Europe. The popes also stopped an attempt by a later emperor, Frederick Barbarossa, to enlarge the empire through the northern part of Italy. It is always good to recall that Voltaire, a key figure of the eighteenth century, remarked that the Holy Roman Empire was "neither holy, nor Roman, nor an empire." Instead, it was secular, German, and a group of states.

Regional Monarchies in France and England
(Themes: Political Structures and Changes and Continuities)

Both the French and English consolidated their feudal estates into the centralized governments of French kings. In France, **Hugh Capet** and his descendents formed a strong monarchy while the English were defeated by a Norman duke from across the English Channel. **William the Conqueror** defeated the Anglo-Saxon King of England in 1066. The Normans reorganized English government and maintained a strong central authority. While both the Capetians and Normans faced internal challenges to their power, successive generations of French and English kings continued to fight each other as well.

Regional States in Italy and Iberia
(Themes: Political Structures and Changes and Continuities)

During this period, Italy was decentralized under a mixture of Catholic states, city-states, and principalities. While the popes influenced most Italian states, they ruled central Italy as the **Papal State**. However, as Italian cities like **Florence, Bologna, Genoa, Milan, and Venice** grew prosperous from trade, they began to dominate the northern region with their own governments and armies. In the south, the powerful **kingdom of Naples** was formed out of former Byzantine and Muslim territories. At the beginning of this period, the Iberian peninsula was split between a small northern Catholic region and the predominant Muslim states in the south. By the thirteenth century, Christian armies had pressed south and conquered the regions that became Castile, Aragon, and Portugal. Only **Granada** remained Muslim.

ECONOMIC GROWTH AND SOCIAL DEVELOPMENT

In the middle of all the political warfare, Europe experienced notable growth in trade which changed the social hierarchy.

Growth of the Agricultural Economy
(Themes: Economics and Demographics)

Economic and social change in Europe was fueled by the new technology mentioned in Chapter 17 such as plows and water mills. The development of **horseshoes and the horse collar** allowed even faster tilling of land. They also began to understand the importance of **field rotation** and animal fertilizer. In addition to this, they experimented with new crops such as legumes and vegetables. The Europeans publicized their findings of agricultural improvements in books and pamphlets in vernacular European languages, rather than the scholarly languages of Latin or Greek. All of these improvements led to significant population growth each century between 1000 and 1300. It grew as much as 36 percent in the thirteenth century alone. The demographic change further fueled the increased rate of urbanization and trade.

The Revival of Towns and Trade
(Themes: Economics and Changes and Continuities)

With the increase in trade and economic activity, peasants made their way to towns. Roman cities like **London, Paris,** and **Toledo** became large regional centers of trade while new towns were founded at advantageous spots. Italy and Flanders in present-day Belgium became important centers of woolen textiles. But Italian cities also prospered mightily from the increased **Mediterranean trade.** Venetian and Genoese merchants established themselves in port cities throughout the eastern Mediterranean in order to deal directly with the Asian market. In northern Europe, the port cities of the Baltic and North Sea formed a trade network known as the **Hanseatic League** and the goods shipped by these merchants were traded in large market towns along the Danube and Rhine rivers. Just as **banking and credit** became a part of the enhanced trade in China and the Islamic world, it became part of the economic life of Europe. European investors also partnered with each other to decrease the risk associated with business.

Social Change
(Themes: Social and Gender Structures and Changes and Continuities)

While the formula for the **three estates** or classes of medieval Europe—those who prayed, those who fought, and those who labored—proves useful for remembering this time period, there were changes in the social system. By the high middle ages, the boorish behavior of the fighting class was calmed considerably by the advent of a **code of chivalry** that governed their manners and actions. The Catholic church even promoted the idea of piety and service to the Christian faith as a part of the code. The code appealed to elite women in particular who promoted its ideals of respect for women and proper behavior. **Troubadours** who traveled between castles sang refined love songs and made up poems based on the sophisticated traditions of Muslim Spain. Their most important patron was **Eleanor of Aquitaine** who also managed to marry both a king of France and a king of England.

As the cities grew, merchants became powerful enough to demand **charters** from the local lords that would exempt them from feudal control. The craftsmen in cities joined together in **guilds** to protect prices and establish uniform standards of production. Guilds also served the social function of providing support and friendship to its members. They served as a sort of social safety net in hard times when a guild member died or became disabled.

The status of women grew with increased urbanization. While rural women continued to work in the same areas of housekeeping and animal husbandry, urban women had opportunities to work the same jobs as men. Women became professionals, bankers, merchants, butchers, and brewers. They dominated the production of clothing and even became members of **female guilds**. In thirteenth-century Paris, there were six all-female guilds that looked after their interests.

EUROPEAN CHRISTIANITY DURING THE HIGH MIDDLE AGES

The Roman Catholic church dominated the lives of medieval Europeans. It served as the major cultural influence on literature and the arts as well as dominating the city scene with its churches and cathedrals. Average Europeans adopted a new form of popular religion that challenged the church while Catholic scholars adopted the long forgotten ideas of Aristotle.

Schools, Universities, and Scholastic Theology
(Theme: Cultural Developments)

As Europeans grew wealthier, education became more available. To be a scholar in any society, one must have wealth in order to have time released from regular labor to pursue academics. Also, the increasingly complex political and religious world demanded more sophisticated and educated workers. Early in the eleventh century, **cathedral schools** were founded in France and northern Italy. By the twelfth century, formal curricula had developed that included the study of Latin, the Bible, and Christian theologians like Saint Augustine. Eventually, **universities** organized by students and teachers in Bologna, Paris, and Salerno offered advanced studies in medicine, law, and theology. Coincidentally, the works of Aristotle were retrieved from Muslim philosophers who had translated his thoughts into Arabic as Byzantine, Spanish, and Sicilian scholars translated them into Latin for European use. Then, a Catholic theologian, **Saint Thomas Aquinas**, wrote books fusing Christianity with the Greek philosophy of Aristotle.

Popular Religion
(Themes: Religious Developments)

While scholars were refining a sophisticated interpretation of Christian theology, the common people were interested in a more vibrant and emotional brand of Christianity that venerated **saints, relics,** and the **Virgin Mary.** Prayers to certain saints could cure illness, guide travelers, and ensure admission to heaven. By far the most popular saint was the mother of Jesus, the Virgin Mary. She was the Christian ideal of womanhood and was believed to have performed many miracles. Also, the veneration of saints required **pilgrimages** to churches where relics (parts of the remains of saints or their clothing and possessions) were located. A sort of travel industry developed around the journeys as inns sprang up along the most famous routes and guidebooks were printed. Of course, there was a good deal of fraud associated with the practice but it comforted medieval Europeans. Devout church attendees became devoted to the seven sacraments as essential rituals of the Catholic church.

Reform Movements and Popular Heresies
(Theme: Religious Developments)

As wealth increased and pilgrimage sites raked in the riches, reformers within the church became concerned with the materialism of the church. **St. Dominic and St. Francis** founded orders of mendicant monks who preached messages of simple faith to audiences and begged for donations of food and clothing for their simple needs. In parts of France and northern Italy, there were those who rejected the Roman church such as the Waldensians who advocated more religious tasks for the lay people and the Cathers who advocated a simple, celibate life on a vegetarian diet. Their appeal disturbed one pope so much that he called for a military campaign against them.

THE MEDIEVAL EXPANSION OF EUROPE

A strengthened medieval Europe began to expand into new regions of the Atlantic, Baltic, and Mediterranean. Colonies were established in Iceland, Greenland, and Canada and Christianity was introduced to the Baltic regions. Christian Spain conquered Muslim Spain and in the most spectacular expression of expansion, the crusades aimed to take back the holy lands from Muslims as well.

Atlantic and Baltic Colonization
(Themes: Demographics, Patterns of Interaction, and Religious Developments)

Once the Vikings of Scandinavia were turned back from continental Europe, they began to expand westward to the islands of the north Atlantic. By the tenth century, they occupied **Iceland** and **Greenland** and around 1000, Leif Ericson established a short-lived community called **Vinland** in eastern Canada.

While the Vikings were exploring, the Scandinavian monarchs converted to Christianity. Although there was considerable resistance among the population, monarchs of Denmark and Norway pressed Christianity on their subjects. A group of fervent Christian soldiers, the **Teutonic Knights**, conquered the Baltic regions of Latvia, Lithuania, and Estonia intent upon conversion as well as conquest. By the fourteenth century, the Roman Catholic church was well-established in all northern regions of Europe.

The Reconquest of Sicily and Spain
(Theme: Patterns of Interaction)

As European interest in the Mediterranean increased, they confronted the Muslim states of Sicily and Granada. In the eleventh century, Normans returned Sicily to Christianity while the *reconquista* of Muslim Spain took considerably longer. However, Christian forces conquered all but the southernmost region of Granada by the mid-thirteenth century. While the conquest of Sicily was driven primarily by military interests, it is apparent that the *reconquista* was driven primarily by religious zeal. Dominican friars played a large part in the conversion of Spaniards to Catholicism.

The Crusades
(Theme: Patterns of Interaction)

Crusade is derived from the Latin word for cross, *crux,* and indeed, that is what crusaders sewed on to their backs. Following the smaller crusades to convert the populations of Scandanavia, the Baltics, Spain, and Sicily, the larger movement of the crusades was started by an appeal from **Pope Urban II** to conquer the holy lands of the Bible. His appeal soon captured the imaginations of medieval Europeans when Peter the Hermit preached the message across France, Germany, and the Low Countries (Holland and Belgium today). Joined by a motley army of commoners and impoverished knights, he set out for the holy lands with few skills but enormous enthusiasm. This prelude to the crusades was a disaster for all concerned with few returning to Europe. The first crusade proper was organized by French and Norman nobles who managed to capture Jerusalem and divide the holy lands into Christian territories. However, these lands were retaken by Muslims necessitating a second crusade. A series of crusades ensued that never achieved the success of the first one but managed to deal the death knell to the Christian Byzantine empire. The upshot of the crusades was that while they were religious in original intent, they quickly became wars of military and political expansion.

Ironically, the consequences of this disastrous European campaign were much more beneficial than harmful. It increased European exposure to Muslim philosophy and theology. Through Muslim scholarship, Europeans also picked up new scientific and mathematical ideas. It increased the trade between the Middle East and Europe while enlarging the choice of goods to include items such as paper, silk, cotton cloth, spices, coffee, granulated sugar, and dates. Europeans also developed a taste for the luxurious goods of Asia and Africa and soon merchants, such as the Polo family, made the decision to go on trading trips themselves. And, it returned the Europeans to full partnership in global trade.

Finished reading the chapter? Be sure you can . . .

- Describe the changes and continuities between the early middle ages and the high middle ages.
- Describe the evolution from feudal governance of the early middle ages to the centralized monarchies of the later period.
- Identify the regions that remained decentralized.
- Demonstrate why the Roman Catholic church retained its significant political and social position.
- Describe the cause and effect of increased urbanization.
- Identify the factors that resulted in the increased status for European women.
- Analyze the shift in Europe from its position isolated from the globe to its reintegration.

Chapter Multiple Choice Questions

1. The establishment of the holy Roman Empire did not settle the question of religious or secular control. In the Investiture Contest,
   a. the Pope ignored the pleas of the Holy Roman Emperor.
   b. Emperor Henry IV proved the might of secular authority.
   c. neither the religious nor secular authorities won.
   d. the Holy Roman Emperor bowed to the will of Pope Gregory VII.
   e. the Pope decided that lay investiture would improve administration.

2. The legacy of William the Conqueror in England was the same as that of Hugh Capet in France. They
   a. concentrated on further conquest of their neighbors.
   b. solidified an efficient centralized administration.
   c. eventually combined the nations into one under French rule.
   d. converted their reluctant subjects to Christianity.
   e. enjoyed enormous popularity and support.

3. Italy remained largely decentralized except in the region of
   a. independent city states in the north.
   b. southern regions under the control of Muslims.
   c. French control of northern Italy.
   d. port cities such as Venice.
   e. papal states of central Italy.

4. Population growth in the high middle ages was enormous due to
   a. increased agricultural yield.
   b. less warfare between nations.
   c. lack of disease in the peasant class.
   d. high birth rates in the nobility.
   e. improved medicine from the Muslims.

5. Which group benefited the most from increased urbanization?
   a. nobility because they could demand tax payments
   b. peasants since they had a place to escape to
   c. soldiers who had increased availability of weapons
   d. merchants because all trade occurred in large cities
   e. townspeople because they obtained charters

6. European women's roles increased in stature during the high middle ages. What development helped the status of more women?
    a. the plow so that only one person was needed to till the soil
    b. the code of chivalry because good manners expanded into all classes
    c. schools and universities because they began to allow women to take classes
    d. recognition for their ability to participate in the economy
    e. recognition of the special status of the Virgin Mary

7. While schools and universities provided education to the elite, participation in pilgrimages was open to all. What other area provided a benefit to all Europeans?
    a. decreased warfare
    b. the military accomplishments
    c. increased trade
    d. the code of chivalry
    e. urbanization

8. The fearsome Vikings of Scandinavia spread their influence far into the Atlantic but were not successful at resisting
    a. the outside influence of religion.
    b. their conquest by the Teutonic Knights.
    c. the reconquest of their countries.
    d. changes to their political scene.
    e. luxury items from the Mediterranean trade.

9. When comparing the expansion of Europeans into Muslim regions of Spain and Sicily, it can most appropriately be said that the former was primarily religious while the latter was primarily
    a. economic.
    b. also religious.
    c. political.
    d. social.
    e. secular.

10. While the crusades were a misguided effort to reconquer the holy lands, they were entirely successful at
    a. defeating the Muslim Byzantine Empire.
    b. uniting the Europeans firmly in a military alliance.
    c. reducing the amount of future warfare.
    d. alleviating national differences.
    e. connecting Europe to the world trade market.

Comprehensive Multiple Choice Questions

1. During the high middle ages in Europe, successful governance was a political mosaic. What is the best explanation for why the Europeans had so many forms of government?
    a. The Europeans had no tradition of empire-building to bind together the disparate states.
    b. There were no superbly talented European leaders who could pull them together.
    c. The Catholic church was too strong to allow the formation of large states.
    d. The strength of church leaders and the profusion of talented leaders led to multiple regional states.
    e. The legacy of decentralized government was too strong to be overcome by any single ruler.

2. In what ways were European women of the high middle ages similar to Mongol women?
    a. European women could also divorce their husbands and determine whom they would marry.
    b. European women in rural areas were also raised to do the same chores as European men.
    c. European women were also raised to take control when men were engaged in long military campaigns.
    d. European women in urban areas also controlled much of the regional commerce.
    e. Elite European women also had a traditional role as the main advisers to their ruling husbands.

3. Refer to the painting on page 515 of your textbook. What were the most important features of Italian city-states, as depicted in the painting of Florence?
    a. The city walls indicate that city-states were independent of the power of regional states.
    b. Due to increased urbanization, city-states were outgrowing their original boundaries.
    c. City-states were heavily under the influence of the Catholic church.
    d. City-states depended on agriculture and fishing more than crafts for prosperity.
    e. The roles of urban women in city commerce were as important as those of urban men.

Primary Source Questions

1. **Examine the manuscript illustrations, Genoese bankers on page 518 and cathedral schools on page 523 of your textbook.**
    a. Both of these illustrations demonstrate growth in European trade and education. What is the point of view of the illustrator?
    b. Are the activities of the people readily apparent?
    c. Describe precisely what you see.
    d. Describe the style.

2. **Read *Sources from the Past: Francesco Balducci Pegolotti on Trade between Europe and China* on page 519 of your textbook.**
    a. What is the point of view?
    b. What areas of foreign trade and travel does Pegolotti address?
    c. What method does he describe at the end that is not available in Europe yet?
    d. What other viewpoints would help you assess European and Chinese trade?

Chapter Multiple Choice Answers

1. **d:** Pope Gregory VII excommunicated Henry IV but rescinded it when Henry had done penance. (p. 512)

2. **b:** Both Hugh Capet and Duke William of Normandy established a strong centralized government. (pp. 512–513)

3. **e:** The Roman Catholic papacy provided a strong central government in the Papal States. (p. 514)

4. **a:** It is an increase in agricultural yield that leads to improved health for all. (p. 517)

5. **e:** The nobility relinquished control of cities so all townspeople benefited from a charter. (p. 521)

6. **d:** Medieval women gained equal status with men in the world of trade and commerce. (p. 522)

7. **c:** Everyone gained from increased trade whether they lived in a town and provided goods or whether they lived in the country and occasionally purchased new goods. (p. 517)

8. **a:** Scandanavian monarchs adopted Christianity and sought conversion among their population. (p. 530)

9. **c:** In Sicily, there was more interest in military conquest and military matters are always political. (p. 531)

10. **e:** The crusades exposed European soldiers to new goods, ideas, and crafts so that Europe came back into direct contact with Asia and the Middle East. (p. 534)

Comprehensive Multiple Choice Answers

1. **d:** The only imperial efforts on the part of Europeans were those in the Holy Roman Empire but just as they were on the cusp of true unification, the emperors vied with the power of the church and lost so they ceded power to other Germanic rulers. Then, the efforts of talented leaders such as Hugh Capet and William of Normandy solidified centralized rule in small regions of western Europe where power was by and large balanced between regional states. Furthermore, Italian city-states had strong leaders who ensured their success. (pp. 510, 512)

2. **d:** Few European women were able to serve as official advisers but in cities, women took on many of the same professions as men and were essential to commerce. The Catholic church did not allow divorce except in extraordinary cases among elite marriages and rural women were relegated to the care of house, children, and smaller livestock. European women did have to take over male responsibilities during the long periods of warfare but they were not raised with that in mind. (p. 522)

3. **b:** The city has outgrown its walls as seen in the clusters of houses outside the walls at the bottom right and left side of the painting. Although Florence was independent, there is nothing in the painting that indicates that. Likewise, the appearance of several churches cannot lead to any conclusions about the church's power in the city. The absence of fields and evidence of fishing does not indicate that crafts were dominant although they probably were. And, since there are no women in the painting, it is impossible to tell what women in Florence did. (p. 515)

Primary Source Answers

1. The manuscript illustrator would have been an educated person but he was a craftsman rather than a scholar. The manuscripts would have been hand-copied and very expensive so it would only be available to wealthy families. European manuscripts often depicted regular life so there is much to be gained from examining them closely. The banking activity is apparent because one can see the bags of coins on the table in the upper picture being taken out of the large chest. In the bottom panel, it is evident that people are settling accounts in some way. One could identify the other illustration as a classroom by the rows of people reading books and listening to the teacher. If you look carefully, there is at least one typical and amusing sleeper during the lecture. As noted in the caption, this is not at all different from some of your classrooms. However, it also could be a church when you notice the pulpit and the gothic windows in the background. Therefore, the most obvious answer is that it is one of the cathedral schools. One can see the status of European women from these pictures. In the banking illustration, you can see how women are well-represented in business as well as men but that is not as true of the educational illustration. But there appears to be at least one woman with a headcovering in the first row. The style is colorful and the figures are somewhat realistic. If you notice how crowded they are, you realize that they have to take up only a small square in a manuscript so the perspective is not accurate. Another aspect that ties them to a manuscript is the decorative edges with pillars that frame the illustration. (pp. 518, 523)

2. Pegolotti was an Italian banker who must be trying to encourage trade with Asia. Although he has never made the journey himself, he is encouraging and matter of fact about it. He addresses personnel issues, concerns about the goods should a merchant die, the cost of the trip, and very specific instructions on what should be traded and used for money at different way stations. Of course, at the end, he also describes the paper money system used in China. As part of a document-based question, you will need to refer to some additional documents that might validate or invalidate the views already presented. In this case, it would be good to have the additional descriptions from European traders who, unlike Pergolotti, had made the journey, or the views of central Asian traders along the route or Chinese traders who had also worked along the silk roads. (p. 519)

CHAPTER 21

WORLDS APART: THE AMERICAS AND OCEANIA

Before you get started: This would be a great chapter for a graphic organizer: charts, *x-y* graphs, Venn diagrams . . . you choose. Two-thirds of this chapter deals with the Aztecs and the Incas, and those two Amerindian empires should demand most of your attention.

Four pages at the end of this chapter discuss Oceania, and there could be a few multiple choice questions about the region on the national exam. The essay portions of the national exam do not address Oceania until the next period, 1450–1750. Be sure to return to these four pages for thorough review before you start Chapter 23. For now, concentrate on the Aztecs and Incas; use that graphic organizer.

STATES AND EMPIRES IN MESOAMERICA AND NORTH AMERICA

The peoples of North and South America, who had only fleeting contact with Asia, Africa, and Europe during the period 1000–1500 C.E., did develop similar empires of highly structured governments, distinctive cultural and religious traditions, and elaborate trade networks. The indigenous peoples of Australia and the Pacific Islands built **self-sufficient societies** and tended to their own needs.

The Toltecs and the Mexica
(Themes: Patterns of Interaction, Trade, War)

The **Toltecs** emerged at the end of the troubled ninth and early tenth centuries as the dominant culture in much of central Mexico. Their capital city, **Tula**, grew to support a population of more than 60,000, due to irrigation from the nearby river which allowed the Toltecs to grow crops of beans, maize, peppers, tomatoes, chilies, and cotton. Their large army helped the Toltecs build a **compact regional empire** supported by subject people and their tribute. Trade networks, which extended to the Gulf of Mexico coast, supplied the Toltecs with luxury goods from across Mesoamerica. The Toltec empire was at its height from 950–1150, but by 1175, they could no longer suppress civil strife between ethnic groups nor could they defend against the nomadic invaders from northwest Mexico.

The **Mexica,** often referred to as the **Aztecs,** arrived in central Mexico about the middle of the thirteenth century. Known as "disorderly" for kidnapping women and seizing lands already cultivated by other groups, the Mexica seemed constantly on the move, as their neighbors quickly grew tired of their disruptions. About 1345, the Mexica settled on a marshy region of **Lake Texcoco** and founded their capital city, **Tenochtitlan.** The site, which offered ample water and abundant wildlife, allowed the Mexica to develop an extremely productive system of agriculture based on raised, floating gardens known as **chinampas.** Good farmers could produce up to seven crops per year of maize, beans, squash, tomatoes, peppers, and chilies from their gardens of rich, lake-bottom muck.

By the early 1400s, the Mexica, under the leadership of Itzcoatl and then **Moctezuma**, began a series of ambitious military campaigns adding portions of southwestern Mexico, then the Gulf coast regions, and finally the high plateaus of central Mexico to their imperial realm. Forming an alliance with two other expansionist allies, the Mexica came to dominate most of Mesoamerica.

The motivation for this expansion was tribute; food crops, textiles, jewelry, obsidian knives, cacao, and rubber balls flowed into the capital for use by the elites or as items for trade outside the region which in turn brought luxuries like translucent jade, emeralds, jaguar skins, and sea shells into the hands of Aztec elites.

Surprisingly, there was no elaborate bureaucracy to administer the Aztec realm. Instead, the Mexica and their allies simply conquered, demanded tribute, and left the managing of local government in local hands. Further, they had no need for a standing army; instead, they simply assembled forces as needed and their reputation for fierceness kept most subject people in line.

Mexica Society
(Theme: Social and Gender Structures)

Mexica society was rigidly **hierarchical** and **patriarchal**. The most elite social group were accomplished warriors who enjoyed great material wealth and fulfilled positions of leadership as their council selected the Mexica ruler, discussed public issues, and filled government positions. A priestly class also ranked among the Mexica elite. These men received a special education in ritual and calendrical lore and presided over religious ceremonies the Mexica viewed as crucial to continuation of the world. On occasion members of this group would become Mexica rulers as in the case of Motecuzoma II. Artisans who worked with gold, silver, cotton textiles, or feathers enjoyed a place of prestige in Mexica society as their work supplied the luxury goods consumed by the elite. Merchants who specialized in long-distance trade were in a prestigious but precarious spot, as they supplied the much-admired luxury goods and even foreign political and military intelligence, but also were constantly suspected of being greedy and tricky. Most Mexica were commoners who lived in hamlets farming the chinampas and other lands allotted to their families by the **calpulli,** organized community groups. The calpulli, which began as ancestor-based groups, evolved into location-based groups which organized their own affairs and allocated land to individual families. In addition to their own calpulli-distributed land, the commoners also worked land for the aristocrats and contributed labor to public building projects such as temples, palaces, roads, and irrigation systems; commoners were also responsible for producing and delivering tribute to the aristocrats. Mexica society also had a significant slave population, most of whom were Mexica, either sold by their families out of financial need or as a result of their own criminal behavior; most slaves were not foreigners.

Though women played little public role in a society so dominated by warriors and military value, they did play significant roles in their families and in their society as the mothers of warriors. Almost all Mexica women married, as tradition taught that a woman's value was first as a mother of warriors and that bearing of children was equivalent to capturing an enemy in battle. Death in childbirth was celebrated as a death on the battlefield.

Mexica Religion
(Themes: Cultural and Religious Developments)

Mexica tradition was built on the foundations of earlier Mesoamerican traditions such as speaking **Nahutal**, adapting the Mayan calendar, and embracing the ball game. Their gods emerged from the traditional Mesoamerican pantheon and included Tezcatlipoca, the giver and taker of life, and Quetzalcoatl, the supporter of the arts, crafts, and agriculture. The gods were believed to have shed their blood to provide life-giving moisture for the earth to ensure continued fertility. Ritualized bloodletting was an integral part of Mexica religious practice. Human sacrifice was seen as essential to the world's survival. When the Mexica warriors adopted Huitzilopochtli as their patron god in the early fourteenth century, the amount of humans sacrificed increased dramatically, as did the Mexica's military victories. The blood of the sacrificed criminals, prisoners of war, or people given in tribute was believed to sustain the sun, secure needed moisture, and perpetuate their society.

Peoples and Societies of the North
(Theme: Political Structures)

The peoples of North America mostly lived in hunting, gathering, and foraging societies which did not support large, dense populations, but they also built some large-scale agricultural societies. The Pueblo and Navajo peoples in the North American southwest built an agricultural society based on maize cultivation. The Iroquois built a complex society based on agriculture in the regions east of the Mississippi. Iroquois culture often included wooden longhouses and compounds surrounded by wooden palisades.

Women took responsibility for village life and men assumed the responsibilities for hunting, fishing, and war. **Mound-building people** in the eastern half of the modern United States built large cities such as the one whose remains are best seen outside St. Louis, Missouri today. Though these people left no written records, archaeological evidence suggests societies linked by trade and characterized by a range of social classes.

STATES AND EMPIRES IN SOUTH AMERICA

Since there was no tradition of writing in South America prior to the Spanish arrival, knowledge about those empires comes mostly from archaeological evidence and from information recorded by Spanish conquerors. Complex societies had existed there since c. 1000 B.C.E.; by 1000 C.E. secular governments were becoming increasingly powerful, and by the end of the fifteenth century, the Incas built the largest empire South America had ever seen.

The Coming of the Incas
(Theme: Patterns of Interaction and Changes and Continuities)

After the demise of the Chavin society in the fourth century B.C.E. and Moche society in the ninth century C.E., a series of small, regional states emerged in Andean South America. The kingdom of Chuchito, which dominated the border region between modern Bolivia and Peru, relied on the terraced production of potatoes and the herding of llamas and alpacas for food and trade items necessary to survive in the high Andes. The kingdom of Chimor or Chimu emerged on the Peruvian coast in the tenth century. Using irrigation networks to tap Andean water, the Chimu and its capital Chanchan emerged as a thriving agricultural society built on abundant maize and sweet potatoes. In the mid-fifteenth century, both the Chuchito and Chimu societies fell under the domination of the Incas who began to expand their realm outside their Lake Titicaca settlements. By the late fifteenth century, the Inca empire stretched from the Pacific to the limits of the Amazon rainforest and from modern Ecuador to Argentina, with a population of more than eleven million people.

Cuzco was the administrative, religious, and ceremonial capital of the empire. Inca royalty, nobility, high priests, and hostages from the conquered people lived in handsome red stone buildings in this city of nearly 300,000. A road system of nearly 10,000 miles tied Cuzco to the rest of the empire and Inca traditions spread throughout the vast empire which they ruled by shrewd use of their power. They encouraged obedience of conquered peoples by using them in their armies and by posting them to bureaucratic positions. They took hostages from the ruling classes and sent their own loyal subjects to colonize difficult regions and they sometimes forced rebelling peoples to relocate in distant parts of their empire. Inca bureaucrats kept detailed records using a mnemonic device called **quipu** to record statistical information such as population, tax rolls and receipts, labor services, and to remember historical information relating to rulers and their deeds.

Inca Society and Religion
(Themes: Social Structures and Cultural and Religious Developments)

The main classes in Inca society were the rulers, aristocrats, priests, and peasants; there was no large merchant class as the Inca government did not permit individuals to become independent merchants. Individual artisans produced goods for local consumption and a few produced specialized goods for the ruling and priestly classes, but goods were bartered on the local level only. In theory, the Inca chief ruler was an absolute and infallible deity descended from the sun, and he owned all the land, livestock, and property in his realm during his lifetime and even after death. The dead rulers, still considered powerful as they were believed to act as intermediaries between the dead and the living, were mummified, cared for, and brought out for ceremonial occasions and when the living Inca ruler needed their counsel. Aristocrats who made up the government bureaucracy wore fine clothes, consumed fine foods, and wore elaborate ear spools as symbols of their authority. Further, these aristocrats staffed the government bureaucracy which allocated the Inca ruler's land which the commoners cultivated on his behalf. Inca priests, who also came from aristocratic families, were responsible for overseeing religious rituals. Common Inca peasants lived in communities called *ayllu,* which consisted of several families who lived together sharing land, tools, animals, crops, and work. Peasants worked together on state lands and the production from these lands went to support the ruling, aristocratic, and priestly classes. The rest of the surplus went into government-held storehouses for distribution during famine and to those people incapable of supporting themselves. Men supplied tribute through their labor and women supplied tribute in the form of textiles, pottery, and jewelry.

THE SOCIETIES OF OCEANIA

The peoples of Oceania built flourishing societies of their own, creating trade networks between hunting and gathering societies.

The Nomadic Foragers of Australia
(Themes: Changes and Continuities and Cultural and Religious Developments)

Life for the aboriginal peoples of Australia changed little after they learned how to exploit the continent's varied resources. Despite knowledge of food cultivated in other lands, they never developed agriculture; instead they relied on their land's regional bounty and on the exchange of surplus foods as they met other mobile and nomadic people during their seasonal migration. Trade goods, like pearly oyster shells, have been found more than one thousand miles inland, having been passed from one group to another rather than being transported by a single individual. Stone axe heads, spears, boomerangs, furs, skins, and fibers were commonly traded items from the interior, and stone clubs, decorative trinkets, exotic plants, and highly prized iron axes indicate that goods entered Australia from New Guinea and the islands of southeast Asia.

Religious traditions among aboriginal people were local and centered on geological features and continuing supplies of plants, animals, and water. These ideas and practices did not spread much beyond the regions inhabited by individual societies.

The Development of Pacific Island Societies
(Themes: Trade, Demographics, Patterns of Interaction, and Social, Religious, and Political Structures)

By 1000 C.E., a surging population prompted social and political development in Pacific Island societies. Because of their proximity, mariners linked island societies in the central and western Pacific regions to develop trade networks for useful and exotic goods as well as foodstuffs like yams. Further, trade and intermarriage between residents of island groups helped to establish political and social relationships among islanders. Yet, because of the vast distances in the eastern Pacific Ocean, regular trade networks did not emerge. Occasional long voyages could have momentous results, as did Polynesian voyages to South America in the fifth century C.E. that introduced the sweet potato to the islands where it quickly became a prominent source of food, especially in New Zealand.

Population growth occurred as islanders built productive agricultural and fishing societies. The cultivation of yams, sweet potatoes, bananas, and other foods and the development of technologies like Hawaiian fishponds both stimulated and responded to rapid population growth. Dense population placed tremendous pressure on natural resources and human institutions. Conflicts like the ones on Easter Island in the early 1500s resulted in eventual disintegration of long-lived societies. Social classes became more stratified, and governments became more centralized. Restrictions on food consumption and on the wearing of particular feathers was part of this stratification of social and political powers. Gods of war and agriculture were common throughout the Pacific Islands, though individual islands and groups had their own deities as well. Structures known as **marae** were built with several terraced floors of rock or coral walls designating the boundaries of a sacred place. In Tonga and Samoa, temples made of timber with thatched roofs were places of worship, sacrifice, and communication with the gods. In eastern Polynesia, ceremonies took place on platforms in open-air courtyards. In Tahiti a step pyramid was constructed for such activities.

Finished the reading the chapter? Be sure you can . . .

- Describe and analyze the social, cultural, economic, and political patterns in the Amerindian world: Aztec and Inca.
- Explain the impact of Aztec and Inca migrations on demographics and the environment.
- Trace the growth and role of cities in the Aztec and Inca empires.
- Compare and contrast the Aztec and Inca empires. (Social hierarchy, religious ideals and practices, economic organization, and political institutions are logical categories to draw from this chapter.)

Chapter Multiple Choice Questions

1. Civil conflict and nomadic incursions are responsible for the fall of what regional empire by the end of the twelfth century?
   a. Toltecs
   b. Mexica
   c. Maya
   d. Oaxaca
   e. Tacuba

2. Why did the Mexica form an alliance with Texcoco and Tlacopan in the mid-fifteenth century?
   a. to avoid civil war and to provide a stronger front against the invading Spanish
   b. to build a military force strong enough to exact tribute from subject peoples
   c. to add another level of bureaucracy to their complex government structure
   d. to gain access to their supplies of rubber and cacao which the Aztecs highly valued
   e. to capture their persuasive merchants and gain access to valuable trade routes

3. Which of the following statements is FALSE regarding Mexica warriors?
   a. All males were viewed as potential warriors, even individuals of common birth.
   b. Warriors wore distinctive clothing and jewelry as a sign of their honors.
   c. Warriors ate rigid diets, severely limiting their intake to keep them hungry for war.
   d. Warriors served on councils to select Mexica rulers.
   e. Warriors received specialized instruction in warfare and military affairs.

4. Why did most Mexica women marry?
   a. In Mexica society, love was a value almost as significant as honor on the battlefield.
   b. In Mexica society, women were not allowed to participate in market or other public duties.
   c. In Mexica society, women would not achieve a glorious afterlife outside of marriage.
   d. In Mexica society, motherhood and homemaking were considered the ideals.
   e. In Mexica society, all of these statements were true.

5. The Mexica placed so much emphasis on human sacrifice because
   a. it was seen as necessary for their victories over the Toltecs and the Mayas.
   b. it was part of the Mayan calendar and ball game tradition which the Mexica adopted.
   c. their military successes in the fourteenth century convinced them of the power of Huitzilopochtli's favor.
   d. it helped them reduce their crime rate and keep control of their military prisoners.
   e. it stimulated their economy through people coming to the cities to attend the rituals.

6. In which of the following North American Indian cultures were women dominant in village domestic affairs?
   a. Pueblo
   b. Navajo
   c. Iroquois
   d. Cahokia
   e. Missouri

7. The Incan *ayllu* is similar to the Mexica *calpulli* in that
   a. both were the basic organizing units of rural society.
   b. both were the main religious tenet of the empires' faith.
   c. both were mnemonic devices used to keep government records.
   d. both were domesticated animals used for meat and wool.
   e. both were the priestly class believed to be responsible for continuity of life in each empire.

8. Why were the llamas and alpacas so important to the Inca?
   a. They served as useful pack animals in the high Andes.
   b. They provided wool for Inca textiles.
   c. They provided hides for leather products.
   d. Their dung could be used as fuel.
   e. All of the above.

9. Both the Chumu and the Chucuito were eclipsed by the rise of what empire in the mid-fifteenth century?
   a. Aztec
   b. Mexica
   c. Inca
   d. Maya
   e. Olmec

10. How were goods traded in aboriginal Australia c. 1000–1500 C.E.?
   a. Overland trade routes and corresponding sea channels much like the silk roads of Eurasia emerged over the centuries.
   b. A small but active class of merchants emerged who were willing to undertake the dangerous overland routes.
   c. Individuals carried small quantities of valuable trade goods from one side of the continent to the other as part of their regular seasonal migrations.
   d. Trade good passed from one aboriginal community to another until they came to rest in distant places.
   e. Polynesian merchants carried the valuable goods in their outrigger canoes from port to port along the Australian coast.

Comprehensive Multiple Choice Questions

1. One commonality in religious practice between the Mexica, the Shang of China, and the Archaic period in Egyptian history is that all three cultures practiced
   a. ritual bloodletting.
   b. human sacrifice.
   c. pyramid building.
   d. ethical monotheism.
   e. female footbinding.

2. Inca roads proved a powerful empire-building tool because
    a. they allowed Incan religious tradition to be easily spread in the empire through an active missionary movement.
    b. they allowed the Inca government to communicate easily with all parts of the empire and to send troops rapidly to problem spots in the empire.
    c. they allowed the merchant classes to travel quickly with goods to markets throughout the Andes.
    d. they made it easy for refugees to be moved from one location to another during times of famine or crisis.
    e. they made it possible for Inca mummies to be displayed throughout the empire and therefore to inspire belief in the supremacy of the Inca ruler.

3. What effect did geography have on the establishment of large kingdoms or empires in Oceania during the period 1000–1500?
    a. Ocean travel, or island hopping, made it easy for a powerful people to overcome their weaker neighbors.
    b. Religious tradition forbade the killing of innocent civilians in battle.
    c. The people of Easter Island came to dominate the eastern Pacific.
    d. Transportation and communication issues made it difficult to establish large centralized states in much of Oceania.
    e. Because there was abundant surplus agricultural production, there was little motivation for wars between island peoples.

Primary Source Questions

1. **Read *Sources from the Past: "Mexica Expectations of Boys and Girls"* on page 545 of your textbook.**
    a. What does the use of animal imagery at a young boy's birth suggest about Mexica culture?
    b. What do the midwife's words indicate about women's roles in Mexica culture?
    c. How might social class impact these expectations?

2. **Examine the quipu photograph on page 553 of your textbook.**
    a. In what ways is quipu well-suited for Inca culture?
    b. Why might the Incas have developed this method using these materials for recording communication?
    c. What parallels exist between quipu technology and modern communication means?

Chapter Multiple Choice Answers

1. **a:** The Toltecs were among the first of these highly compact regional empires located in central Mexico. Their inability to control the conflicting ethnic groups in their realm and pressure from outside nomadic forces from northwest Mexico account for their destruction in 1175. (p. 541)

2. **b:** The Aztecs built a hugely powerful empire through their ability to exact tribute and to inspire fear in their subject peoples. The alliance between the Mexica and their two neighboring allies made both goals possible. (p. 542)

3. **c:** Warriors ate the best foods including vanilla, cacao, and other luxury foods which were, along with elaborate clothing and body decorations, considered a sign of prestige and honor. (p. 544)

4. **d:** The goal of Mexica society was to produce fine warriors so women's roles through marriage, motherhood, and homemaking were highly valued. Love was not a prerequisite for marriage which remained, until very recently, an economic union. (p. 544)

Part IV: An Age of Cross-Cultural Interaction, 1000 to 1500 C.E.

5. **c:** Mexica warriors adopted Huitzilopochtli as their patron god in the mid-fourteenth century, just as their victories over their subjected neighbors began to mount. This occurrence persuaded them that blood sacrifice was necessary to keep the war god appeased. (p. 547)

6. **c:** The Iroquois nation built a complex agricultural society in which women were in charge of the village concerns and men took responsibility for affairs beyond the village. (p. 548)

7. **a:** Both the Mexica's *calpulli* and the Inca *ayllu* were the organizing structures of rural life. They both consisted of several family groups who cooperated to work and manage the land. (pp. 546, 554)

8. **e:** As the only large domesticated beasts in the Americas before the sixteenth century, these animals were an integral part of all aspects of Andean life. (p. 551)

9. **c:** Located in Andean South America, both the Chucuito and the Chimu built large agricultural-based societies until they fell under Inca domination in the mid-fifteenth century. (p. 552)

10. **d:** Peoples in Australia enjoyed access to a wide range of different foods and resources. These goods would be passed from one aboriginal community to another rather than travel with a single individual. (p. 556)

Comprehensive Multiple Choice Answers

1. **b:** Though never as common or as enduring as with the Mexica, during the Archaic period in Egypt and during the Shang Dynasty in China, human sacrifice was practiced in association with the ruler's burial. (pp. 14, 64, 547)

2. **b:** With a road system of nearly 10,000 miles and a system of corps of official runners, news and information could travel to all parts of the empire within days. Likewise, the Inca armies could use either the mountainous road or the Pacific road to reach any site of rebellion within a few days. (p. 553)

3. **d:** Though chiefs in places like Tonga and Hawai'i frequently launched campaigns to bring additional islands under their control, these attempts were usually unsuccessful as large distances and travel hazards made the creation of large centralized states difficult. (p. 559)

Primary Source Answers

1. The animal imagery in the midwife's words to the boy reflects several elements in Mexica culture. First, the assortment of animals mentioned—eagle, ocelot, spoonbill, toupial, and serpent—indicate the complexity of the animal world in the Mexica's land. Second, the animals listed are powerful and beautiful mammals, birds, and reptiles; the inference is that the boy will grow to possess these attributes. The expectation is that the boy will grow up to be someone of great responsibility and honor, beyond the boundaries of his home which is "only the place of arrival," into a more lofty, honorable domain, perhaps even to die in battle, which is the desirable "flowered death."

In direct contrast, expectations for girls are centered only on the hearth and home. Indeed, the boy is supposed to think of home as only a place of arrival, but the girl is to see herself as the home, as the "banked fire" or "the hearth stones," neither of which is easily moved. The expectation is that though this place will require hard work, it is her duty to perform the tasks of grinding, spinning, and weaving which sustain the home.

These words were spoken at the birth of aristocratic children. One wonders to what degree these words might apply to roles for men and women in other Mexica social classes. Though the expecta-

186

tion was that men of common birth might improve their social standing by distinguishing themselves on the battlefield, the reality was that this happened infrequently. Women born into merchant families might become prominent in the marketplace and their home duties may have been reduced through that economic role. Finally, since this record comes through the records of a Spanish Franciscan missionary, one does have to consider the degree to which his recording of the words was influenced by his perceptions and by what women, especially, were willing to share with him.
(p. 545)

2. Inca culture was based on administering a vast, complex empire which included more than eleven million people in widely scattered communities set in some of the harshest terrain on earth. The need to keep accurate, up-to-date records on resources, landholdings, population, labor service, and taxes was essential for the survival of the Inca empire. Therefore, quipu had to be complicated enough to require education and training which would keep the information out of the hands of usurpers; and it had to be clear, so the information would not be misunderstood and wrong actions or responses initiated. Quipu also had to be portable for the set of runners who used the Inca's extensive road system. Clay tablets, fragile papyrus, or other cumbersome textiles could not be transported with the ease or speed of the quipu and certainly were not as durable as the lightweight, flexible, tough knotted cords.

It is interesting to look for parallels between quipu and modern communication technology. Certainly, the reliance on mathematics and codes are obvious parallels. The need for the codes to be understood by only an educated few seems true also, although most people today can understand and use electronic communication at an elemental level without a great deal of training; still, the complexities of modern communication are only fully understood by an elite few. The mobility of the information between the two systems seems parallel as does the ability of the communication to contain information embedded within other information. The Incas relied heavily on "data" to make their decisions, as do governments, corporations, institutions, and sometimes individuals today. (p. 553)

CHAPTER 22

REACHING OUT: CROSS-CULTURAL INTERACTIONS

Before you get started: One of the most important themes in AP World History is the cross-cultural connections made by peoples. At the turn of the first millennium, the Asian trade routes had established connections between the Mediterranean world and Asia. In the fourteenth and fifteenth centuries, many of the trade routes remained the same but activity had increased enormously. Terminus points became different political entities, trade routes were protected by large empires like the Mongols, and improvements in marine technology made the seas safer for travelers. Technology, religions, and diseases also traveled the trade routes, bringing salvation and chaos. From a European viewpoint, this period is known as the age of exploration. In world history, we make note of other travelers and the conditions that allowed the Europeans access around the world.

LONG-DISTANCE TRADE AND TRAVEL

For the first five hundred years of the second millennium, people traveled to establish diplomatic relationships, to spread religion, and to procure valuable market goods.

Patterns of Long-Distance Trade
(Theme: Trade)

Traders in the Eurasian world depended upon two primary routes, the **silk roads** across central Asia and the **sea lanes** of the Indian Ocean with access into the South China Sea. There was also the ocean trade along the Swahili coastline and the Sahara trade in west Africa. The established routes provided the eastern hemisphere with an increasingly regular level of connection. Generally, fine products could travel the silk roads, but items that were heavy such as building materials were transported in ships.

The trade cities along these routes prospered with large communities of foreigners filling neighborhoods. Thriving port cities had strategic locations, guarded their entries, and encouraged trade with lower fees and taxes, like **Melaka** between the Indian Ocean and the South China Sea. By the end of the fifteenth century, Melaka had fifty thousand people speaking more than eighty different languages. On land, the silk road cities grew accustomed to the protection of the Mongols after the thirteenth century and also encouraged trade through lower fees.

The best-known traveler along the Eurasian route was the Venetian trader **Marco Polo.** His father and uncle had already visited China when they took seventeen-year-old Marco with them in 1271. Khubilai Khan encouraged the young man and supported his mercantile interests as well as found him useful for diplomatic missions. All in all, Marco Polo stayed for seventeen years before returning by way of the Indian Ocean routes. When Marco Polo was captured and imprisoned in Genoa, he wrote down his tales. Although some parts of his story are fanciful fiction, there are many accurate depictions of life in the east with an emphasis on trade that sounded so attractive that other Europeans soon traveled the routes.

Political and Diplomatic Travel
(Themes: Political Structures and Patterns of Interaction)

Contact between the Mongols and Europeans intensified after the Mongols attacked the Islamic regions. The Pope began to contemplate an alliance between the Mongols and the Europeans to defeat the Muslims, so he sent envoys to suggest the idea to the Mongols who rejected it and proposed instead that the Europeans surrender immediately. This first round of communications did not result in an alliance, but several years later the ilkhanate sent **Rabban Sauma, a Nestorian Christian priest**, to propose the same type of alliance for the same reason. Rabban Sauma proved to be a charming guest in the courts of France and England but nothing came of this overture either. The point became moot once the next ilkhan converted to Islam.

With the increasing importance of the *sharia* in Muslim lands, it became necessary for legal scholars to visit lands that had converted. Many Islamic intellectuals proceeded to move freely through sub-Saharan Africa, the Swahili states, and into northern India. Among these was the astounding **Ibn Battuta**, arguably the most traveled man in multiple centuries. Born in Morocco, Ibn Battuta traveled and lived at the ends of the trade routes in China, India, and Africa. A *qadi* whose journals are a model of cultural observations, he was a useful adviser on Muslim law and tradition wherever he went. Reread the introduction to the chapter to review his travels.

Missionary Campaigns
(Theme: Religious Developments)

Once again, the **sufi missionaries** proved to be the primary means of Islamic conversion along the trade routes. Their tolerant attitude and fervent devotion impressed foreigners. But **Roman Catholic missionaries** began to travel into Asia as well. Missionaries had accompanied the crusaders and where the Europeans maintained a presence in the Baltics, Spain, Sicily, and the Balkans, the Christian church was secure. Ambitious missionaries even attempted to convert the Mongols and Chinese. One of the best known was John of Montecorvino, a Franciscan who arrived in China during the Mongol rule. He actively sought converts by translating parts of the Bible into Turkish which was the Mongol court language, and he built several churches in China. He may have converted several thousand but, by and large, Roman Catholicism was not of much interest to the Chinese or the Mongols. The church authorities continued to send missionaries but the results were limited in a region that already had sophisticated belief systems.

Long-Distance Travel and Cross-Cultural Exchanges
(Themes: Trade and Technology)

Many cultural ideas passed along the trade routes including arts, philosophy, and scientific knowledge. For example, the troubadours of western Europe borrowed the songs of Muslim performers as they developed their profession. European scientists sought information from their Jewish and Muslim counterparts. Agricultural advances and technology were exchanged profusely during the period between 1000 and 1500. Navigational instruments such as the **Chinese magnetic compass** facilitated steering during long sea voyages. Also, **Chinese gunpowder technology** spread by the Mongols through southwest Asia into Europe. By the mid-thirteenth century, Europeans were using gunpowder rockets that could blow holes in defensive walls.

Asian crops like rice and citrus fruits were introduced to new regions of Europe and sub-Saharan Africa. Cotton was introduced to west Africa and became the leading textile in that region by 1500. Muslims began **large-scale sugarcane production** in the eastern Mediterranean and, once the European crusaders had tasted sugar crystals, they introduced it to Europe to augment honey and fruits as sweeteners. The sugar plantations that were organized on Mediterranean islands required **slave labor** which increased the demand for Muslim war captives and black Africans.

The culture and spread of new food crops enriched diets and caused population growth while cotton production increased the potential of economic development. Improvements in navigation and weapons changed warfare forever.

CRISIS AND RECOVERY

Travelers exchanged not only goods, crops, and ideas but also pathogens. During the fourteenth century, bubonic plague epidemics ravaged the societies along the silk roads and throughout north Africa and

Europe as well. It struck intermittently into the seventeenth century but without the devastating effects of the initial phase.

Bubonic Plague
(Theme: Demographics)

About 1300 C.E., the earth began to cool down into a **little ice age** that made European lives considerably more miserable and even caused the Scandinavians to retreat from their colonies in Greenland. Shorter growing seasons left the population on the edge of starvation when the plague struck.

It is presumed that the **bubonic plague** began in southwestern China where it was picked up by fleas during transmission between rodents in whom the plague was endemic. As the rodent populations declined, the fleas moved on to other hosts and spread the disease to humans. By 1331, an outbreak had killed 90 percent of one Chinese province and continued to spread into all parts of China. The Mongols and travelers brought it with them on the silk roads where it thrived in oases with their great number of available human and animal hosts. By 1346, it had reached the Black Sea and within two years, outbreaks were reported in most European countries.

The symptoms were horrendous: infected lymph nodes in the neck, armpit, and groin areas that would become open purple and black sores as internal hemorrhaging occurred. These "buboes" were the foundation for the European references to **"The Black Death."** Typically, the disease killed up to 70 percent of its victims and could wipe out smaller communities. After the enormous population drop, the birth rate would increase and the disease would then return to claim new victims.

Some areas were spared the worst epidemics, such as Scandinavia which proved too cold to sustain the requisite rodent and flea populations. Also, India and sub-Saharan Africa were largely spared. In the most hard-hit areas, such as China and Europe, there were enormous **population declines.** China had been at eighty-five million but it dropped to seventy-five million in a matter of seventy years. Seventy-nine million Europeans were reduced to sixty million in one hundred years. But both regions recovered and surpassed those initial numbers within a century. Islamic societies suffered terrible losses as well but failed to recover as fast as Europe and China.

The plague took a huge economic and social toll. The epidemics spared no class of citizen which led to **labor shortages** in most regions. Social unrest followed as people looked for work. European cities attempted to keep their craftsmen while rural workers had their freedoms restricted. The growing unhappiness led to a number of **peasant and worker rebellions** that challenged governments and led to further loss of life. Although the epidemics disappeared after the seventeenth century, the plague persisted into the twentieth century and is now controlled by antibiotics.

Recovery in China: The Ming Dynasty
(Themes: Political, Economic, and Cultural Developments)

The Yuan dynasty was weakened so much by fiscal problems and political infighting that by the middle of the fourteenth century, the plague pushed the Chinese into active rebellion. The Mongols departed for the steppes en masse, leaving China in the hands of a Buddhist named **Hongwu.** He proclaimed the **Ming ("brilliant") dynasty** and immediately set out to eliminate Mongol influences and regain China's traditions. He reestablished the Confucian examination system and centralized Chinese government more than ever when he eliminated the position of chief minister so he could rule the country closely and directly. The Ming demanded absolute obedience to central authority and relied on government emissaries known as *mandarins* sent out to direct local administrations. Their other principal government workers were eunuchs since they could not have families and so could not build a power base. In fact, the Ming used **eunuchs** more extensively than any other dynasty had. The strong central government of the Ming persisted almost five hundred years beyond their time in power because the Manchu or Qing dynasty employed the same techniques until their fall in 1911.

Prosperity was a hallmark of the early Ming. The Ming encouraged economic development by conscripting laborers to rebuild irrigation systems and promoted the manufacture of porcelain, lacquerware, silk, and cotton. Agriculture flourished and Chinese merchants enlarged their export trade even though the Ming did not sponsor foreign trade. In addition to the return of a healthy Chinese economy, the Ming promoted Chinese cultural traditions. Of particular note was the emperor **Yongle's encyclopedia** which attempted to anthologize every great Chinese classic of history, philosophy, and literature into twenty-three thousand manuscripts.

Recovery in Western Europe: State Building
(Theme: Political Structures)

Not surprisingly, recovery in Europe took the form of regional states rather than a centralized government. The problems of the fourteenth century initially increased with the continual clashes between the French and English in the **Hundred Years War.** The Holy Roman Empire survived in name but all power was relegated to the states and the Italian city-states. Catholic Spain was able to hold onto Muslim Granada.

By the late fifteenth century, the states began to develop into powerful monarchies driven by new taxes and **standing armies.** State-building began in the Italian states and moved north into France and England. Although England did not have a standing army, both monarchies taxed their populations enormously and were able to retain power over the nobility. But it was in Spain that the monarchies became most powerful. In 1469, **Fernando of Aragon** and **Isabel of Castile** united their kingdoms. Using the sales tax, they built the most powerful standing army in Europe. This army completed the *reconquista* by conquering Granada and they also helped defend southern Italy and soon held that state as well. Spain then turned its attention to the Asian markets.

Competition between European states became so intense that numerous small wars broke out which served to promote new military technologies. These innovations would serve the Europeans well as they launched their global explorations.

Recovery in Western Europe: The Renaissance
(Themes: Intellectual and Cultural Development)

At the same time, the Europeans experienced a cultural flowering that drew inspiration from the Romans and Greeks. **Renaissance** or "rebirth" occurred in art, architecture, scholarship, and literature, all of which heightened the sophistication of urban life.

The Italian city-states led the way again when they began to sponsor art and architecture with their enormous profits from trade. Artists began to study the human form and make more realistic representations, as the Greeks and Romans had. **Leonardo da Vinci** and Masaccio revived the three-point perspective in two-dimensional art while sculptors like Michelangelo sculpted humans into natural poses with an emphasis on the natural action of human muscles. Architects like **Brunelleschi** in Florence designed buildings in simple classical forms and brought back magnificent domes.

Scholars and literary figures known as *humanists* studied philosophy, history, and literature in an attempt to simplify their writing styles from the convoluted efforts of medieval writers. Humanists were generally not secular thinkers but deeply committed Christians like **Erasmus of Rotterdam.** Petrarch, an Italian scholar, unearthed hundreds of classical texts across Europe and offered them to other scholars. With the input of Roman philosophers, humanists began to contemplate a view of moral, secular life that depended upon civic duties. Thus it was fundamentally good for devout Christians to live an honorable, secular life rather than a cloistered religious life.

As Europe became exposed to other cultures, its art began to depict foreign goods such as silk garments, lacquerware, new fruits, and exotic animals and peoples. Wealthy patrons wanted to show their sophistication with their choice of foreign depictions so artists were kept busy producing paintings and sculptures for their homes. Likewise, intellectuals incorporated foreign ideas into their works. Italian scholar Pico della Mirandola used ideas from Islam, Zoroastrianism, and Judaism as well as mystical traditions in his thoughtful work on the place of humans in the cosmos. The interest in foreign culture also piqued the interests of European explorers.

EXPLORATION AND COLONIZATION

China and Europe, the two societies at the end of the trade routes that suffered terribly from the plague, worked hard to reconnect after their relatively swift recoveries. The early Ming accommodated traders and for a brief period sponsored a series of voyages into the Indian Ocean. Meanwhile, European rulers began to sponsor voyages to the southern Atlantic as a route to the riches of Asia. By the end of the fifteenth century, Europeans had opened sea lanes to India and visited the Americas as well.

The Chinese Reconnaissance of the Indian Ocean
(Themes: Trade and Diplomacy)

The Ming Chinese wanted trade but only tolerated foreigners in designated communities along the southeast coast like Guangzhou and Quanzhou. But the early Ming emperors also refurbished the Song dynasty navies and allowed Chinese merchants to trade overseas. Furthermore, the Emperor Yongle organized expeditions to the Indian Ocean basin in an effort to control Chinese trade and demonstrate the power of China to foreign nations.

In 1405, the first huge Chinese fleet sailed into the Indian Ocean. The leader of the expeditions was a Muslim eunuch from Yunnan province in southwestern China, the admiral **Zheng He.** He commanded seven voyages over thirty years that sailed as far away as Swahili ports on the African coastline and into the Persian Gulf. The size of the **expedition fleets** was unimaginably huge with hundreds of vessels and tens of thousands of troops. Chinese shipyards built mammoth "**treasure ships**" that could hold five hundred men to bring back foreign goods. The voyagers carried Chinese gift items but brought back numerous presents and tribute in the form of exotic goods, including zebras and giraffes. The Chinese generally overwhelmed their hosts with the size of the fleet and its army so that military action was rare. Zheng He was an astute diplomat who paid respect to local traditions but employed violence when necessary such as when they suppressed the southeast Asian pirate trade.

Just when China had established its presence in the Indian Ocean, the Ming emperors withdrew support for the endeavor. Possibly as a result of the underlying rivalry between the eunuchs and Confucian advisers, the Ming dynasty made the decision to put their resources toward agriculture instead. There was also a military threat from the northwest that required troops and resources. Thus in 1433, Chinese naval interests abruptly stopped. While Chinese merchants continued to trade in the South China Sea, the navigational maps for the expeditions were destroyed, the huge ships fell apart, and the knowledge of the technology to build such a fleet disappeared.

European Exploration in the Atlantic and Indian Oceans
(Theme: Trade)

As the Chinese fleets explored the Indian Ocean, Europeans began to explore the western coast of Africa in an effort to spread Christianity and gain profit from trade. The **Portuguese** were among the earliest adventurers sponsored by a state. A weak country with rocky soil, Portugal had a seafaring tradition in the northern Atlantic but it took the interest of Prince Henry the Navigator to push the Portuguese into the south Atlantic.

The Portuguese discovered and colonized the Madeiras and Azores as well as other Atlantic islands that had good soil and a mild climate conducive to agriculture. Soon, the Portuguese began to grow **sugarcane** on the islands with the help of Italian investors. As in the eastern Mediterranean, plantations required a large labor source that was provided by Portuguese traders in the form of African slaves purchased with guns, textiles, and other manufactured items. As the Portuguese thrust further south along the west African coastline, the need for slaves increased which formed the foundation of the **Atlantic slave trade** that would transport over twelve million slaves to the Americas in the next four centuries.

Other Portuguese sailors sought a way to profit from the Asian trade by avoiding the Italian and Muslim control of the trade in the Mediterranean. Their efforts to find a sea lane to India proved successful when **Bartolomeu Dias** found his way around the **Cape of Good Hope** in 1488. By 1498, Vasco da Gama had reached Calicut in India, paving the way for direct trade with Asian merchants. The Portuguese, armed with cannons, dominated the trade between Europe and Asia for the next century.

Meanwhile, the Italian mariner **Christopher Columbus** became convinced that sailing west would be a better way to reach the Asian markets. Rejected by the Portuguese monarchs, he gained the support of Ferdinand and Isabel of Spain and in 1492, his small fleet reached the islands off the American continent. Over three more voyages, Columbus remained convinced that he had found Asia but by the end of the fifteenth century other mariners recognized the land as a new continent.

Finished reading the chapter? Be sure you can . . .

- Identify the routes, purpose, and activities of Marco Polo, Rabban Sauma, and Ibn Battuta.
- Analyze the role of cities along the trade routes.
- Describe diplomatic and religious missions along the trade routes of Eurasia.
- Describe technological improvements that aided travel.
- Identify the demographic changes that occurred as a result of the bubonic plague.
- List the social and economic consequences of the bubonic plague.
- Compare the exploration efforts of the Europeans with those of the Chinese.

Chapter Multiple Choice Questions

1. Which of the following would be the best description of foreign merchants in trade cities?
    a. They rarely lived in the cities but stayed in oases near large cities.
    b. They never intermarried but lived separately with their own families.
    c. They formed their own neighborhoods outside the city walls.
    d. They were completely integrated into neighborhoods and societies.
    e. They formed their own neighborhoods but could intermarry with local peoples.

2. Other than Christianity, what did Marco Polo and Rabban Sauma have in common?
    a. They had a religious purpose to their travel.
    b. They were employed by Mongols.
    c. They were committed to commerce and profit.
    d. They came from the Middle East.
    e. They only traveled along the silk roads.

3. What primary purpose did Ibn Battuta serve for his Islamic hosts?
    a. He brought the traditions of other cultures to new places.
    b. He was primarily a trader so he was welcomed enthusiastically.
    c. As a foreign visitor, he proved to be an exotic attraction.
    d. He was a Muslim authority who could interpret Muslim law.
    e. He was a keen observer and a fine diplomat.

4. The compass was a technology derived from which region?
    a. China
    b. Central Asia
    c. India
    d. the Middle East
    e. Greece

5. What earlier change made the plague such a potent destructive force?
    a. Rural populations had grown too large due to good crop seasons.
    b. The climate changed sharply downward leading to poor crop seasons.
    c. Trade became much more prevalent along the land than the sea trade routes.
    d. Plague victims moved eastward escaping the Mongol invasions.
    e. Urban populations had less resistance due to the prevalence of other diseases.

6. The plague caused many social and economic disruptions. Which of the following did NOT occur?
    a. civil unrest
    b. demographic disruptions
    c. labor shortages
    d. structural changes in social classes
    e. political changes

7. What did the first Ming emperor do to reestablish Chinese rule?
    a. He deemphasized the power of the merchants.
    b. He reinstituted Confucian systems of governance.
    c. He eliminated taxes on farmers.
    d. He took on Daoist advisers in government.
    e. He promoted Buddhism and the establishment of monasteries.

8. Europe recovered quickly from the plague and began a period of
    a. increased trade.
    b. centralized government.
    c. stronger nation-states.
    d. increased urbanization.
    e. intensified religiosity.

9. Cultural recovery in Europe was largely based on a return to older traditions. What did the Europeans find appealing about classical philosophy?
    a. its moral foundation of civic duty
    b. its remarkable support of Christianity
    c. its dependence upon intellectual pursuit
    d. its brevity and simplicity of expression
    e. its deep support of military power

10. Both the Chinese and the Europeans initiated maritime exploration. What was the primary difference between them?
    a. Only one was supported by rulers.
    b. One was primarily interested in prestige.
    c. Only one participated in trade.
    d. Only one sought to cut off participation by other nationals.
    e. Only one was primarily interested in exploration.

Comprehensive Multiple Choice Questions

1. Compared with trade networks in the first century, the Asian trade network in the fourteenth century could best be described as which of the following?
   a. The routes were substantially different with the addition of Indian Ocean trade to the silk roads.
   b. Virtually nothing was different except that the volume of basic commodities increased.
   c. The routes were safer and allowed for more travelers and commodities to go farther distances.
   d. Epidemic diseases only spread along the trade routes in the later period.
   e. Once religions had spread along the early trade routes, this was no longer a phenomenon of later trade routes.

2. The cultural recovery of Europe from the ravages of the bubonic plague epidemic was predicated upon an earlier cultural flowering. What was this and how did it form the foundation of the Renaissance?
   a. When medieval Europe began to consolidate into kingdoms, the comparative safety of the times allowed manuscripts to be recovered from monasteries.
   b. When the Catholic church dominated the monarchies of Europe, their libraries were opened to scholars to investigate classical philosophy.
   c. As relationships became less dependent on feudal ties, more nobles turned to art patronage as examples of their power.
   d. After the crusades, the connections between Europe and the Middle East increased which allowed many Christian, Jewish, and Islamic scholars to exchange works including translations of classical literature.
   e. When the Byzantine empire served as Christian allies in the crusades, the Orthodox and Catholic churches shared their histories and literature which provided the entire basis for a later renaissance.

3. The historical tendency of Chinese governments was to reject the attractions of other societies yet the Ming dynasty reached out to the rest of the world for a short period of time with their sponsorship of the treasure fleet. Which of the following circumstances is closest to that relationship?
   a. when the Yuan dynasty imported and employed foreign expertise
   b. when the Han dynasty formed tributary relationships with neighboring states
   c. when the Song dynasty paid tribute to the nomadic Khitan on the northwest border
   d. when the Tang dynasty expanded into Korea, Manchuria, and Vietnam
   e. when the Sui dynasty attempted to suppress rebellions in Korea

Primary Source Questions

1. **Read *Sources from the Past: Ibn Battuta on Customs in the Mali Empire,* fourteenth century, on page 572 of your textbook.**
   a. What is Ibn Battuta's point of view?
   b. What part of Malian culture impresses him the most?
   c. What parts does he criticize?
   d. Make an overall statement of the state of Islam in Mali based on Ibn Battuta's accounts.

2. **Examine the fourteenth-century illustration on page 570, the thirteenth-century illustration on page 575, and the Gentile and Bellini painting on page 584 of your textbook.**
   a. What is the point of view of these three artists?
   b. What content do the three illustrations have in common?
   c. Stylistically, what distinguishes the later painting from the others?

Chapter Multiple Choice Answers

1. **e:** Prosperous trade cities throughout Asia and Africa had neighborhoods filled with foreign traders (p. 567)

2. **b:** In China, Marco Polo was employed by Khubilai Khan while the ilkhanate of Persia sent Rabban Sauma to petition European monarchs. (pp. 570, 571)

3. **d:** Ibn Battuta served as a *qadi* who could interpret law and give direction on faithful adherence to Islamic standards. (p. 571)

4. **a:** The compass was invented in the Tang or Song dynasty and was influencing European mariners by the 1100s. (p. 575)

5. **b:** A little ice age caused a shorter growing season so that populations were already malnourished before the plague arrived. (p. 577)

6. **d:** While political power was challenged and rebellions occurred in many regions, the essential class structure of afflicted societies did not change. (pp. 578, 579)

7. **b:** Hongwu reinstituted the Confucian examination system to provide a new group of Confucian scholar-officials for government service. (p. 579)

8. **c:** Using increased taxes and standing armies, the European rulers increased their power over their states and against their neighbors. (p. 581)

9. **a:** European humanists emphasized the active nature of Roman philosophy which supported a life of civic responsibilities rather than one of quiet contemplation. (p. 584)

10. **b:** China was primarily interested in promoting the prestige of its dynasty while the Portuguese were compelled to find other trade routes due to their location at the far end of Asian trade routes. (pp. 585–587)

Comprehensive Multiple Choice Answers

1. **c:** The Mongol conquests made long-distance travel safer for travelers who by this time included numerous diplomats and missionaries as well as merchants. The Mongols further sent conquered people to various regions of the empire to assist in their administrations. Epidemics including smallpox, measles, and bubonic plague spread along the trade routes during the early period as well as the later period. While the volume of commodities increased in the later period, so did the variety as Europeans eagerly adopted new food crops and textiles. Although the spread of Buddhism, Hinduism, Manichaeism, and Christianity was initiated earlier, they continued to spread along with Islam during the later period. (p. 566)

2. **d:** Even though the answer is found in an earlier chapter, it is important to realize that the so-called renaissance in Europe could not have occurred unless earlier scholars had already recovered the knowledge of antiquities. Political stability, the Catholic church's retention of classical literature, and the art patronage by wealthy men were necessary, but it was the work of scholars throughout the Mediterranean world after the crusades that formed the foundation for later developments. (p. 525)

3. **b:** The Han dynasty set up tributary relationships with neighboring states as did the Tang. The relationship was not one of equality but rather of the inferior country's recognition of China's power and prestige. In the same way, Zheng He's expeditions were designed to demonstrate that same relationship to new countries. The Song relationship with the Khitan is the exact opposite while the Yuan

dynasty is a foreign dynasty importing foreign workers. Zheng He's military did occasionally fight but the purely military actions on the part of the Tang and the Sui did not acknowledge the tributary relationship (although they may have been an attempt to force the tribute states back into submission). (pp. 380, 585)

Primary Source Answers

1. Ibn Battuta was a learned Islamic scholar who brought his knowledge to other cultures so that they might learn how to follow the *sharia*. Thus he constantly evaluated the extent of devotion in regions that he visited outside the core of dar al-Islam. He was enormously impressed by the Malian devotion to prayer, justice, attendance at Friday services, and study of the Quran, but he was quite shocked by the lack of modest clothing in women as well as the failure to have meats slaughtered in a ritual fashion, or as *halal*. It is apparent that while west Africans adopted the basic pillars of Islam, they had chosen to ignore the cultural dictates that clashed with their own traditions. In effect, African Islam was a syncretism of Islam and traditional African practices. (p. 572)

2. All three illustrations were executed by European artists and demonstrate the enormous fascination with foreign cultures that had affected Europe after the twelfth century. Each illustration depicts the interaction between European peoples and peoples of other cultures. (Look carefully at the left foreground and middle background in the painting to see the Italian men.) While the manuscript illustrations are fairly two-dimensional and unrealistic, the Bellini painting reveals the techniques of the Renaissance painters in its three-point perspective which provides a three-dimensional realism to the scene. (pp. 570, 575, 584)

PART V

THE ORIGINS OF GLOBAL INTERDEPENDENCE, 1500–1800

CHAPTER 23

TRANSOCEANIC ENCOUNTERS AND GLOBAL CONNECTIONS

Before you get started: This is an important chapter as it marks the beginning of a new period in world history and in this course: the early modern era c. 1450-1750. Though cross-cultural interactions had taken place for millennia prior to this era, after 1500 these interactions were much more sustained and much more disruptive to all the peoples involved. As you read this chapter, pay particular attention to the impact of technology and trade on political institutions and global interactions. "In fourteen hundred ninety-two, Columbus sailed the ocean blue" is only the beginning of the story. Everything changes from this point forward.

THE EUROPEAN RECONNAISSANCE OF THE WORLD'S OCEANS

Cross-cultural interaction is not a new development, but what is new about this era is that Europe is going to join others like sailors from Ming China or Ottoman mariners whose earlier voyages linked Asia and Africa. What will make Europe different is that European voyages are going to link the eastern hemisphere with the western hemisphere and Oceania. These regular interactions will provide Europe with unparalleled opportunities to increase its power, influence, and wealth. Between 1400 and 1800, European mariners explored all of the earth's oceans except for the extreme polar regions; financed by private investors and some governments, these expensive expeditions used advanced nautical technology to produce valuable results—accurate geographic knowledge, networks of communication and transportation, the commerce of desired products and resources—and the unintentional exchange of diseases. By the nineteenth century, several European nations will have established worldwide empires which will expand and intensify over time.

Motives for Exploration
(Theme: Economics, Patterns of Interaction, and Changes and Continuities)

European exploration was prompted by complex and interacting motivations: a search for basic resources and lands suitable for cultivating cash crops, the need to establish new trade routes outside of Muslim control to reach Asian markets, and the desire to expand the influence of Christianity. These motivations first moved the Portuguese who had relatively poor rocky soil at home to search for new lands and products on islands in the open Atlantic: the Azores, the Madeiras, the Canaries. Soon Portugal established sugar plantations on the central Atlantic islands of Sao Tome, Principe, and Fernando Po as well as the Cape Verde Islands.

In addition to the quest for fresh lands and resources, the desire to reduce costs and increase supplies of products like spices, especially pepper, ginger, and cloves, drove European merchants and monarchs to seek direct routes to Asia and Asian goods and to avoid the expensive services of Muslim merchants who charged mightily for those desirable products. The collapse of the Mongol empire and the spread of bubonic plague made those desired goods increasingly expensive to Europeans. The Europeans were also interested in African goods, especially gold and ivory and eventually slaves to work on the island sugar plantations started by European entrepreneurs. Once again the Muslim intermediaries were to be avoided through European direct access to African markets.

The other motivating factor was religion: the desire to spread Christianity had a biblical foundation. This spread sometimes took peaceful means as through the work of missionaries in India, central Asia, and China, but it could also take military means as in the **reconquista** on the Iberian Peninsula completed in 1492 and in Palestine and the islands of the Mediterranean.

The Technology of Exploration
(Theme: Technology)

Much of the technology needed for the European voyages of exploration came from Chinese or Arabic sources. For example, use of a **stern rudder** developed by the Chinese and diffused into European use through the Arab ships of the Mediterranean and the **triangular lateen sail** which made it possible for a ship to advance against the wind by sailing across it—to "tack"—meant that sturdy European ships could now explore dangerous seas with uncooperative winds. From China, the **magnetic compass** to figure direction, and from Greek and Persian astronomers **the astrolabe** to determine latitude, made these earlier European voyages possible. Soon however, interaction with Arab sailors who used simpler and more serviceable instruments made the **cross staff and back staff** the navigation equipment of choice for European sailors.

European sailors used these "new" technologies to venture out into the uncharted ocean where they began to gather information about winds and currents. This knowledge of wind patterns and currents allowed them to sail almost anywhere on earth. They applied this knowledge in their use of **volta do mar,** a Portuguese phrase meaning "return through the sea"; this strategy allowed them to sail into the open ocean to catch the westerly winds, rather than to fight against the trade winds as they sailed home. Soon all European mariners were relying on this strategy to travel thoughout the world's seas.

Voyages of Exploration: from the Mediterranean to the Atlantic
(Theme: Changes and Continuities)

The Portuguese, and then the Spanish, took the early lead in the European voyages of exploration into the Atlantic. **Prince Henry the Navigator of Portugal** conquered the Moroccan port of Ceuta in 1415 and then sponsored a series of voyages down the west African coast. Soon Portuguese merchants established permanent trading ports where they exchanged horses, leather, textiles, and metalware for gold and slaves. After Henry's death, the voyages of exploration continued with **Bartolomeu Dias** in 1488 who rounded the Cape of Good Hope and entered the Indian Ocean and with Vasco Da Gama who made the round trip to India in 1499 returning with a valuable cargo of pepper and cinnamon. By 1500, the Portuguese had established a trading post in Calcutta and had trading relationships with ports throughout the Indian Ocean basin. Soon the English and the Dutch followed the Portuguese into the Indian Ocean.

The Spanish interest in the Atlantic centered on the desire to reach Asia by sailing west and on inaccurate calculations. Though Genoese mariner **Christopher Columbus** tried to get Portuguese support for his venture, the Portuguese were skeptical of Columbus's mathematics and his concept; they already had a stronger plan going based on Dias's successes. But Columbus found support for his plan with the Spanish monarchs **Ferdinand and Isabella.** Reporting that he had reached the islands of Asia, "the Indies," in the fall of 1492, Columbus managed to get the Spanish monarchs to support three more voyages which were unsuccessful in achieving his goal of reaching Asia. Though these four voyages did not achieve Columbus's dream, they were unintentionally, yet monumentally, successful in establishing Spain as the leader in European exploitation of these new lands, resources, and people.

Voyages of Exploration: from the Atlantic to the Pacific
(Theme: Changes and Continuities)

Even after Columbus's initial failures, some Europeans continued to seek a western route to Asia. **Vasco Nunez de Balboa** first sighted the Pacific Ocean in 1513 while searching for gold in Panama, but he had no idea about its true size: one-third of the earth's surface. Portuguese navigator **Ferdinand Magellan** explored the Pacific and eventually circumnavigated the world, 1519–1522, sailing under the flag of Spain as the Portuguese continued to have little interest in a westerly route to Asia. His three-year voyage, racked by starvation, scurvy, and violence, returned to Spain with only 35 of his original crew of 280 still alive.

Exploration of the vast Pacific was dangerous and delayed. The Spanish concentrated on establishing safe trade routes between Mexico and the Philippines. English mariners determined to find a northwest passage from Europe to Asia inadvertently charted many details of Pacific geography; soon they would be joined by the Norwegians, the French, and eventually the Russians. The most important of these explorers was the Englishman **Captain James Cook** whose three eighteenth-century explorations of the southern and northern Pacific Ocean helped Europeans compile a reasonably accurate understanding of the ocean's basin, land, and peoples.

TRADE AND CONFLICT IN EARLY MODERN ASIA

A key result of the voyages of exploration was the potential for commercial opportunities for European nations who built **trading posts** as footholds in regions where prior commercial powers had dominated for centuries. Lacking the military resources and sheer human numbers to impose their rule in the eastern hemisphere, the Spanish were able to build a small empire in the Philippines and the Dutch were able to establish a small but lucrative empire in Indonesia. On land, Russian commercial interests expanded into the former Mongol lands. These small and eventually competing European claims would eventually lead to the **Seven Years' War** in 1763; the British victory in that worldwide conflict would enable that small nation to dominate world trade and build a vast empire in the nineteenth century.

Trading-Post Empires
(Themes: Economics and Patterns of Interaction)

The Portuguese built the first trading-post empires as they established trading posts from Africa throughout Asia: San Jorge da Mina, Mozambique, Hormuz, Gao, Melaka, Ternate, Macau, and Nagasaki. The goal of this strategy was not to conquer territory but to control trade routes by forcing merchant vessels to stop at fortified trading sites for supplies and to pay duties. **Afonzo d'Alboquerque** was the architect of this aggressive policy and his fleets were very effective at overpowering other crafts they encountered and in using their heavy artillery effectively on shore. He forced merchant ships to purchase safe conduct papers and present them with payment at Portuguese ports of call. Goods would be confiscated and crews imprisoned, ransomed, tortured, and sometimes killed. By the middle of the sixteenth century, Portuguese ships transported half the spices the European nations consumed; the other half continued to be transported on Arab, Indian, and Malay ships. Despite all attempts, the Portuguese simply did not have the manpower or naval power to fully enforce their demands, and, by the end of the sixteenth century, the English and the Dutch began to rival Portuguese domination of the Indian Ocean trade.

English and Dutch merchants also built trading posts in the Indian Ocean region, but they were much more interested in collecting duties on trade rather than controlling ocean shipping. The English concentrated on **India** and built forts at Bombay, Madras, and Calcutta; the Dutch built forts from Cape Town in southern Africa to Colombo, and at **Batavia** on the island of Java.

The English and the Dutch emerged superior to their Portuguese predecessors because they sailed faster, cheaper, and more powerful ships and because they developed an extremely effective and efficient form of commercial organization: **the joint-stock company.** This sophisticated business structure made it possible for investors to make impressive profits while limiting the risk on their investments.

The English **East India Company,** founded in 1600, and the Dutch **United East India Company (VOC)** relied on private merchants who advanced funds to launch the companies; outfit ships with men, equipment, and supplies; and provide commodities and money for travel. Government charters granted these private companies the right to buy and sell goods, build trading posts, and even wage war if it was in the company's interest. Their advanced nautical technology, powerful military arsenal, efficient organization, and untiring pursuit of profit made these companies and the governments who sponsored them very wealthy and helped both England and the Dutch to build a global trade network.

European Conquests in Southeast Asia
(Themes: Patterns of Interaction and Economics)

European interaction in the eastern hemisphere was much different than in the western hemisphere. Unlike in the western hemisphere, where Europeans conquered indigenous peoples and built territorial empires to establish colonies with European settlers, in the east the Europeans were unable to dominate the peoples of larger, more established states. With the decline of the Portuguese influence in the region, other European powers mostly traded peacefully with indigenous peoples and nations with two exceptions: **the Philippines** and **Indonesia.** Though highly populated, neither of these regions was protected by a large centralized power like India or China, so when the heavily armed European powers arrived in the sixteenth century, the indigenous population was no match.

The Spanish goals in the Philippines were clear: **promote trade and Christianity.** Using and at times abusing Chinese merchants, the Spanish relied on these long-established traders to supply silk from China to fill the **Manila galleons.** Spanish authorities approached the spread of Christianity with equal vigor; they built schools and targeted influential Filipino families for conversion. Though meeting some resistance particularly in the rural, mountainous island regions, by the nineteenth century the Philippines were one of the most devout Roman Catholic regions in the world.

The Dutch goals were much more focused: exploit trade and do not be concerned with the spread of Christianity. The desire to control the lucrative spice trade dominated the economic strategy of men like Jan Pieterszoon Coen who established the city of Batavia in 1619 to serve as headquarters for the VOC. Coen and others used local conflicts as an opportunity to gain allies as he pitted one indigenous group against the other. The Dutch, who had neither the manpower nor the military might to exert their control over all of Indonesia, chose to concentrate on specific wealthy **clove-** and **mace**-producing regions; they wanted to control the production of spices, not to rule. To achieve this goal, the Dutch moved spice-bearing plants to islands under their direct control and then mercilessly attacked people who grew spices for trade with non-Dutch merchants. This successful strategy made Holland the wealthiest land in Europe for much of the seventeenth century.

Foundations of the Russian Empire in Asia
(Themes: Trade, Religious Developments, and Patterns of Interaction)

Russian expansion in this era was land-based and took two directions: central Asia and northeastern Eurasia. In central Asia, Russian forces took over previous Mongol khanates which gave them control over the Volga River and offered opportunities for trade in the Ottoman Empire, Iran, and India by way of the Caspian Sea. During the eighteenth century, Russia added much of the Caucasus region to its land empire including the modern-day nations of Georgia, Armenia, and Azerbaijan. In northeastern Eurasia, it was Siberia and its furs which brought Russia great wealth; by 1639, the Russians controlled the region all the way to the Pacific Ocean. This vast region included many different ethnic groups from which the Russians exacted tribute in the form of fur. Some groups resisted Russian domination and the Russians responded with military force, at times nearly wiping out entire cultures. Endemic diseases were an even greater threat to the peoples of Siberia, decimating local communities. There was not a great push for conversion to Russian Orthodox Christianity as conversion removed the requirement for tribute, so most indigenous people of the region retained their traditional beliefs.

Russian settlers in these regions were often individuals who were ostracized from Russian society: social misfits, convicted criminals, and prisoners of war. Often these Russians found working conditions better in Siberia than in Russia proper. Over time, Siberian trading posts developed into Russian towns with populations of Russians often double the population of indigenous people. This rate further increased in the nineteenth century with the discovery of the region's vast mineral wealth.

Commercial Rivalries and the Seven Years' War
(Themes: Trade and War)

The effort to establish markets and monopolies lead to war between the Europeans and the indigenous peoples and also between the European nations themselves. The Dutch, English, Spanish, French, and Portuguese fought each other on land and sea throughout the seventeenth and eighteenth centuries over these trade rivalries. **The Seven Years' War,** also known as the **"great war for empire"** is the most significant of these conflicts as its outcome laid the foundation for 150 years of British imperial domination across the world.

GLOBAL EXCHANGES

The global interactions of this era resulted in an unprecedented volume of exchange in the biological and commercial realms.

The Columbian Exchange
(Themes: Demographics, Patterns of Interaction, and Changes and Continuities)

The Columbian exchange, defined as the "global diffusion of plants, food crops, animals, human populations, and disease pathogens which took place after the voyages of exploration by Columbus and other European mariners," changed the entire world. By creating links between biological zones previously isolated from each other for thousands of years, these voyages triggered a biological exchange which permanently altered the natural environment and human geography all over the world.

In the eastern hemisphere, diseases like smallpox, measles, diphtheria, whooping cough, and influenza claimed a large number of victims, especially children, but left survivors with immunity to the disease through their exposure at an early age. In the western hemisphere, these diseases functioned much differently. Carried by unsuspecting Europeans, when these diseases reached the previously unexposed populations of the western hemisphere, entire societies were annihilated. These imported diseases took their worst toll in densely populated areas like the Aztec and Incan empires, but affected other regions as well, with the disease often reaching the indigenous societies before any direct contact with a European explorer or settler. These epidemic diseases had the same impact in the Pacific Islands as they did in North and South America. Epidemics sparked by the Columbian exchange caused the worst demographic catastrophe in all of human history: in the era 1500–1800, more than 100 million people died as a result of diseases imported into the Pacific Islands and North and South America.

Ironically, though the exchange of disease pathogens decimated populations in the New World, over time the Columbian exchange resulted in an increase in human population due to the introduction of new food crops and animals like wheat, vines, horses, cattle, pigs, sheep, goats, and chickens. American food crops such as maize, beans, tomatoes, peanuts, and especially the potato contributed to a sharp increase in calories available in the Europeans' diets. The world population, after an initial dip due to infectious disease in the fourteenth and fifteenth centuries, grew by 50 percent from 1800 to 1900.

Human populations grew and moved during this period; sometimes these moves were voluntary but often were forced. The largest migration in this era was that of enslaved Africans forcibly transported to North and South America, including the islands of the Caribbean. A sizable group of Europeans migrated to lands in world regions depopulated by disease.

The Origins of Global Trade
(Themes: Trade and Economics)

Due to the trading-post empires established by Portuguese, Dutch, and English merchants, Asian and European markets were linked through goods transported on European ships. Those same ships soon began carrying goods within the Asian markets of the Indian Ocean basin. By the late sixteenth century, European merchants and Arab merchants were nearly equal in the trading patterns in the Indian Ocean basin.

This circumstance laid the groundwork for the emergence of a truly **global trading system** in which mariners from European nations carried goods around the world by way of the Pacific and Atlantic Oceans: **sugar, silver, tobacco, textiles, guns, furs, and enslaved human beings** were carried as valuable cargo from one port to another. **Silver** especially became the desired medium of exchange as it was highly valued in China and easily exploited from South America; likewise, **cowry shells** from India were a highly desirous medium of exchange throughout West Africa. The demand for furs in China, Europe, and North America decimated the ecological balance in fur-producing regions like seventeenth-century Siberia and eighteenth-century North America. Mass markets for commodities like coffee, tea, tobacco, cotton, and especially **sugar** dramatically stimulated the market for enslaved workers. By 1750, all parts of the world, except Australia, participated in this global commercial network with European merchants fulfilling the most prominent roles.

Finished reading the chapter? Be sure you can . . .

- Explain the motivations for European exploration during this era.
- Analyze the impact of technology on the global trading networks during this era (1500–1800).
- Describe and analyze the changes in trade and global interactions as a result of the Columbian exchange.
- Evaluate the demographic and environmental changes resulting from the transoceanic encounters of this era.

Chapter Multiple Choice Questions

1. Why is Vasco Da Gama's voyage in 1499 significant in a global context?
   a. It was the first time any Portuguese mariner had arrived safely in India.
   b. It supported Columbus's claim that the world was round.
   c. It demonstrated that there was a faster passage to Asia than the traditional overland routes.
   d. It showed the south and east Asian empires that Europe was a mighty trading power and foreshadowed Europe's coming dominance.
   e. It opened the doors to direct maritime trading and helped to establish permanent links between Europe and Asia.

2. Which of the following technologies was a western European maritime innovation c. 1400–1800?
   a. astrolabe
   b. sternpost rudder
   c. compass
   d. cross staff and back staff
   e. spring-driven clock to measure longitude

3. The greatest flaw in Columbus's plan to reach Asia by sailing west was that
   a. he drastically underestimated the circumference of the earth and did not know about the existence of the continents of North and South America.
   b. he did not possess the necessary technology to successfully make such a long voyage and to return home safely.
   c. he could not get the better-equipped and better-trained Portuguese mariners to sign on to his plan and help him achieve a successful voyage.
   d. Genoa was too far from Portugal and the differences in language and customs was too great for the two peoples to work together.
   e. he did not have the personal experience to make such a vast voyage and Ferdinand and Isabella refused to finance any additional voyages after his initial failure.

4. Which of the following individuals reported his experiences in this manner?
"So that your highnesses might resolve to . . . Because without a doubt, there is in this land a very great quantity of gold; for not without cause do these Indians that I bring with me say that there are in these islands places where they dig and wear gold and wear it on their chests, on their ears and on their arms. . . . And also, here there is probably a great quantity of cotton and I think it would sell very well here without taking it to Spain but the cities belonging to the Grand Mongol Khan."
   a. Ferdinand Magellan
   b. Vascon Nunez Balboa
   c. Christopher Columbus
   d. Prince Henry of Portugal
   e. Captain James Cook

5. What was a key difference between the Portuguese approach to trading-post empires and the approach taken by the Dutch and the English?
   a. The Portuguese were interested in land and sea territories more than controlling trade routes and custom duties, as were the Dutch and the English.
   b. The Portuguese were interested in controlling trade routes and collecting customs duties, while the Dutch and English were interested in controlling shipping on the high seas.
   c. The Portuguese were interested in militarily controlling trade routes and collecting customs duties while the Dutch and the English were interested in establishing trading posts to sell supplies and collect customs duties.
   d. The Portuguese were more interested in fighting their Spanish rivals than in stopping the English or Dutch merchant companies.
   e. The Portuguese were more interested in the selling of supplies and the trading of gold, salt, and slaves than were the British and the Dutch who were interested in tea and cocoa trade.

6. What common goal(s) did the Dutch and the Spanish have in southeast Asia?
   a. Both wanted to spread Christianity as the dominant faith throughout the world.
   b. Both wanted to dominate trade in the region, but not necessarily to populate the region with European settlers.
   c. Both wanted to spread Christianity and trade throughout their realms by establishing settler colonies.
   d. Both wanted to destroy the power of the Chinese merchants who had dominated the region for centuries.
   e. Both wanted to compete with the English for control of sea routes and markets in the eastern Pacific.

7. Why is the Seven Years' War significant in this era, 1500–1800?
   a. It demonstrated the power of the Prussian army to withstand assault from the west.
   b. It illustrated the importance of the gunpowder empires in Asia.
   c. It showed that the eastern hemisphere could not dominate the western hemisphere in terms of economic and military power.
   d. It placed Britain in a position to dominate world trade for the next 150 years.
   e. It demonstrated the power of joint stock companies to influence governments.

8. Why did disease decimate the indigenous populations of the western hemisphere?
   a. The western hemisphere had developed in relative isolation from Europe, Asia, and Africa for thousands of years, so the people had no natural immunities to diseases from the eastern hemisphere.
   b. The peoples of the western hemisphere did not have access to the more sophisticated medical tradition and practices of the Asians and the Europeans, so they had no way to combat the diseases.
   c. The peoples of the western hemisphere lacked the sanitation and technology needed to prevent the spread of infectious disease acquired from contact with the Europeans, so diseases spread too rapidly to combat.
   d. The peoples of the western hemisphere were weakened from fighting the European invaders, so they were not biologically strong enough to fight the diseases.
   e. The diets of the people of the western hemisphere lacked necessary nutrients, so they were not healthy enough to withstand the European-borne pathogens.

9. Which New World crops added the most calories to European diets and therefore positively impacted sustainable population numbers?
   a. wheat and potatoes
   b. potatoes and maize
   c. maize and beans
   d. tomatoes and peppers
   e. peanuts and manioc

10. What commodity became the most desirous medium of exchange for the Manila galleons of the sixteenth and seventeenth centuries?
   a. gold
   b. sugar
   c. cowry shells
   d. silver
   e. silk

Comprehensive Multiple Choice Questions

1. How did the European mariners of the fifteenth through nineteenth centuries use the westerly winds of the western hemisphere differently than the Indian Ocean mariners used the monsoons?
   a. European mariners relied on "wind wheels" north and south of the Equator to sail both east and west across the Atlantic while the Indian Ocean merchants relied on the changing directions of the monsoons in different seasons to navigate the Indian Ocean.
   b. European mariners relied on their ability to tack, so that they could sail directly into the wind, unlike the Indian Ocean mariners who relied on the sternpost rudder to steer into the winds of the Indian Ocean.
   c. European mariners depended on their smaller, sturdier ships to handle the rough Atlantic seas, while the Indian Ocean mariners built huge ocean-going junks.
   d. European mariners used the change of seasons to follow the "westerlies" while the Indian Ocean merchants avoided monsoon season because of the dangerous storms.
   e. European mariners used the northeast trade winds to sail back to European harbors while Indian Ocean merchants had to rely on the unpredictable monsoons to navigate the Indian Ocean.

2. Columbus was able to convince Ferdinand and Isabella to support his voyages because
   a. they were anxious to follow the routes to Asia already explored by the Portuguese Dias and Da Gama.
   b. based on his mathematical calculations of the earth's circumference, he believed that sailing west from Europe to Asia would be profitable and they recognized the wealth such a route would bring to their kingdom.
   c. he promised them an alliance between the wealthy Italian port city of Genoa and the rising newly unified Spanish kingdom of Aragon and Castile.
   d. he had already made a successful voyage to the islands he called the Indies and he had the gold and natives as specimens to prove it.
   e. he had had the earlier backing of Prince Henry the Navigator of Portugal who died before he could back another voyage and Ferdinand and Isabel wanted to assume that leadership role.

3. The desire to spread Christianity, settle European farmers in new lands, control the trade of specific cash crops, and exploit natural resources is most characteristic of which of the following groups?
   a. the Portuguese in Brazil
   b. the Dutch in Indonesia
   c. the Spanish in the Philippines
   d. the French in Canada
   e. the English in North America

Primary Source Questions

1. **Read *Sources from the Past: Christopher Columbus's First Impressions of American Peoples* on page 607 of your textbook.**
   a. How would you describe Columbus's perceptions of these people?
   b. Why does Columbus believe these people will be "good and intelligent servants"?
   c. How does this excerpt reflect Columbus's motives for exploration?

2. **Examine Map [23.4] on page 615 of your textbook.**
   a. Which two European nations have the greatest number of ports in Africa and Asia in 1700?
   b. Which two European nations have the fewest number of ports in Africa and Asia in 1700?
   c. How might you explain the reasons for the disparity in number of ports between these European nations?

Chapter Multiple Choice Answers

1. **e:** Da Gama's expedition was the first time any Portuguese mariner had successfully sailed to India and returned with an expensive shipload of pepper and cinnamon, but the question asks specifically about global context. The correct answer is "e" because after Da Gama's success, the direct interaction of Europe and Asian merchants was continuous, sustained, and growing. (p. 597)

2. **d:** The cross staff and the back staff were European innovations based on earlier Arab technologies used to measure latitude. Measurement means for longitude were also developed by Europeans but not during the period prescribed in the question. (p. 601)

3. **a:** Columbus believed the circumference of the earth to be about 17,000 nautical miles and that Asia covered about 270 degrees of longitude. Instead, the circumference of the earth is about 25,000 nautical miles and Asia covers only about 140 degrees of longitude. These miscalculations, plus the lack of knowledge of the continents of North and South America, doomed his venture to short-term failure; its benefits would only become clear after his death. (p. 606)

4. **c:** Only Columbus would be making a report back to monarchs Ferdinand and Isabella and only Columbus would be using the term *Indians* as he refers to the ones he brings with him. None of the other explorers listed would be concerned with those standards or issues. Balboa and Magellan are too late for Ferdinand and Isabella, Prince Henry had died much earlier, and Cook was in the service of the English in the eighteenth century. (p. 607)

5. **c:** The Portuguese, under commanders like Alfonso d'Alboquerque, sought to dominate the Indian Ocean by military strength and bravado. The Dutch and the English were much more interested in the income which was derived from customs duties and selling essential supplies to oceangoing vessels and crews. (p. 613)

6. **b:** For the Spanish, the spread of Christianity was a key goal in their domination of the Philippines, but for the more religiously tolerant Dutch, the spread of Christianity was not a concern. Both powers agreed on the desire to control the very lucrative spice trade and neither nation spent much time or energy making their lands a place for European settlers. (p. 616)

7. **d:** The Seven Years' War became a global conflict from which Britain emerged set to dominate the economic and political world for the next 150 years. (p. 620)

8. **a:** The lack of inherited or acquired immunities to diseases like smallpox and measles meant that these diseases could wipe out entire populations or at least enough of a population to make sustaining that population nearly impossible. (p. 621)

9. **b:** Wheat is a food crop from the eastern hemisphere. Peanuts and manioc were most readily adopted in southeast Asia and west Africa. Though it took a while, ultimately maize and especially the potato were adopted by the Europeans resulting ultimately in a significant increase in calories available and a rising population. (p. 622)

10. **d:** Silver was the basis of the Chinese currency and relatively easy access to silver exploited from the Spanish South American mines made the trading of goods around the world possible. (p. 625)

Comprehensive Multiple Choice Answers

1. **a:** In both the Atlantic and Pacific, "wind wheels" affect the westerlies and the easterly tradewinds. Once the European mariners mastered the movements of these winds and their related currents, they understood how to use these winds to sail across both oceans. The monsoons changed in a predictable pattern tied to the seasons; Indian Ocean mariners relied on these steady and predictable winds to navigate the vast Indian Ocean. (pp. 601–604)

2. **b:** Columbus's inaccurate calculations made his theory seem very probable and worth backing as the Spanish monarchs were interested in reaching the shores of Asia more quickly than their Portuguese neighbors and rivals; the potential for wealth made the gamble on Columbus worthwhile. (p. 606)

3. **a:** In the eastern hemisphere, the Spanish and the Dutch did not attempt any large-scale European settler colonies. The French were not initially interested in settler colonies in Canada and the English did not have a direct clearcut goal to promote Christianity in North America. The Portuguese in Brazil, however, had all of these goals. (pp. 615–617)

Primary Source Answers

1. Columbus consistently describes the American people in positive terms. He says they are "well-formed," "handsome," and that they have "good faces." He describes their personalities as positive when he says they do not "know what evil is" and when he calls them "gentle" and says that they became "friends" quite easily. He then begins to record that they learn languages quickly and that they seem to have "no religion." His perceptions of these first Americans remain positive, but not positive as equals, but as potential servants. There is an interesting and enlightening focus in this excerpt because it is clear that Columbus feels no conflict between desiring these people to be converts to Catholicism, servants to the Spaniards, and trading partners. His motivations are very clear and the directness of his comments is chilling in hindsight. He had no problem in recognizing the "potential" in these Americans to bring great "wealth" to the Spanish monarchs and no concern for the morality or immorality in that recognition. (p. 607)

2. The Dutch and the Portuguese both have seven major ports shown on this map while the English only have three, the Spanish have two, and the French only have one port shown. The Portuguese have many Asian ports because they were "given" this hemisphere by the Papal Line of Demarcation in 1494 also known as the **Treaty of Tordesillas;** the Spanish were given the western hemisphere where their trading empire developed. The seventeenth century was the "golden age" for the Dutch commercial empire and their African port at Cape Town was built to supply vessels making the journey to and from Asia. In the early eighteenth century, both the English and the French were concentrating on building their colonial holdings in North America. (p. 615)

CHAPTER 24

THE TRANSFORMATION OF EUROPE

Before you get started: Europe experienced enormous religious, political, commercial, and scientific upheavals in the sixteenth and seventeenth centuries that produced the extensive global expansion by Europeans that we see in later centuries. Extraordinary individuals such as Martin Luther, Ignatius Loyola, Louis XIV, and a panoply of scientists drove these innovations while capitalist market forces affected social life and demographics. These may be familiar to you because they are the basis of modern western society. It will be helpful for you to make a chart divided along religious, political, commercial, and scientific lines with the names of important persons and their ideas or innovations.

THE FRAGMENTATION OF WESTERN CHRISTENDOM

Remember that the Christian church already split earlier between Rome and Byzantium into Catholic and Orthodox sects. Revolts against the Roman Catholic church evolved into the Protestants who further branched into a number of sects according to nationalities and beliefs.

The Protestant Reformation
(Theme: Religious Development)

It all began when German Catholic monk and teacher **Martin Luther** protested the sale of indulgences that had become a method to raise money for the pope's buildings in Rome. With the aid of the invention of the moveable-type **printing press**, Martin Luther, an articulate lecturer and prolific writer, publicized the many abuses in the Catholic church. He advocated a **vernacular Bible**—written in the native language rather than Latin—and an end to priestly authority. The protest soon took on a nationalist bent as almost half of the German states disavowed Catholic practices in favor of Protestantism.

Soon, the Low Countries, modern-day Holland and Belgium, as well as Switzerland, had adopted a strict form of French Protestantism known as **Calvinism.** Its model city, Geneva, was a theocracy with a harsh moral code. In England, the change occurred in a more secular way when English monarch Henry VIII broke with the Catholic church in order to divorce his Spanish wife who had only borne a daughter not eligible for the throne. He established himself as the head of the **Anglican church** and remarried five more times, but little within the church practices changed. His successors proceeded to adopt the more Protestant practices advocated by Martin Luther.

The Catholic Reformation
(Theme: Religious Development)

The Catholic response to the Protestants was to reexamine their doctrine and practices. In essence, they sought to cleanse the church of abuses while investing more into spiritual commitment with the hope that it might persuade lapsed Catholics to return to a reformed church. The reforms were made primarily in the **Council of Trent** with the help of a new order, **the Jesuits**. The Council actually consisted of a series of meetings of the highest church authorities over eighteen years that clarified doctrine, established seminaries, and provided a moral direction for the church. In 1540, Basque nobleman and ex-soldier **Ignatius Loyola** established the Society of Jesus as an order that would hold its recruits to the highest educational and moral standards. Their extraordinary dedication to the faith, combined with their academic brilliance, made them extremely effective missionaries across the globe, gaining converts in the Americas, China, Japan, and the Philippines.

Witch-Hunts and Religious Wars
(Theme: Religious Development)

The effects of religious dissent soon moved into political and social spheres as Europeans sought to adjust to the new split. The most powerful social phenomenon occurred as Europeans hunted **witches** with more fervor than they ever had. Like other cultures, Europeans believed in the power of individuals to mysteriously affect the lives of their neighbors. The hysteria brought some 110,000 people to trial with almost 60 percent killed. While there were male victims, the overwhelming number of accused witches were women, most of whom lived on the margins of society as old, poor widowed or single women. Historians believe that the witch-hunts that persisted in Europe for two centuries were largely indicative of the general stress and strain of profound changes within multiple spheres of society.

Outright war broke out in several places as a result of the Reformation. For thirty-six years, the French Catholics fought the **Huguenot Protestants** for control of the monarchy. It only ended when a Huguenot contender converted to Catholicism. The Spanish monarch tried to persuade England to return to Catholicism first by marrying one queen who died and then attacking the forces of Queen Elizabeth I with an armada. The endeavor proved a spectacular failure for the Spanish who lost forever their chance to re-Catholicize Britain. In addition to that, Spain controlled the Low Countries where the northern provinces were adopting Protestantism. The **Dutch revolt** against the Spanish domination went on for forty years until the provinces gained their independence and became the Netherlands.

The final religious war was the devastating **Thirty Years' War** which was fought on German soil but engaged most European countries in fighting or financing the war. They had political and economic goals but religious allegiances complicated the matter and it became the most destructive war fought on European soil to that point. More than one-third of the German population died while no one state proved its ability to dominate the others.

THE CONSOLIDATION OF SOVEREIGN STATES

Ironically, most monarchs in Europe benefited from religious strife. Established monarchs consolidated their power while ambitious opportunists used the chaos to gain power. The Holy Roman Empire remained decentralized and lost its prominence but almost all other countries gained strength and the ability to compete with each other.

The Attempted Revival of Empire
(Theme: Political Development)

The Holy Roman Empire was a loosely connected federation of German states which appeared to momentarily unite under the Hapsburg ruler **Charles V.** Although a Spaniard, he had inherited the title from his mother's family but he became embroiled in the Lutheran controversy and was unable to consolidate control over the empire. Eventually he had to agree to allow the German princes to choose which religion they would follow. He allowed all the countries he ruled to continue with their separate administrations and only used his military power to subdue rebellions. Furthermore, both the French king and the Ottoman rulers were concerned at the prospect of a large central empire in Europe so they united to work against the Holy Roman Empire. Charles became so defeated at his inability to control his empire that he split the kingdom between his brother and his son and retired to a monastery.

The New Monarchs
(Theme: Political Development)

While Italian states dominated commercial enterprise in Europe, the **new monarchs** of England, France, and Spain increased their political power through taxation, control of the nobility, and strongly centralized administrations.

The Spanish and French monarchs increased the financial stability of their realms with new and increased taxes on sales, households, and salt. Ever since the Magna Carta, the English kings had been reluctant to increase taxation but they did increase royal fees and fines. After **Henry VIII** dissolved the Catholic church, he confiscated church holdings which vastly increased his financial power but also burdened the state with the charitable responsibilities that the church had previously met.

The new monarchs increased the size of their bureaucracy to make tax collection and administration more reliable. Spain and France maintained large standing armies but England's unique position as an island nation did not necessitate the same. The standing armies were so large that they overwhelmed the ability of any nobleman to maintain his own private army which effectively nullified the power of the nobility. In England, the monarch kept the nobility under control by forcing them to comply with royal justice. In addition to these measures, church properties seized by Protestant monarchs gave them increased leverage over their nobility.

In Spain, Ferdinand and Isabel mobilized the Catholic church in the form of the **Spanish Inquisition** to consolidate their power. They obtained a papal license to use it as a royal office to persecute Jews, Muslims, and any incipient Protestant movements. While witch-hunts in northern Europe had addressed the fears and concerns of Protestants, the Inquisition served to expand the power of the Catholic church into every part of Spanish life.

Constitutional States
(Theme: Political Development)

In the seventeenth century, European monarchies began to develop into two distinct types: constitutional and absolute. The rulers of England and Holland shared their power with representative bodies in **constitutional monarchies** while those in France, Spain, Austria, Prussia, and Russia held power tightly within the monarchy itself.

Although they did not have written constitutions, England and the Netherlands evolved into states where political power was vested in the hands of a legislature. However, it did not happen easily. In England, the seventeenth century was a tortuous period of civil war in which one ruler was beheaded and two were deposed in the fight for executive power between the parliament and monarchs. The initial fight over taxation was coupled with religious disagreement between the monarchy's Anglicans and strict Calvinist Puritans in Parliament. Finally, in the bloodless **Glorious Revolution**, British obtained a royal family from Holland who agreed to share power with Parliament.

For the Dutch, a long war of independence waged against the Spanish preceded their republican form of government. As noted earlier, Spanish attempts to suppress the rebellion in the northern provinces of the Low Countries failed and the Dutch gained their independence in 1648. Their government was based on locally elected councils that formed the foundation of the **Dutch Republic.**

Despite little experience with representative government, these two governments were remarkably effective in harnessing popular support while allowing dissenting views. Furthermore, the prosperous merchants who were central to the elected bodies promoted a state policy of maritime trade and overseas empires. Entrepreneurs had remarkably little official interference from government so they became the engine that drove the two small nations to extraordinary prosperity in the late seventeenth and eighteenth centuries. A partnership between merchants and rulers allowed the state to rely on the profits of commerce while the rulers instituted policies to support it.

Absolute Monarchies
(Theme: Political Development)

The **absolute monarchs** of Europe predicated their power on the theoretical basis of the **divine right of kings** which stated that monarchs derived their authority from God while neither commoners nor nobility had any political role. Hypothetically then, disobedience and rebellion were akin to heresy but practically, the monarchs depended upon support from the nobility.

The most fully formed example of the absolute state was found in the court of **Louis XIV** (1643–1715) of France. Based on the earlier work of **Cardinal Richelieu,** adviser to Louis XIII, who destroyed the power of the nobility as well as French Calvinists, the French monarchy was the epitome of tightly centralized absolute monarchy. Louis XIV purportedly declared himself to be the state: "L'etat, c'est moi." He became known as The Sun King for his central and grand position in the French government. As befits an absolute ruler, he turned the royal hunting lodge, **Versailles**, into the largest building in Europe where he was the center of all. This served the purpose of keeping the nobles within the control of the monarchy as they curried favor for themselves. While the nobles concerned themselves with elaborate manners and dress, Louis XIV worked diligently with his ministers to administer his large kingdom. They promoted economic development with improvements to the infrastructure, abolishing internal tariffs, and encouraging exports. Louis XIV also maintained an enormous standing army with which he regularly engaged other European nations.

While the French monarchy was briefly the most successful practitioner of absolutism, the monarchs of Austria, Prussia, and Spain were also embracing its tenets. The **Russian tsars** were particularly adept in absolute policies as the **Romanovs** had already held a tightly controlled government since coming to power in the early seventeenth century. (Note: *Tsar* can be spelled as *czar* and is derived from the Latin word for Caesar.) By 1600, Russia had become a vast empire that spread between the Arctic and Caspian seas. The most important tsar was Peter I, known to all as **Peter the Great** (1682–1725) A veritable storm of energy, the extremely tall young man came to power over a medieval nation that he was determined to pull into the seventeenth century European world. He reformed the army by offering better pay and more professionalism and began to construct a navy. He revised administrative practices to improve tax collection and general administration. Peter even decided that the Russian nobility looked too backward in their long robes and beards so he ordered them to be clean-shaven in western clothing. When faced with active resistance, he personally shaved beards from faces. The crowning achievement of his rule was the construction of **St. Petersburg** along the Baltic as a naval base and capital.

The most talented successor to Peter the Great was an Austrian princess, Catherine, who had married into the Russian royal family. To improve government efficiency, **Catherine the Great** divided Russia into fifty provinces and continued Peter's promotion of development. She did try to help oppressed serfs until a rebellion by disgruntled ex-soldier Pugachev killed numerous nobles and government officials in the steppes north of the Caspian Sea. The rebellion failed but from then on, Catherine vigorously protected authoritarian government.

Later, three absolutist states, Russia, Prussia, and Austria, demonstrated their power by carving up Poland between them in a series of "**partitions.**" It became quite evident that in Europe national survival became dependent on a strong and effective government.

The European States System
(Theme: Political Development)

The new European states were much more powerful than their predecessors and this led to more competition and war. While the Thirty Years' War had been devastating, it was resolved with the **Peace of Westphalia** that granted recognition of sovereignty to each nation and the right of all states to manage their internal affairs.

Nevertheless, Europe continued to engage in rounds of warfare. Most conflicts were small and quickly resolved but occasional wars grew larger, lasted longer, and involved France. Louis XIV engaged in wars to expand into Germany, Spain, and the Spanish Netherlands. Later, a more global conflict, the **Seven Years' War,** had France ally with Austria and Russia against Britain and Prussia. It was fought in India and North America as well as on the European continent. Coalitions that developed could shift as the balance of powers between nations changed. However, it was risky because a coalition could stop one strong state but then see another one rise.

In many ways, the intense competition between European states drained resources but strengthened them as a whole. States developed professional officer corps through military academies while their use of increasingly sophisticated weaponry intensified their firepower. Despite the fact that China, India, and the Islamic lands had used cannons earlier, they never had the incentive to develop more powerful weapons as their military efforts were primarily focused on internal problems rather than confrontation with foreign enemies with their more powerful armaments.

EARLY CAPITALIST SOCIETY

In addition to religious and political changes, Europe also experienced population growth that led to a thriving marketplace. Combined with improvements in communication and transportation, changes in social and economic structure resulted in the development of a broadly based capitalist society. But the effects of wealthy capitalist economies were uneven. The western European countries experienced great economic prosperity while eastern European countries were relegated to providing raw goods such as grain as exports. They remained far away from centers of trade and manufacturing which resulted in little wealth accumulation in the general population. However, wealth had its own wrenching effects on western society.

Population Growth and Urbanization
(Theme: Demographics)

The increased population growth of western Europe was fueled by enriched diets with the advent of new food crops from the **Columbian exchange.** In particular, potatoes provided an increased source of carbohydrates to northern European peasants and laborers who found bread prices to be beyond their means. Some regions adopted American maize as well (polenta in northern Italy) but it was primarily a welcome addition to the feeding of livestock. Tomatoes and peppers provided welcome new tastes to the European palate.

As American crops improved the European diet, better-nourished populations were able to fend off old diseases to an extent that had not been possible before. While smallpox, typhus, dysentery, tuberculosis, and influenza continued to claim victims in all strata of society, the epidemic scourge of bubonic plague began to retreat. The last significant outbreaks were in Marseilles, France and London during the last half of the seventeenth and early part of the eighteenth centuries. After that, Europe was largely free of major epidemic disease.

Decreasing mortality rates helped increase the population at a time when there was no actual rise in the birth rate. In 1500, Europe including Russia had a population of about 81 million. In the next century, the population increased to over 100 million. Despite a decrease by one-third of the German population during the Thirty Years' War, the population recovered and climbed to 120 million by 1700. During the following century, Europe's population grew another 50 percent to 180 million.

Along with the population growth, Europe continued its pattern of **urbanization** that had begun in the late middle ages. Some cities grew as they were designated the site of government. Madrid, for instance, was a town of a few thousand in 1561 when Philip II moved his capital there. By 1600 its population had increased to 65,000 and within thirty years, it reached 170,000. Other cities became commercial and industrial centers. In the mid-sixteenth century, London and Paris had populations of 60,000 and 130,000 respectively; these grew to half a million each in the next century. Amsterdam, Berlin, Copenhagen, Dublin, Stockholm, and Vienna were among other cities that grew significantly if not spectacularly in the early modern era.

Early Capitalism and Protoindustrialization
(Theme: Economic Development)

Population growth and rapid urbanization fostered extraordinary economic growth which coincided with the emergence of **capitalism**—an economic system in which private individuals provide goods in a free market while they bear the costs of production in terms of land, buildings, machinery, tools, equipment, workshops, and raw materials. In capitalism, businessmen hire workers and make the decisions about production rather than depending upon the government or upper classes to direct commerce. However, it can be a risky proposition as the resulting profit or loss is entirely up to the individual.

Individuals accumulating great wealth was common in other regions of the world. In fact, banks, investors, and insurance underwriters had supported private business for over a thousand years in areas like China and the Middle East. However, European merchants transformed their societies during this period in a way no others had. They used efficient networks of communication and transportation to provide their commodities to regions that had the most need and thereby profited enormously. One example was Dutch merchants who imported grain from eastern Europe, stored it in Amsterdam, and sent it to southern Europe when there were crop failures. The Dutch did not produce the grain but they knew how to obtain it cheaply and sell it at the best price.

Europeans began to develop a **banking system** while **insurance companies** underwrote the risks of long-distance trade. Banks not only held funds and granted loans but they published the first business newsletters about the markets. Stock exchanges developed in large cities as capitalists sought investors to fund their ventures. **Joint-stock companies** became essential for the development of overseas trade. The English **East India Company** and the Dutch **Vereenigde Oost-Indische Compagnie (VOC)** spread the risks of distant ventures among many investors while they fueled the extraordinary expansion of European trade into the global market.

As the English and Dutch governments realized the enormous profits and prestige that could be obtained through capitalist venture, they instituted policies that fostered private business. They were encouraged by the presence of merchants in the upper echelons of government. Thus England and Holland protected the individual's right to own property, enforced private contracts, protected financial institutions, and settled disputes. They also chartered the joint-stock companies and granted some of them the right to overseas exploration. As the companies developed colonies to obtain raw materials, the governments took an active interest in their successes, so the concept of imperialism and colonial rule went hand in hand with capitalist expansions into the global market.

As individuals took over the responsibility of business, they began to reorganize their manner of manufacture. The guild structure that had controlled the production of goods for centuries protected its members and decreased competition, while a capitalist economy thrives on competition. So, entrepreneurs avoided guilds by organizing production centers in the countryside rather than in urban settings. In the **"putting-out system,"** raw materials such as wool were given to family households to spin, weave, and be fashioned into garments. Then, the businessman picked it up, paid the family, and sold his goods in town.

The system proved to be very profitable as rural labor was cheap and available. Recognized as an early attempt to organize efficient industrial organizations, some historians call this period the era of **"protoindustrialization"** and it remained in place until the advent of the factory system in the nineteenth century.

Social Change in Early Modern Europe
(Theme: Social Development)

The putting-out system changed life in rural Europe with large infusions of cash that hitherto was unavailable to the peasant class. Western European households acquired more material objects such as cabinets and furnishings while rural people ate and dressed better. With more income, individuals could choose to follow their own pursuits rather than the traditional family pursuits. This became worrisome for older people as they contemplated young adults and women abandoning their agricultural families to follow other lines of work. In eastern Europe, this was not the case as they persisted in traditional agricultural roles, but their landlords pushed them much harder than before so life grew more miserable for peasants in Poland, Russia, and Bohemia.

Conditions were particularly harsh in Russia where the Romanov tsars had restricted the freedom of peasants and tied them to the land as serfs, mimicking what had existed in western Europe in the early middle ages. The Romanov goal was to gain the support of the nobility by guaranteeing that their lands would be worked. Although the legal code of 1649 strictly determined social status and occupation, it did not include a designation of chattel slavery. Yet later nobles bought and sold **serfs** as though it had. All of this provided the landlord with inexpensive labor and huge profits.

The contrast between eastern and western Europe was profound as the east provided raw materials such as grains and timber using an almost enslaved work force and the western Europeans became a thriving capitalist marketplace with its free labor force. The two systems were so interdependent by the early sixteenth century that ironically the development of **capitalist society** was dependent on its non-capitalist counterpart.

Capitalism had moral implications as medieval churches had regarded profit as akin to sinfulness. In particular, interest on loans was considered an immoral profit. Nevertheless, loans and huge profits were the signs of a thriving capitalist economy. Philosophers such as **Adam Smith** (1723–1790) assuaged these concerns by asserting that a prosperous society was the result of individuals pursing profit.

The evolution into a capitalist society was wrenching as people watched their neighbors and family members move away from traditional pursuits while refusing to help them in hard times. The social upheaval was especially evident in the growth in banditry in the countryside and muggers in the cities. Some historians believe that the witchcraft craze also indicates social dislocation and concerns as women moved into new areas and out of the control of husbands and family.

Capitalism appears to have strengthened the nuclear family as an economic and social unit. Traditionally, European couples had married later—in their mid-twenties—in order to set up independent households, and capitalism only enhanced this trend. As the nuclear family grew in economic importance, love became more important in the choice of a spouse instead of value to one's extended families. Furthermore, affection between parents and children took on more importance.

SCIENCE AND ENLIGHTENMENT

Enormous scientific changes took place that ousted the Greek and Roman beliefs and substituted them with mathematics and scientific observation. During the seventeenth and eighteenth centuries, scientists completely revised their understanding of the earth and its universe. Later philosophers decided to apply those concepts to human beings and their political and social endeavors.

The Reconception of the Universe
(Theme: Intellectual Development)

Europeans before the seventeenth century followed the scientific beliefs of Hellenistic scholar Claudius **Ptolemy** of Alexandria. His *Algamest* postulated a motionless earth surrounded by hollow, crystalline, concentric spheres in which were embedded the larger planets, the stars, and the sun. The ninth sphere was the cosmos that provided the spin of the others. Beyond that was heaven. Later scientists added a quality of purity and perfection to the spheres and their heavenly bodies. But there was a problem: the planets did not follow absolutely regular movements. The Greek word *planetes* means "wanderer."

They slowed down, reversed directions, and even appeared to stop which proved hard to explain. Most astronomers attempted to reconcile their observations with the Ptolomaic view. However, in 1543, Polish astronomer **Nicolaus Copernicus** posited that the earth was not the center of the universe and instead that the sun stood at the center with the planets, including the earth, revolving around it. In his treatise, *On the Revolutions of the Heavenly Spheres,* Copernicus completely rejected Ptolemy's view, but this stand threatened both religious views and accepted scientific beliefs. Its implication was that the earth was no better than any other planet and therefore humans were also less significant than was acceptable. And, worst of all, there might be other populations beyond the uniquely God-created ones on earth.

As evidence was accumulated with more precise observations and mathematical calculations, it became clear to scientists that the Copernican view was correct, but it continued to be challenged in other quarters. Scientists and mathematicians began to investigate other possibilities when they applied their analytical methods to mechanics, the branch of science that deals with moving bodies. Two mathematicians, **Johannes Kepler** of Germany and **Galileo Galilei** of Italy, were at the forefront of the research. Kepler demonstrated that the planetary orbits were elliptical which explained some of the anomalies in Copernicus's work. Galileo used the recently invented **telescope** to scan the heavens and determine that there were spots on the sun, mountains on the moon, and distant stars that no one had ever seen before. In addition to astronomy, Galileo proved that the speed of falling objects depended upon their weight rather than the height of their fall; this anticipated an understanding of gravity. He also described the idea of inertia in which a moving body will go in a straight line unless some other force alters it.

In 1687, English mathematician **Isaac Newton** (1642–1727) combined the ideas of astronomy and mechanics in his work, *Mathematical Principles of Natural Philosophy.* He theorized that a great universal system existed in which all bodies were affected by gravitational forces, and he was able to prove mathematically that those forces were exhibited in the movements of bodies on earth. His gravitational theories allowed him to explain a large number of seemingly unrelated phenomena such as the ebb and flow of tides and the oddities in orbits by planets and comets. Until Einstein in the twentieth century, Newton's theories were the framework for all discoveries in the physical sciences.

Newton's ideas which synthesized observation and mathematics provided the foundation for revolutions in every area of the physical sciences. His work was followed by extensive investigation of the natural world in the seventeenth and eighteenth centuries. European scientists used direct observation and mathematics to revise thinking in anatomy, physiology, microbiology, chemistry, and botany.

The Enlightenment
(Theme: Intellectual Development)

Newton's concept that the universe operated under a set of laws that could be observed and explained by scientists soon was applied to the thoughts and actions of human beings themselves. Applying human reason to human problems, philosophers of the **Enlightenment** rejected Aristotelian philosophy, Christian religion, and other traditional authorities.

In their search for natural laws that would govern human society, philosophers went in many different directions. English philosopher **John Locke** (1632–1704) worked on the laws of politics. He attacked divine-right theories and believed that sovereignty lies in the people rather than their rulers. This provided much of theoretical justification for constitutional government and, in particular, the Glorious Revolution. Scottish philosopher Adam Smith turned to a rational explanation of economics which held that the laws of supply and demand determine the actions of the marketplace. The **Baron de Montesquieu** (1689–1755) also took on politics as he attempted to discover the laws that would provide political liberty in a prosperous state.

The center of Enlightenment thought was France, where prominent intellectuals known as *philosophes* publicized the new ideas to an educated public rather than other scholars. Instead of formal philosophical works, the philosophes composed histories, plays, satires, and pamphlets as a form of public discourse on philosophical subjects. In *salons* put on by prominent women, the leading intellectuals could meet and discuss the current thinking within an atmosphere of social refinement. François-Marie Arouet (1694–1778), known as **Voltaire,** was the quintessential French philosophe. He published his first book at seventeen and went on to write some seventy volumes of letters and essays. His works were filled with criticism and stinging wit as he championed individual freedom and attacked the institutions of European society, which included the Catholic church and the French monarchy. When the French monarchy announced it would pare down the number of horses in its barns to reduce costs, Voltaire responded that it would be better to reduce the number of asses who rode the horses. His bitter battle against the Catholic church was exemplified in his cry of *écrasez l'infame* which means "crush the damned thing."

While Voltaire detested organized religion, he was one of many philosophes who were **deists** rather than atheists or conventional Christians. That is to say, they believed in a deity who set the universe in motion and devised the laws that governed it. However, he did not have an interest in its later development, nor did he involve himself in the daily concerns of humanity. God was a watchmaker who manufactured the machine but did not need to interfere as it moved along under natural laws.

The philosophes were an optimistic group who believed that once one had determined the laws of human beings, humanity would move constantly forward. Their belief in **rational progress** became a near ideology that most thought would lead to a state of individual liberty for all and ultimately a just, prosperous, and equitable society. However, despite enormous efforts to attain the ideal, it never came to pass. Nevertheless, the Enlightenment permanently weakened the influence of organized religion, replaced religious thought with secular reasoning, and encouraged political and social experimentation by leaders in order to promote progress. Europe was permanently changed and the influences of the Enlightenment are felt to this day in both Europe and the Americas.

Finished reading the chapter? Be sure you can . . .

- Demonstrate one effect of the Columbian exchange.
- Analyze improvements in European weaponry.
- Explain the evolution of constitutional government in England.
- Explain the evolution of absolute government in France and Russia.
- Describe the Reformation and the Catholic Reformation.
- Discuss the scientific revolution and its effects.
- Describe the Enlightenment and its effects.
- Compare European monarchs with Chinese or Indian empires.
- Describe Russian attempts to westernize.

CHAPTER MULTIPLE CHOICE QUESTIONS

1. When Martin Luther objected to the Catholic church, what was his original issue?
   a. a vernacular Bible
   b. an end to celibacy
   c. the sale of indulgences
   d. the display of relics
   e. priestly authority

2. To what purpose was the Council of Trent convened?
   a. the sale of indulgences
   b. celibacy in priests
   c. as opposition to the Protestant Reformation
   d. the education of priests
   e. all of the above

3. The usual victims of sixteenth- and seventeenth-century witch-hunts were women, but what other characteristic did they share?
   a. a marginalized position in society
   b. a religious threat to the local parish
   c. a prominent and threatening role in society
   d. advocacy of women's rights
   e. a belief in witchcraft

4. Why was Charles V ultimately unable to strengthen the Holy Roman Empire?
   a. He was an inept ruler who depended upon his ministers.
   b. He was confronted with religious and political problems.
   c. The Holy Roman Empire was too loosely connected.
   d. He was Spanish and the Empire was German.
   e. He was distracted by the internal demands of the Spanish government.

5. In addition to enhanced administration and improved finances, the new monarchs needed to
   a. ally themselves with bigger states.
   b. have the support of the nobility.
   c. suppress the power of the nobility.
   d. gain the support of the Catholic church.
   e. satisfy the concerns of the lower classes.

6. Of the following statements, which one is the most accurate in regards to constitutional states?
   a. Constitutional monarchs must follow the rules of a written constitution.
   b. Constitutional monarchs must be sole rulers.
   c. Constitutional monarchs must share power with a representative body.
   d. Constitutional monarchs base their power on divine right.
   e. Constitutional monarchs are always weaker than legislative bodies.

7. The most successful absolute monarchs arguably were Louis XIV of France and Peter the Great of Russia. What did they have in common?
   a. Both forced their people to modernize their customs to conform with western European standards.
   b. Both created new institutions to control the nobility rather than depending on personal power.
   c. Both used enormous sums of money to engage in numerous wars with their rivals.
   d. Both engaged in huge building projects designed to enhance their prestige while adding to their power.
   e. Both ignored administration to concentrate on foreign affairs.

8. Which of the following contributed the most to the enormous growth of the European population during the sixteenth and seventeenth centuries?
   a. the decrease in epidemic disease
   b. new crops from other continents
   c. an increasing birth rate
   d. the move towards the companionate marriage
   e. increased sanitation methods in urban centers

9. What is the best explanation for Isaac Newton's importance to the scientific revolution?
   a. Newton publicized the findings of astronomers to other scientists.
   b. Newton's works were discussed by philosophes in salons.
   c. Newton provided a scientific explanation for human behavior.
   d. Newton proved that the Ptolomaic universe was an error.
   e. Newton provided an explanation of the systematic organization of the universe.

10. Why were the French philosophes important?
    a. They believed that their concepts of individual rights would provide for constant progress.
    b. They explained the theories of the scientific revolution to the public.
    c. They started a religious split that further divided Protestant sects.
    d. They uniformly agreed on the rejection of organized religion.
    e. They allowed intellectual women to participate on an equal basis with men.

Comprehensive Multiple Choice Questions

1. The absolute monarchs of Europe had a philosophy most similar to which of the following rulers?
    a. the Roman emperors
    b. the Incas
    c. the Chinese emperors
    d. the Baghdad caliphate
    e. the pharaohs

2. When comparing the thriving business activities of the Italian city-states during the high middle ages with the flourishing capitalism of Holland and England in the seventeenth and eighteenth centuries, what constitutes the major difference in their practices?
    a. The earlier period was dependent on foreign trade while the latter focused primarily on regional trade.
    b. The Italian governments controlled business practices while the constitutional monarchs ignored them.
    c. The earlier period was more reliant on its own craftsmen than the later period with its putting-out system.
    d. Medieval guilds discouraged competition, but later entrepreneurs depended on competition.
    e. The earlier period had no institutions to support business practices while banks operated in the later period.

3. Which of the following statements best describes the similarities between the Enlightenment and the earlier Renaissance?
    a. Both focused on a philosophy of human behavior.
    b. Both adopted a return to a better, more classical period.
    c. Both allowed women some role in the intellectual world.
    d. Both were a product of recent scientific discoveries.
    e. Both rejected the church for a more humanist view of religion.

Primary Source Questions

Note: The number of gruesome illustrations in this chapter indicates the extent to which Europe was shattered by religious and political events.

1. ***Read Sources from the Past: Adam Smith on the Capitalist Market*, 1776, on page 654 of your textbook.**
    a. What is Adam Smith's point of view?
    b. What is the singular goal of all individuals?
    c. How does that goal affect society as a whole?
    d. What is his opinion of government regulation?

2. **Examine the painting of the Parisian salon of Mme. Geoffrin, c. 1775, 1814, on page 659 of your textbook.**
   a. What is the painter's point of view?
   b. Describe the setting.
   c. Who is at the center of the painting and why?
   d. What do the philosophes appear to be engaged in?
   e. What is the role of women in this illustration?

Chapter Multiple Choice Answers

1. **d:** Outraged by the sale of indulgences, Luther penned his *Ninety-Five Theses* that began the Reformation. (p. 631)

2. **e:** In reaction to the Protestant reformation (choice "c"), the Catholic church reformed all areas of concern in the other three choices. (p. 631)

3. **a:** The witch-hunts claimed some men and prominent women but the primary targets were women weakened by poverty and social position such as widows. (p. 635)

4. **b:** During his reign, Charles V faced the disintegrating Catholic church as well as opposition from the French and the Ottomans. (p. 637)

5. **c:** The primary rivals of the monarchs in England, France, and Spain had always been the nobility so it was necessary to control them. (p. 639)

6. **c:** Constitutional monarchs agree to limited powers and recognize the rights of individuals and legislative bodies. (p. 641)

7. **d:** Louis XIV built Versailles into the center of his power while Peter the Great build St. Petersburg as a capital and naval port. (pp. 644, 645)

8. **b:** New crops, particularly potatoes and maize, increased the carbohydrate levels in peasant diets which provided for a better nourished population more able to fight off disease. (p. 649)

9. **e:** Newton's concept of gravitation and motion was the best explanation for the orderly universe observed by physical scientists. (p. 657)

10. **a:** The philosophes fervently believed that a rational understanding of human behavior would lead to continual progress for all. (p. 659)

Comprehensive Multiple Choice Answers

1. **c:** The absolute monarchs based their power on the notion of divine right, which shares the idea of a form of heavenly sanction of the ruler's role with the Chinese Mandate of Heaven. Both the Incas and the pharaohs were considered actual gods among their people while the Baghdad caliphate was a theocracy in which the secular ruler was also the religious ruler. (pp. 115, 642)

2. **d:** The primary characteristic of capitalism is its encouragement of competition, but the most important goal of guilds was to limit competition by regulating guild members. Capitalist merchants engaged in long-distance trade of grains and other commodities, while Italian city-states were dependent on their participation in the Mediterranean trade. Italian rulers allowed independent business but the later rulers actively sought to encourage private business with charter companies, contract protections, and financial security measures. Lastly, the high middle ages did have banking which they had borrowed from the Islamic world but the capitalist societies also introduced insurance companies to protect investments. (pp. 521, 651)

3. **a:** The Renaissance humanists devoted themselves to the study of the humanities but also supported an active life as moral while the Enlightenment philosophes evaluated the laws of human nature and touted an active moral life as well. The Renaissance scholars looked to classical Greek and Roman societies while the Enlightenment philosophers looked to the newest discoveries and steady progress into a spectacular future. While the philosophes accepted the role of women as facilitators of dynamic philosophical debate, few Renaissance humanists considered women at all. The scientific revolution that preceded the Enlightenment had no parallel in the earlier period and few humanists rejected the Catholic religion for another explanation of God's role as the deists did later on. (pp. 584, 658)

Primary Source Answers

1. Adam Smith was an economic philosopher in one of the most prosperous countries in Europe at the time of this writing. Since capitalism had been promoted by the government for over a century, he would see only the positive effects of private business. Smith goes directly to the core of human nature when he avows that the individual's primary goal is self-interest. Moreover, he states that it is precisely this self-centered single-mindedness that benefits the entire society. Thus he is totally opposed to any type of regulation because market forces are better regulated by the people's response to it than by government. (p. 654)

2. The painter is of a later period, so he is glorifying the Enlightenment despite the fact that the French revolution has already occurred. Many of these people would have lost their heads to the guillotine or become refugees due to their social status. In fact, it was painted at the end of the Napoleonic era (see Chapter 29) when the painter would be eager to hold fast to ideas of French glory and superiority. The setting is a refined room filled with fine paintings in gilt frames, good rugs, and high ceilings, all of which indicate upper-class prosperity. The hostess, the speaker, and a bust of Voltaire are at the center of the painting where they might receive the most attention. As is usual during speeches, the people in the front row closest to the speaker seem fully attentive but other clusters are engaged in discussion with each other. One or two older gentlemen appear to be sleeping. Of the seven women in the painting, only two appear to be paying attention to the speaker. The hostess is fawning over her impressive salon, three women are listening intently to men, and one appears to be daydreaming. From these representations, it is apparent that women were more like accessories to intellectual life than participants. (p. 659)

CHAPTER 25

NEW WORLDS: THE AMERICAS AND OCEANIA

Before you get started: This chapter picks up where Chapter 21 left off, so it merits a quick review of that chapter first. While not especially long, Chapter 25 is an important one focused on three clear ideas: conquest, exploitation, and interaction of cultures. How did the inadequately equipped and vastly outnumbered Spanish subdue the fierce Aztecs and the sophisticated Incas? What type of multicultural society did the Spanish and Portuguese establish in the New World and how did they maintain control so far from home? How did the English, Dutch, and French experiences in North America differ from their European counterparts in South America? Where do Australia and the Pacific Islands fit into these patterns of conquest and exploitation? Above all, this is a great chapter to consider as you think about point of view. How might this story be told much differently from the perspective of the conquered and exploited?

COLLIDING WORLDS

The year 1492 is significant in world history because from that point forward there is permanent and sustained contact between the peoples of the eastern and western hemispheres which brings profound and often violent change to each world; neither realm remains the same and both hemispheres ultimately interact to form a new world. The Europeans brought new technology and devastating disease to the Americas and used existing rivalries to overpower and ultimately destroy existing empires. Eventually, settler colonies would further displace and discard indigenous peoples in both South and North America.

The Spanish Caribbean
(Themes: Patterns of Interaction and Labor Systems)

The islands of the Caribbean had been inhabited by the **Tainos (Arawaks)** since the late centuries B.C.E. when their ancestors sailed in canoes from the Orinoco River valley in South America; by the tenth century C.E. they had settled throughout the region. The Tainos, who lived in small villages under the authority of local chiefs and grew manioc as a primary food source, offered little resistance to Columbus and his men when the Spanish mariners arrived and began to establish a series of forts, originally intended to serve as trading posts for local merchants who would arrive to trade for the anticipated silks, spices, and other goods from the Orient. As it became clear these were not the hoped-for islands of the Orient, the Spanish settlers soon realized they would need to find other ways to make a living. Though they tried gold mining, the Spanish settlers were too few in number and did not desire to physically work as hard as mining required. So the settlers turned to the Tainos to supply the necessary labor; the institution of forced labor known as the **encomienda** developed to compel the Tainos to work in the mines and on the lands now claimed by the Spanish settlers. Theoretically, in return for the Tainos' labor, the Spaniards were to provide for the health and physical welfare of the Indian miners and to attempt to convert them to Christianity. The theory did not translate into practice and a brutal system of exploitation developed. The Tainos did not respond willingly to the encomienda system and the Spanish met their rebellion with steel swords and firearms. The population of available Tainos declined under this harsh physical labor system and, when a smallpox epidemic arrived in 1518, the Tainos population was annihilated. Despite attempts to capture new Tainos people and other indigenous peoples of the region, disease and working conditions eventually wiped out these societies. By the sixteenth century little remained of the Tainos and their Caribbean regional culture.

Thin and dwindling supplies of gold soon made mining in the Caribbean unprofitable and the discovery of vast supplies of silver in **Peru** and **Mexico** shifted the focus of Spanish settlement to the mainland. In the 1640s, English, Dutch, and French settlers began to arrive in the Caribbean, not to mine, but in hopes of producing valuable cash crops like **sugar** and eventually **tobacco.** Plantations require labor and since the Tainos were decimated, these new European settlers desperately needed workers to operate their estates; they began to import **several million slaves from west Africa** to supply that labor. By 1700, the Caribbean was populated by a small class of European planters and large numbers of enslaved Africans.

The Conquest of Mexico and Peru
(Themes: Patterns of Interaction and Technology)

The sparse output of mineral wealth on the islands of the Caribbean soon sent the Spaniards to the mainland in search of minerals to exploit. Conquistadores like **Hernan Cortes** in Mexico and **Francisco Pizarro** in Peru led expeditions of conquest which eventually toppled the Aztec and Incan empires and laid the foundations for colonial regimes that would transform the Americas.

In Mexico, Cortes found a society much different than those of the Caribbean. Making his way from the Gulf coast to the capital city of Tenochtitlan with 450 soldiers, Cortes found a rich and vibrant city with a population well over two hundred thousand people. Initially driven from the city by Aztec forces, Cortes used his superior weaponry and, more significantly, the enmity of other Indian groups, to eventually starve the city into surrender. It was disease, especially smallpox, which sapped the Aztecs in strength and decimated them in number.

Pizarro's experience in Peru was very similar. With a force of no more than six hundred men, he arrived in Peru after a wave of smallpox had seriously weakened the indigenous population. Capitalizing on a bitter fight over succession in the Inca dynasty and exploiting resentments of subjects toward the powerful Incas, Pizarro and his men held the Inca leader for ransom in gold, and then deceived and murdered many of the Inca elite, thus reducing the potential for any serious military resistance. By 1540, the Spanish were firmly established in the Andes.

Iberian Empires in the Americas
(Theme: Patterns of Interaction)

During much of the sixteenth century, Cortes and Pizarro allocated land and labor rights to their troops, but by 1570, **the Spanish Crown** had developed a formal policy of control and administration of justice for these formerly conqistadore-run territories. Spanish administrators established centers of authority in Mexico and in Peru which were each governed by a powerful viceroy who was directly responsible to the Spanish king. The viceroy in Mexico established a new capital, Mexico City, on the ruins of Tenochtitlan, while the viceroy in Peru preferred to establish a new capital city, Lima, in a more hospitable coastal environment than the mountainous Cuzco. To keep these viceroys from becoming too personally powerful, the Spanish monarchy established **audiencias,** review courts staffed by university-educated lawyers whose task it was to review the viceroys' decisions, evaluate their performances, and mete out severe punishments, if needed. Yet, distance from Spain kept the Spanish monarch from being directly involved in administering the Americas, and challenges in transportation and communication even made it difficult for the viceroy to supervise their territories, called **viceroyalties.** Increasingly, Spanish colonists preferred to live in cities, so new cities were established to keep up with the expanding territory in their landed estates. New Spain, administered from Mexico City, reached as far north as St. Augustine in Florida, and New Castile, administered from Lima, reached from Panama to Buenos Aires.

Portugal established an imperial realm in **Brazil** as a result of the 1494 **Treaty of Tordesillas.** This historically curious document divided the world into a Spanish sphere to the west and a Portuguese sphere to the east; the imaginary dividing line included the northeastern tip of South America in the east, which meant Portugal had a New World claim to Brazil. After the voyage of **Pero Alvares Cabral** and a threatened potential land grab by the French and the Dutch, the Portuguese king decided to grant these new Brazil lands to his nobles; he soon sent a governor to oversee their holdings and to implement his royal policy. The establishment of profitable sugar plantations on the coast after 1550 dramatically increased Portuguese interest in Brazil.

The Spanish and Portuguese settlers wanted to live in cities established in a European style; Spanish and Portuguese became the languages of government, society, and business. Indigenous peoples and their cultures survived best in areas removed from European interests, those areas which produced little agricultural surplus. Overall, the Spanish and the Portuguese viewed the New World as a place to exploit resources and make themselves rich rather than as a place to settle and colonize. Yet, between 1500 and 1800, more than five hundred thousand Spanish immigrants and one hundred thousand Portuguese immigrants settled permanently in the Americas.

Settler Colonies in North America
(Theme: Patterns of Interaction)

Spanish explorers ventured north into Florida and Virginia and even toward Maine and Newfoundland along the Atlantic seaboard. In the west, they explored parts of modern Canada, establishing a fort at Vancouver Island. By the mid-sixteenth century, the Dutch, English, and French were regularly venturing to the American coastlines in search of **fish** and the much more elusive **Northwest Passage to Asia**. By the early seventeenth centuries, these explorers began to establish permanent colonies on the North American mainland: French settlements at Port Royal in Nova Scotia in 1604 and Quebec in 1608 and English settlements at Jamestown in Virginia in 1607 and the Massachusetts Bay Colony in 1630. Dutch New Amsterdam, seized by the English in 1664, became New York and part of the growing English colonial holdings spread throughout the east coast of North America. The French settled in eastern Canada and concentrated their exploration for furs and goods along the St. Lawrence, Ohio, and Mississippi Rivers where they built forts all the way to the Gulf of Mexico.

North American settlement life was difficult and often deadly. A focus on the production of valuable **commodities for export** such as fur, pitch, tar, or lumber, rather than on food production, meant these early colonists relied on provisions shipped from Europe, an uncertain and often unrealized hope. Lack of food and disease nearly destroyed the Jamestown settlement as only sixty of the original five hundred settlers survived the first winter.

Numerous differences existed between the English and French colonies and the Iberian territories. The English and French explorations were financed much more often by private capital than were the Iberian explorations which almost always had the backing and control of the monarchs. The French and English colonists, though subject to royal authority, had no audiencias or viceroys to deal with and often had some measure of autonomy through **colonial assemblies.**

Perhaps the greatest difference in the two early settler experiences occurred because of relationships with the indigenous peoples. There were no parallels in North America to the Aztecs or Incas, so the English and French did not find such densely populated, urban traditions. Instead, most of the North American peoples were agricultural, but they often relied on hunting as well and so moved their villages and settlements quite frequently. To the European settlers, this behavior implied that no one "owned" the land and this availability of fertile farmland soon attracted large numbers of European migrants with up to 150,000 English families moving to North America in the seventeenth century; significant numbers of French, Dutch, German, and Irish settlers soon joined them in this quest for free land. These settlers had no real perception of this land as belonging to the indigenous population since it was not farmed, fenced, or occupied in a European manner. Land titles were issued based on English common law, which considered unfarmed land as "unproductive" and therefore available for occupancy and cultivation.

Native peoples recognized this land grab and raided European settlements; these attacks brought reprisals and the conflict ensued. Once again, the indigenous people were ultimately no match for the **weaponry** and especially the **epidemic diseases** of the settlers. Between 1600 and 1800, one million northern European settlers arrived in North America. By 1800, fewer than 600,000 Native Americans lived in North America, with more than five million people of European ancestry and one million slaves of African American ancestry.

COLONIAL SOCIETY IN THE AMERICAS

The history of colonial societies in America is one of interactions of cultures: European, American, African. Mining, fur trapping, and the cultivation of cash crops formed the economic basis of these societies and Christianity emerged as the dominant religion in the western hemisphere. The **mestizo** population, a mixture of European and Euro-American offspring, came to dominate political, economic, and cultural affairs.

The Formation of Multicultural Societies
(Theme: Patterns of Interaction)

European migrants radically transformed the social order in places where they established settler colonies or imperial states; all European territories became places where people of varied ancestry lived in multicultural societies. Because the vast majority of migrants to the Iberian colonies were men, many of these men entered into relationships with native women that produced offspring known as **mestizo** or mixed; this was especially true in Mexico. Women were more prominent in Peru where migrants lived in cities, married among themselves, and kept mostly apart from the native populations. Outside the cities, in Mexico, and other less settled regions, Spanish men associated with native women and gave rise to mestizo society.

Brazil developed as an even more ethnically and racially diverse society than Mexico. In Brazil, where few European women were available, Portuguese men frequently entered into relationships with native women and with African slave women. Various ethnic combinations emerged from these unions including **mestizos, mulattoes** (those born of Portuguese and African parents), **zambos** (those born of indigenous and African parents), and combinations arising from unions within and between these groups.

Peninsulares, the term applied to migrants born in Europe who came to reside in Spanish or Portuguese colonies, stood at the top of the social hierarchy. **Criollos** or **creoles,** individuals born of Iberian parents in the Americas, were next in status. Early in the colonial period, mestizos lived on the fringes of society, but as time passed and their numbers grew, especially in Brazil and Mexico, they were adopted into the social fabric of colonial societies. Mulattoes, zambos, and other people of mixed heritage became prominent in Brazilian society, though always subordinate to anyone of European or European and mixed heritage while slaves and conquered peoples remained at the bottom of the social hierarchy.

In North America, the social structure of French and English colonies developed much differently, in large part because European women were much more numerous among those migrants. Though French fur traders associated with native women to produce offspring known as **metis,** in more settled regions, liaisons between French men and native women were much less common. The English colonies experienced the least mingling of cultures as the English viewed the indigenous people as heathens, too lazy to acquire property or even cultivate the land, and soon extended this scorn to imported Africans who were seen as inferior beings. English settlers strongly discouraged relationships between Europeans and non-Europeans, often refusing to accept or even acknowledge the resulting offspring; these sharp boundaries between groups in the English colonies soon produced virulent racism.

Despite their exclusionary attitudes, the English settlers readily adopted useful cultural elements such as terms and technologies from the indigenous people and from the enslaved Africans. The English settlers adopted names for plants and animals not found in Europe and often the styles of clothing and warfare used by the indigenous people. Likewise, African food crops and agricultural techniques proved useful to the settlers.

Mining and Agriculture in the Spanish Empire
(Themes: Economics, Technology, and Labor Systems)

Though the conquistadores found easy access to gold and silver in the Aztec and Inca empires and, without a thought to artistic or cultural value, melted those looted treasures down into easily transportable ingots, their followers would have to rely on mining to extract the Americas' mineral wealth. Silver, not gold, proved to be the most abundant precious mineral in the Americas in quantity and value. Silver mining was concentrated in two regions: in north Mexico near Zacateas and in the high, cold Bolivian Andes.

Unlike the Mexican mines where many laborers went somewhat willingly to escape the pressures of conquest and disease, many miners at Potosí, in the Andes, fell subject to the draft-labor tradition known as **mita,** which was to fill those jobs deemed too dangerous and thus unacceptable by wage laborers. Developed after the earlier Inca system of draft labor, Spanish administrators required each village to send one-seventh of its male population to work for four months. In theory, the miners were to be paid, fed, and housed during their work period; in reality, wages were low or nonexistent, living conditions were awful, and the work was dangerous and often deadly. Many native men fled to cities or hid in other villages to escape their mita obligations. These patterns of employment influenced settlement patterns throughout the Andean region.

Spain grew wealthy from their silver production in the New World. The Spanish government claimed one-fifth of all silver production for itself; this **quinto** helped the Spanish government build a huge military and a bureaucracy to support it. The silver wealth quickly moved beyond Spain into the rest of Spanish holdings in Europe and eventually into the global markets throughout Asia.

In addition to mining, the principal occupations in Spanish America were farming, raising stock, and craft production. The hacienda, or estate, became the most prominent agricultural and craft production site by the seventeenth century. The hacienda, which relied on indigenous labor, produced crops mostly of European origin such as wheat, grapes, and meat from cattle and pigs. Smaller properties often owned by poorer Spanish migrants or creoles produced similar crops though on a much smaller scale and for local consumption. Indigenous peoples practiced subsistence agriculture and lived in small villages.

At first, these haciendas relied on the **encomienda system** to force indigenous peoples into farm work. Over time however, the payment of **tribute** from indigenous farmers working smaller plots of land proved more profitable than the mita for the Spanish landowners. Still needing laborers to work the hacienda, the Spanish landowners developed another system of exploitation. They loaned money to native peoples so they could buy seed, tools, and supplies, which the indigenous people were to pay off with their labor; of course, the wages were too low to ever repay the loans. Thus, debt peonage produced a captive labor force to work the estates.

The indigenous peoples did resist the Spanish regimes. Sometimes, they tried to work within the Spanish government. Men like **Felipe Guaman Poma de Ayala** sent a 1,200-page letter with four hundred illustrations to King Philip III of Spain detailing the abuse of indigenous peoples and demanding that if Philip wanted to protect his Andean empire he must protect its people. The letter never made it to Spain but somehow ended up hidden in a museum in Denmark until the twentieth century. Other attempts at rebellion were not so tame. In 1680, native groups in northern Mexico, led by a shaman named **Pope,** attacked Spanish estates driving Spanish settlers out of the region for more than twelve years; these uprisings were known as the **Pueblo Revolt.** In Peru, an even larger rebellion occurred in 1780 when a force of 60,000 native people participated in the **Tupac Amaru Rebellion**, which lasted almost two years before it was finally suppressed by Spanish forces.

Sugar and Slavery in Portuguese Brazil
(Themes: Economics, Technology, and Labor Systems)

Portuguese economic and social patterns produced different systems of labor and production in Brazil than the systems in Spanish colonies. Portuguese nobles and entrepreneurs did not have conquistadores like the Spanish had used to subdue the native populations and compel them to work for their conquerors. The Portuguese, instead, relied on imported African people to work as slaves on their sugar plantations; these enslaved migrants rapidly outnumbered their Portuguese captors. Sugar soon became Brazil's most important export and the *engenho,* or sugar mill, became the center of colonial Brazilian life.

While *engenho* originally applied only to the sugar-extracting equipment, the term was soon used to describe the complex land, buildings, animals, equipment, tools, capital, and technical skills necessary to produce molasses and refined sugar from rough cane. Portuguese planters and owners became a privileged class and exercised great political, economic, and social influence in Brazil and Portugal. Royal support for their means and endeavors was guaranteed, so long as their often-risky ventures produced a profit for the entrepreneur and a tax base for the monarchy.

The devastating effects of disease and the non-sedentary nature of the indigenous peoples made them unreliable as a labor source, so the Portuguese plantation managers began to import African laborers as slaves as early as 1530; after 1580, Africans were supplying the vast bulk of labor on the sugar plantations. Tropical heat, disease, overwork, dangerous working conditions, inadequate food and housing, and mistreatment resulted in high death rates—as many as five to ten percent of enslaved peoples each year. The number of deaths exceeded the number of births so the demand for slaves was constantly increasing as the demand for sugar grew. Economically, if a slave lived five or six years, the plantation owner's investment doubled and he could afford to buy a new healthy slave without taking a monetary loss; children of slaves took an economic investment of at least twelve years, which represented a financial loss. It is estimated that every ton of sugar produced cost one human life.

Fur Traders and Settlers in North America
(Themes: Economics, Labor Systems, and Patterns of Interaction)

Fish first brought European mariners to North American shores, but soon fur became the much more lucrative commodity. Initially, fishermen bartered for fur with local peoples, but after the European discovery of the **Hudson Strait and Hudson Bay,** they began the systematic exploitation of northern regions. Royal agents and adventurers built a series of trading posts and forts to connect large portions of the North American interior. Indigenous people would trap the desired animals and then trade those furs for manufactured objects such as woolen blankets, iron pots, firearms, and distilled spirits.

This fur trade created serious conflicts among trappers, native peoples, and Europeans. Individual trappers fought each other over prime territory; native peoples such as the Iroquois and Huron fought over land resources using European-supplied weapons; and Europeans fought each other in the Americas and at home over territorial boundaries.

European trappers soon became settlers and posed a serious threat to native populations as the settler-cultivators turned former trapping grounds into plantations; ironically, these earliest settlers would most likely have perished without the maize, game, and fish supplied by the native peoples. Over time though, the French and English settlers grew more capable of survival and soon were actively seeking to distinguish themselves from their former helpmates. The settlers began to produce cash crops like tobacco, then rice and indigo, and eventually cotton to market in Europe. While they had displaced the indigenous people, the settlers could not subdue enough of them to depend on as the steady supply of labor demanded by the cultivation of these crops. Indentured servants from Europe provided a short-term answer, but most of these laborers died, escaped, or survived to earn their freedom.

In 1619, a group of twenty Africans arrived in Virginia where they worked alongside other European laborers. By 1661, however, Virginia recognized all blacks as slaves, and by 1680, planters were increasingly replacing indentured servants with African slaves. Though slave labor was not profitable in the northern colonies as the land and climate were not suitable for cash crop production, the northern colonies did benefit economically from slavery. Many New England merchants traded in slaves headed for the West Indies, New Yorkers and Philadelphian entrepreneurs made substantial profits on building and supplying slave ships, and New England ports became wealthy off the production of rum manufactured from the slave-produced sugar of the West Indies which was in turn traded for slaves along the West African coast.

Christianity and Native Religions in the Americas
(Themes: Religious and Cultural Developments)

In addition to economic motivations, the desire to spread Christianity traveled to the New World with the European explorers, conquistadores, merchants, and settlers. Missionaries soon followed.

Spanish missionaries from the Dominican, Franciscan, and especially Jesuit orders established schools in towns and villages and were extremely successful in converting the sons of prominent local families to Latin, Spanish, and Christian doctrines. At the same time, the missionaries themselves learned native languages and customs in their attempts to explain Christianity to the indigenous people of Mexico and Peru. Much of the modern knowledge regarding these indigenous cultures comes from the work of men like Franciscan priest Bernardino de Sahagun whose writings chronicled Aztec society, language, customs, history, and literature.

Many native peoples continued to practice their traditional religions even though the Catholic church and the Spanish governments made consistent and sometimes violent attempts to eradicate the worship of pagan deities. When native peoples did adopt Christianity, they frequently blended their own traditions and interests with the faith taught by the Christian missionaries. The reverence for the Virgin of Guadalupe became extremely popular among the mestizo population of Mexico and helped to ensure that Roman Catholicism would dominate Mexican culture.

French and English missionaries found it much more difficult to convert the non-sedentary peoples of North America. English colonists in particular seemed little interested in conversions of indigenous peoples and did not readily welcome native converts into their European, Christian settlements. French missionaries were much more active and found some success in spreading Christianity in the St. Lawrence, Ohio, and Mississippi River valleys.

EUROPEANS IN THE PACIFIC

Though the European mariners explored the islands of the Pacific and Australia after the European migrations began to the Americas, the initial results were very similar, as the Pacific islanders had no immunity to European diseases. The explorations began in the sixteenth to eighteenth centuries, but the European migrant settlements did not begin in most places until the nineteenth century.

Australia and the Larger World
(Theme: Patterns of Interaction)

Many Europeans had speculated for centuries about the existence of an unknown southern land, but it was the Dutch who made the first recorded sighting of Australia in 1606. Though successive Dutch voyagers reported the land as arid and barren and concluded that it could not contain any mineral wealth, the Dutch mariners continued to scout the continent's coastlines as did English Captain James Cook in 1770. These European mariners had only fleeting contact with the aborigines of Australia whom they considered "wretched savages" because the people were nomadic foragers rather than sedentary cultivators. Only after Cook's exploration of Australia's eastern coastline did the Europeans realize that the land was suitable for settlement. After 1788, the English decided to establish a penal colony as the continent's first permanent settlement. It would not be until the nineteenth century that European migrants would begin a steady flow to the continent and begin sustained contact with the aborigines who would not fair well in contact with European settlers and the British government.

The Pacific Islands and the Larger World
(Theme: Patterns of Interaction)

Though European mariners explored the Pacific Ocean basin in the sixteenth and seventeenth centuries, it was not until the late eighteenth century that European merchants and settlers began to arrive in significant numbers. Guam and the Mariana Islands were the only Pacific islands to attract substantial Spanish interest in the sixteenth century. These islands were used as stops for fresh provisions for the Manila galleons, and for nearly a century these interactions were peaceful. In the late seventeenth century, the Spanish authorities decided to impose Spanish control in Guam and the Marianas under direction of the viceroy of Spain in Mexico. Spanish troops were sent to enforce the Crown's rule and to enforce the conversion of the native Chamorro people to Christianity. Military intervention and a smallpox epidemic decimated the Chamorro people and their culture.

By the eighteenth century, European interest and settlement in the Pacific islands was growing. The search for the elusive Northwest Passage and the need to trade for provisions to sustain such long sea voyages promoted interactions between the European mariners and the peoples of the islands. Captain Cook's experience in Hawai`i illustrates a common pattern of relatively peaceful interaction at first, disagreements over sexual behaviors and trade agreements, escalating tensions, and then armed conflict. This time it would be venereal disease carried by the Europeans which would strike the indigenous population. In his 1779 return voyage, Cook died during a skirmish resulting from bitter conflict over thievery between his crew and the formerly welcoming islanders of Hawai`i. Europeans in search of fish, especially whalers, were attracted by Cook's accounts of the islands' wealth and beauty. Rapid and unsettling change began for the islanders during the nineteenth and twentieth centuries.

Finished reading the chapter? Be sure you can . . .

- Describe and analyze the changes in trade, technology, and demographics resulting from the European exploration and settlement of the Americas and Oceania.
- Describe and analyze the impact of European settlements and colonization on slave systems and slave trade.
- Explain the impact of farming, mining industries, sugar production, and fur trapping on demographics and the environment in the Americas.
- Compare and contrast the coercive labor systems of this era.

Chapter Multiple Choice Questions

1. Prior to the arrival of the Europeans, the peoples of the Caribbean made their living by
   a. farming manioc and other crops.
   b. mining for gold and silver.
   c. hunting and trading furs.
   d. herding sheep and goats.
   e. fishing in the Orinoco River.

2. The purpose of the encomienda system was to
   a. convert the Indians into Christians.
   b. provide for the health needs of the Tainos.
   c. guarantee laborers for the Spanish mines.
   d. attract other Europeans to settle in the New World.
   e. support the trading-post system.

3. Why were Cortes and Pizarro able to defeat the Aztecs and the Incas?
   a. The European weapons proved vastly superior against the defenseless Indians who had previously existed peacefully with their neighbors and therefore did not need weapons.
   b. The European conquistadores greatly outnumbered both the small empires of the Aztecs and the Incas.

c. The Europeans used the element of surprise to startle and disorient both Indian groups who were afraid of the white Europeans.

d. The Europeans carried deadly diseases, which decimated the population of both the Aztecs and the Incas and thus undermined their political and military order.

e. The Europeans were able to convince the leaders of both peoples of the benefits of alliances with the European powers who were more interested in doing business than in occupying the land.

4. The production of what cash crop dramatically increased the Portuguese interest in Brazil after 1550?
   a. cotton
   b. tobacco
   c. gold
   d. silver
   e. sugar

5. A key difference between the indigenous peoples of North America and those of South America was
   a. the Indians of North America welcomed the Europeans as fellow farmers, rather than perceiving them as military enemies.
   b. the Indians of North America were farmers and hunters who frequently moved their villages, rather than residents of large centralized empires as in South America.
   c. the Indians of North America were more resistant to European-borne diseases and therefore were better able to resist the European settlers than were the decimated Aztecs and Incas.
   d. the conquistadores were much more interested in claiming individual landownership than were the English farmers.
   e. English common law offered the indigenous peoples of North America more protection than did the viceroys of South America.

6. Why did the Iberian colonies in South America emerge as more ethnically diverse than the French and English colonies of North America?
   a. The Iberian colonists were less racist in their attitudes than the English and especially the French.
   b. The Iberian colonists were more interested in making their fortunes and then returning to Europe than were the French or the English settlers.
   c. Fewer Iberian women migrated to South America than did French and especially English women, forcing the Iberian male migrants to look to other populations for companionship.
   d. The racist French and English did not want to interact in any way with the indigenous peoples or the enslaved Africans.
   e. Though the French and Spanish interacted with great frequency with native populations, the English and the Portuguese developed strong boundaries between themselves and the non-Europeans.

7. What do the encomienda, mita, and debt peonage have in common?
   a. They were all social systems of discriminating between various racial combinations found in Iberian colonies in South America.
   b. They were all economic systems of providing labor for Spanish migrants seeking to make a living in the Iberian colonies of South America.
   c. They were all part of the Spanish system of governing her New World colonies and were designed to enforce royal control of distant lands.
   d. They were all part of the process of conversion among the indigenous peoples of South America to Roman Catholicism.
   e. They were all part of the Spanish military tradition of seeking soldiers among native populations to provide the manpower needed for the growing Spanish army.

8. What was the relationship between Portuguese plantation owners in Brazil and the Portuguese government?
   a. The Portuguese government owned all the land and established a feudal-like system by which the plantation owner used slaves to work the land to produce wealth for the king.
   b. The Portuguese plantation owners owed a *quinto* to the king which represented the principal revenue the crown derived from its American possessions.
   c. The Portuguese government established viceroys to oversee the work of the plantation owners and to make sure that these independent-minded entrepreneurs did not become too independent of royal power.
   d. The Portuguese government was most interested in maximizing the wealth produced by the plantations which came to the government by way of taxes; the government usually supported the planters' wishes and interfered little in their business so long as profits were produced.
   e. The Portuguese plantation owners relied on the Portuguese government to supply the troops and administrative authority necessary to compel the indigenous people to work in the sugar factories.

9. In what way(s), did the northern colonies of North America benefit from the African slave trade?
   a. The northern colonies relied on enslaved African people to provide farm labor necessary to produce cash crops like cotton and sugar.
   b. The northern colonies relied on enslaved Africans to work in the fur trapping, shipbuilding, and textile industries in cities like New York and Philadelphia.
   c. The northern colonies benefited from the African slave trade by the manufacture of slave ships and through the production and sale of rum.
   d. The northern colonies benefited from the African slave trade through the taxes and import duties demanded as slave ships entered the ports of Philadelphia and Jamestown.
   e. The northern colonies benefited from the African slave trade in ALL these ways.

10. Why did Christian missionaries have greater success at conversion of indigenous peoples of Mexico and Peru, than in the North American colonies?
    a. Christian missionaries in Mexico and Peru found it easier to convert the indigenous peoples under Spanish rule because the natives had settled, sedentary urban cultures and thus were much more accessible.
    b. Christian missionaries in North America insisted on a stricter interpretation of Christianity than did their South American counterparts.
    c. Christian missionaries in Mexico and Peru often found willing converts through military action and forced conversions.
    d. Christian missionaries in the North American colonies found it difficult to communicate with the indigenous people of the region who were openly hostile to the European settlers.
    e. The traditional religions of Mexico and Peru were more compatible with Christianity than were the more pagan religions of the Hurons and Iroquois.

Comprehensive Multiple Choice Questions

1. Which of the following statements is FALSE regarding the toppling of the Aztec and Inca empires?
   a. Pizarro manipulated the hatred of subjected peoples toward tax collectors and overlords to gain allies against the Incas; Cortes used a similar strategy against the Aztecs.
   b. Epidemic disease weakened both the Aztec and the Inca resistance to the Iberian conqistadores.
   c. Iberian conquerors starved residents of Tenochtitlan and Cuzco into submission when they could not capture the cities outright.
   d. Both the Aztecs and the Incas had experienced internal political struggles before the conqistadores' arrival, which reduced the efficiency of each empire's response to attack.
   e. Rulers of both the Aztecs and the Incas tried to negotiate a settlement with the conqistadores, but language barriers inhibited successful results and fighting broke out.

2. Which of the following pairings is INCORRECT regarding early European control in the New World?
   a. Dutch: New York
   b. Spain: Peru
   c. Portugal: Brazil
   d. England: Virginia
   e. France: Quebec

3. What is the connection between the *reconquista* and the encomienda system?

   a. The *reconquista* began as sixteenth-century military operations on the Iberian Peninsula, but soon turned into systems of social control throughout the Spanish and Portuguese colonies in South America.
   b. The encomienda system, developed during the *reconquista* in Spain as Christian Spanish conquerors were allowed to extract labor and tribute from the defeated Moorish population, was transferred to the New World as a means of eliciting labor from the indigenous population.
   c. The *reconquista* developed as the conquistadores realized the indigenous peoples of the Americas would not be able to supply the necessary labor to run the Europeans' large estates known as encomiendas.
   d. The *reconquista* was the earliest attempt to recapture the Aztec capital and the encomienda system was the technique that developed to capture Cuzco from the Incas.
   e. The reconquista was an enforced labor system begun in the Caribbean Islands and the encomienda system was the transference of that system to the mining industry at Potosí.

Primary Source Questions

1. **Read *Sources from the Past: First Impressions of Spanish Forces* on page 669 of your textbook.**
   a. What elements of the report seemed most frightening to Motecuzoma?
   b. What does the report indicate about the identity of the Spaniards' troops?

2. **Examine the Potosí Mining Operation illustration on page 678 of your textbook.**
   a. What does this illustration demonstrate about the complexities of the Potosí mining operation?
   b. What could you say about the point of view or perspective in this work?

Chapter Multiple Choice Answers

1. **a:** The Tainos were farmers prior to the coming of the Europeans; the Europeans forced them to mine. (p. 667)

2. **c:** Because the Spanish were too few in number and too opposed to such harsh physical labor required to mine, they needed a steady supply of labor for the dangerous and grueling work. The Tainos resisted and the Spanish responded with force. (pp. 667–668)

3. **d:** While the Europeans had weaponry and firepower not available to the Aztecs and the Incas, it was the spread of deadly disease which weakened the social, political, and military fabric of each indigenous empire and decimated their population. (p. 670)

4. **e:** Gold and silver are not cash crops and cotton and tobacco production developed later in Brazil. (p. 672)

5. **b:** Though indigenous peoples of both groups were decimated by European diseases, the absence of strong centralized powers like the Aztecs and Incas made the occupation of indigenous lands much easier for settlers and their European supporters. (p. 674)

6. **c:** Though there were clear differences in racial attitudes between Iberian migrants and French and English migrants, it was the larger number of French and especially English female migrants which made it possible for the English to retain their strict social boundaries with indigenous and African peoples. (p. 676)

7. **b:** These three terms all refer to economic means of providing cheap indigenous labor to work the mines and lands claimed by Spanish migrants and their descendents. (pp. 679–680)

8. **d:** The Portuguese government was most interested in the money brought into the Portuguese treasury through the sale of sugar and therefore left the planters with a great deal of freedom to run their enterprises as they chose. (pp. 681–682)

9. **c:** Though slavery was never as popular in the northern colonies because the land and climate was not suitable for the production of most of the labor-intensive cash crops, the northern colonies did benefit from the manufacture of slave ships, and the production and sale of rum. (pp. 683–684)

10. **a:** The concentrated population of indigenous peoples in urban settings made it much easier for Christian missionaries to establish and maintain contact with the native peoples of Mexico and Peru. English and French missionaries did not rule over people who lived permanently in cities, towns, and villages. (pp. 685–686)

Comprehensive Multiple Choice Answers

1. **e:** The other four choices all help to explain how these mighty empires ultimately fell to military forces much smaller than their own. There were some feigned negotiations between Pizarro and the Inca, but communication was not the issue. Pizarro was simply trying to capture the Inca as a hostage, which he did. (pp. 669–671)

2. **a:** While the Dutch controlled that region briefly, it became English in 1664. When the Dutch controlled it, it was called New Amsterdam. New York was the name of the English colony. (p. 673)

3. **b:** The *reconquista* refers to the re-claiming of Spain for the Christian monarchs Ferdinand and Isabella. Encomienda developed during that fifteenth-century campaign as a way for the conquerors to extract labor and tribute from the conquered Moors; it was transferred to the New World by the conqistadores and then readily adopted by migrant Spanish landowners in need of cheap labor. (p. 679)

Primary Source Answers

1. Motecuzoma seems especially concerned about the Spanish weapons; specifically guns, armor, and horses. Guns clearly were difficult to describe and the author does his best to describe them in understandable terms based on what he has seen them do. The Spaniards' armor is clearly also a novel item, though the concept of iron is not. The horses, which are described as "deer," are mentioned for their height. The Spaniards' appearance also rates comment and it is interesting to note that the troops must have included Caucasians as well as troops of African ancestry as the soldiers are described as both white and black and their hair is described as yellow and as kinky. (p. 669)

2. This drawing illustrates the complex nature of the mining operations at Potosí. Clearly the mountain from which the silver is mined dominates the drawing in its central placement, and its sheer size dwarfs man, beast, machinery, and buildings. Further, the artist seems to be making a statement about the purpose of this mine, when one realizes that no human or living beings' face is visible in the work. It is the mining process which is illustrated here, not the lives of workers, or even the interaction of workers with work. The focus is on mining and all the "equipment" needed to bring wealth from that mountain. Even the color of the mountain is different from the other black, white, and brown in the work. The only "life" color is a small dark green square which seems to be a small plot of cropland and the blue sky which is even dominated by the mountain's size. (p. 678)

CHAPTER 26

AFRICA AND THE ATLANTIC WORLD

Before you get started: It would be wise to recall the slave labor systems discussed in earlier chapters, such as Mesopotamia, Egypt, Greece, and Rome. Also, review what you know about the rise of savannah states in west Africa as well as the advent of Islam into African societies. Suffice it to say that the trade interactions of Europeans with Africans in the Atlantic trade system were more forceful than what happened on the trans-Saharan routes. This is not surprising if you remember that the conditions existing in the Americas increased the demand for African slaves. Remember that since this is a big history course, it is more important to look at origins and outcomes of the Atlantic slave trade than to dwell on specific people or tactics.

AFRICAN POLITICS AND SOCIETY IN EARLY MODERN TIMES

By 1000 C.E., Bantu speakers had spread through most of Africa establishing villages and clans governed by kinship groups. As their population increased, they went on to form small states and regional kingdoms and with the Muslim trade across the Sahara, empires formed in west Africa. With the Indian Ocean trade in east Africa, city-states were established by the Swahili. After west African maritime trade increased in importance when Europeans arrived on the coast, kingdoms replaced the larger empires while the city-states of east Africa fell to the Portuguese. Stronger trade networks also led regional kingdoms in central and south Africa with Islam and Christianity gaining more prominence.

The States of West Africa and East Africa
(Theme: Political Structures)

As you may recall from Chapter 19, Ghana and its successor Mali were large empires in west Africa that existed between the fifth and sixteenth centuries. Based in the trading city of Gao, **Songhay** had been a small kingdom during the same period but increased its dominance as Mali weakened. In 1464 the Songhay ruler **Sunni Ali** conquered the regions that included Jenne and Timbuktu to dominate the upper Niger River basin. He built an elaborate bureaucracy and professionalized his army into an extremely effective force. His military might combined with the prosperity of the Niger River valley allowed his successors to further expand the empire toward Lake Chad. All the Songhay rulers were Muslims who encouraged the building of schools and mosques yet maintained components of indigenous religion by consulting diviners. Prosperity from trans-Sahara trade made the Songhay extraordinarily wealthy and they dominated the region for a century until Moroccan armies with muskets defeated them in 1591. As the empire crumbled, it devolved into small kingdoms such as Kanem-Bornu and Hausa city-states to the east with the Oyo and Asante in the forested areas and Mande traders along the coast. As Atlantic trade with Europeans increased, the smaller kingdoms prospered but west African nations did not unite into an empire again.

In east Africa, Portuguese explorer **Vasco da Gama** skirmished with local forces in Mozambique and Mombasa on the first journey and demanded tribute from Swahili city-states on the second trip. In 1505, the Portuguese sent naval forces to conquer the cities and went on to build governmental buildings and forts to secure the trade routes for themselves. Although the Portuguese were ultimately unsuccessful, the **Swahili states** had suffered a mortal blow and they never recovered their prominence in Indian Ocean trade.

The Kingdoms of Central Africa and South Africa
(Theme: Political Structures)

As sub-Saharan trade networks increased, new kingdoms came to power. Chief among those in central Africa was the **kingdom of Kongo** which was described extensively in Portuguese records. It emerged in the fourteenth century as a strongly centralized state with a large bureaucracy. By the late fifteenth century Kongo was so successful that it encompassed the present-day countries of the Republic of Congo and Angola.

The Portuguese worked closely with the government once it established trade in the region. Eventually, Portuguese missionaries managed to convert the kings of Kongo to Christianity. Christianity appealed to the rulers by reinforcing the power of monarchs while Christian saints were akin to spirits of the indigenous religion. One ruler, King Nzinga Mbemba, also known as **Alfonso I** (1506–1542), became an exceedingly devout Catholic and the Kongo capital had numerous churches.

The Kongo rulers enjoyed the wealth and foreign recognition but their relationship with the Portuguese actually led to their downfall. Initially, the Portuguese traded weapons, textiles, and craft expertise for gold, ivory, and slaves. Not much later, slaves became an almost singular object of trade which led the Portuguese to ally with and depend on other kingdoms in the interior when the Kongo attempted to limit the slave trade. At first, the Portuguese helped the Kongo defend itself but, eventually they joined other states to defeat the Kongo in 1665. In their quest for better trade, the Portuguese moved south while the kingdom of Kongo disintegrated behind them.

The southern state that had diverted Portuguese attention from Kongo was known as Ndongo or **Angola** from the title of its king, *ngola.* It had grown in power by trading directly with the Portuguese rather than through the Kongo. As they brought more war captives for the slave trade, Angola allied itself with other states in the interior. However, the Portuguese became determined to control the slave trade themselves and sent military forces to defeat the Angolese. A very spirited defense was put up by **Queen Nzinga** (1623–1663), the descendent of a distinguished warrior family. In battle, she led troops and dressed as a male. She even accentuated her "male" persona by traveling with a group of men dressed as her female concubines. One even provided seating for her while in conference with the Portuguese. She allied with states from the interior as well as Dutch mariners who had followed the Portuguese. She was largely successful in controlling Portuguese expansion but was unable to eject them from the country. When she died, her less capable successors were unable to maintain her position, so Angola became the first European colony.

Portuguese records are much less illuminating on the regional kingdoms of south Africa. However, it is apparent that they grew in response to the Swahili trade with the interior. Great Zimbabwe would be an example from the earlier chapter that dominated trade in the region. By the sixteenth century, Portuguese and **Dutch mariners** upset the balance of powers by making alliances with less powerful states and intervening in disputes. After the Dutch built a trading post in **Capetown** in 1652, they conquered and virtually enslaved the hunter-gatherer Khoikhoi people. By 1700, large numbers of Dutch colonists were settling in south Africa and defeating the local peoples.

Islam and Christianity in Early Modern Africa
(Theme: Religious Development)

Indigenous religion continued to be important in African societies despite the active evangelism of Islam and Christianity. While there was a belief in an overarching deity, the major religious concern was with the spirit world of nature—a belief known as **animism**—as well as the spirits of ancestors who could be benign but were often punishing to their descendents. Most Islamic converts continued to observe their indigenous beliefs as well. Although troubling to Muslim travelers such as **Ibn Battuta,** most African Muslims were content with their syncretic religion and saw no problem with female nudity and social activity. However, the **Fulani** herders of west Africa became extremely devout Muslims and attempted to stamp out the heresies. They founded powerful states in today's Guinea, Senegal, Mali, and northern Nigeria where a more devout form of Islam is practiced to this day.

As for Christianity, many Africans believed a Christian priest to be some form of magician with crosses as amulets. However, it was often accepted as a syncretic blend with indigenous beliefs. One interesting development occurred in the early eighteenth century with the **Antonian Movement** in the Kongo which centered around an aristocrat named **Dona Beatriz.** She claimed to be the prophet of thirteenth-century Saint Anthony of Padua—the patron saint of the Portuguese—who regularly communicated through her. She became known for performing miracles and promoted a unique brand of Christianity in which Jesus Christ had been an African. She urged the Kongolese to ignore Portuguese Catholicism and sought to end the widespread warfare in the Kongo. Her movement was such a threat to the Portuguese missionaries that they convinced the king of Kongo to arrest her for heresy for which she was convicted and burned at the stake. But her cult continued to exist after her death and demonstrates the African tendency to blend new religions into their own faith framework.

Social Change in Early Modern Africa
(Themes: Social Development and Changes and Continuities)

Although there was considerable nation-building in Africa, kinship groups still remained important for political and social organization. Within larger states, they administered affairs at the local level, but outside of the states, they allied with each other to control large areas of land. Interaction with Europeans brought changes to this social system as well as many other areas of African life and culture.

European manufactured goods became a part of African life while new food crops became a part of the African diet. From the Americas came manioc, maize, and peanuts that supplemented the African staples of rice, bananas, yams, and millet. In particular, **manioc** was valuable for its adaptation to soils unsuitable for other crops. Bread made from manioc flour led to steady population growth in west and central Africa between 1500 and 1800. It almost doubled in size from thirty-four million to sixty million. The population growth was all the more remarkable since it coincided with the forced migration of millions of Africans into slavery in the Caribbean and the Americas.

THE ATLANTIC SLAVE TRADE

The key link in the Atlantic trade world of the fifteenth to nineteenth centuries was the African slave trade which provided millions of workers for large plantations in the Americas. The Africans received manufactured products, primarily firearms, in return for their slaves, and the weapons were often used to dominate other societies while seeking more slaves.

Foundations of the Slave Trade
(Themes: Economics and Trade)

Slavery had appeared in numerous societies since antiquity as it had in Africa after the Bantu migrations. As in other cultures, most slaves were obtained through warfare but criminals and peoples rejected by their clans also made up the ranks of slaves. A slave lost all legal rights and could be sold and punished at will. Most slaves were cultivators but they were also used as soldiers and administrators. Since the rulers of Songhay did not trust their nobility, they preferred slaves in high places of authority. However, African beliefs about property affected their view of slavery. Rather than private ownership of land which belonged to the community, Africans controlled the labor on that land. Thus, individuals with large numbers of slaves would harvest more crops and attain more prosperity. Africans also purchased slaves to enlarge their families and those slaves could be assimilated into the kinship group where they could earn manumission and kinship rights.

After the eighth century, Muslim traders from Persia, Arabia, and North Africa began to purchase African slaves for distribution in the Middle East and Mediterranean world and as far away as India and China. To keep up with the large demand, merchants began to raid villages and sometimes they were even supported by African governments. The **Islamic slave trade** across the Sahara lasted into the twentieth century and may have involved as many as ten million slaves. By the time the Portuguese ventured to west Africa, the slave trade was well established so they only had to tap into an existing system. Nevertheless, extraordinary labor demands by the western hemisphere resulted in the massive forced migration of millions more into the Atlantic basin in the next four centuries.

Human Cargoes
(Theme: Trade)

The Portuguese slave trade began in 1441 with the seizure of twelve Africans who were taken to Portugal. Fierce resistance to capture made the Portuguese reconsider their methods and soon they joined the more regular slave trade networks. By 1460, they were importing five hundred slaves per year into the fields, mines, and parlors of Iberians. Slaves were also delivered to the island colonies of Portugal off the coast of Africa where sugar planters in the Azores, Canaries, Madeiras, and other islands relied on slave labor. By the 1520s the number was two thousand annually, and this was soon followed by the expansion of African slave labor into the Americas.

Imported diseases of the **Columbian exchange** had devastated the indigenous population and those who remained revolted or fled the labor force so the Spanish and Portuguese turned to Africans who were more resistant to Old World diseases and would have no knowledge of where to go if they did escape. The first shipment arrived in 1518, and the first shipment to the English colonies in North America was in 1619. The importation of African slaves constituted the second leg of what became known as the **triangular trade.** The first leg was the manufactured goods from Europe to Africa, the second was African slaves to the Americas, and the final leg was American commodities taken back to Europe.

The Atlantic slave trade was a brutal and inhumane process infused with violence from start to finish. Most slaves were captured by organized **raiding parties** that relied on surprise. Then they were force-marched to the coast and held in pens awaiting transit. The "**middle passage**" was made in filthy, crowded holds on sailing vessels. Conditions were so bad that slaves attempted to starve themselves or throw themselves overboard. Occasionally, revolts were attempted. The crews used brutal means to keep as many slaves alive as possible since the profit in the Americas was two to three times the initial cost of procuring a slave. Most trans-Atlantic trips took around five weeks which took a toll on the cramped slaves below decks. In the early period of the slave trade, more than fifty percent of the cargo died. As volume grew and it became more profitable, slaves were treated more humanely so mortality rates fell to about five percent. Over the entire time period of the Atlantic slave trade, it is believed that one-quarter of the slaves perished on the voyage.

The Impact of the Slave Trade in Africa
(Theme: Demographics, Political and Social Structures, and Changes and Continuities)

In the fifteenth and sixteenth centuries, it is estimated that two thousand slaves were transported every year. By the end of the next century, it was twenty thousand per annum and at the height of the slave trade in the eighteenth century, more than fifty-five thousand slaves per year made the middle passage. In the 1780s up to one hundred thousand were imported in a single year. Altogether, it is estimated that around twelve million slaves made the involuntary journey and of that number, some four million died.

The impact of the slave trade varied according to society. The interior of central Africa largely escaped its effects while other societies flourished from active participation in it. The **Asante, Oyo,** and **Dahomey** peoples build powerful kingdoms with the firearms that they obtained from the slave trade. Most African societies were adversely affected by the slave trade as they were deprived of millions of individuals. This was especially acute in west Africa between Senegal and Angola. Surprisingly, as already mentioned, population growth continued despite the losses but it often distorted the **gender ratio.** Since young men were the most prized slaves due to their work potential, African societies became skewed towards large female percentages. The gender imbalance pushed Angola to promote polygamy and gave women more duties than in earlier times.

The slave trade also encouraged warfare and violence within and between societies. For instance, as Dahomey obtained Portuguese firearms, it enabled them to attack their unarmed neighbors with great success. Indeed, the Dahomey armies, with a female regiment, became a slave-raiding force in west Africa. And while not in your textbook, societies even made minor criminal offenses punishable by slavery. And sometimes, the whole family was enslaved as well.

THE AFRICAN DIASPORA

While some African slaves worked in mines or as domestic servants, most performed agricultural labor in the cultivation of American cash crops. Passive resistance to slavery was common and active resistance less so. Despite the horrors of slavery, Africans blended new cultures out of their different backgrounds and the cultures they encountered in the Americas. By the nineteenth century, first the slave trade and then slavery itself was abolished. By that time the dispersal (**diaspora**) of Africans across the western hemisphere had established itself as a vibrant part of American life.

Plantation Societies
(Theme: Demographics, and Economic and Social Development)

The first Spanish plantation was established in 1516 on the island of Hispanola in the Caribbean. It was soon followed by plantations in Mexico while the Portuguese organized plantations in Brazil in the 1530s. By the early seventeenth century, the Dutch, English, and French had followed course in North America. Most Caribbean and South American plantations grew sugar but North American **tobacco** became as profitable in the seventeenth century while rice and indigo became the crops of Carolina plantations. By the eighteenth century, cotton and coffee began to emerge as **cash crops.** All were highly profitable and in high demand. Plantations depended almost exclusively on slave labor with a small number of European or Euro-American supervisors directing numerous African slaves.

While plantations themselves were similar, plantation societies differed by region. Caribbean and South American plantations were so harsh due to climate, disease, and an excessively male labor force that they were unable to sustain their slave populations. Thus, they depended upon regular importation of Africans. One-half of all African slaves went to the Caribbean while another third went to Brazil. Only five percent went to North America where there was less disease and where more females were imported. The North American planters also encouraged slaves to form families and have children, especially as slave prices went up in the eighteenth century.

Slaves were not entirely compliant and resisted slavery with slow work in the fields or occasionally by sabotaging plantation equipment. Runaways known as **maroons** formed their own communities in wilderness areas and raided plantations for goods they could not supply themselves. Some maroon societies flourished in several regions of the Americas and persisted for generations. Plantation owners lived in fear of the slave revolt since slaves outnumbered other members of the society. The revolts were violent and destructive but rarely resulted in an end to slavery itself. Only the inhabitants of the French sugar colony of Saint Domingue managed to overthrow its masters and abolish slavery in 1804. The **Haitian revolution** pushed other slave-holding regions to tighten control on their slaves at the same time it inspired slaves to attempt their own unsuccessful revolts.

Many Euro-Americans were utterly dependent on slaves for their economy. Without slaves, mineral riches could not be extracted and cash crops could not be grown. While there was little benefit to the slaves themselves, the region became among the most prosperous and successful in the world.

The Making of African-American Cultural Traditions
(Theme: Cultural Development)

Africans in the Americas maintained some traditions but often had to blend their own with some other African and European traditions. Their experience in the middle passage and on the plantation forced them to associate with other African societies since slaves were procured from different regions of Africa. In addition to that, there were cultural standards enforced by the Euro-American masters and community. The resulting culture was uniquely African-American.

While some African communities held on to their language, usually **creole languages** developed as a combination of African and European languages. In the coastal areas of Georgia and South Carolina where three-quarters of the population were slaves, two languages (Gullah and Geechee) developed.

Religions were syncretic with a basic belief in Christianity fused to African traditions. They met in parish churches and followed Christian ritual but associated saints with African deities and used drumming, dancing, and animal sacrifices in their services. African religious traditions like magic, sorcery, and spiritual possession played a large role. Brazil's Candombe, Cuba's Santeria, and Haiti's **Vodou** attracted numerous followers and continue to this day.

American communities adopted other African cultural influences such as foods and basketry. New hybrid cuisines developed that produced creole dishes. Indeed, both okra and its spicy stew, gumbo, are African words. The low country of Georgia and South Carolina as well as Louisiana proved suitable for **rice cultivation,** a traditional crop of west Africa. **African musical traditions** persisted in plantation life as well and its descendent, jazz, is considered to be the most American of musical forms. Despite early beliefs, African slaves brought their culture, and it has influenced American society widely.

The End of the Slave Trade and the Abolition of Slavery
(Theme: Economic and Social Change)

The cause of abolition was stimulated by the American and French revolutions with their calls for equality and freedom. Abolition had advocates before that time but they had been solitary voices of dissent. Increased **slave revolts** of the eighteenth and nineteenth centuries added to the clamor for reform. Some freed slaves wrote books of their experiences that further popularized the abolitionist cause. One of the most famous was west African **Olaudah Equiano** (1745–1797), who may have been born in Benin, who was captured and worked as a slave in the West Indies, Virginia, and Pennsylvania. A seaman, his accounts of the middle passage experience captivated his audiences and he went on to give speeches and lobby Parliament for abolition. His efforts and other slave narratives strengthened the anti-slavery movement enormously.

However, the economics of slavery contributed enormously to its abolition. In short, it was not very profitable. It was a high-risk venture because of slave rebellions and ocean transport. Also, the slaves were unenthusiastic workers. When sugar prices fell in the late eighteenth century due to overexpansion of plantations combined with the high prices charged for African slaves, slave labor became less economically feasible. Furthermore, as Europeans began to shift into new manufacturing industries, they found that wage labor was less expensive than slave labor. In addition to that, the free laborers had money to spend on the manufactured goods. Leaving Africans in Africa to harvest raw materials made more sense than transportation to new sites.

In 1803 Denmark became the first European nation to give up the slave trade. They were followed by Great Britain in 1807, the United States in 1808, France in 1814, the Netherlands in 1817, and Spain in 1845. However, **abolition** of the slave trade did not stop slavery itself and illegal transport across the Atlantic continued until plantation society disappeared. The last documented slave ship arrived in Cuba in 1867. Emancipation for slaves themselves occurred over a long period with Great Britain in the lead in 1833. The United States engaged in civil war to resolve the issue in 1865 and it was not until the 1880s that Cuba and Brazil abolished slavery. The slave trade persists in Africa to this day but the last countries to officially ban slavery were Saudi Arabia and Angola in the 1960s. Millions still live in servitude illegally through devices such as debt bondage, contract labor, sham adoptions, and servile marriages. The influence of the slave trade on the Americas and Africa was profound and its vestiges are apparent in both regions.

Finished reading the chapter? Be sure you can . . .

- Compare the rise of Songhay with earlier Ghana and Mali and other empires in the world.
- Identify the origins of the African slave trade.
- Analyze the demographic effects of the Columbian exchange on Africa.
- Describe one African kingdom in detail (choose Kongo or Songhay).
- Compare and contrast African governments' responses to Portuguese slave trade.
- Compare and contrast American slave plantation systems.
- Identify the changes in African society due to the Atlantic slave trade.
- Describe the effects of the African diaspora on the Americas.
- Analyze the causes of the abolition of slavery.

Chapter Multiple Choice Questions

1. What was the key to the domination of Songhay's rulers such as Sunni Ali?
   a. diplomatic skills
   b. alliances with north Africans
   c. alliances with Europeans
   d. professional militaries
   e. shared religion

2. The Swahili city-states lost their dominance in the East Indian trade to whom?
   a. Arabs
   b. the Dutch
   c. the Portuguese
   d. Indians
   e. the English

3. What was the role of the kingdom of Kongo in the procurement of slaves for the Portuguese?
   a. They sent armies into the interior to round up their enemies.
   b. They coordinated the slave trade for the Portuguese.
   c. They assisted the Portuguese in slave raiding expeditions.
   d. They allied with other Christian kingdoms to gain rights to the slave trade.
   e. They actively worked to defeat the influence of the Portuguese in the slave trade.

4. Why did the Portuguese slave trade move down the coast to Angola?
   a. The Kongolese began to rebel against Portuguese control.
   b. The Angolans provided more assistance to Portuguese traders.
   c. The Portuguese sought a more profitable region for trade.
   d. Angolan royalty preferred to trade with Portugal rather than the Kongo.
   e. Angolan forces were weaker than those in the Kongo.

5. How do historians account for the fact that despite the pressures of the Atlantic slave trade, west Africa's population continued to grow?
   a. American foods provided greater nourishment to the population.
   b. African diseases were less virulent than European ones.
   c. Fewer young men were taken, so population growth continued.
   d. Young children were more able to live past the age of one year.
   e. Natural mortality rates for females decreased.

6. What role did the Portuguese play in the existing African slave trade?
    a. They brought the concept of agricultural slavery with them.
    b. They competed mightily against the Muslim slave trade.
    c. They conquered coastal kingdoms of west Africa as they did in east Africa.
    d. They brought north Africans with them to negotiate since they had been part of the trans-Sahara trade.
    e. They became another branch of the traditional slave trade.

7. Which of the following effects of the slave trade had the most profound overall effects on Africa?
    a. The gender ratio became distorted.
    b. Some kingdoms that were dependent on it disappeared.
    c. Some states grew rich from the trade.
    d. Some societies converted to Christianity.
    e. Population growth declined severely.

8. To which part of the Americas were the least number of Africans sold?
    a. Caribbean
    b. Brazil
    c. English colonies
    d. French colonies
    e. Spanish colonies

9. What happened to African culture in the western hemisphere?
    a. It was subsumed by European culture so that slave societies were imitations of European culture.
    b. It was maintained in maroon societies where individual African traditions could prosper.
    c. African cultural traditions remained distinct based upon regional differences in the origin of slaves.
    d. African slaves blended their African traditions with other African and European ones.
    e. Music and language were retained but other aspects disappeared.

10. What was the most significant reason for the decline in slavery as a labor system?
    a. It became more profitable to use wage labor.
    b. Disgust in European cultures ended slavery in the Americas.
    c. Anti-slavery groups publicized its wretched conditions.
    d. Sugar produced in the Americas became less desirable.
    e. Slavery was dying out around the globe.

Comprehensive Multiple Choice Questions

1. When comparing the African empire of Songhai with the Mongol empire, which of the following factors was the most similar?
    a. Songhai and Mongol leaders preferred to rule conquered peoples through foreign advisers.
    b. Songhai and Mongol cultures revered their origins in nomadic roots.
    c. Both spread themselves too thinly across their regions to maintain control.
    d. Songhai and Mongol leaders adopted the religion of their conquered populations.
    e. Both relied on a strong military hierarchy to control their conquered regions.

2. In comparing the period of early Islam in west Africa with that of early Christianity, which of the following statements is most accurate?
   a. Islam was spread primarily by traders while Christianity arrived with conquerors.
   b. Africans adopted all tenets of Islam while rejecting some of the tenets of Christianity.
   c. Christian rulers forced Christianity on their subjects while Muslim rulers allowed a variety of beliefs.
   d. Neither religion found recent converts to be complete and exclusive adherents.
   e. Conversion to Christianity was a political decision while conversion to Islam was economic.

3. In comparison with slave labor in earlier Greek and Roman societies, what was the primary difference in African slave labor systems?
   a. European slaves were primarily debtors while African slaves were the result of war.
   b. In Africa, there was no notion of land as private property so slave possession was the highest form of economic power.
   c. European slaves did not work in agricultural roles while African slaves did not work in roles beyond agriculture.
   d. African slaves were sold to very distant places while European societies obtained their slaves from neighboring regions.
   e. African slavery was inherently more harsh than Greek or Roman slavery.

Primary Source Questions

1. **Read *King Alfonso I Protests Slave Trading in the Kingdom of Kongo*, 1526, on page 701 of your textbook.**
   a. What is his point of view?
   b. What is his major concern as to the type of slave that is taken?
   c. What appears to be the reason for the increased slave trade?
   d. What problem did the law passed by the Kongo attempt to resolve?

2. **Examine the bronze plaque of a Portuguese soldier, Benin, sixteenth century, on page 708 of your textbook.**
   a. What is the point of view?
   b. How would you know that this was African in origin?
   c. What makes the figure represented appear to be European?

Chapter Multiple Choice Answers

1. **d:** Songhay ruler Sunni Ali built an efficient administration and effective military hierarchy. (p. 697)

2. **c:** In 1505, the Portuguese sent an enormous naval force that conquered and in some cases destroyed Swahili cities. (p. 699)

3. **b:** They worked so closely with the Portuguese that their monarchs eventually converted to Christianity. (p. 699)

4. **c:** The Portuguese wanted higher profits available south of the kingdom of Kongo. (p. 700)

5. **a:** Manioc from the Americas grew in regions that had been poor producers of foods so the manioc bread provided more nourishment to more Africans. (p. 705)

6. **e:** The Portuguese initially tried to obtain slaves themselves but found that by tapping into the existing network, they could increase their profits and lessen their risks. (p. 707)

7. **a:** Since young men were most desirable for slave labor, the sex ratio became distorted and polygamy increased. (p. 711)

8. **c:** Fewer slaves were sent to the English colonies in North America because the mortality rate was lower as was the number of African women. (p. 713)

9. **d:** Africans came from many different regions, so they had to blend their own traditions with other African ones as well as the dominant European culture of the masters. (p. 715)

10. **a:** Economically, slavery was less profitable than wage labor used in the manufacturing sector of the industrial revolution. (p. 716)

Comprehensive Multiple Choice Answers

1. **e:** In most regions, the Mongols were never completely comfortable in their role as administrators and preferred to return to their military. The rulers of Songhai developed a strong military to keep dominance over conquered regions as well as the initial conquest of those regions. Both had a system of provincial governors to administer government policies but the Songhai were comfortable with their own governors. Songhai was rooted in agriculture rather than nomadism and it did not grow too large to govern. Rather, it was defeated by north Africans with better technology. As for religion, the Mongols tolerated all religions and adopted the tenets of Islam in Persia but Islam had been a part of west African culture well before Songhai rulers and they just continued the Muslim practices of the region. (pp. 472, 697)

2. **d:** In both African Islam and Christianity, the new religion was blended with the indigenous beliefs to form an acceptable belief system. They spread most widely in the context of the trans-Saharan and Atlantic trade systems. African rulers adopted Islam and Christianity for economic and political reasons to increase trade and encourage diplomatic relations. While King Alfonso of the Kongo urged his subjects to convert to Christianity, not all Christian rulers felt the same way. There was a tendency for the elite classes in Africa to adopt new religions while the lower classes maintained their original religion. (pp. 489, 704)

3. **b:** Wealth and power in Africa came from control of labor since property was held communally. As in Africa, large numbers of slaves in Rome and Greece were gained from warfare. Agricultural labor required large numbers of slaves in all three societies and all three used slaves in other roles as well. Greek and Roman slaves were often shopkeepers and educators while slaves in Songhai were members of the government bureaucracy as well. Slaves traveled long distances in all three societies with African slaves ending up in Greece and Rome. Life was exceptionally miserable on the latifundias of Rome and in the mines of Greece so no society held a premium on harsh practices. (pp. 248–249, 275–277, 706)

Primary Source Answers

1. King Alfonso was a Christian and a trading partner with the Portuguese so his view may be skewed by his relationship with them. Also, the letters were written in the period when the Portuguese were considering moving their trade to Angola so he is seeing the desperate attempts to retain it. His major concern is that the people who are being enslaved are of the elite classes rather than the lower classes or from traditional enemies of the Kongo so when he speaks of "depopulation," it is the disappearance of the best people that concerns him. Of course, he also notes that his people have become accustomed to European products and have become willing to grab anyone to trade. Therefore, the new law addressed the problem of free people becoming enslaved by nefarious means and required an investigation by his officials of all slaves before they could be exported. (p. 701)

2. The point of view for this work of art is an African craftsman in the slave trade regions of the Bight of Benin. The artist would surely know that the Portuguese came fully armed to engage in early trade with west Africans and he would certainly view the Portuguese as curious traders. The representation of the Portuguese soldier uses the same facial features of elongated nose and almond-shaped eyes that one sees in African metal sculptures. Indeed, the dog has the same eyes. Furthermore, the incised design on the background appears to be highly intricate as is seen in African art rather than European art. The Portuguese soldier is carrying a musket and wearing a full helmet as was common among European soldiers. Furthermore, he appears to have an intricate protective breastplate, a European-shaped saber, and the skirt that one also sees on European men of the time. The boots even appear to have the hobnail soles of European footwear. There is a rather jaunty feather on his helmet and while he appears to be wary, his little dog moves forward in a confident manner. (p. 708)

CHAPTER 27

TRADITION AND CHANGE IN EAST ASIA

Before you get started: The last time you read much about east Asia was in Chapters 15 and 22, and the section in Chapter 23 that discussed the trading-post empires. Because east Asia is a frequent choice for the comparison/contrast questions as well as for the change-over-time questions on the national exam, this chapter and its related predecessors deserve your thoughtful attention. As the chapter title suggests, the major themes in this chapter are changing political structure, social organization, economic development, and religious tradition in both China and Japan; at the end of each section, be sure to consider what world history themes you might compare and contrast along with what elements changed from the earlier era and what remained the same. Give yourself some extra time with this chapter—read it carefully.

THE QUEST FOR POLITICAL STABILITY

When the **Yuan Dynasty** came to an end in 1368, the **Ming** and then the **Qing** rulers went to great lengths to erase all remains of Mongol cultural elements and to restore Chinese tradition. They built a powerful imperial state, revived and staffed the civil service system with Confucian scholars, and promoted Confucian social precepts. They produced a deeply conservative government whose goal was to maintain stability in a large, agrarian state. They were successful for more than half a millennium.

The Ming Dynasty
(Theme: Political Structures)

The term **Ming** actually means "brilliance" and that is what its founder **Hongwu** hoped to return to Chinese government after nearly three hundred years of Mongol rule under the Yuan dynasty. To rebuild China to its traditional image, Hongwu relied on two specific factions: the **mandarins,** imperial officials who traveled throughout the realm overseeing government policies; and the **eunuchs,** who acted in his name at court and who he believed not to be a threat as they could not father families who might rise to challenge imperial authority.

To eradicate Mongol influence and reestablish traditional Chinese society, the Ming emperors promoted all things Chinese. They revived the Confucian-based civil service exams and schools, they sponsored imperial academies and colleges devoted to studies of the Chinese past, and they encouraged people to abandon Yuan names and dress.

Responding to perceived outside threats to China, **Emperor Yongle** moved the capital to **Beijing** to keep a close watch on the Mongols and other northern invaders. He also launched a series of expensive, but short-lived, naval expeditions throughout the Indian Ocean to demonstrate the superiority of Chinese culture. His successors soon discontinued these journeys, deciding this was money wasted and might even draw undesirable attention to China. Later Ming emperors would restore, rebuild, and refortify the Great Wall to more than 1,500 miles of walls over thirty-five feet high, with watch and signal towers as well as living quarters for deployed Chinese troops.

Ironically, it was internal problems that lead to the decline and fall of the Ming dynasty. Pirates and smugglers disrupted trade and taxes in coastal and even interior provinces. An increasingly extravagant lifestyle occupied Ming emperors' time and attention, and the eunuchs, who had once been thought of as the ideal imperial bureaucrats because they could not breed factions, isolated and manipulated the entire imperial household to enrich their own power and position. Finally, in the mid-seventeenth century, when a series of famines struck China, the Ming emperors were unable to effectively respond. Peasant revolts coupled with invasions from peoples from Manchuria who portrayed themselves as avengers who could save China, led to the Ming's fall. The invading Manchus, who called themselves "pure" or **Qing**, easily displaced the corrupt Ming in 1644.

The Qing Dynasty
(Theme: Political Structures)

The Manchus, who began as pastoral nomads in a region of China north of Korea, had traded and frequently clashed with the Chinese since the Qin dynasty. During the early seventeenth century, under the leadership of a charismatic chieftain named **Nurhaci**, the Manchus were unified into a powerful centralized state and effective military force, and began to challenge and defeat Ming forces, first in Manchuria, then in Korea and Mongolia and finally in China. By the end of the seventeenth century, the Manchus had won the support of many of the Ming military and the Ming Confucian scholars who disliked the luxury-loving Ming emperors and resented the increasingly powerful eunuchs who virtually ran China in the last years of the Ming dynasty.

Though well-schooled in Confucian precepts and Chinese culture and tradition, the conquering Manchus were careful to preserve their own ethnic and cultural identity. They outlawed intermarriage between Manchu and Chinese, forbade the Chinese from traveling to Manchuria or learning the Manchurian language, and imposed the Manchu-style hair queue as a sign of Chinese submission to Manchu rule.

After displacing the Ming, the Qing dynasty ruled China until the early twentieth century due to strong imperial leadership. Manchu emperors had a reputation for effective rule until the nineteenth century, when they eventually succumbed to the lure of luxurious living just as their Ming predecessors had done. **Kangxi,** Qing emperor from 1661–1722, was a Confucian scholar, voracious reader, sometime poet, capable builder and project manager, and a successful conqueror, adding Taiwan, Mongolia, Tibet, and parts of Central Asia to the Chinese realm. His grandson, **Qianlong,** encouraged merchants to settle in China's far western province of Xinjiang, and made Vietnam, Burma, and Nepal vassal states of the Qing Dynasty. Further, Qianlong was a prolific poet and a discerning connoisseur of calligraphy and painting. He ran such an efficient government, he could even afford to cancel taxes four times during his reign. By the end of this reign, however, Qianlong and then his successors began to rely heavily on imperial eunuchs to carry on governmental duties and the golden reign of effective Qing rulers drew to a close.

The Son of Heaven and the Scholar-Bureaucrats
(Theme: Political Structures and Changes and Continuities)

The autocratic state created by **Ming Emperor Hongwu** governed China for more than fifty years. The emperor, as the "**Son of Heaven**," was believed to have been the human designated to maintain order on earth. In practice, that meant he led a privileged life within the walls of the Forbidden City, where everything he did, said, thought, and even wore was closely monitored and protected. The ritual **kowtow** and severe punishment for the most minor perceived infraction were behavioral manifestations of the emperors' power.

The actual running of the empire was dominated by the highly trained **scholar-gentry,** men who passed a series of rigorous examinations grounded in the *Analects* and other Confucian-based works as well as calligraphy, poetry, and essay composition. Stiff quotas restricted the number of candidates who could pass from level to level and physically demanding conditions made the exams a grueling ordeal. Though open to all males regardless of social class or age, the cost of years of preparation as well as studying, travel, and accommodations meant most candidates were from wealthy families; even so, the competition for degrees was fierce—cheating and corruption were not uncommon and even death occurred during the nearly weeklong examinations. Though passing the local or district levels did not assure a high-ranking government position, succeeding on the metropolitan level exams insured the candidate and his family powerful positions in the imperial bureaucracy and society. The structure and the results of these exams meant that Confucianism would be at the heart of state rule and mold the personal values of those who managed day-to-day life in China.

ECONOMIC AND SOCIAL CHANGES

While the Ming and Qing emperors succeeded in their goal of restoring and maintaining Chinese traditional hierarchy and patriarchy, they could not prevent the impact of new food crops from abroad and the impact of global trade on the Chinese economy which produced great wealth, urban growth, and an ensuing boom in population.

The Patriarchal Family
(Themes: Social Structure and Gender Roles)

Like the imperial government, the Chinese family was hierarchal and authoritarian; filial piety, duty to one's family was the essential and most pervasive element of Confucianism in Chinese society. Family values reflected this sense of duty to one's father, the family's eldest males, the familial ancestors, and as extended to one's clan which spanned the social classes. Clans served to transmit Confucian values from the gentry leaders to all social classes within the clan, responsible for local order, public welfare, and the organization of local economic activity. It was the clan who sponsored promising civil service candidates knowing that successful candidates would bring prestige and power to the entire clan.

The Chinese family was also patriarchal and the subordination of women began at an early age. A boy child was a potential exam candidate who could bring great honor and financial opportunity to the family; a girl child was a social and financial liability and so infanticide was not uncommon. Girls of wealthy families or especially pretty female commoners who escaped this early death often suffered from the practice of **footbinding** as an attempt to make them more appealing to potential husbands from wealthy families. Marriage provided little improvement in the lives of women as they became the property of their husband's family and were encouraged to live a subservient and quiet life producing male offspring as frequently as possible. During the Ming and Qing dynasties this patriarchal hold grew even stronger as widows were increasingly discouraged from remarrying and even encouraged to commit suicide to honor their spouse and his line.

Population Growth and Economic Development
(Themes: Demographics, Economics, and Trade)

In the Confucian worldview, the land was the source of everything praiseworthy, which meant farming was the ideal occupation. Yet, only about 11 percent of China's land is arable today, so China had to rely on intensive garden-style agriculture to feed its population. China relied on the cultivation of rice, wheat, and millet until the seventeenth century when Spanish merchants on their way from the Philippines introduced American maize, sweet potatoes, and peanuts. These foods, which could be grown in previously uncultivated soils, dramatically increased the food supply and in turn the population of China. Despite recurring epidemics, China's population rose from 100 million in 1500 to more than 160 million by 1600. Though rebellion and war reduced the population back to 140 million in the mid-seventeenth century, by 1750 the population of China reached more than 225 million.

This increasing population put huge pressures on resources but also offered many opportunities for entrepreneurs. With a large occupationally and geographically mobile population, workers could be hired at low cost to work in China's silk, porcelain, lacquerware, and tea production. An influx of silver from the Americas and Japan in the mid-seventeenth century financed further commercial expansion which brought tremendous prosperity to China.

This economic prosperity took place under tight government controls. Earlier, during Yongle's fifteenth-century reign, eunuch mariner **Zheng He** had demonstrated China's presence by sailing his mighty **"treasure ships"** throughout the Indian Ocean basin. Later Ming emperors had withdrawn imperial support, tried to restrict individual Chinese interaction with foreign peoples, and by the late seventeenth century tried to end maritime activity altogether by evacuating the southern coastal regions. This policy of full isolation was only marginally successful and by the 1680s, its strictest elements were rescinded. Portuguese mariners could trade only through the port of Macau, while the British had to deal through the

Chinese merchant guild at Hangzhou. Chinese merchants exchanged silk and porcelain for American silver through a port in Manila, for spices in Dutch Batavia, and for exotic tropical products throughout southeast Asia.

There was little technological innovation in agriculture or weaponry during the Ming and Qing eras, unlike the earlier and technologically prolific Tang and Song eras. Ming and Qing emperors favored political and social stability over technological innovation which they believed might lead to an unstablizing change. Further, the need for new labor-saving technologies did not exist, as China had plenty of ready and able workers. In the short run, the non-technology, non-development policy was successful in ensuring stability and maintaining economic wealth for China. In the long term, the Europeans would benefit from their own stunning technological innovations and the Chinese would lose.

Gentry, Commoners, Soldiers, and Mean People
(Themes: Social Structure and Gender Roles)

The Chinese social hierarchy was built with the emperor and his family at the most exalted positions, followed by the scholar-bureaucrats and the gentry, then the commoners—peasants, artisans or workers, and merchants—with the soldiers and "mean people"—slaves, indentured servants, entertainers, prostitutes, and beggars—at the bottom.

The scholar-bureaucrats and the gentry were the most fluid groups with educated sons of the gentry often moving into the scholar-bureaucrat level with a successful examination performance. Scholar-bureaucrats and gentry were easily identifiable with their black gowns with blue borders and designs indicating various rankings. These fortunate individuals could anticipate special treatment in judicial courts, exemption from labor services and taxes, and immunity from corporal punishment. After leaving government office, these individuals would reassume their gentry roles in managing local society through projects like water management and public security.

Most Chinese fit into the peasant group that included everyone from the day laborers to tenant farmers to small landlords. Peasant farmers were considered the most honorable of the three subgroups as Confucian tradition taught they were closest to the land and performed the most honest labor.

Likewise, the merchant and artisan class was expansive as well, and though they might enjoy a relatively high income, their labor and their status was considered much more lowly than the farmer. Occasionally, a wealthy merchant's son might score well on the civil service exam and move himself and his family into lofty gentry status. Unlike the seventeenth-century European model of cooperation between merchants and government, the Chinese merchants did not form the political-commercial alliances that proved so profitable for merchants and government alike. Instead, Chinese merchants found little legal protection, frequent demands for bribes, and continued low status and esteem from the Ming and Qing imperial governments which continued to favor stability over innovation.

THE CONFUCIAN TRADITION AND NEW CULTURAL INFLUENCES

The Ming and Qing emperors ensured Confucian traditions and teachings in their governments through support of education and the civil service exam programs. However, changing demographics and rising urban populations encouraged the development of new cultural patterns: urban culture and European traditions.

Neo-Confucianism and Pulp Fiction
(Themes: Changes and Continuities and Patterns of Interaction)

During the Song Dynasty, the work of scholars such as **Zhu Xi** combined the moral, ethical, and political values of Confucianism with the logical rigor and intellectual power of Buddhism to produce **neo-Confucianism.** The resulting focus on filial piety, self-discipline, and obedience to authority made neo-Confucianism exceedingly appealing to Ming and Qing rulers from the fourteenth to the early twentieth century.

To promote neo-Confucianism and its resulting stability, the Ming and Qing emperors supported many educational programs. They funded organizations such as the **Hanlin Academy** which was a research facility for Confucian scholars in Beijing, and they maintained provincial schools throughout China where promising students could study for their exams. They provided generous funding for the publication and distribution of books and encyclopedias which emphasized Chinese cultural traditions.

Literate merchants were not so interested in these Confucian treaties, but were interested in readily available popular novels that dealt with horror, conflict, romance, deception, and even pornography. Some of these novels even dealt with the dynamics of families and the growing interactions between Chinese life and western contacts.

The Return of Christianity to China
(Themes: Religous Developments and Patterns of Interaction)

Though Nestorian Christians had established churches and monasteries in China by the seventh century, and Roman Catholicism had communities in commercial sites since the Yuan dynasty, the plague and the collapse of the Yuan in the fourteenth century had virtually wiped Christianity from China. When sixteenth-century Roman Catholic missionaries arrived in China, they had to start from scratch in their attempt to establish a Christian church there. The Jesuits, under men like Italian Matteo Ricci, were the most prominent among these Christian missionaries. Ricci, a brilliant thinker and gifted linguist, dazzled his Ming hosts with European technology and gadgetry, created Chinese-centered world maps, and supervised the casting of high-quality bronze cannons. Ricci and his fellow Jesuits dazzled the Chinese imperial court with finely ground glass prisms, beautifully crafted harpsichords, and mechanical clocks which the Chinese called "self-ringing bells." The Jesuits' true goal was to attract converts, and they used all means necessary, including translation of Christian classics into Chinese languages and the creation of books which linked Christian theology with Confucian philosophy.

Yet, despite all the bells and whistles and their earnest best efforts, the Jesuits attracted only a tiny portion of the Chinese population to Christianity. By the mid-eighteenth century only approximately 200,000 of the nearly 225 million Chinese had converted to Christianity. Like Islam, Christianity's exclusivity was unappealing to the vast majority of Chinese who easily blended Confucianism, Daoism, and Buddhism and who refused to accept that these faiths were inferior to the European's creed. Further, sectarian squabbles between Jesuits, Dominicans, and Franciscans prompted the Chinese emperor Kangxi to order an end to Christian preaching in China. Though never strictly enforced, the ban weakened the tenuous place of the Christian church in China and by the mid-eighteenth century it was effectively ended.

An unintended consequence of the failed Catholic mission to China was to make China more known in Europe. European monarchs were intrigued with the Chinese civil service exams and bureaucracy. European Enlightenment thinkers found appeal in the logic and ethics of Confucianism as a philosophical tradition. The Jesuits had stimulated a strong European interest in all things east Asian.

THE UNIFICATION OF JAPAN

After nearly four centuries of civil disorder, political unification emerged in Japan in the late sixteenth and early seventeenth centuries. Like their Chinese neighbors, Japanese shoguns would promote the idea of traditional values to lay the foundation for long-term political and social stability but ultimately be unable to withstand foreign influences or restrict commercial interactions.

The Tokugawa Shogunate
(Theme: Political Structures)

Theoretically, the emperor of Japan was the ultimate source of political authority. But from the twelfth through the sixteenth century, the shogun, or "military governor," actually ruled Japan through a series of retainers who supplied him with military support in exchange for political rights and landed estates. This situation led to increasing conflict between shoguns and retainers and by the sixteenth century, Japan was in a state of civil war; this period is known as **sengoku**—"the country at war."

In 1600, a powerful military chieftain **Tokugawa Ieyasu** established a military government known as the **Tokugawa bakufu,** or "tent government" since it was to be a temporary and highly mobile replacement for the emperor's rule. In reality, Tokugawa and his descendents unified and ruled Japan for more than 267 years.

Establishing and maintaining a stable, unified realm was the essential aim of the Tokugawa Shogunate and to do this, they had to control the "great names" called the **daimyo.** The daimyo, a collection of 260 powerful lords who controlled most of Japan through their vast hereditary landholdings, ruled their realms with almost absolute power; they maintained local governments, supported an independent judiciary, circulated money, and established schools throughout their lands. They even negotiated trading agreements with European mariners, from whom they learned how to manufacture and use gunpowder weapons. These weapons played a significant role in the last days of the Sengoku era.

The shoguns governed their own personal domain from the castle town of Edo, the modern city of Tokyo, where they instituted a policy of "alternate attendance" in an attempt to gain some control over the fiercely independent daimyo. This policy required the daimyo to leave his family in residence in Edo and he himself to spend every other year at the Tokugawa court. Further, the shoguns sought to control the daimyo by marriage contracts requiring shogun permission, by construction permits requiring shogun approval, by discouraging daimyo gatherings, and even by requiring shogun permission for any meetings between the daimyo and the emperor.

The shoguns were especially concerned about the impact of European interaction with the daimyo. To prevent such alliances and to reduce the supply of gunpowder weapons available to the daimyo, the shoguns issued a series of edicts throughout the seventeenth century which sharply restricted the interaction of Japanese citizens with foreigners. Japanese were forbidden from traveling abroad, the production of large ships was prohibited, Europeans were expelled from Japan, foreign merchants were forbidden to do business in Japanese ports, and the importation of books was forbidden; breaking these edicts could be punishable by death. Only the harbor of Nagasaki was open to a select few Chinese and Dutch merchants.

Despite their best efforts, it was difficult to fully enforce these restrictions and the policy never achieved the total isolation the shoguns envisioned. Throughout this period, Japan still maintained a strong commercial relationship with China, Korea, Taiwan, and the Ryuku Islands, and even the Dutch merchants brought news of world affairs to Japan.

Economic and Social Change
(Theme: Changes and Continuities)

Though the policies of the Tokugawa shoguns did end civil conflict and maintain political stability and set the stage for economic growth in Japan, ironically, they also encouraged social change that ultimately undermined the very order the bakufu sought to preserve.

Between 1600 and 1700, new crop strains, improved water control and irrigation, and the use of fertilizer resulted in dramatically increasing rice yields. This increase in the food supply caused some villages to move toward market production rather than subsistence farming and brought about significant demographic changes as well. The Japanese population increased by one-third even though many Japanese families were limiting their number of children in an attempt to maintain or raise their standard of living.

"Thinning out the rice shoots" was the euphemism to describe infanticide, which was the principal means of population control; Japanese families felt compelled to limit family size in order to cope with the severely limited amount of land available for farming in that island nation.

Once civil peace had been secured under the Tokugawa shoguns, it was essential to reduce the number of trained professional warriors, so the daimyo and their samurai were to turn their talents to government positions or intellectual or scholarly endeavors. Such occupations could not supply the daimyo or his samurai with the income needed to maintain their positions in society and many fell in to financial difficulty and eventually genteel poverty.

Japanese merchants, however, eventually became quite wealthy as cities like Edo grew. Rice dealers, pawnbrokers, and sake merchants soon controlled more wealth than did the traditional ruling elites. Some especially wealthy merchants purchased rank or arranged marriages for their children with aristocratic families to improve their social status; such behaviors were in direct contradiction to traditional Confucian order.

Neo-Confucianism and Floating Worlds
(Theme: Intellectual Developments and Patterns of Interaction)

The Chinese influence on Japanese society is clear throughout the Tokugawa era. Buddhism had come to Japan through China, Confucian ideals permeated Japanese families and government, formal education began with the Chinese language and its literature, and the ideals of filial piety and loyalty to superiors provided a respectable foundation for the bakufu. Neo-Confucianism was the official ideology of the Tokugawa era.

Some Japanese intellectuals resisted the dominating Chinese ideas. These scholars of "native learning" saw neo-Confucianism and Buddhism as alien cultural imports and instead sought to promote traditional Japanese identity, especially through folk custom and the practices of Japan's indigenous religion, Shinto. By the eighteenth century, these scholars were glorifying the purity of Japanese society before it was affected by Chinese and other foreign influences, sometimes to the extremes of national aggrandizement and even **xenophobia.**

The Japanese middle class in cities like Kyoto, Edo, and Osaka grew dramatically during the Tokugawa Shogunate and with it a new middle-class taste in culture. Teahouses, brothels, theaters, and public baths offered an escape from city life and an opportunity to be released from the social restrictions of the Tokugawa era. Often, these *ukiyo*, or "**floating worlds,**" were in sharp contrast to the strict, solemn, urban public and professional worlds. New forms of prose revolving around episodic stories of love and eroticism appealed to those not enthralled by the heavy neo-Confucian texts. Two new forms of drama emerged: *kabuki,* which included stylized skits involving singing, dancing, and spectacular staging; and *bunraku,* which used elaborate and intricate puppet action to dramatize music and a story. Entertainment and diversion were the desired attractions for these middle-class audiences.

Christianity and Dutch Learning
(Theme: Intellectual Developments and Patterns of Interaction)

Early attempts at conversion to Christianity were quite successful in Japan under the guidance of Jesuits like **Francis Xavier** in the mid-sixteenth century. Christian missionaries were very successful with many of the daimyo and, in turn, their subjects, as the daimyo sometimes saw conversion as a means to establish trade and military alliances; of course, other daimyo experienced genuine conversion and became enthusiastic believers. By 1615, there were an estimated three hundred thousand Japanese Christians and the number was growing. This popularity generated a governmental backlash and much criticism from those Japanese who saw Christianity as another dangerous attack on traditional Japanese religion and culture. The Tokugawa Shogunate restricted European access to Japan for many reasons—foremost out of concern that European Christian powers or even rogue adventurers would form military alliances with the independent daimyo and in turn destabilize Japan and perhaps topple the Shogunate; out of fear for

Buddhist, Shinto, and Confucian traditions as Christianity continued to assert its faith as the only true belief; and out of anger that Japanese Christian converts would not be allowed to become priests or to play leadership roles in a Japanese Catholic church. Starting in 1587 and increasing in number and severity, the shoguns issued decrees halting conversion efforts, commanding Japanese believers to renounce their new faith, and eventually forcing all European missionaries to leave Japan. Failure to obey the pronouncements could result in arrest, torture, and even execution. Tens of thousands of Japanese Christians died as a result of these anti-Christian campaigns at the end of the seventeenth century.

Though the Tokugawa policy was effective in ensuring that Christianity would not soon reappear in Japan, it was not successful in preventing interaction of Japanese with Europeans. The work of Japanese scholars who learned Dutch in order to communicate with Dutch merchants trading through the port of Nagasaki came to be called "**Dutch learning**" and offered the Japanese a glimpse of the world beyond east Asia. After 1720, the Tokugawa Shogunate lifted the ban on foreign books and Dutch learning began to play a significant role in Japanese intellectual life. By the mid-eighteenth century, Tokugawa shoguns themselves became increasingly interested in European art, medicine, technology, and astronomy.

Finished reading the chapter? Be sure you can . . .

- Describe the changes and continuities in Ming and Qing governments.
- Explain the changes in Confucianism during this era.
- Explain the changes and continuities in Chinese economics and society in this era.
- Analyze the interactions of Chinese philosophies and religions with Christianity.
- Explain the process of political unification in Japan during the seventeenth through nineteenth centuries.
- Compare the European monarchy (Chapter 24) with the Chinese and Japanese imperial systems.
- Compare Russia's interaction with the west (Chapter 24) with the Chinese and Japanese interactions during the seventeenth through nineteenth centuries.

Chapter Multiple Choice Questions

1. Which of the following statements is a similarity between Ming and Qing rule in China?
   a. Both were primarily concerned with maintaining stability in a large agricultural society by adopting traditional Chinese political and cultural policies.
   b. Both identified invasions from northern peoples as the primary threat to China's security and so they invested heavily in re-fortifying the Great Wall.
   c. Both sought to expand China's overseas influence by developing a strong navy, which they could use to develop trade connections and to fight the increasing threat from Japanese pirates.
   d. Both sought to preserve Chinese tradition and culture from outside influences like Christianity and Japanese Buddhism by erecting barriers to cultural interactions with the west and the east.
   e. Both were primarily concerned with developing technologies like paper, gunpowder, and the waterwheel as means of expanding Chinese economy and world influence.

2. Which of the following factions proved most effective in usurping the emperors' rule during the Ming and Qing eras?
   a. the military commanders
   b. the pirates and smugglers
   c. the eunuchs
   d. the Indian Ocean merchants
   e. the scholar-gentry

3. Which of the following statements is true regarding the Chinese civil service exams?
   a. They were restricted to family members of existing civil servants as a means of maintaining social stability.
   b. They were based on Confucian, Daoist, and Buddhist teachings and demanded candidates be able to discuss all elements of the three philosophies.
   c. They included a written, oral, and performance element in addition to public testimony as to the candidate's moral and social behaviors.
   d. They were open to all males regardless of age or social class and included district, provincial, and metropolitan levels.
   e. They were an attempt to diffuse the power of the eunuchs and to insure that the other members of the harem would have full access to influential government posts.

4. During the late Ming and Qing dynasties, footbinding was <u>most commonly</u> practiced among
   a. the lower classes seeking to make their female children more appealing.
   b. the middle classes seeking to use their female children to move into the Confucian class.
   c. the upper classes as it demonstrated they could support women who could not accomplish physical labor.
   d. followers of Confucius who were resistant to the freedoms allowed to women under Daoist and Buddhist traditions.
   e. royal concubines and common prostitutes who understood the erotic nature of the practice.

5. According to the social hierarchy of Ming and Qing China, which of the following groups had the highest social status?
   a. wealthy merchants
   b. skilled artisans
   c. urban landlords
   d. tenant farmers
   e. imperial soldiers

6. Why did Ming and Qing emperors embrace neo-Confucianism?
   a. Neo-Confucianism was easily compatible with Christianity as explained by the Jesuits.
   b. Neo-Confucianism promoted the role of merchants and commerce as desirable professions which in turn enriched royal treasuries.
   c. Neo-Confucianism denounced the role of Buddhist monasteries in influencing the imperial bureaucracy.
   d. Neo-Confucianism reduced the powerful eunuchs by stressing the importance of family and family values in guiding the empire.
   e. Neo-Confucianism emphasized self-discipline, filial piety, and obedience to the ruler which paralleled the Ming and Qing emperors' goal of maintaining a stable empire.

7. What changes in popular urban culture developed during the Ming and Qing eras?
   a. fast-paced novels dealing with real human concerns
   b. expansion in the number of urban teahouses
   c. growth in the popularity of wine shops
   d. development of the trickster character in Chinese literature
   e. all of the above

8. In theory the _____ controlled Japan during the twelfth through mid-nineteenth centuries, but in reality it was the _____.
   a. daimyos, shoguns
   b. emperor, shoguns
   c. emperor, merchants
   d. shoguns, emperor
   e. shoguns, eunuchs

9. The concept of "alternative attendance" was conceived to
   a. restore the true power of the emperor.
   b. restrict the powers of the daimyos.
   c. limit the power of the shogun.
   d. protect foreign merchants in Japan.
   e. all of the above

10. What is considered the official ideology of the Tokugawa Shogunate?
    a. xenophobia
    b. Zen Buddhism
    c. Shintoism
    d. neo-Confucianism
    e. Nestorian Christianity

Comprehensive Multiple Choice Questions

1. The use of mandarins who traveled throughout China overseeing the implementation of Ming imperial dictates is most comparable to which of the following non-Chinese imperial institutions?
   a. Charlemagne's missi dominici
   b. Harun al Rashid's caliphs
   c. Harsha's Brahmins
   d. Byzantine Emperor Justinian's themes
   e. Inca's auipu

2. Which of the following statements is true regarding Chinese history and technology?
   a. In the Tang and Song eras, Chinese technological innovation was limited, but during the Ming and Qing eras, China led the world in technological advances.
   b. In the Ming and Qing eras, Chinese technological innovation was limited, but during the Tang and Song dynasties China led the world in technological advances.
   c. In the Ming and Qing eras, Chinese technological innovation was directed to agricultural and silk production rather than maritime technologies of the Tang and Song eras.
   d. In the Tang and Song eras, technological innovation was directly tied to silk and porcelain production, but during the Ming and Qing eras, technology was tied to the expanding maritime trade.
   e. As the world's largest nation, China has always set the mark for technological innovation and progress.

3. Which group is most responsible for bringing social change to China during the Qing era and to Japan during the Tokugawa Shogunate?
   a. peasants
   b. soldiers
   c. merchants
   d. scholar-bureaucrats
   e. farmers

Primary Source Questions

1. **Examine the illustration of the waterfront in eighteenth-century Guangzhou on page 722 of your textbook.**
   a. What do you notice about the placement, location, and number of European-style houses in this illustration?
   b. What do your observations indicate about the influence of these European merchants on eighteenth-century Guangzhou?

2. **Read *Sources from the Past: Fabian Fucan Rejects Christianity* on page 748 of your textbook.**
   a. What adjectives does Fucan use to describe Christianity?
   b. What does his Confucian background teach him to do once he realizes his error?
   c. Why does he fear the Christians in Japan?

Chapter Multiple Choice Answers

1. **a:** Both the Ming and Qing emperors were extremely conservative, seeing tradition as the best way to maintain order in their vast realms. (p. 724)

2. **c:** Ironically, the eunuchs who were originally thought to be the ideal imperial administrators because they could not produce influential families, proved to be the most effective in undermining the emperors' real power either directly, though intrigue and deception, or often through simple distraction or carelessness on the part of inattentive emperors. (pp. 726, 729)

3. **d:** Though most candidates were from wealthy families due to the time and costs involved in preparation, the exams were open to all males regardless of age or social class. The exams were designed in a hierarchy from local, to district, to metropolitan levels. (p. 731)

4. **c:** Though considered erotic and sometimes practiced by middle- and lower-class families in an attempt to make their marriageable daughters more appealing, the practice of footbinding was most common among the upper classes as an outward sign of their wealth and in hopes of making financially advantageous marriages for otherwise expensive daughters. (p. 733)

5. **d:** While merchants, artisans, landlords, and soldiers might make higher incomes, the Confucian focus on the land and on "honest" labor made the social status of a tenant farmer the highest of the groups listed. (p. 737)

6. **e:** Neo-Confucianism was grounded in the essentials of Confucianism and included some intellectual elements of Buddhism which worked together to promote traditional Chinese values, the essential ideology of the Ming and Qing dynasties. (p. 738)

7. **e:** The rapid rise in population and the ensuing rise in urban numbers resulted in many literate city dwellers with leisure time who were not interested in traditional Confucian texts or other stringently intellectual writings. Instead, these people, some of whom had considerable wealth, availed themselves of the popular novels, teahouses, wine shops, and even the occasional historical novel often featuring the trickster character. (p. 739)

8. **b:** The emperor was believed to be the source of all political authority in Japan, but from the twelfth century to 1867, Japan was controlled by the shogun. (p. 741)

9. **b:** The "alternative attendance" policy was one of a series of restrictions placed on the daimyo by the shogun in an attempt to curtail the power of the daimyo and force them to submit to the rule of the shogun. (p. 742)

10. **d:** Despite a surge of national identity and some elements in Japanese society promoting "native learning," it was Chinese neo-Confucianism, with its emphasis on order, loyalty to authority, and obedience to tradition which was the official ideology of the Tokugawa Shogunate. (p. 744)

Comprehensive Multiple Choice Answers

1. **a:** Like the Ming emperors, Charlemagne was seeking to exert imperial control over a vast realm and relied on his "envoys of the lord" to travel throughout his realm and review the accounts of local authorities. (pp. 439, 725)

2. **b:** Given the abundance of capable labor, the relative prosperity of the empire, and the imperial goal to maintain order and stability, the Ming and Qing emperors did not promote technological development as had their predecessors in the Tang and Song eras. This decision would have hugely detrimental effects in China during the nineteenth and much of the twentieth centuries. (p. 735)

3. **c:** In both China and Japan, merchants ushered in the greatest degree of social change, as they were the ones interacting with foreigners. Further, their increasing wealth and exclusion from traditional entertainments and endeavors plus their increasing presence in growing urban settings made them interested in new forms of culture and entertainment. (pp. 735–738, 743–744)

Primary Source Answers

1. The European-style buildings in the illustration are located closest to the water and closest to the bay's docks. The buildings are large, lightly-colored, and reflect the style of architecture one associates with eighteenth-century imperial housing for the French, English, and Dutch, whose flags wave in the open area in front of each building. If one looks closely at the illustration, however, one notices that the European buildings are separated from other buildings in the city by a wall; is it designed to protect the European holdings or to separate the Europeans from the Chinese population or to protect the Chinese from undue interaction with the Europeans? One also notices that the further one examines the buildings outside the wall, the more Chinese they become in appearance, with the tall tower and three forts in the far background overlooking and perhaps protecting the city. While at first glance, the European buildings seem most imposing and most important in the work, if one examines the sheer number of structures and the way the Chinese-style buildings and boats relate to the European structures, it appears much more as though the Chinese are surrounding and encapsulating the Europeans in an attempt to contain them or to block their expansion into China itself. This visual blocking of European expansion reflects the ability to hold back the Europeans from direct influence on east Asian affairs until the nineteenth century. (p. 722)

2. Fucan describes Christianity as a "perverse and cursed faith," as the doctrine being "clever and near reason" but holding "little truth," and as it being the "crooked path of the barbarians." Further, he laments his time as a Christian as shameful and wasted. With insight from a friend, he seeks to apply the Confucian value of recognizing one's error, confronting it, and seeking to remedy it. For that reason, he explains he will write about the dangers of Christianity to Japan and seek to use his knowledge of Christianity to expose its methods of compulsion. He fears the Christians in Japan because he believes they seek to destroy everything Japanese: the idea that Japan is the land of the gods, the belief in the Law of Buddha, and the Way of the Gods. And, he fears the Christians will do this by gaining the support of the "Royal Sway," the rulers who will abandon the gods and the traditions and adopt Christian customs. Fucan recognizes the power of the martyr element of Christianity and describes the depth of Christian conviction as "horrible" and "awful." (p. 748)

CHAPTER 28

THE ISLAMIC EMPIRES

Before you get started: Three Islamic empires were formed during the early modern period and you should concentrate on the Ottomans and Mughals more than the Safavids. Most students find it easy to confuse the Mongols of central Asia and the Mughals of India. The earlier Mongols controlled a larger expanse of Asia, not including India; the later Mughals controlled only India. Furthermore, although Persian Mongols had adopted Islam, the Mughals were Muslim who reigned over a large population of Hindus as well as Muslims. The Ottomans in Anatolia are easier to remember and persisted for seven hundred years over expanses across north Africa and far north into Europe. Sadly, their legacy is still seen today in the enmity that the Balkans hold for Turks. The Safavids ruled Persia.

FORMATION OF THE ISLAMIC EMPIRES

All three Islamic states began as warrior societies in frontier regions. They expanded into neighboring lands and as they grew, so did their administrative apparatuses. With talented rulers, each society prospered and dominated its region politically, economically, and militarily.

The Ottoman Empire
(Theme: Political Structures)

A Turkish-speaking group migrated from central Asia into regions of Anatolia in the thirteenth century under the direction of **Osman Bey.** Osman and his followers intended to be the epitome of the *ghazi,* Muslim religious warriors. Their intent was to purify the conquered regions by eliminating polytheism and protecting the faithful. If they died in battle, it would be as martyrs for the faith.

The **Ottomans** first conquered Bursa, near the Bosporus, and went on to claim Gallipoli and take land in the Balkans. Their success encouraged more men to join the ranks of *ghazi* who furthered their successes by gathering revenues and plunder for the state. Bursa became their first capital and reaped the benefits of the frontier spoils by building shops, schools, libraries, inns, and mosques.

The Ottomans had a formidable military that used light and heavy cavalry as well as a volunteer infantry. Once they had expanded into the Balkans, the Ottomans enslaved Christian boys into an infantry corps through the institution known as the *devshirme.* They forced Christian communities to give up their youth to be converted to Islam and trained into elite corps of military or administrative posts. The soldiers became known as *janissaries* and were trained into the most advanced army in the world with complete loyalty to the Ottoman sultan.

Hastening the end of the Byzantines, **Mehmed the Conqueror** (1451–1481) captured Constantinople in 1453. Its name was changed to Istanbul; its Orthodox cathedral, the **Hagia Sophia**, was converted into a mosque; and the city became a center of commercial activity. With its conquest, Mehmud could truly claim his position as an emperor of two lands (Europe and Asia) as well as two seas (the Black and Mediterranean) rather than as a warrior king. Mehmud continued to work toward expansion into southern Europe, and he even had plans to take Rome but his successors abandoned them.

Expansion continued into the sixteenth century as Selim the Grim took Syria and Egypt. **Süleyman the Magnificent** (1520–1566) ruled during the greatest expansion of the state into modern-day Iraq, the Balkans, and Hungary, and even attempted to take Vienna, Austria. The Ottomans also became a naval power with fleets in the Black Sea, the Aegean Sea, and throughout the Mediterranean. They had inherited the navy of the Mamluks in Egypt and challenged the Spanish and Portuguese in the Mediterranean as well as the Red Sea and the Indian Ocean.

The Safavid Empire
(Theme: Political Structures)

In 1501 an exceptionally young Turk named Ismail, a mere fourteen years old, claimed the throne of Persia. His lineage is somewhat murky but he claimed descent from a thirteenth-century sufi cleric, Safi Al-Din, for whom the dynasty was named. After some time, he accepted the Twelver Shiism branch of Islam as the official religion and forced it upon the largely Sunni population. According to Shia tradition, the twelfth Shiite went into hiding to avoid persecution by the Sunni. Although considered somewhat blasphemous by other Muslims, Ismail's followers wore a distinctive pleated red hat in honor of the twelfth.

Ismail's blend of Turkish militancy with Shia religiosity made the dynasty distinctive and prompted widespread animosity in the region. The Sunni Ottomans were exceptionally concerned and even persecuted the Shia of their empire. The two armies met at the Battle of Chaldiran in 1514 where the gunpowder technology of the Ottomans took on the traditional cavalry of the **Safavids.** Although badly damaged, the Safavids retreated but the Ottomans proved unable to destroy the Safavids completely. They continued to fight each other for the next two centuries.

The Safavids depended upon the existing Persian bureaucracy to run its domains. Although they remained followers of Twelver Shiism, later rulers became more pragmatic and disavowed the semi-divine status that Ismail had claimed for himself. Shah Abbas the Great (1588–1629) reigned over the peak of Safavid power by using gunpowder technology and reforming both government and military. He even allied with Europeans against the Ottomans at one time. His efforts brought Mesopotamia and the Caucuses under the control of the Safavids.

The Mughal Empire
(Theme: Political Structures)

Zahir al-Din Muhammad, a Chagatai Turk—known as **Babur,** "the tiger," (1523–1530)—was the founder of the Mughals. Chagatai was a son of Chingghis Khan, and he claimed descent from both Chingghis and Tamarlane. Furthermore, Mughal is the Persian term for Mongols. Unlike the Safavids or the Ottomans, Babur claimed no specific religious purpose or connection in his conquests. He was just a conqueror following the steps of both Chingghis and Tamarlane. Using modern gunpowder technology, he descended from central Asia into India and took Delhi by 1526. Rather than plunder and return home, Babur chose to stay in India despite the unhappiness of his men. Perhaps he meant to use the riches of India to finance further expansions. By the time he died in 1530, he ruled an expansive empire from Afghanistan across northern India.

As in so many cases in history, the conqueror was followed by a talented administrator, his grandson Akbar (1556–1605). Using harsh methods to overcome his rivals, Akbar came to power and expanded the Mughal empire into southern India by defeating the kingdom of Vijayanagar. Despite his early violence and illiteracy, perhaps due to dyslexia, **Akbar** was a sensitive, tolerant ruler who was deeply interested in religion and philosophy. He devised his own syncretic religion—"divine faith"—that made the ruler the common connection between all religions in his domain.

The height of the Mughal empire came during Aurangzeb's reign (1659–1707) when the Mughal empire encompassed the Indian subcontinent except the southernmost tip. However, his reign was troubled with rebellions and religious tensions. A devout Muslim, **Aurangzeb** eschewed Akbar's tolerance by taxing and persecuting Hindus. While the Muslims were pleased, it deepened the hostility of Hindus for their Mughal rulers.

IMPERIAL ISLAMIC SOCIETY

The three Islamic dynasties are discussed in the same chapter because they shared numerous characteristics. They descended from similar steppe traditions, embraced the same Islamic religion, and adopted similar economic and religious policies for their diverse populations. And, all involved themselves with public welfare, literature, and the arts.

The Dynastic State
(Theme: Political Structures and Functions of States)

The Ottoman, Safavid, and Mughal emperors took personal control of their militaries and administrations and, in theory, owned all land which they divided among their peasant populations. Revenues from the lands financed their governments and militaries. Leadership of the dynasties was based on the success of the ruler who was expected to be militarily competent and personally pious. All three dynasties were associated with the sufis to varying degrees and took pride in their legacy of steppe warrior societies. Furthermore, their style of leadership derived from the steppes as a tradition of independent decision-making regardless of cultural or political traditions. The Ottomans passed large numbers of edicts while both the Safavids and Mughals challenged regional religions. However, the steppe tradition also brought problems in succession. Heirs were expected to compete with each other for the throne. This resulted in frequent murderous struggles in the Mughal and Safavid lines. And while earlier Ottomans avoided the conflicts, later rulers decreed that murder of potential rivals such as brothers was legal and desirable. Even later, imprisonment of all male descendents was common.

Although women were expected to have no role in the public affairs of the Islamic empires due to religious constraints, women in all three dynasties played significant roles. Following the example of Chinggis Khan who revered his mother and his first wife, rulers gave special privileges to women holding those places in their own empires. While the **"rule of women"** was criticized, Süleyman's concubine, Hurrem, was consulted on state affairs, and Mughal empress Nur Jahan ran the government for her husband. One Safavid wife, Mahd-e Olya, grew so powerful that she was assassinated by the outraged *qizilbash*. Even devout Muslim ruler Aurangzeb followed his daughter's advice, while perhaps the world's greatest testament to a ruler's devotion to his wife was the Mughal Shah Jahan's **Taj Mahal.** In addition to the information in the textbook, note that women in imperial households had roles as official wives and concubines but were relegated to the harem where they raised their young children and competed with one another for the ruler's affections and favors. Because succession was an indeterminate matter, imperial struggles for power often began in the harem between competing mothers of potential heirs.

Agriculture and Trade
(Themes: Economics, Demographics, and Trade)

The foundation of the Islamic empires was a strong agricultural base from which they could finance armies and bureaucracies. They relied on the traditional crops of rice and wheat but also grew new crops derived from the Americas such as maize, potatoes, and tomatoes. Some of these filtered into the cuisines of the different regions as in Indian curries while maize became an excellent animal feed. **Coffee** and **tobacco** became the mainstays of social life once they were grown in some quantity in the Americas. Coffeehouses were established by the 1600s despite protests from conservatives concerned about morality and religion. One Ottoman sultan attempted to ban both with the death penalty but had no success. Coffeehouses remain a staple of Middle Eastern life today.

American crops had less effect on the Islamic empires than on Africa. The population of India grew by 85 million to 190 million in 1800 but mainly as the product of intensified farming of traditional crops. The Safavids grew less rapidly while the Ottomans actually declined in population after 1600. But that reflected loss of territory rather than a shrinking population. The central Anatolian growth rate was about one million people each century so that it reached nine million by 1800.

The Islamic empires were prominent in world trade, both on land and sea. The Ottomans were the terminus of the silk routes and also controlled access to the Black Sea while they dominated the eastern Mediterranean. They formed alliances with European states against their competitors, the Spanish and Portuguese. The Safavids made partnerships with the joint-stock companies of northern Europe and got some protection from them. While the Mughals did not actively promote trade, they gained a large amount of their revenue from the trade that came to India with its manufacturing base and its central position in the Indian Ocean trade system.

Religious Affairs in the Islamic Empires
(Theme: Religious Developments)

Maintaining harmony among populations of diverse religions was a common challenge for the Islamic empires. Large numbers of Christians and Jews lived within the extended boundaries of the Ottoman state. Zoroastrians, Christians, and Jews also lived within the Safavid empire while the Mughals ruled over millions of Hindus and fewer Muslims as well as small communities of Christians, Zoroastrians, Jains, and Sikhs.

Jesuits established a Christian mission in Goa and even attracted the interest of Akbar who received them politely but did not convert. Although Akbar drew primarily on Islam as he attempted to establish his own syncretic faith to bind together the diverse populations of his realm, he supported the new Sikh religion and tolerated all faiths. The Ottomans and Safavids made a distinction between the monotheists of Middle Eastern derivation and other faiths by designating Jews and Christians as *dhimmi* (people of the book). They required the payment of a tax to retain their faith as well as some legal autonomy. In the early Mughal empire, the population of other faiths was too large for that system so they forged alliances between the Muslim and Hindu elite classes. Nevertheless, the promotion of religious tolerance disturbed Muslims in India so they insisted that the Mughal empire maintain a Muslim state based on the *sharia*. When Aurangzeb came to the throne, he instituted the tax, persecuted Hindus, and caused permanent enmity between Hindus and Muslims.

Cultural Patronage of the Islamic Emperors
(Theme: Cultural Developments)

The Islamic emperors lavished attention and resources on public welfare and the arts by building magnificent buildings, hospitals, and soup kitchens. They vied for the patronage of the best scholars and artists and sought to bring them to their courts. The Ottomans started a great rebuilding program in **Istanbul** with the magnificent Topkapi palace at its center. Both an administrative center and an imperial residence, it had abundant architectural and artistic treasures. They refashioned the Hagia Sophia into a mosque, and imitated it in a vast religious complex, the Süleymaniye, to honor Islam. The Safavids made their capital Isfahan into a gem of urban planning. An organized plan placed markets, palaces, and mosques around a central core of polo playing fields and an immense public square. There were boulevards to the suburbs, elaborate arcades, and courtyards that were intricately decorated. The Safavid palaces were small and emphasized natural features such as ponds and gardens.

The Mughals blended central Asian features with Hindu architecture as they built numerous mosques, palaces, and forts. They even designed entirely new cities such as Sikri, the gem of Akbar's efforts. It was both an administrative center and a personal retreat but it also glorified religion with a large mosque and mausoleum to a Sufi guru. Unfortunately, it had little water and had to be abandoned. The most famous Mughal edifice is the Taj Mahal, an exquisite mausoleum dedicated to the memory of Shah Jahan's favorite wife. Mughal architecture shows the influence of Islam in its extensive use of arches and arcades. Mughal painting was heavily influenced by Persian painters brought to early Mughal courts. The use of intricate designs and brilliant colors, in particular blue and gold, demonstrates the Persian influence.

THE EMPIRES IN TRANSITION

None of the Islamic empires lasted past the eighteenth century without dramatic changes. In 1722, the Safavids were completely defeated by Afghan tribesmen and disappeared altogether. The Mughals suffered enormous reversals with provincial rebellions and foreign invasions. The Ottomans lost control over Egypt and Lebanon while Russian and European states chipped away at their economic, political, and military spheres.

The Deterioration of Imperial Leadership
(Theme: Changes and Continuities)

The form of government that Islamic empires had chosen was heavily reliant on effective leadership. They each had their share of good emperors, but the dynasties eventually fell into the hands of weak and inefficient leaders who were more dedicated to personal pleasure than efficient government. The Ottomans who had isolated their princes found that the heirs that did come to the throne had no experience and little interest in good governance. One notorious example was Ibrahim the Crazy whose own officials deposed and assassinated him.

Each empire fell into the throes of religious dissension where Muslim clerics pushed for conservative Muslim rule while distrusting the rulers' reliance on sufis, women's roles in government, and religious toleration. In the Ottoman empire, religious students joined with *janissaries* in revolt. The Wahhabi movement in Arabia denounced Ottoman policies and pushed for an extremely conservative form of Islam. Both science and literature were targets of conservative Muslim wrath in the eighteenth century. The Safavids lost power to the Shiite clerics who pushed to eliminate sufism, Sunni Islam, and non-Islamic sects. In the Mughal empire, Aurangzeb's previously mentioned attacks on Hindus and religious tolerance fostered dissension and rebellion.

Economic and Military Decline
(Theme: Changes and Continuities)

The strong base of profitable trade and agriculture was undermined in the later centuries as goods produced elsewhere became dominant commodities. The high cost of intricate administration and vast militaries helped to bring about economic decline. Once the empires stopped expanding, their ability to support their governments could not be augmented by fresh lands and plunder. Long, costly wars by all three states drained their treasuries but resulted in defeats or little gain. The Ottomans suffered seven military revolts when their ability to pay their troops was compromised. The only means by which the rulers attempted to make financial gains was increasing taxation and corruption, so bribery and extortion became common. The empires refused to extend themselves into the world marketplace but merely reaped the benefits of European trading posts in their territories.

Along with the loss in economic initiative, the Islamic empires failed to keep up with changing military technologies. Instead, they purchased European equipment and expertise. However, the technologies they purchased were outdated. Nor did they build on European technology with innovations of their own. By the late eighteenth century the vaunted Ottoman navy no longer built its own ships.

Cultural Conservatism
(Theme: Cultural Developments)

While European travelers and scholars were investigating all aspects of the Islamic worlds, Ottomans, Safavids, and Mughals rarely ventured into the kingdoms of "infidels." Although sixteenth-century Ottoman mariners and geographers such as Piri Reis had charted the Indian Oceans, later mariners depended upon their supposed superiority rather than active exploration.

Innovation was also hugely affected by conservative Muslims who attacked the few European advances that did make it to the Islamic empires; for example, the printing press. Spanish Jews fleeing the Inquisition in the fifteenth century brought printing presses with them. At first, they were banned from printing in Arabic or Turkish, and when it was allowed in 1729, only seventeen books were printed before they were closed down due to religious complaints. Only forty years later was it allowed, leaving the Ottomans almost two centuries behind in the dissemination of scientific and technological knowledge. The Mughals also resisted the printing press introduced by the Jesuits in fifteenth century Goa so that only when the British became dominant were Indian books readily available. To a certain extent, though, aesthetic considerations also played a part in the rejection of the printing press. Muslims viewed the handwritten scripts as preferable to mass-produced copies. Nevertheless, conservative Islamic clerics primarily rejected cheap publishing as an avenue where new and dangerous ideas might sway the public's piety.

The deep conservatism and resistance to innovation left the Islamic empires, as well as imperial China and Tokugawa Japan, desperately backward and weakened when faced with the onslaught of European militaries. Like the Chinese and the Japanese, the Ottomans, Safavids, and Mughals chose stability over the risks of foreign technology.

Finished reading the chapter? Be sure you can . . .

- Describe the effect of the Mongols on the Islamic empires.
- Describe the influence of the expanded world trade network on Islamic regions.
- Describe the shared characteristics of the Ottoman and Mughal empires.
- Explain the roles of women within imperial households.
- Analyze the differing demographics of each region.
- Analyze the influence of Persia, Islam, and central Asia on Mughal art.
- Analyze how the conservative tendencies of the Islamic empires allowed European dominance.
- Describe the extent of Ottoman expansion.

Chapter Multiple Choice Questions

1. In which area of governance did the influence of the Mongols on the Ottoman, Safavid, and Mughal empires prove to be the most problematic?
   a. reliance on a central, dominant military leader
   b. military tactics dependent upon cavalry and siege
   c. independent division of territories as a solution to succession
   d. lack of a clearly designated successor to the imperial throne
   e. separate capitals in far-flung regions designed to improve administrative efficiency

2. Of the following points, which was NOT a factor that explains future European dominance over the Islamic regions?
   a. European attempts to build alliances with Islamic partners
   b. deeply conservative cultural considerations that led to rejection of innovation
   c. failure of agriculture and trade to keep up with the financial demands of administration
   d. refusal to improve upon European technology in armaments
   e. belief in the superiority of cultural and religious traditions

3. In which of the following governmental factors were the Mughals and Ottomans most similar?
   a. the goals and objectives of their founders, Babur and Osman
   b. in both governments, power was shared by religious and secular leaders
   c. rulers were expected to be capable of military command
   d. dependence on troops from conquered regions of the empire
   e. an emphasis on fort construction over construction of administrative buildings

4. Despite the interdiction against public roles for women in the Islamic empires, the mocking "rule of women" was used to describe what phenomenon?
   a. the predominance of women in advisory positions
   b. the large number of women serving as regents for minor children
   c. the dominance of wives over concubines in the harem
   d. the tendency of rulers to confer with female members of the imperial family
   e. women's roles as artistic and cultural advisers to rulers

5. What factor produced large population increases in Mughal India but was missing in the other empires?
   a. increased dependence on American crops as dietary staples
   b. the incidence of disease declined as nutrition increased
   c. the infant mortality rate declined due to increased sanitation
   d. rulers' concern for the public welfare increased medical facilities
   e. a rise in intensive farming practices of traditional crops

6. What were the origins of the Persian influence on the art forms of the Mughals?
   a. Mughal conquerors brought Persian art forms with them when they arrived in India.
   b. Early Mughal emperors imported Persian painters to their court.
   c. The Safavids shared their court artists with the Mughal emperors.
   d. Persian influences predate the Mughal presence in India.
   e. The Mughals hired Persian architects to design their new buildings.

7. Of the following factors, which was the most important in making the world trade network less influential in the Mughal empire?
   a. Geographic position put the Ottomans and Safavids at the crossroads of global trade.
   b. The Ottoman and Safavid governments actively sought to dominate world trade.
   c. European countries preferred to trade with the Ottomans and Safavids.
   d. The Mughals depended on their huge manufacturing capacity rather than trade.
   e. Mughal preeminence in the silk roads led to complacency in trade.

8. To what can one attribute the vast expansion and continued control of Ottoman territories into southern Europe and northern Africa?
   a. They were following the footsteps of earlier Arab conquerors so the territories adopted easily to the Islamic rule of the Ottomans.
   b. The Ottomans combined a strong military presence with an eye to accommodation of local religious traditions.
   c. The Ottomans inherited the Byzantine lands as well as their effective governmental apparatus that enabled the easy incorporation of new lands into the empire.
   d. The Ottomans used a similar form of conquest with autonomy and citizenship privileges as the Romans had while holding those territories.
   e. The conquered lands were in the position to negotiate extended legal and political rights despite the dominance of the Ottoman military.

9. What role did religious tolerance play in the Mughal empire?
   a. Early rulers showed little interest in conversion but later rulers became so focused on it that they persecuted other religions.
   b. Early leaders considered their military role as one of the *ghazi* or spiritual warriors so they pushed strongly for conversion.
   c. Since Islam had been promoted in India by the Sultanate of Delhi, Mughal leaders were content to allow its continued slow spread.
   d. The Mughal persecution of Buddhists and Hindus in the early era was a constant irritant to the dominant population of Hindus.
   e. Mughal leaders carried the tolerant attitude of the Sufi tradition found in the steppes throughout their reign.

10. Examine the photograph of the Süleymaniye mosque on page 768 of your textbook. What does it indicate about the Ottoman empire?
    a. The Ottomans admired the Byzantine architecture of the earlier Constantinople.
    b. The Ottoman rulers valued religious roles over military or secular power.
    c. The Ottomans allowed no other houses of worship in Istanbul.
    d. Ottoman architecture was massive and monumental rather than utilitarian.
    e. Ottoman syncretic religion is reflected in its Muslim minarets and Orthodox domes.

Comprehensive Multiple Choice Questions

1. Which of the following best describes a difference between the Ottoman and Mughal dynasties?
   a. While later Mughal rulers chose to convert Hindus to Islam, the Ottomans did not convert any conquered peoples to Islam.
   b. Ottoman political power depended upon the personal qualities of the ruler while Mughal power rested with the military.
   c. The Ottoman conquerors maintained that they were the epitome of the spiritual warrior while the Mughal conquerors made no claims to religious motives.
   d. The Mughals rarely allowed women to influence their decisions while the Ottoman emperors regularly consulted with influential women in their harem.
   e. The Mughals had considerably fewer problems dealing with their Hindu population than the Ottomans had with the Balkan Christian population.

2. When comparing the domain of the Moghuls with that of earlier states controlled by Muslim conquerors, which of the following is the largest difference?
   a. The Sultanate of Delhi came with more intent to convert Indians to Islam and found greater success at it as well.
   b. Despite the fact that the Sultanate had enormous standing armies, they had much less success in conquering the subcontinent.
   c. Mahmud of Ghazni ruled for a much shorter period of time since the Hindu kingdoms of southern India allied to push the foreigners out.
   d. The Sultanate of Delhi had much more participation in the Indian Ocean trade system than the Mughals since they had a policy of encouraging trade.
   e. Mahmud of Ghazni invaded the northern part of India in order to conquer while Babur was merely interested in plundering and looting.

3. When comparing the Ottoman empire to the imperial achievements of China, which of the following is the best statement?
   a. The Ottoman empire in its early years closely resembled the drive and achievements of most Chinese dynasties.
   b. The Ottoman use of a strong standing army approximates the armies of post Han dynasties as they expanded into other regions of central Asia.
   c. The Ottoman emperor ruled solely from a position of military power and prestige while the Ming emperors ruled from a position of divine right.
   d. The Ottoman imperial household resembled the imperial households of most Chinese emperors with its intention to meet the administrative and personal goals of the emperor.
   e. The Ottomans ruled over a more diverse group of conquered nations and religions than did the Chinese emperors.

Primary Source Questions

Compare the photos of the architecture of each empire in this chapter and you will find that domes, arches, and fine stonework are distinguishing features of each. Likewise, a comparison of the colorful paintings of each has similar masses of figures engaged in common activities with skewed perspectives.

1. **Read *Sources from the Past: A Conqueror and His Conquests: Babur on India* on page 760 of your textbook.**
   a. What is the point of view?
   b. What does Babur believe he can find in India?
   c. Why did his warriors want to leave and why did he wish to stay?

2. **Examine the painting of Sultan Süleyman leading Ottoman forces, on page 756 of your textbook.**
   a. What is the likely point of view?
   b. How can you identify the sultan?
   c. How many different regiments of soldiers can you identify?
   d. What does this tell you about military force in the Ottoman empire?

Chapter Multiple Choice Answers

1. **d:** The Mongol reliance on competition as the solution to succession led to extremes of violence and dynastic instability in the empires. (p. 763)

2. **a:** Their weakening empires could be traced to all other factors but trade alliances could have become routes to dominance had they extended themselves beyond their own boundaries. (p. 774)

3. **c:** Much of a ruler's prestige was based on his successful command of military troops. (p. 762)

4. **d:** While in rare circumstances, women became the sole advisers to rulers, Islamic rulers tended to use their wives, mothers, and daughters as informal advisers. (p. 763)

5. **e:** Expanded cultivation of traditional Indian crops led to a huge increase in the population. (p. 765)

6. **b:** Although Persian influences were apparent in central Asian cultures, it was the importation of Persian painters to the Mughal court that established its influence. (p. 262 of this text)

7. **d:** The Mughals ruled a country of enormous size and manufacturing potential so they neglected to enhance foreign trade opportunities. (p. 766)

8. **b:** Ottoman administration relied heavily on army and naval forces to control the territories while they granted legal and political rights to protected religious classes (the *dhimmi*). (pp. 755, 767)

9. **a:** The conqueror Babur had little interest in religion for any purpose while his grandson Akbar actively sought an integrated spirituality that accepted all Indian religions. But a later ruler, Aurangzeb, was a passionate Muslim who persecuted the followers of other Indian religions. (pp. 761, 762)

10. **a:** In a reflection of the conversion of the Hagia Sophia to a Muslim mosque, the Sülemaniye mosque complex incorporates elements of Byzantine and Islamic architecture. (p. 768)

Comprehensive Multiple Choice Answers

1. **c:** Osman and his warriors claimed affiliation with the *ghazis* as holy warriors engaged in defense of the faith while Babur sought only secular triumphs. Both the Mughals and Ottomans sought to convert others to Islam and the Ottomans used it to fill their armies with a slave corps of converted Christians. Both societies admired the leaders who were active commanders as well as pious observers of the faith. In both societies, some elite women heavily influenced the decisions of the rulers. Finally, resistance and rebellions existed in both empires. (pp. 754, 759)

2. **b:** Akbar and Aurangzeb expanded the Mughal empire to include all but the southern tip of India while neither Mahmud of Gahzni nor the Sultanate of Delhi managed to expand beyond the top third of the subcontinent. Mahmud of Ghazni invaded India seventeen times burning and looting Hindu and Buddhist temples rather than converting the Indians to Islam. The Sultanate conquered and remained but showed little interest in conversion of their Hindu allies since they could rule without mass conversion. At no time in India's history did the southern Hindu kingdoms ally successfully to defeat the

Muslim north. The last two choices are clearly wrong since the Sultanate was far from the fulcrum of Indian Ocean trade, and Mahmud was never interested in ruling any part of India. (pp. 408, 761–762)

3. **d:** As the center of government and the dynasty, both the Topkapi palace in Istanbul and the Forbidden City in Beijing included administrative and personal buildings for the emperors. Offices as well as harems filled with concubines occupied imperial spaces. The Chinese dynasties that most closely resembled the Ottomans in expansion were the Qin and the two foreign dynasties, the Mongol Yuan and the Manchu Qing. Most other dynasties consolidated control over regions of China that had earlier belonged to another dynasty. The Ottoman emperor believed himself to be a spiritual warrior for the faith but that is not the same as having the Mandate of Heaven. Likewise, military prowess was generally more important for the first emperors of Chinese dynasties than later rulers while it remained important to the Turks at least in theory. Lastly, the Chinese ruled over at least as many minority ethnic groups as the Ottomans and held western regions in which Nestorian Christians, Buddhists, and Muslims had settlements. (pp. 729, 763, 768)

Primary Source Answers

1. Babur was a Turkic conqueror who took inspiration from Chinggis Khan and Tamerlane. His perspective is clearly that of a man determined to reap the benefits of a wealthy nation. Thus he is dismissive of the Indian peoples and their culture. Furthermore, written as a memoir, Babur's words needed to show him as an inspirational figure to his people. After listing India's bad qualities, Babur describes his single intent to obtain gold and silver. His Afghan warriors are miserable in the heat of India and concerned about the resistance to their presence but Babur assures them that they should stay since they overcame great obstacles to conquer India and no one would wish to return to the poverty of Afghanistan. As mentioned in the text, it remains somewhat unclear why he settled when he seemed to be the most similar to Mahmud of Ghazni who was content to raid India. (p. 760)

2. The likely painter was a court official commissioned to paint a triumphant picture of Ottoman superiority. The sultan himself is placed in the center of the painting and his importance is indicated by his larger size as well as his position on a horse in the middle of infantry. As indicated by their different costumes, it seems that there are two regiments of cavalry and one infantry division. The extraordinary organization and precision of the Ottoman military is on display in this court painting. (p. 756)

PART VI

AN AGE OF REVOLUTION, INDUSTRY, AND EMPIRE, 1750 TO 1914

CHAPTER 29

REVOLUTIONS AND NATIONAL STATES IN THE ATLANTIC WORLD

Before you get started: This chapter is built on one big idea: Revolution. That concept specifically includes **political revolutions** in the Americas, France, and Haiti, as well as the nations of Latin America; **intellectual revolutions** through the emergence of conservatism and liberalism; and **social revolutions** through changing ideals for the roles of women and the place of slavery in the modern world. The last section of the chapter deals specifically with the creation of nations and the emergence of **nationalism**. You should be much more concerned with the concepts related to nationalism rather than the details in Germany and Italy. As you read this chapter, keep in mind both the comparisons and contrasts you can make among these revolutions and the continuities and changes which occur in these regions as a result of these revolutions and of developing nationalism. This is a prime chapter for essay questions on the national exam.

POPULAR SOVEREIGNTY AND POLITICAL UPHEAVAL

The era of revolutions in the late eighteenth and early nineteenth centuries had two major global results: to spread Enlightenment ideals concerning freedom, equality, and sovereignty, and to fuel the consolidation of nation-states. Neither of these results occurred without upheaval and violence.

The ideal of a just and equitable society built on a government responsive to the needs and interests of its people was based on the Enlightenment principle that legitimate political authority resides with the people, not with a monarch. To realize this Enlightenment ideal would take time and require violence in both of the Americas and in France.

Enlightened and Revolutionary Ideas
(Theme: Intellectual Developments)

Historically, the most common form of government in agricultural, settled societies was rule by a single leader whose sovereignty was most commonly justified by tradition or religion. During the seventeenth and eighteenth centuries, European Enlightenment thinkers began to question these long-held ideals of sovereignty—political supremacy and the authority to rule. **John Locke** went so far as to relocate sovereignty away from the rulers and vest it in the people of a society. Locke's concept of **government as a contract** between the rulers and the ruled held that while people granted political rights to their rulers, they retained the basic rights to life, liberty, and property, and that any ruler who violated these rights could be deposed. Locke went even further to explain that rulers derived their right to rule from their subjects, who could withdraw their consent and replace their rulers. Enlightenment thinkers also addressed ideals of freedom and equality. **Voltaire** used literary satire and harsh direct criticism to call for religious toleration and freedom of expression. **Jean-Jacques Rousseau** demanded legal and political equality and expressed the revolutionary ideal that members of society were collectively the sovereign and thus the general will of the people should rule. These ideals, posited by men of common birth but comfortable means, though revolutionary in content, were not inclusive of women, children, laborers, slaves, or peoples of color. The ideals would spread through violence and social upheaval and take generations to approach fruition.

The American Revolution
(Theme: Intellectual Developments and Changes in Political Identity)

In the mid-eighteenth century, it seemed unlikely that North America would become the center of revolution. The British colonies were economically prosperous and securely British in their tastes and habits.

Yet, after the mid 1760s that identity began to change. High taxes instituted to pay for the **French and Indian War** phase of the **Seven Years' War,** especially the Sugar Act, the Stamp Act, and the Tea Act, and restrictions on commerce through the Townshend Act and the newly revived Navigation Acts did not sit well with the colonists who began to argue that they should govern their own affairs rather than follow instructions from Britain. **"No taxation without representation"** became their motto. They soon followed these arguments with actions such as boycotts, protests like the Boston Tea Party, and the establishment of a **Continental Congress** to coordinate resistance to British policies. By 1775, direct conflict occurred as British troops and colonial militias skirmished at Lexington, near Boston.

On July 4, 1776, the Continental Congress unanimously adopted the **Declaration of Independence** which echoed Locke's ideals of unalienable rights and consent of the governed and carefully listed the specific abuses charged against the British crown. The actual conflict to secure these rights lasted nearly five years, with the original British advantage in troop strength, organization, and experience eventually outweighed by the colonists' home field advantage, reliance on guerilla tactics, and support from European powers who hoped to chip away at British hegemony.

Actually building an independent state based on Enlightenment principles would take a while longer and it was not until 1787 that a constitution for the United States would be drafted which included a federal government based on **popular sovereignty** which guaranteed **individual liberties.** However, these rights and liberties were not granted to all inhabitants; landless men, women, slaves, and indigenous peoples were excluded from the rights and protections of this document. It would take continuous efforts for more than two hundred years for those rights to be extended.

The French Revolution
(Theme: Intellectual Developments and Changes in Political Identity)

The French revolution drew inspiration from the American experience, but it proved much more radical in scope, time frame, and ideals. The French revolutionary ideal was to repudiate the old order, known as the *ancien regime,* and to replace it with new cultural, social, and political structures.

Financial crisis provided the immediate cause for the French revolution. A bankrupt French treasury and a nobility unwilling to give up its historic tax exemption forced King Louis XVI to call into session the *Estates General,* the French national legislature, hoping it would authorize new taxes. This was the first time in more than 150 years that the body had been convened and each faction had a lot to say. Traditionally, France had been divided into the **three estates**—the clergy, the nobility, and the rest of France. This third estate included about twenty-four million Frenchmen including serfs, free peasants, urban poor, laborers, artisans, shopkeepers, attorneys, physicians, and bankers. While the first two estates were much, much smaller in number—100,000 clergy and 400,000 noblemen—nevertheless, each estate had one vote. This system seemed to ensure that the rights of the few would continue despite the wishes and welfare of the many. Yet, this is not the path the revolution would follow.

After several weeks of frustrating debate, members of the Third Estate withdrew from the Estates General and proclaimed themselves to be the rightful **National Assembly.** They met at a large indoor facility—a tennis court—and there took an oath not to disband until France had a written constitution. Public support for their actions included the storming of the **Bastille** prison in Paris on July 14, 1789, as well as growing insurrections in cities throughout France. Taking strength from this popular support, the National Assembly began to pass a series of documents aimed at dismantling the old authority of the *ancien regime.* The most important of these documents was the ***Declaration of the Rights of Man and the Citizen*** which proclaimed the equality of all men, the idea that sovereignty resides in the people, and the principles of liberty, property, and security. The document is very clear in its prohibition against social distinctions which had girded life in France for generations.

With the slogan **"liberty, equality, and fraternity,"** the Assembly began to reconfigure French society, by abolishing the privileges enjoyed by the first two estates, by altering the rule of the Catholic church in

French society, by making the king the nation's chief executive official but depriving him of any legislative authority, and by making France a **limited constitutional monarchy** for men of property.

These changes were not welcomed by members of the traditional nobility or by foreign supporters of the king. The National Assembly used the pretext of foreign aggression to declare war on Austria and Prussia and then on Spain, Britain, and the Netherlands. Threats from abroad and within gave the National Assembly an opportunity to radicalize the revolution by creating a new legislative body, the **Convention**, which abolished the monarchy and declared France a republic based on universal manhood suffrage. The Convention instituted the *levee en mass,* which provided for universal conscription of people and resources to counter the invading foreign forces. To root out enemies at home, the revolution made use of **"terror to root out traitors"** which eventually included the former king, his wife, and anyone else deemed not revolutionary enough to meet the constantly moving standard. Throughout 1793 and 1794, the guillotine was quite busy executing more than 40,000 counterrevolutionaries, and French prisons bulged with more than 300,000 suspected enemies of the revolution. Lawyer **Maximillian Robespierre,** "the Incorruptible," dominated the executive authority of the republic and sought to remake France by providing a secular alternative to Christianity known as the **"cult of reason,"** by granting women the right to inherit property and divorce their husbands, and by reorganizing the work week and even the calendar; all these actions were an attempt to eradicate all remaining elements of the *ancien regime.* By July 1794, the radical revolution began to cannibalize itself as Robespierre himself was arrested and executed. At that point a group of propertied, conservative men seized control of France and sought to rule it through a new institution known as the **Directory.** Unable to resolve France's military or political problems, and unable to successfully follow a middle way between the *ancien regime* and radical revolution, this rule by committee proved ineffectual and eventually corrupt. The timing was perfect for a man with a plan: **Napoleon Bonaparte.**

The Reign of Napoleon
(Theme: Changes in Political Identity)

Making a name for himself on the battlefield and rising as a fervent supporter of the revolution, Napoleon at first joined the Directory and then overthrew it. He imposed a new constitution, initially taking the title of **First Consul** and eventually crowning himself **Emperor.** In part, Napoleon was able to accomplish each of these steps because of his military instincts and his charisma; however, his real appeal was the promise of stability for a people whose lives and nation had been torn apart by revolution and war for more than ten years. Napoleon well understood what the people wanted and began a series of actions to meet those needs. He made peace with the Catholic church by signing the **Concordant of 1801** which recognized Roman Catholic Christianity as the preferred faith of France. At the same time, the concordant also granted some religious freedoms to French Protestants and Jews; this brilliant action brought a degree of religious satisfaction to all French people. He organized the **Civil Code** which affirmed the equality of all adult men, established a merit-based system for education and employment, and he restored some private property lost to aristocrats during the years of revolution. These ideals became the model for civil codes in places throughout the Americas and parts of Europe.

While Napoleon approved of the Enlightenment ideal of equality, he did not extend this ideal to everyone or everything. French women once again became subservient to the male heads of households and they lost all their revolutionary gains in legal and social matters. Napoleon limited free speech and routinely censored newspapers and other publications while making expert use of propaganda. He relied on spies and a secret police force; he arrested suspected political opponents by the thousands and founded a dynasty which set his family above all the people in whose name he ruled.

At the same time that Napoleon was consolidating his powers in France, he continued to make a name for himself on the battlefield. An amazing tactician and strategist, he was able to conquer the Iberian and Italian Peninsulas, occupy the Netherlands, inflict major defeats to the Austrian and Prussian armies, and convince the Russian czar to ally with him, at least for a while.

1812 was not a good year for Napoleon. Though he successfully defied the British, Austrian, and Prussian armies, he was no match for **"General Winter,"** the Russian not-so-secret weapon which reduced Napoleon's Grand Army from 600,000 soldiers to fewer than 30,000 weakened warriors. His disastrous Russian campaign re-energized his enemies who formed a coalition to converge on France and force Napoleon to abdicate in April 1814. His exile to the Mediterranean island of Elba was short-lived as he escaped to remount his empire. However, despite a wild and romantic return to power for one hundred days, he was finally permanently defeated at the battle of **Waterloo** and permanently exiled to the isolated island of St. Helena in the south Atlantic where he died in 1821.

THE INFLUENCE OF REVOLUTION

Freedom, equality, and popular sovereignty appealed to peoples throughout Europe and the Americas and inspired revolutions both political and social. The struggle toward full realization of these Enlightenment ideals continues today in all parts of the world.

The Haitian Revolution
(Themes: Changes and Continuities and Political Structures)

The American and French revolutions paved the way for violent social and political revolution in **Saint-Domingue,** the wealthy French sugar, coffee, and cotton-producing colony located on western **Hispaniola.** Today, that location is the nation of **Haiti.** In 1790, the colony included about forty thousand white French settlers, thirty thousand free people of color known as *gens de coleur,* and about five hundred thousand black slaves, most of whom were born in Africa. Working conditions in Saint-Domingue were brutal, and it was more economical for plantation owners to work their slaves to death and then import replacements than to provide for adequate life-sustaining conditions for the slaves. As a result of this harsh treatment, a substantial number of slaves escaped to the mountainous regions of Haiti. By the late eighteenth century, these escaped slaves, known as **maroons,** had formed their own societies and sometimes attacked plantations in search of food, goods, and new recruits. At the end of the eighteenth century, prices for African slaves increased dramatically.

Also, by the end of the eighteenth century, five hundred *gens de coleur* who had been sent to America to aide in the American revolution returned home ready to reform society there. White planters, fueled by the desire for self-government stemming from the French revolution, wanted self-government for themselves but opposed any attempts to bring social or political equality to the *gens de coleur.* In August 1791, the island descended into chaos as twelve thousand slaves, led by a Voudou priest named **Boukman,** attacked and killed white plantation owners, destroyed their property, and within a few weeks attracted almost one hundred thousand slaves into their ranks. The white factions responded and fought both slave and *gens de coleur* factions. The situation grew more complex as French troops arrived to restore order in 1792 and British and Spanish forces arrived in 1793 in hopes of benefiting from France's colonial problems.

When Boukman died a few weeks into the fighting, he was succeeded by **François-Dominique Toussaint,** who called himself **Louverture,** "the opening," which refers to an opening in the enemy's ranks. Intelligent, educated, and a skilled organizer, Toussaint was also a shrewd judge of character. He used these skills to build a strong, well-disciplined army, to play the French, British, and Spanish troops against each other, and to jockey for power among the other black and mulatto generals. By 1791, his army of twenty thousand controlled most of the island, and, by 1801, he produced a constitution which granted equality and citizenship to all Saint-Domingue residents; he declined to declare full independence from France in hopes of avoiding an invasion by Napoleon's troops. His hopes were unfulfilled, however, as Napoleon sent forty thousand French troops to the island in 1802. Despite Toussaint's attempts at negotiation, the revolutionary was arrested and sent to France, where he died of maltreatment in 1803. However, later that year, an outbreak of yellow fever decimated the French army and Toussaint's successors drove the remaining but sickly French troops from their shores. By January 1, 1804, Haiti had become the second independent republic in the western hemisphere.

Wars of Independence in Latin America
(Themes: Changes and Continuities and Political Structures)

The ideals of the Enlightenment and of revolution spread to the Portuguese and Spanish colonies in the Americas. Conflicts between the ***peninsulares,*** colonial officials from Portugal or Spain, and the ***criollos or creoles***, individuals born in the Americas of Portuguese or Spanish descent, became increasingly common. The less-privileged classes of people of mixed ancestry, indigenous peoples, and black slaves greatly outnumbered either peninsulares or criollos, but lived at the bottom rungs of Latin America's social hierarchy.

The criollos benefited economically throughout the eighteenth century, but they increasingly resented the political and economic restrictions placed on them by the Iberian governments. They wanted to displace the peninsulares and retain their own privileged social status. Between 1810 and 1825, the criollos successfully led independence movements establishing republics in all Spanish colonies in the Americas except Cuba and Puerto Rico.

Independence in Mexico followed a different pattern than in other Spanish colonies. A peasant rebellion began under the leadership of **Father Miguel de Hidalgo.** This parish priest rallied mestizos and indigenous peoples of Mexico against colonial rule and his revolt came to be seen as a social and economic rebellion against all the elites of Mexico. This rebellion by the masses was seen as dangerous by conservative creoles who wanted freedom from Spanish colonial rule, but who also wanted to retain their own privileged status. Father Miguel was captured and executed by these fearful criollos, but his peoples' rebellion continued for three years after his death. Colonial rule finally came to an end in 1821 when creole General Augustin de Iturbide proclaimed independence from Spain. His empire was short-lived though, as creole elites deposed him in 1823 and declared the establishment of a republic. Within two years, the southern end of the republic split to form the **Central American Federation,** and within thirteen years, the independent nations of **Guatemala, El Salvador, Honduras, Nicaragua,** and **Costa Rica** were formed.

Creole elites lead rebellions in South America as well. **Simon Bolivar** led a struggling movement for independence from Spanish rule beginning in 1811. Though the early years of the revolt were difficult, by 1819 Bolivar had assembled an army of more than twenty thousand troops which he used to defeat the Spanish forces first in **Colombia** and then in **Venezuela, Ecuador,** and **Peru.** He coordinated his efforts with **Jose de San Martin** in Argentina and **Bernardo O'Higgins** in Chile. Bolivar hoped to create a great confederation modeled after the United States of America. But, despite early successes, by 1830 it was clear the dream of "**Gran Colombia**" was not going to succeed. Bolivar died on a self-imposed journey to exile in Europe.

Brazilian independence was a much different process. The royal court of Portugal had fled to Brazil to escape Napoleon's Iberian invasion in 1807 and set up a government in exile in Rio de Janeiro. In 1821, the Portuguese court returned home leaving **Prince Pedro** as regent of Brazil. In 1822, when Brazilian creoles demanded independence from Portugal, Pedro agreed and when they sought to curtail his powers, he accepted their offer to become emperor of an independent Brazil. Creole elites dominated this monarchy, just as they did the republics of Brazil's neighbors. Latin American society remained intensely stratified with the creoles replacing the peninsulares as the elite. The new republics and Brazil gave military authority to local strongmen known as **caudillos,** allowed slavery to continue, confirmed the authority and wealth of the Roman Catholic church, and repressed the lower social classes.

The Emergence of Ideologies: Conservatism and Liberalism
(Themes: Intellectual Developments and Political Identity)

The term *ideology* simply means the belief that a particular social and political organization is ideal. That belief is based on a coherent idea of human nature, human society, and the world. Some ideologies seek to justify the status quo, while others are critical of the existing order and promote an alternative order or ideal. Two important ideologies grew out of responses to the American and French revolutions: **conservatism** and **liberalism.**

Conservatives viewed society as a slowly developing organism which must be protected from radical or revolutionary ideas as those beliefs lead to anarchy. Men like **Edmund Burke** of England saw the American revolution as a positive event as it grew naturally from historical events in North America and saw the French revolution as negative as it was a chaotic assault on traditional social order.

Liberals welcomed change which they saw as normal and indeed required in the concept of progress. Change, which should be managed in the best interest of society, would help to bring about the realization of the Enlightenment ideals of equality and freedom, and such ideals would promote higher standards of morality and increased prosperity for all of society. Nineteenth-century liberals generally supported republican forms of government and written constitutions that defined political and social structures based on freedom and equality. **John Stuart Mill** was the most prominent supporter of early liberalism. He supported universal suffrage as the most effective way to advance individual freedom and warned against the tyranny of the majority and of powerful minorities such as wealthy businessmen. Mill even went so far as to call for rights of freedom and equality for women and working-class people.

Testing the Limits of Revolutionary Ideals: Slavery
(Themes: Intellectual Developments and Changes and Continuities)

The ideals of freedom and equality which had survived and evolved during the political revolutions of the late eighteenth and early nineteenth centuries were eventually applied to the issue of slavery. One of the earliest critics of slavery was **Olaudah Equiano,** a former slave who bought his own freedom, traveled the world as a seaman, and eventually made his name and fortune as a writer speaking out against slavery during the last half of the eighteenth century. For more than twenty years, **William Wilberforce** led the fight in Britian's parliament to end slavery; Britain ended her slave trade in 1807. United States followed in 1808, France in 1814, the Netherlands in 1817, and Spain in 1845. But the slave trade died slowly, as illegal trade in African slaves continued until after 1867.

The **abolition** of the slave trade did not end slavery, however, as owners held fast to their "property" rights and were unwilling to let go of such inexpensive labor. Wilberforce and his supporters worked hard to compensate slave owners and abolish slavery throughout the British Empire. In 1833, the British government paid slave owners twenty million pounds sterling in compensation and abolished slavery. France abolished slavery in 1848, the United States in 1865, Cuba in 1886, and Brazil in 1888.

While legal freedom through abolition came to former slaves, **political equality** was much more elusive. Other than in Haiti, African and African-American peoples found little political or economic success as the wealthy white or creole elites were not willing to abandon their roles or to welcome former slaves and their descendents into their ranks.

Testing the Limits of Revolutionary Ideals: Women's Rights
(Themes: Intellectual Developments and Changes and Continuities)

Women had participated in the eighteenth-century political revolutions and in the nineteenth-century abolition movements. From these experiences, they sought to make a case for women's rights as well, but it was not until the twentieth century that these attempts would achieve much success.

Eighteenth-century author **Mary Wollstonecraft** published her famous *A Vindication of the Rights of Woman* in 1792, in which she argued that women possessed all the rights John Locke had said belonged to men. She went further to assert that education would make women better wives and mothers and would enable them to contribute economically and politically to society. Women were essential in the events of the French revolution including the women's march on Versailles in 1789 and their leadership in the sansculottes during the 1790s. Napoleon's ascension and control removed any rights gained by women during the long years of revolution and returned them to their subservient roles under France's patriarchal system. In the Americas, women gained little as a result of the revolutions.

During the nineteenth century, women pressed for the abolition of slavery and the rights of women. American feminist Elizabeth Cady Stanton, enraged after being denied participation in a British anti-slavery conference, returned to the United States and organized a feminist conference in Seneca Falls, New York, in 1848; the delegates issued a series of resolutions demanding women's right to vote, attend public schools, enter professional occupations, and participate in public affairs. Stanton and her successors experienced some success during the nineteenth century, particularly in education, but the opportunity to participate in public affairs or the right to vote would be restricted until the twentieth century.

THE CONSOLIDATION OF NATIONAL STATES IN EUROPE

While the revolutions of the late eighteenth and early nineteenth centuries helped to spread the ideals of freedom, equality, and popular sovereignty, the Napoleonic wars of the same era helped to spread the concept of **nationalism**—the belief that people belong to distinctive national communities based on a shared sense of identity through language, custom, religion, and/or tradition. Nationalism, which promised prosperity and glory to its supporters, often fostered jealousy and distrust of other national groups.

Nations and Nationalism
(Themes: Political Identity and Changes and Continuities)

During the nineteenth century, people increasingly began to identify with their nations—unique communities that shared common identifiable attributes in custom, tradition, values, and experiences. Supporters of nationalism insisted that one's national state boundaries should be reflected in **a shared territory** and **a shared destiny.**

Johann Gottfried von Herder fostered pride in the German heritage by developing the ideal of the **German Volk,** or "people." Herder and his contemporaries believed that this German identity was best revealed through literature and historical scholarship. *Volkgeist*, or the peoples' spirit or essence, could be seen in tales, songs, and poems like those collected by the brothers **Jakob and Wilhelm Grimm.**

Such early nationalism was cultural, but by the third decade of the nineteenth century, nationalism was becoming increasingly political. Loyalty, solidarity, and independence became the goals of such political nationalists as **Guiseppe Mazzini** who resisted Austrian and Spanish controls on the Italian peninsula. His "**Young Italy**" movement inspired similar independence movements in Ireland, Switzerland, and Hungary.

One unintended consequence of nationalist movements was to foster separations between minority groups within the societies and to distinguish those groups from people in other lands. This divisive element is seen in the emergence of **Zionism** at the end of the nineteenth century and continuing into the twentieth century. Suspicion of minority groups fueled historic **anti-Semitism** which in turn led to increased Jewish emigration from much of eastern and central Europe. The case of **Alfred Dreyfus**, a Jewish army officer, unjustly accused, tried, convicted, and imprisoned for spying, became the focus of ugly debate on the 'trustworthiness" of Jews in French society and a key event in the development of Zionism. **Theodor Herzl,** a Jewish journalist from Vienna, witnessed the trial and the mob actions associated with the Dreyfus affair and concluded that anti-Semitism could not be solved by assimilation into any existing nation. Instead, Herzl called for a national homeland for the Jews from all over the world. He organized the **First Zionist Congress** in Basel, Switzerland, in 1897 which resulted in the call for a homeland in **Palestine,** the location of the ancient kingdom of Israel. Jewish migrants began a slow trickle into Palestine over the next fifty years and in 1948, an independent nation of Israel was recognized. An unintended but powerful consequence of that movement was the alienation of Palestinians displaced by the new nation of Israel which has fueled a resentful nationalism among Palestinians and others to this day.

The Emergence of National Communities
(Themes: Political Identity and Changes and Continuities)

The French revolution and the Napoleonic Wars heightened the sense of national identity across Europe and, in turn, instilled fears of nationalism in the hearts of conservative political leaders. French, British, Austrian, Russian, and Prussian conservatives believed that these ideas of national identity and popular sovereignty would undermine European stability, encourage dangerous political experiments, and even further inspire revolutions. To address these concerns and to restore the *ancien regime,* leaders from those five nations met in Vienna in 1814–1815 to remake the map of Europe and restore the "legitimate" rulers displaced by revolution and war. Led by **Klemens von Metternich,** the foreign minister of Austria, the delegates at the **Congress of Vienna** worked to suppress national consciousness which was seen as a clear threat to multinational empires like Austria and Russia. A **balance of power** was restored for a while due to press censorship, secret police, and an extensive spy system, but Metternich's goals would explode in 1914 with the outbreak of World War I.

Metternich and the conservative congressional delegates could not stop national consciousness and ideals of popular sovereignty completely, however. Revolutions in the 1820s on the Balkan peninsula led to **Greek independence from the Ottoman Empire** in 1830. Independence movements gained momentum in Belgium, Italy, and Poland in the 1830s. In 1848, nationalist uprisings brought down the French monarch and threatened the Austrian empire as well as governments in Italy, Prussia, and German states in the Rhineland. Conservative-supported military forces ultimately put down these rebellions by 1849, though their ideals would soon be manifest again in Italy and Germany.

The Unification of Italy and Germany
(Themes: Political Identity and Changes and Continuities)

Since the fall of the Roman empire, Italy and Germany had been disjoined regions, frequently controlled by outside powers such as Spain or Austria or governed under largely ineffective structures such as the Holy Roman Empire. At the Congress of Vienna, much of northern Italy was placed under Austrian control and much of southern Italy remained subject to Spanish authority. Throughout much of the nineteenth century, nationalist movements like Mazzini's Young Italy attracted support from discontented idealists, but despite uprisings in 1820, 1830, and 1848 could not oust foreign rule. It took the combined efforts of practical politicians such as **Camillo di Cavour** and **King Vittore Emmanuele II** of Piedmont, and handsome, dashing revolutionaries like **Guiseppe Garibaldi,** to oust the Spanish and the Austrians, and to create an independent Italy.

Likewise in Germany, it would take shrewd politicians to harness nationalist aspirations. The German Confederation, created by the Congress of Vienna, was dominated by Austria under Metternich who worked hard throughout much of the first half of the nineteenth century to prevent the unification of Germany. In 1862, Prussian King Wilhelm II appointed Otto von Bismarck as prime minister. A wealthy, Prussian landowner, Bismarck was the master of ***Realpolitik,*** "the politics of Reality," and he understood and espoused the idea that **"blood and iron"** would decide the question of German nationalism. Bismarck reformed and expanded the Prussian army and then used it to provoke his enemies one by one into war. With each war, Bismarck used the German people's sentiment to build support for a unified nation embracing all German-speaking people—other than in Switzerland and Austria—into a Second Reich.

The unification of Italy and Germany demonstrated the ability of nationalism built on political, diplomatic, and military leadership to mobilize people who identified with a national kinship. By the end of the nineteenth century, it was the most powerful mode of political organization in Europe and by the mid-twentieth century, it was the dominant political organization around the world.

Finished reading the chapter? Be sure you can . . .

- Compare the Haitian and French revolutions as well as the American and Latin American ones.
- Compare the roles and conditions of women across social classes and nations.
- Discuss the ideals of women's rights and changing ideas on slavery.
- Discuss the development of ideologies: conservatism and liberalism.
- Describe and analyze the causes and outcomes of the wars for independence in Latin America.

Chapter Multiple Choice Questions

1. Why did Olympia de Gouges write *Declaration of the Rights of Woman and the Female Citizen*?
   a. to clarify the place of women in the French government
   b. to appeal for women's inclusion in the rights granted in the French Revolution
   c. to satisfy Marie Antoinette's desire for political power
   d. to plead for her own life during the Reign of Terror and thus avoid execution
   e. to let future generations of French women understand their history

2. Which of the following thinkers would have articulated these ideas: sovereignty resides in the people of a society, government is a social contract between the rulers and the ruled, and individuals have granted political rights to their rulers but always retain their personal rights to life, liberty, and property?
   a. John Locke
   b. Voltaire
   c. Jean-Jacques Rousseau
   d. Olympia de Gouges
   e. Maximillian Robespierre

3. By 1789, the American revolution resulted in a _____ system of government, while by 1791, the French revolution resulted in a _____.
   a. democratic, republic
   b. republican, empire
   c. federal, feudal system
   d. federal, limited constitutional monarchy
   e. constitutional, democracy

4. Which of the followed groups suffered the greatest loss of civil liberties during Napoleon's rule of France?
   a. Roman Catholics
   b. Former aristocrats living in exile
   c. middle-class professionals
   d. women
   e. retired soldiers

5. Why did Toussaint Louverture decide not to declare independence from France in 1801?
   a. He wanted to wait until the French revolution was completely over before declaring independence.
   b. He wanted to wait for assurances from the newly founded United States of America that they would not be sending aid to their French allies.
   c. He hoped to avoid provoking Napoleon into attacking the island.
   d. He decided that the *Declaration of the Rights of Man and the Citizen* provided adequate protection of Haitian civil liberties.
   e. He believed the French government could be reasoned with and hoped to use his skills as a negotiator to avoid direct confrontation.

6. The term *gens de coleur* refers to
   a. escaped slaves.
   b. white plantation owners.
   c. French troops.
   d. free people of color.
   e. mulattoes.

7. Which of the following nations gained its independence through agreement rather than through revolution?
   a. Argentina
   b. Brazil
   c. Colombia
   d. Venezuela
   e. Chile

8. Which of the following nations was the first to abolish the slave trade?
   a. America
   b. Britain
   c. Cuba
   d. Netherlands
   e. France

9. Which of the following individuals is NOT associated with a move to increase the rights of women?
   a. Olympe de Gouges
   b. Elizabeth Cady Stanton
   c. Mary Astell
   d. Olaudah Equiano
   e. Mary Wollstonecraft

10. Which of the following multinational empires provided the greatest impediment to Italian and German unification?
    a. Austria
    b. Britain
    c. Russia
    d. Spain
    e. France

Comprehensive Multiple Choice Questions

1. Victory in the Seven Years' War ensured
   a. the prosperity of British colonies and that Britain would dominate global trade in the coming century
   b. the domination of Britain as a land and sea power and that her colonies would move rapidly toward independence
   c. the demise of Britain as a colonial power and the rise of the United States as the dominant force in global commerce
   d. the rise of European powers as colonial occupiers and the subjugation of the indigenous peoples of North and South America
   e. the demise of European colonial powers and the rise of the Americas as the dominant hemisphere in the eighteenth, nineteenth, and twentieth centuries.

2. This excerpt is most likely from which of the following documents?
   "Men are born and remain free and equal in rights. Social distinction may be based only on common utility. . . . The goal of every political association is the preservation of the natural and inalienable rights of man. These rights are liberty, property, security, and resistance to oppression. . . . The free communication of thoughts and opinions is one of the most precious rights of man; every citizen may thus speak, write and publish freely. . . ."
   a. the Declaration of Independence
   b. *Declaration of the Rights of Woman and the Female Citizen*
   c. *Declaration of the Rights of Man and the Citizen*
   d. the United States Constitution
   e. the Napoleonic Codes

3. In which of the following places was slavery ended with revolution rather than by government decree?
   a. United States
   b. Brazil
   c. Great Britain
   d. Haiti
   e. Mexico

Primary Source Questions

1. **Examine the illustration of a slave rebellion in Saint-Domingue on page 796 of your textbook.**
   a. What differences do you notice between the way blacks are represented and the way whites are represented in this print?
   b. How would you discuss point of view for this print?

2. **Examine the paintings of Liberty leading the people on page 780 and the *Napoleon on Horseback at the St Bernard Pass* painting on page 792 of your textbook.**
   a. What comparisons and contrasts about composition and theme can you make between these two works?

Chapter Multiple Choice Answers

1. **b:** De Gouges believed that the rights granted to men in August 1789 should include women as well. Freedom and equality were inalienable rights to men and women as was the right to vote, to speak freely, and to participate in government. She wrote this document as part of her campaign to raise the standing of women in France and to appeal to the male revolutionaries to include women in the rights of French citizens. (p. 781)

2. **a:** Locke's most essential ideal was that sovereignty resided in the people of a society, not in the tradition or religious claims of any ruler. Locke's ideal of the government as a contract which arises from people banding together to protect their common interests and which can be broken if the ruler does not protect that interest is a basic Enlightenment political concept. (p. 783)

3. **d:** After a minor and unsuccessful flirtation with a confederation of states, the United States became a federal system of government with some powers designated to the national level, some to the state level, and others to the local level. By 1791, France had established a limited constitutional monarchy with the former king at the head, though without any legislative authority. Certainly, after 1791, France would go through a series of attempts at permanent government, but Napoleon would forestall those efforts by the end of the eighteenth century. (pp. 785, 788)

4. **d:** While Napoleon espoused and even practiced some Enlightenment ideals, none of these ideals extended to women who found themselves once again living under a patriarchal order despite their contributions to the revolution. (p. 793)

5. **c:** Toussaint Louverture did not want to provoke Napoleon into attacking the island. His hopes were nearly dashed in 1802 when Napoleon sent forty thousand French troops to restore French authority on the island. But thanks to disease and determined successors, the French troops were driven out of the colony and an independent nation was restored. (p. 795)

6. **d:** This term was used on the island of Haiti to refer to free people of color which included mulattos and freed slaves. (p. 795)

7. **b:** Brazil became a monarchy ruled by the creole elites in 1822. Portuguese Prince Pedro declared Brazil as independent in 1821 and accepted the title of Emperor Pedro I in 1822. (p. 798)

8. **b:** Thanks to the work of men like William Wilberforce, the British Parliament was the first to abolish slavery in 1807. (pp. 800–801)

9. **d:** Olaudah Equiano was a freed African slave who was among the earliest and the most influential critics of slavery. (pp. 799–803)

10. **a:** Austria enjoyed a huge multinational empire for much of the nineteenth century. It benefited economically, politically, and socially from keeping both Italy and Germany as mere "geographic expressions." (pp. 809–811)

Comprehensive Multiple Choice Answers

1. **a:** The Seven Years' War was a contest for imperial supremacy in which the British emerged as victor over their European rivals. That victory set the stage for British colonial and commercial domination throughout the next century. (p. 784)

2. **c:** The direct reference to social distinction identifies this document as French, not American. Further, if the document was an excerpt from Olympia de Gouges' *Declaration of the Rights of Woman and the Female Citizen,* it would refer directly to women. The Napoleonic Codes focused on civil law and did not offer such protection for freedom of speech; actually, they often curtailed it. (p. 789)

3. **d:** Because the revolution in Haiti had such clear connections in cause and leadership with the issue of slavery, when Haiti finally proclaimed her independence from France in 1804, the practice of slavery was outlawed as well. In all the other choices, slavery was ended by government decree and much later than 1804. (pp. 796, 801)

Primary Source Answers

1. More blacks than whites are shown in this work. The black people are shown in positions of aggression and the whites are shown in defensive or even submissive postures. The most compelling representation is that the black people are not shown with any facial features, so they can show no human emotion or individuality. This French print is all about point of view. The representation of the whites as outnumbered, and of the blacks as aggressive, genderless, and faceless, creates the message that the innocent, defenseless, predominantly female whites are overpowered by the aggressive black mob. (p. 796)

2. Both these works deal with the theme of hero, but they approach it in a much different way. In the *Napoleon* work, the hero is clearly Napoleon as the single, powerful warrior wrapped in the red cloak of revolution. In the *Liberty* work, the hero is the ideal of liberty as represented by a woman reminiscent of a Greek goddess but with a distinctive strong French face; however, the ideal of liberty is also seen through the young boy at her side, the wounded sansculottes at her feet and the anonymous crowd behind her. In the first work, hero is a single person; in the second it is an ideal embodied by individuals and groups. (pp. 780, 792)

CHAPTER 30

THE MAKING OF INDUSTRIAL SOCIETY

Before you get started: Industrialization was essential to the modern world and its effects were global. It is tied to demography, urbanization, imperialism, socialism, communism, and the world wars. It also had enormous effects on the economic, domestic, and social spheres of family life. The ghastly stories of the abuse of labor in industrialized workplaces remain compelling. Likewise, the accounts of the abuse of workers on other continents who provided the raw materials are riveting. Once industrialization moves beyond Europe, the manner in which it is adopted is indicative of future economic and political power.

PATTERNS OF INDUSTRIALIZATION

Industrialization is the transformation of agrarian and handcraft industries into reorganized and mechanized systems of production. New technology was the key to producing products by machine rather than hand, and by the end of the nineteenth century factories were the dominant mode of production in Europe, the United States, and Japan. New divisions of labor and the advent of production lines accelerated production while huge investments in expensive equipment fueled the formation of large businesses. The corporations banded together to control trade with trusts and cartels.

Foundations of Industrialization
(Themes: Changes and Continuities, Economics, and Technology)

In the mid-eighteenth century, areas of China, Japan, and Great Britain had dynamic economic systems that were based on agriculture with navigable rivers and canals that facilitated trade. The high agricultural productivity increased the populations leading to increased labor specialization. But the regions also ran into substantial ecological problems such as soil depletion and deforestation that would eventually hinder further economic and demographic expansion. Great Britain and other regions of western Europe turned to coal deposits and natural resources from abroad to overcome the impending ecological problems. The primary fuel of Britain had been wood and charcoal, but the discovery of large coal deposits with available labor and resources to extract it shifted the primary fuel to coal. Water transport and commercial centers provided the additional underpinnings to industrialization. This fortunate confluence of factors put Great Britain into the forefront of industrialization while the lengthy distance between the Yangtze and coal deposits deferred Chinese industrialization to a much later time.

Britain's close association with the Americas further reduced ecological deterioration in Britain by providing the raw materials of the emerging textile industry from America. While the plantation economies were both producers of raw goods and consumers of manufactured goods, later American businesses provided the wood, grain, and beef necessary to build factories and feed laborers. In return, the Americas served as a refuge for the surplus European population left outside the economic mainstream.

Textile mills were the first mechanized industry. A series of new machines were developed to increase the speed of spinning and weaving of cotton cloth which had become popular in the eighteenth century despite the efforts of wool producers. The **flying shuttle** which accelerated weaving was followed by the "mule" which increased spinning production. When powered by steam, the mule could produce a hundred times more thread than a manual spinning wheel. Since the mule produced too much thread for the weavers to keep up with, a clergyman, Edmund Cartwright, invented the first water-powered loom. This was supplanted within two decades by a steam-powered loom and by the 1820s, the era of the hand weaver was over. Industrialization of the textile industry produced huge increases in the availability of cheap cotton cloth while providing thousands with jobs. By the 1830s, the textile industry was the leading business in Britain and accounted for 40 percent of its exports.

Eventually, cheap textile production depended on the **steam engine** which was invented by Scottish engineer James Watt in 1765. Steam engines burned coal to power boilers where steam was generated. The pressure of steam in a piston could turn a wheel which could power any number of machines. The power of the steam engine was measured in terms of *horsepower*, something laymen could understand. By 1800, there were over a thousand steam engines in use. In addition to innovations in power sources, higher-quality iron and steel was produced through the use of coke (a purified form of coal) rather than charcoal. The price of iron dropped considerably so that it became the common material of bridges, buildings, and ships. At the beginning of the nineteenth century, a series of improvements in steel manufacturing known as the Bessemer process produced better and cheaper **steel.** Steel was stronger, harder, and more resilient than iron so it began to replace the earlier ore in manufacturing.

In 1815, George Stephenson successfully tested the first **locomotive,** simply a steam engine on wheels. However, both the Watts engine and the early locomotive engine burned too much coal to power ships successfully, so sailing ships remained the mode of transportation on the oceans until the middle of the nineteenth century. Greater efficiency eventually allowed steamship engines to power ships across the oceans by the 1850s. Since ships and trains had huge carrying capacity, the price of transportation decreased dramatically. Furthermore, dense networks of rail and ship traffic tied regions and their products closer to ports and commercial centers. Steamboats were more effective upriver as they were better able to negotiate twisting, narrow waterways than sailboats. The process of industrialization that began in textile mills had improved the modes of transportation as well.

The Factory System
(Themes: Changes and Continuities and Economics)

In the early capitalist period, the putting-out system was the primary mode of production (Chapter 24). Production was based on the household unit and involved fewer than ten individuals. Increased demand for cotton textiles and the use of water and wind power increased the size of a production unit with many workers under one roof. The largest pre-industrial labor force was slaves and unskilled mine workers.

By the mid-nineteenth century, the **factory system** replaced both of these production modes in industrial economies. Large, complicated machines needed enormous spaces and specialized workers. In a fortunate turn of events, factors such as rural overpopulation, declining job opportunities, and increased financial difficulties for small farmers provided the factories with an abundant labor supply. Specialized new machines required a new form of industrial organization in which each laborer produced one component of the final work. So, rather than one worker making one product, many workers combined to make the single product. Factory managers had more control over their workers, and the quality of the work was completely supervised. The nature of work changed to lessen the craftsmanship of a single individual so workers began to see themselves as mere wage earners. It also produced a new class of wealthy factory owners.

As the quality and consistency of products went up so did the pressures to produce more in a shorter period of time. Rather than working in an environment that responded to the natural cycles as they had in rural work, laborers found themselves working exceedingly long hours, some in artificial light for six days a week. The factory clock and whistle with the pressure of constant supervision filled workers' lives with tension and misery. The work with unprotected machinery was also quite dangerous. In some areas of England, there were violent protests by displaced craftsmen who destroyed machines at night. They were known as **Luddites** and were popular until the government hanged fourteen of them in 1813, which ended the movement.

The Early Spread of Industrialization
(Themes: Changes and Continuities and Economics)

Initially, the English government protected its new industry by forbidding the export of any machines, plans, or workers. However, enterprising entrepreneurs in other countries found other ways to obtain the information, such as bribing or kidnapping workers as well as smuggling plans and machines themselves.

By the mid-nineteenth century, the United States, Belgium, France, and Germany were industrializing and improving methods. Belgium and France were in the forefront of innovation while Germany lagged slightly behind due partially to the instability of many competing German states. By the 1840s, iron and steel production increased dramatically while railroads systems were laid. With German unification in 1871, Bismarck's government sponsored industrialization with magnificent results in mining, armaments, and shipping.

In North America, industry and society were also transformed when industrial innovations were combined with abundant natural resources. In the 1820s, English workers and plans for machines were spirited into New England, which became the textile center of North America. At first, young women from rural areas provided the necessary labor but as the United States became a primary destination for European immigrants, those workers displaced the New Englanders. Other industries like shoes, tools, and handguns were also centered in New England, but later in the century, iron and steel industries arose in Pennsylvania and Alabama where iron and coal deposits were common. By 1900, the United States was an industrial powerhouse while southern Canada had a similar experience.

The vast size of the United States was a treasure trove of natural resources but the transportation of those materials was difficult until states sponsored **canals,** and private investors funded **railroad** and **steamship lines.** As in other regions, transportation and heavy industry complemented each other as both grew.

Industrial Capitalism
(Themes: Changes and Continuities, Economics, and Technology)

After the textile industry flourished, other industries began to **mass-produce** standardized articles. One of the most important contributors to factory production was **Eli Whitney**, inventor of the cotton gin. He invented the process by which each factory worker used a specific machine that made just one part that fit into whatever was being produced. By the end of the nineteenth century, sewing machines, clocks, and everything in between were standardized. In 1913, **Henry Ford** added the idea of an **assembly line** to automobile production. A conveyor belt brought the parts to the workers and the car was assembled as it moved down the line. This mode of manufacturing was so efficient that there were huge increases in productivity, so that prices decreased and ordinary citizens could purchase a car for themselves.

As manufacturing evolved so did the business model. In order to buy the very expensive machinery of the industrial age, it was necessary to find **investors.** As the joint-stock companies had been developed to increase investments while decreasing risk in the sixteenth century, **corporations** were developed to fund the new industries. Hundreds to millions of people bought stock in companies and received the profits in dividends if the company did well. And if the company failed, corporations and their investors were protected by laws that limited the losses. By the late nineteenth century, corporations controlled most businesses involved in large amounts of land, labor, and machinery, such as railroads, shipping lines, and factories. Ancillary industries such as **investment banks** and **brokerage firms** developed to support corporations.

Eventually, some corporations tired of competition and, in **monopolies**, attempted to eliminate all of their competitors by one of two methods. In a method known as **vertical organization**, they purchased companies that fed into and led out of their prime business. For example, a steel company purchased the iron ore mines as well as the rail companies that transported the ore to the factory and carried the steel to its final destination. **John D. Rockefeller** in the United States owned virtually every aspect of the oil business. Or, monopolies attempted **horizontal integration** in which the owner of one steel mill purchased every other one that he could. This occurred in the German firm, **IG Farben**, which controlled almost every aspect of chemical manufacturing. By the end of the century, some governments outlawed monopolies while others did very little to control them.

INDUSTRIAL SOCIETY

Benefits to industrialization included cheap manufactured goods, an increased standard of living, and population growth. However, society changed dramatically in other ways that were less benign. The labor needs of industrialization triggered regional and global migrations. New social classes developed in which people were defined by their position in the workplace: the middle class were managers while the lower class were workers. Families and work habits changed so much that reformers attempted to ameliorate the effects of industrialization on people's lives. Among the reformers, the most influential were the socialists who worked to build a more equitable and just society.

The Fruits of Industry
(Theme: Demographics)

Industry produced **affordable goods** for consumers of all classes. Reductions in the price of clothing meant that more people had more than one change of clothing and washable cotton underwear as well. The price of food staples went down as a result of efficient agricultural machinery and steam-powered railroad transportation. More goods were available to fill homes with furniture and decorative objects. In 1851, as a celebration of the fruits of industrialization, the British set up a Crystal Palace filled with their textiles, iron goods, and machine tools. Also on display were Colt pistols and sewing machines from the United States demonstrating their system of interchangeable parts.

The populations of Europeans and Euro-Americans rose sharply in the industrial age as standards of living increased. Between 1700 and 1800, the European population rose from 105 to 180 million and then doubled in the nineteenth century. The American population increased even more rapidly because of the European migration to that area. From 13 million in 1700, it rose to 24 million a century later. Then, in the nineteenth century, it increased about five times that amount. In pre-industrial societies, fertility was high, but so was child mortality. Due to better nutrition and improved disease control, more children of the industrial age survived to adulthood. Furthermore, as health and sanitation continued to improve, adult mortality also slowed. Britain and Germany experienced the fastest growth in western Europe.

One other population shift occurred: a *demographic transition* where fertility rates began to drop. At first both mortality rates and birth rates declined so population continued to grow, but later on, the declining birth rates led to a slower population increase. Couples in industrial societies began to choose to raise fewer children since more children reached adulthood and the cost of raising children was higher in an industrial society. This type of demographic transition occurred in each country as it industrialized.

Urbanization and Migration
(Theme: Demographics)

As rural workers searched for jobs, they clustered in cities with factories. Thus industrialized cities had spectacular growth in urban areas. In 1800, only one-fifth of British people lived in cities, but by the end of the nineteenth century, three-quarters of the population were living and working in cities. Cities increased in size as well so that by the turn of the twentieth century, the largest four cities in the world had populations topping one million. At six million, London was the largest city in the world.

Increased industry and population caused severe air and water **pollution.** The burning of fuels such as coal and wood filled the air with dense, particulate matter and poisons that combined with certain weather conditions to produce pea-soup fogs in which people could not even see their outspread hands. Human sewage and waste from factories flowed freely into streets, streams, and rivers. Contaminated water supplies were the source of drinking water so diseases such as **cholera** and **typhus** were epidemic. Furthermore, housing for workers was inadequate and squalid, crowding so many people into small spaces that other diseases such as **tuberculosis** were rampant. The horrible living conditions also bred **crime** and **prostitution.** In the latter part of the nineteenth century, city governments began to address their problems by providing clean water sources, enclosed sewage lines, and police forces.

In addition to migration toward cities, millions of European workers chose to find work in the Americas. Upward of fifty million Europeans made **transcontinental migrations** in the nineteenth and early twentieth centuries. Many intended to return home and some did, such as one-third of the Italians, but most made the Americas their new home. In the nineteenth century, the **migration pattern** spread from western Europe to northern Europe in mid-century, followed by southern Europeans. Specific groups were driven by conditions in their home countries, such as the potato famine in Ireland and the pograms against Jews in western Russia. They settled around the new industrial cities such as New York, Cleveland, and Pittsburgh and provided the United States with the constant labor supply necessary to move it into the front ranks of industrialized nations.

Industry and Society
(Themes: Social Developments and Gender Structure)

Industrialization changed the social class organization in most countries. Generally, it eliminated the need for a slave class because slaves did not have the resources to buy what factories produced. New classes of wealthy businesspeople challenged the privileges of the nobility and military. The **middle class** grew to include small business owners, factory managers, accountants, and skilled workers along with professionals such as teachers, physicians, and attorneys. The **working classes** were made up of factory and mine workers who were less skilled than their predecessors had been.

The family went through profound changes as it was no longer the primary production unit in society. In pre-industrial societies, every member of the family contributed to the work of the family and this continued for a short time during industrialization as whole families were hired to work together in the mills. However, it became apparent that strong adults could leave the family to become wage earners, so family members began to live separate lives.

Men's position in society was enhanced by industrial work as they left the home for important jobs while women were relegated to domestic chores. Where men and women had once shared those responsibilities, their lives became separate spheres. Professional men spent their leisure hours in purposeful self-improvement while workers increasingly spent their leisure time at athletic events. Middle-class support of churches and Sunday schools were an attempt to force middle-class values upon workers. Nevertheless, workers resisted the discipline and long hours and continued to engage in base activities such as dog fighting, alcohol consumption in bars, and gambling.

Women's work became increasingly domestic as jobs required workers to leave home. Women were encouraged to devote themselves to raising children, managing households, and preserving traditional family values. Authors such as Mrs. John Sandford encouraged women to accept their place as the "weaker vessel" and focus on the happiness of their families. Lower-class women were required to continue to work, so they often were domestic servants to the increasingly wealthy middle class. Young women often took the positions to earn money for dowries or for funding career training.

Working-class children's roles changed enormously in the industrial age. Where children had once played and worked alongside their parents, they were hired at factories without parents or relatives on hand. They worked extremely long hours for less pay than adults because working families required the additional income. The abuses were so noteworthy that the British Parliament held investigations and passed laws in the 1840s to regulate and restrict **child labor.** Eventually, children were removed from the workplace and began to live lives very separate from their parents in schools. In England, childhood became devoted to education with mandatory school attendance laws in 1881.

The Socialist Challenge
(Themes: Social Development and Economics)

Among the most vocal critics of the abusive labor situations in factories were the socialists. They identified **economic inequity** as the primary problem in capitalism and condemned the working conditions for women and children. Several types of socialists worked to improve the economic and working conditions of laborers. The utopian socialists believed that it was possible to construct a factory system out of a model community in which there were no inequities. To this end, French socialist Charles Fourier and Scottish factory owner Robert Owen planned model communities that were less than successful but led the way to improvements. Americans were particularly drawn to their ideas in the 1840s and 1850s. Numerous communities were founded and subsequently failed despite the best of intentions so it became apparent that there had to be other ways to improve workers' lives.

Freidrich Engels (1820–1895), a factory owner, and **Karl Marx** (1818–1883), a journalist, devised a theory of capitalism that would have profound effects long after their deaths. They rejected utopian socialism and believed that the social problems of industrialized societies were a direct result of capitalism. In their theory, there were only two social classes, the producers (the **proletariet**) and the capitalists (the **bourgeoisie**), who were doomed to struggle with one another. All aspects of modern society from governments to the arts were merely the tools of the bourgeoisie. Marx even referred to organized religion as the "opiate of the masses." In his masterpiece, *Das Kapital,* and the later tract *Manifesto of the Communist Party* written with Engels, Marx aligned himself with communists who advocated the abolition of private property. The conditions of the overworked and abused masses would lead to an inevitable overthrow of the capitalist system leaving a "dictatorship of the proletariat." Eventually, the new system would stabilize and the state would "wither away" forming an entirely just and equitable society. The communist ideology of Marx and Engels grew popular through the nineteenth century but was not accepted by all socialists. Evolutionary socialists believed that a violent revolution was unnecessary so they worked to gain influence in representative governments.

Governments throughout industrialized societies began to respond to the criticisms of socialists and others by expanding the vote (**suffrage** or franchise) to men with less property than previously. The English Parliament equalized representation between urban and rural areas to represent population shifts. In Germany of the 1880s, Otto von Bismarck introduced medical insurance, unemployment compensation, and retirement pensions as a social safety net for workers.

Workers also began to form organizations called **trade unions** to work for better wages and working conditions. However, for most of the century, they were considered illegal by factory owners and governments. The primary weapon of trade unions was the **strike,** which often turned violent as owners hired replacement workers, and police forces battled with the strikers. Eventually, trade unions became legal and led to reforms that lessened the chance that workers would look to communist solutions to their problems.

GLOBAL EFFECTS OF INDUSTRIALIZATION

While early industrialization had occurred in Europe and North America, later in the century the Russian and Japanese governments worked actively to change their economies. The use of raw materials in industry quickly forced the globalization of industrialization as early sources were depleted. Industrialized countries often controlled the countries that had natural resources by buying their raw materials cheaply and returning manufactured goods to those countries.

The Continuing Spread of Industrialization
(Theme: Changes and Continuities, Economics, and Political Development)

After 1870, Russia and Japan began the process of industrialization with strong government support as their governments focused on strengthening their economies and militaries to resist western pressures. In Russia, the tsarist government encouraged the construction of railroads to unify the vast country and link western Europe to east Asia. They added some 35,000 miles of track in forty years. As in North America, railroads stimulated the coal, steel, and iron industries. Count **Sergei Witte** served as the finance minister who promoted industrialization. He pushed to protect infant industries, supported shipping companies, and provided educational institutions for engineers and seamen. He worked to bring in foreign investments and set up savings banks. Witte's remarkable successes included production of half the world's oil and becoming the fourth greatest producer of steel by 1900. Russia also had large coal, iron, and armament industries.

The Japanese government also pushed its economy into industry by hiring thousands of foreign experts for planning and instruction in industrial techniques. They too opened new technical schools, **constructed** railroads, set up a banking system, and opened mines. Soon, Japanese industries were producing ships, armaments, silk, cotton, chemicals, and glass. Once businesses could operate independently, the government sold them to private businessmen who often formed large industrial empires known as *zaibatsu*. Like European and American corporations, zaibatsu soon operated as cartels and trusts. Rather than private investors, zaibatsu were usually run by one family. The Mitsue combine, for example, owned businesses across the economic spectrum. By 1900, Japan was a full-fledged member of industrialized societies and far beyond any other Asian country.

The International Division of Labor
(Themes: Change and Economics)

Beyond the countries that had mechanized early or with governmental support, industrialization was spotty. Entrepreneurs built a thriving hemp industry and a small steel industry in India but had neither government support nor sufficient capital to expand. Industrialization affected other countries primarily with a new division between countries that produced raw materials and those that produced manufactured goods. Large-scale global trade had been in existence since the sixteenth century and the demand for the agricultural products of that trade system had increased due to population growth. In the nineteenth century, demand for new commodities also increased with cotton for the textile industry and rubber for the belts and tires of machines. These commodities were produced in regions of Asia, Africa, and South America.

Two types of national economies developed. Europe and regions that had been settled by Europeans industrialized relatively quickly and became successful. Russia and Japan had good industrial success as well. Most of the rest of the world grew dependent upon demand from industrial nations and failed to industrialize themselves. In **dependent economies**, foreign investors owned the businesses while foreign governments controlled the policies. Companies adopted free trade policies that damaged native industries while workers were paid wages too low to enable them to buy many manufactured goods. The result was wealth concentrated in a small group with little opportunity for economic prosperity.

As a world trade system, division between those who produced raw materials and those who processed and consumed them worked spectacularly well as trade increased and the world's economies were solidly linked to each other.

Finished reading the chapter? Be sure you can . . .

- Describe the pattern of industrialization in European and North American economies.
- Analyze its effects on societies and families.
- Describe the interdependence of producing and manufacturing countries.
- Compare industrialization in England with that in Japan.
- Describe industrialization's effect on demographics.
- Analyze how industrialization contributed to the rise of western dominance.
- Compare European women in the middle classes with women in the lower classes.
- Describe the arguments of the critics of industrial society.

Chapter Multiple Choice Questions

1. Which of the following conditions was LEAST important in the process of industrialization?
   a. a healthy agricultural economy
   b. a navigable system of waterways
   c. an available labor source
   d. innovations in technology
   e. a convenient power source

2. In which industry did the first mechanization occur?
   a. woolen mills as the availability of wool increased
   b. coal mines which provided fuel for the factories
   c. railroad companies as they transported fuel and raw materials
   d. canal companies that profited from increased transportation of goods
   e. cotton factories who benefited from the availability of cotton

3. The advent of steam power enabled increased production and efficiency but in which business was steam power the slowest to develop?
   a. railroads
   b. home heating
   c. coal mining
   d. ocean shipping
   e. steel production

4. Industrialization made profound changes in work responsibilities. Which of the following groups protested the changes first?
   a. socialists because working people had no voice to protest
   b. workers themselves because they resisted being relegated to mere wage earners
   c. Parliament who took note of the abuses before they became national concerns
   d. agricultural landlords because they lost their labor source
   e. city governments who deplored the overcrowding of workers' housing

5. How did other European and American entrepreneurs gain the knowledge to mechanize?
   a. The ideas were in the public domain, so it was easy to borrow them.
   b. The plans were gained through unsavory methods in the earliest cases of industrial espionage.
   c. Foreign visitors were free to wander the factory floors but restrained from talking to engineers.
   d. Trade journals shared plans and systems with their readership.
   e. Factory owners banded together to fund investments in factories in other countries.

6. Industrialization led to global changes in population. What was an example of a demographic transition?
   a. People moved from rural regions into urban regions.
   b. Global migrations occurred as workers moved to new countries.
   c. Declining mortality rates made for a healthier population.
   d. Declining birth rates contributed to a slowing in the population increase.
   e. Better urban sanitation methods contributed to a decrease in mortality.

7. What effect did industrialization have on gender roles?
   a. Men could make higher wages than women so most women looked for jobs as domestic servants.
   b. Women moved into jobs such as teaching that had been relegated to men.
   c. Both men and women found valuable societal roles in separate spheres.
   d. Very few jobs were available for women so most women retired to housekeeping.
   e. As rural men moved into urban jobs, women ran farms on their own.

8. According to Marx and Engels, the final end to a class revolution would
   a. be a multiple class structure giving each class equal opportunities.
   b. elevate the proletariat to the dominant class.
   c. put economic and political power into the hands of all people.
   d. include land reform that allowed each citizen a small plot of land.
   e. be no need for any form of government.

9. Of the following aspects of industrialization, which one clearly underpinned the industrialization of Japan and Russia?
   a. abundant natural resources
   b. a thriving middle class
   c. a large workforce
   d. government support
   e. access to water transport

10. It could be said that global economic forces split countries into two dominant patterns. While one was the manufacturing nations, what was the other form?
    a. nations whose governments received profits for sale of its raw materials
    b. nations in which private citizens benefited from sale of natural resources
    c. nations that exported labor to satisfy the demands in manufacturing countries
    d. nations that were able to remain independent of the manufacturing world
    e. nations that became dependent on manufacturing economies rather than controlling their own

Comprehensive Multiple Choice Questions

1. Which component of the age of proto-industrialization became a key asset for industrialization?
   a. Plantation economies demonstrated the importance of manufactured goods from distant sources.
   b. The putting-out system provided a model of labor that would translate into factory systems.
   c. Cotton as a significant cash crop in American and Asian markets provided the impetus for mechanization of textiles.
   d. Steam power used in processing agricultural products like sugar was transferred to the factories.
   e. The accumulation of enormous fortunes from overseas profits fueled the technological innovations.

2. When comparing the industrialization process of Russia and Japan, which of the following would be most similar in the role of government?
   a. the Dutch government during the commercial boom of the sixteenth and seventeenth centuries
   b. the Inca's participation in the economic production of the high Andes
   c. the laissez-faire practices of nineteenth-century American politics
   d. the role of the Melakkan government after the advent of European trade
   e. the role of the French government in a mercantilist economy

3. When comparing the roles of urban and rural women in the middle ages with those in the industrial age, which of the following is the most accurate description?
   a. Rural women maintained the same roles while urban women became increasingly independent entrepreneurs.
   b. Rural women gained more authority as men left for the cities while urban women lost their autonomy and became completely dependent on men.
   c. Rural women maintained their same roles while urban women continued with a diversity of roles, but there was less opportunity for independent initiative.
   d. Rural women increasingly shouldered both house and work roles while urban women became increasingly relegated to the home.
   e. Rural women began to form cooperatives to market agricultural goods while urban women increasingly depended upon industrial work as the foundation of their economic well-being.

Primary Source Questions

1. **Read *Sources from the Past: Thomas Malthus on Population*, 1803, on page 830 of your textbook.**
   a. What was Malthus's point of view and how did the environment of industrialization contribute to it?
   b. What is the stated problem that he sees?
   c. What does he propose as the solution?

2. **Examine the Japanese Tomioka silk factory, 1870s, on page 840 of your textbook.**
   a. What is the artist's point of view?
   b. What European elements can you find in the print?
   c. What are the implications of those elements?

Chapter Multiple Choice Answers

1. **a:** In fact, overpopulation and economic problems in farming communities increased the labor source for urban areas. (pp. 817–820)

2. **e:** As British consumers had grown fond of cotton Indian calicoes, the demand fueled mechanization of cotton textiles. (p. 818)

3. **d:** Due to excessive use of coal, it took longer to develop steam engines that could power heavily laden ships across the oceans. (p. 819)

4. **b:** The workers themselves were the first to protest in a series of violent attacks on machines by "Luddites." (p. 821)

5. **b:** The newest technologies were kept so secret by factory owners that foreign investors sometimes had to go as far as to smuggle plans and kidnap workers to discover the newest innovations. (p. 821)

6. **d:** The profound demographic transition of the industrial age was a lowering of fertility rates. (p. 827)

7. **c:** Being careful of value judgments, the best answer is that women and men moved into separate spheres of work and home. (pp. 832, 833)

8. **e:** The end to revolution would be the "withering away" of government although it would be preceded by a "dictatorship of the masses." (p. 835)

9. **d:** Without government sponsorship of industrialization, the other factors were insignificant. (p. 837)

10. **e:** When nations exported most of their raw materials they became dependent on their trade partners rather than developing their own resources. (p. 841)

Comprehensive Multiple Choice Answers

1. **c:** While plantation economies did purchase manufactured products from Europe and large fortunes were made, it was the desire for more cost-effective ways to process cotton cloth that drove innovations. Steam power was not first used in sugar processing and the putting-out system revolved around the family as a labor unit. (pp. 817–818)

2. **e:** Japanese and Russian governmental sponsorship of economic development has more in common with the policies of King Louis XIV where the state supported new industries, set up protective tariffs, and constructed improved infrastructure. The Incas collected taxes and tribute but did little to direct economic development. The Melakkans served as middlemen to European traders and the industrialization in the United States occurred in an environment of independent entrepreneurship with little governmental influence. As in England, the Dutch government allowed the business interests of the country almost complete freedom in commerce. (p. 644, 837)

3. **c:** While fewer rural families remained in the country, women's roles remained a combination of indoors and outdoors work. One must remember that urban women were not mostly middle-class artisans and merchants as they had been in the high middle ages but consisted of middle-class women who increasingly stayed at home and working-class women who were responsible for wage earning as factory workers or in domestic service, as well as household responsibilities. The other choices take into account only one group of urban women. (pp. 522, 832–833)

Primary Source Answers

1. Thomas Malthus was a clergyman who studied economics and demography. Living during the period of industrialization, Malthus must have witnessed enormous changes in English society including the growth of cities and the resulting squalor of workers' living conditions. It undoubtedly colored his gloomy prediction of demographic controls. The problem is that the population grows faster than the food supply so that the ultimate result is starvation. He does concede that because humans have rational thought that there is a "preventative" solution to stave off starvation, and that is to refrain from early marriage which he calls moral restraint. The other solution which he somewhat ironically calls "positive checks" is anything that shortens the human life span such as hideous labor conditions, extreme poverty, and large cities with both common and epidemic disease. (p. 830)

2. Printmaking is a traditional Japanese art form and it was always common for the artist to depict everyday work life. There does not seem to be an obvious bias for or against factory work as the print has the elements of Japanese art in its color scheme and sparc lines and a representation of Japanese culture in commanding men and deferring women. European influences are seen in the western brick and wood factory building, the long lines of workers, and the mechanized looms behind them. Also, the male managers are wearing western clothing while the female workers continue in their traditional kimonos perhaps indicating a divide between men's and women's acceptance of western ways. A male in traditional clothing is seated to the left of center; he may be a customer or perhaps the owner since he appears to have status high enough to be seated. (Is that his family we see in the small western-dressed girl and the seated woman in the kimono in the foreground?) This print depicts the extent to which Japan has adopted the European factory system as well as its fashions. (p. 840)

CHAPTER 31

THE AMERICAS IN THE AGE OF INDEPENDENCE

Before you get started: Some parts of this chapter are only tangentially addressed on the national exam, but other parts are crucial. Read the chapter summaries for the United States and Canada elements thoughtfully, but do not sweat the details there. The AP World History course description is careful to say that the United States is included in "relation to its interaction with other societies." Consider how historical patterns in the United States fit with Latin America and other world regions as you read those sections. Don't skip the parts about Canada, but know it is not a single identified region on the exam; it is included in the region for any question regarding North America.

However, the sections on Latin America in this chapter are extremely important as you could be held accountable in several multiple choice questions, in the comparison essay, or in the change-over-time essay from these sections or this time period. There are three Latin American subsections in this chapter: (1) political fragmentation, (2) economic dependence and development, and (3) national identity and gender roles. Major themes, huge region: be sure to read carefully.

THE BUILDING OF AMERICAN STATES

Millions of immigrants came to the United States between 1750 and 1914, some voluntarily and others enslaved. Each, however, contributed to the economic, political, and social development of the new nation and all contributed to the transformation of the Americas.

The United States: Westward Expansion and Civil War
(Themes: Political Identity and Changes and Continuities)

Even after independence from Great Britain, the new United States had several more decisions regarding government structure and popular participation to address. The leaders of the new nation crafted a constitution which outlined a **federal system**, left some responsibilities to the states, and allowed for the admission of new states to the Union. By 1820, most property qualifications for voting had been removed for white males, but issues relating to states' rights and slavery remained unresolved.

Americans began to move west almost as soon as the revolution ended and even before these final constitutional issues were settled. With lands from Britain that stretched from the Appalachian Mountains to the Mississippi River and lands from the Mississippi River to the Rocky Mountains acquired from France under the **Louisiana Purchase** of 1803, the United States rapidly doubled in size. By 1840, the term **manifest destiny** was used to describe the plan to expand westward to build a nation which stretched from the Atlantic to the Pacific Ocean.

Such movement created inevitable conflict between the settlers and government forces and the indigenous people of North America who resisted the attempt to push them from their traditional homeland. Temporary alliances among America's diverse indigenous peoples and occasional native victories on the battlefields slowed westward expansion, but the superiority of the settlers' and government soldiers' weaponry made the conquest inevitable. The **Battle at Wounded Knee** in 1890 marked the place where "a people's dream died," according to a later-day native leader.

Mexico and the United States would also come into conflict over westward expansion. Texas joined the United States in 1845 and the United States began seriously eyeing the rest of Mexico's territory in the southwest. The United States instigated war with Mexico, which was quickly defeated and stripped of her former territory which included most of Texas, California, and New Mexico.

Westward expansion exacerbated problems within the new republic as it aggravated tensions between regions over issues such as **slavery.** Slavery had troubled many of the nation's early leaders and by the nineteenth century, there was a growing abolition movement abroad and in the United States. Divisions hardened between slave and free states and the question of whether settlers could extend slavery into the newly acquired territories had to be resolved. The development of cotton as a cash crop caused a surge in the demand for slaves and as the number of slaves in the United States grew from five hundred thousand in 1770 to nearly two million by 1820, the issue clearly had to be addressed. Legislation such as the **Missouri Compromise of 1820** marked attempts to legislate the dilemma, but the issue was too explosive. After **Abraham Lincoln**, who saw the institution of slavery as immoral, was elected president in 1860, the crisis peaked; the **Civil War** ensued as eleven southern states withdrew from the Union between 1860 and 1861. Though slavery was the center of the war, the conflict, which lasted from 1861–1865, revolved around two key issues: states' rights versus federal government authority and the needs of a growing industrial-capitalist nation pitted against those of a plantation, cash crop economy. Northerners fought against slavery, against the right of states to withdraw from the Union, and for the emerging industrial society. Southerners affirmed their right to withdraw from the union and to support slavery as an economic necessity; they considered themselves agriculturally and economically independent from the north. The industrially superior north was finally victorious in 1865—slavery was abolished in the United States, and the powerful federal Union was upheld. Unlike its European contemporaries who were fighting revolutions of nationalism, ideology, and social class during the mid-nineteenth century, the United States ultimately forged a strong central government to deal with divisive political and social issues.

The Canadian Dominion: Independence without War
(Themes: Political Identity and Changes and Continuities)

Ethnic divisions between French-speaking Roman Catholic Canadians and English-speaking Protestant Canadians might have spilled over into civil war, were it not for the greater threat of United States' expansion. The War of 1812 solidified a Canadian identity as both British and French Canadians joined together to repel invading American forces. That battlefield success forged a sense of Canadian pride and allowed an anti-United States sentiment to supercede the French Canadian/British Canadian split. The British government diffused tensions with French Canadians by allowing increasing amounts of domestic autonomy within Canadian provinces. Fear of westward expansion by the United States stifled internal Canadian dissention and prompted Britain to grant independence to Canada starting in 1867 and reaching full independence in 1931. Canada maintained its ties to Great Britain, protected itself against its powerful southern neighbor, developed as a culturally diverse and politically unified society, and gained independence all without suffering civil war.

Latin America: Fragmentation and Political Experimentation
(Themes: Patterns of Interaction and Changes and Continuities)

Division, conflict, rule by tyrants, rebellion, and civil war would mark much of the nineteenth and early twentieth centuries in Latin America. Though Simon Bolivar had worked to establish a large confederation which could provide Latin America with political, military, and economic strength to avoid foreign encroachment, such hopes proved short-lived as his Gran Colombia broke apart; Venezuela, Colombia, Ecuador, and numerous other independent nations resulted. Though creole elites sought to draft written constitutions for these nations, the process proved difficult and Latin American states experienced failed constitution after failed constitution as various leaders sought to create machineries of government to bring stability to their nations. Creole elites deliberately prevented mass participation in politics and legislated millions of indigenous peoples out of political involvement. Further, there were no institutionalized channels to allow for open public discussion of policies or exploration of contentious issues so violence frequently became the accepted voice of dissent and even the politically active portion of the population found itself sharply divided into competing factions and conflicting ideologies. Sadly, the only real agreement among these elites was the desire to control the land for agriculture and ranching and to further disinherit the indigenous peoples who had managed to survive disease, forced labor, and cultural annihilation through assimilation.

The position of **caudillo,** or regional military leader, emerged out of this unrest to appeal to populist sentiment and to exploit the discontented masses. **Juan Manuel de Rosas,** sometimes called "the Machiavelli of the Pampas," ruled Argentina for nearly twenty years. This "Argentine Nero" relied on terror and brute strength to subdue the other caudillos, stifle opposition, and restore order; he did so by making terror a tool of the government and by ruling as a despot through his own personal army.

In Mexico, there were a series of governments which moved from monarchy to republic to caudillo rule and which eventually produced some liberal reform. After Mexico's humiliating defeat in the Mexican American War, a liberal reform movement attempted to reshape Mexican society under the leadership of **President Benito Juarez**, a Mexican of indigenous ancestry. Juarez sought to curtail the power of the Roman Catholic church in Mexico, limit the power of the Mexican military, grant universal manhood suffrage, promote the development of a rural middle class, and guarantee civil rights such as freedom of the press; such efforts met with intense opposition from Mexico's conservative elites. The fight for control of Mexico reached a peak in 1861 as Juarez sought to lessen Mexico's economic woes by suspending her loan payments to European bankers. France, Britain, and Spain all intervened to protect their investments with France sending tens of thousands of troops to support a proclaimed, but short-lived Emperor, Austrian **Archduke Maximillian.** Juarez eventually regained some control and restored his liberal government, but the rest of his rule was torn by political divisions.

Mexico was moving toward revolution by the early twentieth century. The **Mexican Revolution**, a bitter and bloody conflict that lasted from 1911 to 1920, pitted Mexico's middle class, peasants, and workers against the powerful dictator **Porfirio Diaz** in Latin America's first major attempt to bring equitable land reform. More than 95 percent of peasants in Mexico were landless and they turned increasingly radical as the disparities grew. Revolutionary leaders like **Emiliano Zapata** and **Pancho Villa** organized massive peasant armies fighting for **"tierra y libertad,"** land and liberty. Despite their popularity and growing power, these revolutionaries were no match for the Mexican government or its United States support; over two million Mexicans died in this revolution. Yet, some of their goals were realized in the Mexican Constitution of 1917, which provided for some land distribution, state-supported education, minimum wage, universal suffrage, and some restrictions of foreign economic investments. These provisions were not soon realized in practice, however.

AMERICAN ECONOMIC DEVELOPMENT

While the United States and Canada absorbed vast numbers of migrants during the nineteenth century and built powerful, wealthy industrial societies in part by exploiting British investment, the nations of Latin America did not fare so well. Instead, the fragmented nations of Latin America continued to struggle with vestiges of colonialism, slavery, and economic dependence on plantation-produced cash crops. Migrants in Latin America worked as contract workers or indentured servants, often in conditions not markedly improved from slavery. Freed slaves and their descendents continued to exist at the bottom of society's social and economic hierarchy.

Migration to the Americas
(Themes: Migration and Patterns of Interaction)

There was a mass migration of European and Asian peoples to the Americas during the nineteenth century and there was significant internal migration as many peoples from Latin America moved north in search of work and economic success. The **California Gold Rush** and its ensuing push for support services offered the promise of prosperous American livelihoods to migrants from all over the world. After the mid-nineteenth century, industrial jobs lured migrants and allowed American industry to develop rapidly due to the availability of ready, cheap labor. By the late nineteenth century, it was **eastern and southern European migrants** who dominated the textile and related industries of the American northeast. Asian migrants contributed significantly to the construction of America's transportation infrastructure. Between 1852 and 1875, approximately two hundred thousand **Chinese laborers** migrated to California, most on indentured labor contracts, and five thousand more entered Canada to search for gold in British Columbia or to construct the Canadian Pacific Railroad.

Migrants to Latin America mostly worked on the plantations. These migrants included **Italians** who worked on Brazil's coffee plantations or in Argentina's vast commercial agriculture industry. **Chinese migrants** to Latin America worked in Cuba's sugarcane industry and were joined by **Japanese migrants** in Peru's cotton plantations, guano mining, and railroad projects. **Migrants from India** worked on the island plantations in Jamaica, Trinidad, Tobago and Guyana. Growing United States' interest in Hawai`i in the later nineteenth century brought thousands of east Asians to the sugarcane plantations as indentured servants.

Economic Expansion in the United States
(Themes: Technology, Economics, and Environment)

After the American Civil War, British investors found safe, white-controlled investment opportunities throughout the United States which dramatically stimulated American textile industries, railroad construction, steel mills, and coal and iron mines. These industries grew exponentially, generating significant returns for their British investors and eventually making the United States a rival economic power which would soon outperform Britain.

The construction of transcontinental railroad lines helped to create an integrated, connected national economy as they provided cheap transportation of agricultural commodities, manufactured goods, and individual travelers. Further, the demand for raw materials—coal, iron, steel, timber, glass, and rubber—for railway construction spurred those industries, and the need for support industries and services generated new businesses and towns. By the end of the nineteenth century, the United States had developed new products related to communication and transportation such as electric lights, telegraphs, telephones, typewriters, and electric- and oil-powered motors. The consumer demand for these new products spurred those industries as well. Labor strikes were not unusual, but big business prevailed, though workers did win some rights and protections by the twentieth century.

The railroads and their corresponding industries seriously affected the American environment. The exploitation of land and resources to supply the industries and the pumping of smoke and its emissions into the air produced environmental damage and human suffering to the remaining indigenous peoples and modern workers alike. Even the American sense of time was impacted by the railroads as the United States government adopted "railroad time" in place of local sun time by legally establishing four time zones inside the contiguous United States.

Canadian Prosperity
(Themes: Economics and Patterns of Interaction)

British investment also stimulated the Canadian economy, although there British pounds were used to keep the colony stable and discourage the formation of separatist movements as well as to spur economic development. After the establishment of the Dominion in 1867, politicians developed an economic plan known as the **National Policy,** which was designed to attract migrants, build a national transportation system, and protect Canadian industries. Like the United States, the construction of a continental railroad was essential to developing Canada's economic base and creating a national economic network. Also, like the United States, the indigenous peoples sometimes violently resisted, but were eventually subdued by government troops. The resulting boom in industries drew migrant workers to Canada from Asia and Europe. American investment eventually grew to outpace British investment and the economies of the United States and Canada became increasingly independent.

Latin American Dependence
(Themes: Economics and Patterns of Interaction)

The Latin American experience with industrialization and economic development during the nineteenth century was not like the North American experience. In Latin America, foreign investment did not eventually shift into local hands, but the generated capital and control of industries and exports remained predominately in foreign hands. The investment capital which did make its way to locals was zealously guarded by elites seeking to protect their traditional positions of status and power.

Colonial legacies in economics and politics extinguished or stunted local industries which could not compete with imported European goods. Latin American elites benefited from control of the imports and thus had little incentive to promote economic investment or diversification. British merchants saw limited markets for British goods and British investors were selective in their choices. In Argentina, for example, British investors supported development of sheep and cattle ranching and benefited immensely as the invention of refrigerated cargo ships meant low cost meat could be sold for profit in British markets. European migrants formed the majority of urban workers in Latin America and, though they did not share in the economic benefits of foreign investment, their cultural contributions to rapidly growing cities such as Buenos Aires was significant.

Dictator Porfirio Diaz's attempts to encourage industrialization in Mexico were only partially successful and the profits produced from construction projects, glass, chemical and textile industries, and a small steel industry went into the pockets of the Mexican oligarchy and foreign investors rather than being reinvested in his nation. Little wealth went back into national industrial development and even less went to the urban workers who became increasingly disgruntled. The revolutionary outbreak of 1911 reflects this frustration. Thus foreign investors, especially the British—instead of local people—benefited from Latin America's mining industries and agricultural production.

AMERICAN CULTURAL AND SOCIAL DIVERSITY

American societies experienced much strife during the era 1750–1914. The struggles between diverse peoples with competing and often conflicting goals frequently pitted social class against social class and culture against culture.

Multicultural Society in the United States
(Theme: Social and Gender Structures)

Though the United States was the most culturally diverse nation in the western hemisphere in the late nineteenth century, its economic and political power rested almost exclusively in the hands of elite white males of European descent. Cultural and social tensions existed as indigenous peoples, African-American slaves and their descendants, women, and migrants sought a voice in society and a place in the economic realm.

The United States policy toward indigenous peoples was at first to contain them and then to assimilate them by destroying their bases of native cultural traditions. The destruction of the buffalo, the division of tribal lands into individual holdings, the removal of native children from their families, and their placement in white-controlled boarding schools exemplify this strategy.

Slavery was ended by the Civil War, but equality was not quick to follow for the freed slaves and their descendants. Though civil rights were extended to freed slaves and voting rights to black men during the northern occupation of the south, known as **Reconstruction**, as soon as the northern troops went home, the benefits for southern African-Americans disappeared and a segregated south was created.

Women's concerns for social, political, and economic freedoms had been initially addressed at the **Seneca Falls Convention in 1848,** where feminists had drafted their own "declaration of sentiments." After the

Civil War, some progress was made in education and employment, though meaningful political and economic rights would not be achieved until the twentieth century for women in the United States.

The more than twenty-five million migrants, who came to the United States between 1840 and 1914, brought new foods, religions, traditions, and languages to the United States and contributed much to its cultural richness. However, many white, native-born Americans began to feel threatened by this influx of migrants. Many migrants were eventually forced legally or pushed socially into living in distinct neighborhoods, quite separate from the white regions of cities or towns. White Americans also pressured the government to restrict and eventually halt immigration from China and then Japan.

Canadian Cultural Contrasts
(Theme: Patterns of Interaction)

Canada's political development is often described in terms of divisions between French and British settlers. The indigenous peoples of Canada, however, were an essential aspect of cultural development in that nation. As in the United States, the indigenous peoples of Canada found themselves increasingly pushed out of their own lands as trappers and soon farmers began to settle across Canada, and they became largely isolated from Canada's political and economic development. Slavery also affected the cultural context of Canada, as Canada had allowed slavery until 1833 and escaped slaves from the United States helped to form a population of black Canadians who were not considered equal and were segregated from the Canadian mainstream. Likewise, Asian and eastern European migrants were drawn to Canada as laborers but found themselves also outside the Canadian mainstream which continued to be dominated by descendents of those British and French settlers. Violent conflicts emerged between these groups throughout the 1870s and 1880s as **metis**, descendants of French fur traders, many of whom had intermarried with indigenous peoples, resented the growing westward expansion of British-descended farmers. **Louis Riel** emerged as the leader of the metis and fought to protect the local land rights of people overshadowed by the Canadian Dominion. He even tried to forestall the completion of the Canadian Pacific Railroad; his attempts failed and he was executed for treason. Despite his failed **Northwest Rebellion**, Riel's execution foreshadowed the long-term cultural conflict between Canadians of indigenous, British, and French descent.

Ethnicity, Identity, and Gender in Latin America
(Themes: Patterns of Interaction and Gender Structures)

Latin American countries developed a social hierarchy based on ethnicity and color as a result of both their colonial experiences and as a legacy of slavery. The creoles stood at the top of society; with mestizos, mulattoes, zambos, and castizos occupying the center rungs; and the indigenous peoples and descendants of African slaves at the bottom. Nineteenth-century migrants further complicated this social hierarchy with the addition of East Asians, Indians, and eastern Europeans. Cultural identity for intellectuals in Latin America was either as the heirs to the European enlightenment or as the products of the unique American environment. Argentine President **Domingo Faustino Sarmiento** worked to dismantle the power of the caudillos and to establish his capital, Buenos Aires, as the intellectual fulcrum for Argentina and indeed all of Latin America.

Gaucho culture was one fascinating exception to this race-centered society: to be a gaucho, one simply adopted a gaucho lifestyle. Gaucho tradition was one of the few ethnically egalitarian traditions in Latin America. Gauchos, like the North American cowboys, led independent and self-sufficient lives and came to symbolize bravery and independence from the elaborate hierarchy in Latin American society. Yet, even the brave gauchos could not ultimately resist the inevitable fencing of the grasslands known as the pampas, the pressures from the caudillos to serve in the military, and especially the powers of assimilation. By the late nineteenth century, the gauchos were more romance than reality.

Machismo—the social ethic that honors male strength, courage, aggression, and cunning—was an integral part of life in Latin American tradition. Women were excluded from political life and they could not work or manage estates without male permission. In rural areas, women were especially vulnerable to assault as they were isolated and thus further removed from any semblance of legal protection. In cities, during the later nineteenth century, education became an avenue of opportunity for women, but even there, male domination remained the central characteristic of Latin American society.

Finished reading the chapter? Be sure you can . . .

- Describe and analyze the changes in patterns of global commerce and communication resulting from the building of North American and Latin American states.
- Describe and analyze the reasons for the rise of western dominance.
- Compare and contrast the forms of western intervention in Latin America and in Africa (See Chapters 33 and 36 as well for this one.)
- Describe the changing roles of ethnicity, nationalism, and gender in Latin America.

Chapter Multiple Choice Questions

1. The term "manifest destiny" refers to
   a. the belief held by many United States citizens that their nation was entitled to occupy all of North America from the Atlantic to the Pacific Ocean.
   b. the belief held by many United States citizens that their nation was entitled to occupy Canada and Mexico as a god-given right.
   c. the belief held by many United States citizens that their nation was entitled to occupy the lands of the Louisiana Purchase and the spoils of the Mexican-American War.
   d. the belief held by many United States citizens that their nation was entitled to occupy only those lands rightly won during the war of 1812.
   e. the belief held by many United States citizens that their nation was entitled to occupy all of North and South America.

2. The Trail of Tears in 1838–1839 and the Battle of Wounded Knee in 1890 are significant because they
   a. demonstrate the technological superiority of United States troops over the indigenous peoples of North America.
   b. typify the harsh treatment of native peoples at the hands of the United States government.
   c. exemplify the determination of the American government to bring unity to North America and undermine any attempts at secession.
   d. clarify the United States government's position on slavery and "free soil".
   e. added large portions of land to the United States which had been controlled by foreign powers.

3. Which of the following events shifted the population ratio in Canada from predominately French to predominately British-speaking residents?
   a. the British victory in the Seven Years' War
   b. the American Revolutionary War
   c. the British victory in the War of 1812
   d. the American Civil War
   e. the French and Indian Wars

4. What was the universal goal of the Latin American reform movements of the nineteenth century?
   a. universal manhood suffrage
   b. reduce the power of the Roman Catholic church
   c. undermine the power of the caudillos
   d. land distribution reform
   e. higher pay and reduced working hours

5. Asian migrants to Latin America in the mid-nineteenth century were most likely to work
   a.   in the textile industries.
   b.   in the railroad industries.
   c.   in the mining industry.
   d.   on a sugar or cotton plantation.
   e.   on a tobacco or pineapple plantation.

6. Why were Latin America's elite urban merchants and large landowners reluctant to work toward economic diversification in their nations?
   a.   They were already significantly profiting from European trade and investments.
   b.   They wanted to protect local industries from foreign domination.
   c.   They were controlled by the caudillos and had little economic influence.
   d.   They wanted to develop their nations on a model similar to economic development in the United States and in Canada.
   e.   They wanted to avoid an influx of migrants from Asia and Europe which they believed would destroy their traditional ways of life.

7. What nineteenth-century construction projects provided the greatest boom to economic unification in both the United States and in Canada?
   a.   the building of massive dams and hydroelectric projects
   b.   the building of telephone and telegraph systems
   c.   the building of transcontinental railroads
   d.   the building of cities for business locations
   e.   the building of highways and bridges

8. Economically, which groups comprised the Latin American elite?
   a.   religious officials and businessmen
   b.   caudillos and castizos
   c.   urban merchants and large landowners
   d.   large landowners and foreign investors
   e.   business tycoons and investment bankers

9. What migrant group dominated urban labor in Latin America during much of the nineteenth century?
   a.   Chinese migrants
   b.   Indian migrants
   c.   Japanese migrants
   d.   Turkish migrants
   e.   European migrants

10. Which of the following was the most culturally diverse nation in the western hemisphere by the late nineteenth century?
    a.   Argentina
    b.   Mexico
    c.   Cuba
    d.   Canada
    e.   United States

Comprehensive Multiple Choice Questions

1. Which of the following pairs of political leaders used terror in their respective nations as a nation-building strategy?
   a. Juan Manuel de Rosas and Maximillian Robespierre
   b. Benito Juarez and Niccolo Machiavelli
   c. Pancho Villa and Abraham Lincoln
   d. Emiliano Zapata and Roman Emperor Augustus
   e. Archduke Maximillian and Napoleon Bonaparte

2. What of the following is NOT a parallel which exists between Canadian economic expansion in the nineteenth century and economic expansion in the United States in the same era?
   a. Both were willing to sacrifice indigenous peoples and their cultures for the benefits of economic expansion.
   b. Both benefited from initial British industrial investments to stimulate early economic growth.
   c. Both focused on building a transcontinental railroad to link their vast nations and to create a transportation network essential to stimulating commerce.
   d. Both relied on migrants to provide the cheap labor necessary for rapid industrialization.
   e. Both used government economic policy to encourage national stability and discourage separatist movements.

3. The origins of which of the following Latin American groups equates most fully with the metis of Canada?
   a. mulattoes
   b. creoles
   c. mestizos
   d. peninsulares
   e. migrants

Primary Source Questions

1. **Examine the postcard of Abraham Lincoln on page 852 and the photograph outside Antietam on page 853 of your textbook.**
   a. While both these illustrations relate to the United States Civil War, how is point of view a crucial element to understanding each of these documents?

2. **Read *Sources from the Past: Ponciano Arriaga Calls for Land Reform* on page 858 of your textbook.**
   a. What problems does Arriaga say arise when land is unequally distributed?
   b. What does he mean by the phrase "heavy chains of serfdom"?
   c. What does he say is inevitable if this disparity is not addressed?

Chapter Multiple Choice Answers

1. **a:** Westward expansion was motivated and justified by a belief in the right of the United States to occupy all of North America from the Atlantic to the Pacific. This belief did not specifically include all of Canada or Mexico, however. (p. 849)

2. **b:** Both these tragic events exemplify the United States government's approach to resolving conflicts with the indigenous peoples of North America. Thousands died on the Trail of Tears and two hundred men, women, and children were gunned down at Wounded Knee. (pp. 849–850)

3. **b:** Canada's population remained primarily French based until the late eighteenth century when, as a result of their loss of the American colonies, many British subjects and British supporters left the new United States for Canada. The War of 1812 also brought more British-focused residents to Canada, but choice "c" is historically incorrect as the British did not win the war and 1812 is beyond the end of "late eighteenth century." (pp. 853–854)

4. **d:** Though there was support to varying degrees for each of these choices, it was land reform which drove the revolutionary movements in all of Latin America. (pp. 857–859)

5. **d:** Migrants to Latin America worked predominately on agricultural plantations, especially in sugar and cotton cultivation. (p. 862)

6. **a:** Just as in colonial times, Latin American elites retained control over local economies and they were already profiting handsomely from the existing European trade and investment. They had no motivation to seek other economic policies. (p. 865)

7. **c:** Railroads linked the far reaches of both nations' borders. The construction process in both nations stimulated iron, steel, rubber, glass, and fuel production. Once completed, towns developed to provide necessary supplies and services for businesses and individuals using the rail lines. (pp. 864–865)

8. **c:** Both in colonial times and after independence it was the wealthy urban merchants and the rural large landholders who comprised the economic elite of Latin America. (p. 865)

9. **e:** Though migrants from east and central Asia came to Latin America in search of work, it was European migrants who dominated the urban labor force during much of the nineteenth century. (p. 866)

10. **e:** By the late nineteenth century, the population of the United States included indigenous peoples, Euro-American settlers, Africans and African-Americans, and migrants from virtually every nation. (p. 867)

Comprehensive Multiple Choice Questions

1. **a:** Rosas in Argentina in the mid-nineteenth century and Robespierre in France in 1793–1794 both relied on terror as a way to eradicate opposition and solidify their ideal government, but their visions for their nations' futures were markedly different. (pp. 790, 857)

2. **e:** Choices "a" through "d" are all similarities between Canadian and United States' economic developments throughout the nineteenth century. Choice "e" however, is a distinctly Canadian endeavor, as the United States would resolve its separatist issues in the Civil War. (p. 864)

3. **c:** Since the question specifically asks about origins, "c" is the only possible correct answer. The *metis* of Canada are the offspring of European migrants and indigenous peoples of Canada, while the *mestizo* of Latin America are the offspring of Iberian migrants and indigenous peoples. In both regions, the small number of European women in the early days of European migration to the New World meant that European men entered into relationships with native women which gave rise to both classes. (pp. 676, 870)

Primary Source Answers

1. Understanding point of view is essential in comparing these two documents. In the first document, President Lincoln is speaking, perhaps praying, at a Civil War battlefield, Gettysburg, but the viewer knows it is a battlefield only from the monuments and the wreath. The battlefield at Antietam is strewn with actual bodies, not even laid out in order or in any way covered. The viewer is forced to

confront the ugliness of death in wartime in that photograph, whereas the painting on the Gettysburg postcard is clean, sanitized, and even idealized. The Lincoln postcard shows surviving, well-dressed soldiers whereas the Antietam picture shows only mangled corpses, who are only indicated as soldiers by their weapons and belts. In understanding point of view in these two works, one also has to consider the medium and the purpose. In the Gettysburg illustration, it is a postcard to be sent to someone or kept as a memento of a visit to the site. In the Antietam photograph, the picture was taken to capture the actual event, perhaps as part of a historical record or to publish in a newspaper; it is a primary source unlike the postcard, which is a secondary illustration. (pp. 852, 853)

2. Arriaga lists many problems which arise from unequal land distribution. First, he points out that the great majority of Mexicans "languish in terrible poverty and are denied property, homes, and work" because some individuals possess vast amounts of land which is currently unused but could be used for a much greater good. He calls the current distribution "absurd" and says that it keeps Mexicans from being free and participating fully in the life of their government or even nation. He continues to say that since they do not have land to work, they must either "vegetate in idleness or turn to banditry." He uses the term "heavy chains of serfdom" to describe the situation in which a man must work for another man his whole life with no hope of ever owning his own land or even means to a livelihood. Arriaga says that unless this disparity is remedied, one of two things will happen. Either Mexico will continue as a de facto aristocracy and thus never realize its potential or fulfill its stated goals or the people will achieve the promised land reform and begin to live in full and fruitful democratic equality. (p. 858)

CHAPTER 32

SOCIETIES AT CROSSROADS

Before you get started: As the modern age progressed, some societies adopted to modernization and dominant European values better than others. The rise of modern Japan was positively meteoric while their traditional enemies, the Chinese and Russians, floundered around. Likewise, the Ottomans continued their slide into powerlessness. If you can remember anything about the two world wars, you will realize that this chapter and the next set the scenes for the winners and losers in those wars. A useful exercise would be a chart that compares the way the four societies handled political, economic, and social change.

THE OTTOMAN EMPIRE IN DECLINE

If you recall Chapter 28, the Ottomans suffered military reversals in the nineteenth century so they began to only respond to European challenges rather than direct their interactions with Europeans. As they lost power to Europe, their provinces began to break away and their own population began to demand reforms. The diverse nature of the conquered regions contributed to a desire for independence from the Ottomans.

The Nature of Decline
(Theme: Change and Politics)

Military defeats of the seventeenth century combined with the increasing restlessness of the elite Janissary corps to weaken Ottoman power. The Janissaries engineered palace coups while they neglected military innovation and training. The military declines set the Ottomans into a vulnerable position with their neighbors and lessened the power of the central government as well. Soon provincial officials were forming their own armies while they sent only nominal taxes to the Ottoman government.

The Ottomans began to lose their territories as Russia nibbled away at the Black Sea regions and the Austro-Hungarians carved away the Balkans. Nationalistic movements removed both Greece and Serbia from the Ottoman sphere by the 1840s. After Napoleon attempted to defeat and hold Egypt, the powerful **Muhammad Ali** took control of Egypt with his European-modeled army. He began the process of industrialization with cotton and armaments. However, he never completely broke away from the Ottomans while he gobbled up Syria and Lebanon. He even considered an overthrow of Istanbul before he was stopped by English forces who were determined to protect the Ottomans from Russian dominance.

As Europeans circumvented trade through the eastern Mediterranean, the Ottoman empire's share of trade declined. A flood of cheap European goods resulted in urban riots as craftsmen and artisans felt their income decline. Ottoman exports were largely raw materials such as grain and hemp so they gradually fell into the role of a dependent economy. Economic development grew more dependent on foreign loans as Europeans capitalized Ottoman railroads, utilities, and mines. By 1882, the Ottomans were unable to pay the massive interest on their loans and had to accept foreign administration of their debt. Then, the Ottomans had to make degrading concessions to European power like extraterritoriality where Europeans were exempt from Ottoman laws. The Europeans went on to establish tax-exempt banks and businesses and imposed duties on goods sold in Ottoman ports.

By the twentieth century, the Ottoman government could not even maintain its own bureaucracy. They had to lower wages for the bureaucrats as they increased taxes on the peasants. Neither sector was happy with the solution as bureaucrats turned to corruption and farmers grew fewer crops.

Reform and Reorganization
(Theme: Change and Politics)

The Ottoman response was repeated attempts at reforms starting in the seventeenth century. In the eighteenth century, Sultan Selim III (1789–1807) attempted to reform the army along European lines but that threatened the Janissaries who responded with rebellion and bloodshed as they assassinated all but one of Selim's relatives. That relative, **Mahmud II** (1808–1839), launched his own reforms but since he was politically astute, he first couched them in traditional terms. And when the Janissaries revolted, he massacred them. Mahmud's army followed European models and he instituted military and technical colleges. To bridge elementary mosque schools to colleges, his administration began secondary-level schools for boys. Mahmud tried to transfer power from traditional elites to the central government by taxing the landlords, curbing the religious authorities, and abolishing military land grants. He also instituted postal and telegraph systems and divided his government into ministries. By the time he died, the Ottoman empire was smaller but more efficient.

Continued defeats on the fringes of the empire and in provinces prompted the ruling classes to attempt more reforms in mid-century during a period referred to as the **Tanzimat** ("reorganization period"). Military, legal, and educational reforms were at the forefront as the reformers drew their ideas from the European Enlightenment. With nationalistic and secular fervor, the reformers attacked Ottoman religious law. They adopted elements of the French civil and criminal codes. They also tried to safeguard the rights of citizens with public trials, privacy, and equality regardless of religion or ethnicity. In 1846, a comprehensive elementary and secondary educational system was instituted under a ministry of education. Elementary education was made free and compulsory in 1869.

The Tanzimat had numerous critics; chief among them were the religious authorities who had lost control of law and education. Devout Muslims resented the equality given to Christians and Jews. Younger critics known as the Young Ottomans felt that reforms needed to go farther in individual rights and local autonomy. Many also wanted a constitutional government. The Ottoman bureaucracy itself was displeased with their exclusion from power that had centered in the sultan so they too were determined to impose a constitution and depose the sultan if necessary.

The Young Turk Era
(Theme: Change and Politics)

In 1876, the radical dissidents in the bureaucracy seized power. They forced a constitution upon sultan Abdul Hamid II. Within the year, the sultan had rejected the constitution and retaliated against the reformers. For the next thirty years, he was a complete autocrat, which only served to enflame reformers. In great numbers, those who were educated in the Ottoman school system learned the basic principles of the Enlightenment. Those who were exiled experienced European politics and ideas personally. Most became convinced that the unchecked power of the sultan would ruin the Ottoman empire.

The most active dissident group was the **Young Turk Party** although many members were neither young nor Turkish. An exile group, the Young Turks used newspapers to publicize their positions on universal suffrage, free public education, equal treatment under the law, secularization of the state, and emancipation of women. In 1908, they inspired an army coup that deposed the sultan and turned his descendants into puppet rulers. The Young Turks were also extremely nationalistic so they attempted to institute Turkish as the official language of the empire, but that backfired and aggravated the relationship between the Turks and their subject peoples. Syria and Iraq were particularly resistant Arab provinces proving that despite modern political reforms, the Ottomans continued to face rebellion in the provinces. And, sadly, they also continued to lose territory to other countries.

THE RUSSIAN EMPIRE UNDER PRESSURE

Like the Ottomans, the Russians suffered military defeats to western European armies. It became evident that the Russian military was hopelessly backwards and needed to invest in reforms. The keystone to reform was the emancipation of the serfs who lived lives similar to slaves in other societies. Social reform then paved the way to the industrial reforms mentioned in Chapter 30. However, political reform did not accompany the changes because the tsars refused to yield their autocratic powers. Political oppression led to radical reform groups as it had in the Ottoman empire, but where the Ottomans continued to limp along, the Russians experienced radical revolution in the twentieth century.

Military Defeat and Social Reform
(Themes: War, and Social and Political Development)

The Russian population was large and extremely diverse. Only half of the Russian population could speak Russian and worshipped in the Orthodox church. The Romanov tsars ruled as complete autocrats with the support of the church and the nobility who were exempt from taxation and military duty. Peasants were the bulk of the population and most of those were serfs tied to land. They were almost slaves and could be bought and sold as slaves were but the Russians considered the large peasant class a guarantee of stability.

The vaunted Russian military continued its conquests and expansion into the nineteenth century with gains to the east, south, and southwest. They clashed with the Ottomans in the Balkans and tried to establish a protectorate over the Ottoman empire, but that threatened the European balance of powers and resulted in Russia taking on Britain in the Crimean War. The tsars discovered that where they could defeat the Qing and the Ottomans, European militaries were much more advanced. Clearly the industrialized forces of Europe could triumph over an agrarian society based on unfree labor.

It became apparent that **emancipation** of the serfs was the key but in the past, serf labor had been the bargaining chip for the Romanov tsars to keep their nobility under control. However, it was also a source of concern as rebellions and civil unrest threatened the countryside. Furthermore, it hindered modern economic development which depended upon a free labor source that could congregate around new job sites. In 1861, **Alexander II** (1855–1881), the reformist tsar, abolished serfs under conditions that were more favorable to landowners than former serfs. Landowners were compensated for their loss of labor and land while serfs won few political rights and had to pay a tax for lands that they received. A few peasants prospered but many were very disappointed in the privileges of freedom that left them in debt for the rest of their lives. Alienation and radicalization followed for some.

Other political reforms made by Alexander II were regional assemblies to deal with social issues but they remained subordinate to tsarist authority. He also reformed the legal system along the lines of European courts with trial by jury as its most successful change. The political reforms were less successful than the economic reforms.

Industrialization
(Themes: Change and Economics)

The tsar pushed economic reform as a way to enhance Russia's military power. Governmental policy was far more important to Russian industrialization than private initiative. (Review Chapter 30 for details of Sergei Witte's reforms.) Despite the successes of the industrialization, there were many disappointments centered around worker discontent. Russian workers could not tolerate the low standard of living that came with the early stages of industrialization. Newly freed serfs could not accustom themselves to the strict schedule of factory work. The Russian government made only small concessions like an eleven-and-a-half-hour workday but outlawed trade unions and strikes. The lack of political freedoms caused the formation of underground resistance groups and made workers receptive to radical ideas. However, a growing business class profited too much to be concerned and foreign investors were pleased to participate in a developing economy.

Repression and Revolution
(Themes: Changes and Continuities, and Social and Political Developments)

Anti-government protests increased in the last three decades of the nineteenth century. Peasants were infuriated by their lack of progress while urban workers remained dissatisfied with wage and living conditions. Radical university students and the **intelligentsia** began to agitate for economic and political reform and found western socialism to be better suited to their goals then capitalism. An increasingly radical element emerged who advocated revolution. Russia also became a breeding spot for anarchists who believed in violent means of reform.

The Russian government reacted with harsh prosecution and repression, rounding up hundreds of reformers in the 1870s. They imprisoned many and exiled others to Siberia. The worst tradition of Russian autocracy came into play as authorities used secret police to infiltrate radical groups. In the Baltic provinces dissidents also protested on the grounds of ethnic oppression. They worked for inclusion of their languages in schools and governments and the Russian response was predictably harsh as they suppressed the languages and reserved educational opportunities for loyalists. Jews were persecuted throughout Russian lands with frequent *pograms* (anti-Jewish riots) by neighbors jealous of their business achievements. Hundreds of thousands of Jews fled to western Europe and the Americas in the decades around the turn of the century.

In 1876, the People's Will, a terrorist arm of an anarchist group, assassinated Alexander II which brought an end to all reforms. **Nicholas II** (1894–1917) and his father championed further police control and oppression. He also favored further expansion into Manchuria and Korea which caused a confrontation with expanding Japanese interests. The Russians lost miserably to the Japanese in the **Russo-Japanese War** (1905) with the destruction of their navy.

Military defeats fueled more widespread social and political unrest that began with a violent industrial workers march on the tsar's Winter Palace. Soldiers shot into the crowd killing 130 workers and the incident became known as **Bloody Sunday.** Rebellions, naval mutinies, and student demonstrations ensued as urban workers organized elective councils (soviets) to push for economic reform. The revolutionary activities and pressure from Count Witte forced the tsar to agree to some democratic reforms. Thus, a national legislature was instituted. The **Duma** could change little in government but it was a huge concession on the part of the tsar. However, it did little to slow down discontent as civil unrest continued for the next two years. Finally, the Russian government quelled the unrest with bloody reprisals but the end to the Romanovs was very near.

THE CHINESE EMPIRE UNDER SIEGE

The Qing empire had even more problems than the Ottoman and the Romanovs. When European forces defeated the Chinese in a series of wars, the Qing rulers had to agree to treaties that carved their empire into European spheres of influence. While they were technically independent, the Qing no longer controlled their economy. Internal disruptions and rebellions further weakened the central government so that the ruling elites were forced to make reforms that came too little and too late.

The Opium War and the Unequal Treaties
(Themes: Trade, War, and Change)

In 1759, the Chinese restricted European merchants to warehouses in Guangzhou. Foreign merchants were required to deal with official merchants known as *cohongs*, who were under the strict control of the Chinese government. Since there was little demand for European goods, the merchants paid for silk, porcelain, tea, and lacquerware with silver bullion. British merchants sought another product that would be an alternative to bullion and they found that the **opium trade** was a lucrative, high-demand alternative, but its trade had to be manipulated in criminal ways. The opium was grown in India with Persian and Turkish expertise, and sent to China where company officials exchanged it for Chinese silver coins that flowed back to Britain. Those coins were then made into the bullion that was used for the Guangzhou trade in legitimate goods.

The trade grew quickly as the Chinese population became more addicted to opium. It continued for decades because the Chinese authorities made little attempt to control it. But in the 1830s, the Chinese realized that they had a huge trade deficit and a substantial drug problem as well. In 1838, a Chinese official, Lin Zexu, was charged with cracking down on the opium trade which he did with extraordinary efficiency by seizing and destroying around twenty thousand chests of opium. Sadly, this ignited a war with a humiliating defeat for the Chinese. The **Opium War** (1839–1842) demonstrated how far behind Europeans the Chinese military had fallen. British naval vesssels attacked Chinese coastal cities who could only defend themselves with swords, knives, spears, and some muskets. Despite the defeats and obvious imbalance of firepower, the Chinese refused to capitulate until the British navy moved toward the Grand Canal, China's major north-south waterway. Steam-powered, shallow draft gunboats in a seventy-boat armada steamed swiftly through China's river system. With no other option, China sued for peace. Later in the century, China also lost to combined French and British forces, the French by themselves, and the Japanese as well.

The European nations forced China to sign a series of **unequal peace treaties** that followed the example of the Treaty of Nanjing (1842) which ceded Hong Kong to Britain, opened five Chinese ports to trade, installed Britain with **favored nation status,** and granted **extraterritoriality** status to British citizens. Soon, France, Germany, Denmark, the Netherlands, Spain, Belgium, Austria-Hungary, the United States, and Japan had similar terms. The treaties also added recognition of the rights of Christian missionaries to proselytize as well as legalizing the opium trade and preventing the Chinese government from levying tariffs on imports. They dismantled the Chinese tributary state system as well by releasing Korea, Vietnam, and Myanmar from Chinese control.

The Taiping Rebellion
(Themes: Continuity and War)

As had occurred during the weakened end stage of earlier dynasties, there were internal rebellions as well as foreign defeats. China's population had continued to grow during the nineteenth century from 330 million to 475 million but the amount of land under cultivation had only increased slightly. Peasants strained to make a living, landed elite controlled the resources, while government officials fell into widespread corruption and drug addiction. After 1850, there were four significant rebellions, three of which occurred in separate quadrants, but the last one, the **Taiping rebellion** of 1850, affected most of China. A religious schoolteacher, Hong Xiuquan, called for the destruction of the foreign Qing dynasty and multiple radical reforms. Among the reforms were the abolition of private property and a shared wealth plan to alleviate the distress of peasants. They called for the equality of men and women with the prohibition of footbinding and concubinage, although the Taiping leaders exempted themselves from these ideas by maintaining large harems. Free public education and simplification of written Chinese were proposed to promote literacy for the masses.

After taking over southeastern China, the Taiping settled on Nanjing as their capital and by 1855, they had attacked Beijing but been repelled by the Qing army. But the Taiping were not defeated so they continued to consolidate their control of southeastern China with the conquest of Shanghai. But the Qing realized that their Manchurian forces needed the assistance of the Chinese elite who were alienated by the Taiping program so they raised several regional Chinese armies. Eventually, with European supplies and advisors, the regional armies defeated the Taiping. Hong Xiuquan committed suicide and one hundred thousand supporters were slaughtered. But the overall toll on the population was huge with somewhere between twenty and thirty million lives lost and the rest of the population in the affected areas resorting to starvation diets of weeds and leather.

Reform Frustrated
(Continuity and Political Development)

The Taiping rebellion and foreign domination served notice to the Qing that reforms were necessary. They chose to emphasize a benevolent Confucian form of government while bolstering their military with European technology and tactics. The **Self-Strengthening Movement** (1860–1895) had imperial permission to act as regional governments as they sought to blend Chinese tradition with European industrial technology. They built railroads, shipyards, and steel factories, and founded technological institutes. However, they were unable to bring enough change fast enough to make a difference. And, the Empress Cixi (1835–1908), a former concubine, countered their efforts as she diverted funding for the Chinese navy to build a marble boat in the imperial gardens. Of course, European industrial policies were in direct conflict with Confucian ideals so their program was doomed to fail.

The continued foreign pressures of the 1890s sparked a **Hundred Days reform** movement that had few results. The young emperor accepted a set of reforms which included a constitutional government, a guarantee of civil liberties, public education, military improvements, and an acceptance of European economic advances. The backlash from the Empress **Cixi** and the rest of the imperial forces was swift and determined. She nullified the decrees, imprisoned the emperor, and executed reformers. Then, she threw her support behind the Society of Righteous and Harmonius Fists, or **Boxers**, a violent anti-foreigner group. They rampaged through northern China, killing foreigners, Chinese Christians, and those who had business with foreigners. In 1900, over one hundred thousand Boxers besieged the foreign embassies in Beijing but were defeated by the British, French, German, United States, and Japanese combined military forces. The Chinese were forced to pay for the destruction and allow foreign troops to remain in Chinese cities. Since the empress had been so complicit in the Boxer Rebellion, Chinese revolutionaries rose up against the central government. Once she had died under mysterious circumstances, two-year-old emperor Puyi had no chance to reassert authority as China dissolved the dynasty in 1912.

THE TRANSFORMATION OF JAPAN

After a fleet of American gunships forced the Tokugawa Shogunate to open its trade ports in 1853, the American and European nations also forced the Japanese into unequal treaties that mirrored the Chinese situation. However, the Japanese used its problems as an excuse to overthrow the humiliated government and bring the Meiji emperor into power in 1868. The energetic new ruler instituted the industrial and military changes mentioned in Chapter 30 that brought the Japanese to the forefront of Asian nations.

From Tokugawa to Meiji
(Themes: Change and Political Development)

By the early nineteenth century, Japan's social stability was shaky. The Japanese economy was weakened by crop failures while the rural population suffered heavy taxation and starvation. As the peasants migrated to cities, conditions were hardly better, so the urban poor also lived in extreme poverty. Even the daimyo and samurais suffered hardships as they became more indebted to the rising class of merchants. The misfortunes caused rebellions and protests to which the **Tokugawa** government responded with some conservative reforms such as cancelled debts and forced return of peasants to the countryside. The reforms were inadequate and the government was driven from office.

In addition to economic problems, the Tokugawa government had refused repeated requests for trade from foreign nations other than the Dutch with their tightly controlled offices. Although the government had grown alarmed at foreign persistence and even begun to practice a military defense, when the American fleet under Admiral **Matthew Perry** arrived in Tokyo Bay, the shogun swiftly capitulated to American demands. When the Russians, British, and French demanded similar treatment, the Tokugawa government agreed to unequal treaties with them as well. As in the Qing agreements, they lost control of tariffs and granted extraterritoriality status to foreigners.

Once the shogun had acceded to the humiliating demands, the samurai, daimyo, and emperor's officials in Kyoto banded together to push out the government. In a brief civil war started when the shogunate forcibly retired daimyo and executed disloyal samurai, the dissident armies used European technology and strategy to defeat the shogun. In early January, 1868, the boy emperor, Matsuhito, took over the reins of government calling his reign the **Meiji** ("Enlightened Rule").

Meiji Reforms
(Theme: Change, and Political, Social, and Economic Development)

The Meiji marked the return to imperial government after seven centuries of military rule. Initially, a coalition of samurai, daimyo, and nobility supported a concept of industrialization combined with military might. The government sent students and officials abroad to learn the latest technologies and principles of business. One scholar-official studied constitutional governments, was especially impressed by the recently unified Germans, and returned to set up a new government based on the principles of equality before the law. To do this, it became necessary to revise the old social order.

In a series of land reforms in which the central government convinced the daimyo to yield their lands in return for noble status, the daimyo power was neutralized by the government. Then, the regions were divided into prefectures controlled by governors. It also abolished the **samurai class** and its privileges but compensated them with government bonds. However, inflation rendered the bonds insignificant so most samurai had to seek regular employment instead. A small rebellion that ensued was crushed by the new national army to maintain the reforms. In order to solidify their financial status, the Meiji government revamped the tax system. Where peasants had paid a grain tax, the government changed the method of payment to fixed money instead so that the peasants suffered the vagaries of the market fluctuations rather than the government. The government also taxed according to farming potential which forced poor producers to sell to more efficient producers.

The constitution that was drafted established a constitutional monarchy with a form of parliament (the "Diet") that had a higher body of nobles and an elected lower body of commoners. However, it ceded most authority to the executive branch. The emperor who was declared "sacred and inviolable" could dissolve the Diet, and all ministers reported to him. The Meiji constitution recognized individual liberties but these could be restricted by the government, limited the officeholders to the wealthy, and only 5 percent of the adult male population was eligible to vote in the first election. However, there was more opportunity for debate and dissension than there had ever been in Japanese history. (Review Japan's process of industrialization and the role of its government in Chapter 30.)

In addition to economic reforms, the Meiji government instituted a system of elementary and secondary education as well as a university system that promoted technology and science. The price of industrialization was borne by extremely high peasant taxes and a poorly paid industrial workforce. The peasants rebelled several times in the 1880s but the government responded with mass executions and the condition of the peasants never improved as they sank further into malnutrition and destitution. Those who became part of the industrial labor force remained repressed as well since labor organization was illegal.

Although not discussed in your textbook, the Meiji government promoted westernization of clothing, literature, and art as well as the adoption of western military uniforms and band music. Women stopped shaving their eyebrows and blackening their teeth. Samurai were forbidden from wearing the traditional topknot and carrying swords.

Despite the ills of industrialization, Japan formed itself into an Asian powerhouse in a mere forty years. It ended humiliating treaties, allied with the foreign powers in quelling the Boxer Rebellion, and defeated both the Chinese in 1895 and the Russians in 1905 to become the foremost power in Asia.

Finished reading the chapter? Be sure you can . . .

- Compare the effects of industrialization on the Ottomans, China, Russia, and Japan.
- Compare their political and social reactions to European domination.
- Analyze the economic, social, and political effects of the emancipation of serfs in Russia.
- Compare serf labor with slave labor and free labor.
- Identify and describe westernization in Meiji Japan, as seen in illustrations and primary sources.
- Analyze Japan's successful modernization.

Chapter Multiple Choice Questions

1. What was the role of the military in the gradual decline of the Ottoman empire?
   a. They operated independently but could not finance modernization.
   b. They controlled the government at times and were resistant to modernization.
   c. They were directly subservient to the sultan and attempted to follow his lead.
   d. They were unaware of the extent to which they had fallen behind and did little to modernize.
   e. They supported a religious legal system in order to preserve their position.

2. What allowed European influence to dominate Ottoman economics in the late nineteenth century?
   a. The Ottomans turned to Europe for advice on industrialization, but received inadequate aid.
   b. The Europeans used their military power to dominate trade with the Ottomans.
   c. The Ottomans refused to trade with Asian countries and were entirely dependent upon Europe.
   d. As well as a poor balance of trade, the Ottomans were required to borrow funds from European sources.
   e. There was no interest in modernization in the Ottoman empire so they fell hopelessly in debt.

3. To what extent were the Ottoman people interested in democratic reforms in the nineteenth century?
   a. They were wholly disinterested and looked to their traditional autocratic government for direction.
   b. Small dissonant groups pushed for democratic reforms but were unable to make changes.
   c. Islam was essential to Ottoman power so there were no opportunities to consider political reform.
   d. The population was so insistent that most Ottoman rulers agreed to small permanent changes.
   e. Political pressure resulted in some changes but reform efforts were halted later on.

4. Which of the following descriptions best fits the role of Muhammad Ali in Ottoman history?
   a. He was a loyal Ottoman governor who supported Ottoman policies in Egypt.
   b. He conquered regions of the Ottoman state but never severed the formal subservient relationship.
   c. He challenged Ottoman rulers to reform their laws to grant equality for all conquered groups.
   d. He rebelled against the Ottomans and set up an independent government in Egypt.
   e. He attempted an unsuccessful rebellion against Ottoman power in Egypt.

5. What were the effects of Alexander II's emancipation of serfs in Russia?
   a. Landlords found themselves wholly without labor as former serfs moved away.
   b. While the immediate effect was freedom, disappointed peasants found that their lives changed little.
   c. Industrialization surged forward as factories found an abundant labor force in ex-serfs.
   d. The landed nobility objected hugely and circumvented the new laws to retain their labor.
   e. The tsar became disappointed with the progress of the reform so he rescinded the decree.

6. Despite industrialization and the emancipation of slaves, Russia continued to be subjected to internal problems. Why was there so much discontent?
    a. An autocratic government that brooked no dissent and an economy in which most people were still in traditional jobs led to civil unrest.
    b. Serfs and urban workers banded together to share their problems and work toward better living and working conditions.
    c. The factory owners and government in Russia were much more brutal toward their workers than in other industrialized nations.
    d. In an effort to keep their labor source, the landed nobility passed regional laws that negated all the gains of emancipation.
    e. Serfs in the countryside were traditionally prone to rebellions and they continued to protest against their superiors when emancipated.

7. Of the following factors, which was a weakness in China that allowed Europeans to carve out spheres of influence?
    a. The Chinese had few important trade items to use as a bargaining tool.
    b. The Qing dynasty had devoted itself to the stabilization of relations with the Chinese people.
    c. There were no officials willing to resist the demands of the Europeans.
    d. Asian countries were unwilling to accept ideas from other continents.
    e. The Qing dynasty had an antiquated military and little support from its own citizens.

8. Which of the following is the best example of the extreme extent of the Qing reaction to domination of foreigners?
    a. the Taiping Rebellion
    b. the Opium Wars
    c. the Self-Strengthening Movement
    d. the Boxer Rebellion
    e. the Treaty of Nanjing

9. What key decision did the Meiji government make that changed the longstanding social order in Japan?
    a. It increased the burden of taxation on peasants.
    b. It granted nobility to daimyos in exchange for property.
    c. It elevated scholars to the position of advisers on industry.
    d. It outlawed the samurai class.
    e. It put women workers in industry under the direction of male supervisors.

10. To what extent was the Meiji constitution similar in effectiveness to western constitutions?
    a. It was similar since the ruler had little power beyond his household.
    b. It was similar because the Japanese Diet has the same structure as the British Parliament.
    c. It was different in that it had few checks on executive power.
    d. It was almost completely opposite in its treatment of the nobility.
    e. It was far ahead in its consideration of universal suffrage.

Comprehensive Multiple Choice Questions

1. The nationalist movements of the nineteenth century generally incorporated radical reforms. Which of the following did not include fundamental reforms?
    a. the Tanzimat
    b. the Taiping Rebellion
    c. the Young Turksü
    d. the Boxers
    e. the Meiji Restoration

2. When comparing the early successes of the Qing dynasty under Kangxi with its nineteenth century failures, which of the following has the most similar pattern?
    a. Russia under the early Romanovs and under Alexander II
    b. the Ottomans under Süleyman the Magnificent and during the Tanzimat
    c. India under Akbar and the period of the East India Company
    d. France under Louis XIV and the French Republic of Louis Philippe
    e. South America in the era of Simon Bolivar and the era of caudillos

3. Which one of the following factors most distinguished the Japanese success in attaining modern power from the failure of the Russians, Ottomans, and Chinese to do the same?
    a. a government that worked with business owners to improve the infrastructure
    b. a population that welcomed the changes that industry brought
    c. a government that shared economic power with most people
    d. a pragmatic sense of nationalism that was open to economic, social, and political change
    e. a government that supported research and education to support industrialization

Primary Source Questions

1. **Read *Sources from the Past: Proclamation of the Young Turks*, 1908, on page 886 of your textbook.**
    a. What is the point of view?
    b. Which provisions are nationalistic?
    c. Which provisions are aimed at economic improvements?
    d. Which provisions mirror Enlightenment interests of earlier western constitutions?

2. **Examine the illustration on page 901, Tokugawa audience with United States Ambassador, 1859, and the illustration on page 903, the opening of the Japanese parliament, 1891.**
    a. What are the two points of view and do they differ?
    b. Discuss the differences in dress, people, and place.
    c. What evidence of industrialization is apparent in the later illustration?
    d. Discuss the differences in imperial representations.
    e. Are there differences in artistic style?

Chapter Multiple Choice Answers

1. **b:** The elite corps of Janissaries controlled government policy and even engineered palace coups through much of the nineteenth century. (p. 881)

2. **d:** The Ottomans exported less than they imported and they were forced to borrow heavily from the Europeans as they built a modern infrastructure of railroads and factories. (p. 882)

3. **e:** In the Tanzimat era, legal and educational reforms were made but after Sultan Abdul Hamid II quashed reform, dissident groups such as the Young Turks operated outside the country with few results until the twentieth century. (pp. 884–885)

4. **b:** Muhammad Ali took control of Egypt, conquered further regions of the Ottoman empire, and made Egpyt essentially autonomous but kept his official status within the Ottoman hierarchy. (p. 881)

5. **b:** While the serfs gained freedom and an opportunity to be landowners, tax burdens and debts were too heavy to allow many to do so. (pp. 888–889)

6. **b:** After Alexander II was assassinated, his heirs no longer agreed to reforms and used secret police to crack down on dissenters. Despite the gains of emancipation, life for former serfs continued to be miserable. (p. 891)

7. **e:** Once the European powers sent their naval forces up the Yangtze, it was apparent that the Qing military was hopelessly inadequate. Several small rebellions in addition to the national Taiping rebellion distracted the government as well. (pp. 894, 897)

8. **d:** When Empress Cixi threw her support to the Boxers, it was apparent that the Qing no longer knew how to deal effectively with the outsiders. (p. 899)

9. **d:** While some classes were burdened by different responsibilities, only the samurai were directly removed from the social order. (p. 902)

10. **c:** The Japanese constitution was structured to allow the emperor to effectively control all governmental bodies including the Diet. (p. 903)

Comprehensive Multiple Choice Answers

1. **d:** The Boxer Rebellion was supported by Empress Cixi because it focused its ire on foreigners rather than the unequal economic, political, or social policies. The Tanzimat and Young Turks called for legal, political, and social reforms while the Meiji government went so far as to abolish one social class and institute a constitutional government. Both the Taiping and the Young Turks called for gender equality as well. (p. 899)

2. **c:** The Qing under Kangzi expanded its empire, provided for its people, and promoted its economy, but later Qing had to capitulate to European powers. It agreed to unequal treaties and was divided into spheres of influence. Similarly, the Mughal sovereign Akbar expanded his kingdom, promoted Indian culture, and ruled over a prosperous economy. Mughal power after Aurangzeb deteriorated as the East India Company pressed local authorities into giving up their lands to the company. While China ostensibly ruled its lands, its position was in actuality no better than the Mughals. The Russians, Ottomans, French, and South Americas of the later period were not under the control of foreign powers. (pp. 728, 761, 894, 916)

3. **d:** Where nationalism fueled aspects of the Ottoman, Russian, and Chinese reactions to change, only the Meiji government in Japan embraced those changes with substantive programs. Both Russia and Japan had governments that promoted industrialization. Only some segments of any of the populations, including the Japanese, welcomed the changes. None of the governments shared profits with most segments of society. While both Russia and Japan welcomed foreign expertise and set up schools for technology, neither the Ottomans nor the Chinese did so. (p. 881)

Primary Source Answers

1. The point of view is the Young Turk Party which advocated radical social, political, and economic reforms in order to strengthen Ottoman power. Its tone is formal as that of other constitutions. Nationalistic provisions are those that advocate the use of Turkish as the official language (7) as well as the educational language (17), and all non-Muslims eligible for military service (9). Property rights (14) and secondary educational institutions (17) would form the foundation of economic modernization. The Enlightenment ideals are prominent in the power of the people (1), a legislative body (2), universal suffrage (3), freedom of assembly (4), equality under the law (9), and religious freedom (10). In a free public education (16 and 17), there is evidence of further rights defined by nineteenth-century laws. (p. 886)

2. The artists of both illustrations would have to be sponsored by the courts to have access to the events. It is apparent that they have represented the scenes in a very respectful manner as behooves those whose incomes depend upon the court. The difference between Americans and Japanese are apparent by dress in the early illustration but if there are foreigners at the opening of the Diet, it would be difficult to find them in the sea of western dress. Where women were once not allowed at formal government functions, in the later depiction, there is a viewing gallery for women similar to those in western legislatures of the time. Furthermore, there is additional space for crowded audiences to view the proceedings of the Diet where the earlier drawing has far fewer observers. The government chambers have changed considerably with very traditional Japanese walls and lack of seating in the earlier drawing, and completely western seating, European architectural details, and even western lighting in the later one. The lighting, turned railings, chairs, and perhaps the dress in the later representation demonstrate the influence of an industrialized society. Where the Tokugawa shogun was surrounded by his men in a display of military authority, the Meiji emperor, other than the fact that he is seated, is difficult to distinguish from the other two officials on the dais in the Diet. Where the earlier drawing has a spare, geometric quality, later Japanese art shows the adoption of western principles of perspective and the decorative clutter of the Victorian age. Yet, the men keep the same squared look while women in the later drawing have the graceful, curved quality found in traditional representations of Japanese women. (pp. 901, 903)

CHAPTER 33

THE BUILDING OF GLOBAL EMPIRES

Before you get started: This is a great chapter and in many ways it contains the heart of this whole course: the dynamics of change and continuity and the causes and processes involved in those dynamics. As a student preparing for the national AP World History exam, think about comparisons and contrasts regarding imperialism's impact among world regions and consider what changes occurred within political institutions and economic realms as a result of imperialism.

As a thoughtful human being seeking explanations for many of the complex problems in today's world, this chapter should be high interest for you, and maybe it should be required reading for everyone.

FOUNDATIONS OF EMPIRE

Though imperialism has been part of world history since the days of the earliest Mesopotamians, the events of the nineteenth century brought imperialism to a whole new level. Thanks to strong nationalist sentiments used to motivate the populace, industrialization's output of weaponry and technology, and unparalleled knowledge of world regions and people, European imperial powers quickly established their world hegemony; by the end of the century, the United States and Japan would join those imperial nations.

In many ways, the world grew smaller during this era, as vastly distant regions were brought into tighter economic interaction. Powerful nations were tempted to consider themselves "better" or more "entitled" to the world's resources since they had the means to best exploit them. The legacy of racism developed during this era remains today, as does the power of nationalism to motivate and justify behaviors that ordinarily would be repugnant.

Motives of Imperialism
(Theme: Patterns of Interaction)

The contemporary meaning of the term **imperialism** refers to the domination of European powers over subject lands; the actions of the United States and Japan later would add their nations to the definition. Such domination can come from military actions, but increasingly imperialism resulted from trade, business, and other commercial activities; direct political control was not always necessary for one nation to dominate another.

Colonialism, a term related to imperialism, means not just the sending of colonists to new lands, but the exportation of social, political, economic, and cultural structures which come to dominate the subject lands and seek to supplant similar indigenous or traditional structures. For example, in North and South America, European powers had established settler colonies in the sixteenth through the eighteenth centuries, but in India and southeast Asia colonization occurred without large numbers of migrants from the home societies. Instead, in those regions, European businesspeople and government officials developed foreign and economic policies which integrated the subject lands into the larger network of global capitalism. As a result of this integration, traditional social, economic, political, and military systems were replaced by colonial models.

Imperialism and colonialism were justified in several ways. First and most importantly, the **economic benefits** to the imperial nation were easily apparent. Cheap, readily available raw materials could be used in European factories with the finished products sold back to the colonial subjects. Rubber, cotton, tin, copper, diamonds, gold, and oil were all crucial resources for industrialized nations and were easily exploited from their colonies. Economic justifications also included the necessity for excess population to have a place to migrate, though in reality, most nineteenth-century migrants went to independent states, not colonies. **Political benefits** were also used as justification for imperialism. Strategic locations which offered harbors, ports, and supplies to one European nation over another were seen as advantageous. Simply denying one's rival ease of movement or access to resources around the world was seen as a significant political advantage. Politicians also relied on colonies as an "attractive alternative for civil war." In other words, colonies could become a safety valve for problematic elements within European society. Further, the lure of colonial adventure had huge domestic public relations benefits for European powers. **Cultural justifications** were also used to support colonialism and imperialism. The spread of Christianity, the bringing of education, and the responsibility of the "betters of the world to bring light to their lessers" became easily acceptable romanticized justifications for exploitation. It was the "white man's burden" to fulfill this duty.

Tools of Empire
(Themes: Technology and Patterns of Interaction)

Industrialization brought powerful weapons to the Europeans which enabled the imperial nations to impose their rule throughout the world. **Gunpowder,** and the mass production of advanced tools and military weapons, added to the strong political, economic, and cultural motivations so that the European powers were able to have their way virtually anywhere in the world. Accurate, easy-to-fire **rifles**, machine guns like the **Maxim gun,** and artillery attached to fast-moving ships provided the Europeans with an arsenal vastly superior to any other in the world.

The steamship and railroad expanded the places and ease with which Europeans could stake their imperial claims. New canals, such as the **Suez Canal** completed in 1869 and the **Panama Canal** completed in 1914, enabled naval vessels to travel rapidly between the world's seas and oceans while lowering the cost of trade between subject lands and their imperial overlords. It was now possible for steamships to travel from Britain to India in less than two weeks; such a journey used to take at least four months and was subject to the seasonal monsoon winds of the Indian Ocean. The building of railroads helped the European powers to gain control of local, subject economies and provided a means of expanding European economic and military control far into lands once geographically isolated and thus protected. The application of these "tools of empire" at the battle of **Omdurman** in Sudan in 1898 demonstrated the ease with which these weapons could subdue any local opposition to European imperial will.

Communication technologies also benefited from industrialization. Rapid communication meant imperial troops could be mobilized in moments and businessmen could respond quickly to business and market developments. In the 1830s, telegraph technology began to carry communications over land, by the 1850s engineers had devised reliable submarine telegraph cables, by 1870 telegraph messages were crisscrossing the oceans, and by 1902 the British had telegraph connections with every part of its empire. Access to and monopoly over communication technologies further strengthened European colonial power.

EUROPEAN IMPERIALISM

The second half of the nineteenth century was characterized by a frenzied round of empire building beginning with the British conquest of **India,** European expansion into **central Asia**, the establishment of colonies in **southeast Asia,** and finally a mad "**scramble for Africa**" and the subjugation of **Pacific Ocean territories.**

The British Empire in India
(Theme: Patterns of Interaction)

British control of India grew out of the mercantile activities of the British **East India Company** in the mid-seventeenth century. Ports were established along the coast to garner and warehouse goods moving back and forth between Britain and East Asia; pepper, spices, Chinese silk, and porcelain were soon joined by coffee, tea, and opium as valuable products on route to European markets.

With the demise of the Mughal Empire after 1707, the British East India Company began expanding into the subcontinent to protect their commercial interests and to further their economic opportunities. These inland operations required protection and soon a small number of British soldiers aided by local Indian troops known as **sepoys** were posted to protect East India Company interests. An unnecessarily confusing military directive regarding cartridge coverings and animal fat resulted in the mutiny of Hindu sepoys. The ensuing revolt became an open rebellion as the Indian soldiers, joined by disgruntled local elites and unhappy peasants, slaughtered their British officers; this 1857 **Sepoy Rebellion** nearly drove the British out of India. However, the British responded by using their powerful weapons and communication technology to send troops and equipment to trouble spots. By 1858, the British had crushed the rebellion, exacted bloody revenge, and expanded their authority in India by establishing **direct imperial rule. Queen Victoria** established the office of secretary of state for India, sent a viceroy to India to represent British royal authority and to administer the colony through an **elite civil service** staffed almost exclusively by Englishmen. This imperial structure formulated all foreign and domestic policy in India; Indians served only in low-level bureaucratic positions.

British rule transformed India by extending their rule throughout the subcontinent including Ceylon, now modern Sri Lanka. They cleared forests, redistributed land, and promoted the cultivation of cash crops like tea, coffee, and opium; they built railroads, bridges, roadways, canals, harbors, and irrigation systems. While the British did not seriously try to convert the Indians to Christianity, they did build English-style schools for the children of the elite as a way to guarantee support for British rule and as a way to suppress Indian traditions, like **sati,** the Hindu practice of widows burning themselves on their husband's funeral pyre. Ultimately, these innovations were designed to connect India to the larger global economy and to make Britain very, very rich.

Imperialism in Central Asia and Southeast Asia
(Theme: Patterns of Interaction)

The French and the Russians were envious of Britain's Indian treasure box and each sought to build a similar font of wealth in central Asia. The French revolution and the Napoleonic aftermath stalled the French move, but the Russians had been eyeing central Asia since the early sixteenth century. However, it was only in the nineteenth century, after the weakening of Ottoman and Qing imperial rule, that the Russians began a systematic effort to extend Russian authority south of the Caucasus. By the 1860s, the Russians had gained control of the great caravan cities of the ancient silk roads and were beginning to approach the ill-defined northern frontier of British-controlled India. The "**great game**" for influence and intelligence in central Asia had begun. The spying, mapping, and exploration of lands previously uncharted by Europeans continued until the outbreak of global war in 1914 and the tsarist revolution in Russia in 1917 derailed the envisioned eventual war for India.

Competition for colonial interests continued in southeast Asia as well. The Spanish had gained control of the **Philippines** in the sixteenth century and the Dutch continued to garner great wealth from the sugar, tea, coffee, tobacco, rubber, and tin produced in the islands of the Indonesian archipelago, which they called the **Dutch East Indies.** The British were not to be left out of southeast Asia so they established the port of **Singapore** to serve as the base of British conquest of Malay which in turn allowed them full control of the sea lanes linking the Indian Ocean with the South China Sea and which provided them with abundant supplies of tin and rubber.

Though foiled in India, the French built a huge colonial enterprise in southeast Asia in a region they called **French Indochina;** today those lands would include **Cambodia, Vietnam,** and **Laos.** Like the British, the French used education to train local elites and to garner their support, but unlike the British, the French were active and successful in their attempts to convert the native population to Christianity; **Roman Catholicism** became prominent, especially in Vietnam. Only **Siam,** modern-day Thailand, escaped colonial rule as it was seen as a useful buffer between French and British arenas.

The Scramble for Africa
(Themes: Political Structures, Patterns of Interaction, and Changes and Continuities)

In 1875, European interest in Africa revolved around the exchange of gold, ivory, and palm oil for European textiles, guns, and manufactured goods, and most of these commercial interactions took place within fortified trading posts and a few small coastal colonies. The only sizable European possessions were the Portuguese colonies of Angola and Mozambique, the French colony of Algeria, and the British and Dutch holdings in southern Africa.

By 1900, however, European powers had partitioned and colonized almost all the African continent in the "scramble for Africa" motivated by a quest for resources and nationalistic rivalries. Much of the geographic knowledge of Africa sought by merchants and politicians alike came from European explorers like Dr. David Livingstone, an earnest Scottish missionary who scouted much of southern and central Africa looking for mission sites; Henry Morton Stanley, an American journalist anxious to generate a newspaper-selling tale of his hunt for the "lost" Dr. Livingstone; and Englishmen Richard Burton and John Speke who sought the source of the Nile River in east Africa.

Knowledge of the great African rivers—Nile, Niger, Congo, and Zambezi—meant access to Africa's previously "unknown" interior—unknown to the Europeans, that is. Such knowledge in European hands brought rapid colonization. In the 1870s, King Leopold of Belgium craftily created his own personal colony in the Congo River basin from which he brutally exploited rubber production. It is estimated that four to eight million Africans died on his rubber plantations before the Belgian government took control of the colony in 1908. An ill-fated attempt by Egyptian ruler Muhammad Ali to free his nation from Ottoman rule resulted in British occupation of Egypt in 1882, to protect British economic interests, including the Suez Canal. Dutch holdings in Cape Town, in southern Africa, had become a settler colony in the seventeenth century with farmers, known as **Boers** or **Afrikaners,** claiming that God had destined the land and resources of the Cape for them and their descendents. By the eighteenth century, Dutch, German, and French migrants had joined the Afrikaners to spread northward beyond the Cape into lands held by the Khoikhoi and Xhosa peoples. Disease, warfare, and enslavement decimated these indigenous peoples. The British takeover of the Cape during the Napoleonic wars only further complicated the history of that region. British rule, particularly British law and language, was openly resisted by the Afrikaners. The British prohibition of slavery in 1833 eliminated the primary source of labor for these white farmers and triggered a mass migration of Boers to lands further north, seemingly outside the grasp of the British government. This "Great Trek" became imbedded in Afrikaner folklore as their march to the "Promised Land." However, their promised land was already occupied by Ndebele and Zulu peoples, who, despite fierce resistance, were no match for the superior firepower of these *voortrekkers*, or white pioneers. By the mid-nineteenth century, the voortrekkers and their descendants had created several republics that were independent of British control: Natal, the Orange Free State, and the South African Republic.

The British would not stand for such defiant actions for long, especially after diamonds and minerals were found in those lands in 1867 and 1886, respectively. The South African War (1899–1902), also known as the Boer War, was a brutal conflict between whites and whites, in which white and black Africans died by the thousands on the battlefields and in internment camps. The Afrikaners were defeated, and by 1910, the British government had reconstituted the four Afrikaner colonies as provinces within the Union of South Africa, a large, autonomous British dominion; the British sought to repair damage with their white subjects by supporting white privilege throughout the nation at the expense of black African human rights.

The Berlin Conference of 1884–1885 was the defining political event for the partition of Africa. Without a single African nation present, the European powers delineated acceptable strategies for carving the African continent into European colonies and granted those powers justification for their actions. By the turn of the century, only Ethiopia and Liberia remained independent from European control.

There were problems with colonial occupation, however. The European powers had mistakenly believed that after an initial investment of money and resources, their African colonies would become self-supporting; such perceptions were wrong and colonial rule proved very expensive to maintain. At first, European nations hoped to rule their colonies through "**concessionary companies**" which would rely on private companies to administer each colony. These companies were to undertake all economic activities, including labor recruitment, and to collect taxes for the European colonial power. This system proved problematic as there were humanitarian outcries at the treatment of laborers and, more essentially, the wealth generated for the European nations was not considered sufficient. Concessionary rule was soon replaced by either **direct rule**, as in French colonies, or by **indirect rule**, as was characteristic of British colonies.

Colonies under direct rule featured districts headed by European officials who were responsible for maintaining law and order, organizing labor and military recruitment, and collecting taxes. Direct rule undermined the power of existing kings and other indigenous leaders by redrawing district boundaries and by encouraging the more pliable colonial pawns to embrace the Europeans' "civilizing mission" which effectively undermined local cultures and traditions. Direct rule was hampered by a constant shortage of European administrators, their lack of skill with indigenous languages, and the sheer distance and difficult transport systems within many of these colonies.

Indirect rule was the preferred British system of colonial rule; **Frederick D. Lugard** was its most articulate supporter. He stressed the financial and moral advantages of relying on existing indigenous institutions as the basis for colonial rule. His strategy for control worked well in African regions where strong local states functioned, but in regions where such existing institutions did not fit with colonial needs, indirect rule floundered. Often, colonial leaders would even end up inventing their own definitions of tribal identities or boundaries; these misperceptions would have tragic consequences during the second half of the twentieth century.

European Imperialism in the Pacific
(Themes: Political Structures, Patterns of Interaction, and Changes and Continuities)

Imperialism in the Pacific took two main forms: settler colonies, as in Australia and New Zealand, and commercial bases, as on most of the Pacific Islands. Though aware of the existence of Australia since the early sixteenth century, it was not until the late eighteenth century that European migrants began to settle there seeking their livelihood through sheep herding, farming, and eventually mining. Though the earliest European migrants to the region were convicts, by 1830, the voluntary migrants outnumbered the convicts; the 1851 discovery of gold brought a huge surge in migration to Australia. New Zealand originally attracted fishermen and whalers, but its fertile soil and abundant timber soon attracted European migrants seeking land to cultivate. These European migrants and their diseases decimated local populations and the indigenous survivors found themselves rapidly displaced from their traditional homes. Even when the indigenous peoples openly fought against the European invaders, they were no match for the superior weapons and growing numbers of the aggressors; these resistors often found themselves herded into small, poor, isolated rural communities, far from the prosperous European settlements.

The Pacific islanders suffered greatly from the European diseases, but escaped much of the early troubles of direct occupation. Instead, the Europeans who interacted with the Pacific islanders were usually whalers, fishermen, and missionaries; throughout most of the nineteenth century, the imperialist powers had no desire to establish direct colonial rule over the Pacific islands. In the late nineteenth century, however, the era of global imperialism reached the shores of even the distant Pacific islands, as France claimed **Tahiti**, the Society Islands, and the Marquesas for direct rule by 1880. Likewise, Britain claimed **Fiji**, and Germany claimed the **Marshall Islands. The Berlin Conference** managed to include all the Pacific regions in addition to Africa, so by 1900 only Tonga remained independent and it soon requested British protection out of fear of other European nations.

THE EMERGENCE OF NEW IMPERIAL POWERS

Though much of nineteenth century imperialism was a European affair, rapid industrialization and a fear of being excluded from global influence lead Japan and the United States to seek imperial status.

U.S. Imperialism in Latin America and the Pacific
(Themes: Patterns of Interaction, and Changes and Continuities)

The history of manifest destiny in the treatment of the indigenous peoples of North America is the real and unflattering story of U.S. imperialism. By the nineteenth century, most indigenous peoples of North America had died as a result of European-bred diseases, the survivors had suffered during the years of U.S. westward expansion, and the remainder of these people had been pushed onto marginal lands and reservations.

The Monroe Doctrine (1823) had articulated the U.S. position that all of the Americas were a protectorate and throughout most of the nineteenth century, the U.S. exercised informal control in the Americas and sought predominately to guarantee free trade in the region which benefited U.S. business. By the late nineteenth century, U.S. leaders were increasingly interested in acquiring territory outside the contiguous United States; Alaska was purchased from Russia in 1867, and Hawaii was acquired as a U.S. possession in 1898.

The United States willingly went to war with Spain in 1898 and acquired Cuba, Puerto Rico, and eventually Guam and the Philippines. Instability in other Caribbean and Central American lands prompted U.S. intervention to protect its business interests in Cuba, the Dominican Republic, Nicaragua, Honduras, and Haiti in the early twentieth century. Control in the Philippines, important to U.S. businesspeople and military leaders because of its strategic location, was especially difficult to establish and cost twenty million dollars as well as 4,200 American lives, and the lives of 35,000 Filipinos.

The construction of the **Panama Canal** was a direct result of the need to facilitate transportation and communication between the U.S. interests in the Atlantic and the Pacific Oceans. The ensuing "**Roosevelt Corollary**" (1904) became part of the Monroe Doctrine and stated the United States' right to intervene in the domestic affairs of nations within its hemisphere, if those nations were unable to maintain the security necessary to protect U.S. economic interests.

Imperial Japan
(Themes: Patterns of Interaction, and Changes and Continuities)

Fueled by the demands of industrialization and the dissatisfaction at the treatment by the United States and the European powers in the 1860s, Japan sought to raise its profile in the world and so launched a campaign of imperial expansion.

Starting in the islands of east Asia, Japan claimed hegemony over the islands of Kokkaido, Kurile, Okinawa, and Ryukyu by 1879. Then, using warships purchased from the British, Japan turned its attention to Korea and forced Korean leaders to submit to the same kind of unequal treaty imposed by the U.S. on Japan in 1867. The **Sino-Japanese War** between Japan and China erupted over control of Korea in 1894. By 1895, the war was over and Japan had won overwhelmingly. It gained virtually full control of Korea and Taiwan as well as other formerly Chinese islands in east Asia. Likewise, the Japanese were successful in defeating the Russians in the **Russo-Japanese War** (1904–1905), gaining additional territory in Russian east Asia including major economic interests in Manchuria, and gaining global acknowledgment as a major imperial power.

LEGACIES OF IMPERIALISM

Imperialism and colonialism both tightened the bonds between people across the world and yet also heightened a sense of differences. Likewise, imperialism and colonialism both promoted nationalism while forging independence movements as well.

Empire and Economy
(Themes: Economics and Changes and Continuities)

The desire for natural resources and agricultural products was one of the principal motivations for imperialism. Global trade in products such as timber, rubber, petroleum, gold, silver, diamonds, cotton, cacao, and coffee surged during the nineteenth and twentieth centuries. Colonial policy often changed long-existing production patterns for products like cotton in India or mandated production of crops like tea and coffee in Ceylon or rubber in Malaya and Sumatra with little regard for the impact of such mandates on local traditions or markets.

Labor Migrations
(Themes: Demographics and Technology)

Imperial powers encouraged mass migration of laborers during the nineteenth and early twentieth centuries to exploit the demand for natural resources and agricultural products. Such mass movements of people resulted in depositing people with distinctive ethnic identities far from the lands of their original homes and created a mix of people previously unknown in world history.

Migrants from southern and east Europe went predominately to temperate lands to work as free cultivators in places like Australia or New Zealand or to work as industrial laborers in the growing number of factories in the northeastern United States. These migrations were possible because European and Euro-American peoples had established settler colonies in temperate regions around the world.

Migrants from Africa, Asia, or the Pacific islands moved to tropical or subtropical regions to work as manual laborers on plantations, in mines, or on large-scale construction projects. The abolition of slavery left planters in those regions in need of cheap labor. Many indentured workers, especially those from India, found employment on these distant farms. After the Opium Wars, recruiters found willing Chinese workers to labor in Cuban and Hawaiian sugar plantations; the mines of Peru, Malaya, South Africa, and Australia; and on railroad construction sites in Canada, the United States, and Peru; after the Meiji Restoration, Japanese laborers joined their Chinese counterparts across the globe. These migrations were possible because officials were able to recruit indentured workers and dispatch them to lands with established plantations or open mines.

Empire and Society
(Themes: Cultural Developments and Social Structures)

Colonialism met opposition across the world. The Sepoy Rebellion in India in 1857 was perhaps the most famous revolt, but the Maji Maji Rebellion in Tanganyika, the Mau Mau Rebellion in Kenya, and the Maori King movement in New Zealand all reflected the dissatisfaction of colonized, indigenous peoples.

While the movement of workers produced multicultural societies, it also produced two distinct forms of racism: **scientific racism** and **popular racism.** Scientific racism developed after the 1840s as race theorists assumed that the human species consisted of several distinct racial groups and then began to discuss race as the most important index of human potential. The published works of French nobleman **Joseph Arthur de Gobineau** characterized Africans as lazy and unintelligent, Asians as intelligent but docile, Americans as dull and arrogant, and Europeans as intelligent, noble, and morally superior to all others. Similar works later would seek to link racial identity through skin color, facial features, cranial capacity, and other physical characteristics. After the 1860s, the work of Charles Darwin was used to explain the development of human societies as part of the "survival of the fittest" logic; men like English philosopher

Herbert Spencer justified the domination of European imperialists over subject peoples as the inevitable results of "natural principles."

Popular racism needed no such "scientific" backing. Imperial representatives developed and articulated their racist views based on their personal experiences which became convenient justification for the mistreatment of subject peoples. The morally superior attitude of Europeans was echoed in the U.S. efforts to "Christianize and civilize" in the Philippines and in the Japanese "obligation" to oversee the affairs of their "little Asian brothers."

Nationalism and Anticolonial Movements
(Themes: Patterns of Interaction and Changes and Continuities)

Just as Napoleon's attempted conquest of Europe resulted in a backlash of nationalism across Europe, the response of subjugated peoples to European, American, and Japanese imperialism was to eventually breed anti-colonial responses and ultimately nationalist movements. The father of modern India, **Ram Mohan Roy,** sought to build an India based on European science and enduring Hindu traditions through the publication of newspapers and the founding of nationalist societies to publicize social reform in colonial India. Elite Hindus and Muslims educated at British universities drew inspiration from Enlightenment values and by the end of the nineteenth century had founded the vocal and powerful **Indian National Congress** to express their views on colonial policy. In 1906, the Congress had joined with the **All-India Muslim League** to give distinctive voice to the 25 percent of India's population who were Muslim. By 1947, these organizations would have grown into a successful independence movement. The Indian model of European-educated indigenous elites leading the attack on European colonial rule would become the norm in twentieth century independence movements.

Finished reading the chapter? Be sure you can . . .

- Describe and analyze the changes in global commerce, communication, and technology during this era.
- Explain the demographic changes resulting from imperialism.
- Describe and analyze the rise of western dominance in patterns of imperialism and colonialism in Asia, Latin America, the Pacific, and Africa.
- Explain how patterns of nationalism and anti-colonial movements emerged from this era.

Chapter Multiple Choice Questions

1. Why was Cecil Rhodes so interested in controlling Cape Colony?
   a. He wanted to control the gold mines of South Africa just as he controlled the diamond mines.
   b. He hoped Cape Colony would serve as a base of operations to extend British control of Africa from the Cape to Cairo.
   c. He wanted to prevent German and French intervention in the politics of south Africa.
   d. He hoped to entice the United States back into the British Empire by offering gold and diamonds as incentives.
   e. He wanted to serve as British Prime Minister and saw Cape Colony as a stepping-stone in his political career.

2. Which of the following areas was NOT considered a settler colony in the nineteenth century?
   a. Argentina
   b. Australia
   c. New Zealand
   d. South Africa
   e. India

3. The Suez Canal was constructed to reduce travel time between what two locations?
   a. Britain and Egypt
   b. Britain and Cape Colony
   c. Britain and India
   d. Britain and the United States
   e. Britain and Sudan

4. The outcome of the Sepoy Rebellion was ultimately
   a. the establishment of direct imperial rule in India.
   b. the removal of all Indian troops from Lucknow and Cawnpore.
   c. the inclusion of Sri Lanka as the headquarters of the British East India Company.
   d. the end to British rule in India.
   e. the speedy completion of the Suez Canal.

5. The term "Great Game" is applied to
   a. the struggle between France and Great Britain for control of India.
   b. the struggle between the Ottomans and the Qing to conquer the great caravan cities of Central Asia.
   c. the struggle between the Hindu and Muslim sepoys.
   d. the struggle between the British and Russian adventurers for control of Central Asia.
   e. the struggle for Indian independence from the British East India Company.

6. Which of the following regions did NOT become a European colony during the nineteenth century?
   a. Singapore
   b. Burma
   c. Cambodia
   d. Vietnam
   e. Thailand

7. In which of the following colonies was conversion to Christianity most effective?
   a. Vietnam
   b. India
   c. Indonesia
   d. Malaysia
   e. Burma

8. African colonies where European personnel collected taxes, maintained order, and organized labor and military recruitment were run under which system?
   a. direct rule
   b. indirect rule
   c. concessionary rule
   d. dominion rule
   e. continental rule

9. Scientific racism drew on whose works to support its premise that Europeans were intellectually, culturally, and morally superior to all other peoples?
   a. Ram Mohan Roy
   b. U.S. President McKinley
   c. Charles Darwin
   d. U.S. President Theodore Roosevelt
   e. Rudyard Kipling

10. The Indian National Congress was originally formed
    a. to give Muslims in India a public forum for discussion of nationalist and independence concerns.
    b. as a forum for educated Indians to communicate their views to colonial officials.
    c. to promote the Enlightenment ideals of Herbert Spencer and Ram Mohan Roy.
    d. as a venue to educate and assimilate Indian elites into positions within the colonial government.
    e. as an opportunity for upward mobility for Hindus and Muslims seeking to escape the traditional caste system.

Comprehensive Multiple Choice Questions

1. The imposition of foreign rule provoked nationalist responses in colonized lands in the later nineteenth century, just as nationalism had resulted from
    a. Napoleon's march across Europe in the late eighteenth and early nineteenth centuries.
    b. the United States' nineteenth-century policy of manifest destiny in Latin America.
    c. the expansion of the Roman empire under Augustus in the first century C.E.
    d. Shi Huangdi's building of the Great Wall in the third century B.C.E.
    e. Mansa Musa's pilgrimage to Mecca in the fourteenth century C.E.

2. Both Cecil Rhodes and Otto von Bismarck
    a. insisted that the great questions of history were decided by "blood and iron".
    b. believed overseas expansion benefited both European industrialists and workers.
    c. believed that a Berlin-to-Baghdad railroad was essential for their nation's long-term economic prosperity.
    d. sought to control the mineral wealth of South Africa through the fighting of the Boer War.
    e. were believers in indirect rule as the ideal imperial political structure.

3. Which of the following colonial structures involved the LEAST amount of European governmental involvement?
    a. concessionary company
    b. indirect rule
    c. direct rule
    d. dominion rule
    e. direct occupation

Primary Source Questions

1. **Read *Sources from the Past: Rudyard Kipling on the White Man's Burden* on page 913 of your textbook.**
    a. How might Kipling's life experiences influence his point of view?
    b. What words does Kipling use to describe the non-whites in his poem?
    c. What appeals does he use to justify imperialism?

2. **Read *Sources from the Past: Lord Lugard Justifies Imperialism and Indirect Rule in Africa* on page 924 of your textbook.**
    a. In what ways is Lugard's justification for imperialism different than Kipling's?

Chapter Multiple Choice Answers

1. **b:** Cecil Rhodes had already made his fortune in diamonds and had earned a considerable fortune through the gold mines of southern Africa as well. He was especially interested however in Cape Colony's potential to serve as the southern support for a British-controlled Africa to stretch from Cape Colony to Cairo and ultimately a world dominated by the British empire. (p. 909)

2. **e:** Each of these lands, except India, was populated by settlers sent from European nations' home societies during the nineteenth century. Though some Europeans settled in India during that time, the official policy was to post government officials for a period of time in India, and to encourage businessmen to conduct business there, but large-scale migrations of settlers were not sponsored by the European governments. (p. 911)

3. **c:** India was the "jewel" of the British Crown and the Suez Canal was constructed largely to reduce travel time between Britain and India as well as between Egypt and India. (p. 915)

4. **a:** In order to stabilize economic and military affairs and to forestall any future problems like the Sepoy Rebellion, the British government preempted the East India Company and imposed direct imperial rule in India in 1858. (p. 917)

5. **d:** The Russians and the British struggled for years to gain the upper hand in Central Asia. They mapped uncharted territories, scouted dangerous terrain, and made alliances with local rulers from the Aral Sea to Afghanistan all in an attempt to prepare for the anticipated coming conflict over the northern Indian frontiers. (p. 917)

6. **e:** Siam, modern-day Thailand, avoided colonial rule largely because it was seen as a convenient buffer between French Indochina and British-dominated Burma. (p. 919)

7. **a:** British colonial rule was rarely focused on conversion to Christianity, but in French Indochina, especially in Vietnam, conversion to Roman Catholicism was especially successful. (p. 919)

8. **a:** Direct rule was aimed at removing local kings and leaders from positions of influence and it relied on European administrators working with European selected local pawns to control all aspects of the colony. (p. 922)

9. **c:** Darwin's work, *Origin of the Species*, unintentionally provided the slogan "survival of the fittest" which proved a ready match for the ideas of scientific racists like Herbert Spencer or popular racists like Colonel Francis Younghusband. (p. 934)

10. **b:** The Indian National Congress began with the support of the British government which hoped this forum would allow educated Indians a venue to communicate their views on public affairs. As time went by, however, the INC became the basis for a successful independence movement in India. (p. 937)

Comprehensive Multiple Choice Answers

1. **a:** An unintended consequence of both Napoleons' early nineteenth-century conquests and the conquest of imperialism in the later nineteenth century was the resulting backlash of nationalism. (p. 910)

2. **b:** Fearing pressure or upheaval from communists, socialists, or just disgruntled laborers, both Rhodes and Bismarck saw foreign imperial ventures as a way to ease domestic tension and redirect public attention to a great overseas adventure. (p. 912)

3. **a:** Concessionary companies were private companies which had been granted large concessions of territory and power to rule that territory as they saw fit. This strategy allowed European colonial nations to colonize and exploit immense territories with only a modest investment of capital or personnel. (p. 922)

Primary Source Answers

1. Raised in India and schooled in England, Kipling has some specific life experiences which influence his point of view. Certainly, his early life in India was affluent and though he spoke Hindi, one wonders how much he actually knew of the life of Indians not associated with European colonialists. Kipling appears to have little historical knowledge of India before colonialism. His background gives him one perspective only on India under colonial control. Certainly a non-colonial might have seen India and Indians in a much different light. Kipling's British education shows in his choices of powerful words to describe native peoples: "fluttered folk," "wild," "Half-devil and Half-child," "Sloth and heathen Folly," "silent, sullen peoples." Each of these terms and phrases is laden with connotation and visual images that portray the indigenous people in less than fully human, or civilized, ways. Given these portrayals of indigenous peoples, Kipling uses their lesser status to invest lofty justifications and goals for imperialism: to stop famine, to prevent rule of kings, to improve life for the common man (even when he does not know his life needs improving, because the white way is best even for the world's "lessers"), and, of course, because being superior carries responsibility to "whiten" the world of others. Kipling's words convey a sense of duty and conviction that is difficult to fully understand today. Often, students first reading this poem want to deduce that Kipling was being sarcastic or ironic in his tone; there is no historical evidence to support this interpretation and indeed everything that Kipling wrote about this work and its criticism supports his honest belief that duty and responsibility to serve the less fortunate should drive one's behavior even in the face of criticism and resistance. (p. 913)

2. Lugard's justifications for imperialism and indirect rule in Africa are markedly different from Kipling's reasoning. Whereas Kipling is very concerned with duty and responsibility towards one's "lessers," Lugard is very clear that his motivation toward imperialism in Africa is for an essential advantage to Britain, not solely as a dictate of duty. Lugard thoughtfully explains that the economic rivalry between European powers makes Africa the "last remaining field for enterprise and expansion." He goes further to explain that indirect rule in Africa provides for the growth of trade in Britain, a market for British-produced goods, and an outlet for surplus energy" which translates to elements of the British population seeking to better their economic and social status. Lugard speaks to this rationale when he says, "to provide for our ever-growing population." However, Lugard is wise not to dismiss totally duty as a motivation for imperialism and he is careful to explain that "advantage may run parallel with duty." He proclaims that serving Britain's own national interests will actually help the nations of Africa by training their people "of the right stamp" in the advantages of British-style rule. He concludes by saying that learning British ways will override the "natural inclination" of the African peoples to submit to higher authority. Like Kipling, it does not appear that Lugard intended any irony in such statements and he does not appear to see any parallels between his nation's actions in Africa and the "intolerable tyranny of the dominant tribe." (p. 924)

PART VII

CONTEMPORARY GLOBAL REALIGNMENTS, 1914 TO THE PRESENT

CHAPTER 34

THE GREAT WAR: THE WORLD IN UPHEAVAL

Before you get started: The roots of the First World War were sown in the late nineteenth century as technology and rampant nationalism led to intense competition among European nations. The Great War was played out mostly in Europe but there were episodes in Asia and Africa. Primarily, the war involved troops from colonies around the world so in that sense, it was global. Also, the treaty at the end of the war reshaped the globe, adding countries that had never existed before while eliminating some major global players. The Great War was also a war in which industrialized nations matched technology on the battlefield leading to unimaginable horrors and a completely new method in waging war. There are no tricks to this war other than to remember the two factions: the Central Powers and the Allies. The Central Powers (or Triple Alliance) consisted of Germany and Austria-Hungary with a short commitment by Italy while the Allies were France, England, and Russia with the very late but very effective addition of the United States.

THE DRIFT TOWARD WAR

The spark for the war was the Serbian assassination of the **Archduke Franz Ferdinand** of Austro-Hungary, but its causes were laid down many years before. In Chapter 33, you read about national rivalries, ethnic hatreds, colonial struggles, and technological competition that took over the modern world. They were complicated by a series of secret alliances that would compel the European nations to take sides after the assassination.

Nationalist Aspirations
(Themes: Political Development, Diplomacy, and War)

In the wave of nationalism that spread across Europe after the French revolution, there was a belief that all ethnic groups deserved their own sovereign nations. However, the concept of **self-determination** was a threat to the dominant powers who resisted change and suppressed minorities. Nevertheless, in western Europe, the Belgians gained independence from the Netherlands while both the Germans and Italians united their disparate states into nations. In eastern Europe, the Russian, Austro-Hungarian and Ottoman empires dominated their regions but experienced much internal dissension. As the Ottoman empire shrank, it lost Greece and the Balkan states of Serbia, Bulgaria, and Romania. The Austro-Hungarians had the opposition of the Slavic peoples under its power. The Russian government supported a **pan-Slavic movement** that inspired resistance and rebellion in order to weaken their rival empires. The Slavic Serbians had come under the control of Austro-Hungary so Russia was obligated to back Serbia while, on the other side, the Germans felt compelled to support Austrians with whom they shared heritage and language.

National Rivalries
(Themes: Political Development, Diplomacy, and War)

As the industrialized nations competed for the raw materials, it led to rivalries in the colonies of Asia and Africa. The nineteenth century had seen a series of clashes between western powers over colonial control. Britain and Russia had challenged each other in Persia and Afghanistan while Britain and France had clashed over Siam, Egypt, and the Sudan. In east and southwest Africa, Germany and Britain met head to head while Germany tangled with France in west and northwest Africa. Germany was determined to have its **"place in the sun"** despite the fact that Britain and France had carved up most of the available colonies.

Germany's rapid industrialization had threatened England's dominance. After the turn of the century, Germany had increased its industrial output so that is was the equivalent of England's. In addition to that, steam power had exacerbated shipping and naval rivalries. As European nations became convinced that global dominance depended upon control of the seas, the German challenge to England's traditional superiority was highlighted by its development of the super warship class of **dreadnoughts.**

A series of incidents in Morocco and two small wars in the Balkans predated the Great War. European citizens lined up behind their nation and its allies as public opinion became a driving force toward conflict. The fervor of citizens to "win" all possible competitions from sports to colonies to the race for undiscovered areas such as the South Pole accelerated after the turn of the century. Cheap mass media fueled the excitement by offering vivid accounts and chauvinistic editorials. Diplomats found themselves unable to serve their nations unless they acquiesced to a policy of winning rather than reconciliation.

Understandings and Alliances
(Themes: Political Development, Diplomacy, and War)

Two conflicting series of agreements were reached that entangled most European nations into unbreakable allegiances. Thus the **Triple Alliance** and the **Triple Entente** were set to fall into place should any international crisis occur. The Triple Alliance initially developed when Germany and Austro-Hungary aligned themselves in a defensive pact against Russia and France in 1879. Italy decided to join out of fear of France as well. The Triple Entente formed when France, still smarting from its loss to Germany in the Franco-Prussian War of 1870 and fearful of the Triple Alliance, decided to ally itself with Britain. Since Britain had colonial agreements with Russia, Russia was brought in as the third party.

In addition to the system of alliances, military staffs had developed extensive inflexible war plans. For instance, France had developed an almost completely offensive plan that gave no thought to possible reactions of the enemy. The Germans had developed the **Schlieffen plan** to defeat France swiftly and then turn to meet the Russians. They believed that the Russians would take longer to mobilize so they would have a few weeks to defeat France first. However, the logistics of moving the massive German army were not taken into consideration so the progress would be very slow. Neither France nor Germany had an alternate plan so once the war began, it would play out without revision.

GLOBAL WAR

There were two reactions when war broke out: country folk were shocked and fearful while urban dwellers were euphoric. The forward movement of war very quickly ground to a halt and the war proved closer to the country vision as nations engaged in total war with devastatingly accurate technology. Governments had to grasp dictatorial power in order to sustain the war effort. As increasing numbers of men were required to fight the war, women had to take up the slack in factories and traditional men's occupations. Imperialism brought soldiers of all nationalities to Europe while countries still vied for colonies and eventually the Ottoman Empire, the United States, and Japan were brought into play as well.

The Guns of August
(Themes: Diplomacy and War)

After the assassination of Franz Ferdinand on June 28, the assassins were traced to Serbian nationalist interests. The Austrians decided to teach Serbia a lesson with an almost unacceptable ultimatum that Austrians be allowed to conduct the investigations in Serbia. Since the Serbia reply was not acceptable, the Austrians declared war. After that, an unstoppable series of events pulled all the nations into inevitable war. The Russians mobilized to defend their Serbian allies. They were followed by the Germans with an ultimatum to stop mobilization. When Russia replied negatively, Germany declared war on Russia which pushed the French to mobilize. The Germans declared war on them as well and proceeded to execute the Schlieffen plan across Belgium and into France. With calls for Belgian neutrality and French allegiances in play, Britain entered the war on August 4, 1914.

Mutual Butchery
(Themes: Technology and War)

Most soldiers and civilians expected the war to be brief so they hurried to get into the action before it was over. Every nation was sure of its ability to defeat the enemy swiftly. The Germans moved into France but soon were stopped at the Marne River while both sides built their lines all the way to the English Channel. For the next three years, the western front was virtually stationary as the troops dug into trenches and hacked away at each other in futile offensives. Within a year, the Italians had withdrawn from the **Central Powers** and joined the **Allies** but made no advances north into Austria.

Technological advances of the nineteenth century were largely responsible for the stalemate. **Barbed wire** confined men to their trenches unless they were urged in suicidal charges into the No Man's Land between rolls of it. Continuous **machine-gun fire** ensured that few soldiers made it out of No Man's Land. **Poison gases** were horrifying new weapons that were highly lethal and killed men in slow, agonizing ways weeks after exposure. Some 800,000 men on both sides were killed as there was little control of the gases once they had been expelled into the air. **Life in the trenches** was numbing boredom punctuated by sheer terror. Also, the presence of waist-deep mud, half-decayed corpses, trench rats, and lice made for a grim existence. **Tanks** and **airplanes** were first used in the Great War with few results until strategies were devised for them. The tanks never proved very effective in that war but airplanes became increasingly more sophisticated and effective as "ace flyers" engaged in "dogfights." The German **submarine** was remarkably effective against allied freighters in the Atlantic but Britain and the United States maintained their diesel fleets of subs as well.

In the east, the front line was more fluid. Initially, the Russians did well against the Central Powers but as the war dragged on, its internal weaknesses began to have an effect as its losses mounted. The tsar's popularity sank as revolutionary agitation increased. There were numerous battles on both fronts but the brutal situation on the western front raised casualty rates to the horrific. The Battle of Verdun alone resulted in the deaths of 315,000 Frenchmen and 280,000 Germans. What is worse is that there were only 160,000 identifiable bodies with the rest blown to bits or unrecognizable. The new rules of engagement meant that civilian casualties were high as well. Air warfare could target civilian populations while naval blockades were intended to starve out the enemies' civilians in order to gain capitulation.

Total War: The Home Front
(Themes: War and Gender Structures)

As the Great War became a war of attrition, it became apparent that victory would become more dependent on keeping the armies supplied than on battlefield wins. Thus, the burden of total war fell on the civilian population or the **home front.** Governments took control of civilian industries to maintain the war effort. They abandoned laissez-faire policies and marketplace economics to direct all industry. They established wage and price controls as well as extending work hours. Military service was extended beyond initial enlistment and the countries turned to teenagers and sixty-year-olds to fill their ranks.

As war took men away from jobs, unemployment disappeared and women were required to fill the gaps. They left their homes and domestic service to work in traditional male jobs as well as acting as nurses, physicians, and communications clerks close to the battle lines. The most important work was the production of ammunition. Millions of women were exposed to the hazardous conditions of munitions factories which included explosions and poisonings. Middle- and upper-class women often found war work liberating but lower-class women already knew the experience of hard labor and so were less impressed by the lower wages and longer hours. Women did not stay in those jobs after the war; however, one important consequence to women's war involvement was the extension of the franchise to women. Britain, Germany, Austria, and the United States allowed women to vote soon after the war. Russian women were enfranchised in the Russian revolution of 1917.

In order to maintain the war effort, all governments made extensive use of propaganda and censorship. Governments censored the news and arrested dissidents and pacifists. Posters, pamphlets, and films vilified the enemy with false atrocity stories and racial stereotyping. Eventually, the propaganda became so extreme that people doubted the stories, which would have terrible ramifications in later wars as people had trouble believing reports of the Holocaust and the Rape of Nanjing.

Conflict in East Asia and the Pacific
(Theme: War)

The European war took on global consequences as colonies became embroiled in it, and third parties like the Ottoman Empire, Japan, and the United States got involved. Japan took advantage of Germany's focus on Europe to confiscate German positions in Asia and the Pacific. Declaring war on Germany and allying with the Allies, the Japanese seized a portion of German-leased northeast China and German colonies of the Marshalls, Marianas, Carolines, and Palua. New allies New Zealand and Australia helped the Japanese capture parts of Samoa and New Guinea. Then, Japan went on to issue the secret **Twenty-One Demands** to the Chinese government in an attempt to bring China under its complete control. The Chinese government agreed to most of the demands but leaked the note to the British which helped them maintain their weak autonomy. With these seizures and demands, it became apparent that Japan intended to dominate Asia.

Battles in Africa and Southwest Asia
(Theme: War)

The Allies in Africa had a more difficult time conquering German possessions there. Throughout the war, British, French, and Belgian forces along with African, Arab, and Indian forces engaged in fierce battles with German troops and colonials. Disease killed more troops than the Germans as they fought in jungles, swamps, and deserts.

Fierce fighting also broke out in southwest Asia when the Ottoman Empire aligned itself with the Central Powers. In an attempt to bring the Dardanelles under Allied control, the British navy attacked forts but had to withdraw after severe damage from mines. The British High Command then chose to invade at the poorly chosen site of **Gallipoli** where cliffs prevented easy access to inland areas. They used colonial troops from Australia, New Zealand, and Canada with the royal navy as backup. It was a disaster as the men became pinned down on the beaches, unable to move forward, and unable to get resupplied. The losses for both sides were over 250,000 men and after a nine-month campaign, the British had to withdraw in defeat.

There were long-term consequences to Gallipoli because the colonial troops believed themselves to have been sacrificed to the stupidity of the British military. It ultimately lessened imperial ties and moved the dominions of Canada, Australia, and New Zealand toward autonomy from Britain. On the other side, it elevated the status of one Turkish military officer, Mustafa Kemal, so that, as **Ataturk** ("Father of the Turks"), he would take control of the newly formed Turkey after World War I.

However, Ottoman success was short-lived and, after Gallipoli, they retreated repeatedly from Russian and British forces. An Arab revolt on the Arabian peninsula, aided by British adventurer T.E. Lawrence of Arabia, aided the fall of the Ottoman regime.

THE END OF THE WAR

As civilian populations wearied of the deprivations of war, changes in Allies produced an end to the war. In 1917, the Russians withdrew in the throes of their own revolution while the United States declared war on the Central Powers. In November 1918, an armistice was signed and it held. Peace negotiations took a year to hammer out and proved to be punitive toward the Central Powers while making enormous state-building decisions as well.

Revolution in Russia
(Themes: Political Development and War)

Still demoralized from its defeats at the hands of the Japanese in 1905, the Russian military had few victories and a restive public began to agitate for withdrawal. In 1917, street demonstrations in St. Petersburg were aggravated by military mutinies. Matters got so out of hand that **Nicholas II** became convinced that he had to abdicate the throne, ending three hundred years of Romanov rule.

The revolution spread throughout Russia as political power shifted to the **provisional government** and the socialist soviet worker councils (*soviets*). Soviets sprouted up all over Russia and gained power through their influence on factory workers and the military. While the new government made many liberal reforms, the specter of war still loomed over Russia. Eventually, the power struggle between the provisional government and the Petrograd soviet came to a head as the government continued to support the war and the soviet called for immediate peace.

With remarkably great timing, this was the moment that the Germans sent Marxist leader and anti-war activist, **Vladimir Ilyich Lenin** (1870–1924), back to Russia. Lenin had grown up in a loving, middle-class family but it all came to an end when Russia's secret police arrested and executed his older brother for plotting to assassinate the tsar. Schooled in the law, and banished from his homeland, Lenin went abroad to study international Marxism. He authored political pamphlets and developed a refinement to Marxism that held that the proletariat did not have the ideological knowledge and fervor to be successful leaders and so would need to depend upon a workers' council for firm guidance. Once back in Russia, he and his radical socialists (Bolsheviks) pushed an end to the war and transference of legal authority to the soviets.

The **Bolsheviks** gained control of the Petrograd soviet as the provisional government continued to wage war rather than move toward other reforms. Effective campaigns using slogans like "Peace, Land, and Bread" convinced the workers and peasants that the Bolshevik program was more credible. In October 1917 the Bolsheviks engineered an armed insurrection and stormed the Winter Palace. Virtually bloodless, the coup rendered complete political power to Lenin and his Bolsheviks. Within five months, they had signed the **Treaty of Brest-Litovsk** with Germany to end their participation in the war. And, while the treaty was humiliating for the Russians, the Bolsheviks could move on to its program of remodeling Russia.

U.S. Intervention and Collapse of the Central Powers
(Themes: Diplomacy and War)

When the war started in 1914, the American public was adamantly against participation as they elected **Woodrow Wilson** (1856–1924) who promised nonintervention. As the government promoted a policy of neutrality, by 1917, the public was agitating for warfare. For the first two years of the war, the U.S. went through a severe recession that cleared once businessmen found a role in the war as suppliers and munitions providers to the Allies. Combined with increasing debts on the part of the Allies, it became apparent that the U.S. had a stake in Allied victory. The official reason to declare war was unrestricted submarine warfare on the part of the Germans. The Germans had been sinking neutral vessels in addition to warships without warning, as was called for in international law. When it sank the British liner **Lusitania** in 1915, 128 Americans died and this began the public's movement away from neutrality. Allied propaganda also reinforced Americans' commitment against the Germans.

Wilson declared war in early April 1917 to the resounding approval of the American public. Although it took many months to mobilize, America's entry into the war ended the stalemate. But both Allies and Central Powers were experiencing difficulties. In 1916, Irish revolutionaries unsuccessfully attempted to overthrow the British government. Food shortages as a result of the British blockade made German civilians unhappy enough to demonstrate against the government while German military units began to revolt. The French also experienced an enormous loss of confidence when many of their frontline soldiers mutinied in 1917. In a final assault, the Germans attempted to break through the Allies' line but failed.

Bulgaria, the Ottomans, and Austria-Hungary capitulated before the Germans laid down their weapons on November 11, 1918.

The Paris Peace Conference
(Theme: Diplomacy)

The war was devastating with as many as fifteen million people killed and additional millions dying in the difficult years following the war. The peace conferees in Paris did not know the full cost of the war when they negotiated a treaty in 1919. Despite hopeful expectations, the Versailles treaty exacerbated underlying rivalries and problems. Among the twenty-seven nations that negotiated the treaty were numerous heads of states; however, Woodrow Wilson, **Georges Clemenceau** of France; and **Lloyd George** of Britain were by far the most dominant in the proceedings. Noticeably and regrettably, the Soviet Union was not invited and there were no representatives of the Central Powers. The Allies threatened to resume war if any part of the treaty was rejected; and to keep the pressure on Germany, the British blockade was continued throughout the negotiations.

Woodrow Wilson had forwarded a peacetime proposal to the Germans a full year before the negotiations. His **Fourteen Points** were set on a philosophical foundation of idealism and included open agreements of peace, removal of economic barriers, equal trade opportunities, a reduction in armaments, a solution for colonial disputes, and a "general association of nations." While the Germans had accepted its premises, it felt betrayed by the harsh sanctions in the final treaty. Furthermore, U.S. allies felt betrayed by the settlements of colonial possessions in opposition to secret wartime agreements.

The final form was a series of peace treaties that saved the harshest treatment for the vanquished nations as France pushed to permanently weaken Germany. The Germans were required to accept full responsibility for the war and pay the full costs of the war (**reparations**). It denied a navy and air force for Germany and limited the size of its army to one hundred thousand troops. Territorial break-up of Austria-Hungary was recognized in granting self-determination to some of its regions such as Czechoslovakia and the Balkan nations.

The Ottomans had an even more complicated settlement, losing most of their territories but gaining recognition of the nation of Turkey under Mustafa Kemal in 1920. He immediately instituted a process of secular modernization and economic development that dictated a complete separation of church and state, the emancipation of women, and the adoption of European culture in clothing, law, mathematics, and writing. Although technically a constitutional ruler, Ataturk functioned as a virtual dictator until his death in 1938. Turkey's remarkable successes were exceptions in the outcome of the treaties for the Central Powers. Neither Germany nor Italy's expansionist policies were addressed, nor were those of Japan.

The **League of Nations** was established as an attempt to stave off war but it proved to be largely ineffectual. Its two major flaws were that it had no power to enforce its decisions and that it depended upon collective security to preserve peace, which might have been effective if all the major players had been members at the same time but they never were. The United States itself never joined because the Senate rejected the idea and the peace treaty itself. Germany and Japan left the League in 1933 while Italy resigned after being chided for the invasion of Ethiopia in 1937. The Soviet Union only joined in 1934 but was kicked out in 1940. Despite its weaknesses, the League of Nations laid the foundation for a more effective United Nations after World War II.

The promotion of **self-determination** assuaged the feelings of nationalists everywhere and, in some cases, it functioned quite well. For instance, Czechoslovakia, Poland, and Yugoslavia became independent nations. Nevertheless, even in these countries, it was impossible to draw lines that did not include a large minority population. One-third of all Poles did not even speak Polish while Yugoslavia encompassed Serbs, Croats, and Slovenes in addition to smaller minorities. The German-speaking Austrians and Germans were not allowed to form one state.

Self-determination became more difficult when applied to German colonies and Arab territories. The **mandate system** was devised to protect former colonies as they ostensibly moved toward independence. Of course, the victors only applied it to the defeated Central Powers and conveniently failed to look at their own colonies. Germans saw it as dividing the spoils of war and the Arabs were outraged. Promises had been made to them in exchange for support by British and French leaders during the war that were not carried out. Thus the French established mandates in Lebanon and Syria while the British established them in Palestine and Iraq. Arabs saw the mandate system as a hidden form of imperialism.

Challenges to European Preeminence
(Themes: Political Development and War)

The Great War permanently damaged European prestige and set the stage for decolonization. A commitment to total war had ruined the European economy and left the United States as the primary creditor to the world. Colonial people had viewed the war as a massive, bloody civil war that disproved the superiority of European civilization so the colonials became less inclined to behave as loyal subjects. Self-determination was an appealing notion that had not been extended to the colonies of the victorious nations and revolutionary leaders took note of it. Furthermore, they took inspiration from the Soviet Union which had denounced imperialism. Despite postwar disappointments, the desire for self-rule had become a permanent feature in colonial societies.

Finished reading the chapter? Be sure you can . . .

- Analyze the causes of the Great War.
- Identify the chief combatants and their alliances.
- Identify the roles of women in World War I and the outcome of increased responsibility.
- Identify the roots of the Russian revolution.
- Compare the effects of the World War on areas outside Europe.
- Analyze the successes and failures of the League of Nations.

Chapter Multiple Choice Questions

1. What region of the world was more open to European colonization in the late nineteenth century?
   a. east Asia
   b. south Asia
   c. South America
   d. Africa
   e. southwest Asia

2. Ethnic pride became a part of nationalistic feelings in the nineteenth century. Which group was of most concern to the central European powers?
   a. Belgians
   b. Slavs
   c. Czechs
   d. Jews
   e. Austrians

3. The rapid industrialization of Germany most threatened the dominance of which country?
   a. France
   b. Italy
   c. Britain
   d. Japan
   e. United States

4. What was the chief reason the treaties between countries contributed to the mobilization of war?
    a. They contributed to a sense of security so that governments became complacent.
    b. They obligated allies to come to the assistance of countries when threatened.
    c. They broke down traditional alliances that had existed for centuries.
    d. They were more offensive than defensive which threatened traditional borders.
    e. They supported only sovereign nations with well-defined boundaries.

5. What modern technologies contributed the most to changes in war strategy that endured throughout the war?
    a. barbed wire and airplanes
    b. machine guns and tanks
    c. poison gas and submarines
    d. tanks and airplanes
    e. machine guns and barbed wire

6. What lasting effects occurred when women entered the workforce in support of the total war effort?
    a. Many women persisted in their chosen careers beyond the end of the war.
    b. Many women resented the return of men from the front when they took over jobs.
    c. Most women had to be forced to return to the domestic sphere.
    d. Women's good performance during the war lent validity to the idea of their suffrage.
    e. Unmarried women continued in the industrial workforce as assistants to men.

7. To what extent was the Great War a catalyst for the Russian revolution?
    a. When combined with longstanding socioeconomic problems, the incompetence of war leadership brought down the tsarist government.
    b. War policy had not developed beyond the defeats to the Japanese in 1905, so that was enough to bring down the government.
    c. The war had little effect because the underlying political problems were so significant that the tsarist government would have collapsed anyway.
    d. The revolutionary leaders were so successful in their attacks on war policy that the government collapsed.
    e. The lack of modern technology proved the inherent weakness in the Russian military so that triggered revolution in tsarist opposition.

8. In which region of the globe did the war have the most lasting effect?
    a. Africa where material resources were still needed after war in Europe
    b. the Middle East where oil was needed to wage war in an age of diesel power
    c. Australia and New Zealand who supplied men, material, and supplies to Britain
    d. north Africa which the Germans were determined to control and protect their southern flank
    e. east Asia where Japan formed a useful alliance with the Allies in order to dominate the region

9. What ideological underpinnings of the Paris peace treaties most affected the colonies?
    a. nationalism
    b. acceptance of responsibility
    c. self-determination
    d. gradual independence
    e. global peace

10. Which factor most contributed to the failure of the League of Nations to act as an international force?
    a. Wilson was unable to get the United States to commit as a member nation.
    b. Only weak and insignificant nations signed on as members.
    c. When faced with military force, the League had no way to enforce its decisions.
    d. For any action, over three-quarters of member nations had to vote in agreement.
    e. An association of nations would never be a reasonable approach to world peace.

Comprehensive Multiple Choice Questions

1. When comparing the effects of the First World War on colonies that were settler societies like Australia with those that were simply dependent like India, which of the following is most accurate?
   a. Settler societies continued their remarkable allegiance to Europe while dependent colonies began to break away.
   b. Settler societies were encouraged to seek complete independence while dependent colonies continued to uphold colonial ideals.
   c. Both settler and dependent colonies had contributed men and resources to the war so they were proud of their loyalties to the mother nations.
   d. Neither settler nor dependent colonies wanted to continue their former relationship with colonial masters.
   e. The war effort had required so much loyal colonial participation that both settler and dependent colonies believed that independence would be their reward.

2. When comparing an earlier global war, the Seven Years' War, with the First World War, which of the following statements is the most true?
   a. Unlike the First World War, the combatant nations of Seven Years' War had few alliances.
   b. The First World War was more nationalistic and less economic than the Seven Years' War.
   c. Both wars were the result of intense nationalistic competition in many areas.
   d. Both wars were significant for their use of new weaponry and military strategies.
   e. Neither war was fought much outside Europe but both used colonial troops in Europe.

3. What elements of early modern European society played the greatest part in triggering the Great War?
   a. economic competition as evidenced by guilds
   b. intense state rivalries resulting in frequent wars
   c. a dedication to the development of new technologies
   d. a secular approach to social and economic issues
   e. traditional loyalties that served as military alliances

Primary Source Questions

1. **Examine the cartoon map of Europe, 1914, on page 948 of your textbook.**
   a. What is the artist's point of view?
   b. Which nations are represented in the best way? Is there a possible explanation?
   c. Which nations are represented in the worst way? Is there a possible explanation?
   d. What are the main themes in the cartoon?
   e. What subtle points can you discern?

2. **Read *Sources from the Past: Dulce et Decorum Est*, 1917, on page 957 of your textbook.**
   a. What is the author's point of view?
   b. Describe the interaction of words and rhythm.
   c. How would you classify the words he chose?
   d. Was this poem written at the beginning of the war?

Chapter Multiple Choice Answers

1. **d:** Africa was viewed as open for colonization in particular by Germany who wanted its "Place in the Sun." (p. 948)

2. **b:** The pan-Slavic movement threatened both Austria-Hungary and Germany as it was encouraged by the Russians. (p. 947)

3. **c:** Britain had been a leader in industrialization, so its drop in production vis-a-vis the Germans was threatening. (p. 947)

4. **b:** Once the ultimatums were issued, each nation became obligated to mobilize in support of their allies. (p. 949)

5. **e:** Early use of machine guns and barbed wire forced the armies into trench warfare for the rest of the war. (p. 954)

6. **d:** Women's performance in the domestic labor force during the war was a factor in their enfranchisement in Britain, Germany, and Austria soon after the war. (p. 958)

7. **a:** The lack of military success and civilian war deprivation contributed the final blow to a nation that was wracked by social and economic problems. (p. 962)

8. **e:** While all the resources were still needed after the war, Japan's successful opportunistic expansion into north China laid a significant foundation for the Second World War. (pp. 959–960)

9. **c:** Colonial revolutionary leaders identified self-determination as the key factor in their quest for independence. (p. 972)

10. **c:** While the U.S. failure to join was part of the problem, the lack of enforcement options made the League inconsequential. (p. 970)

Comprehensive Multiple Choice Answers

1. **b:** British dominions were disenchanted with British policies during the war and began to view themselves as autonomous while other colonial dissidents were reinvigorated in their quest for independence by their disenchantment with so-called civilized behavior and the recognition of self-determination as a universal right. (pp. 961, 972)

2. **c:** The Seven Years' War was a war of nationalistic competition for control of colonies and domination of the world, as was the First World War. Both were perpetrated by European nations who formed alliances with one another. Only the Great War had many significant new military technologies that required enormous changes in traditional military strategies. The Seven Years' War was fought in America as the French and Indian War. Furthermore, both wars had military engagements in Asia as well. (pp. 620, 947–948)

3. **b:** The growth of strong regional monarchies during the high middle ages and into the period of absolute monarchies clearly contributed to a legacy of political competition that prefaced the world war. While economic competition was one of the issues, guilds work against competition. Europe's interest in new technologies and science dating from the scientific revolution was certainly important in how the war was waged but was less important as a catalyst for the actual fighting. The tradition of regular warfare in Europe transcends religious and secular periods in European history. Loyalties had played important roles since feudal times, but they were constantly shifting. (pp. 648, 947)

Primary Source Answers

1. The cartoon artist was probably unconnected to a government since this was a period with a relatively independent press—until wartime censorship. Thus it reflects his opinion, which could be a majority or minority opinion in his own country. It is probable that the artist was from the Central Powers since they are represented on the defensive in relatively realistic proportions. In fact, the most favorable depiction is the Austro-Hungarian soldier, a large, handsome man. The Romanian is also

depicted in more realistic terms and seems to be only an observer. The worst representation has to be the gaping mouth of the Russians although unshaven and dirty-looking soldiers are depicted in most other nations. While Austria-Hungary appears to be on the defensive, so do the French who are being literally kicked along by German soldiers. (p. 948)

2. The author's vivid depiction of a gas attack points towards personal experience. There is also a sickened tone of disappointment at the end that points to complete disillusionment with governmental policy. The poem's rhythm mirrors the slow slog through the front at first and then picks up the pace with the actual gas attack. It returns to a slower pace after they have thrown the corpse into a wagon and resumed their trudge. The words that the poet uses could be categorized into disease, exhaustion, panic, and disgust. It would seem that this was written once the war was well under way since there is a familiarity with gas attacks and a weariness that suffuses the poem. Also, the flush of enthusiasm at the beginning of war has disappeared and it ends with a cautionary note about the deceptions of wartime. (p. 957)

CHAPTER 35

AN AGE OF ANXIETY

Before you get started: Some of "the worst of times" and some of "the best of times" coming in the twentieth century are forged in the era discussed in this chapter. Great art, great science, and great thinking all emerge during the eras between the First and Second World Wars but so does the Great Depression, fascist nationalism, and totalitarian communism. This is a chapter to be thinking deeply about actions and consequences, problems and solutions, and of course, comparisons and contrasts. The chapter opens with a compelling explanation of Hitler as a personification of this era; it will help you make sense of the chapter's title, so don't skip that part.

PROBING CULTURAL FRONTIERS

The Great War destroyed much, including long-held beliefs about the superiority of European culture. Building on innovations in science, psychology, art and architecture, changes in those fields reached true revolution in the two decades following the war.

Postwar Pessimism
(Theme: Cultural Developments)

Gertrude Stein coined the phrase **"lost generation"** to describe American intellectuals and literati who flocked to Paris in the postwar years seeking to find some salve for their disillusionment. Those European intellectuals who had managed to survive the massive four-year-long destruction were quickly and profoundly alienated by the brutal realities of industrialized war. Ernest Hemingway's *A Farewell to Arms* and Erich Maria Remarque's *All Quiet on the Western Front* spoke eloquently about the meaningless suffering and ceaseless death their generation experienced in the Great War. Oswald Spengler's *The Decline of the West* and Arnold J. Toynbee's *A Study of History* sought to make sense from the chaos of the war years. Theologians like Karl Barth and Niokolai Berdiaev questioned human potential to realize God's purpose. The very concept of progress was challenged by thinkers who could see little benefit from democracy even as the last vestiges of property and educational restrictions on the right to vote were removed in most European nations. Intellectuals felt these opportunities would lead to a tyranny by the average person and saw democracy as a product of decay, warning against the **"rule of inferiors."**

Revolutions in Physics and Psychology
(Theme: Intellectual Developments)

A revolution in physics occurred during these years led by Albert Einstein whose theory of special relativity showed there was no single spatial and chronological framework for the universe and thus it no longer made sense to speak of time and space as absolutes. To the layperson, such knowledge meant that a commonsense universe had disappeared and so now reality or truth simply was a set of agreed-upon mental constructs. Werner Heisenberg's "uncertainty principle" further undermined accepted notions of cause and effect and brought all notions of truth into question.

Like physics, postwar developments in psychology challenged established values and morals. **Sigmund Freud's** focus on psychological explanations for mental disorders introduced the idea of conflicts between conscious and unconscious mental processes which he believed were often revealed in one's dreams. His theory, known as **psychoanalysis**, was based on the study of mental illness and dreams as manifestations of the repressed consciousness, usually tied to unresolved sexual issues from childhood. Freud's ideas became common themes in art and literature throughout much of the twentieth century.

Experimentation in Art and Architecture
(Theme: Cultural Developments)

The distain for realism and concern for freedom of expression first manifested in the paintings of late-nineteenth-century French avant-garde artists also reached revolutionary proportions in the postwar era. The purpose of painting was to create reality, not to reflect it. A whole range of new schools emerged to "abolish the sovereignty of appearance": les fauves, expressionists, cubists, abstractionists, Dadaists, and surrealists. Painters in these schools were influenced by Pacific, Asian, and African traditions as well. The works of **Edgar Degas, Paul Gauguin,** and **Pablo Picasso** all display influences from these non-European traditions. The existence of a generally accepted definition of "good" and "bad" art had all but disappeared by the 1930s.

Modernist trends in architecture can be seen in the development of the **Bauhaus,** an institution which brought together architects, designers, and painters from several countries to focus on functional design—a marriage of engineering and art—uniquely suited to the urban and industrial twentieth-century landscape. The resulting aesthetic known as **international style** was well-suited to large apartment houses and office complexes, though the public never really warmed to its cold, impersonal style.

GLOBAL DEPRESSION

In 1929, despite postwar hopes for a return to normalcy and prosperity, the world plunged into an economic depression so long-lasting, so severe, and so global that it has come to be called the **Great Depression.** It would take more than ten years, the collapse of the old capitalist systems of trade and commerce, and ultimately another world war to finally return the world to prosperity.

The Great Depression
(Themes: Economics and Patterns of Interaction)

Looks can be deceiving and that was certainly the case of economics in the mid-1920s. It appeared as though prosperity was returning to prewar levels as business sought to repair the damages war had inflicted. However, in reality, this appearance of prosperity was only a thin façade covering a complex and tangled international economy where the flow of dollars from the U.S. to Europe and back to the U.S. was placing an intolerable and unsustainable strain on the world's financial system. Technological advances and improvements in industrial processes reduced the demand for certain raw materials and a drop in prices ensued. Overproduction in agricultural goods meant falling prices there as well. As agricultural production increased, demand declined, and agricultural prices collapsed across the world. By 1929, the price of a bushel of wheat was at its lowest level in four hundred years!

The reduced income of farm families contributed to high inventories in manufactured goods, which caused production cutbacks and labor layoffs across the United States. Coupled with mismanaged and unsustainable stock market practices and sketchy mortgage financing, the U.S. economy and soon the world economy toppled. In October 1929, U.S. investors began to pull out of the stock market, close bank accounts, and call in loans; this economic contraction spread as all business activity, wages, and unemployment slowed, so by 1932, industrial production had fallen to one-half of its 1929 level.

Agricultural economies in Latin American, African, and Asian countries which depended on the export of few products such as coffee, cocoa, sugar, or cotton and raw materials such as minerals, ores, and rubber suffered most. The worldwide depression affected every industrialized society; Japan and Germany suffered the most. Germany was experiencing 35 percent unemployment by 1932 and Japan's dependence on U.S. markets collapsed as the U.S. instituted high tariffs on all foreign imports. The Great Depression destroyed the financial and commercial network of capitalist economies and each country attempted to return to **economic nationalism** from their pre-depression global stance. Economic nationalism as a means to fight the world depression was a huge failure. Between 1929 and 1932, world production dropped by 38 percent and trade dropped more than 66 percent.

Despair and Government Action
(Themes: Economics, Gender Structures, and Social Class)

Unemployment was five times as high in 1933 as it had been in 1929. Economic contraction caused men to lose their jobs. At first, women lost their jobs at a much slower rate as they were paid only about two-thirds of a man's wage; however, the government soon enacted policies to limit female employment, especially married women. "A woman's place was in the home" was the accepted truism, with even Nobel Prize–winners like Charles Richet insisting that both male unemployment and a dangerously low birth rate would be solved by removing women from the workforce.

People were desperate to protect their jobs, homes, savings, and futures and as the years passed for some the struggle for food, clothing, and shelter grew desperate. Like gender roles, social class was a significant variable in understanding the peoples' struggles. Workers and farmers increasingly came to resent the wealthy, who, even with reduced economic resources, still could keep their homes and feed their families. John Steinbeck's *The Grapes of Wrath* captures the economics and the emotions of the times.

Economic Experimentation
(Theme: Economics)

Government responses to the Great Depression were based on **classical economics** which insisted that capitalism was a self-correcting system which operated best when allowed to operate without government interference. At first, governments tried to abide by these ideals, in the belief that the crisis would inevitably resolve itself. However, as the depth of the depression and its misery grew, governments attempted a more corrective role by balancing budgets and by curtailing public spending. Neither approach proved successful and, indeed, it seemed that capitalism was dying.

Noted twentieth-century economist **John Maynard Keynes** proposed a wholly different explanation and response in his 1936 book, *The General Theory of Employment, Interest, and Money*. To Keynes, the big problem was inadequate demand, rather than excessive supply; logically it followed that governments should respond by stimulating the economy by increasing the money supply and thereby encouraging investments, by undertaking public works projects to provide jobs, and by redistributing incomes through tax policy. Keynes even went so far as to say these measures were necessary even if they resulted in unbalanced budgets and deficits. Keynes's ideas did not become fully influential with government policymakers until after World War II.

However, **U.S. President Franklin Roosevelt's** response to the depression paralleled Keynes's ideals in many ways. Roosevelt believed the federal government was justified in intervening to safeguard the social and economic welfare of its citizens. So, he pushed for legislation to prevent the total collapse of the banking system, to provide farm subsidies, to promote jobs in the private and public sectors, to guarantee a minimum wage and decent working conditions, to grant workers the right to organize and bargain collectively, and to provide social security in old age. Roosevelt's approach to government policy and his influence on popular opinion lasted long after the depression years. It was World War II 's economic stimulus, however, which ultimately ended the crisis of the Great Depression.

CHALLENGES TO THE LIBERAL ORDER

The promise of a better tomorrow was the rallying cry for a range of political voices across the world in the post–World War I world. **Marxists** like Lenin and Stalin believed the death of capitalism was inevitable and promised a new and better system based on the rule of the working class. **Fascists** like Mussolini and Hitler found alternative formulas for reconstruction through intense nationalism, militarism, and devotion to a strong leader.

Communism in Russia
(Themes: Economics and Changes and Continuities)

Socialist victory in 1917 had not brought promised peace and prosperity to the Russian workers or to the lands of the former Russian empire. Indeed, Lenin and the Bolsheviks had to spend much of the second decade of the twentieth century defending their "dictatorship of the proletariat" against dissident social-ists, anti-Bolshevik officers and troops, peasant bands, and foreign military forces in a bloody civil war. The **Red Terror**, Lenin's campaign to extinguish all opposition, relied on secret police as well as armed troops to arrest, try, and execute more than two hundred thousand "**Whites**," opponents of the new re-gime. Russia's withdrawal from the Great War and fear of a spreading Marxist revolution inflamed Rus-sia's former allies including the French, British, and Americans who all sent forces to fight against Lenin's troops. When Russia's civil war was finally over in 1920, the Reds were victorious, but at the price of more than ten million Russian lives due to starvation, disease, and battle. An unintended conse-quence of the Russian civil war was the emergence of intense political oppression which would dominate the Soviet state in the decades to come.

Another unintended consequence of the Russian civil war was the implementation of **war communism,** a policy in which the Bolshevik government assumed control of banks, industries, commercial properties, and landed estates, as well as church and monastic holdings. This seizure of private property was un-popular, especially when the government seized crops from peasants in the rural areas to feed the urban populace. Crop production plummeted, and the Bolsheviks were in trouble.

Pragmatic Lenin needed a new plan, so he instituted the **New Economic Plan (NEP),** which temporarily restored the market economy and some private enterprise in Russia, though large industries such as banks, and transportation and communications industries, remained under government control. Peasants were allowed to sell their surplus at free-market prices and the Bolsheviks began a vigorous program of electri-fication for their nation. Lenin died in 1924 and so did not live to see the fruits of his NEP.

Lenin's death produced a bitter power struggle among the Bolshevik leaders. Joseph Stalin annihilated his rivals through treachery, deceit, and violence and emerged as the unchallenged dictator of the Soviet Un-ion by 1928. Stalin supported the ideal of "socialism in one country," and was determined to rapidly build Russia into an industrial powerhouse, no matter the cost in resources or lives. He trashed Lenin's NEP and established his plan for rapid economic development known as the First Five-Year Plan which set targets for increased productivity in all spheres of the economy, but especially in the steel and machinery industries. Stalin's plan for extreme centralization of the entire economy was in sharp contrast to the floundering condition of capitalism in the 1930s.

Stalin's plan for centralization also included the **collectivization of agriculture** which would prove ex-tremely unpopular and problematic even for the "man of steel." Collectivization was enforced most ruth-lessly against peasants who had risen to prosperity during the NEP; known as **kulaks,** they made up less than 5 percent of the Russian peasantry. Even less wealthy peasants were resistant to giving up their small plots of land and few animals. Many of them chose to slaughter their animals and burn their crops rather than to turn these resources over to the government and those who stayed often starved to death on land they had once owned; millions left the land and went to the cities in search of work. It is estimated that at least three million peasants died as a result of the push for collectivization of agriculture. Stalin was forced to abandon the policy in 1931, but he claimed the fiasco as a huge success.

Stalin's First Five-Year Plan also met with "success," although there appears to be some truth to that claim, as the scarcity or absence of any consumer goods was balanced by the construction of steel and hydroelectric plants and by full employment and cheap food and housing. The floundering world of capi-talism made Stalin's centrally planned economy appear somewhat attractive.

Stalin would find it much more problematic to be "successful" with his fellow Communist Party members who recognized the true disaster of agricultural collectivization and questioned Stalin's intellectual abili-ties to be the Party's sole decision maker. Stalin responded to these real, perceived, and imagined threats by ruthlessly "cleansing" any and all real or potential opposition through a series of purges between 1935 and 1938. By 1939, all opposition to Stalin had been silenced as more than three million Soviets were dead and more than eight million others were in labor camps. Stalin seemed to have demonstrated to the world that communism was a viable social and political system, with a few significant flaws.

The Fascist Alternative
(Themes: Political Culture and Political Identity)

Fascism developed as a reaction to both communism and liberal democracy. Taking its name from a bundle of rods strapped around an axe, a symbol of authority in ancient Rome known as **fasces,** fascist parties developed across the world in the 1920s and 1930s; only in Italy and Germany did these parties become powerful enough to overthrow existing parliamentary systems.

Fascism was especially appealing to the middle classes who felt threatened by the communist class conflicts, to those citizens who felt abandoned by their government's unfulfilled promises during the Great War, and to citizens radicalized by economic and social crises of the 1920s and 1930s. Fascists are experts at dedicating themselves to perceived "lost traditions," at promoting the veneration of the state, at "worshipping" a strong leader, and at emphasizing ultranationalism, ethnocentrism, and militarism. The state, not the individual, was the fascists' focus and indeed the individual must always be subordinate to the needs and service of the state.

Italian Fascism
(Themes: Political Culture and Political Identity)

Widespread disillusionment with ineffective government and political leadership, extensive economic turmoil, social discontent, anger at Italy's "mistreatment" at the Versailles Peace Conference, and a growing fear of socialism made Italy ripe for fascism in the years after World War I. Coupled with an arrogant, outspoken, virulent nationalist like Benito Mussolini as its leader, Italian fascism gained wide support after 1920. Mussolini understood the effectiveness of violence to squash opposition and he used the "**Black shirts**" to quell any dissent, or "chaos" as he termed the opposition. In 1922, the mere presence of the fascist black-shirted troops in Rome convinced the Italian king to make Mussolini the prime minister of Italy and to allow him to form a new government, In 1922, Mussolini inaugurated a fascist regime in Italy. Taking the title **Il Duce**, Mussolini moved quickly to eliminate all other political parties, to limit the freedom of the press, to outlaw free speech, and to curb free association. Aligning himself with business interests, Mussolini crushed labor unions and outlawed strikes; he then envisioned an organizing scheme for business which he called "**corporatism**" in which the different interests in society came together under state control. In reality, the **National Council of Corporations** was more a propaganda front than a functioning entity designed to resolve labor and business disputes.

Mussolini's interactions with Hitler began to color Italian fascism after 1936; racism and anti-Semitism became much more emphasized as part of Italian fascism and Mussolini began to speak of a **Rome-Berlin Axis** of world power in 1938, and by 1939, the two men had signed the ten-year **Pact of Steel** to illustrate the strong ties between these two fascist nations.

German National Socialism
(Themes: Political Culture and Political Identity)

The **Nationalist Socialist Party (Nazi)** made its first major public appearance in 1923 when party members, including **Adolph Hitler,** attempted to overthrow the government of the **Weimar Republic** which had been established after 1919. Hitler and his followers were imprisoned for a year, where he had ample time to write and reflect on his tactics once he was released. When freed in 1924, Hitler adopted a "**path of legality**" approach which they effectively used to gain political power and then discarded so that others might not follow their success.

Hitler attracted people who felt alienated from society and frightened by world events and the future. He capitalized on those fears as well as residual anger from the settlement of World War I and found a ready audience among disillusioned Germans, particularly members of the lower middle classes who had lost faith in a democratic system. Further, Hitler masterfully used trumped-up racial doctrines based on "science" to offer excuses and scapegoats for Germany's ills. By 1932, Hitler was selected as Chancellor of Germany who promised a **German Reich** and who delivered on that promise.

Under the cover of a national emergency, Hitler and his Nazi party used all available means to destroy the Weimar Republic and establish a one-party democracy. They outlawed all civil and constitutional rights, suppressed, terrorized, and eventually outlawed all competing political parties and factions, purged the judicial and civil service of any non-Nazis, and firmly established a highly centralized state leaving little local or regional autonomy. Once firmly in power, it was relatively simple to translate their racist ideology into effective practice.

The Nazis effectively touted the science of eugenics to improve the quantity and quality of the "German race." They launched a campaign to increase the births of "racially valuable" children through tax credits, special child allowances, marriage loans, and laws allowing for divorce only on the grounds of sterility; they successfully relegated women to the sole role of wife and mother. Access to information regarding family planning, birth-control devices, and abortions became almost impossible to find. Further, the Nazis instituted a pronatalist propaganda campaign almost as a "cult of motherhood" which included medals for particularly prolific child-producing women.

However, not all people in Germany were encouraged to have children. Indeed there was a parallel campaign to prevent births from people who had been identified as having "hereditarily determined" illnesses, and soon people who were seen as "racial aliens" were added to that effort. Nazi eugenic measures included sterilization, abortion, and soon state-sponsored euthanasia in the mania clothed as "racial health."

Anti-Semitism became the hallmark of Nazi rule. Although theoretically based on nineteenth-century biological race theories, the Nazis skillfully built on deeper underlying religious hatreds to identify who was a Jew. The 1935 Nuremberg Laws deprived Germans of Jewish ancestry of their civil and citizenship rights, which then gave the Nazis unlimited power to deal with the Jews as they wished. The stated official goal was Jewish emigration and the numbers of German Jews seeking to emigrate increased dramatically after ***Kristallnacht***, the "night of broken glass" in November 1938, a clear signal that conditions for Jews in Germany were going to quickly deteriorate.

Finished reading the chapter? Be sure you can . . .

- Discuss the continuities and changes in Germany during the era between wars.
- Describe and analyze the new patterns of nationalism including fascism, racism, and genocide.
- Explain the cultural and political transformations during this era.
- Describe the internationalization of popular culture arising in this era.

Chapter Multiple Choice Questions

1. The term "lost generation" was originally coined to apply to
   a. twentieth-century painters, sculptors, and musicians.
   b. students and followers of Sigmund Freud.
   c. the young people who died in the 1918 flu pandemic.
   d. American intellectuals and literati who gathered in Paris in the postwar years.
   e. Bauhaus designers who valued the cold, impersonal style of the era.

2. Painting in the postwar era was characterized by
   a. attention to detail and realism.
   b. strong anti-war statements through symbolism.
   c. a dislike of realism and a preference for abstraction.
   d. the desire to reflect photographic styles and images.
   e. distrust of non-European cultures and traditions.

3. Sigmund Freud is associated with which theory?
   a. psychoanalysis
   b. Bauhaus
   c. Les Fauves
   d. the uncertainty principle
   e. special relativity

4. Why did Germany and Japan suffer most extensively during the Great Depression?
   a. Both nations relied heavily on the export of manufactured goods to pay for imported fuel and food.
   b. Both were under fascist rule which made it very difficult for the common person to survive.
   c. Neither nation had fully recovered from the physical destruction left from World War I.
   d. Neither peoples were used to living under difficult economic conditions and had few personal resources to draw upon.
   e. Their colonies were unable to supply them with the raw materials to run their factories and so their manufacturing capacity fell.

5. The 1930s themes of official heartlessness and rising political anger are BEST portrayed in which novel?
   a. *All Quiet on the Western Front*
   b. *For Whom the Bell Tolls*
   c. *Origin of the Species*
   d. *The General Theory of Employment, Interest, and Money*
   e. *The Grapes of Wrath*

6. Veneration of the state, devotion to a leader, ultranationalism, ethnocentrism, and militarism are all characteristics of what ideology?
   a. capitalism
   b. fascism
   c. communism
   d. socialism
   e. federalism

7. What event is associated with Stalin's attempt to "cleanse" the Bolshevik party?
   a. National Economic Plan
   b. First Five-Year Plan
   c. the Great Purge
   d. War Communism
   e. Gosplan

8. Italian fascism was different than German fascism in that the Italians
   a. continued to allow differing political parties in their government.
   b. did not rely on secret police or armed enforcers to carry out government mandates.
   c. did not make racism or anti-Semitism a cornerstone of their philosophy.
   d. supported the workers and workers' unions in their government.
   e. appealed mostly to middle-class people who feared communism.

9. The concept of "path of legality" is associated with fascism in
   a. Germany.
   b. Italy.
   c. Japan.
   d. Brazil.
   e. Spain.

10. In which of the following nations did women achieve greater economic success during the 1930s?
    a. Germany
    b. Italy
    c. United States
    d. Russia
    e. Japan

Comprehensive Multiple Choice Questions

1. Which of the following painters was most influenced by African art forms and became the leading proponent of cubism?
   a. Paul Gauguin
   b. Edgar Degas
   c. Claude Monet
   d. Pablo Picasso
   e. Otto Dix

2. Why did Germany manage to rebuild faster than France or Russia after World War I?
   a. No major military engagements had taken place on German soil, so Germany had not suffered the physical destruction of its natural resources, infrastructure, or production capacity as had France and Russia.
   b. Germany benefited from extensive U.S. financial support as part of the Marshall Plan while France and Russia were excluded from the program.
   c. The Nazi Party was incredibly efficient in construction projects as it relied on slave labor rather than wageworkers as France and Russia did.
   d. Both France and Russia experienced internal revolt and revolution during the years of World War I which added to their nations' physical destruction.
   e. France and Russia had used reconstruction funds to rebuild historic sites first, while the Germans had concentrated on rebuilding their economic base.

3. Which of the following nations did NOT have a strong fascist movement during the 1930s?
   a. Argentina
   b. Brazil
   c. Japan
   d. South Africa
   e. Mexico

Primary Source Questions

1. **Examine Otto Dix's painting of the *Seven Deadly Sins* on page 976 of your textbook.**
   a. How might this painting be considered revolutionary?
   b. In what ways is this painting an allegory for the political situation in 1933 Germany?

2. **Read *Sources from the Past: Mein Kampf* on page 998 of your textbook.**
   a. How does Hitler use "science" to justify his racism?
   b. How does Hitler use "history" to justify his claims?

Chapter Multiple Choice Answers

1. **d:** Gertrude Stein coined this term for those disillusioned and disenchanted young American men and women who expressed their dissatisfaction through poetry and fiction as they congregated in Paris in the postwar years. (p. 979)

2. **c:** World War I and its aftermath ushered in a new aesthetic which sought not to mirror reality but to create it, often through pure color and shape. (pp. 979, 982–983)

3. **a:** Freud's theory of psychoanalysis sought to explain human behavior as a manifestation of repressed consciousness. (p. 982)

4. **a:** The manufacturing economies of both Germany and Japan shriveled as they could find no markets for their manufactured goods which they needed to sell in order to import food and fuel. (p. 986)

5. **e:** Steinbeck's story of the Joad family, displaced from their farm by the Oklahoma Dust Bowl and heartless bankers, captures the challenges and struggles faced by many hard-working families during the Great Depression. (p. 988)

6. **b:** Fascism consistently invokes the primacy of the state, is chauvinistic, xenophobic, and extremely ethnocentric. (pp. 994–995)

7. **c:** Stalin turned the Congress of Victors into the Congress of Victims as he identified and then extinguished any real or perceived opposition through the Great Purges of 1935–1938. (p. 994)

8. **c:** It was not until the Italian-German alliance that anti-Semitism became part of Italian fascism. Hitler's influence was immediately apparent in the Italian anti-Semitic laws issued after 1938. (p. 996)

9. **a:** After his year in jail for a failed rebellion, Hitler used the new tactic, "path of legality," to gain power legally through the ballot box and then to dismantle the very path they had used and close it to others. (p. 996)

10. **d:** In Germany, Italy, Japan, and the United States, women were legislatively restricted from employment; in Russia, women were allowed and even required to work. (pp. 986–987, 993–994)

Comprehensive Multiple Choice Answers

1. **d:** Picasso, like many others of his age, was disillusioned with painting reality and increasingly interested in the boldness and power of indigenous art; his special interest in African art forms was reflected in his cubist works. (p. 983)

2. **a:** Though Germany had lost World War I, most of the major fighting and physical destruction in that conflict had taken place in France, Belgium, and Russia. (p. 986)

3. **e:** Though there were fascist movements in many nations, in Latin America, Brazil and Argentina had the most active fascist groups. In Mexico, the communist groups were much more popular. (p. 994)

Primary Source Answers

1. In some ways, this painting is reminiscent of the mid-fifteenth century works of Hieronymus Bosch who painted a work of the same title. Artist Dix would have been familiar with Bosch's work which was likewise painted at a time of great upheaval, during the later years of the European Renaissance

and foreshadowing the great religious upheaval of the upcoming Reformation. Both artists chose to illustrate the conditions of their world through the images of human sins: Anger, Avarice, Envy, Gluttony, Lust, Pride, and Sloth. Bosch painted his sins within the ever-watchful eye of God but God does not appear in Dix's twentieth-century work. Dix is certainly revolutionary when he places the figure of Sloth in the center of the work and its arms and legs are poised like a loose swastika, as if to say that the lack of caring or effort on the part of the German people allowed this sin to come to prominence. Dix clearly recognizes the power of Sloth and even has it holding a scythe, the easily understandable sign of death. Avarice, or greed, is represented as an old woman clutching at money on the ground, Anger is shown as the horned demon behind Sloth, Pride is the enormous head behind the scythe who has an anus for a mouth, Gluttony is the figure with a cooking-pot head, and Lust dances in a lewd way behind Sloth. The figure of Envy is represented by the child face of Hitler, although you should know the mustache was not added to the painting until after the war. The selection of Envy as represented by Hitler clearly demonstrates the artist's understanding of Hitler's personal motives and the motives behind his Nazi supporters. (p. 976)

2. Though not particularly eloquent, Hitler does understand the popular appeal of science and history as justification for his racist arguments. By couching his rationale in those acceptable disciplines, his arguments for racial purity have additional validity, despite the faulty science and distorted history he cites. His discussion of "intrinsic segregation," the "will of nature," and "great civilizations of the past" are clever covers for his unsophisticated readers and those phrases build a gradual base for his real purpose, which is to identify the Jews as a readily explainable evil and as an easily resolvable problem within German society. (p. 998)

CHAPTER 36

NATIONALISM AND POLITICAL IDENTITIES IN ASIA, AFRICA, AND LATIN AMERICA

Before you get started: Although the Great War was planned and led by Europe, its political and economic effects rippled through the global community. Most regions of the globe were affected by the Great Depression as well but all regions that were dominated by Europeans questioned imperialism. While Japan continued to follow expansionist policies, China and India struggled over divisions within their societies that could hinder independence from European control. The Latin American countries sought ways to become less dependent as Africans began to lay the groundwork for decolonization—a key concept in modern history. It would be good to make a chart that shows the process of decolonization from its roots, through the failures and successes and the consequences to both colonies and European nations.

ASIAN PATHS TO AUTONOMY

As mentioned in Chapter 34, the concept of self-determination was a powerful motivator for Asian peoples looking to escape imperialism. They also looked to nationalism and socialism as possible ways to redefine their political and economic roles. Ironically, like Japan, they planned to build nations based on European concepts. Each nation went through a period of disorder as they moved towards independence and unity.

India's Quest for Home Rule
(Theme: Political Development)

The advent of a national rail system combined with an elite class of educated Indians tied the vast subcontinent together with British administrators serving only as policymakers. Indians were educated in a classical European curriculum that exposed them to the Enlightenment ideals of equality, democracy, and individual rights. As a result, a nationalist movement developed. The first and most important organization was the **Indian National Congress** founded in 1885. It stressed collaboration with the British as a way to self-rule and was supported by many prominent Hindus and Muslims. However, the strain between the two dominant religions was demonstrated in 1906 when the **Muslim League** was formed. Muslims had become concerned that the Indian National Congress would replace the British with Hindu leadership.

During the war, partisans had set aside their organizations in order to support Britain's war effort, but, as the war ended, the discontent returned and it was more pronounced. British attempts to quell the protests were harsh, repressive, and ineffective. However, now the independence movement had a figure around whom it could mobilize: Mohandas Kramchand **Gandhi** (1869–1948). Gandhi was a devout Hindu of the merchant middle class who had trained as a lawyer in London, practiced law in South Africa, and returned to India in 1915 with experience in organizing against the social inequalities of Indians in South Africa. During this period, he had refined his philosophy of tolerance and nonviolence and devised a strategy of **passive resistance** to authority. While working with the Indian National Congress, he transformed it into a representative institution of all castes. With his message of equality, he fought particularly hard for the Untouchables. His simple message and personal charisma appealed to the Indian population, and he became revered to many as Mahatma ("Great Soul").

Gandhi and the Indian National Congress organized two mass movements against the British. The first, the Non-Cooperation Movement of 1920–1922, called for the boycott of British goods and a return to homespun cotton clothing. The second, the Civil Disobedience Movement of 1930, pushed even harder for resistance against British authority with a protest against the government's monopoly on salt as the initial event. The Salt March proved the efficacy of civil disobedience. Yet, despite Gandhi's admonition against violence, both British authorities and protesters often resorted to it. However, years of resistance did prove effective when the British passed the Government of India Act that established autonomous legislatures in the provinces, a bicameral national assembly, and an executive under the control of the British. Sadly, it proved unworkable because India's six hundred princes refused to cooperate and Muslims believed it to be an instrument of Hindu nationalism.

It was not surprising that Muslims were concerned because the Great Depression had greatly affected India's economy, particularly in the agricultural sector where Muslims were prominent. As tenant farmers to Hindu landlords, Muslims felt that their economic ills were tied to a Hindu elite that were less effected by economic distress. Support for the Muslim League grew as its head, **Ali Jinnah** (1876–1948), proposed a **two-state solution** to independence where Muslims would be granted their own state.

China's Search for Order
(Theme: Political Development)

The 1911 revolution had thrown out the Qing dynasty before there was a dominant faction to take control. Although **Sun Yatsen** (1866–1925) became the president of a Chinese republic, China sank into political chaos. As common in Chinese history, warlords with private armies soon took control of different regions and vied for national prominence. A few national systems such as the post office were controlled by the national government, but the warlords neglected the infrastructure in favor of a return to the opium trade and corruption. Thus, economic disintegration followed political problems. In addition to internal problems, the national government did not manage its foreign affairs well. It was never able to rid itself of the unequal treaties of the late Qing period.

Nationalist sentiment developed quickly after the war as the Chinese looked to the United States and Europe to grant complete autonomy. However, instead of eliminating the unequal treaties, the peace deliberations gave legitimacy to Japanese seizures during the war. In the May Fourth Movement, the Chinese people made mass protests against the presence of the Japanese to no avail. Some Chinese turned to Marxism and the Soviet Union as an answer to nationalism. Lenin's anti-imperialist rhetoric galvanized some young Chinese like **Mao Zedong** (1893–1976) to form the **Chinese Communist Party (CCP)** in 1921. Mao, a former teacher and librarian, agreed with the radical communist platform that included women's equality and complete social revolution with a dictatorship of the proletariat.

Earlier, Sun Yatsen had attempted to bring the country under the leadership of one party, his **Guomindang** or Nationalist People's Party. At first the communists joined the party and made up one-third of the membership but when the leadership of the party went to **Jiang Jieshe** (Chiang Kai-shek, 1887–1975) after Sun Yatsen's death, the communists were purged from the party in a series of bloody murders. Meanwhile Jiang Jieshe had embarked on a military campaign to bring China under his control. Within one year, he occupied Beijing, set up a capital in Nanjing, and declared the Guomindang to be China's government. The communists retreated to the far southeast corner of China.

China had many political and social challenges, but it managed to avoid the Great Depression as its economy was not closely linked to the industrialized global economy. However, the nationalist government faced three significant challenges in the 1930s. They only controlled part of China, leaving the threat of communists, the remaining warlords, and the Japanese presence in the north. Jiang Jieshi placed a priority on eliminating the communists. Under military pressure from the Guomindang, the CCP made a 6000-mile journey fleeing nationalist forces to northwestern China. In that episode, called the **Long March**, thousands died, and Mao Zedong solidified his role as the leader of the CCP. In Shaanxi province, he devised his own type of Marxist-Leninist philosophy which was uniquely suited to China's configuration. It based a successful social revolution on the peasantry rather than a nonexistent Chinese proletariat.

Imperial and Imperialist Japan
(Theme: Political Development)

Japan's industrialized economy was affected by the Great Depression as it experienced a series of recessions after World War I. In the 1920s, economic unrest fueled political and social demands that liberals attempted to meet with industrial reforms, increased suffrage, and social welfare. After the expansion of the franchise to all males in 1925, conservatives blocked further legislation and espoused either extreme xenophobia or one-party rule. A campaign of political assassinations intimidated their opponents.

Japan had gained status in the First World War and had been treated as one of the "big five" powers in the League of Nations. It also entered into international agreements throughout the 1920s that limited military and naval actions. Nevertheless, Chinese unification under the Guomindang threatened Japan's economic and political interests. China at that time was a tempting target in its weakened state so militarists called upon Japan's martial traditions and distaste for international cooperation to launch an attack on Manchuria. In 1931, the Japanese army blew up a small portion of their Manchurian railroad and blamed it on the Chinese. They used this "**Mukden incident**" as an excuse to attack the Chinese. Despite disapproval from its civilian government, the Japanese forces took control of Manchuria and made it a puppet state. In response to the Japanese invasion, Jiang Jieshi appealed to the League of Nations but they were helpless to do anything more than request withdrawal. The Japanese response to that was to withdraw from the League of Nations. Thus, a pattern of **appeasement** of expansionist nations was born that continued through the 1930s.

AFRICA UNDER COLONIAL DOMINATION

The Great War and the Great Depression made the quest for independence in Africa more difficult. European nations drafted soldiers from Africa to serve in the war and some areas of Africa were battle sites as well. Africans responded with loyalty and resistance, but the resistance was quickly quashed. After the war, African colonies grew more dependent on European economic control so when depression hit, Africa was profoundly affected as well. The tight economic bonds prompted more calls for African independence and led to the rise of nationalist movements.

Africa and The Great War
(Theme: War and Political Development)

Every African colony, except the neutral Spanish-held ones, took part in the Great War. Even the two independent nations of Liberia and Ethiopia aligned themselves: Liberia entered the war with its traditional ties to the United States in 1917 while Ethiopia had originally threw its hat in with Muslim Turkey but realigned with the Allies after a coup. Early in the war, the Allies began to invade Germany's colonies in central and east Africa. While Britain merely wanted to keep German ports out of the war, France intended to take back what it had lost to Germany before the war. Amazingly, fifteen thousand German troops managed to hold off sixty thousand Allied troops for most of the war by using guerilla tactics.

Over a million African troops participated in military campaigns where they saw whites killing whites and were themselves encouraged to kill enemy whites. It was a surprising reversal of what they experienced under colonial control. Even more African men served as support forces for the war effort. Africans were recruited in various ways including volunteerism, impressment, and conscription. There was a uniquely colonial mechanism of recruitment where African leaders were given a quota and they could recruit any way they wished. Eventually, the British and French conscripted all men between certain ages. Ultimately, more than 150,000 Africans were killed, and more were disabled.

As the war continued, more Europeans had to leave the colonies to fight so Africans took advantage of that situation to protest imperialism. The resistance was also complicated by religion, with pan-Islam's stand against the war and a cult in Kenya vowing to kill all Christians. The major resentment that fostered revolt came with compulsory conscription and impressment. All were put down by European authorities but it involved the shifting of valuable military resources.

The Colonial Economy
(Theme: Economic Development)

European nations had two goals for African economies after the war: the export of raw materials and making the colonized pay for their own maintenance. Self-sufficient African economies were erased as European pressure increased in the decades after the war. When the Great Depression occurred, the **dependent colonial economies** suffered severe reversals as commodity prices and trade fell more than 50 percent.

To manage the colonies, Europe had invested in infrastructure in the first decades of the twentieth century. Numerous telegraph wires, port facilities, roads, and railroads had been built with African labor and taxes to primarily benefit Europeans. High taxes had meant that most Africans had to become cash crop farmers or wage laborers on plantations so the indigenous economy virtually disappeared. Cash crops such as cocoa, cotton, peanuts, rubber, and palm oil became the primary crops. In settler societies such as Kenya, Rhodesia, and South Africa, white farmers used indigenous labor to grow export crops. They controlled most of the cropland, as much as 88 percent in South Africa, and so kept the Africans economically marginalized.

Mining became an important sector of colonial economies as European managers hired rural labor and paid minimal wages. This set up a system of labor migration within countries that had the effect of impoverishing the rural areas as the women left behind struggled to feed their families. Outright forced labor and barely disguised slavery existed as well. Colonial administrations gave responsibility to concessionary companies who were allowed to procure labor any way they desired. Railroads were often built this way and the human toll was disastrous as thousands of African workers died of starvation, disease, and maltreatment.

African Nationalism
(Theme: Political Development)

As the war ended, contributions of African troops in combination with ideas of self-determination led Africans to believe that they might be given greater political and social responsibilities. However, African hopes of autonomy were dashed as the colonial system was reinvigorated instead. Ideas of African nationalism persisted with the development of a European-educated urban elite class. They consisted of high-ranking bureaucrats and professionals who spoke and understood the language of the colonizer. **Jomo Kenyatta** (1895–1978), the future president of Kenya, embodied these traits. He spent fifteen years in Europe attending universities as prestigious as the London School of Economics. Those who had not gone abroad were familiar with European ways through study in primary and secondary schools that used European philosophies. The new elite used European languages and adopted European dress but still managed to forge new ideas of African identity.

The new elite saw the European concept of nationhood as a way to forge bonds between disparate African groups. African nationalists had many different concepts about **African nationalism.** Some looked to the precolonial past for inspiration and institutions. Others looked to the concept of the African race as a unifying factor. Interestingly, this idea caught on in the United States and Caribbean as leaders such as Marcus Garvey (1887–1940) preached black pride and a return to Africa. Other nationalists rejected race and looked to geography based on the existing colonial borders. While the ideas percolated, it would take another world war to bring them into fruition.

LATIN AMERICAN STRUGGLES WITH NEOCOLONIALISM

Although most South American nations had shed European colonialism in the nineteenth century, they were still tied economically to dominant colonial interests. Colonial powers also interfered in military and political matters. The biggest change was that Latin American nations were less dependent on former colonial rulers like Spain and Portugal. During the neocolonial period, Britain and the United States moved to the forefront of domination.

The Impact of the Great War and the Great Depression
(Theme: Political Development)

After the Russian revolution and with the ongoing Mexican revolution, disenchanted intellectuals in Latin America began to consider Leninism and Marxism as a solution to the problems of dependent economies and impoverishment in worker classes and among indigenous peoples. The Enlightenment principles that had driven their revolutions had lost credibility in societies where corruption and inequality were so rampant. While nothing was done in this direction, socialist alternatives continued to be viable.

As the United States became the most powerful country in the world after the Great War and Latin Americans felt the direct effect of its power, capitalism came under attack in South America. The first to protest were university students who began to demand reforms. Indeed, South American universities became the breeding ground for future revolutionaries like Fidel Castro (1926–) of Cuba. Radicalism spread into political parties as they embraced anti-imperialist policies as well as Marxism. Peru's Jose Carlos Mariategui of Peru pushed Marxist reforms for the alleviation of the conditions for the poor and indigenous peoples. Peru became a hotbed of revolutionary fervor offering another political party with non-Marxist reforms (the *Alianza Popular Revolucionaria Americana* or APRA). The ruling elite were able to contain the radical reformers but the ideas remained persistently popular.

The ideological yearnings of Latin America were represented in the murals of **Diego Riviera** (1886–1957), a popular Mexican painter. He celebrated indigenous art and pre-Columbian motifs along with socialist ideology in enormous controversial canvasses that he executed for the public. When commissioned to paint murals in the United States, he incorporated all the symbols of American imperialism and oppression to the dismay of the American public.

The Evolution of Economic Imperialism
(Themes: Economy and Trade)

While the United States and Great Britain played a large part in the Latin American economy for decades, the United States now attempted to control all aspects rather than simply the export market. After the Great War, U.S. investments in Latin America more than doubled, primarily by takeovers of mining and oil interests in Chile and Venezuela. The actual beginning to the new relationship occurred before the war and was based on President William Taft's "**dollar diplomacy**" where he encouraged economic investment rather than military intervention.

The Great Depression brought economic growth to a halt as Latin America was completely tied to the foreign trade. Prices of exports in multiple countries dropped precipitously so unemployment rose alarmingly as well. On the plus side, Latin American countries began to support domestic manufacturing as they placed increased tariffs on foreign goods. In Brazil, the dictator president **Getulio Dornelles Vargas** (1830–1945, 1950–1954) pushed industrialization with the support of the military and enacted social welfare reforms for workers.

Conflicts with a "Good Neighbor"
(Themes: Trade and Diplomacy)

In the 1930s the United States decided to increase their economic pressure on Latin America and forgo costly military interventions. In a series of "sweetheart treaties," it guaranteed economic control with a commitment to train domestic police forces. Known as the "**Good Neighbor Policy**," it ensured that the National Guard forces would protect American interests in the nation. The policy did not always work out as it was intended. A case in point was **Nicaragua** where U.S. businesses had long controlled bananas and transportation. An outbreak of civil war in the late twenties led to the intervention of the U.S. Marines as they had in the past. The leader of the rebels was Augusto Cesar Sandino who refused to accept any peace settlement that kept the Marines in the country. The Marines trained a national guard so they could withdraw and the U.S. government supervised an election that brought a new president to power. However, the head of the national guard, Anastacio Somoza Garcia (1896–1956), had Sandino assassinated and took control of the country himself. He remained a loyal friend of the United States while he accumulated the largest fortune in Nicaraguan history and established a political dynasty.

The Good Neighbor Policy did change the U.S. relationship with South America as it led Franklin Roosevelt to rescind the earlier Theodore Roosevelt corollary which had promoted military intervention. The new U.S. approach was tested when Mexican president Lazaro Cardenas (1895–1970) nationalized the Mexican oil industry in 1938. Roosevelt and his administration resisted the calls of big business for military action and negotiated an agreement for the companies to accept a payment in compensation.

It was not just righteousness that drove the agreement because the United States had economic interests in Latin America that they wished to pursue during a time of increasing foreign concerns. It needed to distance itself from European imperialism as global war appeared imminent.

Mexican labor migration into the United States had increased enormously during the period after the first war. Despite calls to restrain cheap labor during the Depression, agribusiness leaders insisted on few border restrictions. In an attempt to repair the bad image of Latin America, even Hollywood came to the fore with support for Brazilian dancing and singing star, Carmen Miranda. In a series of films, she softened stereotypes with amazing headdresses featuring bananas. To soften its own image, the United Fruit Company appropriated her costume to sell fruit with the invention of "Chiquita Banana," a singing cartoon character.

Finished reading the chapter? Be sure you can . . .

- Compare and analyze the differences between the Indian National Congress and the Muslim League.
- Explain the degree to which Marxism became a viable alternative in China and Latin America.
- Compare the impact of the Great Depression in India, China, Japan, Africa, and Latin America.
- Explain the impact of the Great War on Africa.
- Compare postwar economic development in Latin America and Africa.
- Compare Japanese and Chinese nationalism in the 1920s and 1930s.

Chapter Multiple Choice Questions

1. Why did Indian Muslims believe that the Indian National Congress could not meet their needs?
   a. The animosity between Hindus and Muslims had been serious and consistently violent over the last two centuries.
   b. The Muslims generally held a more impoverished position than Hindus so they felt they would never have an equal role.
   c. Muslims believed British concerns that a combined Hindu-Muslim state was not viable.
   e. Hindu caste leaders had made it very clear that they would keep Muslims at the bottom of the caste system after independence.
   e. The Indian National Congress had never allowed Muslims to be in leadership positions despite pleas by prominent businessmen.

2. What influences prompted Gandhi to devise his system of nonviolent protest?
   a. his caste position, his education in England, and a deep-seated pragmatism
   b. British education and experience in segregated South Africa
   c. experience with British bureaucrats and deep-seated pragmatism
   d. British education, South African experience, and mysticism
   e. British education that supported Enlightenment ideals and deep-seated belief in Hinduism

3. At the end of the Qing, what historical pattern did the Chinese fall into?
   a. the rise of a new dynasty
   b. a return to Confucianism
   c. criticism of foreign influences
   d. a period of civil unrest
   e. a division between two separate political entities.

4. After the death of Sun Yatsen, how did the Guomindang treat its communist membership?
   a. It allowed them to remain as silent partners.
   b. It violently purged them from its ranks.
   c. It urged them to form a new political party.
   d. It kept them in to appease its Soviet supporters.
   e. It banished them to southeast China.

5. What three challenges faced the Guomindang in the 1930s?
   a. warlords, Japanese occupation, and European control
   b. the Great Depression, leadership rivalries, and the communists
   c. new political parties, Japanese occupation, and the depression
   d. Japanese occupation, the communists, and warlords
   e. peasant rebellions, warlords, and the communists

6. Who had the most influence over the Japanese government by the mid 1930s?
   a. militant conservatives
   b. liberal legislators
   c. restive shoguns
   d. the imperial household
   e. moderate critics

7. What part of the Great War most changed African thinking toward European colonial powers?
   a. violence in the trenches
   b. forced conscription
   c. poor treatment in the military
   d. fighting in Africa itself
   e. exposure to racist attitudes

8. Which European economic practice most affected the ability of Africans to run their own economies?
   a. forced labor
   b. restrictions on crop choice
   c. divisions among labor force
   d. heavy taxation
   e. white control of cropland

9. Where did reformers learn of radical alternatives to the dependent economies that kept most people impoverished?
   a. Soviet advisors
   b. guerilla fighters
   c. Mexican revolution
   d. universities
   e. capital cities

10. What is the most important reason that the United States moved from a policy of deep involvement to one of being the good neighbor in the 1930s?
   a. It could no longer sustain economic ties during the Great Depression.
   b. It was concerned about the unchallenged rise of Marxism.
   c. It realized that it could no longer sustain costly military incursions.
   d. It wanted to improve its image in the region.
   e. It had given up attempting to control foreign markets and politics.

Comprehensive Multiple Choice Questions

1. When comparing China with Latin America in the 1920s and 1930s, to what extent was Marxism a viable policy?
   a. In Latin America, there were merely discussions in university settings while in China, Marxists vied for control of government.
   b. Both Latin American and Chinese reformers were able to build political parties around Marxist principles.
   c. The Chinese government persecuted Marxists while Latin American Marxists were ignored by their governments.
   d. Neither the Chinese nor Latin American public believed that Marxism offered any improvements for them.
   e. Latin American reformers considered other options more seriously while Chinese reformers backed the Chinese Communist Party.

2. Of the following regions, which one was least affected by the Great Depression and why?
   a. the Middle East because it had oil deposits
   b. Latin America because it had oil deposits
   c. Southern Africa because its economy was so remote
   d. the mainland of East Asia because it was largely agrarian
   e. South Asia because it was largely agrarian

3. Of the following global periods, which one most closely resembles the era after the Great War?
   a. the period after Mongolian expansion
   b. the period at the height of Japanese feudalism
   c. the period after the height of the Roman Empire
   d. the period following the Seven Years War
   e. the period of European exploration

Primary Source Questions

1. **Read *Sources from the Past: Self-Rule Is My Birthright*, Bal Gangadhar Tilak, 1907, on page 1009 of your textbook.**
   a. What is the point of view?
   b. How do the historical references fit into his argument?
   c. What does he propose as the solutions to British rule?

2. **Examine the painting *Imperialism,* Diego Rivera, 1933, on page 1022 of your textbook.**
   a. What is the point of view?
   b. How do the style elements support his view?
   c. What are the predominant motifs and what do they represent?

Chapter Multiple Choice Answers

1. **b:** Muslims traditionally worked as tenant farmers to Hindu landlords so they felt they needed their own advocate. (p. 1008)

2. **d:** Gandhi had unique experiences with British education, South African segregation, and a mystic's adoption of simple living that blended into his philosophies. (p. 1007)

3. **d:** China's dynastic cycle usually involves a period of warlordism between dynasties. (p. 1010)

4. **b:** While initially welcome, Jiang Jieshie turned against them in a series of violent attacks. (p. 1011)

5. **d:** Jiang Jieshie and the Guomindang faced the CCP in the southeast, the Japanese in the north, and warlords in other regions of China. (p. 1012)

6. **a:** Liberal reforms ended after 1925 as militant reformers hardened Japanese policy through legislation and assassination. (p. 1013)

7. **b:** Africans resented forced enlistment above all. (p. 1016)

8. **d:** While each of these answers works for some African colonies, the only one consistent to all is heavy taxation which forced people to plant cash crops or hire themselves out to others. (p. 1017)

9. **d:** Inspired by both the Mexican and Russian revolutions, university students embraced radical solutions like Marxism. (p. 1021)

10. **c:** While image was very important, the United States was concerned about its military in an era when international affairs were becoming more militaristic. (p. 1024)

Comprehensive Multiple Choice Answers

1. **b:** The CCP was formed in China while the APRA was formed in Peru. Neither government was pleased as the Peruvian ruling elite suppressed reform parties and the Guomindang murdered its communist rivals. The CCP was only one of several groups to vie for power in China and, for most of the period, it was a minor group. In both cases, an intellectual elite and peasants were more likely to support Marxist revolutionary movements. (pp. 1010, 1021)

2. **d:** China's agrarianism had a minimal connection to export industries so while India as a colony was a dependent economy, China largely evaded global depression. Having oil deposits did not matter at a time when the global economy was in severe depression. Also, both the Middle East and Latin America were largely dependent on Europe and the United States. Southern Africa was remote but two settler societies connected to world trade existed in this region, South Africa, and Rhodesia. Also, the rest of the region were European colonies attached to the global economy. (p. 1012)

3. **d:** After the Seven Years' War, colonial peoples began to take seriously the ideas of independence but it was also a period of renewed prosperity for the colonial powers. Britain had not yet gained its extraordinary hegemony of the nineteenth century so there were several powers vying for global power as there was after the First World War (only the powers in the modern period included Japan and the

United States as well as Europe). The Mongolians clearly had rebellions but they had more control at their height than any other nation. They influenced trade but they did not control trade as much as they enabled it. The Romans treated their dominions more like colonies but they again were the dominant global power. European exploration began colonialism but did not engender independence movements. Feudalism of any kind had no resemblance to the period after the Great War. (pp. 620, 784)

Primary Source Answers

1. Bal Gangadhar Tilak was an Indian dissident who explained the problem as much as he proposed a solution. The tone is explanatory rather than rabble-rousing. And his references to earlier historical events indicate that he is well-educated. By using historical references to earlier invasions, he set up the dichotomy between savior and invader that the English used so well to convince India of the virtues of membership in the British empire. He did not propose out-and-out revolution but rather a process of attrition where boycotts and resistance would lead to Indian control of their country. (p. 1009)

2. Diego Rivera was an anti-imperialist with a strong message of revolution. He obviously condemned U.S. interference in Latin America. Strong diagonal lines of cannon barrels dominate the mural and contrast nicely with the rounded shapes of Latin Americans below them. The repetition of rounded elements in the United Fruit Company's bundles of bananas draws the eye to the lynched men as well. Rivera has repeated industrial and military elements hanging above the masses that only have their pleading hands and occasional guns to defend themselves against American imperialism. (p. 1022)

CHAPTER 37

NEW CONFLAGRATIONS: WORLD WAR II

Before you get started: Get ready; this is a major chapter. You are probably anxious to finish your textbook reading and to begin reviewing for the national exam, but do not be tempted to skip the reading and to simply rely on your United States history background. This chapter is about World War II (WWII) and its aftermath with a global context, not just a United States focus, so it contains a lot of specific information which may be new to you, though tied to familiar ideas. You can anticipate several specific multiple choice questions drawn from this chapter as well as at least one of the three essays likely building on information contained somewhere in these thirty pages. Consider carefully what you already know about World War II before you start to read; it will help you read faster, with fuller comprehension and greater retention.

ORIGINS OF WORLD WAR II

Although the official starting date for World War II is usually given as **September 1, 1939** when Germany invaded Poland, or even December 7, 1941 when Japan bombed Pearl Harbor, the origins of the war were already clear when Japan invaded **Manchuria** in 1931. Throughout the 1930s, the world was dividing into two camps: the **Axis Powers** of Germany, Italy, and Japan and the **Allied Powers** including Great Britain and the Commonwealth nations, Russia, France, China, the United States, and its Latin American allies.

Japan's War in China
(Themes: Patterns of Interaction and War)

The Japanese conquest of Manchuria in 1931–1932 was the first major step in Japan's process of aggression and expansionism. Militarist factions within Japan's government triumphed over civilian opposition to such aggression, and in 1933 Japan withdrew from the **League of Nations** and began to rapidly pursue its ultranationalist and pro-military policies; Japan began a full-scale invasion of China in 1937.

Japanese conquest and occupation of China was particularly brutal and shockingly foreshadowed the suffering in the World War to come. The 1937 **"Rape of Nanjing,"** in which more than four hundred thousand Chinese residents met death through unimaginable horrors, was perhaps the most gruesome example of brutality tied to an ethos of racial superiority the world had yet seen. Throughout China, the Chinese attempted to resist the much better-equipped, better-trained, and better-lead Japanese armies and, though not successful in defeating the superior Japanese forces, did manage to keep 750,000 Japanese troops tied down and out of other war fronts. The communist faction of the Chinese opposition was particularly effective against the superior Japanese forces as the Chinese used **guerilla tactics** of hit-and-run operations, sabotaged bridges and railroads, and harassed Japanese troops for nearly eight years. Though the communist Chinese faction never defeated the Japanese, they did win the support of the Chinese peasantry which would leave the communists poised to rule China once World War II was over.

Italian and German Aggression
(Themes: Patterns of Interaction and War)

Italy was still smarting from its perceived mistreatment during WWI. It had lost six hundred thousand soldiers and had not been granted expected compensation in colonial territory and reparations, nor received the respect it thought it deserved; further, Italy's postwar economy had never recovered sufficiently for the nation to function as an economic or military equal to other European powers. Mussolini promised to bring glory to Italy and to take the territorial spoils of war denied after the Great War. Italy took **Libya** and **Ethiopia** in 1935–1936, intervened in the **Spanish Civil War** (1936–1939), and annexed

Albania in 1939. The **conquest of Ethiopia** was unnecessarily brutal as 275,000 Ethiopians lost their lives to the Italians tanks, poison gas, and artillery; 2,000 Italian soldiers died in the conflict.

Germany's prewar aggression was ultimately the destroyer of the fragile peace. Hitler came to power in 1933, riding a public wave of resentment at Germany's treatment at the Versailles Peace Conference (1919): the steep reparations, harsh terms of occupation, and the humiliating "war guilt clause." Hitler's blatant disregard for the Versailles Treaty's demilitarization clause and his aggressive foreign policy helped to salve German war shame and depression trauma. After "test running" his troops and war machinery in the Spanish Civil War, Hitler was poised to begin the campaign of aggression which ultimately led to the outbreak of World War II in Europe.

Hitler justified German *Anschluss,* or "forced union," with Austria in 1938 as part of a natural rejoining of German peoples separated by artificial boundaries. Britain and France said little and did nothing in response. Hitler accurately took their silence as proof that they would not seek to stop German expansion and used it to further validate his contempt for democracies. Using the same rationale in 1938, Germany invaded the Sudetenland, a German-speaking region of Czechoslovakia; Britain and France actually tried to convince the Czechoslovakian government that this would be a limited expansion. At the **Munich Conference in September 1938,** the **policy of appeasement** was adopted as Britain and France continued to seek peace, even if it meant acquiescing to Germany's aggressive actions. **British Prime Minister Neville Chamberlain** returned home to joyous crowds waving a document which he ironically said guaranteed "**peace for our time.**"

That time was short, as appeasement was clearly not an effective strategy for blocking fascist aggression or in promoting peace. Germany took the rest of Czechoslovakia in spring 1939 and **Poland** in 1939. Appeasement clearly did not work. Hitler had help in dismantling Poland as he and Joseph Stalin crafted an uneasy pact, the "**Russian-German Treaty of Nonaggression,**" which bought each nation a brief respite against fighting each other, and gave Germany and Russia free hands to divide much of eastern Europe. Stalin had gained temporary accommodation from Hitler and Hitler had gained the green light to conquer Europe.

TOTAL WAR: THE WORLD UNDER FIRE

Even more than the Great War, World War II would involve nations on every continent, the engagement of whole societies within those nations, and the mobilization of all available material and human resources. Only eleven out of nearly two hundred countries in the world avoided direct involvement.

Blitzkrieg: Germany Conquers Europe
(Themes: Technology and War)

Traditionally, nations have made public declarations of war preceding the fighting; World War II would prove different. The Germans perfected a strategy known as *Blitzkrieg*, or "lightning war," in which their superior air force would soften resistance, their swift and highly mobile **Panzer,** or tank units, would roll in, and finally their well-equipped troops would march in to clean up any remaining resistance; they successfully demonstrated this highly effective strategy against the Poles in September 1939. The Germans were also highly successful in their use of **Unterseebootes**, or U-boats or submarines, in the battle of the Atlantic. The Germans relied on these U-boats traveling in "wolf packs" to attack convoys carrying vital imports to Britain while evading British warships and aircraft.

The rapid fall of Belgium, the Netherlands, and especially France in the face of Blitzkrieg tactics gave hope to Germany and to Italy who, now convinced of Germany's inevitable European victory, decided it was time to enter the war and reap the potential benefits of its German alliance. The romantic rescue of stranded Allied troops on the French beaches at **Dunkirk** did little to hide the bleak failure of the democracies against the Reich. The **Battle of Britain,** in which the German air force, the **Luftwaffe,** hoped to defeat Britain almost solely by air attack, resulted in more than forty thousand British civilian deaths before the **British Royal Air Force** could stave off defeat; this allied accomplishment forced Hitler to abandon his plans to invade Britain and refocus his attention eastward toward the **Balkans** and beyond.

The German Invasion of the Soviet Union
(Themes: Patterns of Interaction and War)

The Soviet Union had been a German target for a long time, despite the temporary ruse of the 1939 Nonaggression Pact. The German quest for *Lebensraum,* or "living space," drew Hitler to these lands in which Jews, Slavs, and Bolsheviks could be expelled or exterminated to make way for resettled Germans. The German invasion of the Soviet Union, code-named **Operation Barbarossa,** began in June 1941 and included supporting troops from Hungary, Finland, and Romania who augmented the massive German fighting force of men and equipment. Taking Stalin and his Red Army by surprise, the Germans had captured much of the Russian heartland and reached the gates of Moscow by December 1941. However, the vast Russian expanses reduced the effectiveness of Blitzkrieg tactics, and Stalin's earlier decision to move Russia's industrial heartland to the east coupled with Allied supplies, meant the Germans were not going to roll through Russia as Hitler had predicted. Though the Germans inflicted early heavy losses on the Red Army, Allied-equipped Russian soldiers, helped by an especially brutal Russian winter, were able to halt German advances by December of 1941. The Russians saw this conflict as the "**Great Patriotic War**" and the entire nation mobilized to resist the German army.

Battles in Asia and the Pacific
(Themes: Technology, Patterns of Interaction, and War)

Though the United States did not officially enter the war until December 1941, it had been financing British efforts through the cash-and-carry policy (1939) and the **Lend-Lease Act** (1941), which made American goods and weapons readily available to the Allies. Axis conquests in Europe in 1940 and early 1941 encouraged the Japanese to continue their Asian expansion into **French Indochina;** the United States responded to this occupation by instituting an oil embargo and by freezing Japanese assets in the United States. These actions did not halt Japanese aggression but rather fueled Japanese preparations for war against the United States and Great Britain.

That conflict began on **December 7, 1941** when the Japanese bombed the American Pacific fleet in hopes of destroying American naval capacity in the Pacific and clearing the way for Japanese conquest of all of southeast Asia and the creation of a defensive perimeter to protect the Japanese heartland. Except for the three U.S. aircraft carriers out of the harbor at the time, U.S. naval power in the Pacific was devastated. The United States declared war on Japan on December 8, 1941. Hitler and Mussolini declared war on the United States on December 11, which led the United States to respond by declaring war against Germany and Italy later that same day.

Japan enjoyed a series of rapid victories throughout the Pacific, with the **British surrender of Singapore** being the most humiliating to the British and ending any European myth of military invincibility. The Japanese wisely used anti-European imperialism appeal in the slogan, "**Asia for Asians,**" but conquest and brutal occupation soon made the reality of "**Asia for the Japanese**" all too apparent to the thousands of non-Japanese Asians who died under Japanese occupation.

Defeat of the Axis Powers
(Themes: Technology, Patterns of Interaction, and War)

The addition of personnel reserves and industrial capacity which accompanied Soviet and United States entry into the war were the keys to Allied victory in Asia and in Europe. The Battle of Stalingrad in February 1943 marked the first large-scale victory for Soviet troops. By 1944, the Soviets had pushed Germans back into Hungary, Romania, and Poland, and the German war machine in the east was broken. In the west, Great Britain and France attacked the Germans in north Africa and then through Italy, before launching the major allied offensive through northern France. The D Day offensive beginning on June 6, 1944 was deadly on all sides, but the Germans were overwhelmed. Facing horrific bombing of civilian centers like Dresden, and the unrelenting onslaught of fresh American troops, German resistance collapsed on all fronts and the Germans unconditionally surrendered on May 8, 1945.

The turning point in the Pacific came at the **Battle of Midway** in June 1942, as American aircraft carriers using information gleaned from the newly broken Japanese code sank three Japanese carriers in less than five minutes and a fourth later on the same day. The Allies took the offense and began a carefully crafted policy of "**island hopping**" which allowed the Allies to capture those islands from which they could launch direct air assaults on Japan. The fighting on the islands of Iwo Jima and Okinawa was especially brutal; the **kamikaze** strategy of Japanese pilots using their planes to dive-bomb Allied ships, and the fierce resistance of more than 110,000 Okinawan civilians who refused to surrender convinced many Americans that the Japanese would never give in. By June 1944, the Japanese homeland was in easy reach of U.S. strategic bombers. High-altitude strikes in daylight had failed to do much damage, but the release of **napalm firebombs** in nighttime low-altitude sorties proved devastatingly successful. The United States used new revolutionary **atomic bombs** on **Nagasaki and Hiroshima** resulting in the deaths of more than two hundred thousand people which, coupled with the Russian declaration of war against Japan in August 1945, compelled Japanese **Emperor Hirohito** to surrender unconditionally on September 2, 1945.

LIFE DURING WARTIME

The home front was not a safe place during World War II. Widespread bombing, brutal occupation, and the use of concentration or relocation camps meant that in this total war, civilian lives lost far outnumbered military casualties. The endurance of the human spirit in the face of these brutalities can be seen in the testimony of resistance fighters, and camp and bombing survivors, and in the voices of mobilized women.

Occupation, Collaboration, and the Resistance
(Theme: Social Structures)

Japanese administration of conquered territories varied; often puppet governments were installed as in parts of China, in Burma, and in the Philippines. Sometimes nations like Thailand were simply allowed to align themselves with Japan, but strategic regions like Indochina, the Dutch East Indies, or nations like Singapore or Hong Kong often endured full military occupation.

Likewise, German administration of conquered territories varied between full military occupation as in northern France and the Atlantic coast regions, existing government left in place but under German supervision as in Denmark, or governments of collaboration as in Vichy France. Territories in the east usually were occupied by full military force in preparation for the harsh occupation, economic exploitation, and planned German resettlement.

Whatever the form of occupation, the ultimate goal was always the same: exploit the resources of the lands for Axis benefit, regardless of the impact on conquered peoples. This approach lead to extensive use of slave labor in both Asia and Europe as a means to meet labor shortages in war manufacturing and agricultural production. Conditions were horrific in both realms.

Collaboration was part of the occupations in both Asia and Europe, but in Asia some local populations found little to resent in the change between Asian and European colonial administration. Local notables in both Asia and Europe often joined governments sponsored by the conquerors in hopes of gaining power or at least shielding themselves and their families from the most dire aspects of occupation. Others like businesspeople or corporations cooperated to make money from this foreign rule. Still other people collaborated to settle old scores and resentments.

Resistance movements were dangerous and took many forms; campaigns of sabotage, armed assaults, and assassinations took place throughout Asia and Europe. More subtle, but still dangerous, resistance took the form of intelligence gathering, sheltering and transporting refugees, and producing and distributing clandestine newspapers and books. In Japan and Germany, there was little resistance to their nations' policies as such actions were seen as treasonous and all existing institutions had either been assimilated into the governmental ideology or dismantled and labeled as unpatriotic.

The Holocaust
(Themes: Social Structure, Demographics, Technology, and War)

By the end of World War II, the Nazi regime and its accomplices had annihilated more than twelve million people: Jews, Slavs, Gypsies, homosexuals, physically and mentally handicapped, and anyone else deemed undesirable. The greatest human disaster by far, on a previously incomprehensible scale, was the almost complete destruction of European Jews, with more than six million dead.

Anti-Semitism and organized persecutions were not new ideas or practices, but the Nazi formalization, magnification, and industrialization of those persecutions was unprecedented in the ensuing **genocide.** Initially, the Nazi regime had encouraged Jewish emigration, but many nations outside Germany had limited the numbers of Jews they would accept, especially since the Nazis had previously appropriated much of the migrants' wealth. The Nazis explored the idea of a "reservation" for these Jews in eastern Poland, but this idea proved both impractical and threatening, as the last thing the Nazis wanted was a Jewish nation. Building on the successful extermination of more than a million Jews, Romas (Gypsies), and Slavs by Nazi SS Einsatzgruppen, "action squads," in the western Soviet Union, the Nazi leadership committed to an ideal termed the **"final solution."** Meeting at the Wannsee Conference in January 1942, the members agreed to evacuate all remaining European Jews to camps in eastern Poland where they would be worked to death or executed. With help from collaborating authorities in occupied nations, the Jews of Europe were rounded up and deported to the east, never knowing their destinations, but hearing frightening rumors, nonetheless. Applying their keen organizational skills and their superior technology to their task, the Nazis effectively implemented the planned systematic extermination of the Jews.

Despite prolonged starvation, disease, and mistreatment which sapped the will to live of many, other Jews mounted fierce responses throughout the war years by joining organized resistance movements, by leading rebellions in concentration camps, or by participating in ghetto uprisings.

Women and the War
(Themes: Social and Gender Structures)

Women around the world were affected by the war in many ways. In the United States and Great Britain, women mobilized in great numbers to work in war industries, to fill vital jobs left empty by men gone off to war, and to even enlist in the war itself as nurses, convoy pilots, or clerical help. In Britain, more than 500,000 women enlisted and in the United States that number exceeded 350,000. In China and the Soviet Union women openly took up arms as soldiers or more frequently as members of the resistance.

For women in Britain and the United States in particular, these roles brought new responsibilities and new freedoms previously withheld from women; these new-found freedoms were short-lived however, as women were expected to return willingly to their prewar roles when the conflict was over.

Women were not always involved in the war in such empowering or ennobling ways. The Japanese army enslaved as many as 300,000 women from Taiwan, Manchuria, and most frequently Korea, to work as prostitutes offered as rewards for Japanese soldiers. These **"comfort women"** often serviced thirty to forty men a day; many died of disease, or as casualties of war, or were massacred by Japanese soldiers at the end of the war to cover up these operations. Surviving comfort women experienced deep shame, attempted to hide their past from their families, or acknowledged the treatment and faced shunning by their families.

NEITHER PEACE NOR WAR

The two strongest powers emerging after World War II were the Soviet Union and the United States, each seeking to create a sympathetic world, a system of aligned nations, and world hegemony.

Postwar Settlements and Cold War
(Themes: Patterns of Interaction, and Changes and Continuities)

At least sixty million people perished in World War II: more than twenty million Soviets, fifteen million Chinese, six million Poles, four million Germans, two million Japanese, four hundred thousand British, and three hundred thousand Americans; more than six million Jews died during the Holocaust. Untold millions were displaced by the fighting and perhaps millions more were simply lost in the chaos.

Resettlement and rebuilding would not be simple or cheap. Eight million Germans seeking to escape Russian occupation fled to zones controlled by British or American troops and at least twelve million German and Russian prisoners of war crossed paths on their way home along with death camp survivors and other refugees from the Balkans.

The **cold war** between the Soviet Union and the United States, begun in this confusing context, would come to define the political, ideological, and economic issues for nearly the next fifty years (1947–1991). Although these two superpowers usually refrained from armed conflict, their aligned and non-aligned nations would not.

The unlikely wartime alliance between Great Britain, the United States, and the Soviet Union had held in the face of the greater threat each believed Hitler posed, even though tensions were obvious between the three allies. Differences in postwar visions included war crime trials, redrawn national boundaries, timelines for occupation, and the creation of a **United Nations.** Stalin was insistent on his plans for eastern Europe despite pressure from Churchill and Roosevelt to allow free elections in Poland. Stalin refused, suppressed noncommunist political parties, and prevented free elections in Poland, Czechoslovakia, Hungary, Romania, and Bulgaria; communist governments were installed in all Soviet-occupied regions of eastern Europe, much to the dismay of Great Britain and especially the United States. The Allies did agree on the dismantling of the former Axis nations and their possessions. By the late 1940s, the city of **Berlin,** deep in the Soviet-controlled portion of Germany, remained under uneasy control of all four powers. British Prime Minister Winston Churchill's famous "**iron curtain**" image seemed an apt description of the separation between east and west which characterized Europe for more than forty years. Similarly in Asia, while Japan was occupied only by the United States, **Korea** was occupied by Soviet and American troops.

Conceived in part as a response to growing communist movements in Greece and Turkey, the **Truman Doctrine,** issued in March 1947, crystallized the U.S. perception of the world divided between enslaved and free peoples and unequivocally drew the battle lines of the Cold War. Truman's statement that it "must be the policy of the United States to support free people who are resisting attempted subjugation by armed minorities or outside pressures" clearly articulated the U.S. commitment to an interventionist foreign policy and a policy of "**containment**" of any further communist expansion. The world was now polarized into two armed camps, each equipped, supported, and bankrolled by one of two superpower nations.

Global Reconstruction and the United Nations
(Themes: Patterns of Interaction, and Changes and Continuities)

The **European Recovery Program,** more commonly known as the **Marshall Plan,** was the economic adjunct to the Truman Doctrine and was designed to rebuild European economies through capitalism and cooperation thus neutralizing communism's appeal to struggling peoples. The United States funded more than $13 billion to reconstruct western Europe. The Soviets, seeing the benefits of such a program, refused to allow eastern European nations to participate, instead establishing the **Council for Mutual**

Economic Assistance (COMECON) in 1949 to increase trade within the Soviet sphere and counter the U.S. endeavor. Both programs helped to rebuild Europe and, not coincidentally, also fueled each super-power's economy as well.

The militarization of the Cold War can be seen in the formation of two alliance systems which paralleled the world's division. The **North Atlantic Treaty Association (NATO),** founded in 1949 as a regional military alliance against Soviet aggression, was intended to maintain peace throughout Europe through a collective defense by its members: Belgium, Canada, Denmark, France, Great Britain, Iceland, Italy, Luxembourg, the Netherlands, Norway, Portugal, and the United States. When NATO admitted West Germany in 1955 and allowed it to rearm, the Soviets created the **Warsaw Pact** as a countermove and sought to match NATO's collective defense policies.

The territorial rearrangement of the postwar world gave the United States and the Soviet Union a vast arena in which to compete, and it made each of those nations very wealthy. Yet, despite their many ideological differences, both nations saw the benefit in creating a supranational organization dedicated to keeping world peace. Begun as conversation during the last days of the war and continued in San Francisco in 1945, plans for the **United Nations,** created by delegates from fifty nations, included the goals of maintaining international peace and security and of promoting friendly relations among the world's nations. These ideals offered an alternative for global reconstruction.

Neither the United Nations or any other organization could have foretold how the Cold War would manifest itself in the years to come. With a successful communist revolution in China in 1949, hot spots like Korea, and Soviet development of nuclear weapons, the threat of another war seemed too horrible to contemplate and yet very possible.

Finished reading the chapter? Be sure you can . . .

- Discuss the causes of World War II, its global nature, and its impact on areas outside of Europe.
- Describe and analyze the postwar settlements and the establishment of the United Nations.
- Explain the concept of genocide and apply it to the Holocaust and other twentieth-century examples.
- Discuss the impact of World War II on women's roles.
- Compare high-tech warfare with guerilla warfare.
- Analyze the notion of the "west" and the "east" in the context of Cold War ideology.

Chapter Multiple Choice Questions

1. The first act of aggression which ended the post–Great-War peace was the
   a. German Anschluss with Austria.
   b. Italian invasion of Ethiopia.
   c. Japan's invasion of Manchuria.
   d. Spanish Civil War.
   e. German occupation of the Sudentenland.

2. The phrase "peace for our time" is now associated with
   a. the basis of modern pacifist movements.
   b. the failure of appeasement to halt aggression.
   c. the trauma of the war shame clause in the Versailles Treaty.
   d. the secret protocol of the Russian-German Nonaggression Treaty.
   e. the nonviolence of the Anschluss with Austria.

3. The "Rape of Nanjing" has become the symbol for
   a. the horrors of war passion driven by notions of racial superiority.
   b. the specific problems encountered by women during war and occupation.
   c. the German treatment of non-Germans including Jews, Poles, and gypsies.
   d. the effects of war technologies on civilian populations.
   e. the long-term cost of postwar reparations and indemnities.

4. The success of Blitzkrieg is most effectively seen in
   a. the Battle of Dunkirk.
   b. the Battle of Britain.
   c. the invasion of Czechoslovakia.
   d. the invasion of Poland.
   e. the Battle for the Balkans.

5. The Japanese conquest of Singapore was symbolically significant because
   a. it dealt a blow to British prestige and to European superiority in Asia.
   b. it provided Japan with much needed access to tin, rubber, and petroleum.
   c. it demonstrated Japanese racial superiority over other Asian peoples.
   d. it allowed Japan to demonstrate its abundant and superior technology.
   e. it made the American petroleum embargo obsolete.

6. The use of kamikaze tactics was particularly significant because
   a. they lead to the deaths of hundreds of thousands of Allied civilians.
   b. they were an effective strategy to combat the nighttime allied sorties using napalm fire bombs.
   c. they demonstrated the resolve of the Okinawan civilians not to surrender to Allied forces.
   d. they magnified the growing split between Japanese and Chinese forces.
   e. they convinced many people in the United States that the Japanese would never willingly surrender.

7. Why did some Asian peoples experience little resentment toward Japanese occupation of their countries?
   a. They found little to resent in the change from European colonial occupation to Asian colonial occupation.
   b. The Japanese treated the Asians far better than their European colonial masters.
   c. They were isolated and therefore unaware of the Japanese occupation.
   d. The Japanese occupation offered ready employment for all who wanted to work.
   e. The Japanese occupation did not carry with it the racial ideologies that the European colonial system did.

8. The term "final solution" refers to
   a. the use of kamikaze fighters at the end of World War II.
   b. the use of napalm and atomic bombs at the close of World War II.
   c. the Nazi's attempt to murder every Jew in Europe.
   d. the use of firebombs on German cities like Dresden.
   e. the secret D-Day plans to end the war in Europe.

9. The establishment of comfort houses for Japanese soldiers was
   a. to replace the geisha culture in Japanese tradition.
   b. to prevent mass rape as in the occupation of Nanjing in 1937.
   c. so the emperor could reward glorious Japanese soldiers.
   d. to legalize and administer prostitution.
   e. to shame Korean women and destroy Korean culture.

10. The Warsaw Pact was created to counterbalance the
    a. League of Nations.
    b. North Atlantic Treaty Organization.
    c. COMECON.
    d. United Nations.
    e. Marshall Plan.

Comprehensive Multiple Choice Questions

1. Which of the following was NOT a commonality which existed between Napoleon's invasion of Russia in 1812 and Hitler's invasion of Russia in 1941?
    a. Both Napoleon and Hitler had been formerly allied with Russia.
    b. Both Napoleon and Hitler had the most well-equipped army of their time.
    c. Both Napoleon and Hitler were ill-prepared for the Russian winter.
    d. Both Napoleon and Hitler traveled and fought alongside their troops.
    e. Both Napoleon and Hitler had supporting troops from other nations under their direction.

2. During World War II why did most areas in eastern Europe come under direct military control by German forces?
    a. Puppet governments like in Vichy France proved ineffective in controlling the unruly Slavs and Romanians.
    b. Resistance movements in these areas were particularly strong which warranted this increased enforcement by specially trained German forces.
    c. The Germans were afraid of Russian infiltration in existing governments as the communists had many allies among the Hungarians and the Poles.
    d. These areas were to become part of the greater German empire and therefore required greater attention than the west.
    e. Occupation there was a prelude for the extermination of existing populations and the resettlement of the areas by Germans in the fulfillment of the quest for Lebensraum.

3. Which of the following events is considered genocide?
    a. the execution of the peoples of Palestine at the hands of the Assyrians in the eighth century B.C.E.
    b. Attila the Hun's execution of Visigoths in the fifth century C.E.
    c. the Mongol sack of Baghdad in 1258
    d. the Terror in eighteenth-century France
    e. Cambodia under Pol Pot in the late 1970s

Primary Source Questions

1. **Read *Sources from the Past: A Hiroshima Maiden's Tale,* on page 1045 of your textbook.**
    a. What are the most powerful images in this account?
    b. What reasons can you think of to explain Yamaoka's family's response?

2. **Read *Sources from the Past: "We Will Never Speak about it in Public,"* on page 1051 of your textbook.**
    a. What is the significance of the excerpt's title?
    b. What is the meaning of the phrase "stayed decent"?
    c. What irony do you see in the last sentence of this excerpt?

Chapter Multiple Choice Answers

1. **c:** When Japan invaded Manchuria in 1931, the fragile postwar peace was ended; Japan saw the lack of effective response or reaction as a clear indicator that the nations of the world were more interested in protecting what peace they had than in protecting the rights of others. (p. 1032)

2. **b:** Neville Chamberlain's claim has come to be the haunting reminder that aggressors cannot be satisfied by conciliation or acquiescence. (p. 1037)

3. **a:** More than four hundred thousand Chinese people lost their lives in the most horrific ways imaginable during a six-month period of Japanese occupation of that city. The motivations for the unspeakable brutality were fueled by war frenzy and beliefs of racial superiority. (p. 1034)

4. **d:** The effectiveness of Blitzkrieg was first and most effectively demonstrated in the German invasion of Poland in September 1939. It was repeatedly demonstrated in Belgium, the Netherlands, and France in 1940. (p. 1038)

5. **a:** Because the stem of the question asks specifically for symbolic impact, choice "a" is the only possible correct answer. (p. 1042)

6. **e:** The use of kamikaze tactics included more than nineteen hundred missions during the battle for the island of Okinawa. The unceasing conviction and dedication to honor shown by these young Japanese pilots convinced many Americans that an invasion of Japan proper would cost millions of U.S. soldiers' lives and that the Japanese would never willingly capitulate. (p. 1044)

7. **a:** The Japanese occupation certainly had racial elements, but for many local Asian populations in Japanese-occupied regions, the Japanese were just another colonial power interested in economic exploitation. (p. 1048)

8. **c:** Discussed at the Wannsee Conference in January 1942, the term "final solution" is the phrase used to describe the plan to eradicate Jews from Europe. (pp. 1050–1051)

9. **b:** The Japanese explained the establishment of comfort houses as a response to the Rape of Nanjing in 1937. The degree to which this is a legitimate explanation is questionable, but it was the reason cited at the conclusion of the war. Such an explanation offered little comfort to the three hundred thousand enslaved women. (p. 1055)

10. **b:** The Warsaw Pact was created in 1955 to counterbalance the admission of West Germany to the North Atlantic Treaty Association. (p. 1059)

Comprehensive Multiple Choice Answers

1. **d:** Only Napoleon marched into Russia with his troops which included French troops as well as others from lands he had previously "liberated." Of course, it was "General Winter" which proved the most effective Russian weapon of all. (pp. 793, 1039–1040)

2. **e:** Eastern Europe was populated by Slavs, Russians, Poles, and Jews, all of whom were seen as the lesser races and therefore must be "moved" to allow for resettlement of Germans as part of Hitler's concept of Lebensraum. (p. 1048)

3. **e:** Though each of these examples certainly was an atrocity, only "e" is considered a genocide as defined as the organized killing of members of an identifiable group calculated to bring about its whole physical destruction. (p. 1052)

Primary Source Answers

1. This account is filled with powerful images. Yamaoka's initial description of the bombing seems very detached and clinical and yet descriptive when she says, "There was no sound. . . . I felt colors. It wasn't heat." Those phrases do not fit with any of the images in films or movies where bombing occurs, and, yet, there is no reason to doubt her perspective. One does wonder if the type of bomb or the lethalness of it made it feel or appear different than accounts given by survivors of other non-atomic bombings. Another very powerful image in this account is the section where she describes the injuries to her face, eyes, and lips. The fact that she was a young girl when the bombing occurred makes it very difficult to read about her injuries. Yamaoka's mother's response is very understandable; at first she rescues her daughter and stands by her through her bedridden recovery. However, it must have been very difficult to see one's child so damaged and to know there was to be no real help or hope of recovery. The fact that her more distant family did not embrace the injured girl and her mother makes it easier to see how Yamaoka's mother might consider killing her child to spare her the intense physical and emotional pain that the young girl would have to deal with for as long as she lived. (p. 1045)

2. This powerful speech is twistedly about honor and the actions people will undertake to justify their beliefs. To understand this speech one must always be thinking about point of view. Himmler's audience was an assembly of SS generals and he must have been responding to issues related to the extermination plan. It is in that context that Himmler speaks about the shame in gaining individual wealth from the goods of exterminated Jews and the cowardice in trying to spare "his one decent Jew." The basic premise is that to kill the Jews is necessary for the state to survive. Himmler's perspective is that the extermination of the Jews is a duty to the nation: to enrich oneself at the nations' expense or to save one Jew, even those who tempt officers to consider them good Jews, is to betray duty to the nation. He even says, "We had the moral right, we had the duty toward our people, to destroy these people who wanted to destroy us." The humanity of the Jews or the brutality of the executions is not at all his concern and is not alluded to or considered in any way. Instead, the focus is on morality and honor in fulfilling one's duty, in, as he says, "a spirit of love for our people." The earnest belief in his last words is perhaps the most terrifying aspect of all: "inner being, soul, character" are ideals which he believes are protected by fulfilling his duty to exterminate nearly six million people. (p. 1051)

CHAPTER 38

THE BIPOLAR WORLD

Before you get started: Many of your parents remember this period as the cold war. It only ended in 1989 and we are still affected by it directly today as we worry about dirty bombs and what to do with nuclear waste. The global balance of power was between the United States and the USSR, and their allies, but the actions of nonaligned nations are equally important. The United Nations became increasingly involved as an arbiter and an independent military force. Countries aligned with the Soviet Union are referred to in several ways: "eastern Europe," "Soviet bloc," "Iron Curtain," or "Warsaw Pact." You can identify those countries aligned with the Soviet Union by the use of "democratic" or "people's" in the official name of the country. In the bipolar world, it often means "communist."

THE FORMATION OF A BIPOLAR WORLD

The wartime alliance between the United States and the Soviet Union deteriorated quickly after World War II. Competition for control of Europe combined with earlier competing ideologies of communism and capitalism acted as catalysts to drive the two superpowers apart. It split Europe into separate spheres, then became global with the Korean War.

The Cold War in Europe
(Themes: War and Diplomacy)

Blocs of nations lined up behind the two superpowers and competed economically, politically, and militarily. Western European nations aligned themselves with the interests of the United States while eastern European nations were forced to align themselves with the USSR. Western Europe continued to embrace capitalism and democratic institutions while Eastern European countries became communist under the watchful eyes of occupation armies.

Germany was the first to be divided as the occupation forces carved up the country and its capital, Berlin, into sectors. Access to Berlin was through the Soviet zone which further complicated matters. A very tense relationship built up between the French, American, and British occupiers and their opposing Soviet occupiers and once the western powers decide to merge their zones, it got worse. In an attempt to gain total control of Berlin, the Soviet Union blocked its rail and road access in June 1948. The western forces responded with a year-long **Berlin airlift** of supplies and embargoed products from Soviet-controlled countries. The Soviet Union called off the blockade and the western forces kept their outpost deep within Soviet territory intact. The western sectors became the Federal Republic of Germany with its capital in West Berlin and the eastern sector became known as the German Democratic Republic with East Berlin as its capital.

For the next twelve years, the borders were fairly easy to cross so East Germany lost many citizens to booming West Germany. In 1961, the communists reinforced their border in Berlin with barbed wire that became a wall with watchtowers, mines, and border guards with orders to shoot to kill. The **Berlin Wall** stemmed the flow of immigrants but its reputation was sullied by incidents at the wall where over the years several hundred East Germans lost their lives. It remained a symbol of oppression. In both the Berlin airlift and the Berlin Wall episodes, it became clear that it was possible to avoid a shooting war, so the "cold war" had its moniker.

Quite amazingly, despite the build-up of massive stores of nuclear weapons, the war remained cold. Treaties firmed up the two military alignments with the western powers' **North Atlantic Treaty Organization (NATO)** formed in 1949 and the Soviet-controlled **Warsaw Pact** in response in 1955. Both sides began to amass huge arsenals of nuclear and conventional weapons but not until the 1960s did the Soviet Union approach the number that the west had.

Confrontations in Korea and Cuba
(Themes: War and Diplomacy)

The cold war continued despite outbreaks of conventional warfare like the **Korean War.** The first to challenge the global balance of powers occurred in the summer of 1950, when the People's Democratic Republic of Korea (North Korea) invaded the Republic of Korea (South Korea). After World War II, Korea had been partitioned along the thirty-eighth parallel because the two superpowers could not agree on a timeline for reunification. The international response marked one of the first effective uses of the newly-formed **United Nations** which voted to allow member countries "to provide the Republic of South Korea with all necessary aid to repel the aggressors." The United States with token support from twenty countries responded by pushing the North Koreans back within their borders but as they approached the border with China, they were met by three hundred thousand Chinese forces. The United States and its allies were pushed back to the south and after two years of a stalemate, no peace treaty was ever signed. So Korea remained in a hostile state of potential warfare at the same lines set up in 1949.

The "**containment**" of communist North Korea proved the efficacy of such policies and became the dominant policy of the United States. It began to offer aid to other Asian nations in an effort to contain communism, and it set up an Asian counterpart to NATO, the Southeast Asian Treaty Organization (SEATO). According to President Dwight Eisenhower (1890–1969), Asia was viewed in terms of the "domino theory" which held that if one nation fell to communism, the rest would follow. Subsequent administrations would extend the theory to Latin America and Africa.

Cuba became the focus of U.S. concern in the western hemisphere. In 1959, Cuban revolutionary **Fidel Castro** overthrew the corrupt, U.S.–supported government. He denounced Yankee imperialism, seized businesses, and accepted assistance from the Soviet Union. The U.S. response was to cut off sugar imports and diplomatic ties. In addition to that, the United States began a secret program to take back Cuba. The Soviet Union used its entree into Cuba to set up a large contingent of advisers and military weaponry while Fidel Castro loudly supported its goals in the U.N. General Assembly. President John Kennedy (1917–1963) approved an invasion by anti-Castro Cubans soon after he got into office. The insurgents, backed by the Central Intelligence Agency (CIA), landed on the beach in the **Bay of Pigs** and were quickly captured or killed. The episode diminished U.S. prestige and strengthened Castro's popularity in Cuba.

It also may have been a factor in Castro's decision to accept Soviet nuclear missiles on Cuban shores. The Soviets had other reasons for the assertive move such as protection of the Cuban government, to gain influence in Latin America, and to increase their diplomatic leverage with the United States. At the beginning of the **Cuban missile crisis,** October 1962, President Kennedy announced on television that there were photographs of missiles pointed right at the United States and that the United States would blockade the island until they were removed. The superpowers came as close to nuclear warfare as they ever would, and for one week, disaster seemed imminent. Tense negotiations resulted in **Nikita Khrushchev** (1894–1971) withdrawing the missiles in return for a U.S. promise not to invade Cuba. There was also a secret agreement that the United States would remove its secret missiles from Turkey. The world breathed a collective sigh but it became more evident that nuclear weapons and the tense balance of power could propel the world into a third world war.

Cold War Societies
(Themes: Economic and Cultural Development)

The so-called "kitchen debate" between American vice-president Richard Nixon and Soviet premier Khrushchev personified the differences between the values and attributes of each society and their allies. For example, the United States had wonderful new appliances to simplify women's lives, and on top of that, they did not need to have a job to attain this lifestyle. In contrast, Soviet women had few conveniences and were required to work. Nevertheless, all was not safe and secure as concerns about global communism cast a shadow on American lives and reached a panic level in the early 1950s. Congress began investigations that caused thousands of Americans to be purged from their jobs on suspicion of being members—or having been members—of the Communist Party.

Despite the advantages, more married women worked during the cold war than they had during World War II. Many resented the domestic image on television and some even aligned themselves with the global feminist movement. After involvement in the war and with incipient revolutionary movements, women began to press for more recognition and equality. Books by French author Simone de Beauvoir and American author Betty Friedan put their concerns into words. Women activists also began to use Marxist, anti-imperialist rhetoric like "oppression" and **"women's liberation"** to describe their position in society.

As decolonization became more likely, **black nationalism** became more prominent throughout the globe. In the United States and the Caribbean, citizens of African descent began to identify with Africans in revolutionary battles against colonial powers. Marcus Garvey (Chapter 36), Kwame Nkrumah in Africa (Chapter 39), and Dr. Martin Luther King Jr. (1929–1968) all advocated the unity. The cold war coincided with the civil rights movement in the United States as King also borrowed passive nonresistance strategies from another anti-imperialist movement, that of Gandhi in India.

The southern United States had institutionalized segregation since the Civil War, but in the early 1950s, it was challenged in federal courts and changes began to take place. The first change was *Brown v. the Board of Education* (1954) which ruled against segregation in schools. Then a bus boycott in Montgomery, Alabama resulted in desegregation of interstate transportation. Many changes followed and coincided with African liberation efforts and the cold war.

Huge contrasts existed between the materialism of the western powers and the deprivation of the Warsaw Pact countries. The devastation of World War II had been ameliorated in the west by the U.S. Marshall Plan that granted over $13 billion to rebuild western Europe. The western European economy responded quickly and its gains in the 1950s were enormous, outpacing the United States growth rate during the same period. The only area that the Soviets could compete well in was their space program and sports programs. In 1957, they put the first satellite into space, which horrified the west. Then the Russians sent the first man into space, but with an infusion of government money and force, the Americans were the first to land on the moon in 1969. The **space race** fueled concerns that there was a large "missile gap" and contributed to increased nuclear armament on both sides. The Olympics became the premier venue for the sports competition, as it had been before World War II. During the cold war, both Germanies sent teams while the People's Republic of China boycotted it until Taiwan lost its recognition. Violence even played into it, with pen fighting at a water polo game between the Hungarians and Soviets, and Palestinian terrorists killing the Israeli athletes in 1972. A United States boycott of the games in 1980 was followed by a Soviet boycott in 1984.

Despite competition, the relationship between the superpowers began to temper after Stalin's death and the communist "witch trials" in the United States after 1953. Both governments realized that mutual destruction was a distinct possibility so they began to move toward "peaceful coexistence." The Soviets began to liberalize their relations with their own satellite countries but still exercised severe action when necessary, such as the Hungarian Revolution in 1956, and among its own dissidents. During this period, Khrushchev even toured the United States and proved to be an engaging guest.

CHALLENGES TO SUPERPOWER HEGEMONY

Each side had its challenges as the French decided to challenge NATO and the Yugoslavians simply ignored Soviet wishes and got away with it. In most Soviet satellites, rebels and dissidents were crushed. The People's Republic of China stood up to the USSR and managed to maintain its own Marxist state independently. Both powers suffered setbacks when they took on Vietnam and Afghanistan.

Defiance, Dissent, and Intervention in Europe
(Theme: Diplomacy)

French president **Charles de Gaulle** (1890–1970) envisioned Europe as a third superpower, and to this end, he questioned U.S. policies. He refused to sign a partial nuclear test ban and criticized NATO as he pursued French nuclear equality. Despite nuclear parity, de Gaulle's dream of equal status went unrealized. **Marshall Tito** (1892–1980) of Yugoslovia forged his own brand of communism without aid or direction from the USSR and forged his own alliances with other nonaligned nations.

After Stalin's death, it took several years before the new premier Khrushchev would criticize the Stalin regime. In 1956, he began the process of **de-Stalinization** which ended the rule of terror and atttempted to erase Stalin's name and image from Soviet society. It also liberalized government control enough to permit the publication of anti-government works like the expose of its prison system, *One Day in the Life of Ivan Denisovich* by Alexander Solzhenitsyn. This encouraged satellite governments to liberalize as well. In **Hungary**, the people demanded and reformist leader Imre Nagy (1896–1958) supported a withdrawal from the Warsaw Pact. The Soviets treated it as a serious threat and sent tanks that brutally crushed the uprising. Hungary returned to the fold and Nagy was secretly executed. In 1968, the Czech government supported a loosening of control known as the "**Prague Spring.**" Again, Soviet tanks were sent in and with no bloodshed ended the liberalization. The justification of the invasion was part of the Brezhnev doctrine, named for Khrushchev's successor.

The People's Republic of China
(Themes: Political and Social Development and Diplomacy)

After the defeat of Japan in 1945, China erupted into civil war between the Guomindang and the CCP. Within three years, it was apparent that the communists were winning, so the nationalist government evacuated to Taiwan. Jiang Jieshe proclaimed his government as the legitimate government of China while Mao Zedong proclaimed the new **People's Republic of China**. Initially, Mao set out to reproduce Soviet communism but eventually, he broke with the USSR and proclaimed a uniquely Chinese communism.

The early steps established a form of government and then in 1949, former nationalists were purged from society by imprisonment and execution. The Chinese developed their own **Five-Year Plan** to power rapid industrialization, and, at this point, landowners were purged from society. Collective farms replaced private farms while health care and education were centered around the collectives. Social reforms that benefited women were enacted as well, including banning child marriages, foot binding, granting women access to divorce, and legalizing abortion.

By recognizing Russia's foremost role in global communism, China received enormous military and economic aid. China became the Soviet Union's primary trading partner in the 1950s. However, the Chinese grated under the constant lecturing of their Soviet tutors and resented the unequal quality of the relationship. The USSR required full repayment of its aid during the Korean War before granting more aid, and in 1955, it gave more aid to noncommunist countries like India and Egypt. Moscow even declared neutrality in the rivalry for Tibet between China and India. Finally, small border clashes between China and the USSR exacerbated the deteriorating relationship. In 1964, the two nations broke out into a spate of public name-calling that combined with China's successful nuclear weapons test to finish the split. An unintended result of the rift was that nonaligned countries were able to play the two communist countries off each other as they had earlier with the United States and Russia.

Detente and the Decline of Superpower Influence
(Themes: War and Diplomacy)

By the late 1960s the superpowers had instituted a policy of **detente** or a reduction in hostilities. Their leaders exchanged visits and signed cooperative agreements. The most visible sign of detente were the two Strategic Arms Limitations Talks (SALT) in the 1970s where both sides agreed to reduce their nuclear weapon stores. However, when the United States resumed full diplomatic relations with China and even agreed to sell nuclear weapons to it, detente was over. The relationship was further aggravated by the **Russian invasion of Afghanistan** in 1979. This would prove disastrous for the Soviet Union.

But the prestige of the superpowers had already waned earlier with the U.S. involvement in Vietnam. (See the Chapter 39 summary in the textbook for the decolonization of Vietnam.) After the French left Vietnam and communists had taken control of the north, the United States began to support noncommunist South Vietnam as a part of its containment theory. U.S. presidents from Eisenhower to Lyndon B. Johnson (1908–1973) then militarized the U.S. presence in the south until by 1968 more than a half million U.S. troops were in Vietnam. Still, the south Vietnamese were losing the **Vietnam War,** and the American public became increasingly outraged by U.S. casualties. So, President Richard M. Nixon (1968–1974) began a process of **Vietnamization** where the United States began to hand over the war to the South Vietnamese. An escalation of the war in North Vietnam and an invasion into Cambodia combined with secret talks with the North Vietnamese resulted in U.S. withdrawal in 1973. The **Paris Peace Accords** ended U.S. participation and two years later the communists unified their nation.

In nonaligned Afghanistan, a pro-Soviet coup in 1978 ended its neutrality. The new government issued radical reforms which led to an intense backlash that soon became an armed rebellion. Soviet forces entered Afghanistan to assist the communist government and nine years later had made no headway against the **mujahideen** (Islamic holy warriors) supported by the American, Chinese, Saudi, Pakistani, and Iranian governments. A cease-fire accord withdrew Soviet forces but Afghanistan erupted into civil war two years later. In 1996, the Taliban, an army of religious conservatives, triumphed and installed a rigid, Islamic regime. Both episodes proved the superpowers had overextended themselves and exposed the weaknesses of their militaries and state policies.

In addition to the obvious problems that had been revealed in a bipolar world, young individuals from all countries began to criticize the cold war. A global **countercultural movement** began. In 1968, students in the United States and France protested government policies while Mao supported a complete youth remake of Chinese society, the so-called Cultural Revolution. Rock and roll music which had been merely shocking now became part of the **youth revolution.** One U.S. president, Nixon, was partly brought down by the effects of student protests as he authorized illegal wiretaps on protest leaders and the press. These were revealed in the Watergate hearings and he resigned in disgrace. Even superpower leaders had become vulnerable to public opinion.

THE END OF THE COLD WAR

U.S. President Ronald Reagan (1911–2004) advocated a return to full cold war with a military build up and anti-Soviet rhetoric based on Hollywood imagery, like "the evil empire." However, internal problems had existed in the USSR that led it to collapse before the United States could win the cold war. Economic distress and political reforms brought on by Soviet premier **Mikhail S. Gorbachev** (1931–) prompted multiple revolutions in satellite countries which doomed communist regimes.

Revolutions in Eastern and Central Europe
(Theme: Political Developments)

Despite Soviet influence and tanks, nationalism had failed to fuse with communist ideology in eastern Europe. The early reforms of the Khrushchev era seemed to provide a solution, but after the harsh repression of Hungary, it faded. As he seemed to liberalize again, he was deposed in 1964 by communist hardliners. Again the chance to win over the satellite peoples was lost. However, the hardliners were followed by Gorbachev who was determined to improve the economic and political situation in the Soviet Union. Eastern Europeans greeted his announcements with enthusiasm and soon managed to overthrow the communist regimes of most countries.

In 1989, the Soviet pact countries fell to democratic forces. Poland was the scene of the first change as **Solidarity**, the labor union under Lech Walesa (1943–), a former dockworker and future president, took on the government. In the same year, the Bulgarians overthrew their government while the Hungarians did the same. In Czechoslovakia's "**velvet revolution**," very little violence occurred as the Czechs rejected communist government and three years later divided into two countries, the Czech Republic and Slovakia. A violent uprising in Romania overthrew the harsh dictator Ceausescu who with his wife was executed on television. East Germany's communist leader had objected to the liberal policies of Gorbachev but it too succumbed to revolution in 1989. The sight of the Berlin Wall being torn down became the symbol of the end of communism.

The Collapse of the Soviet Union
(Themes: Economic and Political Development)

By Gorbachev's election in 1985, it had become apparent that the Russian economy was in a state of collapse. It had to import grain to feed its population. Its standard of living was falling, and its health care system was deteriorating. Pollution threatened the country while the educational system lost increasing amounts of funding. Gorbachev decided to restructure (*perestroika*) and that needed to be linked to an increasing openness in government or *glastnost.* Both policies proved to be more difficult to implement than he had foreseen. Decentralization of the economy threatened those dependent on the old system, and open government led to harsh criticism. At the same time, long simmering ethnic resentments bubbled to the surface in the republics.

In 1990, the Soviet economy disintegrated, and the Baltic peoples (Estonians, Latvians, and Lithuanians) rebelled in 1991. In the next year, twelve more republics followed. The Russian republic itself under **Boris Yeltsin** (1931–) led the independence movement. An attempted coup against Gorbachev was stopped but he was forced to resign. Yeltsin went on to dismantle the Communist Party and push Russia toward a market economy. By December 1991, the Soviet Union was no more.

Toward an Uncertain Future
(Theme: Patterns of Interactions)

The cold war, while potentially perilous, had provided a certain comfort in the balance of its powers. An easy familiarity with the forces of good and evil had a certain security as well. With the dismantling of the Soviet Union and its allies, critics and supporters of the cold war were unclear as to the new direction the world would take. The communist model had proved itself to be unworkable even though a few impoverished states—Cuba and North Korea among them—retain the form today. A radical shift in power relations seemed imminent and is still working itself out today.

Finished reading the chapter? Be sure you can . . .

- Describe the alignments of the superpowers and their allies.
- Describe the growth and breakdown of the bipolar system.
- Analyze the breakup of the USSR and its allies.
- Compare the global effects of the cold war policies of the United States and the Soviet Union.

Chapter Multiple Choice Questions

1. How did the Allies of World War II deal with postwar issues in Germany?
   a. an amicable division of Germany
   b. a recognition of the rights of Germany
   c. strict adherence to a plan developed before the end of the war
   d. the Germans were allowed to determine their preferences
   e. division of Germany was not completely determined until well after the war

2. The Korean conflict was characterized by which of the following?
    a. The United States came to the immediate defense of its ally, South Korea.
    b. A multinational force led by the United States received United Nations permission to respond.
    c. The Chinese were allies of North Korea from the beginning.
    d. The containment theory was articulated by the Chinese as they helped defend the North Koreans.
    e. Concern for prior alliances prevented the United States from working with other nations.

3. When Castro came into office, what was one reason that the United States saw Cuba as such a threat?
    a. Castro's revolution had been planned by the Soviet Union.
    b. Castro announced his intention to support revolutions in all Latin American countries.
    c. Cuba's population was fearful of the new government.
    d. The United States had been a longtime supporter of earlier regimes including the one Castro ousted.
    e. Nuclear missiles had been brought in immediately by Cuba's Soviet ally.

4. What actions did Kennedy take and what concessions did he make during the Cuban missile crisis?
    a. Kennedy immediately threatened the USSR with a NATO blockade and agreed to work with Castro.
    b. Kennedy sought European advice and agreed to reduce the U.S. stockpile of weapons.
    c. Kennedy publicized the problem, ordered a blockade, and agreed to remove U.S. missiles in Turkey.
    d. Kennedy refused to speak to Khrushchev, made his decision, and agreed to aid Cuban development.
    e. Kennedy conferred with Castro, aimed NATO missiles at Moscow, and agreed to end the cold war.

5. What rhetoric did the mid-twentieth century women's movement use?
    a. the words of the early twentieth-century suffragists
    b. the language of Enlightenment principles
    c. the phrases of the earliest women's rights advocates
    d. the language of abolitionists
    e. the language of decolonization movements

6. In what way was the civil rights movement of the United States representative of black nationalism?
    a. The protesters were trained by Gandhi under the same philosophy of nonviolence.
    b. It used the strategies of decolonization and a feeling of kinship with other black nationalists.
    c. It wanted independence from the imperialistic control of the United States.
    d. The U.S. movement depended upon a return to Africa as an option.
    e. It led the way with protest strategies that were used by many African nationalists.

7. Before 1980, in which two countries were serious attempts made to break away from Soviet control?
    a. Poland and Czechoslovakia
    b. China and Hungary
    c. Hungary and Poland
    d. China and Poland
    e. Hungary and Czechoslovakia

8. Which issues contributed most to the schism between China and the Soviet Union?
    a. Soviet invasion of Afghanistan
    b. Soviet repression of the Hungarian revolution
    c. Soviet backing of India
    d. Chinese stand on Taiwan
    e. Mao's insistence on a different form of Marxism

9. When comparing the American experience in Vietnam with that of the Soviets in Afghanistan, which was the LEAST similar?
    a. disenchantment of the international community
    b. standard military forces against a guerilla army
    c. a peace treaty after years of futile military effort
    d. a careful withdrawal that took years to negotiate
    e. entry through the invitation of the government in power

10. How did Gorbachev's policies open the way to changes in the USSR?
    a. His perestroika provisions allowed the central economy to reorganize its power.
    b. Perestroika allowed so many western items to come in that the people demanded the same possibilities.
    c. Perestroika underscored the deep problems in the economy and threatened traditional economic power.
    d. Glastnost allowed the government to issue its new policies with a clarity that assuaged the public's worries.
    e. Glastnost was the first time in seventy years that Soviet society experienced a liberalization of policies.

Comprehensive Multiple Choice Questions

1. What legitimate comparisons can be made between the superpowers of the cold war and the Mongolian empire at its height?
    a. The alignment of nations behind the Mongolians was the result of conquest and that was true of one superpower.
    b. The Mongolians were more like the USSR because they directly ruled the same region.
    c. The balance of powers during the cold war acted to encourage trade as Mongolian domination had.
    d. All three superpowers entrusted the rule of allied groups to their own military.
    e. The Mongolians exercised more control over their satellite states than either later superpower.

2. When comparing China's revolution with Russia's 1917 revolution, which area was the LEAST similar?
    a. women's rights
    b. rapid industrialization
    c. dependence on foreign aid
    d. hostility of other nations
    e. social revolution

3. Comparing the results of the twentieth-century world wars, which of the following had the most influence on the development of a cold war?
    a. The first treaties were too unequal to allow the build up of opposing factions.
    b. A successful victory led to an inevitable rebalance of global political power.
    c. There were few animosities among the winners of the Great War.
    d. Global economic power dispersed among many different regions.
    e. No powerful coalition can succeed without an opposing group.

Part VII: Contemporary Global Realignments, 1914 to the Present

Primary Source Questions

1. **Read *Sources from the Past: Nikita Khrushchev on the Capitalist Iron Curtain,* 1961, on page 1074 of your textbook.**
   a. If you did not know who the author was, besides the date, how would you know this was a cold war piece? By its message? By its tone?
   b. How could the iron curtain concept exacerbate the superpower rivalry?
   c. From what you know of the history, to what extent was there truth in what he said?

2. **Examine the photographs on page 1067, Berlin, and page 1079, (troops).**
   a. Is there a point of view in either photo?
   b. How would you characterize the two approaches of repression by the Soviet Union?

Chapter Multiple Choice Answers

1. **e:** It was only after the Berlin airlift that the division of Germany was solidified. (p. 1065)

2. **b:** The Korean conflict was the first major war to benefit from United Nations decisions. (p. 1067)

3. **d:** The United States and American companies had a long history of control over Cuban politics, including the prior government. (p. 1069)

4. **c:** Kennedy wisely brought the world's attention to the problem, issued a blockade, and secretly agreed to eliminate nuclear missiles in Turkey. (p. 1070)

5. **e:** Women's rights advocates picked up the language of dissent found in anti-imperialist movements. (p. 1072)

6. **b:** Moderate U.S. civil rights leaders shared the techniques of black nationalists in other countries. (p. 1073)

7. **e:** The attempts were made in Hungary and Czechoslovakia but China managed to break away successfully. (Sort of a trick question so pay close attention to phrasing.) (p. 1078)

8. **c:** The Soviet aid to India, which was in a dispute with China over Tibet, was a large factor. (p. 1081)

9. **d:** The United States began negotiations for withdrawal and the process of Vietnamization four years before withdrawal, while the Soviet Union withdrew within a year of a United Nations cease-fire. (pp. 1082–1083)

10. **c:** Decentralization of the economy was a fundamental change in Soviet policies so it threatened the communist elite and their positions. (p. 1088)

Comprehensive Multiple Choice Answers

1. **a:** Both the Soviet Union and the Mongols conquered their regions of influence. While the United States conquered part of Germany, it withdrew from the region by 1948. The Mongolians directly ruled areas even further south (Persia) and east (China) than the USSR. While the policies of the United States encouraged trade in the nonaligned world and among their allies, the USSR severely restricted trade within its aligned nations. Neither superpower used its military with its aligned nations unless the problem was very pressing, like Hungary in 1956. The Mongols exacted tribute and taxes rather than directly ruled most regions except China and Persia. (pp. 466, 1056, 1065)

2. **c:** The Russians had few sympathizers as they reformed their society so they received no foreign aid, while the Chinese had the example and encouragement of the Soviet Union. Both governments endorsed women's rights and rapid industrialization in Five-Year Plans. Both also revamped society with the workers and proletariat advanced above former landowners. And, both endured hostility from other countries. Europe and the United States did not support the changes in the USSR or China. (pp. 991, 993, 1080)

3. **b:** In both aftermaths, the balance of power changed: after World War I, the United States emerged as the dominant power, and after World War II, the Soviet Union joined it. The Paris treaties were extremely unequal but that did not prevent the build up of Germany and Italy. The Allies of the Great War did not have the same goals at the end, and indeed one ally, Italy, was compleely cut out of the agreement. After World War I, the imperialist nations retained global economic power, but after World War II, economic power lay mainly in capitalist nations. Over history, there have been empires which have not had strong rivals, such as multiple Chinese dynasties and any empire in an expansion phase. (pp. 972, 1064)

Primary Source Answers

1. The use of "comrade" automatically identifies this as a communist piece. And its discussion of the competing economic models of capitalism and communism also makes it apparent that the author is communist. The references to liberation from imperialism means that decolonization has or is occurring. His scornful tone at the harm in cultural exchanges and his message against the United States identifies him as a top-level Soviet official. The concept of an iron curtain has already exacerbated the situation because it closed the avenues of exchange and discussion between the nations. In fact, the United States was spending millions of dollars to support the activities of the CIA against members it perceived to be a threat, such as Cuba. (p. 1074)

2. There is an obvious NATO and western powers' point of view to the Berlin Wall photo. A Soviet photo would be unlikely to have the barbed wire, a cruel symbol of repression, as the closest object. The Czech photo appears to be more evenhanded although its almost benign treatment of the confrontation between an armored truck and a tank leads one to suspect that it could be a Soviet photo. The first approach emphasizes a policy of containment of potentially dissatisfied populations, while the second emphasizes the Soviet Union's determination to use military solutions to confine dissension. (pp. 1067, 1079)

CHAPTER 39

THE END OF EMPIRE

Before you get started: The national exam objectives related to this chapter are numerous. This chapter requires you to consolidate the thinking you have done about comparisons and contrasts and continuities and changes-over-time regarding Asia, Africa, and Latin America throughout this book. If you've been keeping charts, this will be your last column. If you've created graphic organizers, get extra paper and sharpen your pencils. If you've been keeping lists in your head, check them twice. Do something with this material as you read that will force you to think continuity and change-over-time as well as comparison and contrast since this chapter will figure prominently on the national exam.

INDEPENDENCE IN ASIA

Decolonization, like the cold war, transformed the world after World War II. It sometimes brought newly, independent states autonomy and self-determination; sometimes, however, pressures from cold war superpowers challenged these new nations to choose sides by aligning themselves with either capitalism or communism, often at the expense of their own independence. Achieving national unity, social stability, and economic prosperity would prove a challenging, lengthy, uncertain, and dangerous process. Freedom would come first, security hoped for eventually.

India's Partitioned Independence
(Themes: Patterns of Interaction and Changes and Continuities)

Throughout the 1930s, relentless pressure from the Indian national **Congress Party** and **Mohandas Gandhi,** along with the **Muslim League** lead by **Muhammad Ali Jinnah,** compelled Great Britain to move gradually toward self-rule for its Indian domain. World War II, however, stalled that push. Once World War II was over and a new more liberal Labour government was installed in Britain, moves toward Indian independence proceeded.

As the likelihood of independence grew, so did Muslim fears about their minority status in an independent India dominated by Hindus. Muhammad Ali Jinnah frankly expressed his desire for a separate Muslim state, despite continuing attempts by Gandhi and Jawaharlal Nehru to reassure Muslims and urged all Indians to act and feel as one nation. In August 1946, Muslim leaders called for a Day of Direct Action to push the British closer to granting Indian independence; this demonstration-turned-riot resulted in the death of six thousand Indians and fueled Jinnah's fears. **Communalism**, an ideology which promotes religious identity over national identity, was undermining hopes for a united Indian nation.

As Hindus, perhaps Gandhi and Nehru could not fully understand the Muslim fears of being a minority submerged in a large majority culture. However, their fears of "rivers of blood" resulting from partition came to chilling fruition. More than ten million Muslim and Hindu refugees migrated to either Muslim Pakistan or to Hindu India between 1947 and 1948 and up to one million of those migrants died in the ensuing violence. Hostility between migrating Muslims and Hindus became hostility between nations—Pakistan and India—as the two went to war in 1947 over the contested province of **Kashmir.** Pakistan lost the battle and sought a U.S. alliance to strengthen its position. India responded by accepting aid from the Soviet Union although Nehru insisted on India remaining nonaligned in the superpower standoff. Even Gandhi's assassination in 1948 did not quell the violence.

Though Britain granted full independence to India in August 1947, it chose to rely on its previously tested model of decolonization rather than battle to retain its Asian colonies as the French and the Dutch would painfully and unsuccessfully try to do. Instead, like Canada before them, India and Pakistan became Dominion members of the British Commonwealth and retained English as their first official language.

India set another example for other nations grappling with the issues of decolonization: it zealously protected its nonaligned strategy. One of the most outspoken defenders of nonalignment was Indian prime minister Nehru who warned of the dangers of newly independent nations getting caught in a superpower tug of war. Nehru's and other leaders' stance on nonalignment was clearly articulated at a meeting in April 1955 in **Bandung, Indonesia** dedicated to the struggle against colonialism and racism and promoting the ideal of a "**third path**" as an alternative to aligning with either the United States or with the Soviet Union.

This "third path" proved an elusive reality even as the **Nonaligned Movement** took form. Though the movement's primary goal was to maintain formal neutrality, a constant lack of unity among members and inconsistent and informal ties between nations and superpowers made the movement more theoretical than real.

Nationalist Struggles in Vietnam
(Themes: Patterns of Interaction and Changes and Continuities)

Vietnam's struggle for independence got all tied up in cold war issues. **Ho Chi Minh** had been interested in independence for Vietnam since World War I and had even sought to have his nation's independence discussed at the Versailles peace conference. His hopes were not realized then, nor in the 1920s or 1930s. Ho had helped to oust the Japanese from Vietnam during World War II and again sought independence for Vietnam, this time issuing the **Vietnamese Declaration of Independence** modeled after the founding American document. France, however, still stinging from their resounding loss to the Germans, was anxious to rebuild its international reputation and status as a world power, and so was determined to retain its lucrative prewar colonial holdings, including Vietnam. Using British and U.S. weapons, France recouped Saigon and much of southern Vietnam in 1945, but the northern part of the country proved much more difficult to reclaim; the French mercilessly bombed the cities of Hanoi and Haipong, killing at least ten thousand civilians. By 1947, it appeared that the French had regained control of their colony, so they were unprepared for the guerilla war lead by Ho and General Vo Nguyen Giap. Ho and Giap found willing supporters among the Vietnamese people and after 1949 from the Chinese communists. The humiliating French loss at **Dienbienphu** in 1954 forced the former colonial power to sue for peace.

However, peace would not last. At the **1954 Peace Conference in Geneva**, it was determined that Vietnam would be divided at the seventeenth parallel with Ho and the communists controlling the north, and the south remaining in the hands of the noncommunists. The Geneva Agreement ordered national elections to be held in 1956. However, citing the feared "**domino effect**" of all of southeast Asia falling to communist control if such elections were held, U.S. President Dwight D. Eisenhower avoided the elections and instead installed **Ngo Dinh Diem,** a U.S.-backed leader, as president of South Vietnam. Diem was never popular with the Vietnamese people and Ho found ready support among many Vietnamese in the south. **The National Liberation Front (NLF)** was founded in 1960 in South Vietnam to fight for freedom from U.S.-propped South Vietnamese rule. Supported by Ho's communist government in the north and thus receiving economic and military assistance from China and Russia, the NLF met with continued success against South Vietnamese forces. The United States exponentially increased its support of South Vietnamese forces in 1965, but even that bombing campaign and increasing U.S. troop numbers reached only a draw with the Viet Cong, South Vietnamese supporters of Ho; the U.S., like the French, found itself in a quagmire of successful guerilla warfare against a powerful foe. Ho died in 1969, but the military stalemate in Vietnam continued until 1973, when the U.S. phase of the war ended with the **Paris Peace Accords.** South Vietnam lasted until 1975, and by 1976, Vietnam was a unified country, as Ho had wanted since 1919.

Arab National States and the Problem of Palestine
(Themes: Patterns of Interaction and Changes and Continuities)

First Egypt, then Syria, Iraq, Lebanon, and Jordan gained complete independence after the war. Palestine, however, remained and remains a problem. After World War I and the end of the Ottoman empire, Great Britain had controlled Palestine and made conflicting promises to Palestinian Arabs seeking a nation and to Jews emigrating to Palestine hoping to establish a homeland where they could escape persecution. The **Balfour Doctrine of 1917** had committed the British government to supporting a Jewish homeland in Palestine, and the Zionist dream of a national Jewish state in Palestine had also been supported at the **Versailles Peace Conference in 1919.** In seeking to fulfill both conflicting promises, the British government allowed limited Jewish immigration to Palestine while simultaneously promising to protect the Palestinian Arabs' civil and economic rights.

The British could maintain these conflicting interests only through the use of imperial military forces against many opposing elements. Arab Palestinians rejected British rule as imperial and Jewish immigration as illegal. Mostly of European descent, the Jews expected the British to fulfill their promise. They immigrated to Palestine, purchased land, and established **kibbutzim**, communal farms, which promised to turn the "desert into a garden"; such actions threatened Arab interests in the region. Arab Muslims resented Jews as interlopers on land they considered rightly theirs. Such overlapping conflicts erupted into sporadic open violence in the 1920s and 1930s. An increase in Jewish immigration fleeing Germany and Europe in the late 1930s and 1940s only increased the tension and the complications of the settlement as Zionists in Palestine began to arm themselves to protect Jewish settlers against Arab reprisals.

World War II and its aftermath made the problem more complex. As the surrounding Arab states gained their independence, a sense of Arab nationalism grew to include supporting their Arab kinsmen in Palestine against growing Jewish presence in lands they considered Arab. The Holocaust increased the pressure on the British government and the free world to make good on a promise of a secure homeland for the Jews, especially those who had miraculously survived the Nazi's "final solution." The British could find no answer to this conundrum and so in 1947, they gave up and announced that they were turning the contested lands over to the newly organized United Nations to administer. The United Nations, operating with both U.S. and USSR approval for the plan, announced that two states, one Arab, one Jewish, would be created. The Arabs found this decision unacceptable and civil war broke out almost immediately in 1947. In May 1948, the Jews announced the creation of an independent state, the **modern nation of Israel.**

Almost immediately, Egypt, Jordan, Syria, Lebanon, and Iraq led an attack on Israel in support of the Palestinian Arabs. But their actions were uncoordinated, and they wholly underestimated Israeli determination and military skills. Ironically, the Israelis won the conflict so decisively that they ended up with a nation whose boundaries far exceeded the ones they had originally been defending, far larger than those granted to the Jewish state under the U.N.'s original partition. A truce went into effect in 1949 as did the new partition. Jerusalem and the Jordan River Valley were divided between the new state of Israel and the Kingdom of Jordan, and Israel controlled the coastal regions of Palestine and the Negev Desert to the Red Sea. Thousands of Arabs fled during the fighting, and even after the partition, as they feared life under Jewish political control. Those refugees served, and their descendents serve, as a spur to Arab nations' determination to rid the region of Israel.

Egypt, under the leadership of **Gamal Abdel Nasser** sought to take the lead among Arab nations in opposing Israel. To do so, he and his military supporters abandoned Egypt's new constitutional government and began to use militarism to promote state reform, culminating in a bloodless coup which toppled Egypt's **King Farouk.** Nasser named himself Egyptian prime minister in 1954 and took compete control of the government which he hoped to make the fountainhead of pan-Arab nationalism. Like Nehru, Nasser believed cold war politics were simply a new form of imperialism, and so he adopted an "**internationalist position**" under which Egypt would seek to extract pledges of economic and military support from both the U.S. and the USSR without aligning with either superpower.

Nasser was an anti-imperialist in every sense. He worked to destroy the nation of Israel which he viewed as an imperialist creation. He gave aide to the **Algerians** in their fight to oust the French. He abolished British military rights to the Suez Canal and then decided to nationalize the canal and use the canal's revenues to finance the building of a dam on the Nile River at **Aswan.** When Nasser refused to back down on his attempt to totally control the canal, a combined force of British, French, and Israeli troops simply took control of the canal away from him. However, Nasser did win the diplomatic fight, as the former allies had not consulted with the U.S. before taking action against Egypt, and the U.S. strongly condemned their military actions; the USSR likewise objected forcefully and managed to enhance its image as a strong supporter of Arab nationalism. Oil interests and a sustained U.S. commitment to Israel made a tangle of cold war politics. **Southwest Asia,** popularly called the Middle East, challenged the bipolar view of the world and the orientations of the two superpowers.

DECOLONIZATION IN AFRICA

The cold war also affected decolonization in Africa, a process already complicated by reluctant colonial powers and internal tribal conflicts.

Forcing the French out of North Africa
(Themes: Patterns of Interaction and Changes and Continuities)

The French resisted decolonization, especially in **Algeria.** More than two million French had settled in Algeria by the mid-1940s, and those individuals and their descendents demanded protection for themselves and their property. Beginning with a deadly riot in May 1945 and continuing though the **Algerian War of Independence** (1954–1962), the conflict pitted the **National Liberation Front (NLF)** against more than a half million French soldiers and was especially violent. **Frantz Fanon,** the most famous Algerian revolutionary, supported the use of violence against colonial oppressors as a way of overcoming a history of racist degradation.

Black African Nationalism and Independence
(Themes: Patterns of Interaction and Changes and Continuities)

Nationalism flourished in sub-Saharan Africa before and after World War II. The *Negritude* movement, which celebrated Africa's great poets, writers, traditions, and cultures, was tied to the pan-African movement which was expanding in the United States, the Caribbean, and especially among French-speaking west Africans. Grassroots protests against colonialism became increasingly common among workers in areas like the Gold Coast (modern Ghana) and Northern Rhodesia. The presence of **white settlers** and the pressures from the cold war complicated the process of decolonization, as it was easy for colonial powers to claim subversive communist involvement. **Ghana** was the first sub-Saharan African nation to become independent in March 1957. Many of these new nations took names honoring their **precolonial past:** Zambia, Malawi, and Zimbabwe. Nations like Rwanda, Burundi, and Angola would become independent much later, with much violence and bloodshed sometimes continuing beyond official independence dates.

Freedom and Conflict in Sub-Saharan Africa
(Themes: Patterns of Interaction and Changes and Continuities)

Ghana's early independence and its charismatic leader Kwame Nkrumah inspired other African nationalist movements and symbolized changing times in Africa. But independence was not always peaceful as it had been in Ghana. Decolonization in Kenya, a British colony in east Africa, would be bloody and protracted. In 1947, Kikuyu rebels began an intermittent violent campaign against white settlers and those Africans they deemed "traitorous." The Kikuyu resented the British removal of Kikuyu farmers from their fertile highland farmland and their relocation to "tribal reserves" and their reduced status as wage slaves. The violent interactions continued throughout the 1940s and into the 1950s; members of this Kikuyu movement were either labeled as communists or called **Mau Mau** subversives. In 1952, the British colonial government in Kenya established a state of emergency, and moved to suppress all Kenyan nationalists including **Jomo Kenyatta.** The British then mounted a major military offensive against the rebel forces including the use of artillery, bombers, and jet fighters; by 1956, they had effectively crushed all military resistance in the conflict which claimed more than twelve thousand Africans and one hundred Europeans. By 1959, however, the calls for independence in Kenya from around the world had grown too strong, and, ignoring the calls by white supremacists, the British government lifted the state of emergency; by December 1963, Kenya had negotiated its independence.

AFTER INDEPENDENCE: LONG-TERM STRUGGLES IN THE POSTCOLONIAL ERA

Political and economic stability was elusive in developing nations seeking to avoid domination by more powerful nations. Continued interference by surrounding or superpower nations, local elites trying to maintain their status through imperial ties, or internal divisions prevented development of a clear national identity, caused revolution or war in almost all these postcolonial nations.

Communism and Democracy in Asia
(Themes: Patterns of Interaction and Changes and Continuities)

Most of the developing nations in south, southeast, and east Asia adopted some form of authoritarian or militarist political system after World War II; India and Japan are the exceptions. China, under **Mao Zedong,** served as a model for nations seeking political development away from the paths of their former colonial masters.

Mao transformed communism, a distinctively European ideology, into a distinctly Chinese system of control, bringing unity to China for the first time since the collapse of the Qing dynasty in 1912. He envisioned the **Great Leap Forward** (1958–1961) as a way to push industrial and agricultural production by abolishing all private property and by communalizing all farming and industry. It was a total failure, especially in the agricultural realm where, coupled with bad weather and poor harvests, almost twenty million Chinese died of malnutrition and starvation. In 1966, Mao tried again to mobilize the Chinese populace and reignite their revolutionary spirit; the **Great Proletariat Cultural Revolution** was designed to further the revolution and to root out any revisionists who were seen as traitors or simply not revolutionary enough. This disastrous era cost China more than seven million lives, annihilated China's intellectual elite, and cost China years of stable development. Mao's successor **Deng Xiaoping**, himself imprisoned and persecuted during the Cultural Revolution, moderated Mao's commitment to Chinese self-sufficiency and isolation by encouraging the normalization of relations between China and the west. Deng re-opened China to the west by sending thousands of Chinese students to foreign universities to rebuild China's intellectual elite. An unintended consequence of this western education was the exposure of Chinese youth to the democratic traditions of western Europe and the United States. Deng bloodily crushed their pro-democracy **Tiananmen Square** demonstrations in 1989. The question remains as to how China will reap the benefits of a global economy without compromising its identity and its authoritarian political hold.

While other developing Asian nations developed varying authoritarian rule, India maintained its political stability and its democratic system gained in 1947. **Indira Gandhi,** Nehru's daughter and no relation to Mohandas Gandhi, served as India's second prime minister from 1966 to 1977 and from 1980 to 1984 during a time in which India was beset with problems of food production, overpopulation, and continuing sectarian conflicts. Feeling forced to declare a national emergency, Gandhi attempted to push her programs of population control, including forced sterilizations, on the Indian populace. Riots ensued, population growth did not decrease and Gandhi rapidly lost favor. Faced with a growing Sikh autonomy movement, Gandhi ordered her army to attack the Sikh's sacred **Golden Temple at Amristar** which harbored Sikh extremists. Two months later, two of her Sikh bodyguards assassinated Gandhi. Likewise, her son and successor, Rajiv Gandhi, was assassinated by terrorists in 1991. Brutal assassinations and continued quests for peace and religious tolerance seem to be the pattern in modern India.

Islamic Resurgence in Southwest Asia and North Africa
(Themes: Patterns of Interaction and Changes and Continuities)

The Arab and the Muslim worlds geographically converged in southwest Asia and in north Africa where Arab nationalism became intermingled with the religious force of Islam to provide a model for those nations that wished to fend off U.S. or European influence. The continuing animosity toward Israel provided another linking factor between these Arab nations.

However, pan-Arab unity did not develop, in large part due to cold war splits, jealousies among authoritarian regimes, and religious splits between divergent Sunni and Shia traditions. Israel's resounding defeat of Egypt and Syria in the **Arab-Israeli War** (1967) and in the **Yom Kippur War** (1973) greatly intensified the tensions in the region but ironically also led to a long series of peace negotiations between Israel and Egypt resulting in treaties signed in 1978 and 1980.

Anwar Sadat, the Egyptian leader who had supported those peace negotiations with Israel, was assassinated in 1980 by opponents of his Israeli policies. The **Palestine Liberation Organization (PLO),** which served as the government in exile for Palestinians displaced by Israel, was created and headed by **Yasser Arafat** to promote Palestinian rights. Violent conflicts between the PLO and Israel characterized the 1990s, and yet work by Israeli prime minister **Yitzhak Rabin** and Arafat resulted in a series of agreements designed to advance the notion of a limited Palestinian self-rule in Israeli-occupied territories. Rabin's assassination in 1995 by a Jewish extremist altered that process.

The path toward conciliation was further complicated by the rise of **Islamism**, the term used to describe the desire for reassertion of Islamic values in Muslim politics. Many Muslims had become skeptical of the economic, political, and social values apparent in western, particularly U.S., society. For Islamists, the solution lay in the revival of Islamic identity, values, and power. The vast majority of Islamic activists saw this return to Islamic values as inherently peaceful; however, a minority claimed a mandate from God calling for violent transformation. These extremists took the ideal of **jihad**—which literally means a struggle to protect the faith—and used it to rationalize and legitimize their terrorist actions.

The **1979 Iranian revolution** demonstrated the power of Islam as a means of holding back secular foreign influences. Iranian leader **Shah Mohammed Reza Pahlavi** had come to power in Iran in 1953 with political help from the U.S. CIA, the monies generated by Iran's oil fields, and military support from the U.S. government. Iran became a bastion of anti-communism in the region. By the late 1970s, the shah's secular and very western lifestyle had become increasingly unacceptable to Islamists and especially to Iranian Shias who found his secular regime reprehensible. Iranian small businesspeople resented U.S. influences, and leftist politicians rejected the shah's repressive tactics. The shah was forced to flee Iran in 1979 seeking medical treatment in the U.S., and Islamist Ayatollah Ruhollah Khomeini, who had been maneuvering for the shah's expulsion from many years, assumed power.

The Iranian revolution took a strongly anti-American tact in November 1979, when Shia militants captured sixty-nine hostages at the **U.S. embassy in Tehran** and held fifty-five of them for 444 days, until January 1981; further, Iranian leaders shut down U.S. bases in Iran and confiscated U.S.-owned economic ventures. Though the hostages were eventually freed, the power play against the U.S. inspired other terrorists to undertake similar actions.

Iraq, Iran's neighbor to the west, was also a Muslim nation but Iraq is an Arab nation and Iran is a Persian nation. Those ethnic differences, coupled with differing religious and secular ideals, contributed to the **Iran-Iraq War (1980–1988).** Iraq's leader, Saddam Hussein, believing in the likelihood of a swift victory, attacked Iran in September of 1980. Although Iraqi troops were initially successful and Hussein boasted he would be in Tehran in three days, the Iranians were determined in their counterattack, and the war settled into a long conflict of attrition costing more than a million deaths before the U.N. brokered a halt to the fighting in 1988.

Saddam Hussein was not finished in his attempt to promote Iraq as the leader in the Arab world. He invaded **Kuwait** in 1990, and incited the **Gulf War** in 1991. After the 2004 bombing of the **World Trade Centers**, U.S. President George W. Bush vastly expanded the U.S. war on terror to include a coalition of forces led by the United States who invaded Iraq in order to destroy Hussein's "weapons of mass destruction" and Iraq's capacity to harbor global terrorists. Hussein was captured by American troops in December 2003 and is being tried for his crimes.

Politics and Economics in Latin America
(Themes: Patterns of Interaction and Changes and Continuities)

Nations in Central and South America grappled with the conservative legacies of Spanish and Portuguese colonialism as well as neocolonialism as the United States intervened militarily and economically to "protect its interests." Though the United States may have been a model in the nineteenth-century dreams of liberal democracy, by World War I and after, the United States was increasingly viewed as negative and interfering.

In **Mexico,** only President Lazaro Cardenas sought to apply the reforms granted in the 1917 Mexican Constitution. His attempts at land reforms were not sustained by his successors, and he was unable to resist continuing American influence. Conservative governments promoted one-party rule and Mexican peasants often protested their continuing political oppression.

In **Argentina,** a reasonably expansive economy, the beginnings of an industrial base, and a growing middle-class population composed of mostly European migrants helped that nation remain relatively independent of U.S. control during much of the first half of the twentieth century. During World War II, however, nationalistic military leaders gained power and established a government controlled by the military. **Juan Peron's** military regime was immensely popular with the downtrodden Argentines as he developed his ideology of **nationalistic populism** which called for industrialization, support of the working class, and protection of the economy from foreign control. His popularity was supported by his wife, **Evita,** whose life story was the fulfillment of the rise from poverty to power. Peron remained in power until 1955, with a brief return in the mid-1970s. Argentina, however, soon fell into an era of sinister military rule during the 1970s and 1980s when it waged its own "dirty war" against suspected subversives; between six thousand and twenty-three thousand Argentines disappeared between 1976 and 1983. The inaccurate count indicates the secrecy and chaos which racked Argentina during those years.

Cold war fears, some real and some imagined, put the U.S. at the ready to intervene in Latin America. The U.S. used the CIA to intervene in Guatemala in 1951, as the United Fruit Company feared Guatemalan attempts to gain control of its own economy and redistribute company lands to peasants. The CIA engineered the 1954 ouster of the Jacobo Arbenz Guzman, who had promoted the economic redistribution and supported his replacement. Castillo Armas ruled Guatemala until his assassination in 1957, after which the nation plunged into a civil war which lasted until the 1990s.

Anastacio Somoza Garcia, president of Nicaragua, supported CIA efforts in neighboring Guatemala and throughout the region. His brutal, corrupt, and pro-U.S. stance fostered a growing distrust. In 1979, the Sandinista Front for National Liberation successfully used guerilla tactics to overthrow the Somoza regime. U.S. President Jimmy Carter's commitment to human rights lead to a softening of relations with the Sandinistas and other groups who were fighting to oust oppressive regimes, and to the signing of the **Panama Canal Treaty** in 1979. U.S. President Ronald Reagan abandoned Carter's policies and renewed attacks on communism in Latin America, especially in Nicaragua, including providing weapons for the **Contras,** the rebels fighting the Nicaraguan government.

Latin America's experience with the cold war and with continued U.S. interference produced novel ideologies, attractive to many of the region's peoples. "**Liberation theology**" was developed and supported by members of traditionally conservative institutions like the Roman Catholic church to unit Catholic salvation theology and Marxism to combat the misery of repressive regimes. Existing political regimes arrested hundreds of priests who were preaching this message of liberation: **Archbishop Oscar Romero in El Salvador** in 1980 was the most prominent.

War and Peace in Sub-Saharan Africa
(Themes: Patterns of Interaction and Changes and Continuities)

The impact of colonialism lingered in Africa as it did in Latin America. The optimism with which African nations had approached independence soon waned under social, economic, and political pressures. The boundaries of many African nations were the result of artificial lines drawn by European colonial powers; often these lines did not follow traditional ethnic divisions and people found their real nations divided by political lines. Political institutions failed to thrive amidst inadequate political administration, military pressure, and increasing, grinding poverty. The **Organization of African Unity (OAU)** was established in 1963 to address these issues in hope of preventing intervention by former colonial powers. While the political lines of these African nations have continued, problems and conflicts were not addressed. Military coup and ensuing dictatorial one-party rule became commonplace.

Ironically, South Africa has become a model for multiethnic African transformation. Though the presence of white settlers delayed the arrival of black freedom, in 1994, South Africa was proclaimed "free at last" by its first black president, **Nelson Mandela.** The path to that point include years of "**apartheid**," or separateness, instituted in 1948 when the **Afrikaner National Party** came to power. The government designated over 85 percent of the South African territory for white residents and the remaining as home- lands for black and colored citizens who were designated into a variety of **ethnic classifications**—mixed or colored, Indians, and Bantu—which were then further subdivided into numerous distinct tribal affilia- tions. The system worked well in keeping blacks in positions of political, social, and economic subordi- nation.

Organizations like the **African National Congress (ANC)** labored for decades to wrest their freedom from the white-controlled government who branded all such activists as communists and thus enemies of the state. Massacres such as in **Sharpeville** in 1960 and **Soweto** in 1976 galvanized domestic and interna- tional support for the end of apartheid.

In 1989, when **F. W. de Klerk** became president of South Africa, he began to dismantle the apartheid system, freed Nelson Mandela from jail after more than 27 years, legalized the ANC, and began to nego- tiate for an end to white-only rule. By 1994, the dream had been realized.

South Africa's political stability was not common. The former **Belgian Congo,** reconfigured as **Zaire** in 1971 and renamed the **Democratic Republic of the Congo** in 1997, has seen a litany of rulers all ousted or killed in a series of military coups. The death of **Laurent Kabila** in January 2001 was the most recent.

Most African nations still struggle as developing nations. Though rich in natural resources, an ever- growing population and the lack of capital, technology, foreign markets, and a managerial class slows economic growth. Foreign debt further hinders African economic development.

Finished reading the chapter? Be sure you can . . .

- Compare and contrast the results of decolonialism in Africa, Asia, and India.
- Compare the legacies of colonialism and the patterns of economic development in Africa, Asia, and Latin America.
- Compare nationalist ideologies and movements in contrasting European and colonial environ- ments.
- Compare different types of independence struggles.

Chapter Multiple Choice Questions

1. Which of the following leaders favored partition for Pakistan and India?
   a. Mohandas Gandhi
   b. Jawaharlal Nehru
   c. Indira Gandhi
   d. Muhammad Ali Jinnah
   e. Winston Churchill

2. Which of the following terms is used to describe attempts by newly independent nations to avoid the dangers of being caught in a superpower struggle for influence?
    a.   nonalignment policy
    b.   Truman doctrine
    c.   containment
    d.   domino effect
    e.   partition

3. Which of the following nations had the greatest difficulty in keeping their struggle for independence separate from complications of the cold war?
    a.   South Africa
    b.   Ghana
    c.   China
    d.   India
    e.   Vietnam

4. The concept of partition is associated with the creation of
    a.   Pakistan and Egypt.
    b.   Israel and Egypt.
    c.   Egypt and Vietnam.
    d.   Israel and Pakistan.
    e.   Israel and Jordan.

5. Gamal Abdel Nasser sought to use the revenue generated from control of the Suez Canal to
    a.   finally defeat Israel.
    b.   build the Aswan Dam.
    c.   become the leader of the Arab world.
    d.   provide a homeland for displaced Palestinian Arabs.
    e.   provide help to the Algerians who were fighting to oust the French.

6. The ideology most responsible for the creation of a Jewish homeland is called
    a.   assimilation.
    b.   nonalignment.
    c.   Zionism.
    d.   imperialism.
    e.   decolonialism.

7. The Mau Mau rebellion is associated with the independence movement in what African nation?
    a.   Angola
    b.   Ghana
    c.   Rwanda
    d.   Kenya
    e.   Rhodesia

8. Which two Asia nations did NOT adopt some form of military or authoritarian political system after World War II?
    a.   India and Japan
    b.   China and Japan
    c.   China and India
    d.   Pakistan and India
    e.   Pakistan and China

9. A system of "separateness" or apartheid was instituted in South Africa
   a. by the Afrikaner National Party in 1948.
   b. by the African National Congress in 1912.
   c. by F. W. de Klerk in 1989.
   d. by Nelson Mandela in 1994.
   e. by Laurent Kabila in 2001.

10. Mao Zedong's Great Leap Forward was similar to _____ in its attempt to collectivize agriculture and its failed results.
    a. Joseph Stalin's five-year plans
    b. Lenin's new economic policy
    c. Lenin's communism
    d. Franklin Roosevelt's New Deal
    e. Deng Xiaoping's "Deng's Revolution"

Comprehensive Multiple Choice Questions

1. At which of the following peace conferences would this phrase have been most likely applied:
   ". . . the first international conference of coloured peoples in the history of mankind."
   a. Congress of Berlin, 1884–1985
   b. Versailles Peace Conference, 1919
   c. Geneva Peace Conference, 1954
   d. Bandung Conference, 1955
   e. Paris Peace Conference, 1973

2. Who crafted and delivered this Declaration of Independence in September 1945?
   "All men are created equal. They are endowed by their Creator with certain inalienable rights, among these are Life, Liberty, and the pursuit of Happiness." This immortal statement was made in the Declaration of Independence of the United States of America in 1776. In a broader sense, this means: All the peoples on the earth are equal from birth, all the peoples have a right to live, to be happy and free. The Declaration of the French Revolution made in 1791 on the Rights of Man and the Citizen also states: "All men are born free and with equal rights, and must always remain free and have equal rights." Those are undeniable truths. Nevertheless, for more than eighty years, the French imperialists, abusing the standard of Liberty, Equality, and Fraternity, have violated our Fatherland and oppressed our fellow-citizens. They have acted contrary to the ideals of humanity and justice. In the field of politics, they have deprived our people of every democratic liberty.
   a. Pol Pot
   b. Mao Tse Tung
   c. Ho Chi Minh
   d. Gamal Nasser
   e. Mohandas Gandh

3. Which of the following former British colonies in Africa earned its independence first?
   a. Ghana
   b. Egypt
   c. Zimbabwe
   d. Kenya
   e. Uganda

Primary Source Questions

1. **Read *Sources from the Past: Muhammad Ali Jinnah on the Need for a Muslim Pakistan,* on page 1099 of your textbook.**
   a. What differences does Jinnah cite between Islam and Hinduism?
   b. What historical support does he cite as reasons for separation?
   c. How does Jinnah's background impact his point of view?

2. **Read *Sources from the Past: Kwame Nkrumah on African Unity,* on page 1112 of your textbook.**
   a. Why does Nkrumah believe Africa's problems can best be solved by African unity?
   b. How does he envision Africa fitting into the world order?
   c. What does he believe Africa can offer the modern world?

Chapter Multiple Choice Answers

1. **c:** As a Muslim and thus a minority in a united India, Jinnah spoke reasonably and passionately about the need for partition. (p. 1098)

2. **a:** Nonalignment refers to the attempt to find a "third path," one which did not require choosing between the United States and the Soviet Union. (p. 1101)

3. **e:** The nationalist struggles in Vietnam were complicated by the cold war to a far greater degree than any of the other choices listed. The U.S., the Soviet Union, and Communist China get enmeshed in that nationalist independence conflict. (p. 1102)

4. **d:** The nation of Pakistan was formed as a result of a partition to separate it from India, and the nation of Israel was formed as a result of a partition dividing Palestine into an Arab state and a Jewish state. (pp. 1098, 1100, 1104)

5. **b:** Though Nasser had interests in all of these choices, it was the desire to generate the funds necessary to build the Aswan Dam that motivated his actions to nationalize the Suez Canal. (p. 1106)

6. **c:** Zionism, a movement which developed at the end of the nineteenth century, was always dedicated to the creation of a Jewish homeland. The ideology was strengthened in the early twentieth century with the demise of the Ottoman empire, the Balfour Doctrine, the decolonization movements, and the aftermath of the Holocaust. (pp. 1103–1104)

7. **d:** The term Mau Mau, which may actually be an acronym of sorts for the Swahili phrase, *Mzungu Aende Ulaya—Mwafrika Apate Uhuru,* or *Let the white man go back abroad so the African can get his independence*, is associated with the struggle from 1952 to 1960 for Kenyan independence. (p. 1111)

8. **a:** Authoritarian or militarist rule was the unfortunate norm in Asia after World War II and independence. Only Japan and India avoided such a path. (p. 1113)

9. **a:** Apartheid was created in 1948 as a system of harsh laws to control the black population and resulted from the election of the Afrikaner National Party which had come to power on the platform of squashing any move toward black independence. (p. 1124)

10. **c:** Lenin and Mao both moved to collectivize agriculture early in their rule and both policies met with undesired results. (pp. 991, 1113)

Comprehensive Multiple Choice Answers

1. **d:** Indonesian President Achmad Sukarno proudly made this statement at the Bandung Conference in 1955. The conference was designed to help nonaligned nations find a way to remain neutral in the cold war and to fight a successful struggle against colonialism and racism. (p. 1101)

2. **c:** Ho Chi Minh admired the ideals established in both the American and the French revolutions; it is tragic and ironic that his beliefs somehow conflicted with colonial and cold war ideals and he ended up warring with both nations. (p. 1102)

3. **a:** Ghana was the first British colony in Africa to earn its independence, March 1, 1957. Ghana inspired other African nations to gain independence and, under the leadership of President Kwame Nkrumah, led a movement for pan-African unity. (p. 1109)

Primary Source Answers

1. Muhammad Ali Jinnah worked with Indian Hindus to gain independence from Britain, but as a Muslim and therefore a member of a minority, he came to fear for the rights and freedoms minority Muslims would experience in a democracy where the majority dominates. He cites numerous differences between Muslims and Hindus including different religious philosophies, social customs, and literatures, going so far as to say they are actually two different civilizations which if continued to be yoked together would inevitably lead to discontent. Jinnah cites 1,200 years of tied history as evidence that the two traditions cannot live equally in a single nation and says the only reason this "artificial unity" has worked to date is because of British conquest and at the threat of the "British bayonet." He concludes by expressing his belief that Muslims are a nation and therefore must have their "homelands, their territory, and their state" if they are to develop to their fullest capacity. (p. 1099)

2. Nkrumah is convinced and convincing in his argument that Africa's problems can best be solved by African unity; his argument is that as divided nations, the power of Africans is diminished, but as a united Africa, their power is strong, strong enough, he adds, to be a force for good in the world. The power of unity in Africa would make it possible to bring about "full and effective development of our natural resources" for the benefit of all Africans, he explains. Nkrumah further believes that a successful African union would stand as an example to the world, that in 1961 was divided between the United States and the Soviet Union and each of their aligned nations. He is poetic, optimistic, and a bit romantic as he calls on Africa's "deep-rooted wisdom, innate respect for human lives, intense humanity that is our heritage" to create an African Great Power, not one measured in "stock piles" of atom bombs. He believes this African union could offer the world a positive and compelling alternative to nations which flaunt their wealth and strength; this alternative would be a power not founded on the "expense of others," but on "hope, trust, friendship and directed to the good of all mankind." (p. 1112)

CHAPTER 40

A WORLD WITHOUT BORDERS

Before you get started: This is it. We have reached your lifetime. The AP focus for this chapter is global business, migration, and culture; hence, a world without borders. These are the big issues in the newspapers today and are included in the AP Exam. So, take a deep breath, check out the multiple choice questions first to see how well you do on current events, and pat yourself on the back for finishing the course.

THE GLOBAL ECONOMY

Since the collapse of communism in 1990, a new economic order has been organizing around expansion of trade, global investing, privatization of state economies and deregulation of businesses. Modern technology in the form of computers, the internet, satellites, fiber optics and semiconductors have eliminated national borders and made global business possible.

Economic Globalization
(Theme: Economics)

The **International Monetary Fund** established near the end of World War II has underwritten most of the progress in free trade and market economies. Free trade means that trade occurs without any constraints on it by borders or state-imposed limits. Two other agreements have promoted free trade: the **General Agreement on Tariffs and Trade (GATT)** and its derivative, the **World Trade Organization (WTO).** The WTO, formed in 1994, settles international trade disputes and has the power to enforce its decisions. World trade since the signing of GATT in 1947 has been marked by continued growth.

Global corporations have replaced multinational corporations where business sites operated under the laws of each country. Today, a corporation has a small headquarters staff making decisions with multiple sites around the world producing its products. General Motors and Nestle are examples of companies who have transformed from multinational corporations to global enterprises. Global companies are no longer tied to labor and tax obligations in one country or city; they operate where the costs are lower. In the United States, taxes paid by these companies now generate almost two-thirds less than they once did so not only do workers lose their jobs but governments lose income.

Economic Growth in Asia
(Theme: Economics)

Asia has been the site of several "**economic miracles**" since the second World War. Direct U.S. aid and investments pushed Japan's economy to its prewar levels by 1949 and to the forefront of global economies by the 1970s. Having few natural resources but a good labor source, the Japanese chose to emphasize exports. In the 1960s, they moved from labor-intensive goods like steel and textiles to electronics and motor vehicles. The once derogatory "Made in Japan" label became a guarantee of state-of-the-art manufacturing. By the 1990s, the Japanese economy slowed down and has been in a recession since then.

The successful imitators of Japanese success have been the "**four little tigers**" of South Korea, Hong Kong, Singapore, and Taiwan. They shared the basic problems of few natural resources but an abundant labor force and they too moved into exports. By the 1990s, they were strong competition for Japan in the same commodities. China followed in the 1970s as the disastrous economic plans of communism gave way to foreign trade and investors. Since then, it has gradually been functioning as a socialist market. Its enormous potential has attracted foreign investments and by 2001, it gained entrance into the WTO.

Combined, the **Pacific Rim economies** became hugely successful but there were problems in 1997 as they were affected by a downturn that started in the Asian countries that were just beginning to make economic strides on their own, like Thailand, Malaysia, Indonesia, and the Philippines. Each economy shot downward and recovery has been slow.

Trading Blocs
(Theme: Economics)

Groups of nations have joined together to gain more advantages in the marketplace. **The European Union (EU)** is the foremost among these. Formed by six nations in 1957 as the European Economic Community, it has grown to include all western European nations and many eastern European nations in 2004. The former Soviet republics are still negotiating for membership while the Balkans and Turkey also have high hopes. The EU has agreed on a common currency, the Euro, used by eleven member nations, and it agreed to dismantle all trade barriers between members. It is seeking more ways to magnify its global economic and political power. Southeast Asia has set up its own **Association of Southeast Asian Nations (ASEAN),** and the **North American Free Trade Agreement (NAFTA)** has done the same in the Americas.

The **Organization of Petroleum Exporting Countries (OPEC)** is a cartel formed in 1960 that controls much of the world's oil production. It has reacted to political events by embargoes such as during the Arab-Israeli War of 1973. The result was a global recession that affected not only large countries but much smaller underdeveloped countries as well.

Critics of globalization are often nongovernmental organizations who are interested in indigenous peoples and environmental causes and feel globalization threatens those interests. They claim that only a few benefit and most become impoverished by global business. They believe it threatens the sovereignty of nations by sending political power into the hands of business. They also hold it responsible for the widening gap between rich and poor and the homogenization of world culture.

CROSS-CULTURAL EXCHANGES AND GLOBAL COMMUNICATIONS

While the fall of the Berlin Wall represents a specific example of the disappearance of borders, the process started happening long before that with the erasure of cultural borders brought on by television and consumer products like Coca-Cola. The local traditions of the early twentieth century have been augmented and sometimes replaced by global culture.

Global Barbie
(Theme: Economics)

One has only to look at the American fashion doll, Barbie, in all her global manifestations. In Iran, she has become Sara, in long robes and a *hijab* (headscarf), or Licca in Japan who is younger with doe eyes and a demure smile rather than American Barbie's scary eyes and aggressive toothy smile. The culture may frown upon Barbie's mores but they have found a way to adopt the Barbie concept to another culture.

Consumption and Cultural Interaction
(Theme: Economics)

As industrialization mass-produced products in the nineteenth century, consumption increased. And in the latter part of the twentieth century, consumption went beyond necessities as products became an expression of personality and inclusion in the world cultural scene. People throughout the world drink Coca-Cola, eat at McDonalds, and listen to Usher. At the same time, they have a heightened awareness of local culture; hence, the production of a local Barbie or a local Coca-Cola recipe or vegetarian items on McDonalds menus in India.

Not only do American products have global appeal but so do Swiss watches, Italian designer clothes, and French Perrier water. Another global phenomenon is Argentina's first lady Evita Peron who died in 1953. Revered by Argentines, she has appeared as the heroine of a British rock opera, *Evita*, that was made into a Hollywood movie, and both have been successful around the world. So, while the global culture is American-dominated, it is a manifestation of other cultures as well.

The Age of Access
(Theme: Technology and Change)

From the nineteenth century's communications inventions of the telegraph and the telephone, the twentieth century had an explosion of communications technologies in the radio, television, fax machine, networked computers, and satellite dishes. However, access requires capital expenses, so the more impoverished regions have fallen behind the rest of the world.

Critics of mass communication see it as a form of imperialism, especially since English has become the universal language of global communication. British colonialism had already brought its dominance to parts of the world but the Internet has expanded that. Some places, like China, object so much that they have put up a large firewall in their computer access systems to prevent its spread into China, not unlike the Great Wall in earlier days. Television has been controlled successfully by the most restrictive governments like Myanmar and North Korea, but in most places, satellite dishes have made that virtually impossible. In other places, the ruling party has used it to promote its agenda.

GLOBAL PROBLEMS

Nations are struggling by themselves or in partnerships with not-so-new issues such as coerced labor, poverty, epidemic diseases, terrorism, and human rights.

Population Pressures and Environmental Degradation
(Themes: Demographics and Environment)

Enormous population increases since the nineteenth century due to improvements in sanitation, food crops, and disease control are now a large global problem. The world increased by five times during the twentieth century and that population of 5.5 billion people has put pressure on the world's resources. At first, it seemed that the low mortality rates and high fertility rates would cause population growth to slow down only by voluntary methods. However, the **AIDS crisis** and a falling fertility rate seem to have slowed the growth. It is also interesting to note that in most cases, food production rates have kept up with population growth.

In the last thirty years, scientific groups like the Club of Rome have attempted to calculate the limits of population growth based on the world's resources. They have predicted dire consequences if the growth continues. However, newer statistics seem to indicate that their predictions may be wrong.

It is not only a matter of resources but it is the impact of a huge human population that is also of concern. Human expansion has added more pollution, has eliminated other species, and consumed more resources. Biodiversity is in peril and **global warming** from emissions of greenhouse gases seems evident. As nations enter into more prosperity, they purchase more cars and heat their homes with fossil fuels that contribute to global warming. In 1997, the **Kyoto Agreement** was signed by 159 countries who agreed to cut their emissions. But developing countries, including China and India, the most densely populated countries seeing new prosperity, were not required to cut their emissions.

Population control has been a highly politicized issue as countries have chosen to encourage births or discourage births. China has the one-child policy that has been draconian but effective in reducing population, while Hindu India still sees fertility as a cultural value and has a much harder time reducing its population growth rate. The United Nations and World Trade Organization have population control initiatives that have worked in some countries but not others.

Economic Inequities and Labor Servitude
(Theme: Economics)

Developing areas of the globe have appalling rates of poverty where malnutrition and starvation are common. The poor have been forced to live without adequate hygiene, clean water, and sewage disposal that leaves them exposed to diseases that have disappeared in other regions. Divisions between rich and poor have been a feature of human life but the gap is widening between poor and wealthy nations. There is a misdistribution of the world's resources that favors wealthy nations while population pressures have resulted in ecological degradation of poor nations. Globalization has not helped as it generates more wealth for wealthy nations and less for poor nations.

Labor servitude similar to slavery is a feature of many poor regions. Although legal slavery was finally abolished in the 1960s, forced labor has continued. **Child labor** is particularly abusive in south and southeast Asia where children between five and fourteen work in agriculture, family businesses, domestic service, and the sex trade. Many children are born into their parents' condition of debt servitude or bonded labor where poor people work for low wages and secure borrowed money from their employers with their future labor.

Human trafficking is a form of modern slavery in which people are bought and sold across international borders and within national borders as well. Usually, a person is tricked into servitude with promises of legitimate jobs but find that once they get to their destination, the job does not exist. There is a bustling trade in Russian and Ukrainian women. Most victims are low-status young women who find themselves caught in distant regions as servants or prostitutes with no ability to escape. Often, in south Asia and other areas, impoverished families still find it necessary to sell their family members. Sadly, trafficking is the fastest-growing criminal activity in the world today.

Global Diseases
(Theme: Demographics)

Since the advent of inoculations and antibiotics, it had appeared that the world was on the road to eradication of the diseases that had plagued human society forever. In fact, with the last known case of smallpox in the 1970s, the United Nations called for the elimination of all diseases by the year 2000. They had not reckoned with the appearance of a new epidemic, AIDS, and new diseases such as Ebola fever.

The basis for AIDS (autoimmune deficiency syndrome) is the **human immunodeficiency virus (HIV)** which destroys the immune system leaving it open to other infections. It is spread through sexual intercourse, shared blood products, and from mother to baby during pregnancy and breastfeeding. The factors which have contributed to its spread are poverty, ignorance, sexual promiscuity, and the high cost of drugs. And it is the easy global travel of the modern world that allowed its swift spread. It was first observed in 1981 among homosexual men and in the Haitian immigrant group in New York City and San Francisco. Then, it appeared in epidemic form among men, women, and children in sub-Saharan Africa. It has quickly become a world epidemic and over twenty million deaths can be attributed to it as of 2003.

AIDS is a serious health threat throughout the world and is a demographic plague in sub-Saharan Africa already. It is predicted that there will be a seventy million drop in population by 2010 while life expectancy is expected to fall from fifty-nine to forty-five. Eighty percent of the children living with AIDS in the world are in Africa. There are already ten million orphans and it is expected that there will be forty million unless the pattern is reversed. The social order is expected to be drastically altered as families bankrupt themselves to support sick members and children are forced to grow up without adult guidance.

The drugs that are available in wealthy countries have made HIV a manageable but chronic illness. Those drugs are almost nonexistent in developing nations and the health infrastructure cannot meet the demands of the epidemic. Still, there are some signs that HIV in Africa may stabilize. Successful prevention programs exist in some countries such as Uganda and the pool of the non-infected in some regions is too small to support more infection. However, Asia appears to be the next problem area as the disease crosses India. Some even predict that the situation will be worse than Africa.

Global Terrorism
(Theme: War)

Terrorism has been a useful tactic throughout human history, but in the modern world of swift and easy travel and communications, it has become an international scourge. Improved weaponry and mass media give terrorists the ability to make a bigger statement with more effect. Since World War II, terrorism has become a significant part of world conflicts whether in anticolonial wars, like Vietnam and Afghanistan, or struggles between ethnic groups or religions, like Palestine and Ireland. It has also played a large part in the efforts of revolutionary groups in established nations like the Acehnese in Indonesia or the Tamils in Sri Lanka. A universal definition of terrorism does not exist due to the perspective of the describer but it always includes the deliberate use of violence against civilians with the goal of advancing a cause. Violence magnifies the demands of radical minority groups so that a small group can take on a dominant power. During the last decades of the twentieth century, terrorist groups launched global terror campaigns. International response was neither coordinated nor effective.

On **September 11, 2001,** hijacked airliners hit buildings in New York City and Washington, D.C. The twin towers of the World Trade Center collapsed while the Pentagon was substantially damaged causing thousands of deaths. Television broadcast the event around the world while investigations revealed that it was the work of a militant Islamic group, *al-Qaeda,* and its Saudi leader, **Osama bin Laden.** He had assisted the Afghan mujahideen against the Soviets and later had become disillusioned with American power during the first Gulf War. After Russian withdrawal, Afghanistan had come under the rule of the Taliban who followed a strict interpretation of the sharia. It banished women from the workplace and schools and forbade western clothing. It banned all mass media, movies, photographs, and most music. Its religious police enforced all the rulings.

The United States responded to the events of "9/11" with war on global terrorism and all those countries who supported terrorists. Since Osama bin Laden had remained in Afghanistan, the U.S. and its allies began military operations in Afghanistan in October 2001. In addition to Afghanistan, the U.S. and an international coalition also invaded Iraq on the contention that **Saddam Hussein** harbored terrorists and had amassed nuclear and chemical weapons. This preemptive strike established a dangerous precedent when no weapons and few international terrorists were found. While the Afghanistan operation has gone well despite the failure to capture or kill bin Laden, Operation Iraqi Freedom has had less success although it did manage to capture Saddam Hussein. Deadly resistance and terrorism has persisted in Iraq while the costs have climbed higher. However, as of this writing, elections have been held and the Iraqis are forming a permanent government. There is also concern that the Iraqi action has exacerbated Islamist fervor fanned by Osama bin Laden.

Coping with Global Problems: International Organizations
(Theme: Economics, Demographics, and Political Structures)

National borders have become less significant as global problems have necessitated international solutions.

Nongovernmental organizations (NGOs) have been developed to address significant issues that cross borders. The Geneva Convention signed in 1864 to protect the rights of the wounded and prisoners of war set precedents for the use of NGOs with the formation of the **Red Cross.** Later, its initial charge was extended to noncombatants and then to victims of disaster. Another prominent NGO is **Greenpeace,** an environmental group that has used extraordinary means of confronting whalers with small rubber dinghies to garner the attention of the press and the public.

In 1948 the **United Nations** replaced the ineffective League of Nations and its charge has been to promote world peace and security. It has worked to resolve many international conflicts but has fallen short in places like Somalia, the Iraq-Iran War, and Afghanistan. In other areas, the United Nations has been extraordinarily effective. Its **World Health Organization (WHO)** eradicated smallpox and reduced infant and maternal morality rates more than 50 percent. Other divisions have increased female literacy in Africa to over 50 percent and provided access to safe water supplies to over one billion people; its refugee efforts have been notable.

Human rights organizations have also flourished in the recent past. After World War II, the Nuremberg war crimes trials set a standard for criminality in wartime as well as a standard for human rights. Soon after, the United Nations adopted the **Universal Declaration of Human Rights** which singled out human rights violations such as involuntary servitude and arbitrary arrest as well as discrimination on the basis of race, gender, and religion. New groups such as **Amnesty International** and **Human Rights Watch** continue to monitor human rights around the world.

Although some conflicts have confounded efforts in the United Nations, increased international cooperation has been the only effective model to work toward resolution of international crises.

CROSSING BOUNDARIES

International forces have transformed the world's populations with greater equality for women and mass migrations of workers. In essence, the boundaries between men and women have been crossed as have traditional national borders.

Women's Traditions and Feminist Challenges
(Theme: Gender Structures)

After World War II, the momentum for **women's equality** gained speed as women got increased access to jobs, suffrage, and equal rights. This occurred faster in industrialized nations than developing nations but changes have been instituted in most nations. Employed women in industrialized nations approaches 50 percent while it lags behind at 20 percent in developing nations. In Islamic societies, less than 10 percent of women are employed. In all countries, women generally work in lower-paying and lower-status jobs such as clerks, teachers, and service providers. Forty percent of all farmers are women, particularly in Africa and Asia.

After World War II, discrimination in the workplace stimulated women's equality movements in industrialized countries. By the 1960s, a full-blown feminist movement with revolutionary rhetoric had emerged. Women began to demand control over their reproductive roles so that access to abortion and birth control became primary goals. In most industrialized countries, access was gained but women still suffered discrimination in other areas of society. In the United States, the Civil Rights Act of 1965 banned discrimination on the basis of race or sex but the U.S. failed to pass an equal rights amendment to the Constitution in the 1980s.

In some communist countries women already had equal legal rights. As Mao Zedong declared, "Women hold up half the sky." And the People's Republic of China went on to eliminate the traditional rights of patriarchy. However, the reality has been less promising as women lagged in leadership positions and continued to do most household work while they held menial jobs. (This was the case in communist Russia as well.) Confucian values continue to hold sway as most couples prefer male babies to female. As a result, China's one-child law has caused a statistical **gender imbalance** as parents send away girl children, raise them secretly, or even commit infanticide.

Literacy has been a constant struggle for many women in the developing world. The situation has been changing in the last twenty-five years as girls are catching up with boys in education in Muslim countries. This has also happened in India but women have been hindered by societal norms which dictate women's roles at home. There is also a troubling trend in so-called **dowry deaths.** Dowries are still a requisite part of most Indian marriages but when the husband and his family consider it inadequate or he simply wishes to rid himself of an inconvenient wife, the wife is doused in kerosene and set ablaze. It is reported as a cooking accident. In 1995, the Indian government reported six thousand dowry deaths but some estimates go as high as twenty-five thousand. The practice has also spread to Muslim Pakistan. (Women in some Islamic societies have also been victims of so-called **honor slayings** in which male members of the family have killed their daughters and siblings for slights to the family honor like perceived adultery, loss of virginity, or inappropriate boyfriends.)

Ironically, some of the world's first female political leaders have come from these societies. **Indira Gandhi** (1917–1984) served as prime minister of India while Benazir Bhuto (1953–) led Pakistan before being deposed by military rivals. Both were trained by their politician fathers. Sri Lanka has also had a female head of state. Women have also led powerful opposition to the state such as Daw Aung San Suu Kyi in Myanmar. She won a Nobel Peace Prize for her efforts but was unable to collect it as she endured house arrest and persistent harassment.

Around the world, most women have the vote but despite few leadership positions, they have acted as revolutionaries, human rights activists, and visionaries. For instance, the mothers of Plaza de Maya in Argentina have brought publicity to the "disappeared" of the former regime that has resulted in international trials of its perpetrators.

Migration
(Theme: Demographics)

Humans have always migrated, but around the time of industrialization, demographers have distinguished between two types of migration, internal migration and external or international migration. **Internal migration** describes migration within national borders while **external migration** crosses borders. During industrialization, rural populations moved into cities and they also moved across oceans to America. There are push and pull factors to migration. Lack of resources, overpopulation, and prejudice are push factors, while abundant natural resources, job openings, and freedom from oppression are pull factors. Also, the perceived differences between countries increases the likelihood of migration.

Today's largest migrations are internal as cities attract rural peoples to job opportunities. In North America, parts of South America, western Europe, New Zealand, and Australia, the urban dwellers are more than 75 percent of the population. In Latin America, it is approaching 60 percent, but in Africa and Asia, urbanization is just beginning. The rapid urbanization of rural people has blighted cities with enormous slum areas as jobs never materialize. More than ten million people live in Calcutta, Mexico City, and Cairo, many of them destitute.

Voluntary and forced external migrations have been increasing as well. In the past five hundred years, more than sixty million Europeans colonized other regions of the world. The forced migrations of the Atlantic slave trade moved some twelve million Africans to the Americas. During the second World War, the Nazi regime deported eight million people to labor and extermination camps while the Soviet Union deported ten million ethnic Germans after the war. Refugees fleeing war have made up the bulk of twentieth-century international migrations. The partition of India caused thirteen million Muslims and Hindus to flee their homes. Three to four million Afghanis left in the 1980s. By the end of 2003, the U.N. estimated that ten million refugees were living outside their country of origin.

However, today most international migrations are economic where people flee poor countries for wealthier ones. Generally, that means that they flee developing countries for industrialized countries. Since 1960, around thirteen million "**guest workers**" have moved to western Europe. They come from Turkey, northern Africa, and southern Europe. In the United States, more than ten million migrants from central America have taken up residence. Half of the working population of the oil-producing Middle East is foreign. Over 130 million people work and live outside of their birth country.

Migrants challenge traditional societal norms and they have been treated poorly in many countries. The people of host countries believe that the migrants are taking their jobs and threatening their culture. Many governments are being urged to restrict immigration as the migrants are scapegoated for societal ills. Extreme reactions to foreigners have resulted in violence and racial tension, as when skinheads attacked minority groups in Britain or when neo-Nazis in Germany bombed Turkish community centers. The recent riots in France have pointed to the unequal treatment of the guest workers and their descendents.

Cross-Cultural Travelers
(Theme: Cultural Exchange)

International tourism has been growing for the past century and a half. This form of transient migration has accelerated as transportation has become fast and affordable. In the past, there was usually a religious, economic, or diplomatic purpose to travel. Furthermore, it was extremely expensive and often dangerous. In the 1850s Thomas Cook opened the first international travel agency in England. Around the same time, Karl Baedeker, a German publisher, began to produce travel guides. In the 1800s, wealthy Europeans traveled on extensive trips while working families began to take short excursions to sea resorts.

Today, leisure travel and tourism is the largest industry on earth comprising 10.6 percent of the gross global product and employing 255 million people. It generates jobs and wealth easily but it has a downside since the jobs are generally low-paying, and profits flow to the developed world. And, travel has served as a force for globalization as traditions are turned into commodities so they are sanitized for the tourist trade.

Finished reading the chapter? Be sure you can . . .

- Identify the changes in international business practices.
- Analyze the change in the position of women.
- Compare the effects of globalization on different cultures.
- Compare different economic growth models.
- Analyze the environmental impact of modern societies.
- Describe the growth of international organizations.
- Analyze modern patterns of migration.

Chapter Multiple Choice Questions

1. Which two economic organizations have supported economic globalization?
   a. The UN and GATT
   b. NGOs and WTO
   c. NAFTA and ASEAN
   d. WHO and WTO
   e. NATO and the UN

2. What arguments do critics make against globalization?
   a. Globalization cannot succeed without government support.
   b. Globalization has put political power in the hands of nongovernmental bodies.
   c. Globalization requires the acquiescence of too many laborers.
   d. Single countries are economically stronger than multinational cooperation.
   e. Workers need to be free to follow available labor opportunities.

3. What is the most comparable example to global Barbie?
   a. french fries
   b. Evita Peron
   c. English tea
   d. Chinese textiles
   e. Greenpeace

4. In which of the following ways have strong leaders NOT tried to control electronic content?
   a. They have outright banned it.
   b. They have put filters on it.
   c. They have co-opted it as a form of propaganda.
   d. They have legislated against it.
   e. They have looked to the marketplace to determine content.

5. What factor has been the most important in the slowdown in population growth?
   a. reappearance of old diseases
   b. efforts of international agencies
   c. decreasing fertility
   d. appearance of new diseases
   e. resurgence of warfare

6. As the world comes to grips with increased industrialization, what old effect is still a global problem?
   a. pollution
   b. worker conditions
   c. sanitation
   d. adaptation to new methods
   e. changes in family structure

7. To what extent has coerced labor disappeared?
   a. When slavery was outlawed in the 1960's, coerced labor disappeared.
   b. Coerced labor only appears in developing countries.
   c. Voluntary international migration has virtually replaced it.
   d. Many nations continue to allow child labor and debt bondage.
   e. International organizations are eliminating it.

8. To what can the growth of international nongovernmental organizations be attributed?
   a. a mutual desire of nations to work together
   b. the growth of capitalism and its dependence on private business
   c. the inability of a single state to deal with global problems
   d. the growth in a spirit of volunteerism
   e. a desire to support the solutions provided by nations

9. In which areas have women in developing countries made significant progress?
   a. birth control and legal equality
   b. marriage rights and education
   c. social equality and religious acceptance
   d. political rights and literacy
   e. economic privileges and political leadership

10. What is a social consequence of internal migration?
    a. pressures on transportation systems
    b. increase in governmental assistance
    c. increased tax revenues
    d. increased access to jobs
    e. growth of slums

Comprehensive Multiple Choice Questions

1. In contrast to earlier eras of mass migrations, like the Indian diaspora, modern external migrations have had which of the following?
   a. people seeking economic betterment
   b. fewer government policies to navigate
   c. less actual need of outside labor
   d. modern workers travel as free agents
   e. host countries are more prejudiced against foreigners

2. Which of the following most closely resembles the reaction of the Chinese to the Internet?
   a. the Tokugawa shogunate's response to the growth of Christianity
   b. the Ming dynasty's decision to end global exploration
   c. the Ottoman reaction to the printing press
   d. Dutch learning during the Tokugawa shogunate
   e. Stalin's purges of the 1930s

3. In what way does the AIDS epidemic NOT resemble earlier medieval scourges like the bubonic plague and smallpox?
   a. People's response to epidemics are extreme, at times bizarre.
   b. Ignorance has delayed the response to disease.
   c. Trade and travel have been primary means of spread.
   d. Economic inequities have affected its spread.
   e. All the victims of the modern scourge die without drugs.

Chapter Multiple Choice Answers

1. **c:** NAFTA, ASEAN, the EU, GATT, and the WTO all support economic globalization. (p. 1138)

2. **b:** Economic organizations like the IMF and WTO have the power to shape global economics and politics. (p. 1138)

3. **b:** Evita Peron has been a national and international phenomenon, like Barbie. (p. 1141)

4. **e:** Strong leaders determined to control content in electronic media never allow a free market to determine content. (p. 1142)

5. **c:** Despite the appearance of AIDS, it is still the falling fertility rates that are more important. (p. 1143)

6. **a:** Pollution has taken on a new urgency as it becomes apparent that global warming is one side effect. (p. 1146)

7. **d:** Between child labor and debt bondage, coerced labor is still a problem. Developed countries have the problem of human trafficking. (p. 1149)

8. **c:** Single nations are not as effective with problems that cross international borders. (p. 1153)

9. **d:** In most countries, women can vote and they are making gains in literacy as well. (pp. 1158, 1159)

10. **e:** While the others might occur, only slums are a social phenomenon. (p. 1162)

Comprehensive Multiple Choice Answers

1. **d:** In the days of imperial powers, millions of workers were recruited as indentured servants and traveled between colonies, but today human trafficking is a common feature of forced labor. Earlier, there had been government regulation and people often agreed to it for economic betterment. In both cases, workers are meeting a high demand which has not slowed. There has been open hostility to foreign workers for as long as they have migrated to new countries. (pp. 932, 1162)

2. **c:** The Ottoman's slow adoption of the printing press was a conservative reaction to the dissemination of knowledge, and in that way, it most resembles China's attempts to control the Internet. China has not completely shut off access as was done by the Tokugawa shogunate; nor has it been merely an interdiction against exploring the knowledge of the outside world as in the Ming dynasty. The Stalinist purges were an attempt to eliminate internal rivals rather than address foreign influences. (pp. 773, 1142)

3. **e:** Both bubonic plague and smallpox had extremely high mortality rates when they first occurred in new populations, but some patients recovered and were immune from the disease afterward. In a panic, populations exposed to epidemics have always had extreme reactions ranging from the flagellants of medieval Europe to mass suicides in the Americas. Failure to understand the spread of the disease at first always occurs as do economic inequities that result in higher mortality rates in poorer populations. And, of course, travel brought the bubonic plague to Europe, smallpox to the Americas, and AIDS to the rest of the world. (pp. 475, 577, 1150)

Primary Source Observations

For this final exercise, rather than give you examples of globalization, think of your own experiences.

- Does your supermarket have ethnic food shelves that have grown in your lifetime?
- What kind of ethnic restaurants do you go to?
- Do you put your sandwich contents in tortilla wraps or pita breads?
- Where are your school's spirit wear made?
- Where were your jeans made?
- Do you have a UN or Amnesty club at your school?
- Are you playing sukodo?
- Do you watch anime?
- Have your school English-as-a-second-language classes grown?
- Has soccer become a big sport at your school?
- Do you watch the Olympics or the Tour de France?

The possibilities are endless and include the Advanced Placement* World History course that you have just finished.

SECTION III

THE ESSAYS

THE ESSAYS

The three different essay forms on the test will be covered in this section. You will find descriptions, tips, and model essays. The document-based question (DBQ) is the one that gives students fits at first but the best part about it is that you can do fairly well without knowing the topic since historical detail is only in the expanded core. The average score for the DBQ has been higher than the scores for the other essays which proves that it is easier to do! The comparative and change-over-time essays are actually more difficult because you really do need to know something about the topic. But if you check out the items at the end of each chapter summary in this book, it is more than likely that the topics will be among those.

One last thing to note is that the scoring of the essays is done on a so-called asset model. That is, the scorers want to give you every point that you deserve and are looking for every opportunity to do so. What this means, practically speaking, is that they will read over your errors rather than remove points. So, our message is that you must be daring and do everything that is required and more. Do not let fear of errors hold you back to a timid standard on the AP World History essays. Study the rubrics in this section so that you know what is scored on each essay.

THE DBQ OR DOCUMENT-BASED QUESTION

The Essential Tasks

There are six essential tasks that must be done to be successful at the DBQ. Any essay that does not score all seven points cannot move to the additional eighth and ninth point, no matter how superb it is on all other points.

1. You must write an **acceptable thesis** statement at the beginning of the essay that answers the entire question and gives a clue as to the direction of your answer. Essays in history are not suspense novels; the reader wants to know right at the beginning what you are planning to do. Never save it for the end or have a "ta-dah" moment somewhere in the middle of the essay. If you have trouble, leave a space and return to it when you have finished your essay. Don't forget that you must also address *all parts of the question* in your thesis and your essay. This means that the best theses are usually anywhere from *one to three sentences.* Reread the question to see if you have to do one, two, or three tasks. If there is more than one task, underline each to make sure that you do not miss one. (1 point)

2. You have to demonstrate that you understand **the meaning of the documents.** This means that you need to PARAPHRASE. If you just use quotations, you are in danger of demonstrating that you have no idea what it means and it might make your essay so murky that you could lose your focus (which is to answer the question, not just explain the documents) . We advise that you use every document because you are allowed one misinterpretation. (1 point)

3. If you paraphrase and keep the answer to the question in front of you, you will naturally **use appropriate evidence to support your thesis.** But you must go beyond the mere mention or interpretation to USAGE of the documents. Using the documents includes appropriately grouping them and tying every document or group of documents specifically back to the thesis. You are *not* using the documents if you merely list them with their meanings, or if you just leave them hanging out there without a reference back to the thesis. The College Board gives you two points if you use all or all but one of the documents; it gives you one point for using all but two documents. We absolutely advise that you never leave one out. (1 or 2 points)

4. You have to **analyze point of view** *in at least two documents.* This is why we have asked the point of view question in our primary sources question. As you read the documents, make note of the author, the time period, the audience, the purpose, and the tone. For the author, note nationality, gender, and profession, and note if an aspect of the author invites a slanting of the facts. For the time period, note

whether authors change their views during an earlier or later time period. For the audience, note local or foreign, peer group of author or some other group. For the intent, was the document written to influence someone or some group? Remember that few sources are completely objective; even newspapers have their own point of view. And, for tone, is it upbeat or depressing, is it admiring or disparaging, is it enthusiastic or disinterested? If you are reasonably sure of more than two point of views, we advise you to use all of them in the essay. (1 point)

5. In order to answer the question completely, you must **group them in two or three ways** depending upon factors you identify that will answer the question. The easiest approach appears to be for or against a position but this is almost always too simplistic. It is better to group them into more specific categories based on the issues, point of view, or chronology. Often, there is a change over time or point of view component to the question. Two things happen once you have identified the groups: you have the components for your thesis statement AND you have your paragraph structure for the rest of the essay. (1 point)

6. Determine if **other potential documents** would help answer the question or clarify a point. First, look at point of view. Is there a missing viewpoint? Someone from a different gender, profession, or nationality who might have been there and could have described what they saw? To complete this task well, you have to propose a document and explain why it would be useful. It is not enough to say, there is no woman's point of view. You must explain that an upper-class woman might have contributed a view of an aspect of medieval life that is missing. Also, remember it is not enough to say that there is no lower-class viewpoint because for most of history, literacy was nonexistent at that level of society. Observations of the lower class in the diary or letters of a literate individual or a painting of the lives of lower-class citizens could fulfill this requirement instead. The document does not have to exist but it does have to be possible. You absolutely will not get a point for any document that is similar to any document offered. And, like point of view, we advise that you add as many documents as you can support well. (1 point)

Tasks beyond the Core Points

In brief:

- a thesis statement that analyzes the situation
- particularly insightful analysis of the documents
- very persuasive use of documents
- point of view analyzed in almost every document
- additional groupings, comparisons, or syntheses
- relevant historical details
- explaining why specific additional documents would be useful

The better you write and the more you write—if it is accurate—will gain you additional points.

The Process

Imagine that you have a DBQ in front of you. How do you approach this task successfully? Here's the process:

Prewriting:

1. Jot down **key parts** of the DBQ rubric so you don't leave anything out.

2. **Read the question,** underline the specific tasks, and before you look at any document, STOP! Brainstorm and write down all the information that you know about the topic, no matter how far-fetched. You may figure out some groups but don't worry if you don't. You can still write a strong essay. Pause and contemplate exactly what you need to do.

3. Read the documents one by one and **make notes in the margin** on how they might help you answer the question.

4. Presumably, by the time you have read all the documents, you have begun to form groups or categories in your mind. Remember that a group is at least two documents that address a similar category. So, **group the documents** under categories that you intend to use to answer the question.

Now it is time to write the essay:

5. *First paragraph:* Write a **thesis** that uses the categories you have identified to answer the question. This should be one to three sentences long.

6. *Next three paragraphs:* Write a **topic sentence** that answers the question in a general way using one of your categories. Identify and use each in the group to support your topic sentence. Always refer back to the thesis when you discuss a document because that is the way you use the document. Each paragraph should be three to seven sentences long.

7. Refer to documents by the **author's name** or a **descriptive phrase** (map of . . . , photograph of . . . , drawing of . . .) Make sure that you remember to address **point of view**. We advise you to discuss point of view the first time you use a document. You may do that with a separate sentence, or sometimes just a simple clause after the author's name will suffice.

8. *Possible fifth paragraph:* **Additional documents** may be handled in one of two ways. The more skillful student will weave it into the second to fourth paragraphs, usually as a final sentence. Or you may also put them in a fifth paragraph. Remember to identify at least three other possible documents.

9. If you know some **historical facts** for the era, add them into supporting paragraphs. If you recognize an author, make sure that you describe that person's point of view.

10. Wind up the essay with a **conclusion** that reiterates the thesis. A truly skillful conclusion will expand the question topic into a later period (but never "today"), provide comparisons with a similar situation, or further expand the analysis.

Model Document-Based Question

Note: Due to copyright and time considerations, we have chosen to give you a model DBQ that is more general in nature than the DBQ's have been in the last four AP exams.

Using the documents, analyze the means by which Buddhism, Christianity, and Islam spread into regions outside their place of origin and evaluate their success. What kinds of additional documents would you need to assess the process of conversion?

Document 1

Gregory of Tours on the Conversion of Clovis, sixth century C.E. (p. 438)

The queen [Clotilda] did not cease to urge him [Clovis] to recognize the true God and cease worshiping idols. But he could not be influenced in any way to this belief, until at last a war arose with the Alamanni, in which he was driven by necessity to confess what before he had of his free will denied. It came about that as the two armies were fighting fiercely, there was much slaughter, and Clovis's army began to be in danger of destruction. He saw it and raised his eyes to heaven and with remorse in his heart he burst into tears and cried: "Jesus Christ, . . . I beseech the glory of thy aid . . . if thou wilt grant me victory over these enemies . . . I will believe in thee and and be baptized in thine name . . ." And when he said this, the Alamanni turned their backs, and began to disperse . . . .

And the bishop sent for him secretly and began to urge him to believe . . . But the king said: "I gladly hear you, most holy father, but there remains one thing: the people who follow me cannot endure to abandon their gods . . . " He met with his followers, but before he could speak, the power of God anticipated him, and all the people cried out together: "O pious king, we reject our mortal gods . . . ."

Document 2

Scroll painting depicting the return of the monk Xuanzang to China, 645 C.E. (p. 394)

Document 3

Great Mosque at Córdoba, ninth and tenth centuries C.E. (p. 364)

Document 4

John of Montecorvino on His Mission in China, 1305 (p. 574)
I have built a church in the city of Khanbaliq, in which the king has his chief residence. This I completed six years ago. . . . I have baptized there, as well as I can estimate, up to this time some 6,000 persons. . . . Also I have gradually bought one hundred and fifty boys, the children of pagan parents . . . who had never learned any religion. These boys I have baptized. . . . His Majesty the Emperor moreover delights much to hear them chanting. . . . Indeed if I had but two or three comrades to aid me, it is possible that the emperor khan himself would have been baptized by this time!

Document 5

Ibn Battuta on Customs in the Mali Empire, c. 1351 (p. 572)
When it is Friday, if a man does not come early to the mosque he will not find a place to pray because of the numbers of the crowd. It is their custom for every man to send his boy with his prayer mat. He spreads it for him in a place commensurate with his position and keeps the place until he comes to the mosque. . . .

Among their good qualities is their putting on of good white clothes on Friday . . . Another of their good qualities is their concern for learning the sublime Quran by heart. . . .

Among the bad things which they do—their serving women, slave women and little daughters appear before people naked. . . . I used to see many of them in this state in Ramadan, for it was the custom . . . to break the fast in the sultan's house. . . . And another is that many of them eat animals not ritually slaughtered, and dogs and donkeys.

Document 6

Christopher Columbus's First Impressions of American Peoples, 1492 (p. 607)

And they are credulous and aware that there is a God in heaven and convinced that we come from the heavens; and they say very quickly any prayer that we tell them to say, and they make the sign of the cross. So that Your Highnesses ought to resolve to make them Christians; for I believe that if you begin, in a short time you will end up having converted to our Holy Faith a multitude of peoples and acquiring large dominions and great riches and all of their peoples for Spain.

Document 7

Painting of Virgin of Guadalupe (1530) Primary Source Investigator

MODEL DBQ ESSAY

Below you will find a model DBQ essay that is NOT representative of what could be done in 45 minutes under test conditions. That's right, we have written and reworked it several times so that we may point out the best possible response. An actual essay would be considerably shorter with fewer careful details but could still demonstrate enough proficiency to garner a high score. Read it carefully and then consider how this essay would be scored.

Analyze the means by which Buddhism, Christianity, and Islam spread into regions outside their place of origin and evaluate their success.

A religion might be spread to another society in three ways, each with varying levels of success. The Muslims and Christians often converted themselves or their enemies during periods of conquest but many successful conversions occurred through trade and missionary work as in Buddhism and later examples of Christianity and Islam. However, the varying degrees of compliance with religious standards in the new converts might have given the strictly adherent pause to wonder about their sincerity.

During periods of warfare, there had been active conversion of enemies as seen during the Muslim conquest of Spain three centuries before the Grand Mosque was built (doc. 3). Also it was apparent when Christopher Columbus arrived in the Americas (doc. 6). but surprisingly, sometimes the warriors themselves who had resisted earlier attempts converted on the battlefield, like the Frankish king, Clovis (doc. 1). He went on to effect the mass conversion of his own men and later his descendent Charlemagne spread it throughout Europe. This account has all the elements of miraculous conversion in the face of dire tribulations that is useful for proselytizing on the part of Catholic bishop and later saint, Gregory of Tours. Clovis may have had a battlefield conversion but it is more likely that he forced his men to convert to the faith. As for Columbus, he points out that the Mexica appear to be ripe for conversion. When that statement is combined with the painting of the Virgin of Guadalupe (doc. 7), based on an account of a vision received by a peasant thirty-eight years later, it appears that Columbus was correct. Columbus relates that the Mexica considered the Europeans as gods in flesh from their own pantheon and realized that one of his voiced goals to bring new souls to the Catholic faith, which had been useful in persuading Isabella and Ferdinand to fund his exploration, was within his reach. It would not be surprising if he exaggerated the Mexica response to the Catholic faith in order to please his patrons. The mosque at Cordoba represents the apex of Muslim success in Spain, the end point of the process of conversion stemming from earlier military victory. To investigate the topic of conversion by conquest more closely, it would be important to have additional documents describing actual conversions of the Spanish people to Islam or descriptions of the Christianization of the Baltic region.

Conversion also occurred regularly through trade networks where Buddhist, Muslim, and Christian merchants traveled. It is particularly noteworthy that Muslim traders had good success in conversion of Africans (doc. 5) while Buddhists spread their faith successfully into China, although it was periodically viewed with suspicion by Confucian authorities (doc. 2). To prove the acceptance of Buddhism in Chinese society, Xuanzang's return to China, likely painted by a Buddhist monk, is an exuberant rush of horses with bundles of collected Buddhist items from his long pilgrimage to India. By this time, Buddhist monks and their journeys were very familiar to the Chinese. Also, Nestorian Christians had become firmly planted in the farthest western regions of China. Ibn Battuta, noted world traveler and Muslim cleric, was determined to instruct all converts in the best practices of Islam. He admired the devotion of west Africans to prayer and study of the Quran, but he was continually appalled when the pure faith was not practiced as he believed it should be. And, the freedom of west African women unnerved him. Nevertheless, one can see that Islam had made great inroads into African society in the three centuries since it arrived. Since these accounts are coincidental to conversion along trade routes, it would be helpful to find letters or diaries from Muslim or Buddhist merchants describing incidents in which inquiries on faith were made and actual conversions occurred.

Not only did merchants travel the trade routes, but the Buddhist, Muslim, and Christian hierarchy actively sent missionaries to seek converts along the roads. Xuanzang traveled west along the routes that Buddhist monks had used for centuries while Sufi mystics along with Muslim and Christian clergy moved east along those same routes (docs 2, 4, 5) . Buddhism remained in China for centuries even though there were difficult periods of active persecution. It is fair to say that even Sufi mystics known for their tolerance of local customs made only slight inroads into China but had considerably more success in northern India and central Asia. However, Catholic Christians never achieved much success in regions of east Asia despite claims to the opposite by John of Montecorvino (doc. 4). It is easy to imagine that John of Montecorvino wrote the overly enthusiastic letter to his superiors to persuade them to invest more men and funds into his venture. The fact that he had to purchase young boys to convert to Christianity gives some idea of his lack of success in the general population. Ironically, as the region with fewest missionaries, Africa accepted the tenets of Islam more completely than those regions with active evangelism. Early documents from the few Muslim regions of China might shed some light on conversion, and Buddhist scrolls from monasteries in China might also flesh out the early missionary experiences of Buddhist monks.

By the time that Xuanzang made his pilgrimage to India, Buddhism had been accepted by Tang authorities although it had entered China with Buddhist merchants as early as the Han. Likewise, Muslim merchants in west Africa began the process a few centuries before the arrival of Ibn Battuta. On the other hand, the conversion of Europe went very fast once the Franks had accepted its precepts. Unlike Buddhism, the other religions went through a period of warfare as they spread, but it is clear that their most successful spread occurred along trade routes with merchants and missionaries.

Essay Analysis

What Should a Good DBQ Response Include? Ideally, it should not be necessary to know much history to earn the core points. However, in this essay, you needed to know something about the spread of Buddhism, Islam, and Christianity in order to score enough points to get out of the basic core and maybe even to attain most core points. That has not always been the case since some of the AP DBQs have been more obscure. Then, the bar for proficiency was lowered according to how conversant the students were in that area.

Below is a description of how this essay would be scored based on the generic core-scoring guide.

1. Has an acceptable thesis (1 point)

Here is the thesis of this essay:

> A religion might be spread to another society in three ways, each with varying levels of success. The Muslims and Christians often converted themselves or their enemies during periods of conquest but many successful conversions occurred through trade and missionary work as in Buddhism and later examples of Christianity and Islam. However, the varying degrees of compliance with religious standards in the new converts might have given the strictly adherent pause to wonder about their sincerity.

This thesis is strong because it addresses the required means and success rates for spread of Buddhism, Christianity, and Islam with some hints as to the argument that will be made in the essay. The thesis not only would earn the Basic Core point but would earn the Expanded Core point for thesis because it is "clear, analytical, and comprehensive" which means it is understandable, has a distinct framework, and offers a qualification on the level of devotion to the tenets.

However, three points of caution:

1) The first sentence by itself, while it answers the question, is much too vague to receive the point. You must be more specific even if takes a few sentences.
2) Notice that this is not an introduction. Introductions do not earn you any basic core points. In the case of the DBQ, it is better to get to the body of the piece than to fuss over a well-crafted introduction. It just wastes time.
3) It may be wise to leave a few lines empty to return to if there is time. You could recraft your thesis in that space if you need to.

2. Understands basic meaning of documents (1 point)

This essay gives enough details to indicate that the meanings of the documents are understood.

You will note that there are no quotations in this essay. Remember the admonition about quotations? DON'T! Always paraphrase to indicate that you understand the meaning.

Note the sophistication when meaning is tied into point of view as in the example below:

Ibn Battuta, noted world traveler and Muslim cleric, was determined to instruct all converts in the best practices of Islam. He admired the devotion of west Africans to prayer and study of the Quran, but he was continually appalled when the pure faith was not practiced as he believed it should be. And, the freedom of west African women unnerved him.

However, a simple example is demonstrated below:

As for Columbus, he points out that the Mexica appear to be ripe for conversion.

3. Supports thesis with appropriate evidence from all, or all but one, documents (2 points possible)

This essay uses all the documents to support the thesis. Also, notice that we have included the document number in parentheses (doc. 1) after its first mention to make it easier for the reader. Also, occasionally, they are grouped into parentheses (docs. 2, 4, 5), but you must use each document by itself later to prove use. They may not be discussed as a group to earn that point.

4. Analyzes point of view in at least two documents (1 point)

This essay demonstrates several different ways to earn this point.

A direct discussion of the author and his purpose are in the following three examples:

This account has all the elements of miraculous conversion in the face of dire tribulations that is useful for proselytizing on the part of Catholic bishop and later saint, Gregory of Tours. Clovis may have had a battlefield conversion but it is more likely that he forced his men to convert to the faith.

Columbus relates that the Mexica considered the Europeans as gods in flesh from their own pantheon and realized that one of his voiced goals to bring new souls to the Catholic faith, which had been useful in persuading Isabella and Ferdinand to fund his exploration, was within his reach. It would not surprising if he exaggerated the Mexica response to the Catholic faith in order to please his patrons.

It is easy to imagine that John of Montecorvino wrote the overly enthusiastic letter to his superiors to persuade them to invest more men and funds into his venture. The fact that he had to purchase young boys to convert to Christianity gives some idea of his lack of success in the general population.

One may tie it together with the meaning. Note the use of tone underlined in the next example as well:

Ibn Battuta, noted world traveler and Muslim cleric, was determined to instruct all converts in the best practices of Islam. He admired the devotion of west Africans to prayer and study of the Quran, but he was continually appalled when the pure faith was not practiced as he believed it should be. And, the freedom of west African women unnerved him.

Sometimes visual documents seem difficult to assess but remember that an artist with a point of view crafted it. One may note the tone of the art piece as well.

To prove the acceptance of Buddhism in Chinese society, Xuanzang's return to China, likely painted by a Buddhist monk, is an exuberant rush of horses with bundles of collected Buddhist items from his long pilgrimage to India. By this time, Buddhist monks and their journeys were very familiar to the Chinese.

This essay would earn Expanded Core points for "analyzing point of view in most documents."

5. Analyzes documents by grouping them in two or three ways (1 point)

This essay has grouped the documents into those that spread by military, along trade routes, and through the activities of missionaries. Within these groups are examples of conversion of the armies themselves and their enemies. The spread along trade routes deals with the regions of most successful land trade routes. The missionary group specifically dealt with Christians and Buddhists in the documents but incorporated outside knowledge of the Sufis. So how was this decision made? By recalling what we knew about the topic before we ever started to read the documents. From the course, we knew that there were three ways to spread religious ideas and those are what we focused on when we decided on these groupings.

It might have been grouped less successfully in other ways. One could have split between peaceful and violent means. Two groupings are usually too simplistic to allow for the analysis of small details. Besides, there really is nothing other than the Clovis conversion that referred to battles. Also, one might have been tempted to group them by point of view but that becomes difficult on how to include the visual documents. Would you have grouped them by denomination? That would be barely adequate because you might never get to the three means of spread. You could have earned the grouping point by all these ways but might have missed other significant points.

6. Identifies and explains the need for one type of appropriate additional document (1 point)

At the end of every paragraph are several additional document suggestions that relate directly the paragraph. This is the most effective placement because it reminds you to explain why the documents are needed. For example, as you are writing, you may discover that you can only make inferences with some of the documents that have been given. A good example is the presumption of spread of Buddhism along the central Asian trade routes. After all, if Xuanzang is a Chinese Buddhist and he traveled back to the source of Buddhism in India, then that is how Buddhism spread to China. But there are no documents of actual conversion of Chinese to Buddhism in this DBQ. The end-of-paragraph placement will remind you that as a historian, you would want to clarify the point with further research. If you were to save it for a fifth paragraph, you might forget the problem and end up with a list that does not relate back to why you need them.

Each of the following examples explains precisely what might be found in additional documents:

> To investigate the topic of conversion by conquest more closely, it would be important to have additional documents describing actual conversions of the Spanish people to Islam or descriptions of the Christianization of the Baltic region.

> Since these accounts are coincidental to conversion along trade routes, it would be helpful to find letters or diaries from Muslim or Buddhist merchants describing incidents in which inquiries on faith were made and actual conversions occurred.

> Early documents from the few Muslim regions of China might shed some light on conversion, and Buddhist scrolls from monasteries in China might also flesh out the early missionary experiences of Buddhist monks.

So what score would this essay earn? Probably a 9 because it not only clearly shows competent skills as outlined in the generic scoring guide, but it also has a clear, analytical thesis, provides ample "outside" history, makes several point of view observations, and provides additional documents that would serve a specific purpose.

Practice for Document-Based Questions

Since the document-based question can be on any subject, we do not have any suggestions for topics but encourage you to practice using the following ideas.

1. Be sure that you go over the **primary source questions** in this guide. They are geared to help you analyze any primary document, written or visual.

2. Try a few **other primary sources from your textbook** as well. Look for point of view and think of other documents that would describe the same scene from a different point of view.

3. Try the DBQs in the sample exams, using the **DBQ graphic organizer** on page 400.

4. Beg your teacher to allow you to do more of them and learn to enjoy the DBQ rather than dread it.

Abbreviated Document-Based Question

1. Copy the question:

2. List three topics that will answer the question and group documents BY AUTHOR'S NAME and a very brief summary of meaning.

Topic 1 (Paragraph 2):	Topic 2 (Paragraph 3):	Topic 3 (Paragraph 4):

3. Write a thesis statement.

4. Analyze point of view in **two or more** documents.

5. Suggest additional documents with explanation.

Sample

1. Copy the question.

    Analyze the means by which Buddhism, Christianity, and Islam spread into regions outside their place of origin and evaluate their success.

2. Name three topics that will answer the question and group documents BY AUTHOR'S NAME and a very brief summary of meaning.

Topic 1 (Paragraph 2): *military*	Topic 2 (Paragraph 3): *trade routes*	Topic 3 (Paragraph 4): *missionaries*
Gregory of Tours, conversion of Clovis and army *Great Mosque of Cordoba, Islamic conquest of Iberian peninsula* *Christopher Columbus in Mexico and* *Virgin of Guadalupe: ease of Mexica conversion*	*Anonymous Chinese artist, Xuanzong returns* *Ibn Battuta in Mali: degree of devotion to Islam*	*Anonymous Chinese artist, Xuanzong returns* *John of Montecorvino: success in China*

3. Write a thesis statement.

    A religion might be spread to another society in three ways, each with varying levels of success. The Muslims and Christians often converted themselves or their enemies during periods of conquest but many successful conversions occurred through trade and missionary work as in Buddhism and later examples of Christianity and Islam. However, the varying degrees of compliance with religious standards in the new converts might have given the strictly adherent pause to wonder about their sincerity.

4. Analyze point of view in **two or more** documents.

    Miraculous conversion for proselytizing on the part of Catholic bishop and later saint, Gregory of Tours.

    Columbus wants to bring new souls to the Catholic faith, useful in persuading Isabella and Ferdinand to fund his exploration.

    John of Montecorvino: overly enthusiastic letter to his superiors to persuade them to invest more men and funds into his venture.

5. Suggest additional documents with explanation.

    Conversion by conquest: actual conversions of the Spanish people to Islam or descriptions of the Christianization of the Baltic region.

    Only coincidental to conversion along trade routes: letters or diaries from Muslim or Buddhist merchants describing incidents in which inquiries on faith were made and actual conversions occurred.

THE COMPARATIVE ESSAY

This essay is the easiest to write, but the narrow topic usually makes it difficult to recall on the AP test. Thus, the average scores are lower than the DBQ. Furthermore, there is a temptation to write everything you know about one society first and follow it in another paragraph with everything you know about the other one. DON'T DO IT! You cannot write direct comparisons if you separate the societies into two big lumps of details. You must look for common issues to discuss and deal with both societies on the same issue in the same paragraph.

The Essential Tasks

You must do five tasks; two of them are worth two points each. You must have all seven points to go to eight or nine points.

1. You must write a **thesis** that correctly answers all parts of the question. No problem, we already discussed that. (1 point)

2. **All parts of the question** have to be addressed in the body as well but they do not have to be treated equally. It is acceptable to know more about one area than another but you must discuss all parts. If you only deal with most parts (only differences, for example) you will only receive one point. (1 or 2 points)

3. You must use **accurate historical details** to support the thesis. The more details, the better opportunity for two points. (1 or 2 points)

4. Each essay must have at least **two direct accurate comparisons.** That is, you must compare an aspect of two societies within one sentence, or two sentences that refer back to each other. It is not enough to describe a society in one sentence or paragraph and describe another society in the next sentence or paragraph. They must be explicitly tied to each other because the scorer will not make that connection for you. A good example: "While the paleolithic peoples hunted and gathered, the neolithic peoples settled down into agriculture." A poor example that will gain you no point: "Paleolithic peoples hunted and gathered. Neolithic peoples farmed." (1 point)

5. You must also **analyze why a similarity or difference has occurred.** That is to say, you must state at least one reason for the similarity or difference. Perhaps it can be explained by a natural trend in a region's history, the actions of one individual, a strong break such as a defeat or an invasion, or influence from outsiders. There are possibilities within each topic and you must attempt to explain them. You only need to get it right once, so we advise that you attempt this at least three times in your essay. (1 point)

Tasks beyond the Core Points

-   a thesis statement that analyzes the situation
-   addressing all parts of the question beyond the basics including relevant chronology, connections and interactions between societies, and global themes
-   numerous accurate historical details
-   relates the comparisons to wider global trends and issues
-   makes numerous and consistent direct comparisons throughout the essay
-   makes numerous and consistent analyses of causation

The Process

Prewriting:

1. **Read the question,** underline all the tasks. STOP!

2. **Brainstorm** an answer in the margin. Write down everything that you can recall associated with it.

3. Using your notes, **plan your answer by grouping** with chronology or topic. Ideally you should find three topics or chronologies so that you will have three paragraphs.

4. *First paragraph:* Write a **clear, complete thesis** of one to three sentences about the generalities of your answer and attempt to give an overall reason for similarities and/or differences.

5. *Next three paragraphs:* Taking each topic in the order you planned, write an overall topic sentence followed by **several direct comparisons and similarities**. If you have not done so already, finish with an **explanation for why something was similar or different**. Make sure that you tie each paragraph specifically back to the question.

6. *Final Paragraph:* Write a conclusion that **relates your comparisons to the global context at that time.**

Model Comparative Essay

Below you will find a model comparative essay which is NOT representative of what could be done in 35 minutes under testing conditions. Just as with the other two essays, we have written and reworked this example several times so that we can point out the best elements in a potential response. Your essay will probably be shorter and contain fewer specific details, but it could still demonstrate enough proficiency to garner a high score. Read this essay carefully and then consider how it would be scored.

Compare and contrast European and Japanese feudalism, c. 800–1300 C.E.

After the fall of the western Roman empire in the fifth century C.E., and the demise of the Heian Court in Japan in the twelfth century C.E., both regions struggled unsuccessfully to rebuild a strong centralized governing system. Each region eventually developed a decentralized governing system based on mutual ties and obligations to provide protection for its people: feudalism. Yet, despite emerging out of the same need for security and stability and relying on a noble class to provide protection, feudalism in Europe and Japan differed greatly in attitudes toward women within each system due to the constraints of Christianity and residual patriarchal beliefs which survived the Roman empire.

Feudalism in Europe and Japan developed out of a similar need for security and stability as the previous centralized government in each region fell. In Europe, the western Roman empire had been dying for nearly 200 years as Germanic and Asiatic nomads relentlessly chipped away at the empire's northern and western borders. The peoples of that once mighty power had increasingly abandoned the cities in hopes of finding safety in the countryside. In the ninth century, the search from protection from marauding invaders intensified again as the Norsemen, or Vikings, began to attack western European sea, ocean, and river ports in search of wealth. In Japan, the imperial government had allowed itself to become a pawn of competing family factions who used their wealth and members, especially marriageable daughters, to gain influence at the Imperial Courts. These powerful families, like the Fujiwara, increasingly depended on alliances with local and regional lords to support their efforts to retain imperial influence. By the mid-twelfth century, these conflicts had turned to open feuding between the Taira and Minimoto families. The resulting Gempei Wars, during the twelfth century, marked the beginning of the feudal era in Japan as people sought protection from the rival warlords as the power of the imperial house weakened and the power of the lords grew.

Both European and Japanese feudalism relied on a noble class to provide this protection. In Europe, these nobles, known as knights, fought for their lords in exchange for land, while in Japan, these nobles, known as samurai, fought for their lords in exchange for a living allowance. In Europe, the knights used chain mail armor, broadswords, and lances as weapons in battle, but the Japanese used leather armor and swords, bows, and arrows. Both groups relied on a code of honor which valued bravery and loyalty. But the European knights' code of chivalry was tied to loyalty to God, to a feudal lord, and to a chosen lady, while bushido, the Japanese code, tied this loyalty to the local lord above all.

Though the need for security and the reliance on a noble class to provide that security may have been similar in these two feudal societies, the attitudes toward women within each system were very different. During the European feudal era, most women worked as serfs with their families on a manor and were

---

419

focused on survival. Yet, aristocratic European women probably felt the greatest constraints as women were either idolized as pure and holy or demonized as responsible for the presence of evil in the world. This dichotomy is most clearly seen in the songs of the troubadours whose words contrasted spiritual or courtly love with baser physical love and through the codes of chivalry in which European knights regarded women as weak creatures to be protected and idolized. By the ninth century in Europe, the Christian church had abandoned its earliest traditions of gender equality and, as a result of syncretism with Roman traditions, had become increasingly patriarchal in its attitudes toward women. As Christianity had survived the political fall of Rome and was providing the only sort of centralized "government" in western Europe, it is no wonder that its stance on women would permeate feudal society, especially in those social classes not focused on the barest elements of survival. Unlike the world of aristocratic women in feudal Europe, the Japanese feudal era brought some additional opportunities for women. During the earlier Heian era, women at the imperial court had been expected to be as poised and cultured as their male court counterparts, as Lady Murasaki chronicles in her book *The Tale of Genji.* During the feudal period, Japanese samurai expected their women to live up to the same values of honor and courage as men of that class, so women of those provincial bushi households had learned to ride, shoot, and hunt and had shared in a division of the family estate and inheritance. Hojo Maskao was an early samurai woman and Buddhist who successfully rallied and led the samurai class into standing in support of the Hojo Shogunate. Laws in the early thirteenth century allowed women equal rights for inheritance with their brothers and gave women the right to bequeath property. The expectation of samurai honor and loyalty for women as well as men and the ability to share inheritance greatly enhanced the status of samurai women in feudal Japan, unlike their European counterparts who were restricted by religious constraints to either pedestal or bedroom.

The feudal systems of Europe and Japan both developed as a way to provide safety and security in the absence of a strong, centralized system, and both relied on a noble class to provide that protection; yet, each developed very different attitudes toward women's place in that system. The influence of Christianity and residual patriarchy from the Roman empire account for this difference between women's perception in western Europe and the greater freedoms enjoyed by Japanese women of the feudal era.

Essay Analysis

What Should a Good Comparative Response Include? Clearly, you must know something about feudal Japan and feudal Europe to write a good essay on this topic; there is no way to cheat this system. That is why there are those *"Finished reading the chapter? Be sure you can . . ."* sections at the end of each chapter of this text/test prep book. If you conscientiously use those checks to monitor your understanding, you should face the comparative question on the national exam with something relevant to say.

However, it is very possible to know a lot about feudal Europe and feudal Japan and still not score well on these types of questions, because there is a very clear set of elements that the exam readers are looking for as they evaluate your essay. If you train yourself to write the comparative essay using those elements and can recall and apply accurate, valid historical information, you will score well on this type of essay.

Below is a description of how this essay would be scored based on the generic core-scoring guide used for these questions on the national exam. While the particulars might change slightly depending on the year and the type of responses students submit, the standards will always be high.

1. Has an appropriate thesis (1 point possible)

To earn this point you must address the comparison of the issues or themes specified in the prompt.

Here is the thesis of this essay:

> Yet, despite emerging out of the same need for security and stability and relying on a noble class to provide protection, feudalism in Europe and Japan differed greatly in attitudes toward women within each system due to the constraints of Christianity and residual patriarchal beliefs which survived the Roman empire.

This is a strong thesis because it addresses the required comparison of feudalism in Europe and Japan and identifies three areas of analysis. The thesis not only would earn the Basic Core point but would potentially earn the Expanded Core point for thesis because it is "clear, analytical, and comprehensive" which means it is understandable, has a distinct framework, and offers a "because."

It is best to place your thesis at the end of your introductory paragraph and to try to make it one clear sentence rather than several sentences strung together. That strategy allows the exam readers to know exactly what you are trying to prove in your essay and how you plan to prove it. Further, that clearly articulated one-sentence thesis at the end of your introduction also will guide you as the writer: it keeps you on track and moving forward rather than getting bogged down in unnecessary or irrelevant details and thus running out of time.

However, two points of caution:

1) It is better to have two sentences linked together than to have an incomprehensible or run-on one-sentence thesis.
2) Do not sweat an introduction. It does not earn you any basic core points. A well-crafted introduction may help earn expanded core points in a couple of categories, so many students leave some blank lines in their test booklet, start with their thesis and then return to draft an introduction if there is time left in the writing period.

2. All parts of the question have to be addressed in the body of the essay but not equally. (2 points possible)

This essay would earn both these points because it both compares and contrasts the feudalism in Europe and Japan. To only offer comparisons or to only offer contrasts, despite a wealth of information, would earn only one point, as the prompt directs you to do both. A bit more European information than Japanese information is in this essay but this descriptor allows for that imbalance.

3. Accurate historical details to support the thesis. (2 points possible)

This essay supports all three parts of its thesis: (1) Japanese and European feudalism both emerge out of the same need for security and stability, (2) Japanese and European feudalism both rely on a noble class to provide that protection, and (3) Japanese and European feudalism differ in their attitudes toward women because of the constraints of Christianity and residual patriarchy from the Roman empire.

One of the strengths of this sample essay is the wealth of detail it includes. The writer has a strong grasp of the content and has supplied significant supporting detail for each part of the thesis. The writer includes at least one piece of relevant evidence for Europe and one piece for Japan in each of the body paragraphs; in several sections there is more than one. This essay would earn Expanded Core points for providing ample historical evidence to substantiate the thesis.

4. At least two direct accurate comparisons. (2 points possible)

This essay demonstrates an excellent way to earn both these points; the writer uses direct comparisons as her topic sentences for each body paragraph and then follows up with the details.

> Feudalism in Europe and Japan developed out of a similar need for security and stability as the previous centralized government in each region fell.

Both European and Japanese feudalism relied on a noble class to provide this protection. In Europe, these nobles, known as knights, fought for their lords in exchange for land, while in Japan, these nobles, known as samurai, fought for their lords in exchange for a living allowance.

Though the need for security and the reliance on a noble class to provide that security may have been similar in these two feudal societies, the attitudes toward women within each system were very different.

Clearly, the second box contains the most specific direct comparison of the three topic sentences. The essay also includes other direct comparisons as well.

For example, at the end of the second paragraph:

But, the European knights' code of chivalry was tied to loyalty to God, to a feudal lord, and to a chosen lady, while bushido, the Japanese code, tied this loyalty to the local lord above all.

And, at the end of the third body paragraph:

The expectation of samurai honor and loyalty for women as well as men and the ability to share inheritance greatly enhanced the status of samurai women in feudal Japan, unlike their European counterparts who were restricted by religious constraints to either pedestal or bedroom.

This essay would earn Expanded Core points for making "several direct comparisons consistently between or among societies."

5. Analyzes why a similarity or difference has occurred. (1 point possible)

This essay identifies a reason for the difference between attitudes toward women in feudal Europe and in feudal Japan in the thesis, the third body paragraph, and in the conclusion.

The influence of Christianity and residual patriarchy from the Roman empire account for this difference between women's perception in western Europe and the greater freedoms enjoyed by Japanese women of the feudal era.

So what score would this essay earn? Probably a 9 because it not only clearly shows competent skills and knowledge as outlined in the generic scoring guide, but it also has a clear, analytical thesis, provides ample historical evidence to substantiate the thesis, and it makes several direct comparisons consistently between European and Japanese feudalism.

Practice for Comparative Essays

1. Be sure that you go over the **suggested topics** found at the end of this discussion. They are designed to correspond with the important topics identified by the College Board.

2. Practice writing direct comparisons by **using adjoining chapters.** Look at each category of analysis (political, economic, intellectual, military, beliefs, artistic, and social) and write a direct comparison for each one. For example, using Chapters 2 and 3: "While Mesopotamia was a series of city-states, Egypt had unified under Menes." Note that this example also explains why the centralized state occurred in Egypt and that is one of the essential tasks.

3. Use the **comparison graphic organizer** on p. 423 to work on the adjoining chapters' exercises and suggested comparison topics.

4. Beg your teacher to allow you to do more of them and learn to enjoy the comparison essay rather than dread it.

Abbreviated Comparison Essay

1. Copy the question.

2. Identify three comparative issues and give terms and events for BOTH societies.

Issue #1	Issue #2	Issue #3

3. Write a thesis statement.

4. Write at least TWO directly comparative sentences.

5. Analyze at least one specific similarity and one specific difference.

Sample

1. Copy the question:

    Compare and contrast European and Japanese feudalism, c. 800–1300 C.E.

2. Identify three comparative issues and give terms and events for BOTH societies.

Issue #1 *similar need for security and stability*	Issue #2 *similar noble class to provide this protection*	Issue #3 *different attitudes toward women*
western Roman empire had been dying for nearly 200 years as Germanic and Asiatic nomads *Japan, the imperial government had allowed itself to become a pawn of competing family factions*	*knights; chivalry* *samurai; bushido*	*aristocratic European women pure/impure? troubadours, increasingly patriarchal church* *additional opportunities: Heian era, Lady Murasaki, The Tale of Genji; equal rights for inheritance, samurai roles*

3. Write a thesis statement.

   Despite emerging out of the same need for security and stability and relying on a noble class to provide protection, feudalism in Europe and Japan differed greatly in attitudes toward women within each system due to the constraints of Christianity and residual patriarchal beliefs which survived the Roman empire.

4. Write at least TWO directly comparative sentences.

   Both European and Japanese feudalism relied on a noble class to provide this protection. In Europe, these nobles, known as knights, fought for their lords in exchange for land, while in Japan, these nobles, known as samurai, fought for their lords in exchange for a living allowance.

   But the European knights' code of chivalry was tied to loyalty to God, to a feudal lord, and to a chosen lady, while bushido, the Japanese code, tied this loyalty to the local lord above all.

   The expectation of samurai honor and loyalty for women as well as men and the ability to share inheritance greatly enhanced the status of samurai women in feudal Japan, unlike their European counterparts who were restricted by religious constraints to either pedestal or bedroom.

5. Analyze at least one specific similarity and one specific difference.

   Feudalism in Europe and Japan developed out of a similar need for security and stability as the previous centralized government in each region fell.

   The influence of Christianity and residual patriarchy from the Roman Empire account for this difference between women's perception in western Europe and the greater freedoms enjoyed by Japanese women of the feudal era.

Practice Comparative Questions

Foundations Unit, c. 8000 B.C.E.–600 C.E.

1. Systems of social inequality were common in the ancient and classical worlds. Compare and contrast the caste system in India to ONE other civilization's system of social inequality during the period 8000 B.C.E.–600 C.E.

Choose ONE to compare and contrast with the caste system in India:
Mesopotamia
Egypt
China
Mesoamerica and Andean South America
Classical Mediterranean world

2. Compare and contrast the collapse of the western Roman empire with the collapse of the Han empire in China.

3. Compare and contrast the role of women in TWO of the following belief systems during the period 8000 B.C.E.–600 C.E.
    Hinduism
    Buddhism
    Confucianism
    Christianity

4. Compare and contrast the nature of patriarchal systems in TWO of the following regions during the period 8000 B.C.E.–600 C.E.
    Mesopotamia
    Egypt
    India
    China
    Mesoamerica and Andean South America
    Classical Mediterranean world

5. Compare and contrast development of political institutions in TWO of the following regions during the period 8000 B.C.E.–600 C.E.
    Mesopotamia
    Egypt
    India
    China
    Mesoamerica and Andean South America
    Classical Mediterranean world

6. Compare and contrast the impact of technology on TWO of the following regions during the period 8000 B.C.E.–600 C.E.
    Mesopotamia
    Egypt
    India
    China
    Mesoamerica and Andean South America
    Classical Mediterranean world

7. Compare and contrast the impact of belief systems on social hierarchies in TWO of the following regions during the period 8000 B.C.E.– 600 C.E.
    Mesopotamia
    Egypt
    India
    China
    Mesoamerica and Andean South America
    Classical Mediterranean world

8. Compare and contrast the effects of interregional trading systems on TWO of the following regions during the period 8000 B.C.E.–600 C.E.
   Mesopotamia
   India
   China
   Mesoamerica and Andean South America
   Classical Mediterranean world

Unit II, 600–1450 C.E.

1. Compare and contrast Japanese and European feudalism.

2. Compare and contrast the development of political institutions in eastern and western Europe in the period 600–1450.

3. Compare and contrast the spread of Christianity and Islam during the period 100 C.E.–1450.

4. Compare and contrast the impact of Islam on gender systems in TWO of the following regions c. 600–1450.
   Middle East
   West Africa
   East Africa
   South Asia

5. Compare and contrast the development of political institutions in TWO of the following regions c. 600–1450.
   Mesoamerica
   Andean America
   Eastern Europe
   Western Europe
   East Asia
   Western Africa

6. Compare and contrast the impact of plague pandemics in TWO of the following regions c. 600–1450.
   Western Europe
   Eastern Asia
   South Asia
   Eastern Europe

7. Compare and contrast the opportunities and constraints on women in TWO of the following regions c. 600–1450.
   Mesoamerica
   Andean America
   Eastern Europe
   Western Europe
   East Asia
   Western Africa

Unit III, 1450–1750

1. Compare and contrast the trading patterns in TWO of the following regions c. 1450–1750.
   West Africa
   Latin America
   North America
   East Asia
   South Asia

2. Compare and contrast the political institutions in TWO of the following regions c. 1450–1750.
   Middle East
   South Asia
   West Africa
   Western Europe
   Eastern Europe
   East Asia

3. Compare and contrast the impact of the Columbian exchange on TWO of the following regions.
   North America
   Western Africa
   Latin America
   Western Europe
   East Asia

4. Compare and contrast Russia's interaction with the west with ONE of the following:
   Ottoman empire
   China
   Tokugawa Japan
   Mughal India

Unit IV, 1750–1914
1. Compare and contrast the effects of the industrial revolution in TWO of the following regions c. 1750–1914.
   Western Europe
   South Asia
   East Asia
   Latin America

2. Compare and contrast the impact of the Atlantic slave trade in TWO of the following regions c. 1750–1914.
   Western Africa
   Latin America
   North America

3. Compare and contrast the political revolutions in TWO of the following regions c. 1750–1914.
   Latin America
   North America
   East Asia

4. Compare and contrast the reaction to foreign domination in TWO of the following regions c. 1750–1914.
   East Asia
   South Asia
   Middle East

5. Compare and contrast forms of western intervention in Latin America and in Africa c. 1750–1914.

6. Compare and contrast the roles and conditions of women in the upper/middle classes with the peasantry/working class in western Europe.

7. Compare and contrast the causes and early phases of the industrial revolution in western Europe and Japan c. 1750–1914.

Unit V, 1914–Present

1. Compare and contrast the causes of war in TWO of the following regions c. 1914–2000.
East Asia
South Asia
Southeast Asia
Middle East

2. Compare and contrast the patterns and results of decolonization in Africa and India c. 1914–2000.

3. Compare and contrast the effects of political revolutions on the roles of women in TWO of the following places c. 1914–2000.
Russia
China
Cuba
Iran

4. Compare and contrast the effects of World War I on TWO of the following regions.
Middle East
East Asia
South Asia
Eastern Europe

5. Compare and contrast the effects of World War II on TWO of the following regions.
Middle East
East Asia
South Asia
Eastern Europe

6. Compare and contrast the legacies of colonialism in TWO of the following regions c. 1914–2000.
Africa
Asia
Latin America

7. Compare and contrast the legacies of the cold war in TWO of the following regions.
Eastern Europe
Southeast Asia
South Asia
Middle East

8. Compare and contrast the independence struggles in TWO of the following regions c. 1914–2000.
East Africa
West Africa
North Africa
Southeast Asia
South Asia

9. Compare and contrast the causes for and results of genocide in TWO of the following regions c. 1914–2000.
Europe
Africa
Southeast Asia
East Asia

THE CHANGE-OVER-TIME ESSAY

This has been the most difficult essay to write because the exam questions have often required juggling two or more societies over time. Furthermore, you must identify crucial periods when change occurs or when the situation remains the same. You may be tempted to treat it as a narrative or the story of what happened. DON'T DO IT! You must treat it in the same analytical way that you use in the other essays. The topics are the pivotal points in history. The example we will use is the Little Red Riding Hood story. To gain no points at all, you would tell the story from beginning to end. To gain points, you would set the scene with the initial encounter, tying it to the European fear of wolves and danger in the woods since medieval times. You would then go on to describe the attack and swallowing of granny as a prelude for what could happen to Little Red Riding Hood as well. Many historical events have preceding incidents that presage world events. You would end with the rescue of Little Red Riding Hood and her granny by the woodchopper but tie it into the return to initial conditions which is continuity despite major upheavals. Pivotal events, changes, and continuities should all be a part of your essay.

The Essential Tasks

As in the comparative essay, you must do five tasks and two of them are worth two points. You must have all seven points to go to eight or nine points. The first three tasks are identical to the comparative essay.

1. You must write a **thesis** that correctly answers all parts of the question. No problem, we already discussed that. (1 point)

2. **All parts of the question** have to be addressed in the body as well but they do not have to be treated equally. It is acceptable to know more about one area than another but you must discuss all parts. If you only deal with most parts (only changes when continuities are also required, for example) you will only receive one point. (1 or 2 points)

3. You must use **accurate historical evidence** to support the thesis. For each topic area you plan to discuss, you must have one historical fact that supports it. The more details, the better opportunity for two points. (1 or 2 points)

4. You must **identify global historical events and trends during that time period to explain the change or continuity.** You need to give adequate global history of the time to explain the events you are examining. (1 point)

5. You must **analyze the change process that is occurring during that time span.** This means that you need to break it down into pivotal points of change and identify periods of continuity. You must explicitly identify those moments and periods; it is not enough to tell the story. You should attempt to explain causation at the same time. (1 point)

Tasks beyond the Core Points

- a thesis statement that analyzes the situation and attempts to explain causation
- analyzes all parts of the question accurately by adding causes, effects, chronology, change, continuity, and global context as appropriate
- equal treatment of all parts of the question
- numerous accurate historical details that support the thesis
- makes innovative links to historical themes, events, and trends

The Process

Prewriting:

1. **Read the question**, underline all the tasks. STOP!

2. **Brainstorm** an answer in the margin. Write down everything that you can recall associated with it.

3. Using your notes, **plan your answer by grouping** into chronology and pivotal points. Ideally you should find three topics for discussion so that you will have three paragraphs.

4. *First paragraph:* Write a **clear, complete thesis** of one to three sentences about the generalities of your answer and attempt to give an overall reason for changes and continuities.

5. *Next three paragraphs:* Taking each topic in the order you planned, write an overall topic sentence followed by several sentences describing **the period of change or continuity.** If you have not done so already, finish with an **explanation for why something changed or remained the same.** If possible tie the period into what is happening in the world at the same time. And, as always, make sure that you tie each paragraph specifically back to the question.

6. *Final Paragraph:* Write a conclusion that relates the historical process to the global context or relevant historical trends and themes.

Model Change-Over-Time Essay

Below you will find a model Change-Over-Time essay which is NOT representative of what could be done in 35 minutes under testing conditions. Just as with the other essays, we have written and reworked this example many times to point out the best elements in a potential response. Your essay will probably be shorter and contain fewer specific details, but it could still demonstrate enough proficiency to garner a high score. Read this essay carefully and then consider how it would be scored.

Describe and analyze the changing social response to diseases c. 1200–1920 in ONE of the following regions.
    Latin America
    Western Europe
    Western Africa
    East Asia
    North America

Since human beings first began living, especially in settled, organized communities, they have been making each other sick and looking for someone or something to blame. Societies have responded in a variety of ways to these illnesses: first by seeking religious explanations, then societal ones, and finally scientific ones; whatever the societal response to disease, the response reflects the ideals prevalent at the time. In western Europe, the changing social impact of disease is shown through the religious response to the bubonic plague c. 1347, the public health response to industrialization c. 1800, and the scientific response to the Spanish flu of 1918; each of these social responses had a significant, enduring, economic impact.

The social impact of disease is clearly seen in western Europe's response to the fourteenth-century bubonic plague. The Black Death, as it is often called, began in Asia and traveled along trade routes throughout much of the early fourteenth century, and by 1347, it entered western Europe. In some parts of western Europe, the residents of entire villages died; in other places up to one-half of the population died as a result of the rat-carried bacteria. In addition to the sheer numbers of people affected, the rapidity with which people caught the disease and died and the horror and pain of their deaths served to create a climate of fear. People tried to turn to the Catholic church for answers, but the church was wholly unprepared for such a crisis. The church was involved in its own crisis at the time with the relocation of the seat of the church to southern France in an attempt to loosen the hold of the Italian cardinals on church affairs. The Pope responded to the plague by calling for greater penance and prayers to offer protection as he himself sought refuge in the papal fortress at Avignon. Neither penance nor prayer proved useful in stopping the deaths. Others saw the plague as God's punishment for the sins of humankind and sought his forgiveness by forming groups of flagellants who sought to atone for their own sins and the sins of others by whipping and beating themselves with studded whips and chains. These religious responses not only proved ineffective, but actually may have spread the disease as the fleas which harbored the bacteria also traveled on these misguided religious pilgrims. There were also religious Christians who saw the plague as the work of Jews, and there was a rise in the continuous cycle of Jewish persecutions and murder. Consistent rumors that Jews were poisoning the streams and wells lead to a series of pogroms in western Europe; drowning or burning were often seen as a way of purifying these "non-believers." Though people in western Europe turned to religion to protect them from the plague, religion provided no protection for society. The long-term religious impact would be a weakening in the structure and hold of the church over western Europe and the rise of Protestantism in the sixteenth century. Unlike crises which sometimes draw people together, the bubonic plague of the fourteenth century tore western European society apart.

While the social response to the bubonic plague of the fourteenth century was to turn to religion, the social response to the diseases of nineteenth-century industrialization was to turn to the government for protection. The impact of the enclosure movement and improved farming technologies drove many former farming families to the cities, where Great Britain possessed all the elements necessary for an industrial revolution: land, labor, capital. Further, Great Britain also possessed a government, made stable and useful in the previous century through revolution, which valued the idea of laissez-faire, that the flow of commerce in the world market occurs best without government interference. Great Britain did not have adequate shelter and sanitation for these new industrial workers. There was a lack of clean or even running water, little thought of indoor plumbing, and the factories possessed no safety precautions for equipment or for fire protection; they pumped coal fumes into the air 24 hours a day. These conditions were ripe for cholera and typhoid, waterborne diseases which thrive in filthy cities. It is estimated that during the early years of the industrial revolution the mortality rate due to cholera or typhoid for infants and children under the age of two who lived in cities was 50 percent. Tuberculosis (TB) was another disease of industrialization which affected those who were poorly nourished and lived in dirty or damp housing. In a tightly packed, overcrowded tenement, an infected person could easily spread the disease. It is estimated that TB killed one-third of all those who lived in Great Britain between 1800 and 1850.

When an outbreak of cholera decimated working-class neighborhoods in Manchester in the first decades of the nineteenth century, a few industrialists and some humanitarians such as Edwin Chadwick began to put pressure on the British government to deal with the causes of these deadly diseases. In 1802, the British government passed a series of legislation which limited work hours and required safety inspection of work sites. The Sadler Report, published in 1833, reported on terrible working and living conditions and suggested that reforms must be undertaken to avoid social unrest which, of course, would be bad for business; the Health Act of 1848 reflected this realization. The British government's recognition of the squalid living conditions of workers had much more to do with a fear of social unrest and the feared resulting economic disruption, than it did with the humanitarian needs of its working-class citizens.

Just as western European society had turned to the dominant institution for the fourteenth century, the church, for relief, and the nineteenth-century plea was to government, societal response to disease in the early twentieth century was to science. In 1918, in the last year of the Great War, a particularly virulent form of influenza appeared first in China but rapidly spread west, probably as a result of troop and materials movement associated with the war; more soldiers are estimated to have died from the flu than from the terrible fighting in WWI. In India, it is estimated that 50 out of every 1000 people died of this flu. The first cases in Europe appeared in the spring of 1918, in Spain where eight million people died, including the King of Spain. By late spring, this "Spanish influenza" had spread to the rest of western Europe, wiping out populations in numbers reminiscent of the 14th-century Black Death. Several factors made this disease particularly frightening: the speed and ease with which it spread, the fact that one could be well in the morning, coughing at noon and dead by dinner time, the rate of mutation and possibility of re-infection, and the disease's attraction to young, seemingly healthy people. This strain of flu had the highest mortality rate in people 25 to 30 years old. It is estimated that 40 percent of the world's population became ill with the Spanish flu and up to 100 million people died.

The societal response to this disease was to turn to science. The earlier work of Louis Pasteur and Edmond Koch had developed and clarified the germ theory of disease, and public health and sanitation legislation of the nineteenth century had established norms and practices for dealing with infectious diseases. The medical and scientific communities were developing new theories and applications for prevention. But, while science did not as yet fully understand the causes of the disease, it did understand how to treat the symptoms and how to slow its spread: reduce the pathogen by preventing contact. Close public institutions and ban public gatherings. Local public health departments distributed gauze masks to be worn in public, stores could not hold sales, schools were closed, funerals could not last more than 15 minutes. Some towns in England required good-health passes to ride on the railroads; pubs, dance halls, and cinemas were closed, and programs to push handwashing, good ventilation, and general hygiene were promoted through flu posters and churches. The use of disinfectant and sterilization methods to contain the flu demonstrate society's reliance on science as did a growing interest in the development of a vaccine to prevent infection. Though the disease had run its deadly course by 1919, the quest for a flu vaccine continues today as fears of another flu pandemic intensify.

Each of these diseases elicited a western European societal response that reflects the changing authority of the age: religion, government, and science. Yet each of these societal responses has continuously produced a major economic impact. The economic impact of the black plague was huge; the sheer number of dead and the lack of adequate church response decimated the remaining feudal social structure, spurred an urban movement, and laid the groundwork for the upcoming Reformation. The governmental response to the nineteenth-century diseases of cholera, typhoid, and typhus brought rights and standards to the lives of working people, helped businesses and markets prosper, moved western European governments from a strict laissez-faire stance, and made cities livable again. The societal response to the Spanish flu epidemic of 1918 was to look to science and technology for answers which has directed the growth of science and technology throughout the twentieth century. This resulting economic impact is a continuous process which supports western Europe's changing social response to disease.

Essay Analysis

What Should a Good Change-Over-Time Essay Include? It is best to think of this question as a "Continuity and Change-Over-Time" essay, rather than just a Change-Over-Time. If you look at the AP course description themes and the core-scoring rubric carefully, you will see that a "continuity" may be required based on quality and level of the student responses. Since you always want to score well on this type of essay, you are best served by learning to include the continuity as well as the change elements of these types of questions whenever you write one.

This can be the most difficult of the three essays to write as you must know a depth of content about a single region and a single theme. Further, you must understand solid historical facts, have the background to set that information in historical context, and have had practice in demonstrating that learning under testing conditions. Practice means careful reading, thoughtful discussions, and plenty of well-crafted writing assignments throughout the school year.

For this type of question especially, knowing how to put it together is essential to score well. Think about what stays the same and what changes in each of the eras as you plan your essay. It is essential for you to spend a few moments jotting an outline or visual guide before you start to write. This essay, above the other two, requires you to stay focused on the demands of the question; it is so easy to just begin to tell information in a chronological manner. Think periodization: three distinct time periods, events, or turning points. All sorts of information will earn you only a score of 1 or 2, unless you understand the structural and analytical demands of this essay. Rely on your jottings or outline to save you time and earn you points.

Below is a description of how this sample essay would be scored based on the generic core-scoring guide used for this type of question on the national exam. While the particulars might change slightly depending on the year, the question's focus, and the type of responses students submit, the standards will always be high.

1. Has an appropriate thesis (1 point possible)

To earn this point, you must address the global issues and the time period specified in the question.

Here is the thesis of this essay:

> In western Europe, the changing social impact of disease is shown through the religious response to the bubonic plague c. 1347, the public health response to industrialization c. 1800, and the scientific response to the Spanish flu of 1918; each of these social responses had a significant, enduring economic impact.

This thesis is strong because it addresses the global issue, disease; it selects one of the places listed, western Europe; and it includes three significant time periods, 1347, the early 19th-century, and 1918, which are within the 1200–1920 timeframe. For those reasons, it would earn the Core scoring point for thesis.

This thesis would probably earn the Expanded Core point as well because it is "clear, analytical, and comprehensive." On the Change-Over-Time question, that can mean it includes a "continuity" as well as the changes during this time period, i.e., "each of these social responses had a significant, enduring economic impact."

As in all the essays you will write on this exam, it is best to place your thesis as the last sentence in your introductory paragraph, and to try to make it a single strong sentence. On this essay in particular, that may be difficult to do if you are seeking expanded core points. Remember, you can use a semicolon as the writer did in this sample essay, or you can make it two sentences, one coming right after the other. It is better to have a clear two-sentence thesis than an illogical or totally confusing one. The exam reader is looking for your controlling idea. Be clear. Also, notice that this writer was careful to use the word "changing" and the word "enduring" to clearly indicate that she planned to address continuity and change in this essay.

2. All parts of the question have to be addressed in the body of the essay but not equally. (2 points possible)

You earn both these points by addressing all parts of the question and by addressing change and continuity. This essay would earn both these points because the writer clearly addresses the western European societal response to disease in three distinct time periods or turning points, and she manages to connect them to the continuity of economic impact on society in the final paragraph.

> The economic impact of the black plague was huge; the sheer number of dead and the lack of adequate church response decimated the remaining feudal social structure, spurred an urban movement, and laid the groundwork for the upcoming Reformation. The governmental response to the nineteenth-century diseases of cholera, typhoid, and typhus brought rights and standards to the lives of working people, helped businesses and markets prosper, moved western European governments from a strict laissez-faire stance, and made cities livable again. The societal response to the Spanish flu epidemic of 1918 was to look to science and technology for answers which has directed the growth of science and technology throughout the twentieth century. This resulting economic impact is a continuous process which supports western Europe's changing social response to disease.

3. Accurate historical details to support the thesis. (2 points possible)

These are the points you earn by knowing your content and by sticking to your controlling idea. Often, students fail to earn points here because they tell everything they know about a topic rather than selecting specific historical content to support a controlling idea. In other words, you earn these points through careful selection of historical evidence which supports your thesis. It is not about length here; it is about the accuracy, quality, and applicability of the historical information you choose to include. The time you spend learning and thinking about the content in your textbook and the quality of your coursework over the school year pays off here. You must "know your stuff" to earn these points.

This essay is filled with content for each time period and for each example of change and continuity and so would earn both points. Just to be sure she is clear for the exam reader, the writer uses her topic or closing sentence of each section to lay out her evidence.

> Though people in western Europe turned to religion to protect them from the plague, religion provided no protection for society.

> While the social response to the bubonic plague of the fourteenth century was to turn to religion, the social response to the diseases of nineteenth-century industrialization was to turn to the government for protection.

> Just as western European society had turned to the dominant institution for the fourteenth century, the church, for relief, and the nineteenth century plea was to government, societal response to disease in the early twentieth century was to science.

4. Identify global historical events and trends during that time period to explain the change or continuity. (1 point possible)

This point is earned through the writer's ability to set the stage for the continuities and changes. It is the background or context for the events. Again a rich content background and a clear understanding of the times are essential to earning this point.

In the sample essay, the writer makes two statements which would earn this point. In the first section, she writes:

> The Black Death, as it is often called, began in Asia and traveled along trade routes throughout much of the early fourteenth century, and by 1347, it entered western Europe. In some parts of western Europe, the residents of entire villages died, in other places up to one-half of the population died as a result of the rat-carried bacteria. In addition to the sheer numbers of people affected, the rapidity with which people caught the disease and died and the horror and pain of their deaths served to create a climate of fear. People tried to turn to the church for answers, but the church was wholly unprepared for such a crisis.

In the third section she writes:

> In 1918, in the last year of the Great War, a particularly virulent form of influenza appeared first in China but rapidly spread west, probably as a result of troop and materials movement associated with the war; more soldiers are estimated to have died from the flu than from the terrible fighting in WWI. In India, it is estimated that 50 out of every 1000 people died. The first cases in Europe appeared in the spring of 1918, in Spain where eight million people died, including the King of Spain. By late spring this "Spanish influenza" had spread to the rest of western Europe, wiping out populations in numbers reminiscent of the 14th-century black death.

5. Analyze the change process that is occurring during that time span. (1 point possible)

This point is earned through your ability to explain "how or why this continuity continued and how or why these changes changed." To analyze something is to break it down into understandable parts. This essay does a good job with following the organization laid out in the thesis which sets up the analysis. The writer uses this premise to guide her essay.

In her introduction, the writer says:

> . . . whatever the societal response to disease, the response reflects the ideals prevalent at the time.

In her conclusion, she restates this analysis:

> Each of these diseases elicited a western European societal response that reflects the changing authority of the age: religion, government, and science. Yet each of these societal responses has continuously produced a major economic impact.

The writer has a theory that explains the changes, i.e., that western European societal response to disease reflects the dominant ideas of the particular time period, and the writer has a theory that explains the continuity, i.e., that each differing societal response results in a major economic impact.

So what score would this change-over-time essay earn? Probably a 9 because it demonstrates the historical skills and knowledge necessary to show competence, and it uses its strong, analytical thesis to guide the writing. The solid historical context and the use of ample evidence would help it earn a top score.

Practice

1. Be sure that you go over the **suggested topics** in this guide. They are geared to correspond with the important topics identified by the College Board.

2. Practice change and continuity by taking three of the chapters that describe the same region in different eras and identify key pivotal events when changes or continuities occurred. The question could be in any theme (political, economic, intellectual, military, beliefs, artistic, and social), so write a longitudinal analysis of the most notable ones. (It is unlikely that art will change drastically and this is not an art history course; however, politics, economics, religion, and social issues change and continue.) For instance, with Chapters 4, 9, and 16, you could look at the social scene in India. A good essay would note that "once the caste system was solidified in the Vedic age, it expanded with new subcastes or jatis based on occupation in the Classical period, and even Islam or foreign merchants were incorporated at later times. But throughout India's early history, persons born to a caste remained in that caste whether they prospered economically or not. The explanation for its continuity is that the caste system always accommodated new social and economic conditions and thus was paradoxically flexible." This last sentence incorporates causation, one of the essential tasks.

3. The kicker is that you might be required to deal with **comparisons at the same time,** so to follow our example, add Chapters 5, 8, and 15 on China. "While India expanded its caste system to accommodate new conditions, China largely maintained four social levels associated with professions: scholar-officials, merchants, farmers, and laborers. Unlike India, there was some individual social mobility between classes. Yet, the prestige of classes ebbed and waned according to political policy and economic necessity. For instance, scholar-officials were rejected by the Qin and Yuan but restored to power by the Han and Ming. Merchants were socially disdained while farmers were venerated, but the treatment of those classes was often contrary to their perceived social value."

4. Try the suggested change-over-time essays below.

5. Use the **change-over-time graphic organizer** below to work on the suggested topics or the three-chapter approach described above.

6. Beg your teacher to allow you to do more of them and learn to enjoy the change-over-time essay rather than dread it.

Abbreviated Change-Over-Time Essay

1. Copy the question:

2. Identify three pivotal moments; fill in events, terms, and trends under each one

3. Write a thesis statement.

4. Explain each continuity/change that you identified above with how it reflects global trends.

5. Analyze each continuity/change by looking at causation and the elements that contribute to each one.

Sample

1. Copy the question:

    Describe and analyze the changing social response to diseases c. 1200–1920 in ONE of the following regions.
        Western Europe

2. Identify three pivotal moments; fill in events, terms, and trends under each one

the religious response to the bubonic plague c. 1347	*the public health response to industrialization c. 1800*	*the scientific response to the Spanish flu of 1918*
Neither penance nor prayer proved useful *flagellants* *continuous cycle of Jewish persecutions and murder.*	*no sanitary codes or building controls; no safety precautions for equipment or for fire protection and they pumped coal fumes; cholera or typhoid* *safety inspection of work sites; Adequate ventilation and available fresh water*	*"Spanish influenza" that 40% of the world's population became ill with the Spanish flu and up to 100 million deaths* *germ theory: Louis Pasteur and Edmond Koch* *public health departments* *gauze masks* *disinfectant and sterilization*

3. Write a thesis statement:

    In western Europe, the changing social impact of disease is shown through the religious response to the bubonic plague c. 1347, the public health response to industrialization c. 1800, and the scientific response to the Spanish flu of 1918; each of these social responses had a significant, enduring, economic impact.

4. Explain each continuity/change that you identified above with how it reflects global trends.

    religious: tied to historic persecutions of Jews in the Middle East and Europe

    public health: tied to effect of industrialization throughout the world

    scientific: improvements in western (Europe/Americas) medicine and science in late nineteenth century

5. Analyze each continuity/change by looking at causation and the elements that contribute to each one.

    religious: church weak because the seat of the church had moved to southern France. The Pope sought refuge in the papal fortress at Avignon.

    public health: Sadler Report suggested that reforms must be undertaken to avoid social unrest which, of course, would be bad for business.

    scientific: The earlier work of Louis Pasteur and Edmond Koch had developed and clarified the germ theory of disease.

Practice Change-Over-Time Questions

There are a huge number of potential change-over-time questions, far too many to list completely. However, it is safe to assume that change-over-time questions might include any of the six WH themes applied to world regions across the scope of this course: 8000 B.C.E. to the present. For example, you might see broad questions based on these:

1. Pick one of the following regions and discuss the continuities and changes in belief systems from 8000 B.C.E. to 600 C.E.
   The Middle East
   South Asia
   East Asia
   Europe

2. Pick one of the following regions and discuss the continuities and changes in trade from 8000 B.C.E. to 600 C.E.
   The Middle East
   South Asia
   East Asia
   Europe

3. Pick one of the following regions and discuss the continuities and changes in political structures from 8000 B.C.E. to 600 C.E.
   The Middle East
   North Africa
   East Asia
   Europe

4. Pick one of the following regions and discuss the continuities and changes in social and gender systems from 8000 B.C.E. to 600 C.E.
   The Middle East
   South Asia
   East Asia
   Europe

5. Pick one of the following regions and discuss the continuities and changes in religions from 600 C.E. to 1450.
   The Middle East
   South Asia
   Europe
   North Africa

6. Pick one of the following regions and discuss the continuities and changes in trade from 600 C.E. to 1450.
   The Middle East
   South Asia
   Central Asia
   Europe

7. Pick one of the following regions and discuss the continuities and changes in intellectual and cultural practices from 600 C.E. to 1450.
   The Middle East
   South Asia
   East Asia
   Europe

Or you might see more specific questions such as:

1. Describe and analyze the changing roles for women in ONE of the following regions
c. 1000–2000 C.E.
Middle East
Western Europe
South East Asia
East Asia

2. Describe and analyze the political, social, and economic impact of Christianity in ONE of the
following regions c. 1000–2000 C.E.
Latin America
Sub-Saharan Africa
Eastern Europe

3. Describe and analyze the demographic changes due to migration in ONE of the following places
c. 1000–2000 C.E.
Latin America
North America
West Africa
Western Europe
South Asia
East Asia

4. Describe and analyze the impact of technology on society in ONE of the following places
c. 1450–2000.
Latin America
North America
West Africa
Western Europe
South Asia
East Asia

5. Describe and analyze the impact of political revolution on women's roles in ONE of the following
places c. 1450–2000 C.E.
Latin America
Central Asia
South Asia
North Africa
Eastern Europe

6. Describe and analyze the impact of political revolution on social class in ONE of the following places
c. 1450–2000 C.E.
Latin America
Central Asia
South Asia
East Asia
Eastern Europe

7. Describe and analyze the influence of western dominance on traditional cultures in ONE of the
following places c. 1450–2000 C.E.
North Africa
Sub-Saharan Africa
Latin America
East Asia
South Asia

8. Describe and analyze responses to military aggression in ONE of the following places c. 1750–2000 C.E.
   East Asia
   Western Europe
   Southeast Asia
   Eastern Europe

The list is almost endless if you interchange themes, regions, and time periods.

SECTION IV

PRACTICE TESTS
WITH ANSWERS AND ANALYSIS

PRACTICE EXAM 1

WORLD HISTORY EXAM

You will have three hours and five minutes to complete this exam. The multiple choice section is fifty-five minutes long while the essay section allows two hours and ten minutes.
Ten minutes will be allotted as a mandatory reading and preparation period. The two sections are given equal weight in the final exam score.

Section I
Multiple Choice Question (55 minutes)
70 questions
50 percent of final score

In the real exam, all answers will be done on a separate answer sheet but you will be able to mark up the test booklet. There will be one sample question and answer to indicate how to fill in the answer sheet. There may be a note on random guessing and we advise guessing only when you know something about the question since wrong answers gain a quarter point deduction. The exam will advise that you keep your eye on the clock but aim for accuracy as it is not expected that everyone will answer all the questions in the section.

1. What happened to polytheistic religions in South Asia with the advent of monotheism?
   a. South Asian followers of polytheism were found less in urban centers as they retreated to their origins in the river valleys.
   b. East Asian adherents were adaptable and tended to follow both types of religions at the same time.
   c. In south Asia, there was a tendency for the northern half to convert to monotheism while the southern half remained mostly polytheistic.
   d. Along the Indian Ocean coast, polytheistic peoples did not accept monotheism and held tight to polytheistic beliefs.
   e. The polytheists of central Asia realized that they could enthusiastically accept monotheism by equating one god in their pantheon with the single god of the new religion.

2. The formation of empires such as the Persian and the Roman in the Middle East shared which of the following with the Qin and Han empires in East Asia?
   a. a tendency to subsume the culture of conquered regions into their culture
   b. the strict regulation of trade by foreigners within their borders
   c. the acceptance of all cultural traits that did not contradict their own
   d. maintaining a strong fiscal relationship with conquered regions was the primary goal
   e. each had a strongly decentralized system of governance

3. To what extent did Confucian values influence the treatment of women in China?
   a. It was responsible for the practice of concubinage in the imperial residence.
   b. Its view of proper relationships necessarily made women subservient to men.
   c. As a result of Confucian teachings, women in the Song dynasty began to bind their feet.
   d. It forced women to remain at home with no involvement in the marketplace.
   e. The teachings of Kong Fuxi promoted the practice of female infanticide.

4. All of the following were reasons for the development of major religions EXCEPT
   a. outgrowths of older religions
   b. personal experiences of spiritual awakening
   c. acceptance by a body of the faithful
   d. personal or societal dissatisfaction
   e. governmental mandates in favor of new beliefs

5. To what extent was the spread of medieval Christianity similar to that of early Islam?
   a. They both used vast armies to force conversion to the exclusion of peaceful means.
   b. They relied upon one central authority, either the pope or the caliph, to personally direct its expansion.
   c. They both offered the option of conversion or retention of the older religion with the payment of a tax.
   d. They carried an appealing message of salvation that attracted converts wherever their influence was strong.
   e. They came up against strong resistance from unified leaders of other religions.

6. Which of the following statements best describes the silk roads between 400 and 800 C.E.?
   a. There was thriving commerce between the Middle East, India, and China but very little involvement on the part of Europeans.
   b. Since the Mongols protected the routes, there was more commerce than in the earlier periods.
   c. Since the Roman and Han empires were at the terminal points, the demand for luxury items escalated as did trade.
   d. The routes were so dangerous that most trade moved into the Indian Ocean basin.
   e. While the Chinese were willing to export silk, they were unwilling to import items from other regions.

7. The northwest region of India became a prime route for invaders. Which of the following conquerors did NOT go to India through this region?
   a. Mahmud of Ghazni
   b. Alexander of Macedonia
   c. Alfonso d'Alboquerque
   d. Darius of Persia
   e. Tamarlane

8. To what extent were Europeans involved in manufacturing in the high middle ages?
   a. They remained dedicated to the manorial lifestyle with most products produced locally.
   b. After the crusades, they imported a majority of cloth and steel from the Middle East.
   c. They depended on European trade networks such as the Hanseatic League to provide most manufactured items.
   d. With increased urbanization came sophisticated goods crafted for European use.
   e. As monarchies gained more power, they dictated who and where goods were crafted.

9. The term "diviner" is most similar to which of the following terms?
   a. daimyo
   b. shaman
   c. griot
   d. caliph
   e. cultivator

10. In the period of 600 B.C.. to 200 C.E., some women in Rome could become literate while women of which society would have had the most difficulty attaining literacy?
    a. Greek
    b. Chinese
    c. Egyptian
    d. Indian
    e. Mesopotamian

11. Proximity to China allowed the introduction of Buddhism and Confucianism into which state?
    a. India
    b. Mongolia
    c. Vietnam
    d. Indonesia
    e. The Philippines

12. Mayan and Mesopotamian political traditions are an example of which of the following?
    a. decentralized democracy
    b. centralized oligarchy
    c. decentralized monarchy
    d. centralized theocracy
    e. centralized autocracy

13. Which of the following statements about the fourteenth-century Mali empire is true?
    a. The salt-gold trade was no longer important.
    b. It was considerably smaller than its predecessor.
    c. Its rulers shared its powers with a priestly class.
    d. Women shared political powers
    e. Its rulers encouraged Islam.

14.

The art illustrated above is most likely found in
    a. Islamic mosques
    b. Protestant churches
    c. Hindu temples
    d. Catholic churches
    e. Buddhist temples

15. "Such has been the procedure for many years, although our Celestial Empire possesses all things in prolific abundance and lacks no product within its own borders. There was therefore no need to import the manufactures of outside barbarians in exchange for our own produce."
    The quotation above comes from a 1793 letter sent by whom to the English?
    a. a southeast Asian rajah
    b. the emperor of China
    c. a Japanese shogun
    d. an official of Kongo
    e. the Russian tsar

16. The society of ninth-century Europe was most like that of
    a. second-century Rome.
    b. ninth-century China.
    c. eighth-century Byzantium.
    d. thirteenth-century Japan.
    e. tenth-century Ghana.

17. In the initial expansion of Islam, the last region that Islamic military commanders conquered was
    a. North Africa .
    b. Europe.
    c. Mesopotamia.
    d. India.
    e. Persia.

18.

The photograph above can be found in which region?
    a. Central America
    b. North America
    c. Mesopotamia
    d. North Africa
    e. Southeast Asia

Mounds and Their Interpreters: "Modern archaeological studies have shown definitively that there is no need to imagine exiled Israelites, Phoenicians, or space aliens as mound builders. It is quite clear that the native peoples of North America themselves not only constructed the mounds but also built flourishing settlements around them and relied on them as nodes in wide-ranging networks of communication and exchange. It is also clear that the mounds themselves were the product of careful engineering and architecture: studies of surviving mounds have revealed that their builders used different kinds of soils at different parts of their structures to improve drainage and increase stability."

19. Which of the following is an example of the described mounds?
    a. Teotihuacan
    b. Cahokia
    c. Pueblos
    d. Manchu Picchu
    e. Devil's Tower

20. Which of the following would lend plausible credence to the network of exchange theory?
    a. fragments of Chinese porcelain
    b. European coins
    c. jaguar motifs of jade
    d. sea shells from the Mediterranean
    e. ivory from Africa

21. What cannot be determined by the above explanation?
    a. Mound builders were sophisticated.
    b. Large towns grew up around them.
    c. Numerous people gathered there on occasions.
    d. The mounds were built with slave labor.
    e. The mound builders were careful observers of their environment.

22. Which of the following was the most important factor in the Mongol defeat of the Chinese?
    a. the development of siege weapons
    b. massed cavalry troops
    c. canny leadership and diplomacy
    d. nomadic warrior traditions
    e. traditional Chinese neglect of the military

23. The issues in most South American revolutions generally followed the pattern of the
    a. American revolution.
    b. French revolution.
    c. Haitian revolution.
    d. Iranian revolution.
    e. Russian revolution.

24. "Most of the inhabitants of India are infidels, called Hindus, believing in the transmigration of souls; all artisans, wage-earners and officials are Hindus. In our countries the desert dwellers get tribal names; here people settled in the cultivated villages also get tribal names."
    In this passage, who is most likely to have been the author?
    a. a Baghdad caliph
    b. a Portuguese sea captain
    c. a Mongol commander
    d. a Buddhist monk
    e. a Muslim invader

25. Women's participation in the marketplace in Mongol societies, Medieval Europe, and Africa can be described as
    a. relegated to craft manufacture.
    b. assistants to male merchants.
    c. part of the activities of the entire nuclear family.
    d. a mainstay of commercial activity.
    e. incidental and infrequent due to child-rearing responsibilities.

26. What caused both the Ottomans and Chinese to lag behind small European nations in the eighteenth and nineteenth centuries?
    a. disorganized government administration
    b. a rejection of foreign policy
    c. problems with succession
    d. technological weaknesses
    e. military dissatisfaction and mutinies

27. The European colonization of South Africa has the most in common with the European colonization of
    a. Central America.
    b. North America.
    c. West Africa.
    d. Southeast Asia.
    e. India.

28. Which of the following was not an example of European domination in the nineteenth century?
    a. Opium Wars
    b. Opening of Japan
    c. VOC in Dutch East Indies
    d. Sphere of Influence
    e. Russo-Japanese War

29. The industrialization of Japan compares most closely to its counterpart in
    a. Britain.
    b. China.
    c. Russia.
    d. France.
    e. Germany.

30. Which of the following is the best example of social Darwinism?
    a. the American justification for the invasion of Cuba in 1898
    b. Dutch early development of its East Indies possessions
    c. the belief that Japan should have more control over its more backward neighbors
    d. the explanation for the British defeat of the Boers in South Africa
    e. Spanish attempts to use indigenous labor in the Americas

31. What anticolonial activities proved to be particularly effective in India and Ghana?
    a. guerrilla warfare against the military forces
    b. terrorism against the general population
    c. appeals to neighboring countries for aid
    d. extensive use of mercenaries
    e. strategies of nonviolent mass action

32.

Which of the following best describes the political cartoon printed in *Punch* magazine, 1912?
a. Imperialist nations work to enhance each other's efforts.
b. France and Britain built the Suez Canal.
c. Small victories in North Africa were hoped to deter global warfare.
d. Imperialist control of North Africa was often brutal.
e. The Young Turks were unsuccessful and the Ottomans lost control to Europeans.

33. Of the following revolutions, which one combined a radical change in society with an ideology of independence?
a. American
b. Haitian
c. French
d. Russian
e. South American

34. Which of the following statements describes India after 1946 most accurately?
a. The British were satisfied that the freedoms they had given before the war were adequate.
b. Muslims and Hindus were agitating for different solutions to decolonization.
c. Muslims and Hindus were united in the effort to rid themselves of British control.
d. The British were extremely resistant to Indian independence.
e. The British had a timetable that would allow independence in no less than five years.

35. During the 1950s and 1960s, how was the economic growth of Japan and Germany characterized?
a. Both had growth that was solid and uneventful given their postwar devastation.
b. While Germany was aided by the Marshall Plan, Japan lagged behind.
c. Both Japan and Germany remained economically dependent on the United States.
d. Both Japan and Germany had miraculous recoveries, reaching prewar standards in the 1950s.
e. While Japan began to thrive as a Pacific leader, Germany was slowed by its divided state.

36. Which of the following is most accurate in describing industrialization's effect on demographics?
    a. Countries that industrialize see a drop in population due to lower fertility rates.
    b. Countries that industrialize see a rise in population to satisfy labor shortages.
    c. Countries that industrialize see a drop in population as urban pollution and disease rise.
    d. Countries that industrialize see a rise in population as middle-class women embrace domesticity.
    e. Countries that industrialize see a drop in population as working-class women take on jobs.

37. What have China and Russia had in common since the 1980s?
    a. the desire to maintain central control over the economy while allowing more liberties
    b. a vastly weakened military and concerns over control of their nuclear supply
    c. a desire to transition to a market economy while maintaining a stable government
    d. concerns on how to incorporate former neighbors into their economy and politics
    e. a determination to hold on to regions that are determined to separate

38.

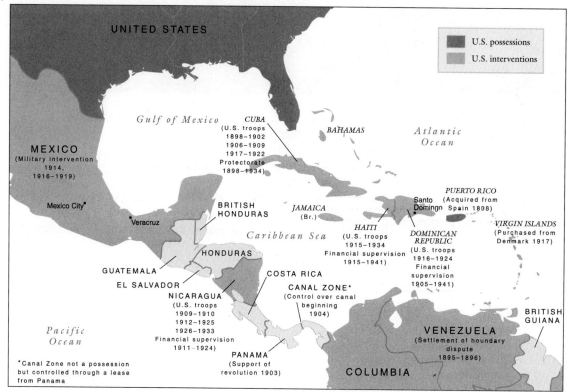

Using the map above, what is the most accurate way to describe the policies of the United States toward Latin America?
a. a good neighbor concerned about stability
b. justified defense of its borders
c. protection of economic interests
d. desire to annex neighboring land
e. defense from outside countries

39.

Bronze Vessel

Which society of the world would have been most likely to produce bronze art like the above?
a. the Mesopotamians who were the first to produce bronze
b. the Hyksos who brought bronze metallurgy to Egypt
c. the Aryans with bronze chariots for warfare
d. the Shang who monopolized bronze production
e. the Mayans who perfected bronze for use as cutting implements

40. Besides Islam, what was the most important unifying institution of dar al-Islam?
a. the military which enforced adherence to law
b. the caliphate which directed policies that were effected across the region
c. the university systems which standardized education
d. merchant roles between the silk roads and the Mediterranean
e. the Arabic language which was used in all sectors of the culture

41. What is the most accurate statement on the social status of mestizos in Iberian colonies in the Americas?
a. They remained on the margins of society, scorned by creoles, slaves, and indigenous people.
b. Mestizo women were likely to carry on indigenous traditions that gave more prestige to women.
c. Although originally marginalized, mestizos became the middle class after fully European elites.
d. Mestizos became a less significant sector of society once more Iberian women migrated.
e. Mestizos never regained their early high status once the colonies were fully settled.

42. Port cities in south India, Melaka, and Hormuz shared which of the following?
a. All were captured by the Portuguese captain, Alfonso d'Alboquerque, to control Indian Ocean trade.
b. They served as clearinghouses of trade between different segments of Indian Ocean trading spheres.
c. They controlled access to the interior where desirable commodities were grown.
d. All were primarily Muslim endeavors and catered to Arabic dhows above other ships.
e. Their success can be assigned to being uniquely unaffected by monsoons.

43. What was the driving force for urbanization in the Tang and Song dynasties?
    a. The Chinese economy became dependent on foreign trade and that brought artisans to primary cities.
    b. There were labor shortages in urban areas that drew workers from the overpopulated countryside.
    c. Chinese artisans chose to move into cities for the opportunity to pursue their craft.
    d. Availability of food from commercial agriculture and a fine distribution system allowed urban growth.
    e. The Chinese during that period revered urban professions so cities attracted large populations.

44. Which of the following statements best sums up the similarities between Song China and dar al-Islam at the end of the first millenium (1000 C.E.)?
    a. a centralized administration, large cities, and a scholarly tradition
    b. xenophobia and a weak military but a thriving economy
    c. a cosmopolitan outlook, a thriving economy, and population growth
    d. a solid agricultural base, thriving foreign trade, and dependence on domestic innovation
    e. multiple provinces and a solid agricultural base around cities

45. What lingering aspects of steppe traditions persisted in the Middle East long after its conquest by Mongols and Turks?
    a. the nomadic tradition of unclear succession
    b. a devotion to military governance over bureaucracy
    c. the acceptance of female authority in the marketplace
    d. a rejection of the arts and scholarship
    e. a belief that clans were the basis for political power

46. Which of the following is the most accurate with regard to the place of elite women in Middle East society?
    a. Often closeted in harems, they were completely subservient to male society.
    b. While secluded from society, elite women could be educated and engage in commerce.
    c. They were completely relegated to the domestic sphere with no recourse to an active life.
    d. In polygamous marriages, they were expected to share all duties and maintained equal status.
    e. They were expected to maintain complete anonymity in life and after death.

47. What were the commercial effects of trans-Sahara trade on Ghana?
    a. It embraced the religion of Islam which arrived with Muslim merchants.
    b. Ghana's position between the gold fields and the Sahara led to increased political power.
    c. As the supplier of gold to traders, Ghana built its commercial presence into the center of trade.
    d. Ghana's success led it to control the Sahara trade routes themselves.
    e. Long-distance trade become more important than local trade so markets were disrupted.

48. Which of the following characterizes the differences between the economies of the Aztecs and the Inca?
    a. The Aztecs had a thriving domestic trade network while the Incas maintained long-distance networks.
    b. Unlike the Incas, Aztecs depended on surrounding peoples to supply them with food and commodities.
    c. Both societies had thriving marketplaces where merchants sold domestic foods and imported crafts.
    d. Incan artisans manufactured goods for foreign trade while Aztec goods were for local use.
    e. Unlike the Aztecs, the Incas did not have a market economy so it did not develop a large artisan class.

49. With the entry of European nations into global trade networks, what was the response of governments in the Middle East?
    a. They focused on internal trade rather than foreign trade.
    b. They increased trade with Africa and central Asia.
    c. They formed alliances with European merchants.
    d. They competed with European traders in the Red Sea and the Persian Gulf.
    e. They formed their own trading companies to compete with European companies.

50. Which of the following did Ibn Battuta feel should be remedied in west Africa?
    a. the economy's dependence on slavery as its basic commodity
    b. the absolute authority of African kings where Islam was their faith
    c. the method of prayer in mosques that was poorly attended and badly led
    d. the dichotomy between devout adherence to faith and persistence of cultural traditions
    e. the failure of Arabs to control trade networks into Muslim areas

51.

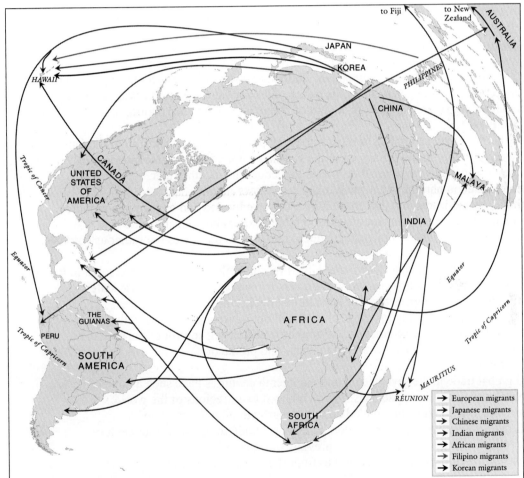

Nineteenth- and Twentieth-Century Imperialism and Migration

In the map above, what accounts for the mass migrations from India and China to Malaya?
    a. the labor shortage in factories
    b. the British movement of its colonials
    c. labor shortages on plantations and in mines
    d. efforts to control population growth
    e. allocation of labor by governments

52. How did the Portuguese maintain their early control of the Atlantic slave trade?
    a. They nurtured close connections with African kingdoms and their traders.
    b. They secured one leg of the triangular trade while the Netherlands and England divided the other two.
    c. Their naval vessels blockaded the African coastline to ships of other nationalities.
    d. The Spanish and British were more concentrated on their plantations.
    e. Africans refused to work with other nations for fear of losing control of the trade.

53. What seventeenth-century method of coerced labor in the Americas found a global resurgence in the nineteenth century?
    a. slavery
    b. serfdom
    c. wage labor
    d. indentured servitude
    e. bonded labor

54. What differences in Dutch and English colonial commerce occurred between the seventeenth century and the nineteenth century?
    a. Control of both production and trade had become directed by Europeans.
    b. Early colonies were more dependent on Europeans than imperial colonies.
    c. Early trade was only through companies while later trade was primarily through governments.
    d. Early commerce was dependent on the ruling elites and later commerce was not.
    e. Colonial peoples were completely cut out of commerce in the later period.

55. Which of the following statements is most true when comparing the expansion of the Ottoman empire in the fifteenth century to the expansion of the Russian empire in the eighteenth century?
    a. Neither had to deal with internal problems that could distract the ruler.
    b. Both chose to emphasize naval forces over land forces.
    c. Both had strong leadership that chose military preparation as a strong initiative.
    d. Both allowed local government officials to retain power and collect tribute.
    e. Neither intended to incorporate the conquered regions as provinces but rather as colonies.

56. In what way did Stalin's dictatorship in the USSR resemble the Romanov tsarist reign in Russia?
    a. Both lost control of its margins to other powers when they challenged those states.
    b. Neither made any progress towards educational opportunities for the masses.
    c. Neither allowed its citizens to travel abroad without governmental approval.
    d. Both were dependent on a large agricultural base and strong control of the elite class.
    e. Both sacrificed culture and the arts to industry and production.

57. Why did global trade in the seventeenth and eighteenth centuries have such a huge effect?
    a. It introduced addictive substances such as tobacco to all regions of the world.
    b. It introduced food crops that fueled population growth on most continents.
    c. It allowed all European nations to dominate world trade for the next four centuries.
    d. It gave residents of Asia and Africa a preview of imperialism.
    e. It marked the first time that trade was as important as political events.

58. In what ways did the kingdom of Kongo accommodate and then lose the Atlantic slave trade?
    a. The Kongo allowed the Portuguese to gain control until the Portuguese deposed its rulers.
    b. By working with the Portuguese to increase the slave trade, the Kongo could not limit it later.
    c. The Kongo lost the trade when their trade partners, the Angolans, invaded.
    d. The Kongo introduced the Portuguese to their enemies who later allied to defeat them.
    e. Since the Kongo did not allow the Portuguese beyond their forts, they lost the trade to more friendly African nations.

59. Which of the following is an accurate depiction of seventeenth century Qing and Tokugawa attitudes or actions toward foreigners?
    a. Foreign trade continued despite strong government controls.
    b. The Qing considered them distasteful while the shogunate considered them dangerous.
    c. Extreme xenophobia characterized both opinions as they persecuted Europeans.
    d. Both the Qing and the shogunate expelled all Christians and refused to trade.
    e. Neither believed that foreigners had anything worthy to trade or communicate.

60. Which of the following was the greatest threat to the Ottoman empire in the nineteenth century?
    a. the Spanish defeat of the Ottoman naval fleet
    b. the Portuguese suppression of Mediterranean trade
    c. India's choice to trade with the Portuguese rather than Arabs
    d. Russian expansionist policies in the Black Sea
    e. the rebellion of Egyptian commander Muhammad Ali

61. In which of the following ways did the Chinese Communist revolution NOT resemble the Russian revolution?
    a. extension of conventional warfare
    b. successful after years of revolutionary activity
    c. revolutionary base in the proletariat working class
    d. led by committed Marxists
    e. collectivization of farms

62. After World War II, British attempts to balance opposing groups attempting to gain independence led to violence. In which two states was this true?
    a. Burma and Ghana
    b. Kenya and Malaya
    c. Palestine and India
    d. Algeria and Tanzania
    e. Iraq and Nigeria

63. Since they had little capital, few natural resources, and overpopulation, in what way did the industrialization of Pacific Rim countries gain success in the global economy?
    a. manufacturing products for internal consumption
    b. manufacturing export goods for the global marketplace
    c. matching the world's needs for communications service workers
    d. becoming the center of research and development
    e. forming a cartel to manage their products

64. In what way has the nineteenth-century pattern of industrialization and urbanization changed in the late twentieth century?
    a. Slums have developed in major cities.
    b. Air and water pollution is a huge problem.
    c. Crime and poverty have increased in cities.
    d. Medicare needs have not been addressed.
    e. Populations can be more than 75 percent urban dwellers.

65. Of the following countries, which one remained the most independent of alignment with the superpowers?
    a. Egypt
    b. Vietnam
    c. Hungary
    d. Ghana
    e. Israel

66. In the twentieth century, which of the following countries made the greatest strides in women's equality in the areas of employment and literacy, and why?
    a. United States and Australia; constitutional rights
    b. Japan and Germany; labor shortages
    c. India and South Korea; unequal gender ratio
    d. Mexico and Venezuela; poverty amelioration
    e. Soviet Union and China; communist ideology

67. In the twentieth century, what has hindered the efforts of South American countries to gain more global status and wealth?
    a. drug and criminal problems
    b. a nonexistent middle class
    c. governmental problems
    d. lack of natural resources
    e. inadequate financial systems

68. In eastern Europe and Africa, the 1950s and 1960s saw the rise of which ideology?
    a. communism
    b. nationalism
    c. democracy
    d. totalitarianism
    e. imperialism

69. Which of the following more clearly expresses the basis for Cuba's alliance with the USSR in the 1960s?
    a. Fidel Castro's personal desire to form a dictatorship
    b. the Soviet Union's desire to put troops in the Americas
    c. Cuba's traditional hatred of U. S. hegemony
    d. Cuban interest in communism as a state policy
    e. the United States' desire to maintain its economic interests

70. The growth of international organizations in the post–cold war era can be best attributed to
    a. a unique period of humanitarian concern in human history.
    b. the inability of governments to meet global challenges.
    c. the growth of wealth that supports the organizations.
    d. increased cooperation by governmental bodies around the world.
    e. decreased interest in purely nationalistic endeavors.

Section II

The mandatory reading period is ten minutes so include that in your practice. That is enough time to read the questions and documents. Jot down notes on both. The suggested writing times are forty minutes for the document-based question and thirty-five minutes for each essay.

Document-Based Question
40 minutes
33-1/3 percent of final score

There will be written reminders to include a thesis, historical evidence, to use all or all but one of the documents, group documents, and to be mindful of point of view.

1. To what extent was the search for equality and independence driven by economic and social forces? What other document(s) might be useful to support your answer?

Historical background: In the eighteenth century, the European Enlightenment gave rise to ideological philosophies that supported just and independent governments. For the next two centuries, many countries used the ideas to support movements for equality and independence.

Document 1

Declaration of the Rights of Man and the Citizen, France, 1789

First Article. Men are born and remain free and equal in rights. Social distinctions may be based only on common utility.
Article 2: The goal of every political association is the preservation of the natural and inalienable rights of man. These rights are liberty, property, security, and resistance to oppression.
Article 17: Property is an inviolable and sacred right.

Document 2

Document 3

Ponciano Arriaga Calls for Land Reform, Mexico, 1856

One of the most deeply rooted evils of our country . . . is the monstrous division of landed property.

While a few individuals possess immense areas of uncultivated land that could support millions of people, the great majority of Mexicans languish in a terrible poverty and are denied property, homes, and work.

Such a people cannot be free, democratic, much less happy, no matter how many constitutions and laws proclaim abstract rights and beautiful but impracticable theories—impracticable by reason of an absurd economic system.

Document 4

Proclamation of The Young Turks, Ottoman Empire, 1908

9. Every citizen will enjoy complete liberty and equality, regardless of nationality or religion, and be submitted to the same obligations. All Ottomans, being equal before the law as regards rights and duties relative to the State, are eligible for government posts, according to their individual capacity and their education. Non-Muslims will be equally liable to the military law.

14. Provided that the property rights of landholders are not infringed upon (for such rights must be respected and must remain intact, according to the law), it will be proposed that peasants be permitted to acquire land, and they will be accorded means to borrow money at a moderate rate . . .

Document 5

The State and Revolution, Russia, V. I. Lenin, 1918

Freedom in capitalist society always remains about the same as it was in ancient Greek republics: freedom for the slave-owners. Owing to the conditions of capitalist exploitation the modern wage slaves are so crushed by want and poverty that "they cannot be bothered with democracy," "they cannot be bothered with politics"; in the ordinary peaceful course of events the majority of the population is debarred from participation in public and political life. . . .

[F]orward development . . . proceeds through the dictatorship of the proletariat; and cannot do otherwise, for the *resistance* of the capitalist exploiters cannot be *broken* by anyone else or in any other way. . . .

Only in Communist society, when the resistance of the capitalists has been completely crushed, when the capitalists have disappeared, when there are no classes, . . . only then the state . . . ceases to exist. . . ."

Document 6

Swaraj (Self-Rule) Is My Birthright, Bal Gangadhar Tilak, India, 1907

Pax Britannica has been established in this country in order that a foreign Government may exploit the country. That this is the effect of this Pax Britannica is being gradually realized these days. . . . Your industries are ruined utterly, ruined by foreign rule; your wealth is going out of the country and you are reduced to the lowest level which no human being can occupy.

Document 7

I Speak of Freedom: A Statement of African Ideology, Kwame Nkrumah, Ghana, 1961

Never before have a people had within their grasp so great an opportunity for developing a continent endowed with so much wealth. Individually, the independent states of Africa, some of them potentially rich, others poor, can do little for their people. Together, by mutual help, they can achieve much. But the economic development of the continent must be planned and pursued as a whole. A loose confederation designed only for economic cooperation would not provide the necessary unity of purpose. Only a strong political union can bring about full and effective development of our natural resources for the benefit of our people.

Section III
Change-Over-Time Question
35 minutes
33-1/3 percent of final score

There will be written reminders to use five minutes for planning, and to include a thesis, historical evidence, address all parts of question, and to show change and continuities using the historical facts.

2. Pick one of the following regions and discuss the continuities and changes
    in religions from 600 C.E. to 1450.
    The Middle East
    South Asia
    Europe
    North Africa

Comparison Question
35 minutes
33-1/3 percent of final score

There will be written reminders to use five minutes for planning, and to include a thesis, historical evidence, address all parts of the question, and to use direct comparisons.

3. Compare and contrast the nature of patriarchal systems in TWO of the
    following regions during the period 8000 B.C.E.–600 C.E.
    Mesopotamia
    Egypt
    India
    China
    Mesoamerica and Andean South America
    Classical Mediterranean world

END OF EXAM

EXAM 1 ANSWERS AND EXPLANATIONS
Section I
Multiple Choice Questions

1. **c:** Since the main route into India was from Muslim regions in the northwest, northern India became Muslim. The conquerors generally did not expand into the south so southern India remained largely Hindu.

2. **d:** None of the empires completely obliterated the regions they conquered but they were interested in financial benefits. Thus Chinese empires maintained tributary status with Korea and Vietnam while Persia and Rome collected taxes from distant provinces.

3. **b:** The Confucian ideal of filial piety underlies Chinese patriarchy but the restriction of women continued into later dynasties. The culmination of women's subservient position was foot binding which started during the Song.

4. **e:** Islam and Christianity are outgrowths of Judaism while Buddhism was derived from Hinduism. All require some form of spiritual awareness, but while some governments adopted new religions eventually, like the Romans, they did not require its worship at first.

5. **d:** Both Islam and Christianity promise rewards after death while some early Christianity was forced upon regions of Europe. Islam always allowed the retention of native religions. Expansion was occasionally led by the religious leader, but often, as with Clovis, a secular leader was responsible for conversion.

6. **a:** Despite being too early for the Mongols and the Han and Roman empires, trade was frequent and prosperous along the silk roads. Thus there was no necessity to move all trade to the Indian Ocean. Europe, on the other hand, was feudal so trade was local and regional.

7. **c:** Alexander, Tamerlane, Mahmud of Ghazni, and Babur were commanders of large land forces, but Alfonso d' Alboquerque was a Portuguese mariner during the period of exploration, who captured Goa.

8. **d:** While the crusades brought new luxury items to the European markets, new cities promoted the professions of talented artisans. They set up shop in the urban areas of Europe and their crafts often dominated the local market.

9. **b:** In Mongol and North American cultures, a shaman makes predictions just as a diviner does in African societies. Caliphs and daimyos are elite ruling members of society while cultivators refers to a peasant class.

10. **d:** While few Greek women would have been educated, elite Egyptian and Mesopotamian women were literate. In India, Sanskrit, the language of the Vedas, was almost exclusively taught to men since women could not serve as priests.

11. **c:** The Vietnamese adopted Confucian practices into its educational system and Buddhism became the predominant religion. India was the home of Buddhism and Indians carried it to southeast Asia as well as China. Some Mongols converted to it but did not adopt Confucianism for long. However, the islands of southeast Asia remained largely exempt from Chinese philosophies but not Chinese trade.

12. **c:** The rulers of Mesopotamia and Mesoamerica ruled from city-states that were surrounded by agricultural lands. Thus they were decentralized and they both maintained monarchies rather than other forms of rule.

13. **e:** Mali was a large Muslim state in west Africa whose rulers, like Mansa Musa, were devout Muslims. Islam technically does not have priests so the kings did not have priestly advisers and, although they encouraged Islam, they did not force it on members of their nation.

14. **c:** No matter the period, Indian art has a busy quality to it with many figures engaged in many activities: And if that is not enough to identify it, the elephant indicates that it can only be Hindu.

15. **b:** The reference to "Celestial Kingdom" indicates a superiority and the use of barbarians is seen only in Japanese, Chinese, and Roman translations. Furthermore, indifference to imported goods is a key to the thinking of the Qing.

16. **b:** In 800 C.E., only two societies in the world had variations of feudalism, and those were Europe and Japan. They shared unique features of feudal society such as landed lords, warrior classes, and social contracts.

17. **a:** The initial expansion of Islam was by military conquest on the Arab peninsula, into the Middle East, and then across north Africa. Muslim armies entered Spain but were defeated in southern France in the Battle of Tours in 732.

18. **a:** This is the Mayan temple complex at Tikal. The stepped pyramidal shape and its steep stairs marks it as Mesoamerican rather than Egyptian or Mesopotamian.

19. **b:** While there were mound builders throughout the Mississippi River valley, Cahokia mound outside of St. Louis is the most extensive mound site found in North America.

20. **c:** South American jade would be the most appropriate evidence of trade because the other goods are derived from places that did not have contact with the Americas yet. The presence of them would actually support the idea that some other culture built the mounds.

21. **d:** All the others are possible through archaeological investigations, but it is impossible to know the social structure of vanished peoples, and who might have built the mounds.

22. **c:** In the Mongol defeat of the Chinese, it is true that the Song leadership had a weak military, but without the leadership of Chingghis Khan, the Mongols would not have been able to organize to make such a stunning conquest.

23. **a:** Despite the inequality between social classes and the existence of slavery, South Americans were primarily motivated toward independence as North Americans had been in the American revolution. The Haitians, Russians, and French were concerned about social classes while the Iranian revolution was focused on American influences and radical Islam.

24. **e:** The use of the word "infidel" refers to nonbelievers of Islam so either the caliph or an invader would make the most sense. Since the Baghdad caliphs did not invade India, it is apparent that the invader was Babur who did not spare his disdain for the Indians he conquered.

25. **d:** Women in those three societies played an essential role in commerce. Mongol women were key to trade in a society where all men were warriors, while African women played equal roles with men in trade. In urban Europe, women were artisans and merchants, even maintaining their own guilds.

26. **d:** The governments of the Ottoman and Chinese were highly organized bureaucracies that failed to foster the development of new military technology. While there were chaotic moments in the Ottoman government, the Qing dynasty was enormously stable. Furthermore, neither the Qing nor the Ottomans completely rejected foreign trade and their relationships with foreign countries.

27. **b:** While the Portuguese were the first to land on the shores of south Africa, the Protestant Dutch actually settled it. The Protestant English settled large areas of coastal North America. Although there was a small group of Puritan separatists, the primary settlers of North America and South Africa had monetary goals.

28. **e:** European domination of Asia was almost complete in the nineteenth century. However, the Meiji government of Japan swiftly adapted European technology so that by 1905, the Japanese navy triumphed over the Russians.

29. **c:** Both the Russians and Japanese threw the weight of the government behind swift industrialization at the end of the nineteenth century. In Britain and France, industrialization was achieved largely outside of government policies while German industrialists worked with their governments rather than under the direction of their governments.

30. **c:** Social Darwinism led to a belief that certain races were more suited for survival of the fittest than others. While Europeans believed that the Japanese were backward at first, the shock of their victory over the Russians led to the belief that they were the natural leaders of the so-called yellow races.

31. **e:** India and Ghana gained independence through peaceful means. After World War II, the British government was ready to end its imperial legacy, so when Gandhi and Nkrumah used pacifist mass actions, they were successful.

32. **d**: The *Punch* cartoon is fairly ghoulish which leads one to suspect that their imperialistic regimes were harsh. The British and French did not collaborate on imperialism but they were proud of their ability to make strong statements of colonial power.

33. **b:** A radical social change is a permanent change in social class such as the abolition of the slave class in Haiti, or the elimination of Russian and French nobility. However, only the Haitian revolution eliminated a social class as well as gaining independence from France.

34. **b:** While the British believed in their empire before World War II, by 1946, they were committed to freeing India. However, Muslim and Hindu activists had become convinced that partition was the only solution that would grant equal rights to their followers.

35. **d:** Both Germany and Japan were considered economic miracles despite the bombing devastation from World War II. They used the aid they received to propel themselves into the forefront of the world's economic leading nations.

36. **a:** During the period of industrialization, a unique demographic transition occurred. A drop in population came initially from decreased mortality rates but was followed by lower fertility rates due to voluntary birth control.

37. **c:** Both Russia and China have entered the world marketplace and so have allowed private enterprise. The attempt to maintain a stable government led Yeltsin to attack the Duma (Russia's parliament) and the Chinese to crack down on dissidents in Tiananmen Square.

38. **c:** The financial supervision of Haiti, the Dominican Republic, and Nicaragua combined with control over the Panama Canal point to the U.S. protection of economic interests. Certainly there have been military incursions but those have been in protection of U.S. economic interests.

39. **d:** The Shang so monopolized the bronze industry that its well-practiced artisans produced bronze items intricately designed and incised. Three-legged vessels are also quite common in Shang art.

40. **e:** The Arabic language allowed the easy transmission of information, trade goods, and coordination of governance throughout dar al-Islam which ranged from Spain to the Middle East.

41. **c:** Since Iberian women never settled in great numbers, marriages with indigenous peoples remained a prominent feature of Iberian colonial life, so the mestizos became accepted as middle class.

42. **b:** Hormuz and Melaka were at the terminus of each end receiving goods from west and east while southern Indian ports served as the pivotal point of trade. It is best to think of the Indian Ocean trade as hemispheric, with India's warehouses at the midpoint.

43. **d:** New crops and agricultural techniques that produced enormous yields combined with the Grand Canal to allow commercial agriculture to deliver goods throughout China. The Chinese also developed financial tools such as "flying money" to allow long-distance commerce. Thus the most urbanized society in the world at that time was the Song dynasty.

44. **c:** Both the Islamic world and Song China had encouraged international trade and communication networks as they developed an agricultural base that could support large cities with their craftspeople, marketplaces, and intellectual innovations. Later, China and Islamic empires became more insular and less innovative.

45. **a:** Ascendance to the throne of the Ottoman empire was often chaotic and usually murderous. It even led to the suppression of rivals in childhood, such as when Suleyman the Magnificent had his first son eliminated.

46. **b:** Islam does not preclude women from business. Elite women in the Middle East were secluded from outsiders but they were often educated, frequently advisers in family business, and even able to own property and run businesses.

47. **c:** Ghana did lie between gold mines in the south and the Sahara so they concentrated on the gold-salt trade with the added commodities of ivory and slaves. They allowed the trans-Saharan trade to be directed by others but profited enormously from it.

48. **e:** The Aztecs had a thriving marketplace with numerous domestic and foreign goods. This led to the formation of a merchant class. The Inca government controlled commerce and did not permit a merchant class to exist.

49. **c:** The Ottomans were the foremost economic power in the Middle East. In an effort to continue their role, they formed alliances with Dutch and English companies to thwart their rival Spanish and Portuguese efforts.

50. **d:** Ibn Battuta was a traveler, trader, and cleric. He believed it to be his responsibility to bring the true practice of Islam to its farthest reaches. He was particularly concerned that devout African Muslims saw nothing wrong with women continuing their traditional social roles.

51. **c:** Since this is a map of the imperialist era, it is apparent that many migrations would have to do with imperial holdings. Thus indentured workers went to British Malaya from British India to work on rubber plantations. Since European-dominated China always had a surfeit of workers, ambitious Chinese signed up to work in Filipino tin mines, American gold mines, and agricultural settings.

52. **a:** The Portuguese not only worked with African nations like the kingdom of Kongo but even used Christianity to encourage a closer relationship. Most Portuguese trade was made through local officials of regional kingdoms, so it was practical to maintain a close relationship.

53. **d:** Indentured servitude which had been the primary means of recruitment for labor in British North America proved to be an excellent method to move labor from Asia to nations around the world a century and a half later.

54. **a:** In the early period, the focus was trade with native intermediaries. At first the Dutch and English were merely two of many nationalities vying for commodities in port cities on the Indian Ocean. In the nineteenth century, the Europeans controlled trade and production of commodities like coffee, tea, and rubber.

55. **c:** Suleyman the Magnificent, Peter the Great, and Catherine the Great emphasized military might to expand their empires. The Ottoman navy was very strong but the Russians had less use for naval forces as they looked to expand across Siberia and Poland.

56. **d:** The retention of serfs satisfied the nobility of the tsarist era while Stalin eliminated his competition as he depended upon state collective farms to support industrialization. The elite class in communist Russia was the Soviet bureaucracy which Stalin periodically persecuted in purges to retain control.

57. **b:** The population grew in most regions of the world, even in Africa despite the Atlantic slave trade. As peoples were introduced to nutritious food crops such as manioc and potatoes, they rapidly incorporated them into their local cuisines.

58. **b:** The Kongo accommodated early Portuguese demands so much that they could no longer acquire the slaves necessary to meet later demands. This led the Portuguese to move their base of operations to Angola.

59. **a:** The Qing dynasty and the Tokugawa shogunate strongly curtailed the trading activities of foreigners but continued to allow select groups of foreign ships to trade in specified cities. The Tokugawa shogunate was more restrictive but the Qing did keep track of foreign traders and attempted to curtail their own ships.

60. **e:** Muhammad Ali's leadership of Egyptian forces was so skilled that the British had to come to the aid of the Ottoman empire to stop his invasion of Anatolia. From that point on, Egypt became an autonomous region within the empire.

61. **c:** The Chinese had very few industries by 1949 so Mao's communist revolutionaries were not part of a proletariat or urban working class. Lenin's proletariat was small also but was the vanguard of revolution nevertheless.

62. **c:** In Palestine the Arabs and Jewish settlers were fighting for control, while in India, it was the Muslims and Hindus. The Jews were granted the state of Israel while the British partitioned India. Both were violent episodes and warfare still remains a possibility.

63. **b:.** The so-called Asian tigers (South Korea, Japan, Singapore, Taiwan, and Hong Kong) concentrated on the export trade which worked remarkably well in a time of globalization.

64. **e:** There is a clear change in the ratio of urban to rural populations in the twentieth century. While in the nineteenth century industrialized countries remained largely rural, today they are overwhelmingly urban. Some countries such as Germany exceed 85 percent while even Latin American countries are close to 50 percent urban.

65. **a:** Egypt's president Gamal Abdel Nasser cleverly received aid from both superpowers while remaining nonaligned. He posited the intellectual basis that alignment with either superpower was a new form of imperialism.

66. **e:** Communist ideology held that women were equal to men and thus they gained high rates of literacy and employment. However, they were also expected to continue most of the domestic work in a household.

67. **c:** Even those countries with strong potential like Argentina, Mexico, and Peru have suffered from military dictatorships or one-party systems that have not fostered adequate economic or social policies.

68. **b:** While democracy might have been their ultimate goal, nationalism was the driving force behind the independence efforts in eastern Europe and Africa. The Hungarian revolt of 1956, Prague Spring in 1968, and Nkrumah's 1960s successes in Ghana demonstrate the power of the idea of nationalism despite repression.

69. **e:** Fidel Castro nationalized all businesses which were mainly U.S.-controlled so the United States was hostile to the regime. When Castro accepted Soviet aid, U.S. hostility grew and drove Cuba permanently into the Soviet sphere.

70. **b:** Nongovernmental organizations such as humanitarian and environmental groups have been formed to address problems that governments have been unable to solve due to their global nature. The example of the United Nations has served as a model for multinational solutions to problems, but sometimes even those efforts have not had great success so private organizations have been founded.

Section II
DBQ Response and Analysis

Every student will write a different DBQ. Most will share some of these variables:

- **Has an acceptable thesis:** This point is earned by dealing with all aspects of the question in a historically viable way. (1 point)

- **Understands the basic meaning of the documents:** The essay is based on an accurate reading of the documents. One misinterpretation is allowed. (1 point)

- **Supports the thesis with appropriate evidence from all or all but one document:** The essay may still earn one point if appropriate evidence comes from all but two of the documents. (2 points)

- **Analyzes point of view (POV) in at least two documents.** (1 point)
Possible Points of View:
Documents 1 and 4: Declarations were devised by political reformers, copying the earlier ideological statements, but the writers were fixed upon political gains, above all.
Document 2: Since it is a French print, the Haitian revolution is shown to be as horrible as possible to convince the French to defend their assets in Haiti.
Document 5: Founder of the USSR, Lenin had been completely impressed by the economic and historical writings of Marx despite the fact that there is only a very small industrialized portion of Russia. Like documents 1 and 4, he is really proposing a political change.
Document 6: An Indian nationalist from India, the "crown jewel" of the British imperial system, Tilak was primarily concerned with political independence.
Document 7: Having gained political independence, Nkrumah puts economics at the core of the postcolonial policy.

- **Analyzes documents by grouping them in two or three ways:**
Possible Groups:
Land for peasants (Documents 1, 3, 4)
Economic profits to workers (Document 3)
Social class change or modification (Documents 1, 2, 4, 5)
States control the profits (Documents 5, 7)

- **Identifies and explains the need for one type of appropriate additional document (AD) or source:**

Possible additional documents:

In France, the Ottoman Empire, Russia, and Ghana, it would be good to have an account by a nonpolitical figure whose main concern is social or economic. For instance, a woman of Paris who participated in bread riots, an Ottoman Christian or Jew's account of the inequity of life under the Ottoman rule, an industrial worker in Moscow, and a former colonial worker in Ghana.

Copies of tax rolls that illustrate the extent to which peasants in France, Mexico, and the Ottoman empire obtained their own land after revolution. An account from a Haitian gens de couleur as to the extent of freedom and prosperity obtained by former slaves.

- **Historical detail beyond the core points:**

Historical details:

Details on events and individuals of the French, Haitian, and Russian Revolutions
Details on events and individuals of Indian and African decolonization
Details on events and individuals in the Reforma (and maybe the later Mexican revolution)
Details on events and individuals in the Young Turk movement

Section III
Change-Over-Time Response and Analysis

From 600–1450 C.E., the Middle East experienced a large religious change with the addition of a major new religion, Islam. Founded on the Arab peninsula, its effects on its neighbors were profound as military conquest and extensive trade supported its spread into other populations. However, some groups of non-believers were able to maintain their original traditions while Christian Europe spent two centuries in attempts to regain influence in the region.

Islam was founded in the seventh century by an Arab merchant. After a series of visions, Muhammad rejected the polytheistic religion of the Arab peninsula for the monotheism of one god, Allah. The first communities to feel the effects of his conversion outside his own clan were the peoples of the peninsula who were conquered and converted by the Muslim armies of the prophet. Muslim military commanders went on to conquer other regions of the Middle East and established a leadership, the caliphate, in Baghdad. While this seemed to consolidate the umma or community of the faithful, fractures appeared around the question of succession to leadership. The Shia claimed leadership through the prophet's family line while the Sunni supported the caliphate which had been established around the advisers of Muhammad. The Persians adopted Shia beliefs while the rest of the Middle East remained Sunni.

The Muslim faith also spread by a branch of traveling Islamic mystics, known as Sufis, who impressed people with their devotion and tolerance. Another avenue of conversion was the complex trade networks of the Middle East, lying at the nexus of Mediterranean, Asian, and Indian Ocean trade. The final method of conversion was the influence of pilgrims as they traveled on the hajj, one of the required Five Pillars. Their piety became a source of admiration and conversion. By the eighth century, the Middle East had become overwhelmingly Muslim.

Some religious communities did not convert to the dominant faith but were able to maintain their faith through the practice of taxation on the dhimmi, or Believers of the Book. Christians and Jews were required to pay a tax to maintain their religious identity. So, neighborhoods and villages of Christians and Jews remained faithful to their religions under the Muslim regime. The most obvious example would be the city of Jerusalem which was a holy site for Christians and Jews and became one for the Muslims as well.

The large group of Orthodox Christian believers on the Anatolian peninsula became justly concerned about the strength of dar al-Islam. So, the Byzantine ruler requested that European Christians come to his aid in the eleventh century. When this coincided with Pope Urban's desire to increase the power of the Catholic church, thousands took up the call which led to a series of crusades to the Holy Land over the next two-and-one-half centuries. Gains made by the Europeans were lost between crusades and the

Middle East remained predominantly Muslim. Eventually, peace treaties allowed the movement of Christian pilgrims through the Holy Lands but did not result in a recapture of Christian eminence.

Islam's profound effect on the Middle East was somewhat mitigated by the retention of communities of other believers. And, despite attempts by militant European Christians four centuries after its founding, Islamic governments retained the region and affected the economic and social life of the region permanently.

Analysis:
This prompt ties to significant and recurring themes in AP World History: religion, continuity, and change. This writer has a strong grasp of this topic and she has a direct understanding of the AP World History criteria for this type of essay. This essay would likely earn the following points:

The thesis is strong, it addresses the issue of change and continuity in the religions of the Middle East, and it is accurately placed at the end of the introduction. Because of its clarity and specifics for analysis, it qualifies as an Expanded Core point as well. (1 point)

This essay answers both parts of the question including both continuities and changes in religions. (2 points)

This essay does an excellent job of substantiating the thesis with historical evidence with more than ten historical facts. (2 points)

This essay sets the question in a global context by addressing the trade networks and European crusades. (1 point)

The analysis point is easily earned in this essay by explaining how Jews and Christians retained their religions, the basis for the Shia-Sunni split in Islam, the sources of Islamic conversions, and the source of the crusades. (1 point)

This essay would earn also earn expanded points for its comprehensive thesis, for its chronological framework, for good causation, for consistent changes and continuities, and for multiple historical facts. This essay would earn a 9.

Comparison Response and Analysis:
Patriarchal systems seem to have evolved with complex societies. In hunting and gathering societies, the two tasks were broken down by gender, but there is little indication that women were vastly subservient to men. In early agricultural societies, gender determined tasks as well but it is only with the development of large settlements with numerous crafts as well as agriculture that patriarchy developed definitively. In India and China, patriarchy became dominant since women were forbidden from significant economic and political roles, and belief systems supported the subordination of women. Nevertheless, there were exceptions in both regions as elite manners and Buddhism evolved.

In India, the Aryan social caste system made strict distinctions between professions so it is not surprising that the division between men and women was strict as well. Written Sanskrit was denied to most women since it was reserved for Hindu priests. The Vedas and later Law of Manu dictated subservience and emphasized faithfulness. However, in China, social divisions were less rigid in that the possibility of social mobility existed, and relations between men and women were somewhat less rigid as well. Unlike most elite women in India, elite women of the Han dynasty were generally well-educated. However, as a book by female author Ban Zhao asserts, women's behavior was also idealized as compliant and subservient.

Social class defined women's status as well. In both societies, lower-class women worked beside men in agriculture, transportation, and trade. However, elite women often led very separate lives. Monogamy was the law in both societies, but in Chinese society, wealthier men were able to include concubines in their households with the official wife at the top of the household hierarchy. Like the Chinese emperor, in India, kings had harems but relationships outside marriage were not sanctioned as an institution in Indian society as it had been in Chinese society. Child marriages and dowries existed in both places, although child marriage was much more common in India by the Gupta era. In India, also, toward the end of this period, the practice of sati became more popular among elite classes as prominent widows were expected to join their husbands in death, rather than suffer a shameful widowhood.

Patriarchy was fully supported by their belief systems. In China, Confucian filial piety and the five important relationships made women subservient to men. Furthermore, it was the responsibility of sons to provide proper care of aging parents as well as proper veneration of ancestors. Combined with the loss of daughter's work when they married, daughters were so undesirable that infanticide of girl babies was common. Infanticide of females was also common in Indian society because they were expensive in terms of dowry and the same loss of work. In the Ramayana and Mahabharata, female deities were depicted as weak and frivolous, a reflection of the opinion of women in Indian society. When Buddhism arose in both regions, options for some women expanded since they were able to become nuns. As in Europe, nuns were often highly educated and revered so their positions were outside the social position of most women.

In China and India, women's lives were determined by their fathers, husbands, and sons. Nevertheless, some women, primarily Chinese, slipped the boundaries of societal expectations. Patriarchy continued as a feature of both cultures, particularly in India. In China, during the later Tang period, elite Chinese women achieved some equality, but then they were severely curtailed in the Song era when foot binding came into fashion.

Analysis:
This prompt ties to significant and recurring themes in AP World History: social structure and gender roles. This writer has a strong grasp of this topic and she has a direct understanding of the AP World History criteria for this type of essay. This essay would likely earn the following points:

The thesis is strong, it addresses the issue of patriarchy in India and China, and it is accurately placed at the end of the introduction. Because of its clarity and specifics for analysis, it qualifies as an Expanded Core point. (1 point)

This essay includes both comparisons and contrasts between the two patriarchal systems, India and China. (2 points)

This essay does an excellent job of substantiating the thesis with historical evidence with more than ten historical facts included. (2 points)

This essay has six direct comparisons between patriarchy in China and in India and so earns the point for comparison. (1 point)

The analysis point is easily earned in this essay. The writer includes several ideas which earn this point: development and maintenance of patriarchy based in religion, the loss of the daughter's labor as the basis of infanticide, the arrival of Buddhism for freeing up some women, and the difference in social class as a basis for some divisions between men and women. (1 point)

This essay would earn also expanded points for its thesis, for regular comparisons, for consistent discussion of causation, for the chronology evident in the structure of the piece, for ample historical evidence, and for global context.

PRACTICE EXAM 2

WORLD HISTORY EXAM

You will have three hours and five minutes to complete this exam. The multiple choice section is fifty-five minutes long while the essay section allows two hours and ten minutes. Ten minutes will be allotted as a mandatory reading and preparation period. The two sections are given equal weight in the final exam score.

Section I
Multiple Choice Questions (55 minutes)
70 questions
50 percent of final score

In the real exam, all answers will be done on a separate answer sheet but you will be able to mark up the test booklet. There will be one sample question and answer to indicate how to fill in the answer sheet. There may be a note on random guessing and we advise guessing only when you know something about the question since wrong answers gain a quarter point deduction. The exam will advise that you keep your eye on the clock but aim for accuracy as it is not expected that everyone will answer all the questions in the section.

1. What purpose do scholars believe paleolithic Venus figures served?
    a. The figures were the idealized form of beauty among paleolithic people.
    b. The figures represent the powerful queen of the paleolithic pantheon, Venus.
    c. The figures reflect a deep interest in fertility necessary for the generation of new life.
    d. The figures represent the attempts of early farmers to insure fertility in their animals.
    e. The figures demonstrate the power of women as rulers in paleolithic society.

2. Why were women probably the first farmers?
    a. Women had more free time than men and therefore had time to experiment.
    b. Women had traditionally been gatherers and therefore understood plant cycles and the effects of sun, rain, and temperature on plant growth.
    c. Women had more patience and therefore were better suited to a farming life which requires farmers to work hard but then wait for the plants to grow.
    d. Women had mastered the raising of animals and now could concentrate on food production.
    e. Women had smaller hands which were necessary to tend and harvest crops which were planted on small hills or tight rows.

3. A key geographic difference between ancient Egyptian, Mesopotamian, Harappan, and Chinese society was that
    a. Egypt and China were more isolated and therefore protected by their environment than were the Mesopotamians or Harappans.
    b. while the Egyptians and Mesopotamians were river valley civilizations, the Harappans and Chinese had to rely on irrigation to produce ample food.
    c. the Mesopotamians and Chinese developed vast trading networks, because their rivers were more navigable than the Nile or the Indus Rivers.
    d. the Chinese and Mesopotamians could produce multiple crops each season because of the steady and predictable flooding of their rivers.
    e. the Egyptians and the Mesopotamians built tall pounded-earth walls to protect their cities because there were few natural barriers to invasion.

4. Which of the following civilizations was governed by a city-state structure?
   a. ancient Egypt and classical Greece
   b. ancient Mesopotamia and ancient Egypt
   c. Classical Rome and Han China
   d. ancient Mesopotamia and Bantu Africa
   e. Classical Greece and ancient Mesopotamia

5. Women in which of the following societies enjoyed the greatest amount of personal freedom?
   a. ancient Egypt
   b. ancient Mesopotamia
   c. Aryan India
   d. Classical Greece
   e. Rome during the republic

6. Which of the following religious traditions relied on a strong missionary movement and was considered a religion of salvation?
   a. Hinduism and Judaism
   b. Buddhism and Daoism
   c. Confucianism and Christianity
   d. Daoism and Christianity
   e. Buddhism and Christianity

7. One key role of the caste system which was unlike other systems of social inequality in the ancient world was that the caste system
   a. had a religious justification rather than one based on race.
   b. served to maintain order and stability as political systems did in Mesopotamia, Egypt, and China.
   c. relied on support from the government to enforce its rules and restrictions unlike the civilizations of Mesopotamia, Egypt, and China.
   d. did not develop further groups and subgroups as did the systems of social equality in classical Greece and Rome.
   e. was denounced in holy texts like the Vedas but remained in Indian tradition because of its economic benefits to the nation.

8. An essential distinction between Confucianism, Daoism, and Buddhism was that
   a. Confucianism is an indigenous religion to China, but Daoism and Buddhism arrived from India.
   b. Confucius was most interested in the structure of the state, while Daoists and Buddhists shunned political involvement.
   c. Confucius's goal was social order while Daoism and Buddhism were much less interested in society.
   d. Confucianism and Buddhism promised a glorious afterlife, but Daoism did not.
   e. Confucius was seen as a god, while Daoism and Buddhism do not rely on deities.

9. One key difference between the fall of the western Roman empire and the fall of Han China was that
   a. Chinese military leaders increasingly usurped political power, while the office of Roman Emperor remained tied to the Senate.
   b. Chinese society suffered from problems of equitable land distribution while Rome managed to support small farmers and large estate owners.
   c. Chinese society was not overrun by invaders as was the western Roman empire.
   d. China eventually rebuilt its imperial power, but Rome never again emerged as an empire.
   e. China experienced a slow demise over several years, but Rome's fall to the Germanic invaders was sudden and unanticipated.

10. Unlike the Legalist tradition of the Qin Dynasty, Roman imperial law
    a. was subject to veto by an advisory body, the Roman Senate.
    b. allowed local autonomy and religious toleration in its provinces.
    c. used forced exile and relocation to deal with difficult subject peoples.
    d. was based on the concept of a *lex talonis*.
    e. insisted on the absolute control of a region by its governor.

11. Which of the following nomadic groups does NOT belong with the others?
    a. Huns
    b. Visigoths
    c. Vandals
    d. Franks
    e. Ostrogoths

12. What accounts for the dramatic population decrease in Rome and China during the second and third centuries C.E.?

    I. large-scale outbreaks of epidemic diseases
    II. war and invasion
    III. deportation and exile of subject populations
    IV. improved technology
    V. persecution of religious minorities

    a. I
    b. I and II
    c. I, II, and III
    d. I, II, and V
    e. III, IV

13. Which of the following empires was NOT associated with the silk roads of the classical era?
    a. Han Empire
    b. Parthian Empire
    c. Roman Empire
    d. Kushan Empire
    e. Andean Empire

14. This excerpt is most reflective of what religious tradition?
    "I call to witness
    the early hours of the morning,
    And the night when dark and still,
    Your Lord has neither left you,
    nor despises you.
    What is to come is better for you
    than what has gone before;
    For your Lord will certainly give you
    And you will be content.
    Did he not find you an orphan
    and take care of you?"

    a. Islam
    b. Buddhism
    c. Christianity
    d. Judaism
    e. Hinduism

15. Which BEST accounts for the rapid spread of Islam in the seventh and eighth centuries C.E.?
    a. The Umayyads were able to regain control from the Abbasids and move the Empire's capital to Baghdad.
    b. The issue of caliph succession had been decided and both the Sunni and Shias were united.
    c. The effectiveness of the Islamic armies coincided with an increase in internal problems in the larger Byzantine and Sasanid empires.
    d. The Muslim armies were better trained and equipped than the Byzantine warriors.
    e. The refusal of Christians to fight in the Byzantine army reduced the number of soldiers available to fight.

16. Why did paper technology affect the Islamic world in the eighth and ninth centuries?
    a. It made Mecca the center of trade and commerce in dar al-Islam, replacing Baghdad in importance.
    b. It was distrusted as coming from the west and infidel world and vellum was still the desired commodity.
    c. It promoted the kidnapping of merchants and technologies from the east.
    d. It facilitated the keeping of administrative and commercial records as well as books and political treatises.
    e. It moved the trade routes from the Mediterranean Sea into the Indian Ocean.

17. Which of the following technologies came to the Arab world from the Hellenistic world?
    a. paper
    b. astrolabe
    c. lateen sail
    d. compass
    e. concept of zero

18. The influence of Islam on medieval western philosophy is most clearly seen in
    a. the development of thirteenth-century scholasticism.
    b. the development of Aristotelian logic.
    c. the work of St. Augustine of Hippo.
    d. the development of the Greek alphabet.
    e. the iconoclast controversy in the Byzantine empire.

19. Which of the following periods represents the greatest period of technological innovation in pre-modern China?
    a. Chin and Han China
    b. Tang and Song China
    c. Yuan and Ming China
    d. Ming and Qin China
    e. Xia and Shang China

20. Which of the following statements is TRUE regarding India after the fall of the Gupta Empire c. 500–1000 C.E.?
    a. India developed strong ties with Islam which served to bring unity to the subcontinent.
    b. Mongol invasions destroyed its historic unity and left it in ruins.
    c. A series of strong rulers like Ashoka and Harsha brought the diverse peoples of India together.
    d. Local rulers turned India into a battleground as each sought to enlarge his realm at the expense of his neighbors.
    e. The Himalayas protected India from nomadic invasion and Indian traditions could develop in protected isolation.

21. Which of the following trade routes relied most heavily on the monsoon winds to facilitate its trade?
    a. Mombassa to Calcutta
    b. Madagascar to Delhi
    c. Kilwa to Baghdad
    d. Aden to Cairo
    e. Hangzhou to Melaka

22. Which of the following trading ports did NOT come into the expanding realm of Islam during the seventh and eighth centuries C.E.?
    a. Hormuz
    b. Zanzibar
    c. Axum
    d. Mogadishu
    e. Aden

23. In India c. 500–1000 what proved to be the most effective agents of conversion from Hinduism to Islam?
    a. marriage of Muslim merchants with local Hindu women
    b. a hope for improved social status after conversion
    c. the use of forced conversions
    d. the work of Sufi mystics
    e. the powerful writings of Harud al Rashid

24. Charlemagne's reign in western Europe was marked by his continual movement throughout his empire in order to maintain control. Which of the following individuals practiced a similar approach to establishing control in his realm?
    a. Ashoka
    b. Harsha
    c. Ibn Battuta
    d. Confucius
    e. Muhammad

25. Norse mariners linked Europe with the Byzantine and Abbasid empires as they
    a. connected with the Indian Ocean trading routes.
    b. traveled down the Russian rivers to the Black Sea ports.
    c. forced the western European Carolingians to find new trade routes to Asia.
    d. developed improved maritime technology resulting from interactions with Indian merchants.
    e. fought for control of the former silk routes connecting Asia and Europe.

26. The adoption of Roman Christianity had what effect on medieval Europe?
    a. It stopped the spread of Islam which was rapidly challenging Christianity in western Europe.
    b. It wiped out the existing pagan traditions and replaced them with a more civilized faith.
    c. It ensured that medieval Europe would inherit classical Roman elements such as the Latin language and the institutions of Roman Catholicism.
    d. It required all kings and queens to swear an oath of loyalty to the Pope.
    e. It established the principle of caesaropapism in western Europe.

27. A tradition of monasticism is most closely associated with which faiths?
    a. Judaism and Christianity
    b. Judaism and Buddhism
    c. Christianity and Buddhism
    d. Hinduism and Islam
    e. Islam and Christianity

28. Why was the Turkish conversion to Islam in the tenth century significant in the spreading of that faith?
    a. As the Turkish people moved into Anatolia and northern India, they expanded the boundaries of the faith.
    b. The Turkish people believed in spreading the faith through the sword and therefore settled inhabitants were required to convert or die.
    c. Because the Turkish people had a written language, it was easier to spread Islam throughout central Asia.
    d. It stopped the spread of Christianity and replaced one monotheistic tradition with another.
    e. It halted the constant tribal warfare in the region and ushered in the Pax Mongolica.

29. What made the Mongol army of Chinggis Khan so effective?
    a. Their skilled use of archers and war elephants struck fear in the hearts of enemies.
    b. Their skilled use of equestrian troops and psychological warfare made them a fierce opponent.
    c. The immense size of their armies and the rapid way the army could move seemed unstoppable.
    d. Their use of gunpowder caught their enemies off guard and unprotected against this new weapon.
    e. Chinggis Khan closely studied the battle strategies of Alexander the Great and Julius Caesar as he carefully plotted each new city siege.

30. In which of the following regions was Kublai Khan a successful conqueror?
    a. Korea
    b. Burma
    c. China
    d. Vietnam
    e. Japan

31. Trade between east Africa and the Indian Ocean merchants had what effect on sub-Saharan Africa?
    a. It wiped out indigenous cultures and replaced them with Swahili-based societies.
    b. It promoted urban development and the adoption of new foods for cultivation.
    c. It promoted the spread of Christianity and Islam and decimated traditional African religions.
    d. It established gold, salt, and slave empires which replaced the traditional stateless societies.
    e. It allowed for small European settlements which would develop into the colonial systems of the nineteenth and twentieth centuries.

32. The institution of privately owned property did NOT exist in what region c. 1000–1500 C.E.?
    a. Western Europe
    b. Eastern Europe
    c. East Asia
    d. North Africa
    e. Sub-Saharan Africa

33. What effect did Islam have on women's roles in sub-Saharan Africa c. 1000–1500?
    a. Islam forced women to veil and seclude themselves from the traditional patterns of community interaction.
    b. Women were given greater freedom in the marketplace as Islam promotes business as a godly profession.
    c. Women were removed from governmental office and required to submit to their husband's rule.
    d. Islam opened up new opportunities to women through education at Islamic schools.
    e. Islam did relatively little to curtail opportunities available to women or to compromise their status in sub-Saharan Africa.

34. Which of the following statements is FALSE regarding slavery in sub-Saharan Africa c. 1000–1500?
    a. Most slaves were captives of war.
    b. Some slaves were debtors, criminals, or suspected witches.
    c. Slaves were considered an important form of personal wealth.
    d. Most slaves worked in urban settings or construction trades.
    e. The Indian Ocean trade stimulated traffic in African slaves.

35. The opening of new lands for cultivation, improved agricultural techniques, the use of new tools and technologies, and the introduction of new crops during the high middle ages had what impact in western Europe?
    a. little impact as the black plague forced the return to manorialism which negated the potential of these developments
    b. little impact as the Roman Catholic church's control on business and commerce had a chilling effect on economic development
    c. some impact, though the constant wars with Islamic neighbors and Viking invaders diverted these resources to paying for the war efforts
    d. great impact as they stimulated the economic and social development in medieval Europe which resulted in great demographic growth
    e. great impact as they immediately lead to the industrial revolution and then global expansion to search for raw materials

36. Which of the following regions was the LAST to return to Christianity as a result of the *reconquista*?
    a. Granada
    b. Sicily
    c. Toledo
    d. Lisbon
    e. Catalonia

37. An unintended consequence of the fourth crusade (1204) was
    a. the surprising success of Peter the Hermit's ragtag army of poor knights and enthusiastic peasants
    b. the sack of Constantinople and the ensuing decline and fall of the Christian Byzantine empire
    c. the spread of epidemic diseases like the black plague which decimated the crusade's soldiers
    d. the introduction of new technologies and weapons into the Muslim world from the western European powers
    e. the development of a code of chivalry for crusaders and Muslim defenders alike

38. Which of the following statements is TRUE about the impact of the crusades on western Europe?
    a. The military victories enjoyed by the western European crusaders established western Europe as the dominant military power in the eastern hemisphere.
    b. The military victories of the western European crusaders brought more and more people back to Christianity and halted the spread of Islam in the eastern hemisphere.
    c. Though the crusades largely failed as a military venture, they helped to reintegrate western Europe into the larger economy of the eastern hemisphere.
    d. Though the crusades were unsuccessful, they did serve to demonstrate the economic power and resources found in the western hemisphere.
    e. The crusades halted the economic and social developments begun after the fall of the Roman empire.

39. The value placed on warriors and the reverence for a military elite is most clearly seen in which of the following societies?
    a. Athens and Rome
    b. Sparta and Mexica
    c. Inca and Maya
    d. Han China and Rome
    e. Zimbabwe and Yuan China

40. Which two groups of people had no indigenous tradition of writing?
    a. South Americans and West Africans
    b. Mesoamericans and South Americans
    c. Mesoamericans and North Africans
    d. Shang Chinese and Harappans
    e. South Americans and Mesopotamians

41. One similarity between the settlement of Siberia by Europeans in the seventeenth and eighteenth centuries and the settlement of Australia by Europeans in the nineteenth century is that
    a. both developed out of state-sponsored programs to promote settler colonies.
    b. both initially attracted social misfits, often including convicted criminals.
    c. both offered the promise of fertile farmland free to settlers who agreed to stay seven or more years.
    d. both were founded with a devotion to Christianity; in Russia it was the Orthodox missionaries, and in Australia, it was Anglican missionaries who provided spiritual guidance.
    e. both depended on the development of cash crops to attract settlers and their families.

42. Which of the following diseases is believed to have claimed more lives than any other malady in world history?
    a. measles
    b. bubonic plague
    c. 1918 Spanish flu
    d. smallpox
    e. whooping cough

43. One key difference between the Spanish conquest of Mexico and Peru and the establishment of English and French colonies in North America was that
    a. the Spanish conquest was the result of individual efforts by freelance adventurers and the English and French presence in North America was established as government or government-chartered endeavors.
    b. the Spanish were interested in converting the indigenous people to Catholicism and the English. and the French were interested in converting the indigenous people to the Protestant tradition.
    c. the Spanish conquest of Mexico and Peru was aided by the power of the mighty Spanish military, but the English and the French colonists had little trouble with the North American natives.
    d. the English and French colonies began as religious effort, but the Spanish effort was focused on gold, silver, and other mineral wealth.
    e. the English and French colonies began as settlement colonies while the Spanish colonies began as trading posts and sugar plantations.

44. Why did a more ethnically diverse society develop in Spanish and Portuguese colonies in the New World than in the English or French colonies?
    a. The Spanish and Portuguese were much less racist than the English or the French.
    b. The Spanish and the Portuguese were interested in producing people who could work on the haciendas and on the plantations while the English and the French preferred to import enslaved Africans to provide the necessary labor.
    c. The English and the French were only interested in making their fortunes in the New World and then returning to Europe while the Spanish and Portuguese were interested in settling the vast amount of uncultivated land in Mexico and Peru.
    d. The English and the French colonies were closer to Europe than were the Iberian colonies, so the northern settlers could return home to marry and raise their families.
    e. The English and the French colonists included more European women in their migrant numbers than did the Spanish or the Portuguese; English and French colonists could mostly marry within their own groups.

45. The cultivation of what crop proved the most deadly for enslaved Africans in the New World?
    a. sugar
    b. tobacco
    c. cotton
    d. indigo
    e. rice

46. The practice of foot binding in Ming and Qing China developed as way to demonstrate
    a. the authority of the emperor to order torture and other such brutal practices.
    b. the power of patriarchal society over lowly women who could not resist.
    c. the ability of wealthy classes to support women who could not perform physical labor.
    d. the depth of erotic desire among men of all social classes.
    e. the desire of women to behave in pleasing ways for men, even if it brought intense pain and disfigurement.

47. The primary reason Japanese shoguns of the seventeenth century forcibly expelled Christianity from Japan was that
    a. they believed it was rapidly replacing Shintoism as the dominant faith in Japan and would thus challenge their authority as spiritual leader.
    b. they feared it could increase the power of the daimyos by leading to alliances with Europeans which would undermine Shogun authority and Japanese tradition.
    c. they had hoped it would undermine the emperor's power and add to theirs by making them head of the Christian church in Japan, but the Pope refused to grant this leadership request.
    d. they claimed to have found evidence that Christian missionaries were working with European monarchs to undermine Shogun influence with the emperor and establish open ports in Japanese cities.
    e. they insisted that Christianity was a lesser faith than Buddhism, Shintoism, or Confucianism and would not agree to let the faiths coexist as part of Japanese philosophical tradition.

48. Looking at the map below, select the most appropriate title from the list provided.

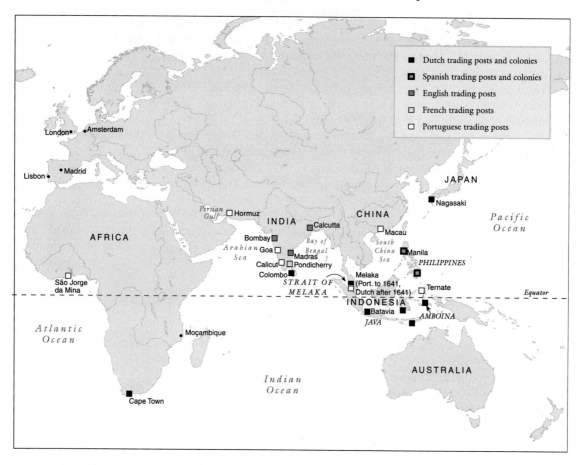

a. Sites of Paleolithic Civilizations c. 500 B.C.E.
b. The Spread of Hinduism in Asia and Africa 500–1000 C.E.
c. Journeys of Ibn Battuta in Asia and Africa c. 1300
d. European Trading Posts in Asia and Africa c. 1700
e. World War II Battle Sites in Asia and Africa c. 1945

49. One reason Christianity and Islam were not more readily adopted in China and Japan was that
   a. both Christianity and Islam claimed to be the only true religion, so conversion implied that Confucianism, Daoism, and Buddhism were false traditions, which was an unacceptable idea to most Chinese and Japanese.
   b. both Christianity and Islam demanded monogamy which was an unacceptable social restriction for most Chinese and Japanese men who were used to having multiple wives necessary for producing the desired number of sons.
   c. both Christianity and Islam required an end to idol worship which was an essential practice in Confucianism, Daoism, and Shinto traditions, and local priests refused to abandon the practice.
   d. both Christianity and Islam fostered a belief in a judgment day and an afterlife which conflicted with the egalitarian beliefs of Confucianism and Shinto tradition.
   e. both Christianity and Islam preached the idea of holy war which was in direct contradiction to the pacifist beliefs of Zen and Chan Buddhists in Japan and China.

50. The intermarriage of Europeans with indigenous peoples c. 1500–1800 was most common in which region?
    a. China
    b. Japan
    c. Australia
    d. North America
    e. Brazil

51. Why could nineteenth-century European conservatives accept the American revolution as just but not the French revolution?
    a. The American revolution had taken place long before the French revolution and the rise of conservatism which saw all revolutions as evil.
    b. The American revolution had only been against the British and not against the other conservative powers at the Congress of Vienna.
    c. The American revolution had not championed the cause "fraternity" which the French revolution had and which the conservatives found most disturbing.
    d. The American revolution was based on Enlightenment ideals, but the French revolution was based on nationalism which the nineteenth-century conservatives viewed as extremely dangerous.
    e. The American revolution was seen as an example of natural historical change and development, but the French revolution was viewed as a chaotic attack on existing society and established social order.

52. Which of the following nineteenth-century individuals sought to extend the rights of freedom and equality to women?
    a. John Stuart Mill
    b. John Locke
    c. Jean-Jacques Rousseau
    d. Theodor Herzl
    e. Simon Bolivar

53. Which of the following modern European nations was built on the principles of "Realpolitik" and "blood and iron"?
    a. The Netherlands
    b. Germany
    c. Italy
    d. France
    e. Great Britain

54. Which of the following events came FIRST?
    a. American revolution
    b. French revolution
    c. Haitian revolution
    d. Congress of Vienna
    e. Mexican revolution

55. Foreign investment in South America during the nineteenth century provided capital for development but
    a. often was controlled by local caudillos and thus did not positively impact working class people.
    b. the resulting wealth as well as control over industries and exports remained in foreign hands.
    c. was squandered in fighting between elites and revolutionaries over economic control and decision making.
    d. unlike the similar investments in North America, soon moved into local hands for reinvestment and diversification.
    e. was used primarily for building railroads and infrastructure rather than steel or textile factories.

56. The British control of Malaya in the 1870s was important because
    a. it halted French expansion in Indochina.
    b. it provided a check against Russian expansion in Central Asia.
    c. it enabled the British Navy to control the sea lanes linking the Indian Ocean and the South China Sea.
    d. it contributed to the dismantling of the Ottoman empire and the Qing empire.
    e. it weakened Spanish claims to the East Indies, especially in the Philippines.

57. Which two nations came LAST to the race for imperial power in the nineteenth century?
    a. Britain and France
    b. Spain and Portugal
    c. China and Russia
    d. The Netherlands and Germany
    e. Japan and the United States

58. Which of the following "documents" was used to justify U.S. imperial incursions into Panama, the Philippines, Nicaragua, and Honduras in the early twentieth century?
    a. United States Constitution
    b. Declaration of Independence
    c. Declaration of the Rights of Man and the Citizen
    d. Roosevelt Corollary
    e. Monroe Doctrine

59. Which of the following conflicts was LEAST tied to nineteenth-century imperial motivations?
    a. the Spanish-Cuban-American War
    b. the Sino-Japanese War
    c. the Russo-Japanese War
    d. the Franco-Prussian War
    e. the South African War

60. John Maynard Keynes would have found most agreement regarding government's role in a capitalist economy with which of the following individuals?
    a. Adam Smith
    b. Franklin Roosevelt
    c. Adolph Hitler
    d. Benito Mussolini
    e. Karl Marx

61. A key motivation for Japanese imperialism in Asia 1931–1945 was
    a. the quest for timber rubber and petroleum available in Indonesia and Malaya.
    b. to secure their holdings in Indochina against further German aggression.
    c. to fulfill their treaty agreement with the other Axis powers.
    d. the quest for additional populations to help them fight the Chinese.
    e. to liberate those regions from European colonialism.

62. The behavior of Japanese soldiers at Nanjing in 1937 was given as the official Japanese reason for the creation of
    a. internment camps for captured resistance fighters and others deemed dangerous by the Japanese authorities.
    b. "comfort houses" where enslaved women from the Japanese-controlled colonies were forced to work as prostitutes.
    c. the United Nations definition of genocide.
    d. war crime tribunals like in Nuremberg from 1945 to 1947.
    e. the League of Nations to prevent further violent aggression.

63. The following statement is part of what larger cold war policy?
    "... it must be the policy of the United States to support free people who are resisting attempted subjugation by armed minorities or by outside pressures."
    a. the United Nations Charter
    b. the rationale for NATO
    c. containment
    d. Monroe Doctrine
    e. Warsaw Pact

64. The formation of the United Nations was motivated by
    a. the earlier successes of the League of Nations.
    b. the Soviet acquisition of atomic bomb technology.
    c. the creation of the nation of Israel.
    d. the firebombing of Dresden and Tokyo.
    e. the desire to keep world peace.

65. Which of these twentieth-century genocides occurred FIRST?
    a. the Armenian genocide
    b. the Holocaust
    c. the Cambodian genocide
    d. the Rwandan genocide
    e. the genocide in Kosovo

66. The most serious challenge to Soviet control in eastern Europe came in
    a. Czechoslovakia in 1968 with the election of Alexander Dubcek.
    b. Afghanistan in the 1990s.
    c. Hungary in 1956.
    d. Yugoslavia in 1945.
    e. Berlin in 1961.

67. Which of the following independence leaders said these words:
    *" It is clear we must find an African solution to our problems, and
    that this can only be found in African unity. Divided we are weak;
    united, Africa could become one of the greatest forces from good
    in the world."*
    a. Nelson Mandela
    b. Kwame Nkrumah
    c. Frantz Fanon
    d. Gamal Abdel Nassar
    e. Jomo Kenyatta

68. Which of the following is NOT a reason that independence came more slowly to African nations than to nations in Asia?
    a. Imperial nations were reluctant to let go of natural resources from their African colonies.
    b. Cold war pressures, especially the pressure to align with one superpower or another, was strong.
    c. Internal conflicts between groups, clans, or tribes sometimes made state building difficult.
    d. African nations themselves could not agree on their joining of ultranational organizations like the Pan-African Union or the United Nations.
    e. ALL of the above are reasons independence came more slowly to African nations than to those in Asia.

69. Which of the following pairs presents the BEST comparison between the policies of Maximillian Robespierre and Mao Zedong?
    a. Both feared counterrevolutionaries and so instituted the Terror and the Great Cultural Revolution.
    b. Both sought to reduce the power of intellectuals and so instituted the Directory and the Gang of Four.
    c. Both valued agriculture as the ideal life profession and so instituted the White Terror and the Great Leap Forward.
    d. Both were religious men and so instituted the Cult of Supreme Being and the Campaign of 100 Flowers.
    e. Both believed in communal living and so instituted the Commune in Paris and the collectivization of agriculture in China.

70. Who said at his trial for treason before facing twenty-seven years in prison:
    "I have cherished the ideal of a democratic and free society in which all persons live together in harmony and with equal opportunities. It is an ideal which I hope to live for and to achieve. But if need be, it is an ideal for which I am prepared to die."
    a. Kwame Nkrumah
    b. Nelson Mandela
    c. Juan Peron
    d. Shah Mohammed Reza Pahlavi
    e. Jacobo Arbenz Guzman

Section II

The mandatory reading period is ten minutes so include that in your practice. That is enough time to read the questions and documents. Jot down notes on both. The suggested writing times are forty minutes for the document-based question and thirty-five minutes for each essay.

Document-based Question
Forty minutes
33-1/3 percent of final score

There will be written reminders to include a thesis, historical evidence, use of all or all but one of the documents, group documents, and to be mindful of point of view.

1. To what extent did labor and business in the period of protoindustrialization set the basis for industrialization?

What other document(s) might be useful to support your answer?

Historical background: In the nineteenth century, Europe, North America, and Japan followed Britain's lead to become industrialized nations. In every country, it was preceded by a period of preparation that enabled the countries to foster industrialization; this period is known as protoindustrialization.

Document 1

Document 2

Document 3

Adam Smith on the Capitalist Market, Britain, 1776 (p. 654)

It is the maxim of every prudent master of a family, never to attempt to make at home what will cost him more to make than to buy. The tailor does not attempt to make his own shoes, but buys them from the shoemaker. The shoemaker does not attempt to make his own clothes, but employs a tailor, The farmer attempts to make neither the one or the other, but employs those different artificers. All of them find it in their interest to employ their whole industry in a way in which they have some advantage over their neighbours, and to purchase with a part of its produce, or, what is the same thing, with the price of a part of it, whatever else they have occasion for.

Document 4

Document 5

Marx and Engels on Bourgeoisie and Proletarians, Britain, 1888 (p. 838)

In proportion as the bourgeoisie, i.e., capital, is developed, in the same proportion is the proletariat, the modern working class, developed—a class of labourers who live only so long as they find work, and who find work only so long as their labour increases capital. These labourers, who must sell themselves piecemeal, are a commodity, like every other article of commerce, and are consequently exposed to all the vicissitudes of competition, to all the fluctuations of the market. . . .
The advance of industry . . . replaces the isolation of the laborers."

Document 6

Section III
Change-Over-Time Question
Thirty-five minutes
33-1/3 percent of final score

There will be written reminders to use five minutes for planning, and to include a thesis, include historical evidence, address all parts of the question, and to show changes and continuities using the historical facts.

2. Pick ONE of the following regions and discuss the changes and continuities in responses to military aggression c. 1000–2000 C.E.
   East Asia
   Eastern Europe
   Southeast Asia
   North Africa
   North America

Comparison Question
Thirty-five minutes
33-1/3 percent of final score

There will be written reminders to use five minutes for planning, and to include a thesis, include historical evidence, address all parts of the question, and use direct comparisons.

3. Compare and contrast the causes of TWO of the following revolutions:
   French (1789)
   Haitian (1791)
   Chinese (1911)
   Russian (1917)
   Cuban (1959)
   Iranian (1979)

END OF EXAM

EXAM 2 ANSWERS AND EXPLANATIONS

1. **c:** The Venus figures represent a deep interest in fertility and the understanding that reproduction of plants, animals, and humans was essential to the survival of paleolithic people.

2. **b:** Throughout the paleolithic era, women had contributed to the clan by gathering plant food necessary for survival. Plants, nuts, roots, and fruits provided the necessary food to supplement the protein supplied by animals hunted by men. When the hunt was unsuccessful, the food gathered by women sustained the group. It is therefore logical that women would understand the natural cycles of plants and attempt cultivation.

3. **a:** The isolation caused by the Sahara and Libyan deserts, the Mediterranean Sea, and cataracts in the Nile River allowed Egypt to develop during the Old Kingdom period in relative security from invasion. Likewise, China was protected from the rest of the world because of the high Himalayas, the forbidding deserts of central Asia, and the rough Yellow Sea and vast Indian Ocean.

4. **e:** Both classical Greece and ancient Mesopotamia relied on a city-state political structure. The other choices were either empires, kingdoms, or stateless societies.

5. **a:** Though certainly a patriarchal society, women in ancient Egypt did serve as regents for young pharaohs, scribes, priestesses, and even an occasional pharaoh herself. Egyptian women could also own property and conduct their own businesses.

6. **e:** Buddhism and Christianity were both spread by strong missionary movements although Buddhism relied on trade as a vehicle for conversion as well. Both religions also offered the promise of salvation not found in most other religions during the Foundations period.

7. **b:** During the Foundations period, systems of social inequality were common. One element which made the Indian caste system unique was that its social hierarchy tied to a religious tradition provided order and stability for society which in most other places was a role filled by the various governments.

8. **c:** Confucianism developed during the "era of warring states" as a response to the social unrest and warfare that characterized the era. Confucius's goal was to create a stable society through a belief in filial piety and the application of principles such as *junzi*.

9. **d:** Though both Rome and Han China fell for similar internal and external reasons, China eventually rebuilt its dynasty under the Sui, Tang, and Song empires. Rome never again rebuilt its imperial power and western Europe was never again unified under a single political structure.

10. **b:** Rome, like the earlier Persians, allowed the conquered subjects in its realm to practice their own religious and cultural traditions without much interference from the imperial government.

11. **a:** The Huns spoke a Turkish language and were probably related to other nomadic groups of western China. Because the Huns put such pressure on all the other Germanic peoples, the Visogoths, Ostrogoths, Franks, and Vandals began to flood across the borders of the Roman empire in larger and larger numbers.

12. **b:** Populations of both empires dropped dramatically in the second and third centuries C.E. as a result of epidemic diseases in combination with war and invasion. By 600 C.E. populations in both regions had fallen by a quarter or more since their classical highs.

13. **e:** The empires in the Andes were located in South America and clearly were not a part of the silk road trading systems which were limited to Eurasia during the classical era.

14. **a:** This is a translation from the Quran. The use of the words *witness, Lord* and *orphan* should have been solid clues, if you did not otherwise recognize the text.

15. **c:** While the Muslim armies were charged with the zeal of new converts, it was internal problems with overtaxed peasants and oppressed minorities in both the Byzantine empire and the Sasanid empire which diverted the larger empire's resources and attention. The Muslim armies took advantage of this situation to build an empire that stretched from India, Central Asia, to north Africa and Iberia.

16. **d:** The Chinese prisoners taken at the Battle of Talas River in 751 brought the technology of paper-making to the Islamic world. With this technology, Baghdad in particular emerged as the administrative, political, and intellectual capital of dar al-Islam. The production of all sorts of paper records and books changed the way people lived, worked, and governed around the world.

17. **b:** Paper and the compass came from China. The lateen sail came from southeast Asia and Indian mariners, and the concept of zero was a Mayan concept, but the astrolabe was a Hellenistic innovation which the Arab and Persian mariners used to calculate latitude.

18. **a:** Thirteenth-century scholasticism was the pinnacle of western philosophy in the medieval Europe. The desire to match reason with faith was an outgrowth of the work of Ibn Rashd, the *qadi* of Seville, who was known in the west as Averroes.

19. **b:** During the Tang and Song dynasties China produced porcelain, improved iron and steel tools and weaponry, gunpowder, printing, and naval technologies.

20. **d:** India was politically fragmented after the fall of the Gupta dynasty. The northern portion of the subcontinent suffered from consistent invasion by nomadic peoples c. 500–1000 C.E. while the south largely escaped invasion but was scarcely more centralized than the north.

21. **a:** The yearly shift of monsoons from November to February and April to September made it possible for goods to travel through the Indian Ocean from Mombassa to Calcutta.

22. **c:** Axum, sometimes spelled Aksum, remained independent and Christian despite attempts by Arab conquerors and merchants to bring it into the expanding realm of Islam in the seventh and eighth centuries.

23. **d:** The personal, emotional, and devotional approach to Islam offered by Sufi mystics had great appeal for many Indians. The fact that Sufis often allowed for the retention of traditional rituals and practices eased the conversion for many former Hindus.

24. **b:** Harsha traveled consistently throughout his realm in order to maintain control of formerly disparate regions in northern India. Further, like Charlemagne, his efforts at unity did not survive long after his death.

25. **b:** Norse merchants relied on the rivers of Russia to reach the Black Sea ports where they could trade with the Byzantines and the Abbasids. They took Scandinavian goods to the Abbasids and traded for silver which they then traded with the Carolingians for glassware, wine, and other European products.

26. **c:** After the adoption of Christianity by Clovis and the Franks, Roman Christianity began to influence all of western Europe, even those areas not easily converted. The use of Latin as the language of government as well as religion and the adoption of Roman institutions helped to ensure that crucial elements from classical Roman society would be preserved.

27. **c:** Both Christianity and Buddhism have a long tradition of monasticism. In both religions, monasteries served as places of refuge, education, and conversions in the beginnings of each faith and continue these traditions today.

28. **a:** In the tenth century Turks living near the Abbasid empire began to convert to Islam. As these people began to migrate and then settle in Anatolia and northern India, they took their newfound faith as well as their political and military influence with them into these new regions added to the Islamic world.

29. **b:** It was the skill of the troops on horseback and the use of terror and intimidation to get their enemies to submit which made the Mongol army so successful.

30. **c:** Though Kublai Khan sought to expand into Korea, Burma, Cambodia, and Japan, none of these military exploits were successful. In China, however, he was successful in expanding Mongol rule and establishing the Yuan dynasty.

31. **b:** In east Africa, the trading networks with Indian Ocean merchants promoted the development of coastal trading cities such as Mombasa and Kilwa and introduced new foodstuffs, like bananas, which provided a new and nutritious supplement to traditional Bantu diets.

32. **e:** Communities in sub-Saharan Africa had a long tradition of lands claimed and used in common. Extended family groups and clans were the dominant social organization and male heads of these families organized the work of their own group.

33. **e:** Women in African societies who converted to Islam during this period continued to appear and work openly in society in ways not always permitted in other Islamic lands. The coming of Islam in this era did little to compromise the status of women in sub-Saharan Africa.

34. **d:** Most slaves in sub-Saharan Africa c. 1000–1500 worked in agriculture.

35. **d:** Just as in China, India, and the Islamic world during the early postclassical era, the dramatic increase in agricultural output was the foundation for economic growth and social developments.

36. **a:** Granada, at the far southern tip of the Iberian Peninsula, managed to hold out against the Christian forces until 1492.

37. **b:** The sack of Constantinople by Christian crusaders in 1204 dealt the city a blow from which it could never recover. Though it did not officially fall to the Ottoman Turks until 1453, the destruction of the city and its infrastructure was ultimately deadly to this Christian empire.

38. **c:** Though the crusades were not a military victory for western Europe, the introduction of new products and the economic stimulation of markets were of huge benefit and brought western Europe back into regular interaction with other regions in the eastern hemisphere.

39. **b:** Both ancient Sparta and the Mexica looked upon all male citizens as potential warriors, and social status was tied to one's service on the battlefield. Spartan and Mexica women earned respect as the mothers of soldiers.

40. **a:** South American peoples and the peoples of west Africa had no indigenous system of writing. The Spanish brought a written script to the peoples of South America in the early sixteenth century and the Muslim merchants of the eighth century brought a written script to west Africa.

41. **b:** Both regions attracted settlers who were social misfits in some way. Often this meant criminals or those seeking to escape unpayable debts. There was not major religious motivation, any significant lure of cash crops, or state-sponsored settler colony programs in either region.

42. **d:** Though each of the disease listed as choices has had a huge demographic impact, smallpox is believed to be the most devastating as there is no cure and survival rates are extremely low, especially among the young, the elderly, and those in poor physical condition.

43. **a:** Though they carried the Spanish flag, conquistadors like Cortes or Pizarro were freelance adventurers out to make their personal fortunes. North American colonies like Jamestown or Massasachusetts Bay Colony began with government support and blessings.

44. **e:** About 85 percent of the Spanish migrants and even a higher percentage of the Portuguese migrants were men, while the English and the French migrants tended to include a much higher percentage of women. The interaction of the Iberian migrants with the indigenous population and the enslaved Africans produced a complex, multiracial society in South America. The same multiethnic result did not occur in North America as the English and French married within their own groups and tended to exclude those offspring which were the result of interracial and interethnic unions.

45. **a:** While all these crops were labor intensive, the production of sugar was the most deadly for enslaved Africans. It is estimated that each ton of sugar exported to Europe cost the life of one enslaved African person.

46. **c:** Although Chinese was a patriarchal society and foot binding joins a list of other traditions which denigrate women, the driving purpose for the practice was to demonstrate that wealthy families did not have to rely on the labor of their women and could afford to support their female members. The erotic element developed over time.

47. **b:** The expulsion of Christianity and persecution of Christians in Japan in the seventeenth century was predominately based on the shoguns' fear that converting daimyo would make alliances with European adventurers and even governments and use that support, especially weaponry, to rival the shogun's control of Japan. Certainly there were fears of loss of Japanese traditions should Christianity become widespread, but it was the availability of weapons and the fear of growing independence among the daimyo which prompted the anti-Christian edicts.

48. **d:** These sites include Dutch, Spanish, English, French, and Portuguese trading ports in Asia and Africa c. 1700.

49. **a:** Christianity and Islam both identify themselves as the one true faith and insist that other traditions are fallacious creeds. For both the Chinese and Japanese peoples, the intertwining of Confucianism, Buddhism, and Daoism, and Shinto tradition in Japan, had produced a stable underlying philosophy for millennium and neither peoples were anxious to abandon those traditions to embrace a new, exclusive faith.

50. **e:** Intermarriage between Europeans and indigenous Chinese, Japanese, Australian, or North American peoples was extremely uncommon during this era. Only in Brazil was intermarriage between Europeans and indigenous peoples the norm.

51. **e:** The American revolution was not challenged by conservatives such as Edmund Burke who saw it as a natural change in the development of North American society. In contrast, nineteenth-century conservatives saw the French revolution as a radical threat to the existing social order which they believed ultimately produced anarchy and violence.

52. **a:** As a nineteenth-century liberal, Mill worked to promote the freedom of individuals to pursue their own economic, social, political, and intellectual interests. Unlike earlier Enlightenment thinkers like Locke or Rousseau, Mill extended these ideals to women as well as working-class people. Herzl was interested in Zionism and Bolivar in nationalism; neither directly addressed women in their agendas.

53. **b:** Realpolitik and "blood and iron" are phrases popularized and utilized by Otto von Bismarck in the formation of the modern state of Germany by 1871.

54. **a:** (Though the specific dates for these events are not essential to remember for the national exam, a sense of chronology and of cause and effect is required.) The American revolution provided inspiration and experience for future revolutionaries to build upon and sometimes even inadvertently contributed to those revolutions as in the bankrupt condition of the French treasury or the experience of the *gens de coleur* in Haiti.

55. **b:** Much of the capital investment in Latin America during the nineteenth century came from foreign investors, and, unlike the situation in North America, the control over industries and exports remained in foreign hands rather than being transferred to local control and reinvested in each nation.

56. **c:** The British conquest of Malaya, modern Malaysia, provided important and abundant supplies of rubber and tin to the British empire, but it was their strategic location linking the Indian Ocean with the South China Sea that proved ultimately most important in maintaining British control of the wealth in the empire.

57. **e:** The rapid industrialism of the United States and Japan, the building of powerful armed forces in both nations, and the fear of being excluded from a position of world influence propelled both Japan and the United States into the imperial realm by the end of the nineteenth century.

58. **d:** The Roosevelt Corollary was drafted to justify the expansion of U.S. interests in Latin America and used throughout the twentieth century in support of U.S. intervention in places where it believed its economic interests were threatened.

59. **d:** Of the choices listed, the Franco-Prussian War is best described as a war related to nation-building or nationalism rather than the clear imperial motivations in the others listed.

60. **b:** Although Keynes would not become extremely influential in U.S. economic policy until after World War II, his ideals about government intervention to promote demand through job programs and encouraging investment are clearly reflected in Roosevelt's New Deal policy.

61. **a:** Japanese imperialism in Asia was directly prompted by their need for natural resources unavailable domestically, but essential to their industrial growth.

62. **b:** Comfort houses, also known as consolation centers, were places of enslavement for up to three hundred thousand women transported from Taiwan, Manchuria, and especially Korea to work as prostitutes. In trying to prevent the horrors of Nanjing from happening again, the Japanese military created a system of imperially sanctioned sex slaves.

63. **c:** This statement is from the Truman Doctrine which was a key element in the U.S cold war policy of containment.

64. **e:** The United Nations grew out of Allied cooperation during World War II, and in 1944 representatives from China, Great Britain, the Soviet Union, and the United States met near Washington, D.C. to finalize proposals approved in 1945 by fifty nations. The stated goal of the United Nations is to maintain international peace and security and promote friendly relations among nations in an attempt to prevent war and promote peace.

65. **a:** The Armenian genocide at the hands of the Turks during the last days of the Ottoman empire is the first genocide of the twentieth century. In the 1930s, when someone asked Adolph Hitler if he did not fear the world's response to his planned extermination of European Jewry, he responded, "who now remembers the Armenians?"

66. **c:** The most serious threat to Soviet control in eastern Europe came in 1956 in Hungary as large numbers of Hungarian citizens embraced de-Stalinization, and demanded democracy and the breaking of ties to Moscow and the Warsaw Pact. The Soviets crushed the uprising by sending in tanks, making massive arrests, executing the rebellion's leaders, and installing a dependable communist leader in his place.

67. **b:** As leader of the first sub-Saharan African nation to gain independence from colonial rule, Nkrumah became a powerful spokesman for pan-African unity. (Though students are not required to recall these specific leaders, they should be able to recognize each and to associate each with a particular aspect of decolonialism)

68. **d:** Though there was some disagreement among African nations regarding their allegiance to a pan-African organization, that disagreement did NOT slow the move toward independence as choices a, b, and c did.

69. **a:** Both Robespierre and Mao were increasingly concerned that their respective revolutions might be sidetracked or halted by those who were traitors or not sufficiently committed to the revolution's ideals. Robespierre relied on the Terror to root out these revisionists and Mao relied on the Cultural Revolution.

70. **b:** Nelson Mandela spoke these words in 1964 on his way to prison on Robben Island in South Africa.

Section II
DBQ Response and Analysis

Every student will write a different DBQ. Most will share some of these variables:

- **Has an acceptable thesis:** This point is earned by dealing with all aspects of the question in a historically viable way. (1 point)

- **Understands the basic meaning of the documents:** The essay is based on an accurate reading of the documents. One misinterpretation is allowed. (1 point)

- **Supports the thesis with appropriate evidence from all or all but one document:** The essay may still earn one point if appropriate evidence comes from all but two of the documents. (2 points)

- **Analyzes point of view (POV) in at least two documents.** (1 point)
Possible Points of View:
Silver mining likely to be depicted to promote the Americas for settlement and profit
Sugar plantation engraving appears to be from an instruction manual
Adam Smith: capitalist in earliest period of industrialization
Engels and Marx: socialist expose of brutality in worker's lives

- **Analyzes documents by grouping them in two or three ways:**
Possible groups:
Mass labor conditions (Documents 1, 2, 4, 6)
Slavery v. free labor (Documents 1, 2, 4, 6)
Control of labor changes from the individual to economic forces (Documents 3, 5)
Use of machines (Documents 2, 4, 6)
Use of foreign labor forces (Documents 2, 6)
Use of domestic labor (Documents 1, 3, 4, 5)
Harsh conditions (Documents 1, 2, 3)
Appearance of less harsh conditions (Documents 1, 2)

- **Identifies and explains the need for one type of appropriate additional document (AD) or source:**

Possible additional documents:

Since both written documents are from higher-class accounts, working-class accounts are needed: newspaper or government investigative accounts of working families who made the transition from rural farms to urban factories

To judge the conditions of work settings: comparative accounts by ex-slaves from plantations and workers in industrial settings

Individual student responses will vary in the Expanded Core category as well. The inclusion of more developed or sophisticated POVs or more explained ADs is the most frequent way to earn these points.

Section III
Change-over-Time Response and Analysis

Pick ONE of the following regions and discuss the changes and continuities in responses to military aggression c. 1000–2000 C.E.

> East Asia
> Eastern Europe
> Southeast Asia
> North Africa
> North America

In the years c. 1000, Vietnam responded to Chinese military aggression by consistently using guerilla tactics to resist while at the same time adopting some Chinese cultural elements, and in the years of French military aggression during the late eighteenth through the early twentieth centuries, Vietnam responded in similar ways. Yet the Vietnamese response to later twentieth-century American military aggression resulted in an enduring civil war and only limited adoption of American culture after the war ended.

The Chinese had been interested in colonizing the lands of Vietnam for more than a thousand years and the Vietnamese had sporadically and violently resisted throughout that millennium, adopting some elements of Chinese tradition and openly rejecting others. The fertile lands of Vietnam and the opportunities for trade first drew the Chinese to northern Vietnam during the Han dynasty and continued until the tenth century C.E. Members of the Vietnamese elite first welcomed the Chinese and hoped to become even wealthier as a result of their interaction with Chinese merchants. This migration resulted in Vietnamese peasants turning to their extended families for protection against this Chinese military aggression and cultural expansion. In particular, Vietnamese women were strongly resistant to the Confucian ideals of women as subservient. One of the most famous Vietnamese campaigns to expel the Chinese from Vietnam was led by women: the Trung sisters in the first century C.E. Though this rebellion was ultimately unsuccessful, it demonstrates the continuously violent response to Chinese military aggression c. 1000 C.E., as Vietnamese peasants consistently resisted Chinese and Sino-Vietnamese attempts to usurp traditional land holdings and change the status enjoyed by Vietnamese women.

The Vietnamese response to French military aggression was remarkably similar to their response to the Chinese: sporadically and violently resist the aggressor while adopting some cultural elements. Though the Chinese had been defeated in a rebellion in 939 C.E. and had not been able to successfully retake Vietnam over the next 900 years, other nations were interested in the wealth an independent Vietnam had to offer; first the Portuguese and soon the French attempted to set up businesses and establish trading arrangements much as the Chinese had done more than one thousand years before. Like the Chinese, the French main goal in Vietnam was economic profit, though the spreading of French culture was also considered important. Catholic missionaries in the eighteenth century were effective in establishing Roman Catholicism among many upper-class Vietnamese. Indeed, to collaborate in religious as well as economic matters meant higher-paying jobs in business and in government for the Vietnamese people. The response of the Vietnamese people to the French military occupation of their nation was to either collaborate with the potential of significant economic gain or to remain poorly paid laborers with few, if any, civil rights. This response would change after World War II.

After the temporary loss of their lucrative rubber, rice, coffee, and mining profits during the Japanese occupation, the French planned to renew their colonial hold in Indochina after World War II. The French did not fully anticipate the Vietnamese reaction to the reassertion of French military control. Ho Chi Minh, like other well-educated, well-traveled young intellectual Vietnamese, was not interested in his homeland returning to colony status; he wanted independence for his nation. But the French had no intention of losing this valuable colony, and Ho had no intention of quitting the fight. Soon the Chinese and the Soviets were supplying Ho with weapons and aid, and the United States was supplying the increasingly unpopular French military. Relying on guerilla techniques much like the Trung sisters had used 1900 years earlier, Ho's forces surrounded the French forces at Dienbienphu and waited them out for almost a year. At that point, French domestic support for the war was gone, the French had lost nearly one hundred thousand troops, and they finally agreed to peace talks. The Vietnamese response to French military aggression was to use guerilla tactics to defeat their larger, better-equipped enemy and to adopt some cultural elements such as religion from those aggressors, a very similar response to the Chinese in the previous millennium.

The Vietnamese response to American military involvement was different than the response to the Chinese or to the French; the Vietnamese response to American military aggression was to fight a war against the aggressors and against their own countrymen who were seen as traitors to the true Vietnam. The United States involvement grew out of the cold war policy of containment and out of the belief in the domino effect, i.e., if Vietnam "falls to the communists, then all of southeast Asia will too." The response of the Vietnamese people was divided. Ho and his supporters saw themselves as the defenders of independence and the true voice of the Vietnamese people. The noncommunist south, led by Ngo Dinh Diem, was backed at first with advisors and supplies, and by 1968, with more than half a million American soldiers. There was little exporting of American culture, no correlation with Confucianism or Roman Catholicism. Even when the U.S. finally withdrew in 1973, the fighting continued between Vietnamese factions, until Saigon fell to North Vietnamese forces in 1975; it took a Vietnamese civil war to resolve this military aggression.

The continuity in response to military aggression in Vietnam was to use guerilla tactics to drive out the foreign invaders; the changes are in the impact the invading cultures had on Vietnamese culture. With the Chinese and the French, the cultural and religious acceptance of Confucianism and Roman Catholicism and their integration into the traditional Buddhist religious practices is very similar. The U.S. military aggression did not have that religious or cultural impact, but today Vietnam is increasingly embracing capitalism. Perhaps that economic tie is the ultimate American cultural legacy in Vietnam's response to U.S. military aggression.

Analysis:
Patterns of interaction, including cultural transformation resulting from wars, is an AP World History theme and a specified type of knowledge students are expected to have in the course curriculum. For this essay, the student has chosen southeast Asia and correctly identified Vietnam as a nation in that region. This is a solid essay as the writer knows her content and she has crafted her essay to follow the scoring guide. This essay would likely earn the following points:

This essay gets a point for the thesis which addresses the global issue of responses to military aggression c. 1000–2000 C.E.; note that the writer does not include an introduction, but lets her thesis stand alone. This is an expanded core thesis. (1 point)

This essay addresses all parts of the question, though not necessarily thoroughly or evenly. The writer has three distinct periods in the same world region. (2 points)

This essay substantiates the thesis with appropriate historical evidence. This essay has good information in the second and third sections; the earliest section c. 1000 C.E. is the weakest as the Trung sisters example is way before the time period prescribed in the prompt. The last sentence of that paragraph would be enough, however, to earn both these points. (2 points)

This essay earns a point for relevant world context in the section on American military aggression. The inclusion of containment and the domino effect would be considered world context. (1 point)

This essay earns a point for analyzing the processes of change and/or continuity. The student's comments in the last paragraph address the processes of both change and continuity in all three eras. (1 point)

Because of the expanded core thesis, this essay would earn an 8.

Comparative Response and Analysis:
Compare and contrast the causes of the French (1789) and Haitian (1791) revolutions.

The revolutions in France and Haiti were similar in that both began in societies based on legalized privilege, and both were triggered by acts of popular violence, but they differed in the importance of outside influences in propelling the revolutions.

The concept of legalized privilege was an important cause for the French and the Haitian revolutions. In France, the *ancien regime* was divided into three estates: the Roman Catholic clergy, the nobility, and everyone else. That political and social distinction meant the clergy, about 1 percent of the population, had one vote in the Estates General; the nobility, less than 3 percent of the population, had another vote; and the Third Estate, which included everyone else in France from the wealthiest, best-educated lawyer to the lowliest serf—about 95 population of the population—also had one vote. Since the Estates General operated on the principle of one vote per estate, that meant that 95 percent of France's population was consistently outvoted by 3 percent as the first two estates almost always voted together. This legalized privilege was determined by birth and there was little, if any, opportunity to change estates; you stayed where you were born. In Haiti, in 1791, legalized privilege was the rule of order also, but in that plantation nation, race was the discriminating factor. In 1791, the population of Haiti was divided into three main groups: about 40,000 wealthy, white French settlers; about 30,000 free people of color, known as gens de couleur, who worked smaller plots of lands or who were artisans; and more than 500,000 black slaves, most born in Africa, who worked in awful conditions on Haiti's sugar, coffee, or cotton plantations. A person did not change status despite financial successes; your racial origins determined your social status and did not change. In both France and Haiti, being a member of the privileged class carried with it special legal, political, and economic benefits which were unavailable to "lessers" in each society. This legalized inequality was a key cause of both revolutions.

The causes for the French and Haitian revolutions were also similar in that both revolutions were triggered by acts of violence. In France, the storming of the Bastille in 1789 by the Parisian mob in search of weapons is often cited as the beginning of that revolution. The Bastille, actually a prison holding only a few prisoners at the time, was a symbol of the king and the crowd grew so agitated after being fired upon by the prison guards that they actually hacked the defenders to death. This model of mob action and violence would be a recurring pattern in the ongoing events of the French revolution. Likewise in Haiti, violence marked the beginning of that revolution and became part of its cause. In 1791, a Vodou priest led 12,000 Haitian slaves in revolt against the white planters; within a month more than 100,000 slaves were drawn into the violence which killed whites and gens de coleur alike. This violence, like in France, marked the beginning of the Haitian revolution and kept it going.

Though the Haitian and French revolutions were both caused by legalized privilege and continuing "mob" violence, the two revolutions were different in the role outside nations played in causing the revolutions. In France, the revolution began largely inside the nation. The unhappiness of the Third Estate at their lack of social or political input into their country's governance began the French revolution; only after the revolution had spread outside the borders of France did Austria, Prussia, and Great Britain become involved. In Haiti, the fear of spreading slave rebellion and the opportunity to damage the French while they fought to retain their valuable colonial economic resources brought French troops and then British and Spanish troops to the island. Outside forces became almost immediately involved in the Haitian revolution, but not in the French.

The French revolution can be considered a domestic revolution as its causes—class distinctions—began and remained almost completely internal, until those causes spilled into neighboring nations. As a French colony, the long-term causes for the revolution in Haiti were likewise internal: in this case, racial privilege. So, it was the strict racial inequity, the rapid and widespread violence, and ensuing external foreign intervention which caused the Haitian slave revolt and the eventual creation of the second independent republic in the western hemisphere.

Analysis:
This topic is one you could easily see on the AP Exam. The causes of revolutions figure prominently in the course guide and are likely comparative topics on the national exam. This is a solid essay; clearly, the writer knows content related to both the French and Haitian revolutions and has paid attention to the scoring guide in crafting the essay. This essay would likely earn the following points:

The student has an acceptable thesis placed appropriately in the paper. Note that she does not have an introduction, but simply begins her paper with her thesis. This is a fine exam strategy, as students do not earn points for an introduction, but must have a thesis, preferably as the opening sentence of an essay which does not have an introduction or as the last sentence of an essay with an introductory paragraph. This thesis would earn the Expanded Core thesis point as the thesis is clear, deals with all aspects of the question, and is analytical in that it sets up specific areas of comparison and contrast. (1 point)

The student addresses all parts of the question dealing with both comparisons and contrasts between the two revolutions, though the comparisons seem stronger than the contrast paragraph. (2 points)

The student does substantiate the thesis with appropriate historical evidence. She has at least one example for France and one example for Haiti in each body paragraph. (2 points)

The student has wisely used her topic sentences to make relevant, direct comparisons between France and Haiti. (2 points)

The student has not done a thorough job in analyzing a reason for a similarity or difference in a direct comparison. She does say, in her conclusion, "As a French colony, the long-term causes for the revolution in Haiti were likewise internal." "Likewise" refers to the previous sentence about the French revolution and so could be considered a reason for the similarities: both nations were either French or a French colony and so that is why the causes for their revolutions are initially internal. A "because . . ." in her thesis or a stronger explanation of reason in her conclusion would have made the difference. She is close to this point, but it probably would not be assessed. What she has written is not a strong piece of analysis, and so probably would not earn this Basic Core point.

Thus, this essay, though beginning with a strong thesis, including ample historical evidence, and doing an excellent job with making several direct comparisons between the revolutions, would earn a 6 on the 9 point scale, as the reason for the similarities or differences is not analyzed but only suggested.